THE COLLECTED WORKS OF

ABRAHAM LINCOLN

THE COLLECTED WORKS OF
ABRAHAM LINCOLN

THE ABRAHAM LINCOLN ASSOCIATION
SPRINGFIELD, ILLINOIS

II

ROY P. BASLER, *EDITOR*

MARION DOLORES PRATT AND LLOYD A. DUNLAP

ASSISTANT EDITORS

RUTGERS UNIVERSITY PRESS
NEW BRUNSWICK, NEW JERSEY

SOURCES
AND LOCATION SYMBOLS

DESCRIPTION OF SOURCES

THE following symbols provide a description of sources as cited at the beginning of the first footnote to each item. In addition to the customary symbols for describing manuscripts, the editors have employed symbols or single words to identify other sources which have been cited repeatedly in the first footnote.

AD	Autograph Document
ADS	Autograph Document Signed
ADf	Autograph Draft
ADfS	Autograph Draft Signed
AE	Autograph Endorsement
AES	Autograph Endorsement Signed
AL	Autograph Letter
ALS	Autograph Letter Signed
ALS copy	Autograph Letter Signed, copied by Lincoln and preserved in his papers
Copy	Copy not by Lincoln
D	Document
DS	Document Signed
Df	Draft
DfS	Draft Signed
ES	Endorsement Signed
F	Facsimile—following any of the preceding symbols
LS	Letter Signed
P	Photostat—following any of the preceding symbols

Angle — *New Letters and Papers of Lincoln.* Compiled by Paul M. Angle. Boston and New York: Houghton Mifflin Company, 1930.

Herndon — *Herndon's Lincoln: The True Story of a Great Life.* By William H. Herndon and Jesse W. Weik. 3 volumes. Chicago, New York, and San Francisco: Belford, Clarke & Company, [1889].

Hertz — *Abraham Lincoln: A New Portrait.* By Emanuel Hertz. 2 volumes. New York: Horace Liveright, Inc., 1931.

Lapsley — *The Writings of Abraham Lincoln.* Edited by Arthur Brooks Lapsley. 8 volumes. New York: P. F. Collier and Son, 1905.

NH   *Complete Works of Abraham Lincoln.* Edited by John G. Nicolay and John Hay. 12 volumes. New York: Francis D. Tandy Company, 1905.

OR   *The War of the Rebellion: A Compilation of the Official Records of the Union and Confederate Armies.* 4 series; 70 "volumes"; 128 books. Washington: Government Printing Office, 1880-1901. Roman numerals are used for Series, Volume, and Part (if any); pages are in arabic.

Tarbell   *The Life of Abraham Lincoln. . . .* By Ida M. Tarbell. 2 volumes. New York: The Doubleday & McClure Company, 1900.

Tracy   *Uncollected Letters of Abraham Lincoln.* Edited by Gilbert A. Tracy. Boston and New York: Houghton Mifflin Company, 1917.

Wilson   *Uncollected Works of Abraham Lincoln.* Edited by Rufus Rockwell Wilson. 2 volumes. Elmira, New York: Primavera Press, 1947-1948.

LOCATION SYMBOLS

CCamStJ   St. John's Seminary Library, Camarillo, Calif.

CLCM   Los Angeles County Museum Library, Los Angeles, Calif.

CSmH   Henry E. Huntington Library, San Marino, Calif.

CoHi   State Historical Society of Colorado, Denver, Colo.

CoU   University of Colorado Library, Boulder, Colo.

Ct   Connecticut State Library, Hartford, Conn.

CtHi   Connecticut Historical Society, Hartford, Conn.

CtLHi   Litchfield Historical Society, Litchfield, Conn.

CtSoP   Pequot Library, Southport, Conn.

CtWat   Watertown Library Association, Watertown, Conn.

CtY   Yale University Library, New Haven, Conn.

DLC   Library of Congress, Washington, D. C.

DLC-HW   Herndon-Weik Collection, Library of Congress

DLC-RTL   The Robert Todd Lincoln Collection of the Papers of Abraham Lincoln, Library of Congress

DLM   Lincoln Museum, Ford's Theatre, National Park Service, Washington, D. C.

DNA   National Archives, Washington, D. C. All additional abbreviations and numbers given with this symbol are those employed by the National Archives at the time the manuscript was located.

DNM   National Museum Library, Washington, D. C.

DeHi	Historical Society of Delaware Library, Wilmington, Del.
DeWI	Wilmington Institute Free Library, Wilmington, Del.
I-Ar	Archives Division, Illinois State Library, Springfield, Ill.
IBloHi	McLean County Historical Society, Bloomington, Ill.
ICHi	Chicago Historical Society, Chicago, Ill.
ICU	University of Chicago Library, Chicago, Ill.
IDecJ	James Millikin University Library, Decatur, Ill.
IFre	Freeport Public Library, Freeport, Ill.
IHi	Illinois State Historical Library, Springfield, Ill.
IJI	Illinois College Library, Jacksonville, Ill.
ISLA	The Abraham Lincoln Association, Springfield, Ill.
IU	University of Illinois Library, Urbana, Ill.
IaCrM	Iowa Masonic Library, Cedar Rapids, Iowa
IaDaM	Davenport Public Museum, Davenport, Iowa
IaHA	Iowa State Department of History and Archives, Des Moines, Iowa
In	Indiana State Library, Indianapolis, Ind.
InFtwL	Lincoln National Life Foundation, Fort Wayne, Ind.
InHi	Indiana Historical Society, Indianapolis, Ind.
InLTHi	Tippecanoe County Historical Association, Lafayette, Ind.
InU	Indiana University Library, Bloomington, Ind.
KyBC	Berea College Library, Berea, Ky.
KyU	University of Kentucky Library, Lexington, Ky.
LU	Louisiana State University Library, Baton Rouge, La.
MB	Boston Public Library, Boston, Mass.
MCon	Free Public Library, Concord, Mass.
MFai	Millicent Library, Fairhaven, Mass.
MH	Harvard University Library, Cambridge, Mass.
MHi	Massachusetts Historical Society, Boston, Mass.
MS	Springfield Library Association, Springfield, Mass.
MSHi	Connecticut Valley Historical Society, Springfield, Mass.
MdAA	Hall of Records, State of Maryland, Annapolis, Md.
MdHi	Maryland Historical Society, Baltimore, Md.
MeHi	Maine Historical Society, Portland, Me.
MiD	Detroit Public Library, Detroit, Mich.
MiK-M	Kalamazoo Public Library Museum, Kalamazoo, Mich.
MiU-C	William L. Clements Library, University of Michigan, Ann Arbor, Mich.

MiU-Hi   Michigan Historical Collection, University of Michigan, Ann Arbor, Mich.
MnHi   Minnesota Historical Society, St. Paul, Minn.
MnSM   Macalester College Library, St. Paul, Minn.
MoHi   State Historical Society of Missouri, Columbia, Mo.
MoSHi   Missouri Historical Society, St. Louis, Mo.
N   New York State Library, Albany, N. Y.
NAuE   Fred L. Emerson Foundation, Auburn, N. Y.
NBLiHi   Long Island Historical Society, Brooklyn, N. Y.
NBuG   Grosvenor Library, Buffalo, New York
NBuHi   Buffalo Historical Society, Buffalo, N. Y.
NDry   Southworth Library, Dryden, N. Y.
NHi   New-York Historical Society, New York City
NIC   Cornell University Library, Ithaca, N. Y.
NN   New York Public Library, New York City
NNC   Columbia University Library, New York City
NNP   Pierpont Morgan Library, New York City
NRU   University of Rochester Library, Rochester, N. Y.
NSh   John Jermain Memorial Library, Sag Harbor, N. Y.
NSk   Skaneateles Library Association, Skaneateles, N. Y.
NWM   U. S. Military Academy Library, West Point, N. Y.
NbO   Omaha Public Library, Omaha, Nebr.
NcGu   Guilford College Library, Guilford, N. C.
NhExP   Phillips Exeter Academy, Exeter, N. H.
NjP   Princeton University Library, Princeton, N. J.
OCHP   Historical and Philosophical Society of Ohio, Cincinnati, Ohio
OClCS   Case Institute of Technology, Cleveland, Ohio
OClWHi   Western Reserve Historical Society, Cleveland, Ohio
OFH   Hayes Memorial Library, Fremont, Ohio
OMC   Marietta College Library, Marietta, Ohio
ORB   Oliver R. Barrett Collection, Chicago, Ill.*
OSHi   Clark County Historical Society, Springfield, Ohio
OrHi   Oregon Historical Society, Portland, Ore.
PHC   Haverford College Library, Haverford, Pa.
PHi   Historical Society of Pennsylvania, Philadelphia, Pa.

---

* After the *Collected Works* was in press, the collection of the late Oliver R. Barrett was sold at auction by Parke-Bernet Galleries (Catalog 1315) on February 19-20, 1952. It has been impossible to trace all new owners of the more than two hundred items, and impracticable to change the source citations for those which are known, but many of the more important items went to such well-known collections as those in the Library of Congress (Debates Scrapbook, purchased for the Alfred Whital Stern Collection) and Illinois State Historical Library (letters to Joshua F. Speed, etc.).

PMA	Allegheny College Library, Meadville, Pa.
PP	Free Library of Philadelphia, Philadelphia, Pa.
PPDrop	Dropsie College Library, Philadelphia, Pa.
PSt	Pennsylvania State College Library, State College, Pa.
PU	University of Pennsylvania Library, Philadelphia, Pa.
RPAB	Annmary Brown Memorial Library, Providence, R. I.
RPB	Brown University Library, Providence, R. I.
THaroL	Lincoln Memorial University, Harrogate, Tenn.
THi	Tennessee Historical Society, Nashville, Tenn.
ViU	University of Virginia Library, Charlottesville, Va.
VtU	University of Vermont Library, Burlington, Vt.
WBeloHi	Beloit Historical Society, Beloit, Wis.
WHi	State Historical Society of Wisconsin, Madison, Wis.
WvU	West Virginia University Library, Morgantown, W. Va.

FEBRUARY 28, 1857 (*c.*)
By Alexander Hesler

THE COLLECTED WORKS OF
ABRAHAM LINCOLN

THE COLLECTED WORKS OF
ABRAHAM LINCOLN

To Thaddeus Stevens[1]

Hon: Thaddeus Stevens   Washington,
Dear Sir: Sept. 3. 1848

You may possibly remember seeing me at the Philadelphia Convention—introduced to you as the lone whig star of Illinois. Since the adjournment, I have remained here, so long, in the Whig document room. I am now about to start for home; and I desire the undisguised opinion of some experienced and sagacious Pennsylvania politician, as to how the vote of that state, for governor, and president, is likely to go. In casting about for such a man, I have settled upon you; and I shall be much obliged if you will write me at Springfield, Illinois.

The news we are receiving here now, by letters from all quarters is steadily on the rise; we have none lately of a discouraging character. This is the sum, without giving particulars. Yours truly

A LINCOLN

[1] ALS, DLC. Stevens was elected to the Thirty-first Congress on the Whig ticket in 1848.

Speech at Worcester, Massachusetts[1]

September 12, 1848

Mr. Kellogg[2] then introduced to the meeting the Hon. ABRAM LINCOLN, whig member of Congress from Illinois, a representative of *free soil.*

Mr. LINCOLN has a very tall and thin figure, with an intellectual face, showing a searching mind, and a cool judgment. He spoke in a clear and cool, and very eloquent manner, for an hour and a half,

[1] Boston *Daily Advertiser*, September 14, 1848. The Whig state convention was to meet in Worcester on September 13, and Lincoln spoke on the preceding evening to an assembly of delegates and other Whigs.
[2] Ensign H. Kellogg of Pittsfield, Massachusetts, chairman of the meeting.

[1]

carrying the audience with him in his able arguments and brilliant illustrations—only interrupted by warm and frequent applause. He began by expressing a real feeling of modesty in addressing an audience "this side of the mountains," a part of the country where, in the opinion of the people of his section, everybody was supposed to be instructed and wise. But he had devoted his attention to the question of the coming Presidential election, and was not unwilling to exchange with all whom he might meet the ideas to which he had arrived.

He then began to show the fallacy of some of the arguments against Gen. Taylor, making his chief theme the fashionable statement of all those who oppose him, ("the old Locofocos as well as the new") that he *has no principles*, and that the whig party have abandoned their principles by adopting him as their candidate. He maintained that Gen. Taylor occupied a high and unexceptionable whig ground, and took for his first instance and proof of this his statement in the Allison letter[3]—with regard to the Bank, Tariff, Rivers and Harbors, &c.—that the will of the people should produce its own results, without Executive influence. The principle that the people should do what—under the constitution—they please, is a whig principle. All that Gen. Taylor does is not only to consent, but to appeal to the people to judge and act for themselves. And this was no new doctrine for Whigs. It was the "platform" on which they had fought all their battles, the resistance of Executive influence, and the principle of enabling the people to frame the government according to their will. Gen. Taylor consents to be the candidate, and to assist the people to do what they think to be their duty, and think to be best in their natural affairs, but because *he don't want to tell what we ought to do*, he is accused of having no principles. The Whigs here [have?] maintained for years that neither the influence, the duress, or the prohibition of the Executive should control the legitimately expressed will of the people; and now that on that very ground, Gen. Taylor says that he should use the power given him by the people to do, to the best of his judgment, the will of the people, he is accused of want of principle, and of inconsistency in position.

Mr. Lincoln proceeded to examine the absurdity of an attempt to make a platform or creed for a national party, to *all* parts of which *all* must consent and agree, when it was clearly the inten-

[3] General Taylor's letter of April 22, 1848, ostensibly addressed to his brother-in-law, Captain J. S. Allison of Louisville, Kentucky, was in fact a political letter originally drafted in Washington by John J. Crittenden, Alexander Stephens, and Robert Toombs, and carried to Taylor's headquarters by Major William W. S. Bliss. It was widely printed by the Whig press as a campaign document.

tion and the true philosophy of our government, that in Congress all opinions and principles should be represented, and that when the wisdom of all had been compared and united, the will of the majority should be carried out. On this ground he conceived (and the audience seemed to go with him) that General Taylor held correct, sound republican principles.

Mr. Lincoln then passed to the subject of slavery in the States, saying that the people of Illinois agreed entirely with the people of Massachusetts on this subject, except perhaps that they did not keep so constantly thinking about it. All agreed that slavery was an evil, but that we were not responsible for it and cannot affect it in States of this Union where we do not live. But, the question of the *extension* of slavery to new territories of this country, is a part of our responsibility and care, and is under our control. In opposition to this Mr. L. believed that the self named "Free Soil" party, was far behind the Whigs. Both parties opposed the extension. As he understood it the new party had no principle except this opposition. If their platform held any other, it was in such a general way that it was like the pair of pantaloons the Yankee pedler offered for sale, "large enough for any man, small enough for any boy." They therefore had taken a position calculated to break down their single important declared object. They were working for the election of either Gen. Cass or Gen. Taylor.

The Speaker then went on to show, clearly and eloquently, the danger of extension of slavery, likely to result from the election of General Cass. To unite with those who annexed the new territory to prevent the extension of slavery in that territory seemed to him to be in the highest degree absurd and ridiculous. Suppose these gentlemen succeed in electing Mr. Van Buren, they had no specific means to *prevent* the extension of slavery to New Mexico and California, and Gen. Taylor, he confidently believed, would not encourage it, and would not prohibit its restriction. But if Gen. Cass was elected, he felt certain that the plans of farther extension of territory would be encouraged, and those of the extension of slavery would meet no check.

The "Free Soil" men in claiming that name indirectly attempted a deception, by implying the Whigs were *not* Free Soil men. In declaring that they would "do their duty and leave the consequences to God," merely gave an excuse for taking a course that they were not able to maintain by a fair and full argument. To make this declaration did not show what their duty was. If it did we should have no use for judgment, we might as well be made without intellect, and when divine or human law does not clearly point out what *is* our duty, we have no means of finding out what it is by using our most intelligent judgment of the consequences. If there were divine law, or human law for voting for Martin Van Buren, or if a fair examination of the consequences and first reasoning would show that voting for him would bring about the ends they pretended to wish—then he would give up the argument. But since there was no fixed law on the subject, and since the whole probable result of their action would be an assistance in electing Gen. CASS, he must say that they were behind the Whigs in their advocacy of the freedom of the soil.

Mr. Lincoln proceeded to rally the Buffalo Convention[4] for forbearing to say anything—after all the previous declarations of those members who were formerly Whigs—on the subject of the Mexican war, because the Van Burens had been known to have supported it. He declared that of all the parties asking the confidence of the country, this new one had *less* of principle than any other.

He wondered whether it was still the opinion of these Free Soil gentlemen, as declared in the "whereas" at Buffalo, that the whig and democratic parties were both entirely dissolved and absorbed into their own body. Had the *Vermont election* given them any light? They had calculated on making as great an impression in that State as in any part of the Union, and there their attempts had been wholly ineffectual. Their failure there was a greater success than they would find in any other part of the Union.

Mr. Lincoln went on to say that he honestly believed that all those who wished to keep up the character of the Union; who did not believe in enlarging our field, but in keeping our fences where they are and cultivating our present possession, making it a garden, improving the morals and education of the people; devoting the administration to this purpose; all real Whigs, friends of good honest government;—the race was ours. He had opportunities of hearing from almost every part of the Union from reliable sources, and had not heard of a country [county?] in which he had not received accessions from other parties. If the true Whigs come forward and join these new friends, they need not have a doubt. We had a candidate whose personal character and principles he had already described, whom he could not eulogize if he would. Gen. Taylor had been constantly, perseveringly, quietly standing up, *doing his duty*, and asking no praise or reward for it. He was and must be just the man to whom the interests, principles and pros-

[4] The Free Soil Party was organized at Buffalo, New York, on August 9, 1848.

perity of the country might be safely intrusted. He had never failed in anything he had undertaken, although many of his duties had been considered almost impossible.

Mr. Lincoln then went into a terse though rapid review of the origin of the Mexican war and the connection of the administration and of General Taylor with it, from which he deduced a strong appeal to the Whigs present to do their duty in the support of General Taylor, and closed with the warmest aspirations for and confidence in a deserved success.

At the close of this truly masterly and convincing speech, the audience gave three enthusiastic cheers for Illinois, and three more for the eloquent Whig member from that State.[5]

[5] On the next morning Lincoln was one of several impromptu speakers at "an enthusiastic meeting near the Rail Road station, where the different delegations had assembled" to meet incoming delegations. Lincoln was "interrupted by the arrival of the train from Boston, and a procession was then formed and moved to the Town Hall." (Boston *Daily Advertiser*, September 14, 1848.)

Speech at Boston, Massachusetts[1]

September 15, 1848

BOSTON WHIG CLUB.—A full and enthusiastic meeting of this Club was held last evening at Washingtonian Hall, Bromfield street. They were addressed by the Hon. Abraham Lincoln, of Illinois, in a speech of an hour and a half, which, for sound reasoning, cogent argument and keen satire, we have seldom heard equalled. He defended General Taylor from the charge that he had no principles, by showing conclusively that his avowed and well known principles were, that the people's will should be obeyed, and not frustrated by Executive usurpation and the interposition of the veto power.

He pointed out the absurdity of men who professed Whig principles supporting Van Buren, with all his Locofocoism, while the Whigs were as much opposed to the extension of slavery as were the Van Buren party. His remarks were frequently interrupted by rounds of applause. As soon as he had concluded, the audience gave three cheers for Taylor and Fillmore, and three more for Mr. Lincoln, the Lone Star of Illinois, and then adjourned. It was a glorious meeting.

[1] Boston *Atlas*, September 16, 1848. A brief mention of this speech quoting the Boston *Chronotype* appears in the *Illinois State Register*, October 13, 1848. Following the report in the *Atlas* is an announcement that Lincoln will speak in Dorchester on Monday, September 18. There is no other record of this speech.

Speech at Lowell Massachusetts[1]

September 16, 1848

. . . . Mr. Woodman[2] introduced the Hon. Abraham Lincoln, of Illinois. It would be doing injustice to his speech to endeavor to give a sketch of it. It was replete with good sense, sound reasoning, and irresistible argument, and spoken with that perfect command of manner and matter which so eminently distinguishes the Western orators. He disabused the public of the erroneous suppositions that Taylor was not a *Whig;* that Van Buren was anything more than a thorough Locofoco, on all subjects other than Free Territory, and hardly safe on that—and showed up, in a masterly manner, the inconsistency and folly of those Whigs, who, being drawn off from the true and oldest free soil organization known among the parties of the Union, would now lend their influence and votes to help Mr. Van Buren into the Presidential chair. His speech was interrupted by the cheers of the audience, evincing the truth of the great supposition that the *dead* can speak.

[1] Lowell *Daily Journal*, September 18, 1848.
[2] George Woodman of Boston.

Speech at Taunton, Massachusetts[1]

September [21?] 1848

The Taylor men were well entertained Wednesday evening, the 20th inst.,[2] at Union Hall, by an address from the Hon. Abraham Lincoln of Illinois. The address as well as the speaker was such as to give unlimited satisfaction to the disheartened Taylorites. Such a treat it is indeed seldom their good luck to get, and they were in ecstacies. At former meetings their spirits were too low for a good hearty cheer, but on this occasion "the steam was up." It was reviving to hear a man speak as if he believed what he was saying and had a grain or two of feeling mixed up with it; one who could not only speak highly of Taylor, but could occasionally swell with indignation or burst in hatred on the Free Soilers. When political spite runs high nothing can be too pungent or severe, and the speaker is appreciated in proportion as his statements are rash and unscrupulous. So it was on this occasion. The speaker was far inferior

[1] *National Magazine*, Vol. XXXI, No. 5, pp. 523-25, account taken from *Bristol County Democrat*, September 29, 1848. Although politically unsympathetic, this is the most extensive account of Lincoln's speech available.

[2] Since Lincoln spoke in Cambridge on Wednesday evening, September 20, this date is in error. The Taunton *Daily Gazette*, September 23, 1848, mentions the speech in Taunton and assigns September 21 as the date.

as a reasoner to others who hold the same views, but then he was more unscrupulous, more facetious and with his sneers he mixed up a good deal of humor. His awkward gesticulations, the ludicrous management of his voice and the comical expression of his countenance, all conspired to make his hearers laugh at the mere anticipation of the joke before it appeared. But enough concerning the speaker; let us examine his arguments.

General Taylor, he argued, *has* principles, though he has not given expression to them on the Tariff, Bank and other questions of policy. This, however, is in direct contradiction of Taylor, himself, who in his letter to Delany writes, "As regards the second and third inquiries (about a bank and tariff), I am not prepared to answer them. *I could only do so after investigating them.* I am no politician; near forty years of my life have been passed on the Western frontier and in the Indian count[r]y." The speaker next discussed the veto question and said that Taylor was the first Whig candidate that had come fully up to the Whig platform in this point, because unlike all other candidates before him he had not even claimed the right to advise Congress on matters of policy. The proper limitation of the veto, he contended, was the Whig platform itself, and General Taylor by his equivocal silence had come up to it better than the great parent of Whig principles—Henry Clay. He did not know that General Taylor had professed that he would *not* veto the Wilmot proviso, but *believed* that he would not, because General Taylor had promised not to veto any measure unless it was unconstitutional or passed in haste and acknowledged that to be constitutional which had been established by long usage and acquiesced in by the people. As the constitutionality of the Wilmot Proviso he said "had never been disputed," it was therefore acquiesced in by the people and consequently Taylor was bound not to veto it.

He subsequently admitted in speaking of Cass, that in the Nicholson letter the constitutional power of Congress to exclude slavery from any territory in the Union was denied. Yet he seemed to forget this when he said that the constitutionality of the Proviso had never been disputed. He seemed to be entirely ignorant that every propagandist of slavery in existence, with John C. Calhoun at their head, claimed the right, under the Constitution, and independent of Congress, to carry their "property" into any part of the United States territory and there to hold it.

Calhoun said in the Senate that when the South consented to the Missouri Compromise the rights of the South granted by the Constitution were given up but belonged to the South the same as if no compromise had been made. Thomas Corwin said in his speech on the Compromise Bill introduced in the Senate last session of Congress that the constitutionality of any measure excluding slavery from the territories could not with safety be left to the decision of the Supreme Court. The House of Representatives had the same views and rejected the bill. None of these facts did the speaker allude to, but instead uttered the stupendous falsehood that the "constitutionality of the Proviso" had never been disputed. Without this "whopper," however, the argument would have been defective. There would have been a gap in it, so the lie was made big enough to fill the gap that the argument might thereby be made sound and conclusive.

He related a conversation which he overheard at the dinner table of a house in Lowell between two Free Soilers. One of them remarked that the reasoning of the Taylor men was not logical, for it certainly was illogical to say, "General Taylor is a slaveholder, therefore we go for him to prevent the extension of slavery." He thought this was an unfair statement of the case and gave what he deemed the correct one in the form of a syllogism as follows: "General Taylor is a slaveholder, but he will do more to prevent the extension of slavery than any other man whom it is possible to elect, therefore we go for Taylor."

It needs no argument to prove that the major proposition does not include the minor o[n]e and has nothing to do with it. But let that pass. The minor proposition asserts that General Taylor will do *"more"* to prevent the extension of slavery than any other man it is possible to elect, and this assertion is made before the logician has even attempted to prove that General Taylor was opposed to the extension of slavery at all! The attempt is made to prove that he will do *more* than any other man before it is proved that he will do the first thing. But taking for granted that General Taylor will not veto the Proviso (a position founded on a lie) is that a proof that he will do anything to prevent the extension of slavery? He may never have a chance to veto the Proviso even if elected in November. The slave states are equal with the free states in the Senate and before the Proviso can pass that body one or two of the Southern Senators must yield.

Under such circumstances, is it likely that any Senator from the South will be influenced to vote for the Proviso by the executive patronage of the unrepentant slaveholder, Zachary Taylor? Is it not more probable that it would be brought to bear on some Northern doughface? It would be quite safe for Taylor to make an equivocal promise not to veto the Proviso, but he has not even done so much as that. The speaker contended that Van Buren had approved the policy of the Mexican War and the annexation of new territory. This he did not prove from Van Buren's letter written in 1844. If he had read that letter to his hearers they would have found that Van Buren wrote *against* annexation, partly because it would produce war. The proof he gave was the fact that some of the same individuals who supported Van Buren in 1844 had since voted both for Texas and war.

He said in another part of his speech that the Northern Democrats were opposed to the annexation of Texas in 1844. Yet he undertook to prove that Van Buren was in favor of annexation and war from the fact that these men once supported him and that at the very time they themselves were opposed to annexation. But why should Van Buren be held responsible for all his friends? Where is the proof that he ever favored the extension of slavery in all his life? Is General Taylor responsible for all who now support him? Are the sins of Berrien Mangum and other propagandists of slavery to be laid to his charge? He has enough to answer for his own account if we acquit him of all guilt connected with the Native Church burning of Philadelphia.

To show the recklessness and audacity of the honorable gentleman and the low estimate he had formed of his hearers, it will suffice to give but one specimen. Speaking of Van Buren, he said, "he (Van Buren) won't have an electoral vote in the nation nor as many as all others in any county in the nation." The reasoning adopted by the Whig Free Soilers he gave in the form of a syllogism as follows: "We can't go for General Taylor because he is not a Whig. Van Buren is not a Whig; therefore, we go for him." This dishonest statement of the case elicited warm applause from his truth-loving hearers. The syllogism should have stood thus: We can't vote for a man without principles. General Taylor has got none, and Van Buren has, at least, got one good Whig principle; therefore, we go for Van Buren against Taylor.

For the benefit of those who are like the speaker, always misrepresenting the Free Soil Party, I will define our position in a prosyllogism. The abolition of slavery in the territory of the United States can never be accomplished unless the North is united. But the North cannot be united until old party lines are broken down. But these lines cannot be broken down unless every man is willing to sacrifice his attachment to minor questions and make opposition to slavery the leading idea; therefore, we have come out of the old pro-slavery parties and formed the United Party of the North.

[9]

Fragment: Niagara Falls[1]

[c. September 25-30, 1848]

Niagara-Falls! By what mysterious power is it that millions and millions, are drawn from all parts of the world, to gaze upon Niagara Falls? There is no mystery about the thing itself. Every effect is just such as any inteligent man knowing the causes, would anticipate, without [seeing] it. If the water moving onward in a great river, reaches a point where there is a perpendicular jog, of a hundred feet in descent, in the bottom of the river,—it is plain the water will have a violent and continuous plunge at that point. It is also plain the water, thus plunging, will foam, and roar, and send up a mist, continuously, in which last, during sunshine, there will be perpetual rain-bows. The mere physical of Niagara Falls is only this. Yet this is really a very small part of that world's wonder. It's power to excite reflection, and emotion, is it's great charm. The geologist will demonstrate that the plunge, or fall, was once at Lake Ontario, and has worn it's way back to it's present position; he will ascertain how *fast* it is wearing now, and so get a basis for determining how *long* it has been wearing back from Lake Ontario, and finally demonstrate by it that this world is at least fourteen thousand years old. A philosopher of a slightly different turn will say Niagara Falls is only the lip of the basin out of which pours all the surplus water which rains down on two or three hundred thousand square miles of the earth's surface. He will estim[ate with] approximate accuracy, that five hundred thousand [to]ns of water, falls with it's full weight, a distance of a hundred feet each minute— thus exerting a force equal to the lifting of the same weight, through the same space, in the same time. And then the further reflection comes that this vast amount of water, constantly pouring *down*, is supplied by an equal amount constantly *lifted up*, by the sun; and still he says, "If this much is lifted up, for *this one* space of two or three hundred thousand square miles, an equal amount must be lifted for every other equal space; and he is overwhelmed in the contemplation of the vast power the sun is constantly exerting in quiet, noiseless opperation of lifting water *up* to be rained *down* again.

But still there is more. It calls up the indefinite past. When Columbus first sought this continent—when Christ suffered on the cross—when Moses led Israel through the Red-Sea—nay, even, when Adam first came from the hand of his Maker—then as now, Niagara was roaring here. The eyes of that species of extinct giants, whose bones fill the mounds of America, have gazed on Niagara, as ours do now. Co[n]temporary with the whole race of men, and older than the first man, Niagara is strong, and fresh to-day as ten thousand years ago. The Mammoth and Mastadon—now so long dead, that fragments of their monstrous bones, alone testify, that they ever lived, have gazed on Niagara. In that long—long time, never still for a single moment. Never dried, never froze, never slept, never rested,

1 AD, DLC-RTL. The dating of this document by Nicolay and Hay [July 1, 1850?] has been rejected because the editors can find no reason for so dating it. The date, c. September 25-30, 1848, is based on two principal facts: (1) Lincoln visited Niagara Falls en route from Boston to Chicago, September 23-October 5, 1848; (2) the document is in appearance of paper and handwriting contemporary with the documents of speeches written in 1848 in Washington. The content suggests the sort of meditation and recapitulation of observations and reflections which would be psychologically apropos following a visit to the Falls, and one suspects that Lincoln's boat trip from Buffalo provided the leisure to begin, if not to conclude, the meditation. Nicolay and Hay entitle the piece "Notes for a Lecture," but the subject itself should suffice. The manuscript stops abruptly with an unfinished sentence.

Speech at Chicago, Illinois[1]

October 6, 1848

Mr. Lincoln's speech occupied about two hours, which time he devoted to a most earnest, candid and logical examination of the great questions involved in the present Presidential canvass. He clearly and conclusively showed that the defeat of Gen. Taylor would be a verdict of the American people, against any restriction or restraint to the extension and perpetuation of slavery in newly acquired territory. In this he resorted to no special pleading, but with well arranged and pertinent facts, and sincere arguments he fully demonstrated it. During his speech he introduced several humorous, but very appropriate illustrations.

1 *Illinois Gazette* (Lacon), October 14, 1848, quoting the Chicago *Commercial Advertiser*.

Debate at Jacksonville, Illinois[1]
October 21, 1848

Jacksonville, Oct. 24

GENTS: On Friday night, Mr. Lincoln, member of Congress from this district, had an appointment to speak in Jacksonville, but gave way to the other branch of the whig family—the barnburner-abolition-free-negro party. On Saturday night, he renewed his ap-

[11]

pointment, and Mr. McConnel,[2] having arrived from the north, gave notice that he would be with him. The consequence was that a general rally took place.

The debators were confined to an hour each. . . . Lincoln spent his first hour in persecuting his free-negro friends, that their object of promoting freedom would be easier and better attained by voting for Taylor, the owner of three hundred negro slaves, because Taylor would not veto the Wilmot proviso if passed by Congress. It is true, said L., that *Taylor has not pledged himself to that effect*, but he had pledged himself generally against the exercise of the veto power.

McConnel enquired of L. why the Taylor faction of the whig party did not go over to the free-negro faction, and then they would be sure to have a man . . . about whom, in relation to the free-soil question, there was no doubt. To this Lincoln said he would have no objection, if there were not other questions about which Taylor and Van Buren disagreed. But when McConnel thrust the question upon him: in what do they disagree, what is Taylor for or against? Lincoln could not answer, and was most palpably exposed before his friends. . . .

Mr. Lincoln in his second hour, made a weak attempt at a justification of his course, but the flood of authorities thrust upon him by Mr. McConnel, were evidently new to him. . . .

Lincoln then took a turn at the veto power, and attempted to show that Taylor was against it generally, and against executive patronage especially, but in this he was equally unhappy as in his efforts upon the slavery question. . . .

At the close of this debate a rather exciting scene occurred. Mr. Lincoln charged that Mr. Polk had constantly been trying to drive Wentworth[3] to vote upon certain subjects in accordance with the democratic platform, and to misrepresent his constituents and vote contrary to their wishes.

Mr. McConnel denied the charge, and called on Lincoln for his authority. He gave Mr. Wentworth as his informant, and then pronounced the conduct of Mr. Polk, and the democratic party, anti-democratic and wrong, and said it was the duty of every representative truly to represent his constituents.

Mr. McConnel then took up a copy of the journal of the House of Representatives . . . of January last, and showed that Mr. Lincoln *had refused to vote for a resolution of thanks to General Taylor and his brave comrades for his and their conduct at the battle of Buena Vista, until he had first voted an amendment thereto*, that this battle was fought in a war *unconstitutionally and unneces-*

sarily begun by the President. . . . He asked if Mr. Lincoln did not know when he gave that vote that he was *misrepresenting* the wishes of the patriotic people of this district, and did he do so by the influence of Mr. Polk or some whig leader. In the midst of the shower of fire that fell around him, Lincoln cried out, "No, I did not know it, and don't believe it yet.". . . . Lincoln crouched in silence beneath the blows that fell thick and fast around him, and his friends held down their heads with shame.

Lincoln has made nothing by coming to this part of the country to make speeches. He had better have stayed away. Yours, &c.,

J. H.

[1] *Illinois State Register*, October 27, 1848. The only account available.
[2] Murray McConnel, Morgan County Democrat.
[3] John Wentworth, Democrat and congressman from Illinois, fourth district.

Warranty Deed of Lincoln and Jayne to Armstrong and Yardly[1]

October 27, 1848

This Indenture made this twentyseventh day of October in the year of our Lord one thousand, eight hundred and fortyeight, by and between Gershom Jayne and Sibyl Jayne,[2] his wife, and Abraham Lincoln, and Mary Lincoln his wife, all of the city of Springfield, in the State of Illinois, party of the first part; and Pleasant Armstrong and John Yardly of the county of Menard and State aforesaid, party of the second part, Witnesseth:

That the said party of the first part, for, and in consideration of the sum of one hundred dollars to them in hand paid, by the said party of the second part, the receipt whereof is hereby acknowledged, have granted, bargained and sold; and by these presents do grant bargain and sell unto the said party of the second part, the following described tract or parcel of land, towit: The North part of the North West fractional quarter of Section Three in Township Nineteen North of Range Seven West, of the Third Principal Meridian, situated in the county of Mason, and State aforesaid, containing fortyseven acres more or less.[3]

To have and to hold to the said party of the second part, their heirs and assigns forever, the above described tract of land, together with all and singular the previleges and appurtenances thereunto belonging. And the said party of the first part, for themselves and their heirs, do covenant to and with the said party of the second part, that they are lawfully seized, have full right to convey, and will warrant and forever defend the title of said land against the claim or claims of themselves, their heirs, and of any and all persons whomsoever.

In testimony whereof the said party of the first part have hereunto set their hands and seals this day and year first above written.

GERSHOM JAYNE (SEAL)   A. LINCOLN (SEAL)

SIBYL JAYNE (SEAL)   M. LINCOLN (SEAL)

[1] ADS, CoU. The document carries also the certificates of James W. Keyes, J. P., and Noah W. Matheny, clerk.

[2] The father and mother of Mary Todd Lincoln's close friend Julia Jayne, who married Lyman Trumbull.

[3] This piece of land had been purchased by Lincoln in 1836. On May 9, 1837, he sold an undivided half interest to Jayne, who was one of the proprietors of the nearby town of Huron, surveyed by Lincoln in 1836.

Speech at Lacon, Illinois[1]

November 1, 1848

Mr. Lincoln followed him,[2] with one of his most brilliant efforts. His main purpose was to show that the peace and prosperity of the country, and the limitation of slavery depended upon the election of a Whig Congress and Gen. Taylor; that the Old Hero, whose fidelity to whig principles none should now doubt, had pledged himself to carry out the will of the people, through their representatives, without interposing the veto power. He declared that the contest was between Taylor and Cass—that he doubted that Van Buren would get even one State, except perhaps the little state of Wisconsin; and admonished all "Liberty" or Van Buren men, by the history of Texan Annexation to cast their votes for Gen. Taylor, and *not* indirectly for Gen. Cass, who has avowed his favor of the unlimited exercise of the veto power, and as a probable consequence if elected, to the unbounded extension of slavery, &c. He scored with the most scathing language, that *"consistency"* of the Abolitionists, which, while they professed great horror at the proposed extension of slave territory, they aided in the election of Mr. Polk; for which, and its disastrous consequences, they were responsible, as they held the balance of power.

[1] *Illinois Gazette* (Lacon), November 4, 1848.

[2] Dr. Anson G. Henry preceded Lincoln on the platform.

To Amos Williams[1]

Dear Sir: Washington, Decr. 8 1848

Your letter of Novr. 27, was here for me when I arrived on yesterday. I also received the one addressed me at Springfield; but seeing I could do nothing in the matter *then & there,* and being very busy with the Presidential election, I threw it by, and forgot it. I shall do better now. Herewith I send you a document of "Information &c." which you can examine; and then if you think fit, to file a caveat, you can send me a description and drawing of your "invention" or "improvement" together with $20 in money, and I will file it for you. Nothing can be done, by caveat; or by exam-[in]ing the models here, as you request without having a *description* of your invention. You perceive the reason of this. Yours as ever   A. LINCOLN

¹ ALS, owned by the Woodbury family of Danville, Illinois. Amos Williams was a resident of Danville, who served for many years as clerk of the Circuit Court of Vermilion County.

Endorsement Concerning Joseph Newman¹

[December 14? 1848]

Please examine the within, and return your answer to me.

A. LINCOLN

¹ AES, RPB, Lincoln's endorsement, probably addressed to the War Department, appears on the envelope in which the first portion of a letter dated December 14, 1848 is enclosed, the remainder containing the signature being lost. Internal evidence establishes the probability that the letter was from Henry Newman, concerning back pay due his son Joseph who was killed in the war with Mexico (*vide infra,* affidavit concerning Joseph Newman, January 4, 1849).

To Thomas Lincoln and John D. Johnston¹

My dear father: Washington, Decr. 24th. 1848–

Your letter of the 7th.² was received night before last. I very cheerfully send you the twenty dollars, which sum you say is necessary to save your land from sale. It is singular that you should have forgotten a judgment against you; and it is more singular that the plaintiff should have let you forget it so long, particularly as I suppose you have always had property enough to satisfy a judgment of that amount. Before you pay it, it would be well to be sure you have not paid it; or, at least, that you can not prove you have paid it. Give my love to Mother, and all the connections. Affectionately your Son   A. LINCOLN

Dear Johnston:

Your request for eighty dollars, I do not think it best, to comply with now. At the various times when I have helped you a little, you have said to me "We can get along very well now" but in a very short time I find you in the same difficulty again. Now this can only happen by some defect in your *conduct*. What that defect is, I think I know. You are not *lazy*, and still you *are* an *idler*. I doubt whether since I saw you, you have done a good whole day's work, in any one day. You do not very much dislike to work; and still you do not work much, merely because it does not seem to you that you could get much for it. This habit of uselessly wasting time, is the whole difficulty; and it is vastly important to you, and still more so to your children that you should break this habit. It is more important to them, because they have longer to live, and can keep out of an idle habit before they are in it; easier than they can get out after they are in.

You are now in need of some ready money; and what I propose is, that you shall go to work, "tooth and nails" for some body who will give you money [for] it. Let father and your boys take charge of things at home—prepare for a crop, and make the crop; and you go to work for the best money wages, or in discharge of any debt you owe, that you can get. And to secure you a fair reward for your labor, I now promise you, that for every dollar you will, between this and the first of next May, get for your own labor, either in money, or in your own indebtedness, I will then give you one other dollar. By this, if you hire yourself at ten dolla[rs] a month, from me you will get ten more, making twenty dollars a month for your work. In this, I do not mean you shall go off to St. Louis, or the lead mines, or the gold mines, in Calif[ornia,] but I [mean for you to go at it for the best wages you] can get close to home [in] Coles county. Now if you will do this, you will soon be out of debt, and what is better, you will have a habit that will keep you from getting in debt again. But if I should now clear you out, next year you will be just as deep in as ever. You say you would almost give your place in Heaven for $70 or $80. Then you value your place in Heaven very cheaply for I am sure you can with the offer I make you get the seventy or eighty dollars for four or five months work. You say if I furnish you the money you will deed me the land, and, if you dont pay the money back, you will deliver possession. Nonsense! If you cant now live *with* the land, how will you then live without it? You have always been [kind] to me, and I do not now mean to be unkind to you. On the contrary, if you will but follow my advice, you will find it worth more than eight times eighty dollars to you. Affectionately Your brother   A. LINCOLN

[1] ALS, CSmH. This letter and the one to John D. Johnston (*infra*) are parts of the same document, the letter to Johnston beginning on the bottom of the letter to Thomas Lincoln.

1849

Johnston had written the letter for Thomas Lincoln and followed it with a letter of his own on the same sheet. Due to the fact that Nicolay and Hay (II, 144-46) printed the letter to Johnston under the erroneous date of January [2?] 1851, Beveridge (I, 479) states erroneously that Lincoln "ignored" Johnston's request for money.

To Joshua F. Speed[1]

Dear Speed: Washington, Dec. 25. 1848

While I was at Springfield last fall, Wm. Herndon showed me a couple of letters of yours concerning your note against Judge Browne.[2] I suppose you and we (Logan & I) feel alike about the matter; that is, neither side likes to lose the money. You think the loss comes of our fault, and that therefore we should bear it; but we do not think it comes of our fault. We do not remember ever having had the note after you received the Auditor's warrants; and, after the most thorough search, we can no where find it. We *know* we have never received any thing on it. In what you say, as to the note being left with us, we do not question your veracity, but we think you may be mistaken, because we do not remember it ourselves, and because we can not find it. We, like you, would rather lose it, than have any hard thoughts. Now, whatever you are short of your due upon the note Judge Browne still owes, and he must be made to pay it. You mention in your letter that you have our receipt for the note. I wish you would, at once, send a copy of the receipt to Logan. Browne will most likely be at Springfield this winter, and I wish Logan to see by the receipt, whether he or I, could, by reference to it, sufficiently describe the note, on oath, to recover on it as a lost instrument. If he decides we can, he will have a writ served on him while he is there, unless he will voluntarily pay it. Dont neglect to do this at once.

Nothing of consequence new here, beyond what you see in the papers. Present my kind regards to Mrs. Speed. Yours as ever

A. LINCOLN.

[1] ALS, ORB.   [2] Thomas C. Browne.

Fragment of a Letter[1]

[1849]

he *lied* in his *heart*, when he said he was not an ultra whig, and he desired General Taylor to be so informed

This is our information on the subject   Your Obt. Servt.

A. LINCOLN

E. D. BAKER

[17]

[1] ADS, ORB. The date supplied for this fragment rests on the assumption that the entire letter of which this is the last page was probably written by Lincoln during the scramble for patronage that followed the inauguration of Zachary Taylor. Lincoln's other correspondence of this period affords ample ground for conjecturing the name of the Whig to whom Lincoln and Baker were referring. Baker had moved to Galena, Illinois, following the Mexican War and had been elected to the Thirty-first Congress, thus following Lincoln as the lone Whig of Illinois.

Affidavit Concerning Joseph Newman[1]

January 4, 1849

This day came before me the Hon. A. Lincoln and Oliver Dieffendorf[2] and made oath that they were well acquainted with Joseph Newman, deceased, who was a private in Col. Baker's regiment of Illinois volunteers who died in Mexico, in Battle, and also with Henry Newman, his father, of Sangamon County, Ill. They state that the deceased was very young, and never married, to the best of their knowledge and belief.   A. LINCOLN.

[1] DS as advertised by F. H. Sweet, List No. 52 (1939), No. 109. The only text available; may be incomplete. *Vide supra,* endorsement concerning Joseph Newman, December [14?] 1848.

[2] Oliver Dieffendorf, resident of Springfield, was commissioned first lieutenant in Company D, Fourth Illinois Infantry, under Colonel Edward D. Baker. Presumably Dieffendorf and Lincoln appeared together at the War Department to give testimony.

To Walter Davis[1]

Friend Walter: Washington, Jan: 5. 1849

Your letter is received. When I last saw you I said, that if the distribution of the offices should fall into my hands, you should have *something;* and I now say as much, but can say no more. I know no more now than I knew when you saw me, as to whether the present officers will be removed, or, if they shall, whether *I* shall be allowed to name the persons to fill them. It will perhaps be better for both you and me, for you to say nothing about this.

I shall do what I can about the Land claim on your brother Thomas' account. Yours as ever   A. LINCOLN

[1] ALS-P, ISLA.

To William H. Herndon[1]

Dear William   Washington, Jan. 5. 1849

Your two letters were received last night. I have a great many letters to write, and so can not write very long ones. There must be some mistake about Walter Davis saying I promised him the Post-Office; I did not so promise him. I did tell him, that if the distribution of the offices should fall into my hands, he should have *something;* and if I shall be convinced he has said any more than this, I shall be disappointed. I said this much to him, because, as I understand, he is of *good character,* is one of the *young* men, is of the *mechanics,*[2] an always *faithful,* and never *troublesome* whig, and is *poor,* with the support of a widow mother thrown almost exclusively on him by the death of his brother. If these are wrong reasons, then I have been wrong; but I have certainly not been selfish in it; because in my greatest need of friends he was against me and for Baker. Yours as ever   A. LINCOLN

P. S. Let the above be confidential

[1] ALS, PHi.   [2] Springfield Mechanics Union.

To C. U. Schlater[1]

Mr. C. U. Schlater: Washington,
Dear Sir: Jan: 5. 1849

Your note, requesting my "signature with a sentiment" was received, and should have been answered long since, but that it was mislaid. I am not a very sentimental man; and the best sentiment I can think of is, that if you collect the signatures of all persons who are no less distinguished than I, you will have a very undistinguishing mass of names. Very respectfully   A. LINCOLN

[1] ALS, PHi. No C. U. Schlater has been identified, but a "C. M. Schlater, clerk," is in the Philadelphia, Pennsylvania, Directory for 1853, and a "C. W. Schlater, clerk" is listed in 1854. Perhaps both Lincoln and the compiler of the Directory were puzzled by Schlater's middle initial.

Remarks in United States House of Representatives[1]

January 6, 1849

Mr. LINCOLN, (addressing the Chair). I have had information brought to me in relation to the record of my vote on the bill which has just been passed.[2] I desire to be informed by the clerk how my vote is recorded.

The CLERK. The vote is recorded in the negative.

Mr. LINCOLN. That is right.

[1] *Congressional Globe,* Thirtieth Congress, Second Session, p. 177.
[2] A bill establishing a board for adjudication of private claims.

[19]

Remarks and Resolution
Introduced in United States House of Representatives Concerning Abolition of Slavery in the District of Columbia[1]

January 10, 1849

Mr. LINCOLN appealed to his colleague [Mr. WENTWORTH][2] to withdraw his motion, to enable him to read a proposition which he intended to submit, if the vote should be reconsidered.

Mr. WENTWORTH again withdrew his motion for that purpose.

Mr. LINCOLN said, that by the courtesy of his colleague, he would say, that if the vote on the resolution was reconsidered, he should make an effort to introduce an amendment, which he should now read.

And Mr. L. read as follows:

Strike out all before and after the word "Resolved" and insert the following, towit: That the Committee on the District of Columbia be instructed to report a bill in substance as follows, towit:[3]

Section 1 Be it enacted by the Senate and House of Representatives of the United States of America, in Congress assembled: That no person not now within the District of Columbia, nor now owned by any person or persons now resident within it, nor hereafter born within it, shall ever be held in slavery within said District.

Section 2. That no person now within said District, or now owned by any person, or persons now resident within the same, or hereafter born within it, shall ever be held in slavery without the limits of said District: *Provided*, that officers of the government of the United States, being citizens of the slave-holding states, coming into said District on public business, and remaining only so long as may be reasonably necessary for that object, may be attended into, and out of, said District, and while there, by the necessary servants of themselves and their families, without their right to hold such servants in service, being thereby impaired.

---

[1] *Congressional Globe*, Thirtieth Congress, Second Session, p. 212. Also ADf, DLC-RTL. The remarks are taken from the *Congressional Globe*, but the proposed bill has been corrected additionally from the autograph draft in the Lincoln Papers.

[2] John Wentworth of Illinois, who had moved to table a motion to reconsider the resolution, adopted on December 21, 1848, on motion of Daniel Gott of New York, instructing the committee for the District of Columbia to report a bill prohibiting slavery in the District.

[3] In the autograph draft the bill carries the following title: "A bill for an act to abolish slavery in the District of Columbia, by the consent of the free white people of said District, and with compensation to owners."

Section 3. That all children born of slave mothers within said District on, or after the first day of January in the year of our Lord one thousand, eight hundred and fifty shall be free; but shall be reasonably supported and educated, by the respective owners of their mothers or by their heirs or representatives, and shall owe reasonable service, as apprentices, to such owners, heirs and representatives until they respectively arrive at the age of —— years when they shall be entirely free; and the municipal authorities of Washington and Georgetown, within their respective jurisdictional limits, are hereby empowered and required to make all suitable and necessary provisions for enforcing obedience to this section, on the part of both masters and apprentices.

Section 4. That all persons now within said District lawfully held as slaves, or now owned by any person or persons now resident within said District, shall remain such, at the will of their respective owners, their heirs and legal representatives: *Provided* that any such owner, or his legal representative, may at any time receive from the treasury of the United States the full value of his or her slave, of the class in this section mentioned, upon which such slave shall be forthwith and forever free: and *provided further* that the President of the United States, the Secretary of State, and the Secretary of the Treasury shall be a board for determining the value of such slaves as their owners may desire to emancipate under this section; and whose duty it shall be to hold a session for the purpose, on the first monday of each calendar month; to receive all applications; and, on satisfactory evidence in each case, that the person presented for valuation, is a slave, and of the class in this section mentioned, and is owned by the applicant, shall value such slave at his or her full cash value, and give to the applicant an order on the treasury for the amount; and also to such slave a certificate of freedom.

Section 5 That the municipal authorities of Washington and Georgetown, within their respective jurisdictional limits, are hereby empowered and required to provide active and efficient means to arrest, and deliver up to their owners, all fugitive slaves escaping into said District.

Section 6 That the election officers within said District of Columbia, are hereby empowered and required to open polls at all the usual places of holding elections, on the first monday of April next, and receive the vote of every free white male citizen above the age of twentyone years, having resided within said District for the period of one year or more next preceding the time of such voting, for, or against this act; to proceed, in taking said votes, in all respects not herein specified, as at elections under the municipal laws; and, with as little delay as possible, to transmit correct statements of the votes so cast to the President of the United States. And it shall be the duty of the President to canvass said votes immediately, and, if a majority of them be found to be for this act, to forthwith issue his proclamation giving notice of the fact; and this act shall only be in full force and effect on, and after the day of such proclamation.

Section 7. That involuntary servitude for the punishment of crime, whereof the party shall have been duly convicted shall in no wise be prohibited by this act.

Section 8. That for all the purposes of this act the jurisdictional limits of Washington are extended to all parts of the District of Columbia not now included within the present limits of Georgetown.

Mr. LINCOLN then said, that he was authorized to say, that of about fifteen of the leading citizens of the District of Columbia to whom this proposition had been submitted, there was not one but who approved of the adoption of such a proposition. He did not wish to be misunderstood. He did not know whether or not they would vote for this bill on the first Monday of April; but he repeated, that out of fifteen persons to whom it had been submitted, he had authority to say that every one of them desired that some proposition like this should pass.[4]

[4] Three days later, on January 13, Lincoln gave notice of his intention to introduce the bill himself, his earlier effort having come to nothing. He never followed the announcement, however, and the document in the Lincoln Papers is doubtless the actual copy made for that purpose. Years later, in 1861, Lincoln explained that upon "finding that I was abandoned by my former backers and having little personal influence, I *dropped* the matter knowing that it was useless to prosecute the business at that time." (James Quay Howard's Notes on Lincoln, DLC-RTL).

To James M. McLean[1]

Friend McLean: Washington, Jan: 11. 1849.

Yours of the 1st. Inst. was received last night. I know [nothing?] as to what course the new administration will pursue in regard to the offices. I shall lay your letter by; and if the disposition of these offices falls into my hands, in whole or in part, you shall have a fair hearing. I believe you are the first who has written me in relation to the offices at Palestine. Yours truly   A. LINCOLN

[1] ALS, IHi. James M. McLean, Lawrence County Whig who had been in the legislature with Lincoln in 1840-1841.

To John Bennett[1]

Dear Bennett: Washington, Jan: 15 1849.
    Your letter of the 2nd. was received last night. I do not know
yet what places there may be to dispose of in California, nor what
share I may be allowed in disposing of them when the time comes,
but I shall especially remember you, and do something for you if
I can.

[1] AL, THaroL. The bottom of the page has been torn off this manuscript.

To James Berdan[1]

Dear Sir: Washington, Jany. 15. 1849
    Your letter of the 2nd. was received last night. I went this morn-
ing to the folding room, and made enquiry for the documents you
desire. They told me (what I had forgot) that our House has ordered the printing of 10.000 copies of Emory's and Abert's reports[2]
together, and that 8 copies for each member will be ready in about
two weeks. The first lot I receive, I will provide you and Mr. Harkness[3] out of. I was very glad to receive your letter, and shall be
pleased at any time to have another. We have the news here, that
Shields[4] was *nominated* for the Senate, from which we infer, that
he was elected, as a matter of course. How do you suppose this, as
a fruit of the glorious Mexican war, tastes to Breese, McClernand[5]
et al?. Do you suppose they are in a mood of *blessing* the war
about now?
    Write me again. Yours as ever—   A. LINCOLN

[1] ALS, RPB.
[2] Lieutenant William H. Emory and Lieutenant John J. Abert, "Notes of a
Military Reconnaissance, from Fort Leavenworth, in Missouri [*sic*], to San
Diego, in California, and Map of Lieutenant Abert. . . ." Thirtieth Congress, *House Executive Document No. 41.*
[3] Probably James Harkness, a Jacksonville Whig.
[4] James Shields, who served as brigadier general of volunteers, was elected
to the Senate on January 13.
[5] Sidney Breese and John A. McClernand, also Democrats.

To Josiah B. Herrick[1]

Dear Doctor: Washington, Jan: 19. 1849
    Your letter from Chicago, recommending Wm. M. Black,[2] for
Register of the Land office at Vandalia, is received. Two others,
both good men, have applied for the same office before. I have made
no pledge; but if the matter falls into my hands, I shall, when the
time comes, try to do right, in view of all the lights then before

me. I do not feel authorized to advise any one of the applicants what course to pursue. Yours truly   A. LINCOLN

1 ALS-P, ISLA. Josiah B. Herrick had resided in Vandalia, but accepted a position on the faculty of the Rush Medical College in Chicago, where his brother William B. Herrick was professor of anatomy. He was succeeded in 1850 by Dr. Joseph W. Freer in his position as "demonstrator of anatomy."
2 James M. Davis, not William M. Black, received the appointment.

To Joseph Gales and William W. Seaton[1]

Messrs Gales & Seaton: House of Representatives
Gentlemen: Jan: 22. 1849

   Two drafts, one for $743 37/100 the other for $733 33/100, drawn by Thomas French,[2] and accepted by you, have been sent to me for collection. Please let me hear from you on the subject. Yours truly
                                          A. LINCOLN

1 ALS, CSmH. Gales and Seaton were publishers in Washington of the *National Intelligencer*, leading Whig newspaper.
2 French has not been identified.

To Henry E. Dummer[1]

Dear Dummer: [January 23? 1849]

   Your letter was received by me; and a copy of the body of it sent to the P.O.D. Then came the above & accompanying, which you will readily understand   A. LINCOLN

1 ALS, owned by Rev. Thomas W. Smith, San Carlos, California. This note is written on the bottom of a letter from R. A. Lacey of the Post Office Department Appointment Office, dated January 22, 1849. Lacey requests Lincoln to transmit enclosures concerning appointment of a new postmaster at Beardstown, Illinois, to "some neighboring Postmaster—or other reliable person," who will notify citizens to send in expressions of their wishes concerning a new appointment.

To John Murray[1]

My dear Sir: Washington, Jan: 27– 1849–

   Your letter, in relation to the office of Marshall, was received last night. You are not mistaken, in so far as you may suppose, I entertain the strongest personal friendship for you; but I have more than one application for the same office, before yours, appealing to my feelings in the same way. I know not what control of this matter may fall into my hands; and I can only say now that I will lay your letter by, and, when the time comes, give your claim, among others, that consideration, which is due to impartiality, fairness, and friendship. Yours as ever   A. LINCOLN—

1 ALS, owned by Mrs. H. L. Murray, Minneapolis, Minnesota. John Murray was a Whig of Belleville, Illinois, who served in the Illinois Senate in 1836-1840.

To William Schouler[1]

Friend Schooler: Washington, Feb. 2. 1849

In these days of Cabinet making, we out West are awake as well as others. The accompanying article is from the Illinois Journal,[2] our leading whig paper; and while it expresses what all,[3] the whigs of the Legislatures of Illinois, Iowa, and Wisconsin have expressed —a preference for Col. Baker—I think it is fair and magnanamous to the other Western aspirants; and, on the whole shows by sound argument, that the West is not only entitled to, but is in need of, one member of the cabinet. Desiring to turn public attention, in some measure to this point, I shall be obliged if you will give the article a place in your paper, with or without comments, according to your own sense of propriety.

Our acquaintance, though short, has been very cordial; and I therefore venture to hope you will not consider my request presumptious, whether you shall or shall not think proper to grant it.

This I intend as private and confidential. Yours truly

A. LINCOLN

1 ADfS, DLC-RTL.
2 Articles promoting Baker for a cabinet post appeared in the *Journal* for December 20, 1848, and January 3 and 24, 1849.
3 A phrase is deleted at this point as follows: "or at least nearly all the Illinois whigs feel"—and the phrase inserted as it stands.

To William A. Crafts[1]

Wm. A. Crafts, Esq   Washington,
Dear Sir: Feb. 6. 1849

Yours of the 31st. of Jany. was received two or three days since. I know Mr. Asahel Thayer,[2] and have the impression that he is not able to pay any thing. Besides his brother Martin Thayer, of Philadelphia, he has a brother, Joseph Thayer, at Springfield, Illinois, who is pecuniarily, in good circumstances. Still, my impression of Asahel is as I have stated; but, lest I be mistaken, I send your letter to a friend in Springfield, with the request that he will ascertain the material facts and write you. Your Obt. Servt.

A. LINCOLN

1 ALS, MH. There are two docketings on the verso: "F.D. Crafts matter" and "Crafts & Thayer." Efforts to identify Crafts have been unsuccessful.
2 Asahel Thayer resided in Morgan County, Illinois.

Remarks in U. S. House of Representatives
Concerning Disposal of the Public Lands[1]

February 13, 1849

Mr. LINCOLN said he had not risen for the purpose of making a speech, but only for the purpose of meeting some of the objections to the bill.[2] If he understood those objections, the first was, that if the bill were to become a law, it would be used to lock large portions of the public lands from sale, without at last effecting the ostensible object of the bill—the construction of railroads in the new States; and secondly, that Congress would be forced to the abandonment of large portions of the public lands to the States for which they might be reserved, without their paying for them. This he understood to be the substance of the objections of the gentleman from Ohio[3] to the passage of the bill.

If he could get the attention of the House for a few minutes, he would ask gentlemen to tell us what motive could induce any State Legislature, or individual, or company of individuals, of the new States to expend money in surveying roads which they might know they could not make? [A VOICE: They are not required to make the road.]

Mr. LINCOLN, (continuing.) That was not the case he was making. What motive would tempt any set of men to go into an expensive survey of a railroad, which they did not intend to make? What good would it do? Did men act without motive? Did business men commonly go into an expenditure of money, which could be of no account to them? He generally found that men who have money were disposed to hold on to it, unless they could see something to be made by its investment. He could not see what motive of advantage to the new States could be subserved by merely keeping the public lands out of market, and preventing their settlement. As far as he could see, the new States were wholly without any motive to do such a thing. This, then, he took to be a good answer to the first objection.

In relation to the fact assumed, that, after a while, the new States having got hold of the public lands to a certain extent, they would turn round and compel Congress to relinquish all claim to them, he had a word to say, by way of recurring to the history of the past. When was the time to come (he asked) when the States in which the public lands were situated would compose a majority of the representation in Congress, or anything like it? A majority of Representatives would very soon reside west of the mountains, he admitted; but would they all come from States in which the

[26]

public lands were situated? They certainly would not; for, as these western States grew strong in Congress, the public lands passed away from them, and they got on the other side of the question: and the gentleman from Ohio [Mr. VINTON] was an example attesting that fact.

Mr. VINTON interrupted here to say, that he had stood upon this question just where he was now, for five-and-twenty years.

Mr. LINCOLN was not making an argument for the purpose of convicting the gentleman of any impropriety at all. He was speaking of a fact in history, of which his State was an example. He was referring to a plain principle in the nature of things. The State of Ohio had now grown to be a giant. She had a large delegation on that floor; but was she now in favor of granting lands to the new States, as she used to be? The New England States, New York, and the Old Thirteen, were all rather quiet upon the subject; and it was seen just now that a member from one of the new States was the first man to rise up in opposition. And so it would be with the history of this question for the future. There never would come a time when the people residing in the States embracing the public lands would have the entire control of this subject; and so it was a matter of certainty that Congress would never do more in this respect than what would be dictated by a just liberality. The apprehension, therefore, that the public lands were in danger of being wrested from the General Government by the strength of the delegation in Congress from the new States, was utterly futile. There never could be such a thing. If we take these lands (said he) it will not be without your consent. We can never outnumber you. The result is, that all fear of the new States turning against the right of Congress to the public domain must be effectually quelled, as those who are opposed to that interest must always hold a vast majority here, and they will never surrender the whole or any part of the public lands unless they themselves choose so to do. That was all he desired to say.

[1] *Congressional Globe*, Thirtieth Congress, Second Session, p. 533.
[2] Senate bill No. 415, "An act to grant the right of way across the public lands, and to dispose of said land in aid of the several States in the construction of railroads and canals."　[3] Samuel F. Vinton.

To William Brown and Richard Yates[1]

Messrs. Brown & Yates　　　　　　　　　　　　Washington,
Gentlemen:　　　　　　　　　　　　　　　　　Feb. 19. 1849

Your letter, enclosing the papers for Bounty land & Extra pay for Mrs. Eliza Pearson, was received saturday night. This (monday) morning I went to the Pension office, filed the Bounty land papers; went to the Pay Master, and had the claim for extra pay rejected, because the proof of *two* witnesses that Mrs. Pearson, is the widow of the soldier—which proof, they say, is indispensable. I went back to the Pension office to see if the papers left there might not supply the proof, but the office was so full, I could get no chance. I shall try it again tomorrow morning. Yours as ever

A. LINCOLN

1 ALS, owned by E. Warfield Brown, Jacksonville, Illinois.

Endorsement on a Petition Concerning Conrad Summers[1]

[February 19, 1849]

The petition of citizens of Woodford county Illinois, in behalf of Conrad Summers—

I personally know Conrad Summers, named in, this petition, that he is blind, and that most of the statements of said petition are true.

A LINCOLN

1 AES, DNA RG 233, HR 30A F 18 (6), Committee on Public Lands.

To Joshua F. Speed[1]

Dear Speed: Washington, Feb: 20. 1849.

Your letter of the 13th. was received yesterday. I showed it to Baker.[2] I did this because he knew I had written you, and was expecting an answer; and he still enquired what I had received; so that I could not well keep it a secret. Besides this, I knew the contents of the letter would not affect him as you seemed to think it would. He knows he did not make a favorable impression while in Congress, and he and I had talked it over frequently. He tells me to write you that he has too much self-esteem to be put out of humor with himself by the opinion of any man who does not know him better than Mr. Crittenden[3] does; and that he thinks you ought to have known it. The letter will not affect him the least in regard to either Mr. Crittenden or you. He understands you to have acted the part of a discreet friend; and he intends to make Mr. Crittenden think better of him, hereafter. I am flattered to learn that Mr. Crittenden has any recollection of me which is not unfavorable; and for the manifestation of your kindness towards me, I sincerely thank you. Still there is nothing about me which would authorize me to think of a first class office; and a second class one would not compensate me for being snarled at by others who want it for themselves. I believe that, so far as the whigs in congress, are concerned, I could have the Genl. Land office almost by common consent; but then Sweet,[4] and Don: Morrison,[5] and Browning,[6] and Cyrus Edwards all want it. And what is worse, while I think I could easily take it myself, I fear I shall have trouble to get it for any other man in Illinois. The reason is, that McGaughey,[7] an Indiana ex-member of congress is here after it; and being personally known, he will be hard to beat by any one who is not.

Baker showed me your letter, in which you make a passing allusion to the Louisville Post-Office. I have told Garnett Duncan[8] I am for you. I like to open a letter of yours, and I therefore hope you will write me again on the receipt of this.

Give my love, to Mrs. Speed. Yours as ever   A. LINCOLN

P.S. I have not read the Frankfort papers this winter; and consequently do not know whether you have made a speech. If you have, and it has been printed send me a copy.   A. L.

[1] ALS, MeHi.   [2] Edward D. Baker.   [3] John J. Crittenden.
[4] Martin P. Sweet, a Whig of Freeport, Illinois.
[5] James L. D. Morrison, a St. Clair County Whig who had been United States representative in the Twenty-eighth Congress.
[6] Orville H. Browning.   [7] Edward W. McGaughey.
[8] William Garnett Duncan, representative from Kentucky.

To Charles R. Welles[1]

C. R. Welles, Esq.   Washington,
Dear Sir: Feb: 20. 1849

This is tuesday evening, and your letter enclosing the one of Young & Brothers[2] to you, saying the money you sent by me to them had not been received, came to hand last saturday night. The facts, which are perfectly fresh in my recollection, are these: you gave me the money in a letter (open I believe) directed to Young & Brothers. To make it more secure than it would be in my hat, where I carry most all my packages, I put it in my trunk. I had a great many jobs to do in St. Louis; and by the very extra care I had taken of yours, overlooked it. On the Steam Boat near the mouth of the Ohio, I opened the trunk, and discovered the letter. I then began to cast about for some safe hand to send it back by. Mr. Yeatman,[3] Judge Pope's son-in-law, and step-son of Mr. Bell of Tennessee, was on board, and was to return immediately to St. Louis from the Mouth of Cumberland. At my request, he took the letter and promised to deliver it—and I heard no more about it till I received your letter on saturday. It so happens that Mr. Yeatman is now in this city; I called on him last night about it; he said he remembered my giving him the letter, and he could remember nothing more of it. He told me he would try to refresh his memory, and see me again concerning it to-day—which however he has not done. I will try to see him to-morrow and write you again. He is a young man, as I understand, of unquestioned, and unquestionable character; and this makes me fear some pick-pocket on the boat may have seen me give him the letter, and slipped it from him. In this way, never seeing the letter again, he would, naturally enough, never think of it again. Yours truly   A. LINCOLN

¹ ALS, IHi. Charles R. Welles was a lawyer and land agent in Springfield, representing John Grigg of Philadelphia, investor in western lands.
² A St. Louis banking firm.
³ Prominent St. Louis business men, Thomas Yeatman and James E. Yeatman were brothers who married the sisters Lucretia and Cynthia Ann Pope, daughters of Judge Nathaniel Pope. The widowed mother of the Yeatman brothers had married Senator John Bell. Since, according to the *Dictionary of American Biography*, James did not marry Cynthia until May 5, 1851, it would seem that Lincoln here refers to Thomas Yeatman.

To Zachary Taylor¹

Gen. Taylor.   House of Representatives
Dear Sir: Feb: 27. 1849
    Yesterday you were so kind as to say it would be convenient for you to receive the papers reccommending Col. Baker for a Cabinet appointment, through the mail. I herewith transmit them in that way, with the request, that my name be considered as added to the recommendation. Your Obt. Servt.   A. LINCOLN

¹ ALS, DNA FS RG 59, Appointment Papers.

To Zachary Taylor¹

[c. February 27, 1849]
I have such evidence as enables me to say I know the within recommendation was signed by all the Whig members of the Illinois Legislature   A. LINCOLN

¹ AES, DNA FS RG 59, Appointment Papers. Lincoln's endorsement is written on a letter signed by Whig members of the Illinois legislature, January 1, 1849, recommending Edward D. Baker for appointment to the cabinet.

To John M. Clayton[1]

Hon: John M. Clayton   Washington,
Secretary of State.   March 8. 1849

Dear Sir: On the other half of this sheet is a copy of a recommendation, that Anson G. Henry of Springfield, Illinois, be appointed Secretary of the Teritory of Minesota. In their confidence and kindness in and for Col. Baker and myself, fortynine of the whig members of the H.R. have signed it, they being nearly all to whom it was presented. I am *exceedingly* anxious, the appointment of Dr. Henry shall be made; and fearing the place may be filled before I can see you personally, must be my excuse for troubling you in this way. On other matters I am anxious to a common degree; but on *this,* my solicitude is extreme. Your Obt. Servt.

A. LINCOLN.

[1] ALS, DNA FS RG 59, Appointments. See further, Lincoln to Clayton, November 25, *infra.*

To John M. Clayton[1]

Hon: John M. Clayton   Washington,
Secretary of State.   March 8. 1849

Dear Sir: We recommend that Archibald Williams, of Quincy, Illinois, be appointed U.S. District Attorney for the District of Illinois, when that office shall become vacant. Your Obt. Servts.

A. LINCOLN

[1] ALS, DNA FS RG 59, Appointment Papers. On the bottom of this letter is the following endorsement: "I beg leave to urge this particularly E D Baker." Williams received the appointment.

To Thomas Ewing[1]

Hon: Thomas Ewing   Washington,
Secretary of the Home Department: March 9. 1849

Dear Sir: We recommend that Matthew Gillespie[2] be appointed to fill the Land-office now, or soon to be, vacant at Edwardsville, Illinois. Your Obt. Servts.

A. LINCOLN

E. D. BAKER

[1] ALS, IHi.
[2] An older brother of Lincoln's friend Joseph Gillespie. He received the appointment.

[31]

To William M. Meredith[1]

COPY.

Hon: Secretary of the Treasury.   Washington,

Dear Sir: March. 9. 1849.

 Col. E. D. Baker and myself are the only Whig members of congress from Illinois—I, of the 30th. & he of the 31st. We have reason to think the whigs of that state hold us responsible, to some extent, for the appointments which may be made of our citizens. We do not know you personally; and our efforts to see you have, so far, been unavailing. I therefore hope I am not obtrusive in saying, in this way, for him and myself, that when a citizen of Illinois is to be appointed in your Department to an office either in or out of the state, we most respectfully ask to be heard. Your Obt. Servt.

             A. LINCOLN

 [1] ADfS, DLC-RTL.

Application for Patent
on an Improved Method of Lifting Vessels over Shoals[1]

            March 10, 1849

To the Commissioner of Patents.[2]

 The Petition of Abraham Lincoln, of Springfield in the county of Sangamon & State of Illinois

 Respectfully represents.

 That your petitioner has invented a new and improved manner of combining adjustable buoyant chambers with steam boats or other vessels which has not, as he verily believes been heretofore used or known, and that he is desirous that Letters Patent of the United States may be granted to him therefor, securing to him and to his legal representatives, the exclusive right of making and using, and of vending to others the privilege to make or use, the same, agreeably to the provisions of the Acts of Congress in that case made and provided, he having paid thirty dollars into the Treasury of the United States, and complied with other provisions of the said Acts.

 And he hereby authorises and empowers his Agent and Attorney, Z. C. ROBBINS, to alter or modify the within specification and claim as he may deem expedient, and to receive his patent; and

 [1] DS, DNA IR RG 241, Records of the Patent Office, Patented File, No. 6469. Only Lincoln's signatures are in his hand. The drawing is now missing from the file, but is reproduced from Nicolay and Hay, *Abraham Lincoln: A History.*
 [2] Edmund Burke was Commissioner of Patents.

also to receive back any moneys which he may be entitled to withdraw, and to receipt for the same.   A. LINCOLN.

County of Washington ⎱
District of Columbia ⎰ SS.

On this 10th. day of March 1849 before the subscriber, a Jus Peace in and for the said county personally appeared the within named Abraham Lincoln and made solemn oath according to law, that he believes himself to be the original and first inventor of the within described improved manner of combining buoyant chambers with steam boats or other vessels and that he does not know or believe that the same has been before used or known; and that he is a citizen of the United States.   I L. SMITH, JP

To all whom it may concern:

Be it known that I, Abraham Lincoln, of Springfield, in the county of Sangamon, in the state of Illinois, have invented a new and improved manner of combining adjustable buoyant air chambers with a steam boat or other vessel for the purpose of enabling their draught of water to be readily lessened to enable them to pass over bars, or through shallow water, without discharging their cargoes; and I do hereby declare the following to be a full, clear, and exact description thereof, reference being had to the accompanying drawings making a part of this specification. Similar letters indicate like parts in all the figures.

The buoyant chambers A. A. which I employ, are constructed in such a manner that they can be expanded so as to hold a large volume of air when required for use, and can be contracted, into a very small space and safely secured as soon as their services can be dispensed with.

Fig. 1. is a side elevation of a vessel with the buoyant chambers combined therewith, expanded;

Fig. 2. is a transverse section of the same with the buoyant chambers contracted.

Fig. 3. is a longitud[i]nal vertical section through the centre of one of the buoyant chambers, and the box B. for receiving it when contracted, which is secured to the lower guard of the vessel.

The top g, and bottom h, of each buoyant chamber, is composed of plank or metal, of suitable strength and stiffness, and the flexible sides and ends of the chambers, are composed of india-rubber cloth, or other suitable water proof fabric, securely united to the edges and ends of the top and bottom of the chambers.

The sides of the chambers may be stayed and supported centrally by a frame k,—as shown in Fig. 3,—or as many stays may be combined with them as may be necessary to give them the requisite fullness and strength when expanded.

The buoyant chambers are suspended and operated as follows: a suitable number of vertical shafts or spars D.D. are combined with each of the chambers, as represented in Fig. 1, 2 & 3; to wit: the shafts work freely in apertures formed in the upper sides of the chambers, and their lower ends are permanently secured to the under sides of the chambers: the vertical shafts or spars (D.D.) pass up through the top of the boxes B.B. on the lower guards of the vessel, and then through its upper guards, or some other suitable support, to keep them in a vertical position.

The vertical shaft (D.D.) are connected to the main shaft C, which passes longitudinally through the centre of the vessel—just below its upper deck,—by endless ropes f. f. as represented in Fig 2: the said ropes f.f. being wound several times around the main shaft C, then passing outwards over sheaves or rollers attached to the upper deck or guards of the vessel, from which they descend along the inner sides of the vertical shafts or spars D. D. to sheaves or rollers connected to the boxes B. B. and thence rise to the main shaft (C,) again.

The ropes f.f. are connected to the vertical shafts at i.i. as shown in Figs. 1. & 2. It will therefore be perceived, that by turning the main shaft C. in one direction, the buoyant chambers will be expanded into the position shown in Fig. 1; and by turning the shaft in an opposite direction, the chamber will be contracted into the position shown in Fig. 2.

In Fig. 3. e,e, are check ropes made fast to the tops of the boxes B, B, and to the upper sides of the buoyant chambers; which ropes catch and retain the upper sides of the chambers when their lower sides are forced down, and cause the chambers to be expanded to their full capacity. By varying the length of the check ropes, the depth of immersion of the buoyant chambers can be governed. A suitable number of openings m, m, are formed in the upper sides of the buoyant chambers, for the admission and emission of air when the chambers are expanded and contracted.

The ropes f.f. that connect the main shaft C, with the shafts or spars D. D. (rising from the buoyant chambers,) may be passed from one to the other in any direction that may be deemed best, and that will least incommode the deck of the vessel; or other mechanical means may be employed as the medium of communication between the main shaft and the buoyant chambers, if it should be found expedient. I shall generally make the main shaft C. in as many parts as there are corresponding pairs of buoyant chambers, so that by coupling the sections of the shaft together, the whole of

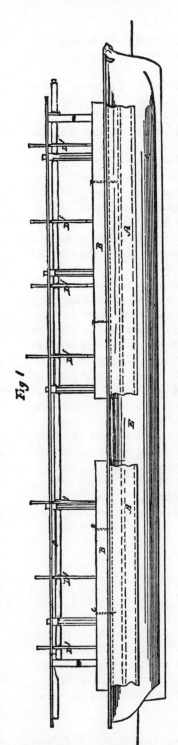

Fig 1

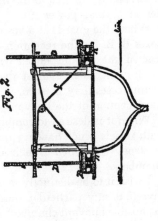

Fig 3

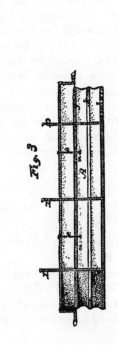

Fig 2

A LINCOLN'S IMP'd MANNER OF BUOYING VESSELS.—

Patented 22 May 1849.—

From Nicolay and Hay, *Abraham Lincoln: A History*

the chambers can be expanded at the same time, and by disconnecting them, either pair of chambers can be expanded, separately from the others as circumstances may require.

The buoyant chambers may be operated by the power of the steam engine applied to the main shaft C, in any convenient manner, or by man power.

Where the guards of a vessel are very high above the water, the boxes B. B. for the reception of the buoyant chambers when contracted, may be dispenced with, and the chambers be contracted by drawing them against the under side of the guards. Or, protecting cases may be secured to the under sides of the guards for the reception of the buoyant chambers when contracted.

When it is desired to combine my expansible buoyant chambers with vessels which have no projecting guards; shelves or cases must be strongly fastened to their sides for the reception of the buoyant chambers.

I wish it to be distinctly understood, that I do not intend to limit myself to any particular mechanical arrangement, in combining expansible buoyant chambers with a vessel, but shall vary the same as I may deem expedient, whilst I attain the same end by substantially the same means. What I claim as my invention and desire to secure by letters patent, is the combination of expansible buoyant chambers placed at the sides of a vessel, with the main shaft or shafts C, by means of the sliding spars, or shafts D, which pass down through the buoyant chambers and are made fast to their bottoms, and the series of ropes and pullies, or their equivalents, in such a manner that by turning the main shaft or shafts in one direction, the buoyant chambers will be forced downwards into the water and at the same time expanded and filled with air for buoying up the vessel by the displacement of water; and by turning the shaft in an opposite direction, the buoyant chambers will be contracted into a small space and secured against injury.

Witness   z. c. robbins   A. Lincoln
           h. h. sylvester

To John M. Clayton[1]

COPY.

Hon: Secretary of State   Washington,
Dear Sir: March 10. 1849

There are several applicants for the office of U. S. Marshall for the District of Illinois, among the most prominent of whom are Benjamin Bond, Esq. of Carlyle, and ——— Thomas,[2] Esq, of Galena. Mr. Bond I know to be, personally, every way worthy of the office;

and he is very numerously, and most respectably recommended. His papers I send to you; and I solicit for his claims, a full and fair consideration. Having said this much, I add that in my individual judgment, the appointment of Mr. Thomas would be the better. Your Obt. Servt. A. LINCOLN

(Endorsed on Mr. Bond's papers)

In this and the accompanying envelope, are the recommendations of about 200 good citizens of all parts of Illinois that *Benjamin Bond* be appointed Marshall for that District. They include the names of nearly all our whigs who now are, or have ever been, members of the state Legislature, besides 46 of the democratic members of the present Legislature, and many other good citizens. I add that, from personal knowledge, I consider Mr. Bond every way worthy of the office, and qualified to fill it. Holding the individual opinion that the appointment of a different gentleman would be better, I ask *especial* attention and consideration for his claims, and for the opinions expressed in his favor, by those over whom I can claim no superiority. A. LINCOLN

1 ADfS, DLC-RTL; ADS, DNA FS RG 59, Appointments. In addition to this letter and document, there is in the Lincoln Papers a second copy of the letter in Lincoln's hand bearing the date March 11, but without the additional statement "Endorsed on Mr. Bond's papers." The letter of March 11 was intended to accompany the endorsed envelope for the Secretary of State, but was withheld, purposely or unintentionally, when the accompanying endorsed envelope containing recommendations was sent.

2 Charles G. Thomas. See Lincoln's receipt to the Department of Interior, June 22, 1849, *infra*, Appendix I, volume VIII. Benjamin Bond received the appointment, but not until 1850.

Endorsement
Edward D. Baker to Nathaniel G. Wilcox[1]

[March 14, 1849]

If Mr. Wilcox[2] can receive the appointment above indicated, I shall be truly and heartily gratified. From at least one severe test, I have seen him subjected to, I consider him a gentleman of the highest sense of honor, besides possessing all the other requisite qualifications. A. LINCOLN.

1 Certified copy, ICU. Lincoln's endorsement was written on the bottom of Baker's letter to Wilcox, March 14, 1849, which stated "We desire this to stand as our recommendation of your appointment to a Pursership in the Navy." The original document has not been located; on December 9, 1865, it was in the possession of Wilcox. Certification of the copy, dated February 23, 1861, is signed by W. W. Lester, acting chief clerk, Department of the Interior.

2 Nathaniel G. Wilcox was a Schuyler County, Illinois, Whig, unsuccessful candidate for lieutenant governor (1846) and congress (1847).

Endorsement: Edward D. Baker to
John M. Clayton[1]

[March 20, 1849]

Private & confidential

I have heard the foregoing letter of Col. Baker read; and from a long personal & intimate acquaintance with him, if the plan he proposes is at all practicable, I think, he would be the very man to execute it. [Your Obt. Servt.   A. LINCOLN[2]]

Hon. J. M. Clayton.

[1] AE, DLC-John M. Clayton Papers. Baker wrote from Louisville, Kentucky, on March 20, 1849, proposing that a reliable Whig should be sent to California to assist in organizing the territory and gaining its admission to the Union *"at once,"* as a Whig state. He set forth his own qualifications and expressed his willingness to go.

[2] Close and signature have been cut off but copied below in pencil, presumably by the autograph collector.

To John M. Clayton[1]

Hon J. M. Clayton   St. Louis, Mo.
Secretary of State   March 26. 1849

Dear Sir: I take great pleasure in introducing to your acquaintance my good personal and political friend Benjamin Bond Esq. He is an applicant for the office of Marshall for Illinois; and previous to leaving Washington, I filed his recommendations, with my indorsement upon them to which I refer you. What I there say in his favor, I take great pleasure in repeating. Your obt. Servt.

A. LINCOLN.

[1] ALS, DNA FS RG 59, Appointments. See Lincoln to Clayton, March 10, *supra.*

To John M. Johnson[1]

[c. March 26, 1849]

Post-Master of the H.R.   St. Louis, Mo.

Dear Sir: The bearer of this, Benjamin Bond, Esq, supposes that some letters addressed to me and Col. Baker, or to me alone by him, may now be in your office. I therefore request you will permit him to look over all letters in your hands, to me or to me & Baker, and deliver to him all such as he may say are addressed in his hand writing. Your obt. Servt.   A LINCOLN

[1] ALS, DNA FS RG 59, Appointments.

Petition For Appointment of Robert Allen[1]

[c. April, 1849]

The undersigned Members of the Bar of the State of Illinois desire and would respectfully recommend Col: Robert Allen the appointment of U: S: Marshal for the District of Illinois aforesaid

A. Lincoln (If new appointment is made).

[1] DS, DNA FS RG 59, Appointments. Sixteen signatures appear on the petition, of which Lincoln's signature and endorsement are in fourth place. Lincoln must have signed this petition some time after his return to Springfield on March 31.

To Jacob Collamer[1]

C O P Y.

Hon: Post-Master-General: Springfield, Ills.
Dear Sir: April 7, 1849

I recommend that Abner Y. Ellis[2] be appointed Post-Master at this place, whenever there shall be a vacancy. J. R. Diller, the present incumbent, I can not say has failed in the proper discharge of any of the duties of the office. He, however, has been an active partizan in opposition to us. Located at the Seat of Government of the State, he has been, for part, if not the whole of the time he has held the office, a member of the Democratic State Central Committee, signing his name to their addresses and manifestos; and has been, as I understand, re-appointed by Mr. Polk since Gen: Taylor's election. These are the facts of the case as I understand them, and I give no opinion of mine as to whether he should or should not be removed. My wish is that the Department may adopt some proper general rule for such cases, and that Mr. Diller may not be made an exception to it, one way or the other. Your Obt. Servt.

A LINCOLN

P.S. This office, with it's delivery, is entirely within my district; so that Col. Baker, the other whig representative, claims no voice in the appointment.   A. L.

[1] ADfS, DLC-RTL.
[2] Ellis received the appointment as Lincoln recommended.

To Thomas Ewing[1]

Hon: Secretary of the Home Department: Springfield, Ills,
Dear Sir: April 7. 1849

I recommend that William Butler be appointed Pension Agent, for the Illinois agency, when the place shall be vacant. Mr. Hurst,[2]

[39]

the present incumbent, I believe has performed the duties very well. He is a decided partazan, and, I believe, expects to be removed. Whether he shall, I submit to the Department. This office is not confined to my District, but pertains to the whole state; so that Col. Baker has an equal right with myself to be heard concerning it. However, the office is located here; and I think it is not probable any one would desire to remove from a distance to take it. Your Obt. Servt.   A. LINCOLN

1 ALS (copy?), DLC-RTL. This document may be a copy or may be the original letter not sent. See memorandum of May 1 and letter to Ewing, May 10, *infra.*   2 Charles R. Hurst.

To Thomas Ewing[1]

Hon: Secretary of the Home Department: Springfield, Ills.
Dear Sir: April 7. 1849
I recommend that Walter Davis be appointed Receiver of the Land Office at this place, whenever there shall be a vacancy. I can not say that Mr. Herndon,[2] the present incumbent, has failed in the proper discharge of any of the duties of the office. He is a very warm partizan; and openly & actively opposed the election of Gen: Taylor. I also understand that since Gen: Taylor's election, he has received a re-appointment from Mr. Polk, his old commission not having expired. Whether this is true, the records of the Department will show. I may add that the whigs here, almost universally desire his removal. I give no opinion of my own, but state the facts, and express the hope that the Department will act in this, as in all other cases, on some proper general rule. Your Obt. Servt.
                                                                   A. LINCOLN
P.S. The land district to which this office belongs, is very nearly if not entirely within my district; so that Col. Baker, the other whig representative, claims no voice in the appointment.
                                                                   A. L.

1ALS, IHi; also ADfS, DLC-RTL.   2 Archer G. Herndon.

To Thomas Ewing[1]

Hon: Secretary of the Home Department: Springfield, Ills.
Dear Sir: April 7. 1849
I recommend that Turner R. King, now of Pekin, Ills be appointed Register of the Land-Office at this place, whenever there shall be a vacancy. I do not know that Mr. Barret,[2] the present

incumbent, has failed in the proper discharge of any of his duties in the office. He is a decided partazan, and openly and actively opposed the election of Gen: Taylor. I understand, too, that since the election of Gen: Taylor, Mr. Barret has received a reappointment from Mr. Polk, his old commission not having expired. Whether this be true, the records of the Department will show. Whether he should be removed I give no opinion; but merely express the wish that the Department may act upon some proper general rule, and that Mr. Barret's case may not be made an exception to it. Your Obt. Servt.   A. LINCOLN

P.S. The land district to which this office belongs is very nearly if not entirely within my district; so that Col. Baker, the other whig representative, claims no voice in the appointment.   A.L.

1 ALS, The Rosenbach Company, Philadelphia and New York; also ALS copy, DLC-RTL.   2 James W. Barrett held the office from 1842 to 1849.

To William B. Warren and Others[1]

Gentlemen: Springfield, Ills. April 7. 1849

In answer to your note concerning the General Land-Office I have to say that, if the office can be secured to Illinois by my consent to accept it, and not otherwise, I give that consent. Some months since I gave my word to secure the appointment to that office of Mr. Cyrus Edwards, if in my power, in case of a vacancy; and more recently I stipulated with Col. Baker that if Mr. Edwards and Col. J. L. D. Morrison could arrange with each other for one of them to withdraw, we would jointly recommend the other. In relation to these pledges, I must not only be chaste but above suspicion. If the office shall be tendered to me, I must be permitted to say "Give it to Mr. Edwards, or, if so agreed by them, to Col. Morrison, and I decline it; if not, I accept." With this understanding, you are at liberty to procure me the offer of the appointment if you can; and I shall feel complimented by your effort, and still more by it's success. It should not be overlooked that Col. Baker's position entitles him to a large share of control in this matter; however, one of your number, Col. Warren, knows that Baker has at all times been ready to recommend me, if I would consent. It must also be understood that if at any time, previous to an appointment being made, I shall learn that Mr. Edwards & Col. Morrison have agreed, I shall at once carry out my stipulation with Col. Baker, as above stated. Yours truly

Col. W. B. Warren, & others.   A. LINCOLN

[1] ALS copy, DLC-RTL. William B. Warren, Morgan County Whig, was distinguished as a major of militia in the Mormon War, and as major and lieutenant colonel of the First Regiment of Illinois Volunteers in the Mexican War.

To Thomas Ewing[1]

Hon: Secretary of the Home Department   Springfield, Ills.
Dear Sir: April 10. 1849

I have been requested to say something to the Department in relation to the Land offices and officers at Kaskaskia in this state. They are a great distance from me, and not in my district; so that my information is too limited to enable me to speak properly on the question. Cols. J. L. D. Morrison, and R. B. Servant[2] are two good and true men residing in the district; and I have concluded to indorse in advance, whatever they may concur in saying to the Department in relation to those offices. Your Obt. Servt.

    A. LINCOLN

[1] ALS, ORB.
[2] Richard B. Servant, who had been state senator from Randolph County when Lincoln was in the legislature.

To Thomas Ewing[1]

Hon: Secretary of the Home Department: Springfield, Ills.
Dear Sir: April 13– 1849

Under date of the 7th. Inst. I forwarded to you, in separate letters, recommendations that Walter Davis be *Receiver*, and Turner R. King *Register*, of the Land Office at this place. For a personal reason, of no consequence to the Department, I now wish to transpose those recommendations; so that Davis may stand for *Register*, and King for *Receiver*. Your Obt. Servt.   A LINCOLN

[1] ALS, IHi.

To William B. Preston[1]

Hon: W. B. Preston: Springfield, Ills.
Dear Sir: April 20. 1849.

No member of the cabinet knows so well as yourself, the great anxiety I felt for Gen: Taylor's election, and consequently none could so well appreciate my anxiety for the success of his administration. Therefore I address you. It is seen here that the government advertising, or a great part of it, is given to the Democratic papers. This gives offence to the Whig papers; and, if persisted in, will leave the administration without any newspaper support whatever. It causes, or will cause, the Whig editors to fall off, while the Democratic ones will not be brought in by it. I suppose Gen: Taylor, because both of his declarations, and his inclination, will not go the doctrine of removals very strongly; and hence the greater reason, when an office or a job is not already in democratic hands, that it should be given to a Whig. Even at this, full half the government patronage will still be in the hands of our opponents at the end of four years; and if still *less* than this is done for our friends, I think they will have just cause to complain, and I verily believe the administration can not be sustained. The enclosed paragraph is from the leading Whig paper in this state. I think it is injudicious, and should not have appeared; still there is no keeping men silent when they feel they are wronged by their friends. As the subject of this paragraph pertains to the War Department, I would have written Mr. Crawford,[2] but that it might have appeared obtrusive, I having no personal acquaintance with him. I am sure *you* will not be offended. Your Obt. Servt.

A. LINCOLN—

1 ALS, The Rosenbach Company, Philadelphia and New York.
2 George W. Crawford was secretary of war; William B. Preston, secretary of the navy.

To Josiah M. Lucas[1]

J. M. Lucas, Esq   Springfield Ills. April 25, 1849.

Dear Sir: Your letter of the 15th is just received. Like you, I fear the Land Office is not going as it should; but I know nothing I can do. In my letter written three days ago,[2] I told you the Department understands my wishes. As to Butterfield,[3] he is my personal friend, and is qualified to do the duties of the office; but of the quite one hundred Illinoisians, equally well qualified, I do not know one with less claims to it. In the first place, what you say about Lisle Smith,[4] is the first intimation I have had of any one man in Illinois desiring Butterfield to have any office. Now, I think if any thing be given the state, it should be so given as to gratify our friends, and to stimulate them to future exertions. As to Mr. Clay having recommended him, that is *"quid pro quo."* He fought for Mr. Clay against Gen Taylor to the bitter end as I understand; and I do not believe I misunderstand. Lisle Smith too, was a Clay delegate at Philadelphia; and against my most earnest entreaties, took the lead in filling two vacancies, from my own district with Clay men. It will now mortify me deeply if Gen.

Taylors administration shall trample all my wishes in the dust merely to gratify these men. Yours as ever   A. LINCOLN.

1 Copy, DLC-RTL. Copy bears Nicolay's endorsement: "A true copy J. G. N." Josiah M. Lucas was a clerk in the Land Office in Washington. He had former-ly resided in Jacksonville, Illinois, where he published the Whig paper, *Illinoisan*, and served one term as recorder of Morgan County.
2 Letter not extant.   3 Justin Butterfield of Chicago.
4 S. Lisle Smith, attorney and prominent Whig of Chicago.

To Philo H. Thompson[1]

Dear Thompson: Springfield April 25, 1849

A tirade is still kept up against me here for recommending T. R. King. This morning it is openly avowed that my supposed influence at Washington, shall be broken down generally, and King's prospects defeated in particular. Now what I have done in this matter, I have done at the request of you and some other friends in Tazewell; and I therefore ask you to either admit it is wrong, or come forward and sustain me. If the truth will permit, I propose that you sustain me in the following manner—copy the enclosed scrap in your own hand-writing, and get everybody (not three or four but three or four hundred) to sign it and then send it to me.[2] Also have six, eight or ten of our best known whig friends there, to write me individual letters, stating the truth in this matter, as they understand it. Dont neglect or delay in the matter. I understand information of an indictment having been found against him about three years ago, for gaming or keeping a gaming house has been sent to the Department. I shall try to take care of it at the Department till your action can be had and forwarded on. Yours as ever   A. LINCOLN

1 Copy, DLC-HW. Present location of original letter is not known; copy enclosed in letter of Thompson's son (Charles H.) to William H. Herndon, October 12, 1866. Philo H. Thompson was a merchant of Pekin, Illinois.
2 See letter to Thomas Ewing of May 10, 1849.

To Thomas Ewing[1]

Hon: Secretary of Home Department   Springfield, Ills.
Dear Sir: April 26 1849

Some time since I recommended to your Department, the appointment of Turner R. King and Walter Davis, to the Land Offices in this place. Several persons here, who desired these offices themselves, are finding great fault with the recommendations; and I learned this morning that charges against King have been, or are to be, forwarded to your Department. I write this to request that, if in this, or any other case, charges shall be sent against persons I have recommended, you will suspend action, and notify me. I will take pains to avoid imposing any unworthy man on the Department. Mr. King resides in the Land District, but sixty miles distant from me; and I recommended him to you, on the recommendation of his neighbors to me. I know him personally, and think him a good man; still my acquaintance with him is not intimate enough to warrant me in totally disregarding a charge against him. Accordingly I am making particular enquiry in the matter, and the Department shall know the result. I am not the less anxious in this matter because of knowing the principal object of the fault-finders, to be to stab me. Your Obt. Servt.

A. LINCOLN

[1] ALS-F, ISLA.

Memorandum Concerning John R. Jeffries[1]

[May 1, 1849?]

Tell Bond[2] that Linder[3] wishes John R. Jeffries appointed Deputy to take census for Coles.

[1] AD, DLC-RTL. This and the memorandum concerning William S. Wallace (*infra*) are pinned to the same sheet containing the notation, not in Lincoln's hand, "about May 1st 1849." With this sheet is a "true copy" initialed by Nicolay.　　[2] Probably Benjamin Bond.　　[3] Usher F. Linder.

Memorandum Concerning Orville Paddock and William S. Wallace[1]

[May 1, 1849?]

I have already recommended W. S. Wallace[2] for Pension Agent at this place. It is, however, due the truth, to say that Orville Paddock,[3] above recommended, is every way qualified for the office; and that the persons recommending him, are of our business men, and best whig citizens.

[1] AD, DLC-RTL. This slip of paper may have been a draft of an endorsement which Lincoln wrote on the bottom of a petition in favor of Paddock which he forwarded to the commissioner of pensions.

[2] Lincoln's recommendation of Wallace has not been found, the document having disappeared from the Interior Department files, but the covering jacket which remains in the file indicates that Wallace was appointed May 31, 1849. The letter recommending William Butler (*supra*, April 7) may never have been sent, Butler having refused the recommendation in hopes of obtaining the receivership of the land office for which Lincoln would not recommend him, and Lincoln's recommendation of Wallace may have been made instead of Butler.　　[3] Orville Paddock was a resident of Springfield.

To Caleb B. Smith[1]

Hon. C. B. Smith: Springfield, Ills.
Dear Sir: May 1. 1849

You remember my anxiety that Dr. A. G. Henry of this place, should be appointed Register of the Land Office at Minesota.

Since I left Washington, I have heard nothing of the matter. I suppose Mr. Evans[2] of Maine, and yourself are constantly together now. I incline to believe he remembers me, and would not hesitate to oblige me, where he conveniently could.

Now I will do twice as much for both of you, some time, if he and you will take some leisure moment to call on Mr. Ewing, and, in as graceful a way as possible, urge on him the appointment of Henry. I have always had a tolerably high hope that Mr. Ewing will appoint Henry, if he does not forget my peculiar anxiety about it.

Write me soon. Your friend as ever   A. LINCOLN

[1] ALS, CSmH.
[2] George Evans, ex-senator from Maine, and Caleb B. Smith, ex-representative from Indiana, were appointed by President Taylor to a board investigating claims of American citizens against Mexico.

To George W. Rives[1]

Hon: G. W. Rives   Springfield,
Dear Sir: May 7. 1849

Your letter of the 25th. ult was received on the 1st. Inst. You overrate my capacity to serve you. Not one man recommended by me has yet been appointed to any thing, little or big, except a few who had no opposition.

Besides this, at the very inauguration I commenced trying to get a Minesota appointment for Dr. Henry, and have not yet succeeded; and I would not now, lessen his chance, by recommending any living man for any thing in that Teritory. It is my recollection that you sent me an application to be P.M. at Paris. Am I mistaken? Very truly Yours   A. LINCOLN

[1] ALS, The American Academy of Arts and Letters, New York City. George W. Rives of Edgar County was seeking appointment as register of the land office in Minnesota.

To Thomas Ewing[1]

Hon: Secretary of the Interior—   Springfield, Ills.
Dear Sir: May 10th. 1849

I regret troubling you so often in relation to the Land Offices here; but I hope you will perceive the necessity of it, and excuse me. On the 7th. April I wrote you recommending Turner R. King for Register, and Walter Davis for Receiver. Subsequently I wrote you that, for a private reason, I had concluded to transpose them. That private reason was the request of an old personal friend,[2] who himself desired to be Receiver, but whom I felt it my duty to refuse a recommendation. He said if I would transpose King & Davis, he would be satisfied; I thought it a whim, but anxious to oblige him, I consented. Immediately he commenced an assault upon King's character, intending as I suppose, to defeat his appointment, and thereby secure another chance for himself. This double offence of bad faith to me, and slander upon a good man, is so totally outrageous, that I now ask to have King and Davis placed as I originally recommended—that is, King for Register and Davis for Receiver.

An effort is being made now to have Mr. Barret [sic], the present Register, retained. I have already said he has done the duties of the office well; and I now add he is a gentleman in the true sense. Still he submits to be the instrument of his party to injure us. His high character enables him to do this more effectually. Last year he presided at the convention which nominated the democratic candidate for congress in this District; and afterwards ran for the state Senate himself, not desiring the seat, but avowedly to aid and strengthen his party. He made speech after speech, with a degree of fierceness and coarseness, against Gen: Taylor, not quite consistent with his habitually gentlemanly deportment. At least one (& I think more) of those who are now trying to have him retained, was himself an applicant for this very office; and failing to get my recommendation, now takes this turn.

In writing you a third time in relation to these offices, I stated that I supposed charges had been forwarded to you against King, and that I would enquire into the truth of them. I now send you herewith what I suppose will be an ample defence against any such charges. I ask attention to all the papers, but particularly to the letter of Mr. David Mark[3] & the paper with the long list of names. *There is no mistake about King's being a good man.*[4] After the unjust assault upon him, and considering the just claims of Tazewell county, as indicated in the letters I enclose you, it would, in my opinon, be injustice, and withall, a blunder, not to appoint him, at least as soon as any one is appointed to either of the offices here. Your Obt. Servt.   A. LINCOLN

[1] ALS, DNA NR RG 48, Appointments; copy, DLC-RTL.
[2] See the letters to Ewing written on April 7 (*supra*). Presumably Lincoln refers to William Butler, who wanted the receivership, but was recommended for pension agent. Herndon relates (Herndon to Weik, January 15, 1886, DLC-HW) that as a result of this disagreement Butler and Lincoln did not speak for years.   [3] David Mark was a resident of Pekin, Illinois, King's home.
[4] See letter to Philo H. Thompson of April 25 (*supra*).

To John M. Clayton[1]

Hon: J. M. Clayton   Springfield, Ills.
Dear Sir: May 13. 1849

Permit me to introduce to your acquaintance my esteemed friend
Charles H. Constable, Esq. Mr. Constable is a Marylander by birth,
who came to our state ten years ago, has fought the whig battles
faithfully with us ever since, and is now a favorite with us all. He
thinks of being an applicant for Charge d' Affaires to one of the
South American States[2] and should he succeed, I, and I believe the
other whigs of the state, will be much gratified. Your Obt. Servt.

A. LINCOLN

[1] ALS, DNA FS RG 59, Appointment Papers. Charles H. Constable of Wayne
County, Illinois, had been Whig senator in the Illinois legislature 1844-1848.
Constable was not appointed.

[2] "Charge d'Affaires to one of the South American States" is not in Lincoln's
handwriting.

To John M. Clayton[1]

Hon: Secretary of State   Springfield, Ills.
Dear Sir: May 16. 1849

I learn that E. P. Oliphant, of Union Town, Pa. is a candidate for
the appointment of Chargé to Denmark. Several years ago Mr. Oliphant was a citizen of our town, and was a fellow soldier with us
in the "famed Black Hawk War." His success would afford me
sincere satisfaction. Your Obt. Servt.   A. LINCOLN

[1] ALS, DNA FS RG 59, Appointment Papers. Ethelbert P. Oliphant wrote
Lincoln from Union Town, Pennsylvania, on May 8, "I have the pleasure to
be informed by your letter of Jany 24th ult. that it will afford you great pleasure to aid me in the matter I have in view, to wit the chargé to Denmark. That
aid would come very seasonably at this time, as I am about to visit Washington
City, to see something in relation to that matter. If you and Mr Stuart could
feel at liberty to do me the favour to write to Genl. Taylor & forward it to him
or the Secy of State direct from your place you will place me under lasting obligations." (DLC-RTL). Lincoln's letter of January 24, 1849, is presumably not
extant. No record has been found of Oliphant's appointment.

To William B. Preston[1]

Hon: W. B. Preston: Springfield, Ills.
Dear Sir: May 16. 1849

It is a delicate matter to oppose the wishes of a friend; and consequently I address you on the subject I now do, with no little hesitation. Last night I received letters from different persons at Washington assuring me it was not improbable that Justin Butterfield,

of Chicago, Ills, would be appointed Commissioner of the Genl. Land-Office. It was to avert this very thing, that I called on you at your rooms one sunday evening shortly after you were installed, and besought you that, so far as in your power, no man from Illinois should be appointed to any high office, without my being at least heard on the question. You were kind enough to say you thought my request a reasonable one. Mr. Butterfield is my friend, is well qualified, and, I suppose, would be faithful in the office. So far, good. But now for the objections. In 1840 we fought a fierce and laborious battle in Illinois, many of us spending almost the entire year in the contest. The general victory came, and with it, the appointment of a set of drones, including this same Butterfield, who had never spent a dollar or lifted a finger in the fight. The place he got was that of District Attorney. The defection of Tyler came, and then B. played off and on, and kept the office till after Polk's election. Again, winter and spring before the last, when you and I were almost sweating blood to have Genl. Taylor nominated, this same man was ridiculing the idea, and going for Mr. Clay; and when Gen: T. was nominated, if he went out of the city of Chicago to aid in his election, it is more than I ever heard, or believe. Yet, when the election is secured, by other men's labor, and even against his effort, why, he is the first man on hand for the best office that our state lays any claim to. Shall this thing be? Our whigs will throw down their arms, and fight no more, if the fruit of their labor is thus disposed of. If there is one man in this state who desires B's appointment to any thing, I declare I have not heard of him. What influence opperates for him, I can not conceive. Your position makes it a matter of peculiar interest to you, that the administration shall be successful; and be assured, nothing can more endanger it, than making appointments through old-hawker foreign influences, which offend, rather than gratify, the people immediately interested in the offices.

Can you not find time to write me, even half as long a letter as this? I shall be much gratified if you will. Your Obt. Servt.

A. LINCOLN

1 ALS, The Rosenbach Company, Philadelphia and New York.

To Duff Green[1]

Dear General: Springfield, Ills. May 18. 1849

I learn from Washington that a man by the name of Butterfield will probably be appointed Commissioner of the General Land-Office. This ought not to be. That is about the only crumb of patronage which Illinois expects; and I am sure the mass of Gen: Taylor's friends here, would quite as lief see it go East of the Alleghanies, or West of the Rocky mountains, as into that man's hands. They are already sore on the subject of his getting office. In the great contest of /40 he was not seen or heard of; but when the victory came, three or four old drones, including him, got all the valuable offices, through what influence no one has yet been able to tell. I believe the only time he has been very active, was last spring a year [ago], in opposition to Gen: Taylor's nomination.

Now can not you get the ear of Gen: Taylor? Ewing is for B; and therefore he must be avoided. Preston I think will favor you. Mr. Edwards[2] has written me offering to decline, but I advised him not to do so. Some kind friends think I ought to be an applicant; but I am for Mr. Edwards. Try to defeat B; and in doing so, use Mr. Edwards, J. L. D. Morrison, or myself, whichever you can to best advantage. Write me, and let this be confidential. Yours truly

A. LINCOLN

[1] ALS, CSmH. The ubiquitous Duff Green was living in Washington at this time and had been lately appointed agent for the United States in settling payments to Mexico under the treaty of Guadalupe Hidalgo.
[2] Cyrus Edwards.

To Joseph Gillespie[1]

Dear Gillespie: Springfield, Ills. May 19. 1849

Butterfield will be Commissioner of the Genl. Land Office, unless prevented by strong and speedy efforts. Ewing is for him; and he is only not appointed yet because Old Zach hangs fire. I have reliable information of this. Now, if you agree with me, that his appointment would *dissatisfy*, rather than gratify the whigs of this state; that it would slacken their energies in future contests, that his appointment in /41 is an old sore with them which they will not patiently have re-opened—in a word, that his appointment now would be a fatal blunder to the administration, and our political ruin here in Ills—write Mr. Crittenden to that effect. He can control the matter. Were you to write Ewing, I fear the President would never hear of your letter. This may be mere suspicion. You might write directly to Old Zach; you will be the judge of the propriety of that. Not a moment's time is to be lost. Let this be confidential, except with Mr. Edwards & a few others, whom you know I would trust just as I do you. Yours as ever   A. LINCOLN

[1] ALS, RPB.

To Elisha Embree[1]

CONFIDENTIAL

Hon E. Embree   Springfield, Ills.
Dear Sir: May 25– 1849

I am about to ask a favor of you—one which, I hope will not cost you much. I understand the General Land Office is about to be given to Illinois; and that Mr. Ewing desires Justin Butterfield, of Chicago, to be the man. I give you my word, the appointment of Mr. B. will be an egregious political blunder. It will give offence to the whole whig party here, and be worse than a dead loss to the administration, of so much of it's patronage. Now, if you can conscientiously do so, I wish you to write General Taylor at once, saying that either *I, or the man I recommend*, should, in your opinion, be appointed to that office, if any one from Illinois shall be. I restrict my request to Ills. because you may have a man of your own, in your own state; and I do not ask to interfere with that. Your friend as ever   A. LINCOLN

1 ALS, owned by Mrs. Howard Taylor, Temecula, California. Elisha Embree was an Indiana Whig, member with Lincoln of the Thirtieth Congress.

To Richard W. Thompson[1]

CONFIDENTIAL

Hon: R. W. Thompson: Springfield, Ills.
Dear Sir.   May 25. 1849—

I am about to ask a favor of you—one which, I hope, will not cost you much. I understand the General Land-Office is about to be given to Illinois; and that Mr. Ewing desires Justin Butterfield of Chicago to be the man. I will not trouble you with particulars, but will assure you, that the appointment of Mr. Butterfield will be an egregious political blunder. I believe it will gratify no single whig in the state, except it be Mr. B. himself. Now, the favor I wish of you is, that you will write Gen: Taylor at once, saying that in your opinion, either *I, or the man I recommend*, should be appointed to that office, if any one from Illinois, shall be. I restrict my request to Illinois, because I think it probable you have already recommended some one, probably from your own state; and I do not wish to interfere with that. Yours truly   A. LINCOLN

1 ALS, ORB. "Colonel Dick" Thompson was a Whig member of Congress from Terre Haute, Indiana.

To Thomas Ewing[1]

Hon: Secretary of the Interior   Springfield, Ills.
Dear Sir: June 3. 1849

Vandalia, the Receivers office at which place is the subject of the within, is not in my District; and I have been much perplexed to express any preference between Dr. Stapp[2] & Mr. Remann.[3] If any one man is better qualified for such an office than all others, Dr. Stapp is that man; still I believe a large majority of the whigs of the District prefer Mr. Remann, who also is a good man. Perhaps the papers on file, will enable you to judge better than I can. The writers of the within are good men, residing within the Land District. Your Obt. Servt.   A. LINCOLN

[1] ALS, IHi.   [2] James T. B. Stapp.
[3] Frederick Remann of Vandalia, Illinois. A letter, bearing signatures of eight Whigs of Decatur, Illinois, which Lincoln forwarded, expressed strong preference for Remann.

To Josiah B. Herrick[1]

Dr. J. B. Herrick   Springfield,
Dear Sir: June 3. 1849

It is now certain that either Mr. Butterfield or I will be Commissioner of the General Land-Office. If you are willing to give me the preference, please write me to that effect, at Washington, whither I am going. There is not a moment of time to be lost. Yours truly   A. LINCOLN

[1] ALS-P, ISLA.

Form Letter [To James M. McLean?][1]

Dear Sir.   Springfield June 3. 1849–

It is now certain that either Mr. Butterfield or I will be commissioner of the General Land office. If you are willing to give me the preference, please write me to that effect, at Washington, whither I go, in a few days. Not a moment of time to be lost. Yours truly

A LINCOLN.

[1] Copy by Mary Todd Lincoln, ICU. This copy is annotated "presumably to J. M. McLean at Lawrenceville, Ill." Probably Mary Lincoln penned other copies which have not survived. See the similar form letter to D. G. [Duff Green], June 5, *infra*.

To Robert C. Schenck[1]

Hon: R. C. Schenck
Dear Sir:

Springfield Ills,
June 3. 1849

As between Illinoians, would you not as soon I should be Commissioner of the General Land Office as any other? If so, write me to that effect, at Washington, whither I intend going in a few days. No time to be lost. Your Obt. Servt.   A. LINCOLN

[1] ALS, IHi. Robert C. Schenck was a Whig congressman from Ohio.

To Willie P. Mangum[1]

Hon: Willie P. Mangum:
Dear Sir:

Springfield, Ills.
June 4th. 1849

I understand the President has determined to give the General Land Office to Illinois; and if you would quite as soon I should have it as any other Illinoian, I shall be grateful if you will write me to that effect at Washington, where I expect to be soon.

A private despach from thence, tells me the appointment has been postponed three weeks from the first Inst. for my benefit. No time to lose. Your Obt. Servt.   A. LINCOLN

[1] ALS, MH. Mangum was senator from North Carolina.

Form Letter [To Duff Green][1]

Dear Sir   Springfield Ills. June 5. '49

Would you as soon I should have the Genl. Land Office as any other Illinoian?[2] If you would, write me to that effect at Washington where I shall be soon. No time to loose. Yours in haste
                                        A. LINCOLN

[1] Copy, DLC-RTL. Not in Lincoln's hand, this copy was presumably one of many sent out. It was returned with the following endorsement: "I most sincerely wish you success/DG." The same letter addressed to William Nelson, representative from New York, under same date, and another copy without name of addressee, under date of June 4, are printed in Hertz, II, p. 599.
[2] Written in at this point by Green: "A. Yes."

To Nathaniel Pope[1]

COPY.

Hon: N. Pope:
Dear Sir:

Springfield,
June 8. 1849

I do not *know* that it would, but I can well enough conceive it *might*, embarrass you to *now* give a letter reccommending me for

the General Land Office. Could you not, however, without embarrassment, or any impropriety, so far vindicate the truth of history, as to briefly state to me, in a letter, what you *did* say to me last spring on my arrival here from Washington, in relation to my becoming an applicant for that office? Having at last concluded to be an applicant, I have thought it is perhaps due me, to be enabled to show the influences which brought me to the conclusion—among which influences the wishes and opinions you expressed were not the least. Your Obt. Servt.   A. LINCOLN

[1] ALS, DLC-RTL. Nathaniel Pope was United States Judge for the district of Illinois.

Memorandum to Zachary Taylor[1]

June [15?] 1849

Nothing in my papers questions Mr. B.'s competency or honesty, and, I presume, nothing in his questions mine. Being equal so far, if it does not appear I am preferred by the Whigs of Illinois, I lay no claim to the office.

But if it does appear I am preferred, it will be argued that the whole Northwest, and not Illinois alone, should be heard. I answer I am as strongly recommended by Ohio and Indiana, as well as Illinois; and further, that when the many appointments were made for Ohio, as for the Northwest, Illinois was not consulted. When an Indianian was nominated for Governor of Minnesota, and another appointed for Commissioner of Mexican claims, as for the Northwest, Illinois was not consulted. When a citizen of Iowa was appointed Second Assistant Postmaster General and another to a Land Office in Minnesota, Illinois was not consulted. Of none of these have I ever complained. In each of them, the State whose citizen was appointed was allowed to control, and I think rightly. I only ask that Illinois be not cut off with less deference.

It will be argued that all the Illinois appointments, so far, have been South, and that therefore this should go North. I answer, that of the local appointments every part has had its share, and Chicago far the best share of any. Of the transitory, the Marshall and Attorney are all; and neither of these is within a hundred miles of me, the former being South and the latter North of West. I am in the center. Is the center nothing?—that center which alone has ever given you a Whig representative? On the score of locality, I admit the claim of the North is no worse, and I deny that it is any better than that of the center.

[1] Joseph H. Barrett, *Abraham Lincoln and His Presidency*, I, 107-108.

To Thomas Ewing[1]

(COPY.)

Hon. T. Ewing,   Washington,
Secretary, &c.   June 19, 1849.

Sir: My friend, N. G. Wilcox, is an applicant to be Receiver of
the Land Office at Stillwater, Minesota; and I sincerely hope he
may succeed. He is every way worthy of the office. I have once
seen his devotion to principle put to the severest test, and come out
unshaken. My confidence in him unlimited. Your Obt. Svt,

                                                  A. LINCOLN.

[1] Certified copy, ICU. As in the case of Lincoln's endorsement of Wilcox
(March 14, 1849), *supra*, the copy is certified by W. W. Lester, acting chief
clerk, Department of the Interior. The original document has not been located,
but an endorsement on this copy indicates that it passed from the Interior Department into the possession of Wilcox. Wilcox received the appointment as
receiver at Stillwater.

To Thomas Ewing[1]

Hon: Secretary of the Interior   Washington,
Sir: June 22. 1849

Please transmit to me the papers on file in your Dept. recommending me for Comr. of Genl. Land office, if not inconsistent with
the rules of the Department. Your Obt. Servt.   A. LINCOLN

[1] ALS, DLC. On the preceding day, Justin Butterfield had been appointed
commissioner of the General Land Office by President Taylor.

Endorsement: William Porter to Lincoln[1]

                                                  June [23] 1849

The writer of this is a man of excellent bussiness qualifications, and
particularly versed in the business of the Land offices. If he could
get the job of examiner as he desires, I should be much gratified. I
know no other applicant   A LINCOLN

[1] AES, DNA NR RG 48. A resident of Sangamon County who had known
Lincoln from his New Salem days, William Porter wrote a letter of application on June 10, assuming that Lincoln would certainly be appointed commissioner. Lincoln carried the letter to Washington, where he added his endorsement and filed the letter on June 23. See also Lincoln to Ewing, July 5, 1849,
infra.

To William B. Preston[1]

Hon: Secretary of the Navy   Washington,
Dear Sir: June 24, 1849

I understand my personal friend and fellow Illinoian, A. F. Patrick,[2] has been removed from a clerkship in your Department, on some charge implicating his capacity or business habits as a clerk. In such an implication I suspect injustice has been done him, not by you, but by those on whose information you acted. If this be so, you can ascertain it; and I shall be much obliged if you will wipe the injurious stigma from him. This is one thing; another is that if not inconsistant, I much wish he could have some temporary employment till about the meeting of Congress. When I say "if not inconsistent" I mean that I wish you to be consistent in all things; and that if obliging Mr. Patrick, democrat as he is, in the matter of temporary employment, would at all interfere with your consistency," I wish you not to do it. Your Obt. Servt

                                                             A. LINCOLN

[1] ALS, The Rosenbach Company, Philadelphia and New York.
[2] Lincoln first wrote the initials "S.G.," then crossed them out and inserted "A.F." Amos F. Patrick had practiced law in Will County, Illinois, and was a clerk in the General Land Office in 1847-1849.

To John M. Clayton[1]

Hon. Secretary of State   Springfield, Ills.
Dear Sir.   July 4. 1849

I understand the name of our excellent friend Hon. R. W. Thompson, of Indiana, is before you for some diplomatic appointment. It needs no one to tell you who he is, and I wish to say, as matter of substance, and not of form merely, that I sincerely desire he may be successful. Your Obt. Servt   A. LINCOLN

P.S. This letter is unsolicited by Mr. Thompson, and wholly voluntary on my part   A. L.

[1] ALS-P, ISLA.

To Thomas Ewing[1]

Hon: Secretary of the Interior: Springfield,
Dear Sir: July 5. 1849

I have a friend here, William Porter, who desires the job of examining the Land Offices in the North-West, if such a job is to be given out. I also desire him to have it; and while at Washington I filed a letter of his, with my indorsement upon it to that effect.[2] I

[56]

do not know that a citizen of my district, or even of Illinois, is to receive this little favor, and if not, I have no preference to express between applicants elsewhere. What I do ask is, that, if any citizen of my district, and *particularly* of my own town, is to receive it, Mr. Porter may be the man. Your Obt. Servt   A. LINCOLN.

[1] ALS, DLC-Ewing Papers.   [2] June 23, *vide supra.*

To Joseph Gillespie[1]

Dear Gillespie: Springfield, Ills, July 13th. 1849

Your letter of the 9th. of June in which you manifest some apprehension that your writing directly to Gen: Taylor had been regarded as improper, was received by me at Washington. I feel I owe you an apology for not answering it sooner. You committed no error in writing directly to the President; half the letters, or nearly so, on the subject of appointments, are so addressed. The President assorts them, and sends them to the Departments to which they belong respectively. Whether he reads them first, or only so far as to ascertain what subject they are on, I have not learned.

Mr. Edwards[2] is angry with me; and, in which, he is wronging me very much. He wrote a letter against me & in favor of Butterfield, which was filed in the Department. Ever since I discovered this, I have had a conflict of feeling, whether to write him or not; and, so far, I have remained silent. If he knew of your letters to me of the 9th. of May, and to the President of the 23rd. I suspect he would be angry with you too. Both those letters would help defend me with him; but I will not hazzard your interest by letting him know of them. To avoid that, I write you a separate letter which I wish you would show him when it may be convenient.

You will please accept my sincere thanks for the very flattering terms in which you speak of me in your letter to the President. I withdrew the papers on file in my behalf, by which means your letter is now in my possession. Yours as ever   A. LINCOLN

[1] ALS, owned by Charles S. Gillespie, Edwardsville, Illinois.
[2] Cyrus Edwards.

To Joseph Gillespie[1]

Dear Gillespie: Springfield, July 13. 1849.

Mr. Edwards[2] is unquestionably offended with me, in connection with the matter of the General Land-Office. He wrote a letter against me, which was filed at the Department. The better part of one's life consists of his friendships; and, of these, mine with Mr.

Edwards was one of the most cherished. I have not been false to it. At a word, I could I [*sic*] have had the office any time before the Department was committed to Mr. Butterfield—at least Mr. Ewing & the President say as much. That word I forebore to speak, partly for other reasons, but chiefly for Mr. Edwards' sake. Losing the office that he might gain it, I was always for; but to lose his *friendship* by the effort for him, would oppress me very much, were I not sustained by the utmost consciousness of rectitude. I first determined to be an applicant, unconditionally, on the 2nd. of June; and I did so then upon being informed by a Telegraphic despach, that the question was narrowed down to Mr. B. and myself, and that the Cabinet had postponed the appointment three weeks for my benefit. Not doubting, that Mr. Edwards was wholly out of the question, I nevertheless would not then have become an applicant, had I supposed he would thereby be brought to suspect me of treachery to him. Two or three days afterwards a conversation with Levi Davis convinced me Mr. E. was dissatisfied; but I was then too far in to get out. His own letter, written on the 25th. of April, after I had fully informed him of all that had passed up to within a few days of that time, gave assurance I had that entire confidence from him, which I felt my uniform and strong friendship for him entitled me to. Among other things it says "whatever course your judgment may dictate as proper to be pursued, shall never be excepted to by me." I also had had a letter from Washington, saying Chambers[3] of the Republican had brought a rumor then that, Mr. E. had declined in my favor, which rumor I judged came from Mr. E himself, as I had not then breathed of his letter, to any living creature.

In saying I had never before the 2nd. of June determined to be an applicant, *unconditionally*, I mean to admit that before then, I had said substantially I would take the office rather than it should be lost to the state, or given to one in the state whom the whigs did not want; but I aver that in every instance in which I spoke of myself, I intended to keep, and now believe I did keep, Mr. E. ahead of myself. Mr. Edwards' first suspicion was that I had allowed Baker[4] to over-reach me, as his friend, in behalf of Don: Morrison. I knew this was a mistake; and the result has proved it. I understand his view now is, that if I had gone to open war with Baker I could have ridden him down, and had the thing all my own way. I believe no such thing. With Baker & some strong men from the Military tract, & elsewhere for Morrison; and we and some strong men from the Wabash & elsewhere for Mr. E, it was not possible for either to succeed. I *believed* this in March, and I *know* it now.

The only thing which gave either any chance was the very thing Baker & I proposed—an adjustment with themselves.

You may wish to know how Butterfield finally beat me. I can not tell you particulars now, but will, when I see you. In the mean time let it be understood I am not greatly dissatisfied. I wish the office had been so bestowed as to encourage our friends in future contests, and I regret exceedingly Mr. Edwards' feelings towards me. These two things away, I should have no regrets—at least I think I would not.

Write me soon. Your friend, as ever   A. LINCOLN—

1 ALS, owned by Charles S. Gillespie, Edwardsville, Illinois.
2 Cyrus Edwards.
3 Colonel A. B. Chambers, editor and publisher of the St. Louis *Republican*.
4 Edward D. Baker.

To John Addison[1]

Dear Addison: Springfield, Ills. July 22. 1849

On the other half of this sheet is what I hope may be both satisfactory and serviceable to you.[2] If any thing I have written *for* any body should be turned to your disadvantage, I could hardly ever forgive myself for the carelessness of so writing. Give my respects to my friends about you, particularly Lucas;[3] and tell him I am truly glad he is at a good understanding with the new Commissioner.[4] If letters have come to the Dept. in my favor since the appointment, may they not be sent to me? I should like to see them. I have now about forty such, nineteen (I believe) of which are from M.C.'s

I shall write Berdan to-day[5] on the matter of which you speak concerning him. He is as much of a gentleman as lives. Yours very truly   A. LINCOLN—

1 ALS, owned by Mrs. F. de L. Robinson, Greenport, New York. John Addison was a clerk in the Interior Department.
2 Presumably this was a letter of recommendation which Addison tore off and used in its appropriate place. The original has not been located.
3 Josiah M. Lucas.   4 Justin Butterfield.   5 *Vide infra.*

To James Berdan[1]

James Berdan, Esq   Springfield,
My dear Sir: July 22. 1849

Last night I received a Washington letter from Mr. John Addison, in which, among other things he says: "Lucas tells me this morning that Mr. Butterfield was making very particular enquiries about our friend *Berdan*, & expressed a wish to have his services in the Dept., remarking that he considered him one of the best land lawyers in the West &c. Would he like an appt.? I feel satisfied that he could obtain a good one if he applied"

I took the precaution to withdraw the letters filed in my favor for Comr.; so that the very pretty one you wrote for me, can not rise in judgment against you, if, indeed, being seen, it would affect Mr. B's feelings towards you. Now, my dear Sir, I do not know whether you have thought of going to Washington, or, if you have, whether my friendship would *help* or *hurt* you with Mr. B; still I write this to put myself at your service in the matter, and to say I shall be pleased to act as you may desire. Please write me by return mail[.] Your friend as ever   A. LINCOLN

1 ALS, owned by Morrison Worthington, Chicago, Illinois.

To John M. Clayton[1]

Hon. J. M. Clayton.   Springfield, Ill., July 28, 1849.

Dear Sir: It is with some hesitation I presume to address this letter—and yet I wish not only you, but the whole cabinet, and the President too, would consider the subject matter of it. My being among the People while you and they are not, will excuse the apparent presumption. It is understood that the President at first adopted, as a general rule, to throw the responsibility of the appointments upon the respective Departments; and that such rule is adhered to and practised upon. This course I at first thought proper; and, of course, I am not now complaining of it. Still I am disappointed with the effect of it on the public mind. It is fixing for the President the unjust and ruinous character of being a mere man of straw. This must be arrested, or it will damn us all inevitably. It is said Gen. Taylor and his officers held a council of war, at Palo Alto (I believe); and that he then fought the battle against unanimous opinion of those officers. This fact (no matter whether rightfully or wrongfully) gives him more popularity than ten thousand submissions, however really wise and magnanimous those submissions may be.

The appointments need be no better than they have been, but the public must be brought to understand, that they are the *President's* appointments. He must occasionally say, or seem to say, "by the Eternal," "I take the responsibility." Those phrases were the "Samson's locks" of Gen. Jackson, and we dare not disregard the lessons of experience. Your Ob't Sev't   A. LINCOLN

1 Tracy, 39-40.

To John M. Clayton[1]

Hon: Secretary of State   Springfield,
Dear Sir: Augt. 12. 1849

When I was about leaving Washington last I told you an anecdote by way of impressing on your memory the application of Allen Francis to be Consul at Glasgow, Scotland. I very much wish he could be obliged. He is part editor of the oldest paper in the state; and, being a practical printer, has worked constantly, setting type for it, eighteen years. He is tired, and has a right to be. His wife is a "Scotchman" and wishes to visit her father-land. Your Obt. Servt   A. LINCOLN

1 ALS, DNA FS RG 59, Appointment Papers. Allen Francis, brother of Simeon and Josiah Francis, was a partner with Simeon in publishing the *Illinois Journal*. Allen Francis was not appointed.

To John M. Clayton[1]

Hon: J. M. Clayton,   Springfield, Illinois,
Secretary of State.   Augt. 21st. 1849

Dear Sir: Your letter of the 10th. Inst., notifying me of my appointment as Secretary of the Teritory of Oregon, and accompanied by a Commission, has been duly received. I respectfully decline the office.

I shall be greatly obliged if the place be offered to Simeon Francis, of this place. He will accept it, is capable, and would be faithful in the discharge of it's duties. He is the principal editor of the oldest, and what I think may be fairly called, the leading Whig paper of the state,—the Illinois Journal. His good business habits are proved by the facts, that the paper has existed eighteen years, all the time weekly, and part of it, tri-weekly, and daily, and has not failed to issue regularly in a single instance.

Some time in May last, I think, Mr. Francis addressed a letter to Mr. Ewing, which, I was informed while at Washington in June, had been seen by the cabinet, and very highly approved. You possibly may remember it. He has, for a long time desired to go to Oregon; and I think his appointment would give general satisfaction   Your Obt. Servt.   A. LINCOLN—

1 ALS, DNA FS RG 59, Appointment Papers. See Lincoln to Clayton September 27, *infra*. Lincoln's letters to Clayton of August 21, September 12, 15, and 16, *infra*, seem to have been misplaced in the Department of State. The present letter is marked "Rec'd 29 Augt."

Resolutions of Sympathy
with the Cause of Hungarian Freedom[1]

September 6, 1849

Resolved, That in their present glorious struggle for liberty, the Hungarians, command our highest admiration, and have our warmest sympathy.

Resolved, That they have our most ardent prayers for their speedy triumph and final success.

Resolved, That the Government of the United States should acknowledge the Independence of Hungary as [a] Nation of freemen, at the very earliest moment consistent with our amicable relations with that Government, against which they are contending.

Resolved, That in the opinion of this meeting, the immediate acknowledgment of the independence of Hungary by our government, is due from American freemen, to their struggling brethren, to the general cause of Republican liberty, and not a violation of the just rights of any Nation or people.

[1] *Illinois Journal*, September 7, 1849. "At a large meeting of citizens (at which many ladies were present,) . . . being called to order by S. FRANCIS, Esq., the Hon. DAVID DAVIS . . . was elected President. . . . On motion, the President appointed citizens John Todd, Wm. Carpenter, Abraham Lincoln, E. H. Merryman, Thomas Lewis, and David B. Campbell, [a] committee to draw up resolutions to express the sentiments of the members of this meeting in relation to the war now progressing in Hungary." *Ibid.*

To John M. Clayton[1]

Hon: Secretary of State   Springfield, Ills.
Dear Sir: Sept. 12. 1849.

You perceive the object of the inclosed paper. I personally know Majr. Fellows to be worthy of either of the offices mentioned. The signers of the paper are of the "tip top" whigs of Illinois. One of them is now a circuit judge, one other has been such, one is now U.S. District Attorney, and the others are all lawyers of high standing. I fully indorse Majr. Fellows and them, reserving only, that I have already recommended S. Francis for the Secretaryship of Oregon. Your Obt. Servt.   A. LINCOLN

[1] ALS, DNA FS RG 59, Appointment Papers. This letter is marked "Rec'd 20 Sept." The enclosure is a letter to Lincoln signed by Orville H. Browning and others September 6, 1849, recommending Major Hart Fellows of Schuyler County for appointment to a federal judgeship or as secretary of Oregon Territory. Fellows did not receive either appointment, but in 1851 he was surveyor of the Port of San Francisco.

To Elisha Embree[1]

Dear Judge   Springfield, Ills. Sept. 12. 1849

Your letter asking my aid in behalf of your friend Stickney[2] has been received. I had already made a recommendation for the Secretaryship of Oregon; I however mentioned that, and then endorsed you and Webb[3] in the strongest terms I could and sent your letters to Mr. Clayton. Please accept my thanks for your kind letter to the President in my behalf; and also the expression of my deep regret for your failure in the late congressional contest. I did not, however, dare to hope for your success. There was too much against you. Your friend as ever   A. LINCOLN

[1] ALS, In.   [2] Lyman D. Stickney of New Harmony, Indiana.
[3] Possibly Lincoln's old friend Edwin B. Webb of nearby White County, Illinois.

To William Fithian[1]

Dear Doctor   Springfield, Sept. 14. 1849—

Your letter of the 9th. was received a day or two ago. The notes and mortgage you enclosed me were duly received. I also got the original Blanchard[2] mortgage from Antrim Campbell, with whom Blanchard had left it for you. I got a decree of foreclosure on the whole; but owing to their being no redemption on the sale to be under the Blanchard mortgage the court allowed Mobley[3] till the first of March to pay the money, before advertising for sale. Stuart was empowered by Mobley to appear for him, and I had to take such decree as he would consent to or none at all. I cast the matter about in my mind, and concluded, that as I could not get a decree before March at any rate, and as taking a decree now would put the accrued interest at interest, and thereby more than match the fact of throwing the Blanchard debt back from 12 to 6. per cent, it was better to do it. This is the present state of the case.

I can well enough understand and appreciate your suggestions about the Land-Office at Danville; but in my present condition, I can do nothing. Yours as ever   A. LINCOLN

[1] ALS-P, ISLA. William Fithian resided at Danville, Illinois. He was a leading Whig, elected representative (1834) and senator (1838, 1842) in the state legislature.   [2] William W. Blanchard of Wheeling, Virginia.
[3] Mordecai Mobley, former resident of Sangamon County who had removed to Dubuque, Iowa, where he was appointed receiver for the land office in 1849.

To John M. Clayton[1]

Hon: J. M. Clayton   Springfield, Illinois,
Secretary of State—   Sept. 15th. 1849

Sir: Understanding that Simeon Francis, of this city would accept the office of Secretary of the Teritory of Oregon, and that his name has been presented to you for that appointment, we most cheerfully join in bearing testimony to his worth and qualifications, and in the expression of a desire that the place may be conferred upon him.

John T. Stuart   Ben: Bond
Turner R. King   A. Y. Ellis
Walter Davis   Wm. S. Wallace.

John T. Stuart, Whig member of the 26th. & 27th. Congresses.
Turner R. King —Present Register of the Land office here.
Walter Davis   —Present Receiver of Public Monies here.
Ben: Bond   —Present U.S. Marshal of this state.
A. Y. Ellis   —Present Post-Master here
Wm. S. Wallace—Present Pension Agent of this state.

LINCOLN

[1] ALS, DNA FS RG 59, Appointment Papers. This communication is in Lincoln's handwriting except for the other signatures. See Lincoln to Clayton, September 27, *infra.*

To John M. Clayton[1]

Hon J. M. Clayton.   Springfield, Illinois,
Secretary of State   Sept. 16– 1849

Dear Sir: I send you a paper recommending Simeon Francis for the appointment of Secretary for the Oregon Teritory.

I know I have no right to claim the disposal of the office; but I do think, under all the circumstances, that he ought to receive the appointment. If a long course of uniform and efficient action as a whig editor; if an honesty unimpeached, and qualifications undisputed; if the fact that he has advanced to the meridian of life without ever before asking for an office, be considerations of importance with the Administration, I can not but feel that the appointment, while it will do him justice, will also do honor to the Administration. Your Obt. Servt.   A. LINCOLN

[1] ALS, DNA FS RG 59, Appointment Papers. This letter is marked "Rec'd 24 Sept." See Lincoln to Clayton, September 27, *infra.*

To John Addison[1]

Springfield, Illinois,
John Addison, Esq.   September 27, 1849.

My dear Sir: Your letter is received. I can not but be grateful to you and all other friends who have interested themselves in having the governorship of Oregon offered to me; but on as much reflection as I have had time to give the subject, I cannot consent to accept it. I have an ever abiding wish to serve you; but as to the secretaryship, I have already recommended our friend Simeon Francis, of the "Journal." Please present my respects to G. T. M. Davis[2] generally, and my thanks especially for his kindness in the Oregon matter. Yours as ever,   A. LINCOLN.

[1] NH, 129-30.
[2] George T. M. Davis, formerly of Alton, Illinois, at the end of the Mexican War had accepted a chief clerkship in the War Department.

To John M. Clayton[1]

Hon: J. M. Clayton   Springfield, Illinois.
Secretary of State   Sept. 27. 1849

Dear Sir: Your letter of the 17th. Inst. saying you had received no answer to yours informing me of my appointment as Secretary of Oregon, is received, and surprises me very much. I received that letter, accompanied by the commission, in due course of mail, and answered it two days after, declining the office, and warmly recommending Simeon Francis for it. I have also written you several letters since,[2] alluding to the same matter, all of which ought to have reached you before the date of your last letter. Your Obt. Servt.

A. LINCOLN—

[1] ALS, owned by Richard Helms, Chevy Chase, Maryland.
[2] Most, if not all, of these letters have recently been discovered. See Lincoln to Clayton, August 21 and September 12, 15, and 16, *supra*.

To Thomas Ewing[1]

Hon Thomas Ewing   Springfield Sept. 27th. 1849.

I respectfully decline Governorship of Oregon; I am still anxious that, Simeon Frances shall be secretary of that Territory

A. LINCOLN

[1] Copy, DLC-Ewing Papers. Not in Lincoln's hand but presumably in the hand of the operator, this telegram is written on a form of the North American Telegraph Company.

To Thomas Ewing[1]

Hon: T. Ewing, Secretary &c.   Springfield, Illinois,
Dear Sir: Sept. 27. 1849

    Some discrepancy may appear between my letter of the 23rd.[2] and my Telegraphic despatch of to-day, to explain which I write this. As I told [y]ou in that letter, I sent a dispatch the same [d]ay to a friend at Springfield to be forwarded [to] you; but that friend and some others, supposing [I] had decided hastily, witheld the despatch, and [wr]ote me again. On receiving their letter, I came to Springfield, and now Telegraph you myself. Your Obt. Servt.

                                    A. LINCOLN—

[1] ALS, DLC-Ewing Papers.   [2] This letter is presumably not extant.

To Isaac Onstott[1]

Dear Isaac: Springfield, Oct. 14. 1849

    I have but a moment to say your letter is received; and that when a Petition comes to me in relation to your Post-Master it shall be attended to at once. Give my respects to your father and mother, and believe me ever: Your friend   A. LINCOLN

[1] ALS, owned by John Onstott, Petersburg, Illinois. Isaac Onstott was the son of Lincoln's old friend Henry Onstott, the village cooper at New Salem. Isaac was interested in the postmastership at Havana, Illinois.

To William B. Preston[1]

Hon: W. B. Preston   Lexington, Ky.
Secretary of the Navy.   Novr. 5. 1849

    Dear Sir: Being here in Kentucky on private business,[2] I have learned that the name of Dr. John T. Parker[3] is before you as an applicant for the Hemp Agency of the State. I understand that his name has been presented in accordance with the wish of the hemp-growers, rather than his own. I personally know him to be a gentle-man of high character, of excellent general information, and, withal, an experienced hemp grower himself. I disclaim all right of interference as to the offices out of my own state; still I suppose there is no impr[opr]iety in my stating the facts as above; and I will venture to add that I shall be much gratified, if Dr. Parker shall receive the appointment. Your Obt. Servt.   A. LINCOLN—

[1] ALS, RPB.   [2] Lincoln's business was the lawsuit Todd *v.* Wickliffe.
[3] An uncle of Mary Todd Lincoln.

To Thomas Ewing[1]

Hon. Thos. Ewing:—   Springfield Novr. 17th. 1849.

I most anxiously desire that Simeon Francis be appointed Surveyor General of Oregon.   ABRAHAM LINCOLN.

[1] Copy, DLC-Ewing Papers. Delivered copy of a telegram.

To Josiah M. Lucas[1]

J. M. Lucas   Springfield,
Dear Sir: Novr. 17. 1849

I have been from home a month, so that your letter of the 17th. of October was not received by me till yesterday. I regret that the elections in the states have gone so badly; but I think there is some reason for hoping that this year has been the administration's "darkest hour." The appointments were it's most difficult task; and this year it has necessarily been viewed in connection with them alone. These are pretty much through with, and next we can get on grounds of *measures*—policy—where we can unite & rally again. At least, I hope so. I am sorry Don: Morrison has thought fit to assail you; and exceedingly glad Mr. Ewing has sustained you. I am glad of this, for your sake and my own—*my own*, because I think it shows Mr. Ewing is keeping faith with me in regard to my friends. By the way, I have a better opinion of Mr. Ewing than you, perhaps, suppose I have.

As to the suppression of some of my letters of recommendation for the Genl. Land Office, Addison[2] never said or wrote a word to me, or I to him. After the appointment was made I requested my letters to be returned to me, upon which a sealed bundle was sent to my room. I took it, or rather, brought it home unopened. Some days after I reached here I opened it, and discovered that two letters were missing which I knew ought to be in it. I did not make the matter public here, and I wrote to no one concerning it elsewhere, except Mr. Ewing himself. He answered my letter, and that subject has been dropped for at least three months. Till you mention it, I did not suppose Addison had any knowledge of it. I dont perceive that it would do any harm to any one, but perhaps it will be more prudent for you not to speak of my having mentioned the subject to you. Your friend as ever   A. LINCOLN

[1] ALS, CSmH.   [2] John Addison.

To the Editor of the *Chicago Journal*[1]

Editor of the Chicago Journal:

Springfield,
Nov. 21, 1849.

Dear Sir—Some person, probably yourself, has sent me the number of your paper containing an extract of a supposed speech of Mr. Linder, together with your editorial comments.[2] As my name is mentioned, both in the speech and in the comments, and as my attention is directed to the article by a special mark in the paper sent me, it is perhaps expected that I should take some notice of it. I have to say, then, that I was absent, from before the commencement, till after the close of the late session of the legislature, and that the fact of such a speech having been delivered never came to my knowledge, till I saw a notice of your article, in the Illinois Journal, one day before your paper reached me. Had the intention of any whig to deliver such a speech been known to me, I should, to the utmost of my ability, have endeavored to prevent it. When Mr. Butterfield was appointed commissioner of the land office, I expected him to be a faithful and able officer, and nothing has since come to my knowledge disappointing that expectation. As to Mr. Ewing, his position has been one of great difficulty. I believe him, too, to be an able and faithful officer. A more intimate acquaintance with him, would probably change the views of most of those who have complained of him. Your ob't serv't,

A. LINCOLN.

[1] *Illinois State Register*, December 1, 1849. The Democratic *Register*, in reprinting this letter, editorialized that Lincoln "does not touch the principal point at issue . . . that Messrs. Ewing and Butterfield are popular with their own party in this state. The reverse of this assumption is too notoriously true to be deliberately disputed, by even as ardent a whig politician as Mr. Lincoln. Having been, and doubtless being, an applicant for the favors of the cabinet, he could not *prudently* say less than he has done in the above letter. . . . Hence his certificate amounts to nothing. . . ."

[2] The Chicago *Journal*, November 14, printed a portion of a speech delivered by Usher F. Linder in the legislature on November 2, attacking Thomas Ewing as an aristocrat "unsuited to wield the immense patronage placed in his hands." He expressed the general sentiment of Illinois Whigs against the appointment of Justin Butterfield as commissioner of the General Land Office in disregard of the "almost unanimous wish of . . . the whig people of Illinois." The editor of the Chicago *Journal* was Charles L. Wilson.

To John M. Clayton[1]

Hon: J. M. Clayton.
Secretary of State

Springfield, Ills.
Novr. 25 1849

Dear Sir   Allow me to introduce our friend, Dr. A. G. Henry of this place. I solicit for him your kindness and confidence; and this

I do, not cerimoniously merely, but in all sincerety. You may perhaps remember his name, as that of the first person in whose behalf I made an appeal to you immediately after the inaugeration
of Genl. Taylor. Your Obt. Servt.   A. LINCOLN

1 ALS, IHi. See Lincoln to Clayton, March 8, *supra*.

To George W. Rives[1]

G. W. Rives, Esq   Springfield,
Dear Sir: Decr. 15– 1849
    On my return from Kentucky, I found your letter of the 7th. of
November, and have delayed answering it till now, for the reason
I now briefly state. From the beginning of our acquaintance I had
felt the greatest kindness for you, and had supposed it was recipro-
cated on your part. Last summer, under circumstances which I
mentioned to you, I was painfully constrained to withhold a recommendation which you desired;[2] and shortly afterwards I
learned, in such way as to believe it, that you were indulging open
abuse of me. Of course my feelings were wounded. On receiving
your last letter, the question occurred whether you were attempting to *use* me, at the same time you would *injure* me, or whether
you might not have been misrepresented to me. If the former, I
ought not to answer you; if the latter I ought, and so I have remained in suspense. I now enclose you a letter[3] which you may
use if you think fit. Yours &c.   A. LINCOLN

1 ALS, The Rosenbach Company, Philadelphia and New York. See Lincoln
to Rives, May 7, 1849, *supra*.
2 Presumably because he was recommending his friend Anson G. Henry for
the same office.
3 This letter of recommendation is presumably not extant.

To David M. Irwin[1]

[1850?]

The Heirs of Payne
            To Logan & Lincoln   Dr.
1844.   To attending to Ejectment suit
            against Hall in Sangamon
            Circuit Court. $20.00.
    Same
            To A Lincoln   Dr.
1845-6.   To attending same suit in
            Supreme Court $10.00

Same

To Lincoln & Herndon   Dr.

1846.7-8-9. & 50. To attending to Chancery
suit between same par-
ties in Sangamon Cir-
cuit Court. $10.00.

"40.00

D. M. Irwin:

Dear Sir. Above is the Bill as you requested me to send you.
Logan only attended the first trial in the circuit court. I, alone, that
is without any partner attended the case in the Supreme court. In
the Chancery case, Mr. Herndon was my partner. I mention all
this to explain the three separate bills. Yours &c. A. LINCOLN

¹ ALS, CSmH. David M. Irwin was a merchant of Virginia City, Cass County,
Illinois, who had been engaged in the mercantile business in Springfield
(1841-1845) and in St. Louis, Missouri (1845-1848). In 1853 he moved his
business to Beardstown, Illinois.

Memorandum to Joseph Ledlie¹

[c.1850]

In 1826, I believe it was, Elijah Iles conveyed a parcel of ground
to Thomas M. Neale, by the following description—

"Beginning at a stake in the East line of Daniel P. Cook's sixteen
acre tract, 330 feet from Madison Street—thence North with said
Cook's line to his corner—thence at right angles to James Adams'
corner—thence South with his line to another of his corners—
thence East to John Taylor's corner of his Eleven acre tract—
thence South with said Taylor's line to another of his corners on
Madison Street—thence West to a corner on said Street of Beach-
er's Block of lots—thence North and West with the lines of said
Block of lots to the beginning, containing about Eleven acres."
Book B– 128

Afterwards Neale conveyed away part of the tract by the following description,

"Beginning at the South West corner of Joseph Millers purchase
from John Taylor—thence N 88° W. 1 chain & 20 links—thence
N 2° E. 4 chains & 92 links—thence N 88° W. 4 chains & 80 links
—thence N 2° E 7 chains & 25 links—thence S 88° E. 6 chains—
thence S 2° W 12 chains & 17 links to the beginning." Book B. 218

Also another part by the following description—

"Beginning at the North West corner of the tract last above described—thence N 2° E. 4 chains & 48 links—thence N 89 E 4

chains & 30 links—thence North 48 links—thence East 2 chains & 20 links—thence S 2° W. 4 chains & 96 links—thence West 4.° 48 chs. to the beginning." These conveyances were to Edward Mitchell. Neale also made a conveyance to J. R. Saunders by the following description—Book E. 421

"Beginning at the N.W. corner of James Adams' ten acre lot— thence with the quarter Section West 3 chains & 31 links—thence at right angles with D. P. Cook's East line to a stake opposite the S.W. corner of said Adams' field—thence at right angles to last mentioned corner—thence with Adams' line to the beginning." Book B. 144. Whether this last is intended as part of the tract bought of Iles I am not sure; but I think probably it is.

Mrs. Neale, now for ten years a widow,[2] and very necessitous, thinks there is some small part of the Iles purchase which is not included by the conveyances of her husband. If so, it can only be ascertained by a Survey. If Mr. Ledley will take an occasion to carefully make such survey, and thus ascertain the truth, I will do as much or more for him, in the line of my profession, at his order. I am not expecting any compensation from Mrs. Neale.

A. LINCOLN

[1] ADS, ICU.
[2] Harriet Blakemore Neale. Thomas M. Neale died August 7, 1840. Lincoln had served as deputy surveyor to Neale, who succeeded John Calhoun as county surveyor in 1835.

To Zachary Taylor[1]

His Excellency
The President of the U.S.

Springfield, Ills.
Jany 25– 1850.

Dear Sir: In a letter to you of this date I have strongly recommended Hon Stephen T. Logan for U.S. Judge of the District Court for Illinois.[2] Understanding that a portion of our good whig friends are recommending Hon: Samuel D. Lockwood for the same office, I mean not to abate in the least my recommendation of Judge Logan, when I say that Judge Lockwood too is most worthy of such an appointment. His moral worth, and legal ability are above all question. For about twentyfive years he was a judge of our Supreme Court; and his opinions, extending through nearly all our books of Reports, are a sufficient guarranty of his capacity, to all who may not personally know him. His appointment, I think, would give very general satisfaction. Your Obt. Servt. A. LINCOLN.

[1] ALS, DNA FS RG 59, Appointment Papers. Neither Stephen T. Logan nor Samuel D. Lockwood received the appointment. See Lincoln to Browning, January 29, *infra*. [2] This letter has not been located.

[71]

To Orville H. Browning[1]

Dear Browning: Springfield, Jany. 29: 1850–

Yours of the 26th. was received last night. As you anticipate, I had already recommended Judge Logan for District Judge; and more, I had already said all I could consistently with this, in favor of Judge Lockwood.[2] I certainly esteem Mr. Bushnell[3] as being every way worthy of such an office. In moral character, and legal attainments, he is entirely sound and sufficient. If you think this letter can be used to any advantage, you are at liberty to so use it. What I here say, I say most cheerfully; and more I could not now say consistently. Yours as ever.   A. LINCOLN

[1] ALS, RPB. See Lincoln to Zachary Taylor, January 25, *supra*.
[2] Samuel D. Lockwood. District Judge Nathaniel Pope died on January 22.
[3] Nehemiah Bushnell of Quincy, Illinois, Browning's partner.

To Thomas J. Turner[1]

Hon: T. J. Turner   Springfield,
Dear Sir: Feb: 8. 1850.

I have been examining your Bill, and studdying the case some to-day. There is some confusion in the description of the land, as given in the Bill, which I suppose comes by mistake. To enable me to correct this, before filing the Bill, send me an exactly accurate description of all the tracts. I do not think any Injunction will be necessary pending the suit; and consequently no bond is necessary except the ordinary bond for cost, a blank for which I herewith send you. Have the bond filled, and executed by some one for whose responsibility you can vouch, and send it back to me.

Were our men actually in possession of the land at the time it was conveyed by Denny to Bradshaw? Are we *obliged* to put Bradshaw on his oath? Can we not *prove* our case without?

Please answer these questions when you write me. Yours as ever

A. LINCOLN

[1] ALS, owned by Mrs. J. B. Woodworth, Dixon, Illinois. Lincoln's correspondence with Turner about this case continues over several years, and letters to Adam Adams (June 23, 1853) and Solon Cumins (February 14, 1853) also are concerned with it. Since records of the United States District Court for this period are not extant, efforts to identify circumstances and participants have in most instances been futile.

To Sylvester Emmons[1]

S. Emmons, Esq   Springfield,
Dear Sir: Feb: 9. 1850

Yours of the 2nd. was not received till yesterday. I shall be entirely satisfied for you to receive the appointment you desire; still

I know, by conversations with the Marshal,[2] that he will look to the wishes of the people of your county, rather than to mine, as to who shall have the appointment. Therefore as your friend, I advise you to get the recommendation of some of your prominent whigs— Dummer, Dick Thomas—Arenz,[3] and such men, and I will most cheerfully present them to the Marshall when he shall be here. Very truly your friend.   A. LINCOLN

[1] ALS, Herbert W. Fay Collection. Emmons was a resident of Beardstown, Illinois.   [2] Benjamin Bond.
[3] Henry E. Dummer, Richard S. Thomas, Francis Arenz.

To John Tillson[1]

Mr. John Tilson   Springfield,
Dear Sir: Feb: 15. 1850

A Mrs. Stout, formerly a Miss Huldah Briggs, of Vandalia, and who says she knows you, has become a near and favorite neighbor of ours. She thinks that some relatives of hers in Bond county have not done exactly right with her in relation to the estates of her grand-father & grand-mother, and that you have some knowledge on the subject.

The out-line of her narative is, that her father, Charles Briggs died in Mass. in 1822 or thereabouts; that her grand-father, Richard Briggs, died at Boston about 1833, leaving some property; that her grand-mother removed to Bond county, Ills, bringing her husbands means with her, and acquiring some herself by means of a pension, & divided some $5000 out to her five *living* children, giving nothing to Mrs. Stout, or to the children of another deceased child. In 1842 her grand-mother also died, leaving some property, as Mrs. Stout thinks, but of which she still got nothing.

If you can, please answer me these questions—

Did her grand-father make a Will? & if so what was the substance of it?

Did her grand-mother bring means of her grand-father to this country? & if so what went with it? Did her grand-mother make a Will? & if so, what was the substance of it?

Has there been an administration on either estate.

Any thing further which you may know. I shall be much obliged if you will do this. Yours truly   A. LINCOLN

[1] ALS, IHi. John Tillson, whose name Lincoln misspells, was a wealthy and prominent citizen of Hillsboro, Illinois, until 1843, when he removed to Quincy in the interest of his business investments.

To William Fithian[1]

Dr. W. Fithian: Springfield,
Dear Sir: Feb: 16. 1850

I now undertake to answer your enquiries. According to the opinion and information of Mr. Higby,[2] the agent who has attended to the property for Majr. Mobley:[3]

The piece near *Butler's*[4] is worth $900 or $1000—is rented at six dollars per month, to terminate at the end of any month.

The piece near *Dr. Henry's*[5] is worth $300, is rented at $2.75 per month, to terminate the first of April.

The piece near *Burkhardt's*[6] is worth $400, is rented at $2.50 per month, to terminate any time.

The piece near the *Governor's house* is worth $800, is rented at $5.00 per month, to terminate the first of April.

My partner, Mr. Herndon, has been to Menard to see the land there; and he reports it as worth about $3.25 cents per acre, that it will sell best in 40 acre lots, and probably would bring $4. per acre, if it could be sold on a credit. There are 200 acres of it. The time of sale will be about the 1st. of April, but is not yet fixed; when fixed, I will write you. The sale will be piece by piece, applying the proceeds first to the Blanchard debt, and so much as it takes to pay it will be without redemption, & the purchaser will get immediate possession. The remainder will be subject to redemption, & immediate possession will not be given.

Majr. Mobley writes me that he shall try to be here at the sale; and I think it will be to your interest to be here also. Both being present, you can by agreement, sell a piece on credit whenever you see any thing can be made, or saved by it. Besides, R. Latham[7] who owns one undivided half of the piece near *Burkhardt's* says he wants to either buy or sell. In giving the value, I mean, the *undivided half*, mortgaged to you, is worth $400 & rents for $2.50.
Yours as ever   A. LINCOLN

1 ALS, IHi.   2 Lemuel Higby.   3 Mordecai Mobley.
4 William Butler.   5 Anson G. Henry.   6 John M. Burkhardt.
7 Robert B. Latham.

To George W. Crawford[1]

[February 20, 1850]

To the Honorable, The Secretary of War, of the United States.

Sir: The undersigned, citizens of the State of Illinois, beg leave to recommend to your consideration the name of *Napoleon Koscialowski,* for the appointment of *Major,* should there be a disposable post of that rank, in one of the Regiments to be raised for the protection of the U. S. frontier. We make this recommendation more earnestly, because we believe that your Department cannot possibly make a better appointment. Mr. Koscialowski is a native of Poland, and has been bred and has served as a soldier. He entered a military school at Warsaw at the age of sixteen, and having graduated then served three years in the Body-Guard of the Emperor of Russia. He quitted that corps and joined his national banner in the year 1830, when the Poles made their bold but unfortunate attempt to regain their national independence. After several years' imprisonment, consequent upon the failure of the revolt, he with some others succeeded in making his escape to this country, and became a citizen of the U. S. in 1834. In 1846, when War was declared against Mexico, he volunteered and having raised a company in St Louis, was elected captain and served as such until discharged. He then volunteered again for the Term of During the War, and commanded a company on the Western frontier until Peace was concluded and he was discharged. In the course of this service, he has necessarily acquired much experience in the kind of warfare to which the frontier Regiments are destined—and we think, and so respectfully represent, that this experience added to his education in a regular Military Academy, peculiarly fits him for the station to which we recommend him. As an accomplished civil engineer, also, we are the more confident that his services will be valuable to his adopted country. Mr. Koscialowski is a resident of Jacksonville, Illinois.[2]

Saml D. Lockwood	David L Gregg	M. McConnel
Wm Brown	Aug C. French	W. B. Warren
J. L. McConnel	Tho H Campbell	A. Lincoln
Jas. Berdan	Jas L D Morrison	Wm. Pickering
Wm. H. Snyder	John Moore	N M Knapp
Wm. Thomas	William McMurtry	Wm H. Bissell
A Dunlap	E R Roe	B. F. Bristow
	Richd Yates	

[1] DS, IHi.

[2] Among Lincoln's co-signers the following have not been previously identified: John L. McConnel of Jacksonville, best known for his "Western Characters or Types of Border Life" (1850-1853); William H. Snyder of Belleville, elected to the legislature in 1850; Adam, or Alva, Dunlap, both of Rushville; David L. Gregg of Cook County, elected secretary of state on the Democratic ticket in 1850; Thomas H. Campbell of Randolph County, state auditor; John Moore of McLean County, state treasurer; Edward R. Roe, Jacksonville physician and editor of the *Morgan Journal;* Murray McConnel, Morgan County Democrat formerly a member of the legislature, and father of John L. McConnel; William Pickering, Edwards County Whig in the legislature; Nathan M. Knapp, Scott County Whig elected to the legislature in 1850; Benjamin F. Bristow, Morgan County Whig elected to the legislature in 1850.

To George W. Crawford[1]

Hon: Secretary of War—   Springfield, Illinois.
Sir: Feb: 20 1850

Capt. Koscialowski, who will present you this letter, is an applicant for an appointment of Major in the new Regiments proposed to be raised by congress. I have already placed my name, among others, to a general recommendation of him for that appointment; but I now desire to say, a little more specifically, that I shall be much gratified if he shall be successful in his application. He is every way a gentleman, a great favorite with his acquaintances here, and, (as I understand, without any capacity for deciding myself,) has a military education, fitting him peculiarly for the position he seeks. Your Obt. Servt.   A. LINCOLN

[1] ALS, IHi.

To Abram Bale[1]

Mr. Abraham Bale: Springfield,
Dear Sir: Feb: 22. 1850

I understand Mr. Hickox[2] will go, or send to Petersburg tomorrow, for the purpose of meeting you to settle the difficulty about the wheat. I sincerely hope you will settle it. I think you *can* if you *will*, for I have always found Mr. Hickox a fair man in his dealings. If you settle, I will charge nothing for what I have done, and thank you to boot. By settling, you will most likely get your money sooner; and with much less trouble & expense. Yours truly
A. LINCOLN—

[1] ALS, IHi. Abram Bale was a Baptist preacher residing at Petersburg, Illinois. Lincoln misspells his first name.
[2] Addison or Horace Hickox, brothers who operated a mill to which Bale probably took his wheat. Virgil Hickox was a prominent Springfield merchant.

To John D. Johnston[1]

Dear Brother   Springfield, Feb. 23 1850

Your letter about a mail contract was received yesterday. I have made out a bid for you at $120, guaranteed it myself, got our PM here to certify it, and sent it on. Your former letter, concerning some man's claim for a pension was also received. I had the claim examined by those who are practised in such matters, & they decide he can can [*sic*] not get a pension.

As you make no mention of it, I suppose you had not learned that

we lost our little boy. He was sick fiftytwo days & died the morning of the first day of this month. It was not our *first,* but our second child.[2] We miss him very much. Your Brother in haste

A. LINCOLN

[1] ALS-P, ISLA.   [2] Edward Baker Lincoln.

To John Murray[1]

Hon: John Murray   Springfield, Ills.
Dear Sir   Feb: 25. 1850

Ninian[2] handed me your letter, in consequence of which I have written the accompanying letter, which as you see, Ninian & Stuart[3] have also signed. I addressed it to the President,[4] because you can then send it to whom you please to present to him; and because Baker & Butterfield[5] I believe are not very cordial with one another. Either alone would do better. Yours as ever   A LINCOLN

[1] ALS, owned by Mrs. H. L. Murray, Minneapolis, Minnesota. John Murray of Belleville, Illinois, had served as state senator from St. Clair County 1836-1840.   [2] Ninian W. Edwards.   [3] John T. Stuart.
[4] This letter is presumably not extant.
[5] Edward D. Baker and Justin Butterfield.

To Augustus C. French:
Petition for Appointment of William B. Fondey[1]

March 7, 1850

Hon. A. C. French—Governor of Illinois.

Sir.   The undersigned your petitioners legal voters of the City of Springfield would respectfully request that your Excellency appoint Wm. B. Fondey as an additional Notary Public for this City. and as in duty bound &c.   March 7th 1850[2]

[1] DS-P, ISLA. The verso bears the following endorsement: "You will appoint Mr. Fondey for the City of Springfield/ A C French."
[2] Signed by Lincoln and fifty-four others.

To Zachary Taylor[1]

His Excellency the President &c.   Springfield, Ills.
Dear Sir: March 15. 1850

I understand some one of our Ohio friends will probably be appointed Minister to Brazil; and if so, I hope Hon: Robert C. Schenck may be the man. In expressing a preference for Mr. Schenck over others of his own State, I do not mean to say that he

[77]

is less worthy than any out of his state; but were I to not limit myself as I do, I should probably come in collision with some recommendation of my own, formerly made; or, perhaps with the interests of some friend of my own state. Your Obt. Servt.

A. LINCOLN

[1] ALS, DNA FS RG 59, Appointment Papers. Robert C. Schenck served as U.S. representative 1843-1851 and was minister to Brazil, also accredited to Uruguay, Paraguay, and the Argentine, 1851-1853.

To Thomas Ewing[1]

Hon. Thomas Ewing: Springfield, Ills.
Secretary &c.   March 22. 1850

Dear Sir: I understand you have under consideration the question of appointing Dr. A. G. Henry to some Indian Agency. I wish now merely to say that of all those whom I have desired should receive appointments from this Administration, Dr. Henry was at first, has always been, and still is, No. One with me. I believe, nay, I *know*, he has done more disinterested labor in the Whig cause, than any other one, two, or three men in the state. Your Obt. Servt.

A. LINCOLN

[1] ALS, The Rosenbach Company, Philadelphia and New York.

Resolutions on the Death of Nathaniel Pope[1]

June 3, 1850

The Hon Nathaniel Pope District Judge of the United States Court for the District of Illinois having departed this life, during the late vacation of said Court and the members of the Bar of said Court entertaining the hig[h]est veneration of his memory, a profound respect for his ability, great experience and learning as a Judge, and cherishing for his memory virtues, public and private, his earnest simplicity of character, and unostentatious deportment, both in his public and private relations, the most lively and affectionate recollections, have resolved.

That as a manifestation of their deep sense of the loss which has been sustained in his death they will wear the usual badge of mourning during the residue of the Term.

That the Chairman communicate to the family of the deceased a copy of these proceedings, with an assurance of our sincere condolence on account of their heavy bereavement.

That the Hon: A. Williams District Attorney of this Court be

requested in behalf of this meeting to present these proceedings to
the Circuit Court and respectfully to ask that they may be entered
on the records   SAMUEL H TREAT
    E. N. POWELL   Chairman
    Secretary

¹ Copy, IHi. "Proceedings of the Circuit and District Courts of the United
States at Springfield Illinois on the death of Judge Nathaniel Pope. . . ." On the
opening of court, June 3, 1850, Lincoln "suggested the death of the Hon. Nathaniel Pope" and the court adjourned "until tomorrow morning." On the evening of June 3 a meeting of the bar was held in memory of Judge Pope and
a committee composed of Lincoln, Stephen T. Logan, Norman H. Purple,
David L. Gregg, and George W. Meeker, represented by Logan, presented the
resolutions as adopted and recorded in the proceedings of the court. There is a
discrepancy of dates in the court proceedings, in as much as under date of June
5 the proceedings of the bar meeting are designated as "held yesterday" (June
4), but the *Illinois State Register,* June 4, confirms that the bar meeting was
held on June 3.

To the Editors of the *Illinois Journal*¹

Editors of the Illinois Journal: Springfield,
Gentlemen—   June 5, 1850.
    An article in the Tazewell Mirror in which my name is promi-
nently used, makes me fear that my position, with reference to the
next Congressional election in this District, is misunderstood, and
that such misunderstanding may work injury to the cause of our
friends. I therefore take occasion to say that I neither seek, expect,
or desire a nomination for a seat in the next Congress; that I prefer
my name should not be brought forward in that connection; and
that I would now peremptorily forbid the use of it, could I feel entirely at liberty to do so. I will add, that in my opinion, the whigs
of the district have several other men, any one of whom they *can*
elect, and that too quite as *easily* as they could elect me. I therefore
shall be obliged, if any such as may entertain a preference for me,
will, at once turn their attention to making a choice from others.
Let a Convention be held at a suitable time, and in good feeling,
make a nomination; and I venture the prediction we will show the
District once more *right side up.* Your obd't servant,
                                                    A. LINCOLN.

¹ *Illinois Journal,* June 7, 1850.

To Nathaniel Hay¹

Mr. N. Hay: Springfield, June 11th. 1850
    I wish to build a front fence, on a brick foundation, at my house.
I therefore shall be obliged, if you will, as soon as possible, deliver

me bricks of suitable quality, and sufficient number to build such foundation, fifty feet long; of proper width, and depth, under ground, and about two feet above ground. Yours &c.

A. LINCOLN

1 ALS, owned by Mrs. Logan Hay, Springfield, Illinois. Nathaniel Hay was in the brick-making business with his father John Hay (grandfather of Lincoln's secretary) and also engaged in a lumber business with his brother-in-law, Joshua F. Amos.

To Richard S. Thomas[1]

Dear Thomas: Springfield, June 27. 1850

I am ashamed of not sooner answering your letter, herewith returned; and, my only appologies are, first, that I have been very busy in the U.S. court; and second, that when I received the letter I put it in my old hat, and buying a new one the next day, the old one was set aside, and so, the letter lost sight of for a time.

Either of the forms you give (the latter rather preferable) would do, I think, if it were proper to frame a suit on the *bond,* in which sureties as well as principal are to be held, on the 27th. Section. But, after a good deal of reflection, I think suits under the 27th. section are to be brought only against the offender *himself* for *penalties* incurred, & not against him *and* his sureties on his bond. If you sue on the bond, you can go for nothing but what is covered by the *condition* of the bond; and what is so covered? "that the applicant will keep an orderly house, and that he will not permit any unlawful gaming or riotous conduct in his house." Now look quite through the Chapter, and find what *penalty* is given for "disorderly house" "unlawful gaming" or "riotous conduct" or for all three together. The first eight sections say nothing about grocery keepers; the ninth provides for granting the license & taking the bond—the tenth, eleventh, twelfth, thirteenth & fourteenth, give no *penalty* or *penalties;* the fifteenth can not apply to this case, because it relates to selling *without* license—the sixteenth gives a penalty, but not for any of the *causes* covered by the bond—the seventeenth has nothing to the purposes—the eighteenth goes to the *causes* covered by the bond, but no *pecuniary* penalty is given by it—the 19th. 20th. & 21st. do not touch the causes covered by the bond, & with those sections, the chapter ends as to grocery keepers. Now I think you are to bring just such a suit on the bond, taken under the ninth section, as you would bring if the 27th. section had no existence.

Bring the suit in the name of whoever, on the face of the bond, is made the obligee, and for the use of whoever is entitled to the

money when collected—that is if the bond is given to the People of
the state of Illinois—your first heading, which I mark (A) is right
—if the bond is given to an individual, let his name, stand in place
of that of the People. Yours as ever   A. LINCOLN

1 ALS, owned by Richard S. T. Marsh, Washington, D. C.

Fragment: Notes for a Law Lecture[1]

[July 1, 1850?]

I am not an accomplished lawyer. I find quite as much material
for a lecture in those points wherein I have failed, as in those
wherein I have been moderately successful. The leading rule for
the lawyer, as for the man of every other calling, is diligence.
Leave nothing for to-morrow which can be done to-day. Never let
your correspondence fall behind. Whatever piece of business you
have in hand, before stopping, do all the labor pertaining to it
which can then be done. When you bring a common-law suit, if
you have the facts for doing so, write the declaration at once. If a
law point be involved, examine the books, and note the authority
you rely on upon the declaration itself, where you are sure to find
it when wanted. The same of defenses and pleas. In business not
likely to be litigated,—ordinary collection cases, foreclosures, par-
titions, and the like,—make all examinations of titles, and note
them, and even draft orders and decrees in advance. This course
has a triple advantage; it avoids omissions and neglect, saves your
labor when once done, performs the labor out of court when you
have leisure, rather than in court when you have not. Extempora-
neous speaking should be practised and cultivated. It is the lawyer's
avenue to the public. However able and faithful he may be in other
respects, people are slow to bring him business if he cannot make
a speech. And yet there is not a more fatal error to young lawyers
than relying too much on speech-making. If any one, upon his rare
powers of speaking, shall claim an exemption from the drudgery
of the law, his case is a failure in advance.

Discourage litigation. Persuade your neighbors to compromise
whenever you can. Point out to them how the nominal winner is
often a real loser—in fees, expenses, and waste of time. As a peace-
maker the lawyer has a superior opportunity of being a good man.
There will still be business enough.

Never stir up litigation. A worse man can scarcely be found than
one who does this. Who can be more nearly a fiend than he who
habitually overhauls the register of deeds in search of defects in

titles, whereon to stir up strife, and put money in his pocket? A moral tone ought to be infused into the profession which should drive such men out of it.

The matter of fees is important, far beyond the mere question of bread and butter involved. Properly attended to, fuller justice is done to both lawyer and client. An exorbitant fee should never be claimed. As a general rule never take your whole fee in advance, nor any more than a small retainer. When fully paid beforehand, you are more than a common mortal if you can feel the same interest in the case, as if something was still in prospect for you, as well as for your client. And when you lack interest in the case the job will very likely lack skill and diligence in the performance. Settle the amount of fee and take a note in advance. Then you will feel that you are working for something, and you are sure to do your work faithfully and well. Never sell a fee note—at least not before the consideration service is performed. It leads to negligence and dishonesty—negligence by losing interest in the case, and dishonesty in refusing to refund when you have allowed the consideration to fail.

There is a vague popular belief that lawyers are necessarily dishonest. I say vague, because when we consider to what extent confidence and honors are reposed in and conferred upon lawyers by the people, it appears improbable that their impression of dishonesty is very distinct and vivid. Yet the impression is common, almost universal. Let no young man choosing the law for a calling for a moment yield to the popular belief—resolve to be honest at all events; and if in your own judgment you cannot be an honest lawyer, resolve to be honest without being a lawyer. Choose some other occupation, rather than one in the choosing of which you do, in advance, consent to be a knave.

[1] NH, II, 140-43. The date assigned to this piece by Nicolay and Hay has been retained in the absence of satisfactory evidence to the contrary, but it seems probable that Lincoln wrote these observations on the legal profession several years later.

To Lewis C. Kercheval and Others[1]

Gentlemen:—   Chicago, Ill., July 24, 1850.

Yours of the 22nd inviting me to deliver an address to the citizens of this city upon the life of Z. Taylor deceased, late President of the United States was duly received. The want of time for preparation will make the task, for me, a very difficult one to perform, in any degree satisfactory to others or to myself. Still I do not feel at

liberty to decline the invitation; and therefore I will fix to-morrow
as the time. The hour may be any, you think proper, after 12
o'clock, M.   Your Ob't Serv't,   A. LINCOLN

Messrs. L. C. Kercheval, B. S. Morris,
Geo. W. Dole, John H. Kinzie, W. L. Newberry.[2]

[1] Chicago *Daily Journal*, July 24, 1850; Chicago *Weekly Journal*, July 29,
1850. Lincoln was attending the U.S. District Court in Chicago, representing
the defendant in Parker *v.* Hoyt, a patent case involving a waterwheel. Lincoln
won the case on July 24.

[2] Members of the two committees, one appointed by the Common Council the
other by a citizens meeting. Those not previously identified, are as follows: Lewis
C. Kercheval, famed in the annals of early Chicago as an eccentric but impartial
justice of the peace; John H. Kinzie, businessman and financier who was one
of the sons of the pioneer trader of Chicago, John Kinzie; Walter L. Newberry,
merchant, banker, and philanthropist who founded the Newberry Library.

Eulogy on Zachary Taylor[1]

EULOGY PRONOUNCED

BY HON. A. LINCOLN,

ON THE LIFE AND SERVICES OF THE LATE

PRESIDENT OF THE UNITED STATES,

At Chicago, July 25th, 1850

GENERAL ZACHARY TAYLOR, the eleventh elected President of the
United States, is dead. He was born Nov. 2nd,[2] 1784, in Orange
county, Virginia; and died July the 9th 1850, in the sixty-sixth
year of his age, at the White House in Washington City. He was
the second[3] son of Richard Taylor, a Colonel in the army of the
Revolution. His youth was passed among the pioneers of Kentucky,
whither his parents emigrated soon after his birth; and where his
taste for military life, probably inherited, was greatly stimulated.
Near the commencement of our last war with Great Britain, he was
appointed by President Jefferson, a lieutenant in the 7th regiment
of Infantry. During the war, he served under Gen. Harrison in
his North Western campaign against the Indians; and, having been
promoted to a captaincy, was intrusted with the defence of Fort
Harrison, with fifty men, half of them unfit for duty. A strong

[1] Chicago *Weekly Journal*, August 5, 1850; also in Chicago *Daily Journal*,
July 27, 1850.

[2] November 24 is the correct date. The haste with which Lincoln was forced
to prepare his eulogy and the unreliable data in the 1848 biographies are to
blame for Lincoln's errors. In later paragraphs, where Lincoln follows closely
Taylor's own reports and dispatches as printed in *Niles' Register* and the *House
Executive Documents*, his accuracy improves.

[3] Zachary Taylor was not the second, but the third son of Richard Taylor.

party of Indians, under the Prophet, brother of Tecumseh, made a midnight attack on the Fort; but Taylor, though weak in his force, and without preparation, was resolute, and on the alert; and, after a battle, which lasted till after daylight, completely repulsed them. Soon after, he took a prominent part in the expedition under Major Gen. Hopkins against the Prophet's town; and, on his return, found a letter from President Madison, who had succeeded Mr. Jefferson, conferring on him a major's brevet for his gallant defence of Fort Harrison.

After the close of the British war, he remained in the frontier service of the West, till 1818. He was then transferred to the Southern frontier, where he remained, most of the time in active service till 1826. In 1819, and during his service in the South, he was promoted to the rank of lieutenant colonel. In 1826 he was again sent to the North West, where he continued until 1836. In 1832, he was promoted to the rank of a colonel. In 1836 he was ordered to the South to engage in what is well known as the Florida War. In the autumn of 1837, he fought and conquered in the memorable battle of Okeechobee, one of the most desperate struggles known to the annals of Indian warfare. For this, he was honored with the rank of Brigadier General; and, in 1838 was appointed to succeed Gen. Jessup in command of the forces in Florida. In 1841 he was ordered to Fort Gibson to take command of the Second Military department of the United States; and in September, 1844, was directed to hold the troops between the Red River and the Sabine in readiness to march as might be indicated by the Charge of the United States, near Texas. In 1845 his forces were concentrated at Corpus Christi.

In obedience to orders, in March 1846, he planted his troops on the Rio Grande opposite Mattamoras. Soon after this, and near this place, a small detachment of Gen. Taylor's forces, under Captain Thornton, was cut to pieces by a party of Mexicans. Open hostilities being thus commenced, and Gen. Taylor being constantly menaced by Mexican forces vastly superior to his own, in numbers, his position became exceedingly critical. Having erected a fort, he might defend himself against great odds while he could remain within it; but his provisions had failed, and there was no supply nearer than Point Isabel, between which and the new fort, the country was open to, and full of, armed Mexicans. His resolution was at once taken. He garrisoned Fort Brown, (the new fort) with a force of about four hundred; and, putting himself at the head of the main body of his troops, marched forthwith for Point Isabel. He met no resistance on his march. Having obtained his supplies, he began his return march, to the relief of Fort Brown, which he at first knew, would be, and then knew had been besieged by the enemy, immediately upon his leaving it. On the first or second day of this return march, the Mexican General, Arista, met General Taylor in front, and offered battle. The Mexicans numbered six or eight thousand, opposed to whom were about two thousand Americans. The moment was a trying one. Comparatively, Taylor's forces were but a handful; and few, of either officers or men, had ever been under fire. A brief council was held; and the result was, the battle commenced. The issue of that contest all remember—remember with mingled sensations of pride and sorrow, that then, American valor and powers triumphed, and then the gallant and accomplished, and noble Ringgold fell.

The Americans passed the night on the field. The General knew the enemy was still in his fort; and the question rose upon him, whether to advance or retreat. A council was again held; and, it is said, the General overruled the majority, and resolved to advance. Accordingly in the morning, he moved rapidly forward. At about four or five miles from Fort Brown he again met the enemy in force, who had selected his position, and made some hasty fortification. Again the battle commenced, and raged till toward nightfall, when the Mexicans were entirely routed, and the General with his fatigued and bleeding, and reduced battalions marched into Fort Brown. There was a joyous meeting. A brief hour before, whether all *within* the fort had perished, all *without* feared, but none could tell—while the incessant roar of artillery, wrought those *within* to the highest pitch of apprehension, that their brethren *without* were being massacred to the last man. And now the din of battle nears the fort and sweeps obliquely by; a gleam of hope flies through the half imprisoned few; they fly to the wall; every eye is strained—it is—it is—the stars and stripes are still aloft! Anon the anxious brethren meet; and while hand strikes hand, the heavens are rent with a loud, long, glorious, gushing cry of victory! victory!! victory!!!

Soon after these two battles, Gen. Taylor was breveted a Major General in the U.S. Army.

In the mean time, war having been declared to exist between the United States and Mexico, provisions were made to reinforce Gen. Taylor; and he was ordered to march into the interior of Mexico. He next marched upon Monterey, arriving there on the 19th of September. He commenced an assault upon the city, on the 21st, and on the 23d was about carrying it at the point of the bayonet, when Gen. Ampudia capitulated. Taylor's forces consisted of 425 officers, and 9,220 men. His artillery consisted of one 10 inch mortar, two 24 pound Howitzers, and four light field batteries of four guns—the mortar being the only piece serviceable for the siege. The Mexican works were armed with forty-two pieces of cannon, and manned with a force of at least 7000 troops of the line, and from 2000 to 3000 irregulars.

Next we find him advancing farther into the interior of Mexico, at the head of 5,400 men, not more than 600 being regular troops.

At Agua Nueva he received intelligence that Santa Anna, the greatest military chieftain of Mexico, was advancing after him; and he fell back to Buena Vista, a strong position a few miles in advance of Saltillo. On the 22nd of Feb., 1847, the battle, now called the battle of Buena Vista, was commenced by Santa Anna at the head of 20,000 well appointed soldiers. This was Gen. Taylor's great battle. The particulars of it are familiar to all. It continued through the 23d; and although Gen. Taylor's defeat seemed to be inevitable, yet he succeeded by skill, and by the courage and devotion of his officers and men, in repulsing the overwhelming forces of the enemy, and throwing them back into the desert. This was the battle of the chiefest interest fought during the Mexican war. At the time it was fought, and for some weeks after, Gen. Taylor's communication with the United States was cut off; and the road was in possession of parties of the enemy. For many days after full intelligence of it, should have been in all parts of this country, nothing certain, concerning it, was known, while vague and painful rumors were afloat, that a great battle had been fought, and that Gen. Taylor, and his whole force had been annihilated.

At length the truth came, with its thrilling details of victory and blood—of glory and grief. A bright and glowing page was added to our Nation's history; but then too, in eternal silence, lay Clay, and Mc'Kee, and Yell, and Lincoln, and our own beloved Hardin.

This also was Gen. Taylor's *last* battle. He remained in active service in Mexico, till the autumn of the same year, when he returned to the United States.

Passing in review, Gen. Taylor's military history, some striking peculiarities will appear. No one of the six battles which he fought, excepting perhaps, that of Monterey, presented a field, which would have been selected by an ambitious captain upon which to gather laurels. So far as fame was concerned, the prospect—the promise in advance, was, "you may lose, but you can not win." Yet Taylor, in his blunt business-like view of things, seems never to have thought of this.

It did not happen to Gen. Taylor once in his life, to fight a battle on equal terms, or on terms advantageous to himself—and yet he was never beaten, and never retreated. In *all*, the odds was greatly against him; in each, defeat seemed inevitable; and yet *in all*, he triumphed. Wherever he has led, while the battle still raged, the issue was painfully doubtful; yet in *each* and *all*, when the din had ceased, and the smoke had blown away, our country's flag was still seen, fluttering in the breeze.

Gen. Taylor's battles were not distinguished for brilliant military manoeuvers; but in all, he seems rather to have conquered by the exercise of a sober and steady judgment, coupled with a dogged incapacity to understand that defeat was possible. His rarest military trait, was a combination of negatives—absence of *excitement* and absence of *fear*. He could not be *flurried*, and he could not be *scared*.

In connection with Gen. Taylor's military character, may be mentioned his relations with his brother officers, and his soldiers. Terrible as he was to his country's enemies, no man was so little disposed to have difficulty with his friends. During the period of his life, *duelling* was a practice not quite uncommon among gentlemen in the peaceful avocations of life, and still more common, among the officers of the Army and Navy. Yet, so far as I can learn, a *duel* with Gen. Taylor, has never been talked of.

He was alike averse to *sudden*, and to *startling* quarrels; and he pursued no man with *revenge*. A notable, and a noble instance of this, is found in his conduct to the gallant and now lamented Gen. Worth. A short while before the battles of the 8th and 9th of May, some questions of precedence arose between Worth, (then a colonel) and some other officer, which question it seems Gen. Taylor's duty to decide. He decided against Worth. Worth was greatly offended, left the Army, came to the United States, and tendered his resignation to the authorities at Washington. It is said, that in his passionate feeling, he hesitated not to speak harshly and disparagingly of Gen. Taylor. He was an officer of the highest character; and his word, on military subjects, and about military men, could not, with the country, pass for nothing. In this absence from the army of Col. Worth, the unexpected turn of things brought on the battles of the 8th and 9th. He was deeply mortified—in almost absolute desperation—at having lost the opportunity of being present, and taking part in those battles. The laurels won by his previous service, in his own eyes, seemed withering away. The Government, both *wisely* and *generously*, I think, declined accepting his resignation; and he returned to Gen. Taylor. Then came Gen. Taylor's *opportunity* for revenge. The battle of Monterey was approaching, and even at hand. Taylor *could* if he *would,* so place Worth in that battle, that his name would scarcely be noticed in the report. But no. He felt it was due to the service, to assign the real post of honor to some one of the best officers; he knew Worth was one of the best, and he felt that it was *generous* to allow him, then and there, to retrieve his secret loss. Accordingly he assigned to Col. Worth in that assault, what was *par excellence,* the post of honor; and, the duties of which, he executed so well, and so brilliantly, as to eclipse, in that battle, even Gen. Taylor himself.

As to Gen. Taylor's relations with his soldiers, details would be endless. It is perhaps enough to say—and it is far from the *least* of his honors that we can *truly* say—that of the many who served with him through the long course of forty years, all testify to the uniform kindness, and his constant care for, and hearty sympathy with, their every want and every suffering; while none can be found to declare, that he was ever a tyrant anywhere, in anything.

Going back a little in point of time, it is proper to say that so soon as the news of the battles of the 8th and 9th of May 1846, had fairly reached the United States, Gen. Taylor began to be named for the next Presidency, by letter writers, newspapers, public meetings and conventions in various parts of the country.

These nominations were generally put forth as being of a no-party character. Up to this time I think it highly probable—nay, almost certain, that Gen. Taylor had never thought of the Presidency in connection with himself. And there is reason for believing that the first intelligence of these nominations rather *amused* than *seriously* interested him. Yet I should be insincere, were I not to confess, that in my opinion, the repeated, and steady manifestations in his favor, *did* beget in his mind a laudable ambition to reach the high distinction of the Presidential chair.

As the time for the Presidential canvass approached, it was seen that general nominations, combining anything near the number of votes necessary to an election, could not be made without some pretty strong and decided reference to party politics. Accordingly, in the month of May, 1848, the great Democratic party nominated as their candidate, an able and distinguished member of their own party, on strictly party grounds. Almost immediately following this, the Whig party, in general convention, nominated Gen. Taylor as their candidate. The election came off in the November following; and though there was also a third candidate, the two former only, received any vote in the electoral college. Gen. Taylor, having the majority of them was duly elected; and he entered on the duties of that high and responsible office, March 5th, 1849. The incidents of his administration up to the time of his death, are too familiar and too fresh to require any direct repetition.

The Presidency, even to the most experienced politicians, is no bed of roses; and Gen. Taylor like others, found thorns within it. No human being can fill that station and escape censure. Still I hope and believe when Gen. Taylor's official conduct shall come to be viewed in the calm light of history, he will be found to have *deserved* as little as any who have succeeded him.

Upon the death of Gen. Taylor, as it would in the case of the death of any President, we are naturally led to consider what will be its effect, politically, upon the country. I will not pretend to believe that all the wisdom, or all the patriotism of the country, died with Gen. Taylor. But we know that *wisdom* and *patriotism*, in a public office, under institutions like ours, are wholly inefficient and worthless, unless they are sustained by the confidence and devotion of the people. And I confess my apprehensions, that in the death of the late President, we have lost a degree of that confidence and devotion, which will not soon again pertain to any successor. Between public measures regarded as antagonistic, there is often less real difference in its bearing on the public weal, than there is between the dispute being *kept up*, or being *settled* either way. I fear the one *great* question of the day, is not now so likely to be partially acquiesced in by the different sections of the Union, as it would have been, could Gen. Taylor have been spared to us. Yet, under all circumstances, trusting to our Maker, and through his wisdom and beneficence, to the great body of our people, we will not despair, nor despond.

In Gen. Taylor's general public relation to his country, what will strongly impress a close observer, was his unostentatious, self-sacrificing, long enduring devotion to his *duty*. He indulged in no recreations, he visited no public places, seeking applause; but quietly, as the earth in its orbit, he was always at his post. Along our whole Indian frontier, thro' summer and winter, in sunshine and storm, like a sleepless sentinel, *he* has *watched*, while *we* have *slept* for forty long years. How well might the dying hero say at last, "I have done my duty, I am ready to go."

Nor can I help thinking that the American people, in electing Gen. Taylor to the presidency, thereby showing their high appreciation, of his sterling, but unobtrusive qualities, did their *country* a service, and *themselves* an imperishable honor. It is *much* for the young to know, that treading the hard path of duty, as he trod it, *will* be noticed, and *will* lead to high places.

But he is gone. The conqueror at last is conquered. The fruits of his labor, his name, his memory and example, are all that is left us—his example, verifying the great truth, that "he that humbleth himself, shall be exalted" teaching, that to serve one's country with a singleness of purpose, gives assurance of that country's gratitude, secures its best honors, and makes "a dying bed, soft as downy pillows are."

The death of the late President may not be without its use, in reminding us, that *we*, too, must die. Death, abstractly considered, is the same with the high as with the low; but practically, we are not so much aroused to the contemplation of our own mortal natures, by the fall of *many* undistinguished, as that of *one* great, and well known, name. By the latter, we are forced to muse, and ponder, sadly.

"Oh, why should the spirit of mortal be proud"

So the multitude goes, like the flower or the weed,
That withers away to let others succeed;
So the multitude comes, even those we behold,
To repeat every tale that has often been told.

For we are the same, our fathers have been,
We see the same sights our fathers have seen;
We drink the same streams and see the same sun
And run the same course our fathers have run.

They loved; but the story *we* cannot unfold;
They scorned, but the heart of the haughty is cold;
They grieved, but no wail from their slumbers will come,
They joyed, but the tongue of their gladness is dumb.

They died! Aye, they died; we things that are now;
That work on the turf that lies on their brow,
And make in their dwellings a transient abode,
Meet the things that they met on their pilgrimage road.

Yea! hope and despondency, pleasure and pain,
Are mingled together in sun-shine and rain;
And the smile and the tear, and the song and the dirge,
Still follow each other, like surge upon surge.

'Tis the wink of an eye, 'tis the draught of a breath,
From the blossoms of health, to the paleness of death.
From the gilded saloon, to the bier and the shroud.
Oh, why should the spirit of mortal be proud!

To Lewis C. Kercheval and Richard J. Hamilton[1]

Gentlemen: Chicago, July 26, 1850.

Your polite note of yesterday, requesting, for publication, a copy of the address on the life and public services of Gen. Taylor, is received; and I comply with the request very cheerfully. Accompanying this, I send you the original manuscript. Your ob't serv't.

Messrs. L. C. Kercheval.   A. LINCOLN.
     R. J. Hamilton.[2]

[1] Chicago *Daily Journal*, July 27, 1850; Chicago *Weekly Journal*, August 5, 1850.
[2] Richard J. Hamilton, representing the Common Council, City of Chicago, was a prominent lawyer and Democrat who held various public offices.

To Edwin W. Bakewell[1]

E. W. Bakewell, Esq   Springfield,
Dear Sir: Augt. 1. 1850

I have at last found time to draw up a Bill in your case. Inclosed you have it. Get from the Recorder's office a copy of Cole's deed to Campbell, mark it thus: (A) and put it with the Bill, as part of it. Then fill properly the blank date in the bond at the end of the Bill, have some good man to sign his name to the bond, and file the whole with the clerk of the circuit court. Yours truly

                                                   A. LINCOLN

[1] ALS, owned by Charles W. Olsen, Chicago, Illinois. The enclosures are no longer with the letter, and the case has not been positively identified, but see Lincoln's letter to Robert E. Williams, August 15, 1857, *infra*. Bakewell was a resident of Bloomington, Illinois.

To John Addison[1]

John Addison, Esq-   Springfield,
Dear Sir: Augt. 9. 1850

Your letter of the 31st. of July was received yesterday. The substance of the matter you speak of, in detail, has long been known to me; and I have supposed, if I *would*, I *could* make it entirely plain to the world. But my high regard for some of the members of the late cabinet; my great devotion to Gen: Taylor personally; and, above all, my fidelity to the great whig cause, have induced me to be silent; and this especially, as I have felt, and do feel, entirely independent of the government, and therefore above the power of it's

[91]

persecution. I also have long suspected that you were being persecuted on account of this piece of villiany, by, or for the benefit of, the original villian; and, I own, this fills me with indignation.[2] A public expose, however, though it might confound the guilty, I fear might also injure some who are innocent; to some extent, disparage a good cause; reflect no credit upon me, and result in no advantage to you.

Mr. Bates[3] I see declines a place in the Cabinet; so that it is not yet apparant how I can serve you, which I am anxious to do so soon as I shall perceive the way. Write me again.

One part of your letter induces me to say I would not now accept the Land Office, if it were offered to me. Yours as ever

A. LINCOLN

[1] ALS, InFtwL.
[2] Lincoln probably alludes to the suppression of some of his letters of recommendation for the Land Office. See his letter to Josiah M. Lucas, November 17, 1849, *supra*.
[3] Edward Bates of Missouri, to whom President Millard Fillmore offered the secretaryship of the War Department.

To Samuel R. Lowry[1]

Mr. S. R. Lowry.   Springfield,
Dear Sir: August 17. 1850

Your letter of the 13th. was received a day or two ago, and I now proceed to answer it. Your first question is "What is lacking to perfect a title on the part of the defendants?" Answer—The defendants, so far as I know, do not claim to have any title, except a tax-title; and this the court has decided to be insufficient; and I know nothing the defendants *can* do to perfect this title. I do not know what you mean by "the conveyances sent by mail." The deed purporting to be made some years ago, at St. Louis, by Page (the Patentee) to Ryan, we had at the trial, and still have. That deed, in the hands of these defendants, was sought to be used as evidence of what the lawyers call an outstanding title—that is, a title owned by neither plaintiff nor defendants. The trouble with this deed was, that the plaintiff proved it to be a forgery; and I see no way in which the defendants can ever succeed unless they can somehow prove that this deed is *not* a forgery. This is the whole story. The case can not be gained by *much* talking.

A new trial was allowed upon the payment of costs; and, until the costs are paid, the defendants are liable to be put out of possession at any moment the plaintiff may see fit to order out a writ;

which, however, he has not yet done. The amount of the cost is $25-82 cents, as the clerk informs me. Yours &c   A. LINCOLN—

1 ALS, owned by Horace Lowry, Minneapolis, Minnesota. Samuel R. Lowry was a resident of Peoria, Illinois. The case referred to has not been identified.

To Thomas Corwin[1]

Springfield, Ill., Sept 1 [1850]

Hon Thomas Corwin: This will introduce to your acquaintance my friend Simeon Francis, editor of the *Illinois Journal*. He will desire an interview with the new Secretary of the Interior,[2] with whom I am not acquainted. I shall be greatly obliged if you will procure him a favorable introduction to that gentleman, and show him any other attention which the press of your duties will permit. Your Ob't. Serv't,   A. LINCOLN

1 Tracy, p. 44. Senator Thomas Corwin of Ohio resigned his seat in the Senate, July 20, 1850, to accept President Fillmore's appointment to the secretaryship of the Treasury Department.   2 Alexander H. H. Stuart of Virginia.

To John J. Crittenden and Thomas Corwin[1]

Hon: John J. Crittenden, &   Springfield, Illinois,
Hon: Thomas Corwin—   Sept. 2. 1850.

I suppose both of you have a slight general recollection of me; though nothing more, I am aware. My friend, John Addison, who will present this, desires a clerkship; and, for a reason which I do not wish to commit to paper, or even to speak of particularly, I very much wish he could be gratified.[2] I will only say, it will be righting him in a point, in which, I feel quite sure, he has been greatly wronged. As to his capacity and faithfulness, he will find abundant testimonials in Washington. Your Obt. Servt.   A. LINCOLN

1 ALS, PHC. President Fillmore appointed Governor Crittenden attorney general. Crittenden resigned as governor of Kentucky on July 22, 1850.
2 See letter to Addison, August 9, 1850, *supra*.

To John Addison[1]

John Addison, Esq   Springfield, Illinois,
Sir: Sept. 9. 1850

There are some letters remaining at the Department of the Interior, which were placed there as recommendations of myself for Comr. of the Genl. Land Office. I will thank you to withdraw them, and forward them to me. Truly Yours   A. LINCOLN

1 ALS, DLC.

Endorsement: Petition for Pardon of Henry Heath[1]

[September 27, 1850]

The signers to this petition are excellent citizens

A. LINCOLN

[1] AES, I-Ar. Sixty citizens of Tazewell County signed the petition to Governor Augustus C. French sent with accompanying letter of David Davis, dated September 27, 1850.

To Isaac Onstott[1]

Dear Isaac: Springfield, Nov: 6. 1850

I have been absent on the circuit seven weeks, only getting home to the election; so that I could not answer your letter of the 16th. of Octr. till now. I am for you; and have written to the Department, that if the recommendations from your own county place *you* on very nearly equal ground with the best of your competitors, I desire that you may be appointed. I send the letter directly to the Department thinking it may be best not to lose the time of sending it to you first. Your friend as ever,   A. LINCOLN

[1] ALS-P, ISLA. Onstott was appointed postmaster at Havana, Illinois, on November 7, 1850.

Family Record Written by Abraham Lincoln[1]

[1851?]

[Thos. Lincoln was born Jan. the 6th A.D. 1778 and was married June 12th 1806 to Nancy Hanks who was born Feb 5th 1784.

Sarah, Lincoln Daughter of Thos. and] Nancy Lincoln, was born Feb. 10th. 1807.

Abraham Lincoln, Son of Thos. & Nancy Lincoln, was born Feb. 12th. 1809.

Sarah Bush, first married to Daniel Johnston, and afterwards second wife of Thos. Lincoln, was born Decr. 13th. 1788.

John D. Johnston, Son of Daniel & Sarah Johnston, was born May [10]th. 18[15] married to Mary Bar[ker] October 13th. 1834—who was born July 22nd. 1816.

Thomas L. D. Johnston, Son of John [D.] and Mary Johnston, was born January 10th. 1837.

Abraham L. B. Johnston, Son of same parents, was born March 27th. 1838.

Marietta, Sarah Jane Johnston, Daughter [of] same parents, was born January 21[st.] 1840.

Squire H. Johnston, son of same parents, was born, December 15th. 1841.

Richard M. Johnston, son of same parents, was born, October 26th. [*sic*] 1843.[2]

Dennis F. Johnston, son of same parents, was born, November 18th. 1845.

Daniel W. Johnston, son of same parents, was born, December 13th. 1847.

Nancy Jane Williams, was born, March 18, 1836.[3]

Thomas Lincoln married to Sarah Johnston, Decr. 2nd. 1819.

Sarah Lincoln, daughter of Thos. Lincoln, was married to Aaron Grigsby, Aug. 1826.

Abraham Lincoln, son of Thos. Lincoln, was married to Mary Todd, Novr. 4th. 1842.

John D. Johnston was married to his second wife, Nancy Jane Williams, March 5. 1851.[4]

Nancy Lincoln wife of Thos. Lincoln, died October 5th. 1818.

Sarah, daughter of Thos. Lincoln, wife of Aaron Grigsby, died [Jan]uary 20th. 1828.

Thomas Lincoln, died, January 17 [1851] aged 73 years & 11 days.

Daniel W. Johnston, Son of John D. & Mary Johnston, died July 5th. 184 [8 or 9?][5]

1 AD, ORB. Three record pages of Thomas Lincoln's family Bible were filled in by Abraham Lincoln, probably in 1851 after his father's death. The pages are worn and tattered at the edges and portions are illegible or torn off. Fortunately it is possible to restore illegible and missing portions from other sources. A contemporary copy made by John D. Johnston (also in the Barrett Collection) provides the missing portion torn from the top of the first page. All editorial restorations are bracketed.

2 Purported facsimile reproductions of this page in the Bible record have been printed showing that Lincoln wrote "October 31st" for the date of Richard M. Johnston's birth. These facsimiles have been "doctored" to give the "31st" in place of Lincoln's "26th."

3 The verso of this first page of the manuscript contains no entries, but has been used for arithmetic.

4 An additional entry on this page, was written by John D. Johnston recording the birth of his son John D., Jr., on April 11, 1854.

5 Further entries written in pencil on this page are not in Lincoln's hand. They read as follows:

"Mary Johnston be[loved] wife of John D. Johnston died Sept. 21st. 1850 a bout ½ hour before Sun down.

"Marietta Sary Jane Johnston Daughter of John D. & Mary Johnston Died Apr. the 8th. 1853."

Memorandum of Births in the Hall Family[1]

[1851?]

Elizabeth Jane Hall, was born August 14th, 1829.
Alfred L. Hall, was born August 12th 1839.
Sarah Louisa Hall, was born August 12th 1841.

[1] AD, ORB. The slip of paper containing these entries is presumably contemporary with the record in the family Bible. All three were children of Lincoln's stepsister, Matilda Johnston, who married Squire Hall.

To ——— Wilson[1]

Mr. Wilson: Springfield Illinois January 1851
    Take care of this boy until to-morrow, or longer if the weather is bad, and send the bill to me.   A. LINCOLN.

[1] Tracy, p. 45. The boy is identified by Tracy as "Gilbert J. Greene, who set type in the *New York Tribune* office." The originals of this note and the one to Wallace (*infra*) have not been found. Advertisements in the *Illinois Journal* of this period list the proprietors of the Globe Tavern in Springfield as "Chamblin & Wilson."

To ——— Wallace[1]

Mr. Wallace, Peoria: Springfield, Ill. Jan. 1851.
    Dear Sir: This boy wants to reach the Rock River country somewhere near Beloit. If he needs any assistance so you can help him in any way, it will be appreciated, and I will be responsible. Yours,
                                             A. LINCOLN

[1] Tracy, p. 45.

To John D. Johnston[1]

Dear Brother: Springfield, Jany. 12. 1851—
    On the day before yesterday I received a letter from Harriett,[2] written at Greenup. She says she has just returned from your house; and that Father [is very] low, and will hardly recover. She also s[ays] you have written me two letters; and that [although] you do not expect me to come now, yo[u wonder] that I do not write. I received both your [letters, and] although I have not answered them, it is no[t because] I have forgotten them, or been uninterested about them—but because it appeared to me I could write nothing which could do any good. You already know I desire that neither Father or Mother shall be in want of any comfort either in health or sickness while they live; and I feel sure you

[96]

have not failed to use my name, if necessary, to procure a doctor, or any thing else for Father in his present sickness. My business is such that I could hardly leave home now, if it were not, as it is, that my own wife is sick-abed. (It is a case of baby-sickness, and I suppose is not dangerous.) I sincerely hope Father may yet recover his health; but at all events tell him to remember to call upon, and confide in, our great, and good, and merciful Maker; who will not turn away from him in any extremity. He notes the fall of a sparrow, and numbers the hairs of our heads; and He will not forget the dying man, who puts his trust in Him. Say to him that if we could meet now, it is doubtful whether it would not be more painful than pleasant; but that if it be his lot to go now, he will soon have a joyous [meeting] with many loved ones gone before; and where [the rest] of us, through the help of God, hope ere-long [to join] them.

Write me again when you receive this. Affectionately

A. LINCOLN

1 ALS, ORB. The letter is damaged on one edge. Bracketed words are taken from Nicolay and Hay.

2 Harriett Hanks Chapman, the daughter of Dennis Hanks and Lincoln's stepsister Elizabeth Johnston Hanks, who had married Augustus H. Chapman.

To James A. Pearce[1]

Hon: James A. Pearce: Springfield,
Sir: Jany. 13. 1851.

It is believed here, by myself & some others, that your influence, if we could enlist it, would secure the appointment of Charles H. Constable to a Judgeship in Oregon. Mr. Constable is a native of Maryland; and I understand you have some personal acquaintance with him, or his family. He is now, and for several years has been, a resident of this State. He is well qualified to do the duties of a Judgeship; and I believe it would give universal satisfaction to the whigs of this State for him to receive such an appointment. I shall be greatly obliged, if you shall find it agreeable to interest yourself in his behalf.

You will probably not remember me; and therefore, as an appology for addressing you, I have to say that I had an introduction to you while I was a member of the H.R. of the 30th. Congress. Your Obt. Servt   A. LINCOLN

1 ALS, DNA FS RG 59, Appointment Papers. Lincoln's letter was enclosed with one by David Davis of the same date to Senator James A. Pearce of Maryland recommending Constable. Constable did not receive the appointment.

To William Martin[1]

Hon: William Martin: Springfield, Feb: 19. 1851

The Legislature having got out of the way, I at last find time to attend to the business you left with me on behalf of the Alton and Sangamon Railroad Company.

As to your first question "Is there or is there not, a legal liability, raised in favor of the Company, against a *subscriber* under the 1st. and 14th. sections of their charter, independent of any special contract, upon which a suit may be sustained for instalments called for under said 14th. section?["]

Supposing you use the word *"subscriber"* as synonamous with *"stockholder"* I answer that in my opinion, such legal liability is raised, upon which such suit may be sustained.

The reason I note the word *subscriber* is, that I think a person might *subscribe;* and yet if he did not make the *advance payment,* he would not be fixed as a stockholder, and no suit for calls would lie [be?] against him.

Second question. "If there be such legal liability, how far is it affected by that clause of Sec: 14 which declares that all instalments shall be paid as the Directors may deem fit 'under the penalty of the forfeiture of all previous payments thereon' (meaning all previous payments made on each share of said stock)?["]

I find several decisions that this matter of forfeiture is a merely cumulative remedy given the Company, and that it does not at all affect the right of the Company to maintain a suit against a delinquent stock-holder. This I believe to be the law.

Third question. "To sustain an action on this legal liability (if any exists) what material facts should be stated in the declaration? and what will be legal and competent proof to sustain them?"

As to the declaration. Upon this subject I have examined the books, and reflected a good deal; and my conclusion is that nothing more than a common count is necessary. You will find a very apt precedent for such a count in 2. Chitty's Pleading, 52. Notwithstanding this conclusion of mine, I have, through great caution, inserted two special counts in the declarations I have drawn. In the first of these, I state accurately, the creation of the Company by the Legislature, the opening of subscription books, the subscription and payment of five per cent by the defendant, the subsequent organization of the Company, and the calls for the instalments by the

---

[1] ALS, owned by Kingman Brewster, Washington, D. C. William Martin of Alton, Illinois, was one of the commissioners for the sale of stock in the Alton & Sangamon Railroad Company, which had retained Lincoln in suits to compel stockholders to pay past-due installments on their shares of stock.

Directors. In the other, I state the written article in the book, as a conditional promise of the defendant, with averments, of the performance of the conditions. I am bringing four suits;[2] and in the two most important, for the special counts, I file complete copies of the books, signatures and all; in the other two I risk it with copies of the article, *without the names*. For the common counts, I file accounts for the calls in all the cases.

As to the proof. To be entirely safe, we must prove

1. The creation of the Corporation
2. That the defendant is a Stockholder
3. That the Corporation has been organized
4. That the calls have been made
5. That due notice of calls has been given.

The first will be proved by the production of the charter.

The second, by the production of the subscription book with the defendant's name, and proof of the genuineness of his signature, together with any competent parol or written evidence, that he made the advance payment.

The third may be proved by the production of the book, containing the record entry of the organization; and it may also be proved by parol evidence that the Company is, in fact, doing business as an organized corporation.

The fourth can be proved by the production of the book, in which the orders for the calls are recorded, together with proof, in person or by deposition, that the book produced is the book of the corporation—*and it can be proved in no other way*, unless it can be first proved, that no *record* entry of the calls was made; or being made, has been lost or destroyed. Knowing the inconvenience of this, in these cases, I have labored hard to find the law otherwise; but it is vain.

The fifth may be proved by the common printer's or publisher's certificate, under our general statute of "Advertisements."

I am satisfied, from several adjudged cases, that a Stockholder is a competent witness for the company in these cases.

Gillespie and Stuart[3] have both told me that some law passed at this session making Stockholders competent witnesses, and also touching the evidence as to corporation records; but they can not tell the title of the act, and after considerable search, I have not found it.

[2] But see the last sentence of this letter. Only two cases came to trial before the Sangamon Circuit Court in August, against Joseph Klein and James A. Barret, respectively. For other letters concerning these suits, *vide infra* February 24, 26, March 6, June 23, July 19, 26, 31, and August 29, 1851.

[3] Joseph Gillespie and John T. Stuart.

Send me the name of the keeper of the records (Secretary or Clerk.) in New-York.

One of my men "caved in" & paid his instalments yesterday[4] Yours truly   A. LINCOLN

4 John M. Burkhardt.

To David A. Smith[1]

D. A. Smith, Esq   Springfield,
Dear Sir: Feb: 20. 1851

I learn that Caldwell[2] has execu[ted his] bond and qualified under the decree. I am now anxio[us to] know whether the arrangement has been made *to your sat[isfac]tion;* and I do not like to ask Caldwell. Will you write [me] by return mail?. Yours as ever   A. LINCOL[N]

1 ALS, ICHi. The letter is damaged on one edge. Bracketed words are reconstructed by Angle, p. 78. David A. Smith was a lawyer of Jacksonville, Illinois.

2 Albert G. Caldwell, defendant in Atwood *v.* Caldwell pending in the state supreme court, was a Democrat, at the time representative in the legislature from Gallatin County.

To William Martin[1]

Hon: Wm. Martin   Springfield,
Dear Sir: Feb: 24. 1851

Your letter of the 21st. is received. I have examined the cases refered to by you, in 21st. Wend: 5 Ala. 3 Do. & 5 B. Monroe; and I fear to rely on them to sustain us in our question. We have sued for payments which *we say* the Directors have required. We must prove that the Directors *did* require them. Our exact question is "Can we prove this without producing the books containing the orders requiring the payments?" This question seems to me not [to] have been decided in any of the cases refered to. In the case in Wendell "The plaintiffs proved calls for payments &c." p. 297. This was probably done by the production of the books. The only question then was whether the defendant had been sufficiently notified of the *plan* of making payment. The Alabama cases, though excellent on other points, do not seem to me to approach our question. In the Kentucky case, the Court themselves say, "and the only objection made to it" (the declaration) "being that it does not show a sufficient *notice* or *publication* of the calls made by the board of directors or managers, upon the subscribers for stock, *we shall confine our attention to that point."* This clearly is not our point.

On the 5th. point, *I* thought the "printer's certificate["] would be sufficient; but Mr. Herndon doubted at the time; and as I find you doubt also, I will not be so arrogant as to insist that you are both wrong. Let us then be prepared to have the printer, in person, or his deposition, together with the papers, in open court.

As to making a "Stockholder a witness" I can not send you the authorities just now; because I have not preserved a list of them— but I will send them in a few days. Neither have I yet been able to find the new statute we have been speaking of.

Send me one of your blank declarations, and if I need more, I will write you. Yours as ever   A. LINCOLN

1 ALS, owned by Kingman Brewster, Washington, D. C.

To Isaac Gibson[1]

Secretary of the Alton and   Springfield, Illinois
Sangamon Railroad Company   Feb. 26th. 1851

Sir   Under the direction of William Martin of Alton, I have commenced suits against three of your Stockholders who refuse to pay their calls. I suppose it is a matter of interest to the Company that we should not fail in these suits, as such failures might encourage others to stop payments. The cases will be fiercely contested at all points. Among other things, we shall be obliged to prove that the *calls* for instalments were made by the Directors under the 14th. Section of the charter. This proof we can not legally make without the *production* of the Book or Books, in which the orders for these calls are entered.

Knowing the inconvenience of producing these Books I have struggled hard to convince myself that we could in some way dispense with them, but in vain. The Books *must* be here, together with some person, or deposition to certify them as the Books of the Company. Our Court, at which these cases stand for trial, commences its term on Monday the 17th. of March next. Now what I wish is, that you will put that Book in your trunk, and bring it here to court. This may be a little troublesome, but I believe it will prevent a greater amount of trouble in future. Please write on receipt of this. Respectfully   A. LINCOLN

1 Copy, IHi. Accompanying the contemporary copy of Lincoln's letter are copies of Gibson's telegram and letter in reply, dated March 15, 1851, explaining that in view of the fact that he could not leave New York at the time it would be necessary to postpone the suits.

To William Martin[1]

Hon: Wm. Martin   Springfield,
Dear Sir: March 6. 1851.

Yours of March —— with it's inclosures, was received yesterday.
I agree with the New-York lawyer, that it is best not to amend the
minutes. In my view, if there were no minutes—no entries in
writing—of the calls, then we could prove by *parol* that the Directors required the payments, and procured the publication of notices
of them in the papers. My difficulty was that the calls *being entered
of record*, and that fact getting out in evidence, we could not proceed without producing the record. If I am right in this, it follows
that if the records, when produced, are defective, the defects can
be supplied by parol.

If any of my cases are brought [to] trial at the ensuing term, I
shall need the minutes of the Commissioners, together with the
witness to identify them as you suggest. I shall also want the print-
ers' certificate, and if not too inconvenient, a living witness also, to
prove the publication for the calls. The reason I say *if*, is, that another of my victims, J. M. Burkhardt, has "caved in" and paid his
instalments—still another, Joseph Klein, probably will; and the
remaining one, James A. Barret,[2] as I wrote you, is proposing
terms. In addition to all this, I can not be ready unless the Secretary comes on with his books. If I find I shall need the proof from
Alton I will write you again.

As to Barret, if the Board think they have the power, I rather
think they would better accept his terms. Mr. Lyon[3] thinks the
change of the location of road makes a serious question as to the
release of stock-holders, and Barret is the only one I have heard of
who is disposed to make the question. I think, Mr. Lyon's opinion
notwithstanding, that the change will not work a release; but still
it is better to get along peaceably if possible. I have not time *now*
to review your declaration as you desire, but I have no doubt it is
right, or at least as nearly right as I could make it, before I get
some rubbing by an adversary in court.

Your despach is just here. On the question of the competency of
a Stockholder to testify in these suits I send you 4 Watts & Serg:
393. This book is not here, & I find a reference to it in the Septr.
U.S. Dig: Vol. 2 page 976, Sec. 405.

I also send you 7 Dana 99. This case is full and plump; and is,
perhaps, the only reported case, exactly in point. There is no case
against us. There are many deciding that a Stockholder is incompetent for the corporation; but they are all in cases where *strangers*

& not *members* of the corporation, were suing or being sued. Yours
as ever   A. LINCOLN

¹ ALS, IHi.
² James A. Barret, a leading citizen and agriculturist of Springfield, whose
name appears in contemporary sources with either one or two *t*'s.
³ Efforts to identify Lyon have been unsuccessful.

To Millard Fillmore¹

His Excellency   Springfield, Illinois,
The President of the U.S.   March 11. 1851.

Sir: We have a highly valued friend here, Francis Arenz, who is
a native of ———.² He is an educated gentleman, of unquestioned
integrity, and excellent business capacities and habits. He has resided in this country, and within what is now our sole whig District
in Illinois, nearly a quarter of a century, during most of which
time we have known him personally and intimately. In our political contests he has ever been our firm and efficient friend; and,
disabusing the minds of his own countrymen among us, of those
prejudices they generally entertain against us as a party, he has
done as much as—perhaps more than,—any other one man, in preserving the integrity of our District. Through this long period he
has acted a most disinterested part, never claiming any thing for
himself. He now wishes to visit his native country; and *we* would
be much gratified if the government would find him some honorable employment which would enable him to do so without pecuniary loss. We know not enough of the employments abroad, to
enable us to designate; yet we make this appeal, not formally, but
in all sincerety and earnestness. Your Obt. Servts.

JOHN T. STUART

A. LINCOLN

¹ ALS, DNA FS RG 59, Appointment Papers. Francis Arenz, a native of
Prussia and resident of Beardstown, Illinois, had served as representative in the
Illinois House of Representatives 1845-1847. He was appointed as "bearer of
dispatches to Prussia and Austria."
² The blank was left unfilled in the letter.

To Orville H. Browning and Nehemiah Bushnell¹

Messrs Browning & Bushnell   Springfield,
Gentlemen   March 28. 1851

Your letter is received. I have made the arrangement to use the
Hoyt evidence² in the other cases.

The new Act of Congress provides that all cases begun here shall

[103]

be tried here, & not go to Chicago at all. All our Patent cases were begun here.

It also fixes the summer term here in July,[3] instead of June as heretofore. So no trouble is created in our Patent cases by the new law. In haste Yours as ever   A. LINCOLN

[1] ALS, IHi.

[2] Parker *v.* Hoyt, a patent case involving a waterwheel, which Lincoln won for the defendant in the U.S. District Court, July 24, 1850.

[3] The U.S. Circuit Court convened July 7, and on July 10 continued Lincoln's patent cases.

To David A. Smith[1]

Dear Smith   Springfield, March 28. 1851–

On yesterday evening we argued and su[bmit]ted the Bank Certificate question.[2] I learn that Da[vis][3] will probably not decide it for a week or [so] when he will send the decision down from [the] circuit. Logan entered his motion[4] merely [to get] satisfaction to the extent of the notes & certif[icates] received, taking no notice of the tender. [This] I suppose will test the question just a[s] well. He also thinks there may be a dif[fer]ence between *notes* and *certificates;* and therefore urged me, and I consented, that you should ascertain the exact separate am[ounts] of each, which you have received, and send it up, so that it can be got into the record. He also pressed me to agree that the certificates are in the *form* given in the [11?] Sec: of the Act of 1843. I agreed to this, [on] condition that my agreement should go for nothing, if the fact is really otherwise. W[e agree] on all this.

One other little matter. I am short of [funds] and intended to ask Col. Dunlap for my [fee] in the case in the U.S. court, but he lef[t sooner] than I expected. He is in no default wi[th me,] for he once mentioned the subject to me, a[nd I] passed it by. But I now need the money [and] I will take it as a favor if you will s[how] him this note & get him to send it to me. We never agreed on the amount; but I cl[aim] $50. which I suppose neither he or you will think unreasonable. Yours truly   A. LINCOLN

[1] ALS, owned by Mrs. Thomas S. Noyes, Chicago, Illinois. One edge of the letter is burned. Bracketed portions are given as reconstructed in Angle and revised by the present editors.

[2] David A. Smith and George A. Dunlap as assignees of the defunct Bank of Illinois were suing James M. Dunlap, brother of George, for payment of debts owed the bank. The case had been decided previously against James Dunlap in the Sangamon County Circuit Court and Illinois Supreme Court, and was now back in the Circuit Court in James Dunlap's effort to get the court to credit partial satisfaction of the judgment by reason of payments received by the as-

signees in notes and certificates of the bank. Judge Davis later granted an appeal to the State Supreme Court. On July 7 The Supreme Court decided in favor of James Dunlap, allowing his claim to discharge his debt in notes and certificates of the bank. ³ Judge David Davis.

⁴ Stephen T. Logan, counsel for the defense, entered a motion for an order from Judge Davis requiring the assignees to accept notes and certificates of the bank. Judge Davis denied the motion.

To Lewis M. Hays[1]

Dear Sir: Mount Pulaski, Ills. April 23. 1851

I this day commence the suit against Turley.[2] It will not be for trial till October.[3] I return you the Letters. You see a certificate I have written in blank, which you must have filled and signed by the present presiding judge of the Probate Court. Be sure that the blanks are all filled, and the signature added. Then return the paper to me at Springfield, Ills. Yours &c.   A. LINCOLN

¹ ALS-P, ISLA. Lewis M. Hays was a resident of Gosport, Indiana.
² George W. Turley was one of the founders of Mt. Pulaski, Illinois.
³ Lincoln finally got judgment for Hays and collected the debt September 7, 1853. For further correspondence about this case see letters to Hays, October 27, 1852, and September 8, 1853, *infra*.

To Orville H. Browning and Nehemiah Bushnell[1]

Messrs Browning & Bushnell   Springfield,
Gentlemen   June 5. 1851

I reached home from the circuit yesterday, after an absence; and hence your letter of May the 8th. was not sooner answered. The arrangement to use the Hoyt evidence,[2] in the Rock-Island cases, was made before the adjournment of the Legislature, and I so informed our clients then. This I believe is all you seek to know.
Yours truly   A. LINCOLN

¹ ALS, owned by Robert Barton, Foxboro, Massachusetts.
² *Vide supra*, letter of March 28 and note.

To William Martin[1]

Hon: Wm. Martin   Springfield,
Dear Sir: June 23. 1851

What points, in our Rail Road cases,[2] were decided at the Spring term of your Circuit Court? and how were they decided?

Will the Secretary, with his Books, be out here at our fall terms? or will we be driven to try to prove the ordering of the calls, by depositions? Our next term of Court commences on the fourth monday of August.

Please write me on the receipt of this. Truly Yours

A. LINCOLN

¹ ALS, IHi.
² See other letters to Martin, beginning February 19, 1851, concerning the Alton & Sangamon Railroad cases.

To Andrew McCallen¹

Andrew McCallen.   Springfield, Ills.
Dear Sir: July. 4. 1851.

I have news from Ottawa, that we *win* our Galatin & Saline county case.² As the dutch Justice said, when he married folks "Now, vere ish my hundred tollars" Yours truly   A. LINCOLN

¹ ALS, ORB.
² On July 3, the Illinois Supreme Court held invalid the act of the legislature (February 11, 1851) by which Gallatin and Saline counties were united making Equality the county seat. The Saline County Court, claiming the act to be unconstitutional, had applied for a mandamus to compel Samuel S. Marshall, the circuit judge, to hold the regular term of court at Raleigh in Saline County.

To William Martin¹

Dear Sir: Springfield, July 19– 1851.

Yours of the 17th. is received, and I have just been to the Telegraph-office with it. The operator, after a long examination, declares that no such despach ever went from this office—at least, never in the months of February or March last. He then got up a correspondence with the operator at Alton, who, he says, tells him no such despach was ever, received there—that he has seen what purports to be the despach in the hands of you or your client, and that he will swear he never wrote it.

I do not see that I can do any more. Yours truly   A. LINCOLN

¹ ALS, owned by Kingman Brewster, Washington, D. C. On the verso Martin has noted: "One to M[E]AGHER/ 25.th January 1851." Below this notation he has copied the following, presumably the telegram which Thomas Meagher had sent: "To Michael McCormack/care of James Lamb./ Springfield Ill, 24 Jan 1851./ Your [horse?] is bad. Cannot/ work any longer He is sick/ dont want to keep him any/ longer/ Thos Meagher." As Lincoln's letter of July 26 (*infra*) indicates, he found the telegram to Meagher later, but could not identify the writer. James L. Lamb was a prominent merchant of Springfield. Thomas F. Meagher, the Irish patriot, seems an extremely unlikely candidate for the authorship of the telegram but he is the only Meagher mentioned in contemporary newspapers. Michael McCormack likewise has not been identified.

To William Dickson[1]

Mr. Wm. Dickson   Springfield, Ill.
Dear Sir: July 21, 1851

Most of the business at the late term of the U. S. Court, and your case with the rest, was continued over without a trial. Of course we can tell you nothing new about it. Yours truly   A. LINCOLN

[1] ALS, KyBC. The letter is addressed to William Dickson at Camden Mills, Rock Island County, Illinois. Dickson's case has not been identified.

To William Martin[1]

Hon: Wm. Martin   Springfield,
Dear Sir: July 26, 1851

I received yours of the 22nd. yesterday. I went to the Telegraph office & found the despach as you say, of Jany. 25th. It is in pencil; and the operator says he does not know whose handwriting it is; but that he does know it is not the writing of the operator who was here at that date. I took Mr. James L. Lamb to see it, who at first said it was not McCormack's nor his own writing; but that he thought he knew who wrote it, and would enquire. Just now he has told me that the man he thought had written it, denies doing so, and that he, Lamb, now has no idea who did write it. He says it is a much better hand than McCormack himself can write. I do not see any clew to the handwriting. Can you not set it up in pleading so as to be relieved from proving it's execution unless McCormack denies it under oath? Yours as ever   A. LINCOLN

[1] ALS, IHi. See Lincoln to Martin, July 19 and note.

To William Martin[1]

Hon: Wm. Martin   Springfield,
Dear Sir: July 31. 1851

Yours of the 29th. is received. The present operator here says, that the operator who was here on Jany. 25. 1851 is C. P. Rosser; and that he has no knowledge of his present whereabouts—that previous to being here, he had been in the Telegraph office at Burlington, Iowa; but that he knows nothing of him since he left here. This is all I can learn. Yours as ever   A. LINCOLN

[1] ALS, IHi.

Affidavit Concerning David H. Rutledge[1]

State of Illinois   ss.   August 5, 1851
Sangamon County

Personally appeared before the undersigned, Clerk of the County Court, in and for the County aforesaid, Abraham Lincoln, who, being first duly sworn, deposes and says that David H. Rutledge, now deceased, did in the year 1832, serve in the war against the indians, commonly called the "Black-Hawk war" for a period of about forty days; that said Rutledge entered the service on or about the 21st. day of April 1832, on Richland creek in the County aforesaid; and was honorably discharged therefrom, about the last of May of the same year, at or near Ottawa in said State—that said Rutledge so served as a private, or non-commissioned officer,[2] deponent thinks the[3]   in a company commanded by deponent, in the 4th. Regiment commanded by Col. Samuel M. Thompson.

A. LINCOLN[4]

[1] ADS, DNA RG 15A Veterans Records, Bundle 52, Box 27, Elizabeth Rutledge, widow of David Rutledge.
[2] Captain Lincoln signed Private David Rutledge's certificate of service on August 30, 1832, specifying forty days of service after enlistment on April 21, 1832.   [3] Blank not filled in.
[4] The attestation by N. W. Matheny at bottom of the sheet, dated August 5, 1851, has been omitted.

Deed to John D. Johnston[1]

August 12, 1851

This Indenture made this twelfth day of August in the year of our Lord one thousand eight hundred and fiftyone, by and between Abraham Lincoln and Mary Lincoln, his wife, of the City of Springfield, county of Sangamon, and State of Illinois, party of the first part, and John D. Johnston, of the county of Coles and State aforesaid, party of the second part, Witnesseth:

That the said party of the first part, for, and in consideration of the sum of one dollar to them in hand paid, the receipt whereof is hereby acknowledged have remised, released, and forever quit claimed, and by these presents do remise, release, and forever quitclaim to, and in favor of the said party of the second part, his heirs and assigns forever, all the right, title, interest and estate, which the said party of the first part have in and to the North West quarter of the South East quarter; and the North East quarter of the South West quarter, both of Section Twentyone, in Township Eleven North, of Range Nine East of the Third Principal Meridian, situated in the said county of Coles, and together containing eighty acres more or less—the interest of the said party of the first part in and to said lands, being that derived as sole heir at law of the late Thomas Lincoln, now deceased, and subject to the right of Dower of Sarah Lincoln, widow of the said Thomas Lincoln deceased.

To have and to hold to the said party of the second part, and to his heirs and assigns forever, the interest aforesaid, in and to the above described lands, together with all and singular the previleges and appurtenances thereunto belonging.

In testimony whereof the said party of the first part have hereunto set their hands and seals the day and year first above written.

A. LINCOLN

M. LINCOLN

1 ADS, CSmH. The deed is attested by N. W. Matheny. Lincoln enclosed the document with his letter to John D. Johnston, August 31, 1851 (*infra*); it was filed September 4, examined and recorded on September 6.

Promissory Note Drawn for Daniel E. Ruckel, with Lincoln's Receipts[1]

Springfield, August 15– 1851

On or before the 25th. day of December 1854, I promise to pay Abraham Lincoln three hundred dollars, together with interest thereon at the rate of ten per cent per annum, from the 25th. day of December next until paid, the interest payable annually, and on any default in the payment of interest, the principal to be due, for value received.   D. E. RUCKEL

[VERSO]

Received, Jany. 3, 1854– on settlement of D. E. Ruckel; account against me, seventynine dollars. ($79.00.)   A. LINCOLN

Dec. 25– 1854. Received nine dollars and ten cents, leaving remainder of interest now due to rentors the original principal of $300.   A. LINCOLN

Jany. 26. 1856. Received of R. H. Beach, administrator thirty, dollars, being entered up to Christmas last   A LINCOLN

Jany. 2. 1857. Received of R. H. Beach, administrator, &c. thirty dollars, being interest up to Christmas last   A. LINCOLN

1 AD and AES, RPB. To secure this note Ruckel, a cabinetmaker, gave Lincoln a mortgage on four lots and an interest in another lot. The mortgage record carries two notations by Lincoln, July 7, 1853 and September 28, 1857 (*vide infra*).

To William Martin[1]

Hon: Wm. Martin   Springfield,
Dear Sir: Aug: 25. 1851.

Our New-York depositions are here; and our court commences to-day. Send me, *instanter*, the minutes of organization, the newspaper publications of the calls, and a witness to prove all by. Mr. Ferguson[2] is thought to be the person for a witness. I telegraph you now; but lest there should be a slip, I write also. Yours as ever

                                                  A. LINCOLN

[1] ALS-P, ISLA.
[2] Robert Ferguson of Alton, Illinois, a merchant and commissioner and director of the Alton & Sangamon Railroad.

To William Martin[1]

Hon: Wm. Martin   Springfield,
Dear Sir: Aug: 29. 1851

I have just seen a letter of yours to Mr. Hickox,[2] in which you *reiterate* that the publications for the calls were all made in the [*sic*] both the city papers at Springfield. May be they were; *but I tell you if they were, neither I, nor the editors or publisher's of the papers can find them.* All we can find is a publication made in *time,* for the *first* call, & one for the second, not in time. Surely you can not suppose I would be so pertenaceously urging you to send the publications, if I had them here already.

You also say "If we had been informed that these books & witness were needed a week ago &c"

Well, nearly or quite six months ago,[3] you & I by our correspondence, had it distinctly settled that I should need this book, witness & newspapers, when the trials of my cases should come on; and you had distinctly promised me that you would send them up *whenever* I should want them. Now, send them at once, if you shall not have done so already. Yours as ever   A. LINCOLN

[1] ALS, IHi.   [2] Virgil Hickox.
[3] See letters of February 19 and June 23, 1851, *supra*.

To John D. Johnston[1]

                                    Springfield, August 31, 1851.

Dear Brother: Inclosed is the deed for the land.[2] We are all well, and have nothing in the way of news. We have had no cholera here for about two weeks. Give my love to all, and especially to mother. Yours as ever,   A. LINCOLN.

[1] NH, II, 149-50.   [2] *Vide supra*, August 12.

To Robert Dunlap[1]

Mr. Robt. Dunlap.   Springfield,
Present.   Sept. 2. 1851

Dear Sir: The moment you reach Alton procure and send me
by mail an Alton Newspaper, having in it a publication of *"the
notice for opening the books for subscription to the capital stock"* of
the Alton & Sangamon Railroad Company. Dont omit this for a
moment; and be sure you do not send a wrong paper. Yours truly
                                                     A. LINCOLN

[1] ALS, IHi. Dunlap was a resident of Alton, Illinois, and commissioner of
the Alton & Sangamon Railroad.

To John D. Johnston[1]

Dear Brother: Shelbyville, Novr. 4. 1851

When I came into Charleston day-before yesterday I learned
that you are anxious to sell the land where you live, and move to
Missouri. I have been thinking of this ever since; and can not but
think such a notion is utterly foolish. What can you do in Missouri,
better than here? Is the land any richer? Can you there, any more
than here, raise corn, & wheat & oats, without work? Will any body
there, any more than here, do your work for you? If you intend to
go to work, there is no better place than right where you are; if you
do not intend to go to work, you can not get along any where.
Squirming & crawling about from place to place can do no good.
You have raised no crop this year, and what you really want is to
sell the land, get the money and spend it—part with the land you
have, and my life upon it, you will never after, own a spot big
enough to bury you in. Half you will get for the land, you spend in
moving to Missouri, and the other half you will eat and drink, and
wear out, & no foot of land will be bought. Now I feel it is my duty
to have no hand in such a piece of foolery. I feel that it is so even
on your own account; and particularly on *Mother's* account. The
Eastern forty acres I intend to keep for Mother while she lives—if
you *will not cultivate it;* it will rent for enough to support her—at
least it will rent for something. Her Dower in the other two forties,
she can let you have, and no thanks to [me].

Now do not misunderstand this letter. I do not write it in any un-
kindness. I write it in order, if possible, to get you to *face* the truth
—which truth is, you are destitute because you have *idled* away all
your time. Your thousand pretences for not getting along better,
are all non-sense—they deceive no body but yourself. *Go to work* is
the only cure for your case.

A word for Mother:

Chapman[2] tells me he wants you to go and live with him. If I were you I would try it awhile. If you get tired of it (as I think you will not) you can return to your own home. Chapman feels very kindly to you; and I have no doubt he will make your situation very pleasant. Sincerely your Son   A. LINCOLN

1 ALS, ORB.

2 Augustus H. Chapman, who had married Harriett Hanks, daughter of Dennis Hanks and granddaughter of Lincoln's stepmother.

To John D. Johnston[1]

Dear Brother: Shelbyville, Novr. 9. 1851

When I wrote you before I had not received your letter. I still think as I did; but if the land can be sold so that I get three hundred dollars to put to interest for mother, I will not object if she does not. But before I will make a deed, the money must be had, or secured, beyond all doubt, at ten per cent.

As to Abram,[2] I do not want him *on my own account;* but I understand he wants to live with me so that he can go to school, and get a fair start in the world, which I very much wish him to have. When I reach home, if I can make it convenient to take him, I will take him, provided there is no mistake between us as to the object and terms of my taking him. In haste As ever   A. LINCOLN

1 ALS, MeHi.

2 John D. Johnston's thirteen-year-old son, whose name Lincoln spelled "Abraham" in the Family Record, [1851?], *supra.*

To Joseph S. McIntyre[1]

J. S. Mc.Intire, Esq   Decatur,
Dear Sir: Novr. 14th. 1851

I am here now at court, and Shoaff[2] has spoken to me about that suit of his against Thompson.[3] In order for you to get a trial at the next term, you must get a copy of Thompson's Bill for Discovery, and send it to Shoaff at once, so that he can answer it. Dont neglect this a single day, but get the copy at once, and send it to Shoaff at this place by mail. Yours truly   A. LINCOLN

1 ALS, IDecJ. Joseph S. McIntyre was an attorney in Pekin, Illinois. Lincoln's spelling of the name seems to be a variant.

2 Probably James Shoaf, editor of the Decatur *Weekly Gazette.*

3 Thompson has not been identified.

To John D. Johnston[1]

Dear Brother   Springfield, Novr. 25. 1851.

Your letter of the 22nd. is just received. Your proposal about selling the East forty acres of land is all that I want or could claim for *myself;* but I am not satisfied with it on *Mother's* account. I want her to have her living, and I feel that it is my duty, to some extent, to see that she is not wronged. She had a right of Dower (that is, the use of one third for life) in the other two forties; but, it seems, she has already let you take that, hook and line. She now has the use of the whole of the East forty, as long as she lives; and if it be sold, of course, she is intitled to the interest on *all* the money it brings, as long as she lives; but you propose to sell it for three hundred dollars, take one hundred away with you, and leave her two hundred, at 8 per cent, making her the *enormous* sum of 16 dollars a year. Now, if you are satisfied with treating her in that way, I am not. It is true, that you are to have that forty for two hundred dollars, *at* Mother's death; but you are not to have it *before.* I am confident that land can be made to produce for Mother, at least $30 a year, and I can not, to oblige any living person, consent that she shall be put on an allowance of sixteen dollars a year. Yours &c

           A. LINCOLN

[1] ALS-P, ISLA.

Call for Whig Convention[1]

November 29, 1851

WHIG STATE CONVENTION.

The whigs of the State of Illinois are respectfully requested to meet in Convention at SPRINGFIELD, on the FOURTH MONDAY OF DECEMBER NEXT, to take into consideration such action as upon consultation and deliberation may be deemed necessary, proper and effective, for the best interests of the party, and to secure a more thorough organization of the Whig party at an early day. (Signed.)[2]

Abraham Lincoln	Isaac Hardy	O. H. Browning
J. T. Stuart	Horace Miller	C. W. Craig
J. C. Conklin[g]	E. B. Washburne	J. L. Wilson
H. O. Merriman	Henry Waterman	B. G. Wheeler
Geo W. Meeker	Ezra Griffith	H. D. Risley
J. O. Norton	Samuel Haller	Levi Davis
Churchill Coffing	Joseph T. Eccles	B. S. Edwards
Joseph Gillespie	Jas. W. Singleton	And many others.

[1] *Illinois Journal*, November 29, 1851.

[2] Signers not previously identified: George W. Meeker, Chicago attorney;

Jesse O. Norton, representative in the legislature from Will County; Churchill Coffing of Peru; Isaac Hardy, hotel proprietor of LaSalle; Horace Miller, representative in the legislature from Winnebago County; Elihu B. Washburne of Galena, later a member of Congress and long a close political associate of Lincoln's; Henry Waterman (unidentified); Ezra Griffith of Fayette County; Samuel Haller of Montgomery County; Joseph T. Eccles of Montgomery County; James W. Singleton of Brown County; C. W. Craig of McHenry County; John L. Wilson of Will County; B. G. Wheeler (unidentified); Hamilton D. Risley of Will County.

Endorsement on Mortgage from John Hay[1]

December 6, 1851

This mortgage is satisfied in full this 6th day of December 1851.

A. LINCOLN.

[1] AES, Sangamon County Record Book CC, 43. The mortgage on 150 acres in Sangamon County secured a loan of $500, May 7, 1849, payable six months after date.

Arbitration Award in Dispute
between David Spear and Isaac P. Spear[1]

December 6, 1851

We, Stephen T. Logan and Abraham Lincoln, to whom a certain matter in dispute between David Spear and Isaac P. Spear was this day, in writing, submitted for our decision and award, having heard and considered the allegations and proofs of the parties, so far as the same were offered, do award that, to entitle the said Isaac P. Spear, to a conveyance of the land mentioned in the said submission, and particularly described in a written obligation of the said David to the said Isaac P. of date May 22.nd. 1840, he is to pay to the said David Spear, six thousand five hundred and fiftyseven dollars and thirtyeight cents, less by the sum of three thousand five hundred and two dollars, and seventyeight cents, the value of the said Isaac P. Spear's half of a stock of goods lately transferred to the said David Spear, and leaving now to be paid to the said David, by the Isaac P. the nett sum of three thousand and fiftyfour dollars and sixty cents.[2] Given under our hands and seals this 6th. day of December 1851 STEPHEN T. LOGAN (SEAL)

ABRAHAM LINCOLN (SEAL)

[1] ADS-F, ISLA. The document is in Lincoln's hand except for the last sentence and Stephen T. Logan's signature. David and Isaac P. Spear were partners in the mercantile business in Springfield for many years but dissolved their partnership in August, 1851.

[2] Lincoln had written "thirtyeight" and Logan deleted it and substituted "sixty."

Call for a Kossuth Meeting[1]

January 5, 1852

HUNGARIAN MEETING.

It is proposed that a Kossuth meeting be held by the citizens and others now visiting the seat of government, on the 8th of January inst., at 7 o'clock P. M., at the court-house in Springfield. All are invited to attend, and to express their views freely.

A. Lincoln,	L. Trumbull,
E. Peck,	Thos. L. Harris,
Arch. Williams,	R. S. Blackwell,
W. H. Herndon,	G. Edmunds, Jr.,
W. I. Ferguson.	

January 5, 1852.

[1] *Illinois State Register*, January 6, 1852; *Illinois Journal*, January 6, 1852. The only major variation in the two printings is that the call is dated January 6 in the *Journal*. Two of the signers, who have not been previously identified, are: Ebenezer Peck, Chicago attorney, and William I. Ferguson, a Springfield attorney who was occasionally associated with Lincoln as legal counsel.

Resolutions in Behalf of Hungarian Freedom[1]

January 9, 1852

Whereas, in the opinion of this meeting, the arrival of Kossuth in our country, in connection with the recent events in Hungary, and with the appeal he is now making in behalf of his country, presents an occasion upon which we, the American people, cannot remain silent, without justifying an inference against our continued devotion to the principles of our free institutions, therefore,

Resolved, 1. That it is the right of any people, sufficiently numerous for national independence, to throw off, to revolutionize, their existing form of government, and to establish such other in its stead as they may choose.

2. That it is the duty of our government to neither foment, nor assist, such revolutions in other governments.

3. That, as we may not legally or warrantably interfere abroad, *to aid*, so no other government may interfere abroad, *to suppress* such revolutions; and that we should at once, announce to the world, our determinations to insist upon this *mutuality* of non-intervention, as a sacred principle of the international law.

4. That the late interference of Russia in the Hungarian struggle was, in our opinion, such illegal and unwarrantable interference.

5. That to have resisted Russia in that case, or to resist any power

[115]

in a like case, would be no violation of our own cherished principles of non-intervention, but, on the contrary, would be ever meritorious, in us, or any independent nation.

6. That whether we will, in fact, interfere in such case, is purely a question of policy, to be decided when the exigency arrives.

7. That we recognize in Governor Kossuth of Hungary the most worthy and distinguished representative of the cause of civil and religious liberty on the continent of Europe. A cause for which he and his nation struggled until they were overwhelmed by the armed intervention of a foreign despot, in violation of the more sacred principles of the laws of nature and of nations—principles held dear by the friends of freedom everywhere, and more especially by the people of these United States.

8. That the sympathies of this country, and the benefits of its position, should be exerted in favor of the people of every nation struggling to be free; and whilst we meet to do honor to Kossuth and Hungary, we should not fail to pour out the tribute of our praise and approbation to the patriotic efforts of the Irish, the Germans and the French, who have unsuccessfully fought to establish in their several governments the supremacy of the people.

9. That there is nothing in the past history of the British government, or in its present expressed policy, to encourage the belief that she will aid, in any manner, in the delivery of continental Europe from the yoke of despotism; and that her treatment of Ireland, of O'Brien, Mitchell, and other worthy patriots, forces the conclusion that she will join her efforts to the despots of Europe in suppressing every effort of the people to establish free governments, based upon the principles of true religious and civil liberty.

---

[1] *Illinois Journal*, January 12, 1852. Lincoln spoke to the meeting on the 8th in favor of sympathy but non-intervention. Following considerable debate, a committee composed of Lincoln, Samuel S. Marshall, Ebenezer Peck, Lyman Trumbull, Archibald Williams, William I. Ferguson, and Anson G. Henry, was appointed to report resolutions the following evening, and the meeting adjourned. Lincoln reported the resolutions the next evening. Interventionists objected to the resolutions and added the following amendments, which were also adopted:

"Resolved, That it is the duty of the United States not to do any act, or lay down any principle in regard to non-intervention, that shall prevent this Nation at any time, from interfering in favor of any people who may be struggling for liberty in any part of the world, when a proper occasion shall arrive.

"Resolved, That the people of Ireland are as much entitled to the sympathies of the people of the United States, as the people of Hungary; and we here cordially tender to the people of Ireland, and to all other oppressed people who are struggling for liberty, the sincere sympathies of this meeting."

A further resolution was adopted instructing the officers to have the resolutions published and copies sent to Louis Kossuth and to each Illinois member of Congress.

To Hezekiah M. Wead[1]

H. M. Weed Esq.   Springfield,
Dear Sir: Jany. 22. 1852.

Your letter, inquiring for your case, was duly received. We finished arguing, and submitted the case yesterday afternoon, and it is not yet decided. We had a two days trial of it—and they are pressing us very hard on one or two points. I should not wonder if the case is decided against us. One of the hard points is, that our deed of Jany. 1820 is under the act of 1819, fraudulent & void as against their deed of Augt. 1820, because it was not proved or acknowledged according to that act, and because their deed was not defeated by a subsequent recording, the *only* mode of defeasance known to that law, and because it was incompetent to the Legislature to defeat it in any *other* mode, as they apparantly do by the act of Decr. 1822. This is the only dangerous point, as I think, on their *old* deed.

As to the tax deed, they do not rely on it as a perfect title, nor as a basis for the limitation act of 1839, but only as a basis for the limitation act of 1835. To our objection, that the law was repealed under which the sale was made, they insist that as the new law only repeals all laws coming within the *purview* and *meaning* of it, and as the uncollected taxes of 1838 were not within the purview of the new law, so far, the old law itself was not within the purview of the new, & so far was not repealed. This position of theirs seems absurd to me; and I found several authorities against it; but they find one *for it* and, worse than all, the judge[2] intimates that he is with them. If they get this deed in, their next step is to show "actual residence[.]" On this they introduced but one authority, which clearly *is not* in point, and the judge has given no intimation on this point.

Thus stands the case. I will write you so soon as it shall be decided. Yours truly   A. LINCOLN

1 ALS, PU. Wead was an attorney at Lewistown, Illinois. The records of the United States District Court are not extant for this period, and nothing further is known of the case in question.   2 Judge Thomas Drummond.

To Orville H. Browning[1]

Dear Browning: Springfield, Jany. 26. 1852

The case of Smith vs Gardner is decided *for* the plaintiff. It went off on two points only. First, that defendant's deed from patentee, of Aug: 1820, not having been recorded until after the *curing* act of 1822, could not take precedence of our deed of Jany. 1820 & recorded in June 1820, but defectively; but which defect, the court holds to be cured by the act of 1822.

Secondly, that the Revenue act of 1839 did repeal all former laws on the subject, and *did not* retain them for finishing up the collections of the revenue for 1838; and therefore, that a sale made under the old laws, *after* their repeal, was void. This is all. Yours as ever

A. LINCOLN—

[1] ALS, Adams County Historical Society, Quincy, Illinois. There is no further record of this case available.

Call for Kossuth Meeting[1]

January 26, 1852

KOSSUTH MEETING.

We, the undersigned citizens of Springfield, understanding that GOVERNOR KOSSUTH will probably soon be in Indianapolis, Indiana, on his way to St. Louis, respectfully request the citizens of Springfield, to meet at the Court House, on Monday (THIS) Evening, 26th inst., for the purpose of taking measures to invite him to Springfield.

[1] *Illinois Journal*, January 26, 1852. The names of sixty-three citizens, including Lincoln's, are appended to the notice. Lincoln was appointed one of a committee of thirteen instructed to extend the invitation. When the meeting reconvened the next day, none of the committee appeared, and a second committee of nine, including Lincoln, was appointed. This committee met on January 29. There are no further references in the *Journal*.

To Hezekiah M. Wead[1]

H. M. Wead, Esq.   Springfield
Dear Sir—   Febry 7 1852

Your letter enclosing ten dollars was received today. I have just called on Logan and he tells me they have paid the costs and will take a new trial. Be sure, therefore to send the brief, with the authorities on it. It might be well for you to re-record your old deed from the patentee, with the new certificate in it. Yours truly

A. LINCOLN.

[1] Hertz, II, 610.

To Henry Prather[1]

February 14, 1852

State of Illinois⎫ SS.   Of the June Term of the Macon County
Macon County ⎭   Circuit Court— A.D. 1852.

Trustees of Schools of Township Sixteen North of Range One East of the Third Principal Meridian, in the County of Macon

[118]

aforesaid, for the use of the inhabitants of said Township, for School purposes, plaintiffs, complain of Henry Prather, defendant, in custody &c. of complaint of Trespass in Ejectment.

For that heretofore, towit on the first day of January in the year of our Lord one thousand eight hundred and fiftytwo, at the county aforesaid, the said plaintiffs were, for the use aforesaid, possessed of certain parts of Section Sixteen, in the Township and Range aforesaid, which parts are known and designated as Lots Eight, Nine, and Sixteen, of said Section, & which parts or Lots the plaintiffs claim in fee, for the use aforesaid, and being so possessed thereof, the said defendant afterwards, towit on the day and year aforesaid, entered into such Lots or premises, and unlawfully withholds from the plaintiffs the possession thereof, to their damage of one hundred dollars, and therefore they bring their suit &c.

LINCOLN, for Plffs.

Mr. Henry Prather

Sir: You are hereby notified that the above declaration will be filed in the Macon county circuit court, on the second day[2] of the next term thereof—that, upon filing the same, a rule will be entered requiring you to appear and plead to said declaration, within twenty days after the entry of such rule; and, that if you neglect so to appear and plead, a judgment by default will be entered against you, and the plaintiffs will recover possession of the premises.

Feby. 14, 1852.   LINCOLN, for Plffs.

State of Illinois⎱ SS
Macon County⎰

Michael L. Devin, being first duly sworn states on oath that on the   day of April A.D. 1852, at the county aforesaid, he did serve the within declaration and notice upon Henry Prather, the defendant named therein, by then & there delivering to him, a true copy of said declaration and notice.

Subscribed & sworn to before   M. L. DEVIN
me on 3d June 1852
    Wm Prather clk

1 AD and ALS, DLC-HW. All of the two-page document is in Lincoln's handwriting except the signature of Devin and the attestation by William Prather, clerk of the Macon County Circuit Court.
2 Lincoln filed the declaration on June 4, 1852.

To J. C. Louderman and Company[1]

Messrs. J. C. Louderman & Co   Springfield, Ills.
St. Louis: Mo.   March 14. 1852

    Gentlemen: Mr. Bunn[2] has returned to Springfield, saying he took the sample of our carpet to you, and afterwards forgot to give the matter any further attention. He also says he handed you your own letter to us, with a memorandum of mine at the bottom of it. I must now ask the favor of you to send us back the sample, (as, to lose it will spoil the carpet we have) and with it, if it matches, the quantity, or number of yards (35 I believe) of the new, mentioned in the memorandum. The expense, at all events, and price of the new carpet, if it matches & you send it, I will pay promptly to your order—and shall feel under great obligation, besides. Very Respectfully   A. LINCOLN—

  [1] ALS, The Rosenbach Company, Philadelphia and New York.
  [2] Jacob Bunn, the leading merchant of Springfield.

Call for a Whig Meeting[1]

WHIG CITY MEETING.

       Springfield, April 7th, 1852.

    The Whigs of this city are requested to meet at the court house on Wednesday, this evening at 7 o'clock to nominate candidates for the coming city election.

  [1] *Illinois Journal*, April 7, 1852. Signed by one hundred and ninety-nine Springfield Whigs, including Lincoln.

To Onslow Peters[1]

Onslow Peters, Esq   Springfield,
Dear Sir   June 25. 1852

    Yours of the 23rd. is just received. I can not recollect John W. Gere[2] by name, but if it is the case I had in hand once, Gere had no *legal* claim or title papers, but on speculation had made an arrangement with one of the Shurtluffs,[3] to share expenses & profits in an attempt to get the land under Shurtluffs' claim. At my own expense I went to Jacksonville once, and investigated the claim, & decided it to be valueless. The case was this. While Shurtluff was a minor, his father entered the land in the minors name; then wishing to change residence, as guardian of the minor, applied to the Morgan circuit court (in which county the land lies) for an order to sell the land and to invest the proceeds in other lands for the minor. Judge Lockwood[4] was Judge of the circuit court then; & he conducted the case with great caution. He allowed the sale of land, (which had in fact been previously negociated) to be confirmed only after taking proof that it had been sold for it[s] full value, and the proceeds, or rather, an equal amount of money, already invested in other lands, in the minors name, in Tazewell county—deeds executed & recorded, for the Tazewell lands, & evidence of it brought into the Morgan court, before the decree confirming the sale of the Waverly land was allowed to pass. The quantity of the Tazewell land was greater (as I remember) than that of the Waverly land—the former 3. 80's the other 160. I believe there were *two* minors instead of one, but this does not change the principle. One died under circumstances that made the other sole heir. After the survivor came of age he took & appropriated the Tazewell land. Yours as ever   A LINCOLN

1 ALS, owned by E. C. Crampton, Raton, New Mexico. Onslow Peters was an attorney of Peoria, Illinois.

2 Neither John W. Gere nor the case referred to has been identified.

3 Possibly Milton Shurtleff, a son of Benjamin Shurtleff, founder of Shurtleff College, Alton, Illinois.   4 Samuel D. Lockwood.

Eulogy on Henry Clay[1]

July 6, 1852

HONORS TO HENRY CLAY

On the fourth day of July, 1776, the people of a few feeble and oppressed colonies of Great Britain, inhabiting a portion of the Atlantic coast of North America, publicly declared their national independence, and made their appeal to the justice of their cause, and to the God of battles, for the maintainance of that declaration. That people were few in numbers, and without resources, save only their own wise heads and stout hearts. Within the first year of that declared independence, and while its maintainance was yet problematical—while the bloody struggle between those resolute rebels, and their haughty would-be-masters, was still waging, of undistinguished parents, and in an obscure district of one of those colonies, Henry Clay was born. The infant nation, and the infant child began the race of life together. For three quarters of a century they have

1 *Illinois Weekly Journal*, July 21, 1852. Henry Clay died June 29 at Washington, D.C. On July 6, citizens of Springfield held two memorial meetings. The first was conducted at the Episcopal Church by the Reverend Charles Dresser; afterwards a procession moved to the Hall of Representatives, where Lincoln delivered his eulogy. "During the proceedings business was suspended, stores closed, and everything announced the general sorrow at the great national bereavement." (*Journal*, July 9).

travelled hand in hand. They have been companions ever. The nation has passed its perils, and is free, prosperous, and powerful. The child has reached his manhood, his middle age, his old age, and is dead. In all that has concerned the nation the man ever sympathised; and now the nation mourns for the man.

The day after his death, one of the public Journals, opposed to him politically, held the following pathetic and beautiful language, which I adopt, partly because such high and exclusive eulogy, originating with a political friend, might offend good taste, but chiefly, because I could not, in any language of my own, so well express my thoughts—

"Alas! who can realize that Henry Clay is dead! Who can realize that never again that majestic form shall rise in the council-chambers of his country to beat back the storms of anarchy which may threaten, or pour the oil of peace upon the troubled billows as they rage and menace around? Who can realize, that the workings of that mighty mind have ceased—that the throbbings of that gallant heart are stilled—that the mighty sweep of that graceful arm will be felt no more, and the magic of that eloquent tongue, which spake as spake no other tongue besides, is hushed—hushed forever! Who can realize that freedom's champion—the champion of a civilized world, and of all tongues and kindreds and people, has indeed fallen! Alas, in those dark hours, which, as they come in the history of all nations, must come in ours—those hours of peril and dread which our land has experienced, and which she may be called to experience again—to whom now may her people look up for that council [counsel] and advice, which only wisdom and experience and patriotism can give, and which only the undoubting confidence of a nation will receive? Perchance, in the whole circle of the great and gifted of our land, there remains but one on whose shoulders the mighty mantle of the departed statesman may fall —one, while we now write, is doubtless pouring his tears over the bier of his brother and his friend—brother, friend ever, yet in political sentiment, as far apart as party could make them. Ah, it is at times like these, that the petty distinctions of mere party disappear. We see only the great, the grand, the noble features of the departed statesman; and we do not even beg permission to bow at his feet and mingle our tears with those who have ever been his political adherents—we do [not?] beg this permission—we claim it as a right, though we feel it as a privilege. Henry Clay belonged to his country—to the world, mere party cannot claim men like him. His career has been national—his fame has filled the earth— his memory will endure to 'the last syllable of recorded time.'

"Henry Clay is dead!—He breathed his last on yesterday at twenty minutes after eleven, in his chamber at Washington. To those who followed his lead in public affairs, it more appropriately belongs to pronounce his eulogy, and pay specific honors to the memory of the illustrious dead—but all Americans may show the grief which his death inspires, for, his character and fame are national property. As on a question of liberty, he knew no North, no South, no East, no West, but only the Union, which held them all in its sacred circle, so now his countrymen will know no grief, that is not as wide-spread as the bounds of the confederacy. The career of Henry Clay was a public career. From his youth he has been devoted to the public service, at a period too, in the world's history justly regarded as a remarkable era in human affairs. He witnessed in the beginning the throes of the French Revolution. He saw the rise and fall of Napoleon. He was called upon to legislate for America, and direct her policy when all Europe was the battle-field of contending dynasties, and when the struggle for supremacy imperilled the rights of all neutral nations. His voice, spoke war and peace in the contest with Great Britain.

"When Greece rose against the Turks and struck for liberty, his name was mingled with the battle-cry of freedom. When South America threw off the thraldom of Spain, his speeches were read at the head of her armies by Bolivar. His name has been, and will continue to be, hallowed in two hemispheres, for it is—

'One of the few the immortal names
That were not born to die,'

"To the ardent patriot and profound statesman, he added a quality possessed by few of the gifted on earth. His eloquence has not been surpassed. In the effective power to move the heart of man, Clay was without an equal, and the heaven born endowment, in the spirit of its origin, has been most conspicuously exhibited against intestine feud. On at least three important occasions, he has quelled our civil commotions, by a power and influence, which belonged to no other statesman of his age and times. And in our last internal discord, when this Union trembled to its center—in old age, he left the shades of private life and gave the death blow to fraternal strife, with the vigor of his earlier years in a series of Senatorial efforts, which in themselves would bring immortality, by challenging comparison with the efforts of any statesman in any age. He exorcised the demon which possessed the body politic, and gave peace to a distracted land. Alas! the achievement cost him his life! He sank day by day to the tomb—his pale, but noble brow, bound with a triple wreath, put there by a grateful country. May his ashes rest in peace, while his spirit goes to take its station among the great and good men who preceded him!"

While it is customary, and proper, upon occasions like the present, to give a brief sketch of the life of the deceased; in the case of Mr. Clay, it is less necessary than most others; for his biography has been written and re-written, and read, and re-read, for the last twenty-five years; so that, with the exception of a few of the latest incidents of his life, all is as well known, as it can be. The short sketch which I give is, therefore merely to maintain the connection of this discourse.

Henry Clay was born on the 12th of April 1777, in Hanover county, Virginia. Of his father, who died in the fourth or fifth year of Henry's age, little seems to be known, except that he was a respectable man, and a preacher of the baptist persuasion. Mr. Clay's education, to the end of his life, was comparatively limited. I say *"to the end of his life,"* because I have understood that, from time to time, he added something to his education during the greater part of his whole life. Mr. Clay's lack of a more perfect early education, however it may be regretted generally, teaches at least one profitable lesson; it teaches that in this country, one can scarcely be so poor, but that, if he *will,* he *can* acquire sufficient education to get through the world respectably. In his twenty-third year Mr. Clay was licenced to practice law, and emigrated to Lexington, Kentucky. Here he commenced and continued the practice till the year 1803, when he was first elected to the Kentucky Legislature. By successive elections he was continued in the Legislature till the latter part of 1806, when he was elected to fill a vacancy, of a single session, in the United States Senate. In 1807 he was again elected to the Kentucky House of Representatives, and by that body, chosen its speaker. In 1808 he was re-elected to the same body. In 1809 he was again chosen to fill a vacancy of two years in the United States Senate. In 1811 he was elected to the United States House of Representatives, and on the first day of taking his seat in that body, he was chosen its speaker. In 1813 he was again elected Speaker. Early in 1814, being the period of our last British war, Mr. Clay was sent as commissioner, with others, to negotiate a treaty of peace, which treaty was concluded in the latter part of the same year. On his return from Europe he was again elected to the lower branch of Congress, and on taking his seat in December 1815 was called to his old post—the speaker's chair, a position in which he was retained, by successive elections, with one brief intermission, till the inauguration of John Q. Adams in March 1825. He was then appointed Secretary of State, and occupied that important station till the inauguration of Gen. Jackson in March 1829. After this he returned to Kentucky, resumed the practice of the law, and continued it till the Autumn of 1831, when he was by the Legislature of Kentucky, again placed in the United States Senate. By a re-election he was continued in the Senate till he resigned his seat, and retired, in March 1842. In December 1849 he again took his seat in the Senate, which he again resigned only a few months before his death.

By the foregoing it is perceived that the period from the beginning of Mr. Clay's official life, in 1803, to the end of it in 1852, is but one year short of half a century; and that the sum of all the intervals in it, will not amount to ten years. But mere duration of time in office, constitutes the smallest part of Mr. Clay's history. Throughout that long period, he has constantly been the most loved, and most implicitly followed by friends, and the most dreaded by opponents, of all living American politicians. In all the great questions which have agitated the country, and particularly in those great and fearful crises, the Missouri question—the Nullification question, and the late slavery question, as connected with the newly acquired territory, involving and endangering the stability of the Union, his has been the leading and most conspicuous part. In 1824 he was first a candidate for the Presidency, and was defeated; and, although he was successively defeated for the same office in 1832, and in 1844, there has never been a moment since 1824 till after 1848 when a very large portion of the American people did not cling to him with an enthusiastic hope and purpose of still elevating him to the Presidency. With other men, to be defeated, was to be forgotten; but to him, defeat was but a trifling incident, neither changing him, or the world's estimate of him. Even those of both political parties, who have been preferred to him for the highest office, have run far briefer courses than he, and left him, still shining, high in the heavens of the political world. Jackson, Van Buren, Harrison, Polk, and Taylor, all rose *after*, and set long before him. The spell—the long enduring spell—with which the souls of men were bound to him, is a miracle. Who can compass it? It is probably true he owed his pre-eminence to no one quality, but to a fortunate combination of several. He was surpassingly eloquent; but many eloquent men fail utterly; and they are not, as a class, generally successful. His judgment was excellent; but many men of good judgment, live and die unnoticed. His will was indomitable; but this quality often secures to its owner nothing better than a character for useless obstinacy. These then were Mr. Clay's leading qualities. No one of them is very uncommon; but all taken together are rarely combined in a single individual; and this is probably the reason why such men as Henry Clay are so rare in the world.

Mr. Clay's eloquence did not consist, as many fine specimens of eloquence does [do], of types and figures—of antithesis, and elegant arrangement of words and sentences; but rather of that deeply earnest and impassioned tone, and manner, which can proceed only from great sincerity and a thorough conviction, in the speaker of the justice and importance of his cause. This it is, that truly touches the chords of human sympathy; and those who heard Mr. Clay, never failed to be moved by it, or ever afterwards, forgot the impression. All his efforts were made for practical effect. He never spoke merely to be heard. He never delivered a Fourth of July Oration, or an eulogy on an occasion like this. As a politician or statesman, no one was so habitually careful to avoid all sectional ground. Whatever he did, he did for the whole country. In the construction of his measures he ever carefully surveyed every part of the field, and duly weighed every conflicting interest. Feeling, as he did, and as the truth surely is, that the world's best hope depended on the continued Union of these States, he was ever jealous of, and watchful for, whatever might have the slightest tendency to separate them.

Mr. Clay's predominant sentiment, from first to last, was a deep devotion to the cause of human liberty—a strong sympathy with the oppressed every where, and an ardent wish for their elevation. With him, this was a primary and all controlling passion. Subsidiary to this was the conduct of his whole life. He loved his country partly because it was his own country, but mostly because it was a free country; and he burned with a zeal for its advancement, prosperity and glory, because he saw in such, the advancement, prosperity and glory, of human liberty, human right and human nature. He desired the prosperity of his countrymen partly because they were his countrymen, but chiefly to show to the world that freemen could be prosperous.

That his views and measures were always the wisest, needs not to be affirmed; nor should it be, on this occasion, where so many, thinking differently, join in doing honor to his memory. A free people, in times of peace and quiet—when pressed by no common danger—naturally divide into parties. At such times, the man who is of neither party, is not—cannot be, of any consequence. Mr. Clay, therefore, was of a party. Taking a prominent part, as he did, in all the great political questions of his country for the last half century, the wisdom of his course on many, is doubted and denied by a large portion of his countrymen; and of such it is not now proper to speak particularly. But there are many others, about his course upon which, there is little or no disagreement amongst intelligent and patriotic Americans. Of these last are the War of 1812, the Missouri question, Nullification, and the now recent compromise measures. In 1812 Mr. Clay, though not unknown, was still a young man. Whether we should go to war with Great Britain, being the question of the day, a minority opposed the declaration of war by Congress, while the majority, though apparently inclining to war, had, for years, wavered, and hesitated to act decisively. Meanwhile British aggressions multiplied, and grew more daring and aggravated. By Mr. Clay, more than any other man, the struggle was brought to a decision in Congress. The question, being now fully before congress, came up, in a variety of ways, in rapid succession, on most of which occasions Mr. Clay spoke. Adding to all the logic, of which the subject was susceptible, that noble inspiration, which came to him as it came to no other, he aroused, and nerved, and inspired his friends, and confounded and bore-down all opposition. Several of his speeches, on these occasions, were reported, and are still extant; but the best of these all never was. During its delivery the reporters forgot their vocations, dropped their pens, and sat enchanted from near the beginning to quite the close. The speech now lives only in the memory of a few old men; and the enthusiasm with which they cherish their recollection of it is absolutely astonishing. The precise language of this speech we shall never know; but we do know—we cannot help knowing, that, with deep pathos, it pleaded the cause of the injured sailor—that it invoked the genius of the revolution—that it apostrophised the names of Otis, of Henry and of Washington—that it appealed to the interest, the pride, the honor and the glory of the nation—that it shamed and taunted the timidity of friends—that it scorned, and scouted, and withered the temerity of domestic foes—that it bearded and defied the British Lion—and rising, and swelling, and maddening in its course, it sounded the onset, till the charge, the shock, the steady struggle, and the glorious victory, all passed in vivid review before the entranced hearers.

Important and exciting as was the War question, of 1812, it never so alarmed the sagacious statesmen of the country for the safety of the republic, as afterwards did the Missouri question. This sprang from that unfortunate source of discord—negro slavery. When our Federal Constitution was adopted, we owned no territory beyond the limits or ownership of the states, except the territory North-West of the River Ohio, and East of the Mississippi. What has since been formed into the States of Maine, Kentucky, and Tennessee, was, I believe, within the limits of or owned by Massachusetts, Virginia, and North Carolina. As to the North Western Territory, provision had been made, even before the adoption of the Constitution, that slavery should never go there. On the admission of the States into the Union carved from the territory we owned before the constitution, no question—or at most, no considerable question—arose about slavery—those which were within the limits of or owned by the old states, following, respectively, the condition of the parent state, and those within the North West territory, following the previously made provision. But in 1803 we purchased Louisiana of the French; and it included with much more, what has since been formed into the State of Missouri. With regard to it, nothing had been done to forestall the question of slavery. When, therefore, in 1819, Missouri, having formed a State constitution, without excluding slavery, and with slavery already actually existing within its limits, knocked at the door of the Union for admission, almost the entire representation of the non-slaveholding states, objected. A fearful and angry struggle instantly followed. This alarmed thinking men, more than any previous question, because, unlike all the former, it divided the country by geographical lines. Other questions had their opposing partizans in all localities of the country and in almost every family; so that no division of the Union could follow such, without a separation of friends, to quite as great an extent, as that of opponents. Not so with the Missouri question. On this a geographical line could be traced which, in the main, would separate opponents only. This was the danger. Mr. Jefferson, then in retirement wrote:

"I had for a long time ceased to read newspapers, or to pay any attention to public affairs, confident they were in good hands, and content to be a passenger in our bark to the shore from which I am not distant. But this momentous question, like a fire bell in the night, awakened, and filled me with terror. I considered it at once as the knell of the Union. It is hushed, indeed, for the moment. But this is a reprieve only, not a final sentence. A geographical line, co-inciding with a marked principle, moral and political, once conceived, and held up to the angry passions of men, will never be obliterated; and every irritation will mark it deeper and deeper. I can say, with conscious truth, that there is not a man on earth who would sacrifice more than I would to relieve us from this heavy reproach, in any *practicable* way. The cession of that kind of property, for so it is misnamed, is a bagatelle which would not cost me a second thought, if, in that way, a general emancipation, and *ex-*

patriation could be effected; and, gradually, and with due sacrifices I think it might be. But as it is, we have the wolf by the ears and we can neither hold him, nor safely let him go. Justice is in one scale, and self-preservation in the other."

Mr. Clay was in congress, and, perceiving the danger, at once engaged his whole energies to avert it. It began, as I have said, in 1819; and it did not terminate till 1821. Missouri would not yield the point; and congress—that is, a majority in congress—by repeated votes, showed a determination to not admit the state unless it should yield. After several failures, and great labor on the part of Mr. Clay to so present the question that a majority could consent to the admission, it was, by a vote, rejected, and as all seemed to think, finally. A sullen gloom hung over the nation. All felt that the rejection of Missouri, was equivalent to a dissolution of the Union: because those states which already had, what Missouri was rejected for refusing to relinquish, would go with Missouri. All deprecated and deplored this, but none saw how to avert it. For the judgment of Members to be convinced of the necessity of yielding, was not the whole difficulty; each had a constituency to meet, and to answer to. Mr. Clay, though worn down, and exhausted, was appealed to by members, to renew his efforts at compromise. He did so, and by some judicious modifications of his plan, coupled with laborious efforts with individual members, and his own over-mastering eloquence upon the floor, he finally secured the admission of the State. Brightly, and captivating as it had previously shown, it was now perceived that his great eloquence, was a mere embellishment, or, at most, but a helping hand to his inventive genius, and his devotion to his country in the day of her extreme peril.

After the settlement of the Missouri question, although a portion of the American people have differed with Mr. Clay, and a majority even, appear generally to have been opposed to him on questions of ordinary administration, he seems constantly to have been regarded by all, as *the* man for a crisis. Accordingly, in the days of Nullification, and more recently in the re-appearance of the slavery question, connected with our territory newly acquired of Mexico, the task of devising a mode of adjustment, seems to have been cast upon Mr. Clay, by common consent—and his performance of the task, in each case, was little else than a literal fulfilment of the public expectation.

Mr. Clay's efforts in behalf of the South Americans, and afterwards, in behalf of the Greeks, in the times of their respective struggles for civil liberty are among the finest on record, upon the noblest of all themes; and bear ample corroboration of what I have said was his ruling passion—a love of liberty and right, unselfishly, and for their own sakes.

Having been led to allude to domestic slavery so frequently already, I am unwilling to close without referring more particularly to Mr. Clay's views and conduct in regard to it. He ever was, on principle and in feeling, opposed to slavery. The very earliest, and one of the latest public efforts of his life, separated by a period of more than fifty years, were both made in favor of gradual emancipation of the slaves in Kentucky. He did not perceive, that on a question of human right, the negroes were to be excepted from the human race. And yet Mr. Clay was the owner of slaves. Cast into life where slavery was already widely spread and deeply seated, he did not perceive, as I think no wise man has perceived, how it could be at *once* eradicated, without producing a greater evil, even to the cause of human liberty itself. His feeling and his judgment, therefore, ever led him to oppose both extremes of opinion on the subject. Those who would shiver into fragments the Union of these States; tear to tatters its now venerated constitution; and even burn the last copy of the Bible, rather than slavery should continue a single hour, together with all their more halting sympathisers, have received, and are receiving their just execration; and the name, and opinions, and influence of Mr. Clay, are fully, and, as I trust, effectually and enduringly, arrayed against them. But I would also, if I could, array his name, opinions, and influence against the opposite extreme—against a few, but an increasing number of men, who, for the sake of perpetuating slavery, are beginning to assail and to ridicule the white-man's charter of freedom—the declaration that "all men are created free and equal." So far as I have learned, the first American, of any note, to do or attempt this, was the late John C. Calhoun; and if I mistake not, it soon after found its way into some of the messages of the Governors of South Carolina. We, however, look for, and are not much shocked by, political eccentricities and heresies in South Carolina. But, only last year, I saw with astonishment, what purported to be a letter of a very distinguished and influential clergyman of Virginia, copied, with apparent approbation, into a St. Louis newspaper, containing the following, to me, very extraordinary language—

"I am fully aware that there is a text in some Bibles that is not in mine. Professional abolitionists have made more use of it, than of any passage in the Bible. It came, however, as I trace it, from Saint Voltaire, and was baptized by Thomas Jefferson, and since almost universally regarded as canonical authority *'All men are born free and equal.'*

"This is a genuine coin in the political currency of our generation. I am sorry to say that I have never seen two men of whom it is true. But I must admit I never saw the Siamese twins, and therefore will not dogmatically say that no man ever saw a proof of this sage aphorism."

This sounds strangely in republican America. The like was not heard in the fresher days of the Republic. Let us contrast with it the language of that truly national man, whose life and death we now commemorate and lament. I quote from a speech of Mr. Clay delivered before the American Colonization Society in 1827.

"We are reproached with doing mischief by the agitation of this question. The society goes into no household to disturb its domestic tranquility; it addresses itself to no slaves to weaken their obligations of obedience. It seeks to affect no man's property. It neither has the power nor the will to affect the property of any one contrary to his consent. The execution of its scheme would augment instead of diminishing the value of the property left behind. The society, composed of free men, concerns itself only with the free. Collateral consequences we are not responsible for. It is not this society which has produced the great moral revolution which the age exhibits. What would they, who thus reproach us, have done? If they would repress all tendencies towards liberty, and ultimate emancipation, they must do more than put down the benevolent efforts of this society. They must go back to the era of our liberty and independence, and muzzle the cannon which thunders its annual joyous return. They must renew the slave trade with all its train of atrocities. They must suppress the workings of British philanthropy, seeking to meliorate the condition of the unfortunate West Indian slave. They must arrest the career of South American deliverance from thraldom. They must blow out the moral lights around us, and extinguish that greatest torch of all which America presents to a benighted world—pointing the way to their rights, their liberties, and their happiness. And when they have achieved all those purposes their work will be yet incomplete. They must penetrate the human soul, and eradicate the light of reason, and the love of liberty. Then, and not till then, when universal darkness and despair prevail, can you perpetuate slavery, and repress all sympathy, and all humane, and benevolent efforts among free men, in behalf of the unhappy portion of our race doomed to bondage."

The American Colonization Society was organized in 1816. Mr.

Clay, though not its projector, was one of its earliest members; and he died, as for the many preceding years he had been, its President. It was one of the most cherished objects of his direct care and consideration; and the association of his name with it has probably been its very greatest collateral support. He considered it no demerit in the society, that it tended to relieve slave-holders from the troublesome presence of the free negroes; but this was far from being its whole merit in his estimation. In the same speech from which I have quoted he says: "There is a moral fitness in the idea of returning to Africa her children, whose ancestors have been torn from her by the ruthless hand of fraud and violence. Transplanted in a foreign land, they will carry back to their native soil the rich fruits of religion, civilization, law and liberty. May it not be one of the great designs of the Ruler of the universe, (whose ways are often inscrutable by short-sighted mortals,) thus to transform an original crime, into a signal blessing to that most unfortunate portion of the globe?" This suggestion of the possible ultimate redemption of the African race and African continent, was made twenty-five years ago. Every succeeding year has added strength to the hope of its realization. May it indeed be realized! Pharaoh's country was cursed with plagues, and his hosts were drowned in the Red Sea for striving to retain a captive people who had already served them more than four hundred years. May like disasters never befall us! If as the friends of colonization hope, the present and coming generations of our countrymen shall by any means, succeed in freeing our land from the dangerous presence of slavery; and, at the same time, in restoring a captive people to their long-lost father-land, with bright prospects for the future; and this too, so gradually, that neither races nor individuals shall have suffered by the change, it will indeed be a glorious consummation. And if, to such a consummation, the efforts of Mr. Clay shall have contributed, it will be what he most ardently wished, and none of his labors will have been more valuable to his country and his kind.

But Henry Clay is dead. His long and eventful life is closed. Our country is prosperous and powerful; but could it have been quite all it has been, and is, and is to be, without Henry Clay? Such a man the times have demanded, and such, in the providence of God was given us. But he is gone. Let us strive to deserve, as far as mortals may, the continued care of Divine Providence, trusting that, in future national emergencies, He will not fail to provide us the instruments of safety and security.

Notice of Meeting of Commissioners
of the Springfield and Terre Haute Railroad[1]

July 9, 1852

SPRINGFIELD AND TERRE HAUTE RAILROAD.

NOTICE is hereby given, that a meeting of the Commissioners appointed in the "act approved June 22d, 1852, for the location of the Springfield and Terre Haute Railroad," will be held at the Courthouse, in Charleston, Coles county, Illinois, on the eighteenth day of August next, (1852) for the purpose of organizing and opening Books for the subscription of stock, as required by said act. At which meeting it is hoped a full board of said Commissioners will be present.

Marshall. July 9th. 1852.

1 *Illinois Journal*, July 9, 10, 12, 1852. Thirty-eight names including Lincoln's are appended to the notice. Lincoln was one of the incorporators of this railroad.

To Mrs. Catharine Nance[1]

Mrs. Catharine Nance   Springfield,
Dear Madam: July 21. 1852

This morning I received an affidavit of yours, inclosed with a letter of L. B. Wynne,[2] for the purpose of getting a Patent from the Land Office. Herewith is the Patent. Please accept my respects.
Yours truly   A. LINCOLN—

1 ALS, owned by Mrs. Fern Nance Pond, Petersburg, Illinois. Mrs. Catharine Nance was the widow of Thomas J. Nance.
2 Lewis B. Wynne of Petersburg, Illinois.

To Adam Adams and John Bovey[1]

Messrs. Adams & Bovey   Springfield,
Gentlemen: Augt. 2 1852

The court is about to adjourn; and it does not decide our case, but takes it under advisement—till next term, I suppose. It appears to me, however, that the signs are against us. What I mean by this is, that I have entire confidence that the law is with us on the Statute of Limitations, and yet it seems, I can not get the judge to remember that this is a question in the case at all. This morning he said he had a pretty decided opinion on *"the question"* already; but as it was a new, and very important one, he would consider it further. The *"the question"* he spoke of, was evidently, the question as to a lien on after acquired lands, & not the act of limitations. Now, as to the question of Limitations, we must have a hearing on

[133]

it, even if we have to go to the Supreme Court of the U.S. for it—
that is, if the other question shall be decided against us. Be patient.
They have not got your land yet. Write me. Yours truly

A. LINCOLN

¹ ALS, ORB. John Bovey, Ogle County pioneer and farmer, was the man
addressed. The case to which Lincoln refers was tried in the United States District Court and records for this period are not extant. See other letters to Adam
Adams and Thomas J. Turner, *supra* and *infra*.

To Justin Butterfield¹

Hon J Butterfield   Springfield Illinois
Commr of the Gen Land office   August 10 1852
Washington City

Dear Sir   When the Land office was opened here on the 26th
July last for the entry of lands which had been withdrawn from
market in consequence of the Central RailRoad more than one application was made for nearly or quite every tract so that a public
auction had to take place[.] At this auction, a large number of
tracts were run up very high some to between nine & ten Dollars
per acre and struck off it being well understood at the time that the
successful bidders had no intention of taking the lands and paying
for them at their bids[.] The next day or two after the last day of
this Public auction to wit on the 31st July 1852, John T. Stuart who
had made no application before applied to the Register to enter at
the minimum price of the lands bid off and forfeited as above the
South half of Section 28 the W½ of Sec 29 the entire Sec 32 and
the N½ of Sec 33 all in township No 20 North of Range No 2 West
of the 3d principal meredian—and tendered payment for the
same[.] The Register refused to allow the entry & purchase but
gave Stuart a certificate of the facts of the application and tender[.]
No other application was made for these lands on that day[.] Some
days after this these lands were again put up at public auction and
all bid off at a Dollar & twenty five cents per acre under a combination doubtless among those who were concerned in making and
forfeiting the former exorbitant bids. These last sales the Register
& Receiver have ratified so far as in them lies and Stuart and I as
interested with him wish to contest their legality and to insist on
Stuarts legal right to have the lands upon his application[.]

Will you please *do* or advise us how *to do* what ever may be necessary to insure us a fair hearing of our case. Your obt servant

A. LINCOLN

P.S Lest I be misunderstood I wish to say I do not intend by any
thing I have said in the above letter to cast any censure upon the
Register or Receiver² here   A. L.

Again since writing the above I have been applied to by Mr. William J Black[3] who made an application and tender on the same day precisely as Stuart did (and whose claim in all respects is like Stuarts) for the entire Sec 27 the South half of Sec 33 and the entire Sec 34 in the same township & Range as Stuarts application[.] I wish his case to be considered with Stuarts[4] Yours &c

A LINCOLN

[1] Copy, DNA RG 49, Land Office Files, Miscellaneous Letters Received, B37823. The original letter is missing, but a copy was enclosed by Richard M. Young, attorney for William J. Black, in a letter addressed to John Wilson, the new commissioner, on February 10, 1853.

[2] The register of the Springfield office was Turner R. King; the receiver was Walter Davis.

[3] William J. Black was clerk and attorney for the City of Springfield.

[4] The decision in this case is recorded in John Wilson's letter to the Register and Receiver at Springfield, May 2, 1854 (ibid., Register and Receiver Letter Record, Vol. 42), which reads in part as follows: "That on the interval between the first and second offerings, Mr. Stuart applied to purchase at private entry, a portion of the lands for which application had been received on the 25th July, the bid forfeited, and which, according to notices given, were again to be offered on the 5th August. The Attorney General in an opinion given on the 14th July, 1837, says that 'one of the most important points to be observed in the execution of the law is the securing to all persons a fair and equal opportunity to become purchasers of the public lands.' To carry out the principle, the necessity and propriety of the instructions given by this Office to the District Land Officers for bringing these lands into market, cannot be questioned. If Mr. Stuart's application had been entertained, this important principle would have been wholly violated, hence his application is void in itself, independent of the action of the officers in relation to the other applications. The only errors of the land officers were first, in permitting a party to bid who had forfeited his bid. Second, in permitting others to bid than those who had applied. Under the peculiar circumstances of the case, perhaps the only mode to carry out the opinion of the Attorney General was that adopted by them; at all events, the only persons who had a right to complain of this course were those who had applied, and for whom the circle of competition was thus enlarged. There is no evidence to show that there was any combination to prevent fair competition of the sale of 5th August. Hence the land officers were correct in refusing Mr. Stuart's application, and in permitting the entries as made."

Speech to the Springfield Scott Club[1]

August 14, 26, 1852

HON. A. LINCOLN'S ADDRESS, BEFORE THE SPRINGFIELD SCOTT
CLUB, IN REPLY TO JUDGE DOUGLAS' RICHMOND SPEECH

[Published by desire of the Club.][2]

GENTLEMEN:—Unlike our young friend[3] who has just taken his seat, I do not appear before you on a flattering invitation, or on any

[1] *Illinois Weekly Journal*, September 22, 1852. The speech had previously appeared in the *Daily Journal* in installments, September 15-21.

[2] Brackets are in the source.

[3] Tompkins Bush had been invited to speak to the club but asked to be excused because of a recent severe illness (*Journal*, August 17).

invitation at all; but, on the contrary I am about to address you, by your permission, given me at my own special request. Soon after the Democratic nomination for President and vice-President in June last at Baltimore, it was announced somewhat ostentatiously, as it seemed to me, that Judge Douglas would, previous to the election, make speeches in favor of those nominations, in twenty-eight of the thirty-one States.[4] Since then, and as I suppose, in part performance of this undertaking, he has actually made one speech at Richmond, Virginia.[5] This speech has been published, with high commendations, in at least one of the democratic papers in this state, and I suppose it has been, and will be, in most of the others. When I first saw it, and read it, I was reminded of old times—of the times when Judge Douglas was not so much greater man than all the rest of us, as he now is—of the Harrison campaign, twelve years ago, when I used to hear, and *try* to answer many of his speeches; and believing that the Richmond speech though marked with the same species of "shirks and quirks" as the old ones, was not marked with any greater ability, I was seized with a strong inclination to attempt an answer to it; and this inclination it was that prompted me to seek the privilege of addressing you on this occasion. In the speech, so far as I propose noticing it now, the Judge rebukes the whigs for calling Gen. Pierce "a fainting General;" eulogizes Gen. Scott's military character; denounces the whig platform, except as to the slavery question, which he says is a plank stolen from the democratic platform; charges that Gen. Scott's nomination was forced on the South by the North on a sectional issue; charges Gen. Scott with duplicity, and intent to deceive in his letter of acceptance; attempts to ridicule Gen. Scott's views on naturalization; charges that Gen. Scott, in his letter of acceptance, has pledged himself to proscription; denounces as dangerous the election of military men to the Presidency; says the hand of Providence saved us from our first and only military administration; speaks of Mr. Fillmore and his administration. In addition to these specific points, a constant repetition of something more than insinuations and yet something less than direct charges, that Gen. Scott is wholly under the control of Seward of New York; and that abolitionism is controlling the whole whig party, forms a sort of key-note to the whole speech. As a further characteristic of the speech, it may be noted that a very small portion of it is devoted to Pierce, and almost the whole of it to attacks upon Scott.

[4] Stephen A. Douglas had attracted a considerable national following among the Democrats since his election to the Senate in 1847, and had received strong support for the party nomination at the Baltimore convention.

[5] The speech was made on July 9.

As I desire to say something on each of these matters, and as the evening is already partially spent, I propose going only about half-way through, reserving the remainder for a subsequent meeting. As to the Judge's rebuke of the whigs for calling Pierce "a fainting General," in which he insists that they mean to impute cowardice to Gen. Pierce, and that it is cowardly and false in them to cast such an imputation, I have only to say that, Gen. Pierce's history being as it is, the attempt to set him up as a great General, is simply ludicrous and laughable; and that the free merry people of the country have laughed at it, and will continue to laugh at it, in spite of the querulous scolding of Judge Douglas or of anybody else; and further, that if the Judge has any real honest indignation against unjust imputations of cowardice, he will find a much ampler field for the indulgence of it against his own friends, who are every-where seeking by reference to an old affair with Gen. Jackson, to throw such an imputation upon Gen. Scott.

As to the Judge's eulogy on Gen. Scott's military character, in which he says "I will not depreciate his merits as a soldier, because truth and honor forbid it," I have but to remark that whoever will read the speech through and carefully note the imputations imply-ing ignorance and stupidity, and duplicity and knavery, against Gen. Scott in almost every paragraph, will I think, conclude that the eulogy on his military character, was dictated quite as much by the Judge's view of the party impolicy of assailing that character, as by a love of truth and honor.

In denouncing the whig platform generally, the Judge gives no reason other than that it is "a whig concern" and that all democrats are presumed to be opposed to it. This needs no answer other than that for the same reason all whigs are presumed to be in favor of it. But as to the slavery question, the Judge says it was a plank stolen from the democratic platform.[6] On what authority does he make this declaration? Upon what fact, or what reasoning from facts does he base it? I had understood and now understand, as the indelibly written history of the country, that the compromise measures were not party measures—that for praise or blame, they belonged to neither party to the exclusion of the other; but that the chief lead-ers in their origin and adoption were whigs and not democrats. I had thought that the pen of history had written, acknowledged, and recorded it as facts, that Henry Clay, more than any other man, or perhaps more than any other ten men, was the originator of that system of measures; and that he together with Webster and Pearce[7]

6 Both platforms endorsed the Compromise of 1850, but the Democrats adopted theirs a few days earlier than the Whigs.
7 James A. Pearce, U.S. representative (1835-1839) and senator (1843-1862).

of Maryland, (not Gen. Pierce,) were its most efficient supporters in its progress. I knew, or supposed I knew, that democrats, numerous and distinguished, gave it able and efficient support; and I have not sought, or known of any whig seeking to deprive them of the credit of it. Among these last Judge Douglas himself was not the least. After the close of the session of Congress at which these measures were passed, Judge Douglas visited Chicago, in this State, and the measures, if not the Judge himself, were there clamorously assailed. He succeeded in getting a hearing at a public meeting, and made a speech which silenced his adversaries, and gave him a triumph most complete. It was afterwards written out and published. I saw a copy, and read it once hastily, and glanced over it a second time. I do not now remember seeing anything in it to condemn, and I do remember that I considered it a very able production—by far superior to any thing I had ever seen from Judge Douglas, and comparing favorably with any thing from any source, which I had seen, on that general subject. The reading of it afforded me a good deal of pleasure; and I never said, or inclined to say any thing in disparagement of it. But as the Judge, in his Richmond speech, has thought fit to speak so confidently, and, in my judgment so unjustly, of stealing, I will venture to suggest that if he had stolen none of the ideas of Henry Clay and Daniel Webster, and other whigs, which he had been listening to for the last preceding six or eight months, he might not have been able to get up quite so creditable a speech at Chicago as he did.

But the Judge asserts in substance, that the nomination of Scott was forced on the south by the north, on a sectional issue; and he argues that such a nomination is exceedingly perilous to the safety of the Union. As evidence that the nomination was forced on the south by the north, the Judge says, "every southern delegation voted against him more than fifty times, day after day, and night after night." This is not quite correct, for one, two, or more of the Virginia delegation voted for Scott every ballot after the first; but call it substantially correct to say that the Southern delegations did not vote for Scott, does it follow, in the sense the Judge would have us to understand, that they voted *against* Scott? If so, then, by the same rule, in the democratic Convention, every delegation north and south, voted against Gen. Pierce thirty-four times.

Now, according to the Judge's logic, the nomination of Pierce was *forced* on the whole country by some mysterious and invisible agency, "a defiance of the thirty-four times repeated protest and remonstrance of the delegates from ALL the States of the Union represented in the Convention." Still the Judge thinks the nomination

of Scott, made in compliance with the original preference of nearly
half the whig convention, is extremely perilous to the safety of the
Union; but that the nomination of Pierce, made contrary to the
original preference of every man in the democratic Convention
(and every man out of it, I presume) is to be the very salvation of
the Union!!! It may be said that although every member of the
democratic convention preferred some other man, finally they all
honorably surrendered their preferences and united on Pierce.
Very well, if the whole democratic convention could honorably,
and without being forced, go over to Pierce, why could not HALF
the whig convention, as honorably and as free from force, go over
to Scott?

But, according to the Judge's view, Scott's nomination was not only
forced upon the south, but was forced upon it, *on a sectional issue*.
Now, in point of fact, at the time the nomination was made, there
was no issue, except as to who should be the *men* to lead the campaign upon a set of principles previously put in writing and acquiesced in by the whole convention; and those principles, too, being
precisely such as the south demanded. When the platform, which I
understand to be just such as the south desired, was voted upon by
the convention—the whole south, and more than half the north
voted for, and adopted it, by a vote of 226 to 66; those who voted
against it made no further opposition to it. On the adoption of the
platform arose the only sectional issue which came before the convention, and by the vote it passed from an issue into a decision, and
left no issue before the convention, except as to men. It is proper
to notice too, that on the first ballot for a candidate for the presidency, Scott's vote only lacked one of doubling the numbers of all
the votes cast against the platform; so that of Scott's original friends
in the convention, more than half *may* have been, and within one
of half *must* have been original platform men. If Scott should
throw himself into the hands exclusively of those who originally
preferred him, to be controlled by the majority of them, in utter
disregard of all those who originally preferred others, it is still
probable that the majority would lead him to adopt the platform
or union view of the slavery question.

But the gist of all the Judge's views is, that Scott's nomination,
made as it was, is more perilous to the safety of the Union, than
all the scenes through which we have recently passed in connection
with the slavery question. Well, we ought all to be startled at the
view of "peril to the Union," but it may be a little difficult for some
shortsighted mortals to perceive such peril in the *nomination of*
Scott. Mark you, it is the *nomination* and not the *election*, which

produces the peril. The Judge does not say the election, and he cannot mean the election, because he constantly assures us there is no prospect of Scott's election. He could not be so alarmed at what he is so sure will never happen. In plain truth I suppose he did mean the election, so far as he meant anything; but feeling that his whole proposition was mere nonsense, he did not think of it distinctly enough to enable him to speak with any precision.

As one point in support of his charge of duplicity against Gen. Scott, Judge Douglas attempts to show that Gen. Scott in his letter of acceptance, framed language studiously for the purpose of enabling men north and south to read it one way or the other, as the public pulse should beat in their particular localities, and he insists that the language so designed will be so used. He quotes Scott's language as follows, "I accept the nomination, with the resolutions annexed," and then he criticises it as follows: "Now gentlemen I desire to know what is the meaning of the words 'with the resolutions annexed.' Does he mean that he approves the resolutions? If so, why did he not say so, as the candidate for the Vice Presidency, Mr. Graham,[8] did in his letter of acceptance? Or why did he not do as that gallant and honest man, Frank Pierce did, and say, 'I accept the nomination upon the platform adopted by the convention, not because this is expected of me as a candidate, but because the principles *it* embraces command the approbation of my judgement.'

"There you have (continues the Judge) an honest man speaking from an honest heart, without any equivocation, dissimulation, or mental reservation. Here you find that Gen. Scott accepts the nomination with the resolution annexed—that is to say, using language susceptible of two constructions—one at the North, and another at the South. In the North it will be said he accepts the nomination notwithstanding the platform; that he accepts it although he defies the platform; that he accepts it although he spits upon the platform. At the South it will be said he accepts it with the approval of the platform. I submit the question to you whether that language was not framed studiously for the purpose of enabling men, North and South to read it one way or the other as the public pulse should beat in their particular localities. Again, I submit to you, was it the General-in-chief of the armies who fought the battles in Mexico, that conceived this part of the letter, or was it his commander-in-chief, Gen. Seward, who dictated it?" [Great applause.]

What wonderful acumen the Judge displays on the construction

8 William A. Graham of North Carolina, who had served as secretary of the navy in President Fillmore's cabinet.

of language!!! According to this criticism of his, the word "with" is equivalent to the word "notwithstanding," and also to the phrases, "although I defy," and "although I spit upon." Verily these are wonderful substitutes for the word "with." When the builders of the tower of Babel got into difficulty about language, if they had just called on Judge Douglas, he would, at once, have construed away the difficulty, and enabled them to finish the structure, upon the truly democratic platform on which they were building. Suppose, gentlemen, you were to amuse yourselves some leisure hour, by selecting sentences, from well known compositions, each containing the word "with" and by striking it out, and inserting alternately, the Judge's substitutes, and then testing whether the sense is changed.

As an example, take a sentence from an old and well known book, not much suspected for duplicity, or equivocal language; which sentence is as follows:

"And Enoch walked *with* God; and he was not, for God took him."

Try, for yourselves, how Judge Douglas' substitutes for the word "with" will affect this sentence. Let Judge Douglas be brought to understand that he can advance the interest of a locofoco candidate for the presidency by criticising this sentence; and forthwith he will hie away to the African church in Richmond, Virginia, and make a great speech, in which he will find great difficulty in understanding the meaning of the words "walked with God." He will contrast it, greatly to its disadvantage, with the language of that *gallant* and *honest* man, Frank Pierce! He will show that it is, and was designed to be, susceptible of two constructions, one at the North, and another at the South; that at the North the word "with" will be read "NOTWITHSTANDING," "ALTHOUGH HE DEFIES," "ALTHOUGH HE SPITS UPON;" and finally he will thrill, and electrify, and throw into spasms of ecstasy his African church auditors by suggesting that such monstrous duplicity could not have been conceived by Enoch or Moses, but must have been dictated by Gen. Seward!!!

As another example, take from Judge Douglas' ratification speech a sentence in relation to the democratic platform and the democratic ticket, Pierce and King, which is as follows:

"With such a platform, and with such a ticket, a glorious victory awaits us."

Now according to the Judge's rule of criticising Gen. Scott's language, the above sentence of his will, without perversion of meaning admit of being read in each of the following ways:

"NOTWITHSTANDING such a platform, and notwithstanding such a ticket, a glorious victory awaits us."

"ALTHOUGH WE DEFY such a platform, and although we defy such a ticket, a glorious victory awaits us."

"ALTHOUGH WE SPIT UPON such a platform, and although we spit upon such a ticket, a glorious victory awaits us."

Similar examples might be found without end; but the foregoing are enough, if indeed anything was wanting to show the utter absurdity of the Judge's criticism. Can any two fair minded men differ about the meaning of this part of Gen. Scott's letter? Do his friends, north and south, read it differently, as Judge Douglas asserts they will? Nothing is too absurd for the malice of his fault finding enemies; but where among his millions of friends can a single one be found who is supporting him because he understands him to defy, and spit upon the Whig platform?

Judge Douglas also perceives the same duplicity in Gen. Scott's language about the Public Lands, and about Naturalization; but his criticisms upon it, are so similar to that which I have already reviewed, that I am willing to trust my review of the one, to stand as answer to the whole.

But, in addition to the charge of duplicity, the Judge also seizes upon what Gen. Scott says about naturalization, on which to base a charge of ignorance and stupidity against Gen. Scott. Scott, in his letter of acceptance, suggests the propriety of so altering the naturalization laws as to admit to the rights of citizenship, such foreigners as may serve one year in time of war, in the land or naval service of the United States. The Judge insists that it is uncertain whether the General means this to be an *addition* to the present laws on the subject, or a *substitute* for them; but by a few brief dashes, he argues himself into the belief that the General means his proposition to be a substitute—to embrace the *only* law on naturalization; and then the Judge bewails the supposed condition of things, when the numbers of the army and navy must either be swelled to a million, or the bulk of the foreigners must remain unnaturalized, and without rights of citizenship among us. He admits the General does not say that he intends his proposition to embrace the only law; but inasmuch as he does not say the contrary, he must so mean it, because, the Judge argues, to maintain the present laws, and such as Scott proposes, *together*, would be unconstitutional. He quotes from the constitution, and shows that there can be but *one* uniform rule of naturalization; and swelling with indignation, he grows severe on Gen. Scott, and asks, "Is it possible that this candidate for the presidency never read the constitution?"

He insists that to add Scott's proposition to the present laws, would establish *two* rules because it would admit one person on one set of reasons and another person on another; and hence the unconstitutionality. Now it so happens that the first Congress which ever sat under the constitution, composed in a great part of the same men who made the constitution, passed a naturalization law, in which it was provided that adult aliens should come in on one set of reasons; that their minor children should come in on another set; and that such particular foreigners as had been proscribed by any State, should come in, if at all, on still another set. Will Judge Douglas sneeringly ask if the framers of *this law* never read the Constitution? Since the passage of the first law, there have been some half a dozen acts modifying, adding to, and substituting, the preceding acts; and there has never been a moment from that day to this, when, by the existing system, different persons might not have become naturalized on different sets of reasons.

Would it be discourteous to Judge Douglas to retort his question upon him, and ask, "Is it possible that this candidate for a nomination to the Presidency never read the naturalization laws?" Cases under these laws, have frequently arisen in the courts, and some of them have gone to and passed through, the Supreme Court of the United States. Certainly in some, probably in every one of these cases, one of the parties could have gained his suit by establishing that the laws were unconstitutional; and yet I believe Judge Douglas is the first man who has been found wise enough or enough otherwise, as the case may be, to even suggest their unconstitutionality.

Even those adopted citizens, whose votes have given Judge Douglas all his consequence,[9] came in under these very laws. Would not the Judge have considered the holding those laws unconstitutional, and those particular votes illegal, as more deplorable, than even an army and navy, a million strong?

If the Judge finds no cause to regret this part of his assault, upon the General, I certainly think that the General needs not.

> The man recovered of the bite,
> The dog it was that died.

[The Club adjourned to Wednesday evening August 26, on which evening the Speech was concluded as follows:][10]

When I spoke on a previous evening, I was not aware of what I

---

[9] A solid block of Irish votes were regularly garnered by the Democrats, and were largely responsible for the election of Stephen A. Douglas as well as other Democratic candidates.   [10] Bracketed in the source.

have since learned, that Mr. Edwards,[11] in his address to you, had, to some extent, reviewed Judge Douglas' Richmond speech. Had I known this, I probably should [have] abstained from selecting it as the subject of my remarks; because I dislike the appearance of unfairness of two attacking one. After all, however, as the Judge is a giant, and Edwards and I are but common mortals, it may not be very unfair. And then it is to be considered too, that in attempting to answer the Judge, we do not assail him personally; but we are only trying to meet his mode of conducting the assault which the whole party are making upon Gen. Scott.

Taking up the Richmond speech at the point where I left it, the next charge is that Gen. Scott has pledged himself to a course of proscription. This charge the Judge makes in the following language—

"Gen. Scott, in his letter of acceptance,—in cunning and adroit language—solemnly pledges himself that no democrat shall ever hold office under his administration; but that abolition whigs may do so without the slightest hindrance."

Upon this the Judge indulges himself in a long comment, in the course of which he falls into a strain of wailing pathos which Jeremiah in his last days might envy, for the old soldier democrats to be turned out of office by Gen. Scott. And finally he winds up with the use of Clayton's name in such connection, as to insinuate that he, as Secretary of State under Gen. Taylor, had been exceedingly proscriptive.

In the first place, I think it will be in vain, [that] any fair minded man will search for any such solemn pledge in the letter of acceptance, as Judge Douglas attributes to it. Indeed, the Judge himself seems to have thought it would not be quite safe to his reputation to leave his allegation without furnishing it the means of escape from a charge which might be brought against it; for he immediately adds, "This is my translation of that part of his letter." He then quotes from the letter, as follows—

"In regard to the general policy of the administration, if elected I should, of course, look among those who may approve that policy for the agents to carry it into execution; and I should seek to cultivate harmony and fraternal sentiments throughout the whig party, without attempting to reduce its members by proscription to exact conformity to my own views."

Now it appears to me the Judge's translation of this may be called a very *free* translation—a translation enjoying a perfect

11 Ninian W. Edwards and James C. Conkling addressed the club on the evening of July 31.

freedom from all the restraint of justice and fair dealing. So far from having solemnly pledged himself that no democrat should ever hold office, the evident sense of the sentence shows that he was not speaking or thinking of the democrats at all—that he was merely giving an assurance that difference of opinion among whigs should not be regarded, except in the higher offices through which the general policy of the administration is to be conducted.

But suppose the translation is correct, I still should like to hear from the Judge where are the democratic office holders who are to be made to "walk the plank" by Gen. Scott, after having told us in this very speech that the Taylor and Fillmore administrations have proscribed nearly every democrat in office. The Judge's pathos on this subject reminds me of a little rumor I heard at Washington about the time of Gen. Taylor's inauguration. The Senate was democratic and could reject all the nominations. The rumor was that the democratic clerks from Illinois, appealed to our democratic delegation to save them their places if possible; but that the delegation told them no; "we prefer your heads should fall; the sight of your blood will aid us to regain our lost power." Judge Douglas was then at the head of our delegation, and will know better than I whether the rumor was true.

A word now about Clayton, and his proscriptive disposition and practices, as insinuated by Judge Douglas. It is matter of public history, that on Saturday night before Taylor was inaugurated Monday, Mr. Polk nominated Edward Hannegan, a democrat, as minister to Prussia, and that the Senate confirmed the nomination; and that Clayton, a few days after becoming Secretary of State, to which department such appointments belong, allowed him to go, and receive the outfit and salary of $18,000. This is public history, about which there is no disputing. But the more private history, as I have heard and believe it, and as I believe Judge Douglas, knows it, is still more favorable to Clayton's character for generosity. It is that Mr. Clayton induced Mr. Polk to make the appointment, by an assurance that the new administration would not revoke it. Hannegan had been a Senator from Indiana six years, and, in that time, had done his state some credit, and gained some reputation for himself; but in the end, was undermined and superseded by a man who will never do either. He was the son of an Irishman, with a bit of the brogue still lingering on his tongue; and with a very large share of that sprightliness and generous feeling, which generally characterize Irishmen who have had anything of a fair chance in the world. He was personally a great favorite with Senators, and particularly so with Mr. Clayton, although of opposite politics. He was now broken down politically and pecuniarily; and Mr. Clayton, disregarding the ties of party came to his relief. With a knowledge of the exact truth on this subject, how could Judge Douglas find it in his heart to so try to prejudice the nation against John M. Clayton? Poor Hannegan![12] Since his return, in a heated, and unguarded moment, he spilled the life of a favorite brother-in-law, and for which he is now enduring the tortures of deepest mental agony; yet I greatly mistake his nature, if, ever to be released from his extreme misery, he could be induced to assail John M. Clayton, as one wanting in liberality and generosity.

Next Judge Douglas runs a tilt at Gen. Scott as a military politician, commencing with the interrogatory "Why has the whig party forgotten with an oblivion so complete all that it once said about military politicians?" I retort the question, and ask, why has the *democratic* party forgotten with an oblivion so complete all that *it* once said about military politicians?

But the Judge proceeds to contrast Scott with General Pierce and with all our General presidents, except Taylor; and he succeeds in showing that Scott differs from them, in having held a military commission longer than any of them; in holding such a commission when nominated for the presidency, in not having been a physician or farmer and in not having held civil office. He does not stop to point *how* any of these differences is material to the question of his qualification for the presidency; but he seems to assume that disqualification must necessarily follow from these facts. Let us not adopt this conclusion too hastily. Let us examine the premises. He has held a military commission a long time—over forty years. If you assert that this has bred in him a thirst for war, and a distaste for peace, "the known incidents of a long public life" abundantly prove the contrary. Among them are his successful efforts for peace and against war in the South Carolina Nullification question, on the burning of the Caroline, and on the Maine boundary question.[13] The mere fact that he held a military commission when he was nominated, I presume no one will se-

[12] In a drunken quarrel, Hannegan stabbed his brother-in-law John R. Duncan. Before dying, Duncan absolved Hannegan of the primary blame.

[13] Scott commanded the federal forces in Charleston harbor in 1832, and his tactful but firm handling of the situation was widely credited with having averted armed conflict. Likewise, the near conflict with Britain in 1839, over the burning of the *Caroline* on the Niagara River (December 29, 1837) by Canadian troops engaged in suppressing the remnant of William L. McKenzie's rebellion, and over the disputed boundary between Maine and New Brunswick, was averted by Scott, who was in command of the American forces. Both questions were settled more or less amicably by the Webster-Ashburton Treaty in 1842.

riously contend proves anything to the point. Nor is it perceived how the being a physician or farmer, should qualify a man for office. Whatever of sound views of government is acquired by the physician and farmer, is acquired not in their regular occupations, but by reading and reflection in the hours of relaxation from their regular occupations. It is probable that the leisure time for such reading and reflection would, in time of peace, be quite as abundant with an officer of the army, as with a physician or farmer.

But Gen. Scott has not held civil office, and General Pierce has; and this is the great point. Well, let us examine this too. Gen. Pierce has been in the State Legislature and in congress; and I misread his history if it does not show him to have had just sufficient capacity, and no more, of setting his foot down in the track, as his partizan leader lifted his out of it—and so trudging along in the party team without a single original tho't or independent action. Scott, on the contrary, has on many occasions, been placed in the lead, when originality of thought and independence of action, both of the highest order, have been indispensable to success; and yet he failed in none. What he has performed in these stations bears much stronger resemblance to the duties he would have to perform as president, than any thing Gen. Pierce has ever done. Indeed they were literally, in every instance, executive duties—functions delegated to Gen. Scott by the president, because the president could not perform them in person. Is it not great folly to suppose that the manner of performing them is any less a test of his capacity for civil administration than it would be if he had held a civil office at the time? They say we rely solely on Gen. Scott's military reputation. Throw it aside then. In comparing the candidates let no consideration be given to military reputations. Let it be alike forgotten that Gen. Pierce ever fainted, or that Gen. Scott ever made a "fuss" or wore a "feather." Let them be placed in the scales solely on what they have done, giving evidence of capacity for civil administration; and let him kick the beam who is found lightest.

But, we cannot help observing the fact, that the democrats, with all their present horror of military candidates, have themselves put a general on the track. Why is this? It must have been by *accident* or by *design;* and it could not have been by accident, because I understand the party has become very philosophical, and it would be very unphilosophical to do such a thing by *accident*. It was by design, then. Let us try to trace it. They made their nomination before we made ours; but they knew we *ought*, and therefore concluded we *would*, not nominate Gen. Scott, and they shaped their course accordingly. They said "confound these old generals, is there no way of beating them? In 1840 we thought it would be mere sport to beat Harrison. We charged that his friends kept him in a cage; that he was an abolitionist, so far as he had sense enough to be anything; and we called him a petticoat general, and an old granny; but the election showed we had not hit upon the true philosophy. Again when Taylor was put up, we did not venture to call him an old granny, but we insisted he was not a whig; and, to help along, we put up a general against him, relying on our accustomed confidence in the capacity of the people to *not see* the difference between one who *is* a general, and one who is *called* a general, but we failed again. History is philosophy teaching by example, and if we regard the examples it has given us, we must try something new, before we can succeed in beating a general for the presidency."

Accordingly they nominated Pierce. It soon came to light that the first thing ever urged in his favor as a candidate was his having given a strange boy a cent to buy candy with. An examination of the official reports of his doings as a general in Mexico, showed him to have been the victim of a most extraordinary scene of mishap, which though it might by possibility have so happened with a brave and skillful general, left no considerable evidence that he was such. Forthwith also appears a biographical sketch of him,[14] in which he is represented, at the age of seventeen, to have spelled "but" for his father, who was unable to spell it for himself. By the way I *do* wish Frank had not been present on that trying occasion. I have a great curiosity to know how "old dad" would have spelled that difficult word, if he had been left entirely to himself. But the biography also represents him as cutting at the enemy's flying cannon balls with his sword in the battles of Mexico, and calling out, "Boys there's a game of ball for you;" and finally that he added enough to a balance due him to raise the whole to three hundred dollars, and treated his men.

When I first saw these things I suspected they had been put forward by mischievous whigs; but very soon I saw the biography published at length in a veritable democratic paper, conducted by a man whose party fidelity and intelligent co-operation with his party, I know to be beyond suspicion. Then I was puzzled. But now

[14] *Life and Services of Gen. Pierce, Respectfully Dedicated to Gen'l Lewis Cass* (Concord: Gazette Press, 1852). As has been pointed out by Elwin L. Page (*The Abraham Lincoln Quarterly*, December, 1949, pp. 458-59), this anonymous satirical pamphlet purported to come from the press of a Democratic organ but was "probably printed in the office of Charles L. Wheler's *Tribune*, a grossly virulent Whig campaign paper." Page observes, however, that "Pierce's over-zealous friends had retailed the very stories upon which the burlesque was built."

we have a letter from Gen. Shields,[15] in which, speaking of Pierce and himself, he says, "As we approached the enemy's position, directly under his fire, we encountered a deep ditch, or rather a deep narrow, slimy canal, which had been previously used for the purpose of irrigation. It was no time to hesitate, so we both plunged in. The horse I happened to ride that day was a light active Mexican horse. This circumstance operated in my favor, and enabled me to extricate myself and horse after considerable difficulty. Pierce, on the contrary, was mounted on a large, heavy American horse, and man and horse both sank down and rolled over in the ditch. There I was compelled to leave him . . . After struggling there, I cannot say how long, he extricated himself from his horse, and hurried on foot to join his command, &c."

Now, what right had a brigadier general, when approaching the enemy's position, and directly under his fire, to sink down and roll over in a deep slimy canal and struggle there before he got out, how long, another brigadier general cannot tell, when the whole of both their brigades got across that same "slimy canal," without any difficulty worth mentioning? I say, Judge Douglas, "Is *this* manoeuvre sanctioned by Scott's Infantry Tactics as adopted in the army?" This ludicrous scene in Gen. Pierce's career had not been told of before; and the telling of it by Gen. Shields, looks very much like a pertinacious purpose to "pile up" the ridiculous. This explains the new plan or system of tactics adopted by the democracy. It is to ridicule and burlesque the whole military character out of credit; and this [thus?] to kill Gen. Scott with vexation. Being philosophical and literary men, they have read, and remembered, how the institution of chivalry was ridiculed out of existence by its fictitious votary Don Quixote. They also remember how our own "militia trainings" have been "laughed to death" by fantastic parades and caricatures upon them. We remember one of these parades ourselves here, at the head of which, on horse-back, figured our old friend Gordon Abrams,[16] with a pine wood sword, about nine feet long, and a paste-board cocked hat, from front to rear about the length of an ox yoke, and very much the shape of one turned bottom upwards; and with spurs having rowels as large as the bottom of a teacup, and shanks a foot and a half long. That was the last militia muster here. Among the rules and regulations, no man is to wear more than five pounds of cod-fish for epaulets, or more than thirty yards of bologna sausages for a sash; and no two men are to

15 Written on August 5 to H. B. McGinnis and others at Galena, Illinois, James Shields' letter was published in the *Illinois State Register*, August 23, 1852. 16 Further identification of Gordon Abrams is not available.

dress alike, and if any two should dress alike the one that dresses most alike is to be fined, (I forget how much). Flags they had too, with devices and mottoes, one of which latter is, "We'll fight till we run, and we'll run till we die."

Now, in the language of Judge Douglas, "I submit to you gentlemen," whether there is not great cause to fear that on some occasion when Gen. Scott suspects no danger, suddenly Gen. Pierce will be discovered charging upon him, holding a huge roll of candy in one hand for a spy-glass; with B U T labelled on some appropriate part of his person; with Abrams' long pine sword cutting in the air at imaginary cannon balls, and calling out "boys there's a game of ball for you," and over all streaming the flag, with the motto, "We'll fight till we faint, and I'll treat when it's over."

It is calculated that such opposition will take "Old Fuss and Feathers" by surprise. He has thought of, and prepared himself for, all the ordinary modes of assault—for over-reachings, and under-minings; for fires in front and fires in the rear; but I guess this would be a fire on the "blind side"—totally unlooked for by him. Unless the opposition should, once more sink down, and roll over, in that deep slimy canal, I cannot conceive what is [to] save Gen. Scott.

But Judge Douglas alluding to the death of General Taylor says it was the hand of Providence which saved us from our first and only military administration. This reminds me of Judge Douglas' so much wanted [vaunted?] confidence in the people. The people had elected Gen. Taylor; and, as is appointed to all men once to do, he died. Douglas chooses to consider this a special interference of Providence, against the people, and in favor of Locofocoism. After all, his confidence in the people seems to go no farther than this, that they may be safely trusted with their own affairs, provided Providence retains, and exercises a sort of veto upon their acts, whenever they fall into the "marvelous hallucination," as the Judge calls it, of electing some one to office contrary to the dictation of a democratic convention. The people have fallen into this hallucination in two of the presidential elections of the four since the retirement of Gen. Jackson. The present struggle is for the best three in five. Let us stand by our candidate as faithfully as he has always stood by our country, and I much doubt if we do not perceive a slight abatement in Judge Douglas' confidence in Providence, as well as in the people. I suspect that confidence is not more firmly fixed with the Judge than it was with the old woman, whose horse ran away with her in a buggy. She said she trusted in Providence till the britchen broke; and then she didn't know what on airth *to* do. The chance is the Judge will see the breechen break, and then he can at his leisure, bewail the fate of locofocoism, as the victim of misplaced confidence.

Speaking of Mr. Fillmore, the Judge calls him, "a man who, previous to that time (his accession to the presidency) had never furnished such proofs of superiority of statesmanship as to cause him to be looked to as a candidate for the first office." O ho! Judge; it is you, is it, that thinks a man should furnish *proof of superiority of statesmanship,* before he is looked to as a candidate for the first office? Do please show us those proofs in the case of your "gallant and honest man, Frank Pierce." Do please name a single one that you consider such. What good thing, or even *part* of good thing has the country ever enjoyed, which originated with him? What evil thing has ever been averted by him? Compare his proofs of statesmanship with those of Mr. Fillmore, up to the ·times respectively when their names were first connected with presidential elections. Mr. Fillmore, if I remember rightly, had not been in Congress so long as Mr. or Gen. Pierce; yet he did acquire the distinction of being placed at the head of one of the most important Committees;[17] and as its Chairman, was the principal member of the H.R. in maturing the tariff of 1842. On the other hand, Gen. Pierce was in Congress six whole years, without being the chairman of any committee at all; and it was at the beginning of his seventh year when he was first placed at the head of one;[18] and then it was a comparatively unimportant one. To show by comparison, to the people of Illinois, the estimate in which Mr. Pierce was held, let me mention, that Douglas and McClernand[19] were each, placed at the head of an important committee, at the commencement of their second term; while it was not till the commencement of Pierce's fourth term, or rather of the fourth congress of which he had been a member, that he was admitted to the head of a less important one. I have no doubt that Col. McClernand is as much the superior of Pierce as this difference in the estimation in which they were held in Congress, would indicate. I have glanced over the Journals a little to ascertain if I could, what it is, or was, that Gen. Pierce had originated; and the most noted of any thing I could see, was a proposition to plead the Statute of Limitations against certain Revolution-

17 Fillmore was chairman of the ways and means committee of the Twenty-seventh Congress. He had been a member of three previous Congresses. Lincoln was somewhat inaccurate in contrasting the length of time elapsing before the respective Congressmen attained the distinction of committee chairmanships.

18 Pierce was chairman of the judiciary committee.

19 Douglas was chairman of the committee on territories; McClernand was chairman of the committee on public lands.

ary claims; and even this I believe he did not succeed in having adopted. There is one good democrat in our town who I apprehend would turn against Pierce if he only knew of this; for I have several times heard him insist that there is nothing but unmitigated rascality in Statutes of Limitation.

Judge Douglas says Mr. Fillmore, as president, "did no harm to the country," and he says this in such connection as to show that he regards it a disparagement to an administration to be able to say no more for it, than that it "did no harm to the country." And please Judge, is not an administration that "does no harm," the very *beau ideal* of a democratic administration? Is not the very idea of *beneficence*, unjust, inexpedient, and unconstitutional, in your view? Take the present democratic platform, and it does not propose to do a single thing. It is full of declarations as to what ought *not* to be done, but names no one to be done. If there is in it, even an inference in favor of any positive action by the democracy, should they again get into power, it only extends to the collecting a sufficient revenue to pay their own salaries, including perhaps, constructive mileage to Senators. Propose a course of policy that shall ultimately supplant the monstrous folly of bringing untold millions of iron, thousands of miles across water and land, which [while?] our own hills and mountains are groaning with the best quality in the world, and in quantity sufficient for ten such worlds, and the cry instantly is "no." Propose to remove a snag, a rock, or a sand-bar from a lake or river, and the cry still is "no."

I have seen in a dirty little democratic issue, called "papers for the people," what is there called a "democratic Battle Hymn." The first stanza of the delectable production runs as follows:

> "Sturdy and strong, we march along,
>   Millions on millions of freemen bold;
> Raising the dead, with our iron tread—
>   The noble dead, of the days of old!"

Now I do not wish to disturb the poet's delicious reverie, but I will thank him to inform me, at his earliest convenience, whether among the "noble dead" he saw "stirred up" there were any from the hulls of flats and keels, and brigs, and steam boats, which had gone to the bottom on questions of constitutionality?

After speaking rather kindly of Mr. Fillmore, the Judge proceeds to find fault with "certain features" of his administration, for which, he says, the Whig party is responsible, even more than Mr. Fillmore. This is palpably absurd. The Whigs hold no department of the government but the executive, and that is in the hands

of Mr. Fillmore. What can they be responsible for which he is not?
What led the Judge to make this absurd declaration is equally
plain. He knew the Whigs of Virginia were partial to Mr. Fillmore,
and he supposed to hold him up as a good man sacrificed, might excite his friends against Scott; but suddenly it occurs to him it will
not do to leave the thing in such shape, as that the Whig party may
claim it as an indorsement, to any extent, of a Whig administration. It was with some regret, that the Judge could do no more for
lack of time than merely glance at these "certain features." He had
before, in his ratification speech at Washington, glanced at the same
features, not having sufficient *time* to consider them at length. It is
to be hoped that in some one of the twenty-seven speeches yet to
come, he will find *time* to be a little more specific.

One of these "certain features" is that the proper satisfaction was
not insisted upon, for the shooting of the Americans in Cuba last
year. He says that, whether they were right or wrong, they were,
by a treaty stipulation, entitled to a trial, which was not given them.
Now whether there is a treaty stipulation that American citizens
shall not be punished in the Spanish dominions, without a fair trial,
I know not; but it strikes me as most remarkable that there should
be. Without any express treaty stipulation, it would seem to me to
be a plain principle of public law. The question is, did the principle
apply to these fifty men? Were they "American citizens" in the
sense of that principle? The position they had assumed was, that
they were oppressed Spanish subjects, and as such, had a right to
revolutionize the Spanish government in Cuba. They had re-
nounced our authority and our protection; and we had no more legal right to demand satisfaction for their treatment, than if they
had been native born Cubans. Their butchery was, as it seemed to
me, most unnecessary, and inhuman. They were fighting against
one of the worst governments in the world; but their fault was, that
the real people of Cuba had not asked for their assistance; were
neither desirous of, nor fit for civil liberty.

But suppose I am mistaken, and that satisfaction should have
been demanded of Spain for the shooting of the fifty in Cuba. What
should have been the nature of the satisfaction? Not pecuniary certainly? A disavowal of the act by the government, with the punishment of perpetrators? The very nature of the case made this impossible. The satisfaction, if sought at all, must have been sought
in war. If Judge Douglas thought it cause for war, upon him rests
the responsibility of not bringing a proposition before the Senate to
declare war. I suppose he knows that under the constitution, Congress, and not the president, declares war. Does not his omission to

move in the matter, in Congress, coupled with his greediness to agitate it before ratification meetings, and African church audiences, prove that he feels much greater concern for a presidential election, than he does to vindicate the honor of the nation, or to avenge the blood of its citizens?

The extravagant expenditures of the present administration is another of the Judge's "certain features." On this subject his language is very general, for want of *time* no doubt. At the "ratification" he says, "You find the expenditures nearly doubled, running up to about sixty millions of dollars a year, in times of profound peace." At Richmond he says, "I should like to know why a whig administration costs more in a profound peace than a democratic administration does during a great war." I have not had the opportunity to investigate this subject as I would like to do before undertaking to speak upon it; but I have learned enough to feel confident that the expenditures (of 1850-51 for instance) have not, by any plausible mode of estimating them, amounted to sixty millions, or to more than the expenditures of a "democratic administration in a great war," by at least ten millions of dollars.

I take the following from a paper which, is not often misled, and never intentionally misleads others—the National Intelligencer:—

"In the discussions which have taken place, in the newspaper and elsewhere, on the financial question, an attempt has been made to hold the present administration responsible for an alleged large *increase* of the expenditures of the Government. With the growth of the Government, and the additional cost of governing newly acquired and distant territories, it could not well be otherwise than that the expenses of the Government must be somewhat increased, but not to anything like the amount at which it has been stated; as, for example in the "Union" of a few days ago, in which the expenditures of Government were charged to have reached fifty two millions of dollars, instead of the thirty seven millions which they had reached at one period of the Van Buren administration.

"Let us briefly analyze this sweeping charge. It is not true, in the first place, that the expenditures of the Government last year amounted so high as fifty millions. In so large an expenditure, however, a few millions more or less would by some persons be thought to make little difference. But the *actual* payments during the year amounted to only forty eight millions of dollars, instead of fifty two millions (or fifty millions, as estimated by others,) as will be seen by the following statement, made up from authentic materials:

"The *payment* (net expenses) of the Government for fiscal year
1850 and 1851 were $48 005,878

From which *deduct*—

One Mexican instalment...

......$3 242 400

Mexican indemnity claims..

..... 2 516 691   5 759,091

42 246,787

Duties *refunded* on sugar and molasses
wrongfully collected (see decisions of
Supreme Court)....

..... $513 850

Debentures 867 268

Excess of duties 896 024

Expenses of collecting the revenues and
sales of lands.....

..... 2 051 708   4 328,845

38 917,936

Census expenses 672 500

Three and five per cent. funds to states,
and repayment of lands erroneously
sold 74 345

Smithsonian Institution 30 910   777,755

37 140 177

And mail service—Navy Department 1 303,365

35,837 812

Payments to volunteers 635 380

$35,201,432

"Of the expenditures of the last year nearly six millions of dollars, it will be seen, went to pay in part for our little property in California.

"The duties refunded, and the expenses of collecting the revenues, &c., amounting to more than four millions of dollars, would, under *former Administrations*, according to the then existing laws, have been paid by and deducted from the revenue by collectors. Now every thing is paid into the Treasury and repaid to the employees, &c.

"The items under the third division of the above statement are surely not 'ordinary expenses' of Government.

"The revenue from the Ocean Mail Steamers not appearing in

the *receipts* of the Treasury, the fourth item of the above should not be added to the expenses.

"The volunteers (comprising the fifth item) ought to have been paid years ago. Why, then, does that hold a place in the account of 'ordinary expenses' of the Government?

"A just computation of the 'ordinary' expenditures of the Government for the year 1851 is, therefore, by this analysis, reduced to little more than thirty five millions of dollars, being a less annual amount, as before stated, than the Government expenditure had risen to before the Whigs had ever had any effective share in the administration of the General Government."

By this it appears that in this twice made assault upon the administration, Judge Douglas is only mistaken about twenty five millions of dollars—a mere trifle for a giant!

I come now to the key-notes of the Richmond speech—Seward—Abolition—free soil, &c. &c. It is amusing to observe what a "Raw Head and Bloody Bones" Seward is to universal Locofocoism. That they do really hate him there is no mistake; but that they do not choose to tell the true reason of their hatred, is manifest from the vagueness of their attacks upon him. His supposed proclamation of a "higher law"[20] is the only specific charge I have seen for a long time. I never read the speech in which that proclamation is said to have been made; so that I cannot by its connection, judge of its import and purpose; and I therefore have only to say of it now, that in so far as it may attempt to foment a disobedience to the constitution, or to the constitutional laws of the country, it has my unqualified condemnation. But this is not the true ground of democratic hatred to Seward; else they would not so fondly cherish so many "higher law" men in their own ranks. The real secret is this: whoever does not get the State of New York will not be elected president. In 1848, in New York, Taylor had 218 538 votes—Cass 114 319, and free soilism, under Van Buren 120 497, Taylor only lacking 16 234 of beating them both. Now in 1852, the free soil organization is broken up, Van Buren has gone back to Locofocoism, and his 120 thousand votes are the stakes for which the game in New York is being played. If Scott can get nine thousand of them he carries the State, and is elected; while Pierce is beaten unless he can get about one hundred and eleven thousand of them. Pierce has all the leaders, and can carry a majority; but that won't do—he cannot live unless he gets nearly all. Standing in the way

[20] Senator William H. Seward's speech in favor of the admission of California into the Union (March 11, 1850) maintained that slavery should be excluded because of a "higher law" than the Constitution.

of this Seward is thought to be the greatest obstacle. In this division of free soil effects, they greatly fear he may be able to get as many as nine out of each hundred, which is more than they can bear; and hence their insane malice against him. The indispensable necessity with the democrats of getting these New York free soil votes, to my mind, explains why they nominated a man who "loathes the Fugitive Slave Law." In December or January[21] last Gen. Pierce made a speech, in which, according to two different news paper reports, published at the time in his vicinity and never questioned by him or any one else till after the nomination, he publicly declared his loathing of the Slave law. Now we shall allow ourselves to be very green, if we conclude the democratic convention did not know of this when they nominated him. On the contrary, its suposed efficacy to win free soil votes, was the very thing that secured his nomination. His Southern allies will continue to bluster and pretend to disbelieve the report, but they would not, for any consideration, have him to contradict it. And he will not contradict it—mark me, *he will not contradict it.* I see by the despatches he has already written a letter on the subject; but I have not seen the letter, or any quotation from it. When we shall see it, we shall also see it does not contradict the report—that is, it will not specifically deny the charge that he declared his loathing for the Fugitive Slave Law. I know it will not, because I know the *necessity* of the party will not permit it to be done. The letter will deal in generalities, and will be framed with a view of having it to pass at the South for a denial; but the specific point will not be made and met.

And this being the necessity of the party, and its action and attitude in relation to it, is it not particularly bright—in Judge Douglas to stand up before a slave-holding audience, and make flings at the Whigs about free soil and abolition! Why Pierce's only chance for presidency, is to be born into it, as a cross between New York old hunkerism, and free soilism, the latter predominating in the offspring. Marryat,[22] in some one of his books, describes the sailors, weighing anchor, and singing:

> "Sally is a bright Mullatter,
>   Oh Sally Brown—
> Pretty gal, but can't get at her,
>   Oh, Sally Brown."

Now, should Pierce ever be President, he will, politically speaking, not only be a mulatto; but he will be a good deal darker one than Sally Brown.

[21] In his speech at New Boston, January 2, 1852.　　[22] Frederick Marryat.

Speech at Peoria, Illinois[1]

September 17, 1852

The people of this city were addressed at the court house on Friday evening last, by Hon. A. LINCOLN, of Springfield. He showed up the inconsistency of the sham democracy on the question of internal improvements in such a manner that it is not to be wondered at that the friends of Pierce and King were dissatisfied. On the subject of the tariff he advocated the American side of the question, asking why, instead of sending a distance of 4,000 miles for our railroad iron, the immense iron beds of Missouri were not worked, affording a better article than that of English manufacture, and giving employment to American labor. On this point, he agreed with that distinguished democrat, Benton,[2] who does not believe with the President of the Peoria Pierce Club, that a protective tariff is a tax on the poor for the benefit of the rich. After alluding to the evasiveness exhibited in the celebrated platform adopted by the Democratic National Convention, the speaker contrasted the claims of the respective candidates to the support of the American people. Gen. Pierce had been a member of the U.S. Senate for five years and of the Lower House four years, and if he is the possessor of the great civil qualifications claimed for him by his friends, where is the evidence? Instead of possessing eminent civil abilities, said Mr. LINCOLN, did not an examination of the record prove that he is not worthy of the extravagant praises now bestowed upon him by his partizan friends. His votes show that he was the steady, consistent enemy of western improvements, and judging of the future by the past, should Mr. Pierce be elected he would surely veto such internal improvement bills as the one recently passed by Congress. The speaker also contended that as Mr. Pierce was a member of Congress a number of years without being appointed on any important committee, it was evidence of the estimation in which he was held in Washington, and was democratic testimony against his claims to great civil attainments. As a legislator he was noted for his bitter opposition to western interests, showing his hatred of the west, by voting with a minority of three or four congenial spirits against western measures. The speaker next alluded to the evidences of the civil qualifications of WINFIELD SCOTT as exhibited in his settlement of the troubles growing out of the Canadian Patriot war, the North-Eastern Boundary question, the Nullification excitement, and the removal of the Cherokee Indians. In this connexion, Mr. L. read extracts from several "democratic" papers applying opprobrious epithets to Gen. Scott, and among others a paragraph from an organ of *the* party calling Gen. SCOTT a fool. "Can it be possible," said he,

[158]

"that Gen. Jackson appointed a FOOL to the important duties connected with the settlement of the South Carolina difficulty, where, as the agent of the General Government those duties were performed in such a manner as to win the thanks of Gen. Lewis Cass, Andrew Jackson's Secretary of War? Can it be possible that the man selected by President Van Buren to adjust the difficulties on the Northern frontier is a fool? Is it true that the noble hearted man and Christian gentleman who as the agent of a democratic administration, removed the Cherokee Indians from their homes to the west of the Mississippi in such a manner as to gain the applause of the great and good of the land, is a fool?" Mr. L. also, in substantiating the claims of Scott spoke of his successful effort in procuring the enactment of a law by Congress authorizing retaliation on the part of our authorities in the event of the execution of the twenty-three Irishmen who were taken prisoners with Scott at the battle of Queenstown.[3]

On the conclusion of the speech an excellent song, composed by a member of the Glee Club, was sung, and the meeting adjourned with three cheers for Winfield Scott and three more for Abram Lincoln.

We understand that Mr. L. will visit us again previous to the election and address the people.

[1] Peoria *Weekly Republican,* September 24, 1852. This is the only report of the speech available, but the Peoria *Democratic Press,* September 22, 1852, devoted a paragraph to ridiculing it as "little worthy of attention" and suggested that "if Mr. Lincoln has made no better speeches during the campaign, he had better '*rub out,* and begin again.' "   [2] Thomas H. Benton.
[3] October 13, 1812.

To Charles R. Welles[1]

C. R. Welles, Esq.   Bloomington,
Dear Sir   Sept. 27. 1852.

I am in a little trouble here. I am trying to get a decree for our "Billy the Barber"[2] for the conveyance of certain town lots sold to him by Allen, Gridly and Prickett.[3] I made you a party, as administrator of Prickett, but the Clerk omitted to put your name in the writ, and so you are not served. Billy will blame me, if I do not get the thing fixed up this time. If, therefore, you will be so kind as to sign the authority below, and send it to me by *return mail,* I shall be greatly obliged, and will be careful that you shall not be involved, or your rights invaded by it. Yours as ever   A. LINCOLN

[1] ALS, IHi.
[2] William Florville, a Negro barber residing in Springfield, had failed to record his deed to the lots and had lost the deed.
[3] James Allin and Asahel Gridley were partners of David Prickett, who died in 1847.

To Lewis M. Hays[1]

L. M. Hays Esq.   Springfield,
Dear Sir: Oct. 27. 1852

Yours of Sept. 30th. just received. At our court, just past; I could have got a judgment against Turley, if I had pressed to the utmost; but I am really sorry for him—*poor* and a *cripple* as he is. He begged time to try to find evidence to prove that the deceased on his death bed, ordered the note to be given up to him or destroyed. I do not suppose he will get any such evidence, but I allowed him till next court to try. Yours &c   A LINCOLN

[1] ALS-P, ISLA. See letter to Hays, April 23, 1851, *supra.*

Opinion on Election Laws[1]

Springfield, Nov. 1, 1852.

A leading article in the Daily Register of this morning has induced some of our friends to request our opinion on the election laws, as applicable to challenged votes. We have examined the present Constitution of the State, the election law of 1849, and the unrepealed parts of the election law in the Revised code of 1848; and we are of opinion that any person taking the oath prescribed in the act of 1849, is entitled to vote, unless counter proof be made, satisfying a majority of the Judges that such oath is untrue, and that for the purpose of obtaining such counter proof, the proposed voter may be asked questions in the way of cross-examination, and other independent testimony may be received. We base our opinion as to receiving counter proof, upon the unrepealed Section Nineteen of the election Law in the Revised code.   A. LINCOLN,

B. S. EDWARDS,

S. T. LOGAN.

I concur in the foregoing opinion,

S. H. TREAT.

[1] *Illinois Journal,* November 2, 1852. The opinion is prefaced by the following: "The Register of yesterday morning assumes that the whigs will attempt to prevent our adopted citizens from voting to-day; and it advises them *not* to take their naturalization papers to the polls. By the opinion of three whig lawyers and one democratic Judge, which we publish this morning, it seems the having the Naturalization papers at the polls is not indispensably necessary; but notwithstanding this, we would advise our friends among the adopted citizens to take their papers with them, as the shortest and easiest way of doing the thing up, in case of a controversy."

Endorsement: Anson L. Brewer to Lincoln[1]

[c. November 17, 1852]

[Last sp]ring I commenced a suit in [the case] within mentioned, for the October [term of] the Logan Co. Circuit court; & [when the] term came, behold, the Sheriff had not served the process. I ordered an alias for the next April term. It was all I could do.

A. LINCOLN

1 AES, RPB. The document has a square cut out which removes portions of the writing. The reconstruction is the editors'. Anson L. Brewer, an attorney of New Lisbon, Ohio, wrote on November 17, 1852, "I should like very much to hear how you are getting along in the collection of the claim of Kelly *v.* Blackledge." Lincoln's endorsement probably represents the substance of his answer. Further reference to the case of James Kelly *v.* Jesse D. Blackledge will be found in Lincoln's letters to Brewer on March 16, July 27, and November 5, 1855, *infra.* Kelly was a building contractor and Blackledge a well-to-do resident of Pickawa County, Ohio, who had removed to Logan County, Illinois.

Petition to Augustus C. French
for Pardon of John A. L. Crockett[1]

[November 22, 1852]

To His Excellency, the Governor of the State of Illinois.

We, the undersigned, chiefly citizens of Moultrie and Shelby counties, respectfully represent that one John A. L. Crockett, a man of about twentysix years of age, has been found guilty of the crime of manslaughter by a jury in the circuit court of said Moultrie county, and has been sentenced to the Penitentiary for the term of two years. We further represent that said Crockett has been, from his infancy, only not quite an ideot, being at least, of the very lowest grade of intellect above absolute ideocy. We, therefore, (several of us being jurors who sat on the trial) believing that his punishment can result in no public good, respectfully recommend that he be pardoned.

1 AD, I-Ar. This petition drawn by Lincoln bears more than one hundred names. Although undated, it accompanies the letter of Anthony Thornton, *infra,* which bears Lincoln's endorsement.

Endorsement: Anthony Thornton
to Augustus C. French[1]

[c. November 22, 1852]

I assisted in the defence of J. A. L. Crockett; and, of course, heard and noted the evidence; and I concur generally with the state-

[161]

ment of Mr. Thornton, above. I think him, most clearly, a proper
subject of the Executive Clemency.   A. LINCOLN—

[1] AES, I-Ar. Thornton's letter of November 22, 1852, elaborates on the substance of the petition *supra*. In addition to this endorsement Lincoln has written an explanatory footnote on the second page of Thornton's letter, as follows:
"His [Crockett's] fathers residence is near where the three counties join." The
file contains several other letters and petitions.

Endorsement on Mortgage
from Thomas Cantrall and Elizabeth Cantrall[1]

Satisfied in full, this 29th day of November 1852. Witness my
hand and seal   A. LINCOLN

[1] Sangamon County Mortgage Records, Book HH, 148. To secure a note for
$600, payable two years from date with interest at ten per cent, Lincoln took
a mortgage on Cantrall's eighty-acre farm on November 28, 1851.

Report of Commissioners Appointed to Investigate the Illinois and Michigan Canal Claims[1]

To His Excellency,   January 7, 1853
   the Governor[2] of the State of Illinois:

We, the undersigned, two of the commissioners appointed by
the act of the general assembly of the state of Illinois, entitled "An
act to constitute a commission to take evidence in relation to certain claims," approved June 22, 1852, report that the Hon. Hugh
T. Dickey,[3] the other commissioner named in said act, having declined to act, we caused a notice to be published in more than one
newspaper in Chicago, in one at Joliet, and in one at Ottawa, more
than thirty days before the 3d day of December, 1852, that on
said third day of December, we would meet at Ottawa, for the purpose of taking evidence according to said act, an exact copy of
which publication is as follows, to wit:

*"Notice to claimants against the state, on account of the Illinois
and Michigan canal.*—All claimants within the provisions of an
act of the general assembly of the state of Illinois, entitled 'An act
to constitute a commission to take evidence in relation to certain

[1] *Reports Made to the Eighteenth General Assembly of The State of Illinois*
(1853), House Reports, pp. 4-24.   [2] Augustus C. French.
[3] Hugh T. Dickey was a Chicago attorney and judge of the Seventh Judicial
Circuit Court.

claims,' approved June 22, 1852, are hereby notified that the undersigned, two of the commissioners named in said act, will meet on the third day of December next at Ottawa, on the line of said canal, for the purpose of taking evidence according to said act.

November 2, 1852.   NOAH JOHNSTON,[4]

                                                          A. LINCOLN."

That, accordingly, we did, on said third day of December, 1852, at Ottawa, take the oath prescribed in said act, which was administered to us by the Hon. Edwin S. Leland, judge of the ninth judicial circuit of the state of Illinois, and did proceed at once to the taking of said evidence.

On motion of counsel for claimants, and against the objection of Mr. Edwards,[5] counsel for the state, it was ordered by the board that the original papers filed at the seat of government, and then in the control of the board, should be subject to the inspection of the counsel for the claimants as well as the counsel for the state, but that said papers was not to be taken from the room where the board might be sitting, nor to be inspected by witnesses.

Mr. Edwards, counsel for the state, gave notice to claimants for damages to real estate, that title papers must be produced.

Roswell D. Lyman, whose claim has been presented to the legislature, offered evidence, which, together with the cross-examination by counsel for the state, is as follows:

[See Plat A.][6]

Joseph H. Wagner, being duly sworn, says he is acquainted with sec. 6, T. 33 N., R. 4 E., that the plat marked "R. D. Lyman, No. 1," fairly represents said section, that witness is county surveyor, and made the plat from actual survey and the original field notes of the United States survey. Notes at the bottom of the plat are correct, there are coal beds between the river and the feeder on the northeastern subdivision of the section; extent of these beds from S.W. to N.E. about forty rods, and from the river to and under the feeder; so much of the coal as lies under the feeder, and also so much as lies near adjacent to the feeder, cannot be worked without injury to the feeder, and the breakage of the feeder is some detriment to the working of the remainder; the strata of coal is about two feet thick; all the subdivisions of said section which

4 Noah Johnston (or Johnson, both spellings appearing throughout this and other contemporary records) was a Mount Vernon attorney who had served several terms in the Illinois legislature, both House and Senate.

5 Ninian W. Edwards.   6 Brackets in the source.

are marked "Lyman" are inclosed and the greater part cultivated as farm land; Lyman's residence is on said land at the point where the word "house" is written on the plat. To travel from Lyman's residence to the coal bed he must go a mile and a half further than he would if the feeder were not there, unless he should ford the feeder, which is impracticable, and the same distance to reach that part of his farm lying south of the feeder; the residence of Lyman a mile and a quarter from Ottawa, and the coal land one and three quarters. From 8 to 12, south of where the east and west line passing through the middle of said section crosses said feeder, there is a waste weir or place for surplus water to escape. The water runs a distance of about twelve rods over another coal bed into the river. This last mentioned coal bed has a stratum of about two feet, it is opened about four rods one way and thirty or forty feet the other, doubtless extends further, but how far is not known. So far, witness thinks, the waste water aforesaid has facilitated the raising of coal from the bed, but thinks it will ultimately be an injury to it. Thinks Lyman's farm is, at this time, worth from twenty to twenty-five dollars per acre.

Cross-Examination.—In the winter of 1842-3 thinks the land was worth eight dollars per acre. The town of Ottawa was laid out on state canal land, part on a donation by the state to the county, and part as a state's addition to the town; the proximity of Lyman's land to Ottawa has something to do with its enhanced value. The construction of the canal has enhanced the value of all lands on the line, and Lyman's with the rest, and witness thinks if Lyman's land had been his, would have preferred having the canal, without compensation, to not having it at all.

Re-examined.—Lyman's land derives no particular advantage from the canal, but only the common advantage with other lands on the line. The feeder, witness considers a decided disadvantage to Lyman's farm, on the whole, though it gives a small advantage of bringing stock water more convenient to him. Witness thinks the lands lying along the Illinois river are as much benefitted by the canal as those immediately on the line. The feeder, witness thinks, indispensably necessary to the canal, but that it might have been constructed at less expense, just as beneficial for the canal and less injurious to Lyman's land.

George H. Norris, by Mr. Edwards, for the state, says he has and is prosecuting a claim against the state, for damage done by the canal on one tract and by a feeder on another.

By Lyman's counsel.—Lyman's land is not cut by the main canal, it is a half mile distant, and Fox river is between at the nearest point. Witness thinks Lyman's farm is now worth twenty-five dollars per acre; Lyman has occupied and possessed said farm for near fifteen years. Witness knew Downey Buchanan, who testified for Lyman on his original application, and knows that he is now dead, and with good opportunities for knowing, he does not believe he had any interest in this or any similar claim. Witness thinks that Lyman's coal beds, taken separately from the other land, is worth four or five hundred dollars per acre. Feeder is not navigable with canal boats freighted; tried it several times and failed.

State of Illinois, ⎱
   La Salle county, ⎰ ss.

Henry J. Reed, being first duly sworn, says that he is well acquainted with the farm of R. D. Lyman, on the west fraction of the north-east quarter of sec. six (6,) town. 33, range 4, east of the third principal meridian; that he has been acquainted with said land about eighteen years; that Roswell D. Lyman has been in possession of the same since about 1839, claiming title; that said land is an improved and cultivated farm; that there is on said tract of land a valuable coal bed on the north-east corner of the fraction. Said feeder runs across said coal bed for forty rods or more; said coal bed is of a good quality and the strata of coal about two feet thick. I think the coal on that land is worth two cents a bushel. The coal bed cannot be worked nearer than almost twelve feet of the base of the feeder bank. To get to this coal bed or to that part of his land which is across the feeder from his house, Lyman has to travel at least one mile and a half further than he would have to do if the feeder was not there. On that piece of land which is marked "Cushman and Lyman," on the plat, there is a bank on each side of the feeder 75 feet wide, making 150 feet in width, exclusive of the bed of the feeder, which is rendered utterly useless by reason of the deposit of earth and sand excavated from the feeder. On the same land, on the north side of the feeder, about three acres are overflowed by water setting back from the feeder. On the south side of the feeder about six acres of land is rendered useless, by reason of the drainage from the feeder. On the same land is a coal bed of a good quality, about two feet thick, over which the feeder runs. I believe there is coal under the bed of the feeder in its whole length on section six aforesaid. Affiant knows that when the feeder was dug, coal was found in various places for the whole distance, and coal was raised from the feeder very near the waste weir hereafter mentioned, at a time when there was a break in the feeder. There is a waste weir of that land where the water runs from the feeder, and that water will render it difficult to get the coal. Lyman has been obliged to dig a drain to carry the water around that part of the coal bed where coal is now being raised. I believe the coal land to be worth four hundred dollars an acre for the coal that is upon it. And that the farm of Lyman, and the land of Cushman and Lyman, is worth less by one-fourth than it would be if the feeder did not cross it at all.

Cross-Examination.—The feeder mentioned was constructed in 1838, 1839, and 1840. Does not know whether Lyman made any objection to the construction of feeder. Witness knew there was coal on Lyman's land before feeder was located; thinks some coal was dug there in the fall of 1834. Boats can pass on the feeder now and take coal from the bank. Thinks Lyman's whole farm now worth from twenty to twenty-five dollars per acre. Knows of contiguous canal lands being appraised at one hundred dollars per acre; thinks this canal land mentioned, worth more than Lyman's by ten dollars per acre. Has no interest in this or any similar question.

Re-examination.—Witness thinks the appraisement of the canal lands as above stated was very much above the true value; thinks thirty dollars per acre about the true value. Witness thinks the said canal lands more valuable than Lyman's, because it is not cut by the feeder, the quality of the land is very similar, the canal lands are also nearer the town of Ottawa. Before the construction of the feeder Lyman's land was all dry and fit for cultivation; about nine acres of that part of the land marked on the plat as "Lyman and Cushman," is flooded by the feeder, this being the same mentioned in the direct examination. On reflection, witness does not remember to have ever seen a common canal boat on said feeder, and is not sure the feeder is navigable for such boats.

Re-Cross-Examination.—Witness thinks the lands marked "Lyman," on the plat, is not as much damaged by the feeder as that marked "Lyman and Cushman." Thinks this land was worth about twenty dollars per acre as early as 1839.

Re-examination.—Thinks that while the feeder injures Lyman's land, as before stated, it does not benefit it in any particular. Thinks the canal is of benefit to the state generally, and also supposes it may be of some greater benefit to the lands now contiguous to it.[7]

[7] Footnote in source: "NOTE.—Mr. Edwards objected to all the proof, in the case of R. D. Lyman, in relation to coal and coal banks, as being an increase of a claim."

Abstract W. fr. S. E. ¼ Sec. 6, 33, 4.

Allen H. Howland and Henry Green, W. fr. S. E. ¼ 6,33,
4. Filed October 21, 1835, ... A.500
Henry Green, etrx. Henry L. Brush, deed, und. ½ same.
March 3, 1836, ... C.118
United States patent, Henry Green, W. fr. S. E. ¼ sec. 6,
33, 4. March 24, 1840, ... 5.159
Henry Green, etrx. deed, W. H. W. Cushman, und. ½ W.
fr. S. E. ¼ 6, 33, 4. March 17, 1841, ... 7.176
Henry L. Brush, etrx. deed, R. D. Lyman, und. ½ W. fr.
as above. May 15, 1841, ... 7.300
Henry Green, etrx. deed, W. H. W. Cushman, und. ½ W.
fr. as above. March 29, 1842, ... 8.93
Joseph O. Glover, etrx. deed, W. H. W. Cushman, und. ½
same. March 23, 1842. . . . . . . 9.07
R. D. Lyman, mort. John Vahort, November 15, 1844, und.
½ same tract, ... 10.443
R. D. Lyman, mort. W. H. W. Cushman, und. ½ same
tract. April 25, 1846, ... 12.349
Henry Green, etrx, trust deed, Aaron Reed, W.fr.S. E. ¼
sec. 6, as above. Filed March 24, 1847, . . . 13.537

State of Illinois, ⎤
  La Salle county, ⎦ ss.

I, Philo Lindley, clerk of the circuit court, and *ex officio* recorder in and for said county, do hereby certify that the within
is a correct abstract of conveyances of west fr. of S. E. ¼, sec. 6,
T. 33, R. 4, as shown by the tract book in my office, and that the
dates given herein are the dates of filing for record.

In witness whereof I have hereunto set my hand
and affixed the seal of said court, this 4th
[L.S.]   day of December, A.D. 1852.
P. LINDLEY, *Clerk and*
                                  ex officio Recorder.

The record shows that the consideration mentioned in the deed
from Henry L. Brush to R. D. Lyman, was three hundred dollars.
The date of the deed, April 30, 1841, book 7, page 300.

The consideration in the deed from Henry Green to H. L. Brush,
of date 31st August, 1835, was sixty-three dollars, book C, page 118.

George H. Norris, on one claim which had been presented to
the legislature, offered evidence, which, together with the cross-examination by counsel for the state, is as follows, to wit:

Henry J. Reed, being first duly sworn, saith that he is well acquainted with the west fraction of the south-west quarter of section thirty-two, in township thirty-four north, of range four, east of the third principal meridian. The Fox river feeder of the Illinois and Michigan canal enters said tract on the north line of said tract, and following the base of the bluff runs diagonally through said tract about a half a mile, in a south-west direction, leaving twenty-five acres of said land in a strip, over a half mile long, between Fox river and the feeder, and the remainder of the tract in a three cornered form on the other side of the feeder. There is a coal bed on said tract. In my judgment, at least two acres of the coal land on said tract is taken up by the said feeder and its banks. That to get from one part of said land to the other, it would be necessary to travel at least two and one half miles. The construction of the feeder injures the land for farming purposes, and makes it a great deal more difficult to get the coal to market. Affiant agrees in his opinion in relation to these last matters with the statements of J. H. Wagner, this day made in this case. I have known this land some eighteen years. In my opinion the injury to the coal bed alone, and the amount of the coal taken, damage the land one thousand dollars.

Cross-Examination.—This land is immediately above and corners with section six. From 1838 to 1840 the land was worth from ten to fifteen dollars per acre. This land is not so valuable as that of Mr. Lyman's. This land is, from 1848 till now, worth from fifteen to twenty dollars per acre. The general value of the lands for four or five miles up the feeder, and up the canal, is from fifteen to twenty-five dollars per acre.

Re-examination.—The piece of land joining Norris, on the west, was in 1839 worth twelve dollars per acre, and in witness' estimation it is now worth more per acre than Norris'. In estimating Norris' land at from ten to twelve dollars per acre from 1838 to 1849 witness did not intend to estimate the coal upon it at that time. Witness knew there was some coal there, but did not know the extent of it. Witness now regards the coal as of more value than the land would be independent of it.

Re-Cross-Examination.—In answer to the question, what was the market value of Norris' land from 1838 to 1840, witness says, if that land had been put up for sale I should not have given more than ten dollars per acre. In answer to the question, what is it now worth as a market value, he says, from fifteen to twenty dollars per acre.

Re-examination.—Witness thinks Norris' land, as it is, is worth twenty-five dollars, and that it would be worth ten dollars more with the feeder off from it.

Joseph H. Wagner, being duly sworn, deposes and says, that he is acquainted with the situation of the W. fraction of S. W. ¼ sec. 32, T. 34, R. 4 E. That the feeder of the Illinois and Michigan canal runs through said tract from the north to the south end, rendering it almost valueless for farming purposes; that there is a bed of coal to the extent of several acres on said land, part of which is covered by said feeder and its banks, that the coal land is materially injured in value by the leakage from the feeder rendering it more difficult and expensive excavating the coal; the only way to haul coal from that portion of the land lying east of the feeder is by hauling it either on the bank of the feeder, or across Fox river, which in the winter season is difficult and sometimes dangerous; there is no bridge by which a team can cross from one portion of the land to the other, without traveling at least two and a half miles. Aside from the damage done the land for farming purposes, in my opinion the value of the land lessens by the construction of the feeder, one thousand dollars.

Cross-Examination.—This land was worth in 1842, from eight to ten dollars; was not in the country before 1842. The lands up the feeder its whole length, four miles, excepting sections one and two, which are now worth from twenty-five to thirty dollars per acre in 1842 suppose they were worth from six to ten dollars per acre, though was not so well acquainted then; sections one and two are now valuable; section one is canal land and section two is not. Witness is county surveyor.

Re-examination.—If the feeder was not there the coal bed would be worth a cent and a half per square foot as it is; that which is accessible is not worth more than half as much, to say nothing of that which is covered by the feeder and banks. That part of the land west of the feeder is, for farming purposes, worth twenty-five dollars per acre; that between the feeder and river is, for farming purposes, worthless; the land between the feeder and river is some wetter in consequence of the feeder, but would still be good meadow land if it were accessible; as it is not, without a bridge, and it would not be so convenient even with a bridge, the land between the feeder and river, including the coal bed, is worth ten dollars per acre. The cost of a bridge to reach the land between the feeder and river, would be more than the value of the land. The feeder is not navigable for ordinary canal boats, but witness has seen it navigated by small flat boats drawing ten inches water, in transporting flour and bran from the Dayton mills.

The deed for the land to Norris is dated December 4, 1847, consideration $575, quantity 73.17-100 acres.

George H. Norris, on another claim which had been presented

to the legislature, offered evidence which, together with the cross-examination by counsel for the state, is as follows, to wit:

Norris' deed for this land is dated August, 1835, consideration $10 per acre.

John H. Wagner, produced by the claimant and examined by the attorney for the state, says that cattle cross the canal and feeder. Does not know that there is coal on sec. 10, 33, 3, but sec. 2, where the feeder crosses, there is coal, which is from seven to eleven feet under ground, and is worth from one and a half to two cents per bushel in the bed.

Cross-Examination.—That the canal trustees claim to control on each side of the canal ninety feet in width; that the ground occupied by the spoils banks is worthless, rendered so by the occupation of this earth, and that the spoils banks occupy the ninety feet, or nearly so, and that the trustees of the canal have forbidden the adjoining proprietors from removing said earth.

Henry Green, being first duly sworn, saith that he is acquainted with sec. 12, town. 33 north, range 3 east, and has known it for nineteen years. The W. ½ of N. E. ¼, and und. ½ of E. ½ of same quarter, is claimed by W. H. W. Cushman. The Illinois and Michigan canal runs through the whole quarter section from the east line to the west line of the quarter section; that through the west half of the said north-east quarter, said canal is one hundred feet wide, except about twelve rods on the west side, which is sixty feet, exclusive of the spoil banks; there is a coal bed on said quarter, which is worked upon the W. ½ of said quarter at different points, and coal exhibits itself nearly the whole width of the quarter and on both sides of the canal, and I have no doubt that the bed of coal underlies the whole bed of the canal on that quarter, except about ten or twelve rods next to Fox river; the strata of coal on that land is from eighteen to twenty inches thick, so far as opened, and is worth at least one cent per bushel in the bed; between three and four acres on the west half of said quarter had been stripped to the depth of from three to four feet, so as to render the same entirely valueless for farming purposes, and said last named tract is mostly in such a situation in reference to the canal that the coal cannot be removed from it, so that it is for the most part entirely valueless.[8]

[8] Footnote in source: "NOTE.—Mr. Edwards, counsel for the state, objects to so much of the above statement as relates to coal, because it is an increase of claim, which objection the board sustain, but allowed the statement to be placed on file for the inspection of the legislature, on the ground that the evidence in relation to coal is rejected. Mr. Edwards declines to cross-examine the witness, or to introduce proof upon the point. Mr. Edwards admits the sufficiency of the title to all the tracts in this claim."

Reddick and Brush, each making a separate claim for damage to the E. ½ of S. E. ¼ of sec. 2, T. 33 N., R. 3 east, presented their title papers, to which Mr. Edwards, counsel for the state, raised no objection. The consideration in one of the deeds shows this land to have been worth $60 per acre in September, 1848.

Henry L. Brush, on a claim for damages to S. ½ of W. ½ of N. E. ¼ of sec. 10, T. 33 N., R. 3 east, also for E. ½ of N. E. ¼ of same section, presented title papers, to which counsel for the state raised no objections. The deed to Brush, in this case, dated July 14, 1837, consideration $2.50 per acre; also proved by Joseph H. Wagner that he considers Brush's land on sec. 10, worth seventy-five dollars per acre.

On the claim of Henry L. Brush for the undivided half of E. ½ of S. E. ¼ of sec. 2, and for the whole of the S. ½ of W. ½ of N. E. of sec. 10, and E. ½ of N. E. 10, all in T. 33 N., R. 3 E., counsel for the state offers the parol testimony of Joseph H. Wagner, which is as follows, to wit:

Joseph H. Wagner sworn, says he considers the E. ½ of S. E. ¼ of sec. 2, 33 N., R. 3 east, worth five hundred dollars per acre, and thinks the coal on it increases the valuation one half; considers Brush's land on sec. 10 worth seventy-five dollars per acre.[9]

On the claim of J. C. Chaplin and others, for damages to the W. ½ of S. E. ¼ of sec. 2, T. 33 N., R. 3 E., counsel for the state offered the parol testimony which follows, to wit:

Joseph H. Wagner sworn, says that he considers the W. ½ S. E. ¼ sec. 2, 33, 3, worth now, the south forty acres, one thousand dollars per acre, the north forty acres, two hundred and fifty dollars per acre. Witness thinks that there is ten acres out of the south forty acres worth only fifty dollars per acre; said ten acres lies in the south-west corner of said forty. Witness has been a civil engineer since 1835, and employed on the Utica and Schenectady Railroad, firstly as rodman and leveller, and on the Canojoharie and Catskill Railroad, as assistant engineer, and is acquainted with the land, and has been for several years. Does not know that the feeder could have been constructed so as to have injured that land much less than it is. Witness thinks that material for construction of the feeder banks might have been obtained at other points, so as to have not injured that land as much, but to have done this it would have been more expensive to the canal. Witness thinks that the material for these embankments might have been taken from one acre of ground, but to have done so would have been more ex-

[9] Footnote in source: "NOTE.—This evidence, as to the first tract, applies equally to the claim of Mr. Reddick."

pensive, but such additional expense would not equal the additional damage done the land by extending over the surface.

Springfield, December, 1852.

R. E. Goodell states on oath, that he has resided in the town of Ottawa eighteen years last past, during which time the Fox river feeder of the Illinois and Michigan canal was constructed; that since the construction of said feeder he has been well acquainted with the value of real estate in the state's addition to Ottawa and the adjoining lands; that in his opinion the state's addition to said town has increased as much in value, since the construction of said feeder, as any part of section number two, adjoining the same. The town of Ottawa is situated on section eleven, and most of the part I refer to, to wit, the state's addition to Ottawa, is nearer the court house than any part of section two. The increased value of section eleven has been caused, in my opinion, by the nearer location it has to the business part of the town, and the completion of the canal. I think that the valuation of section two in a body has been increased by the completion of the canal. At the time the canal was completed, I think I would rather have the land in section two with the canal than without it. The land which is used on the W. ½ S. E. ¼ for the feeder, I consider worth at least six hundred dollars per acre. The land overflowed by the feeder and the canal I think in a body valueless. The injury done by the overflowing the eighty acres with the feeder I consider not less than eight thousand dollars. By the construction of the canal without the feeder, unless the state built a culvert so as to let the water pass off, there would have been nearly the same amount of land overflowed; this would have been in consequence of the construction of the canal. The plat herewith filed, marked "Plat of lands near Ottawa," is a correct map.

The following plat, proved to be correct, was introduced by counsel for the state, and filed for reference in all cases to which it applies:

[*See Plat B.*][10]

The trustees of the United States Bank, whose claim had been presented to the legislature, offered the exhibit herewith, marked "U.S. Bank, No. 1," which, together with explanatory parol testimony, was received, as follows, on the condition stated: Samuel Staats Taylor, produced by the attorney of the United States Bank, and sworn. The witness holding in hand the account herewith

[10] Brackets in the source.

filed, marked "U.S. Bank, No. 1," offered to give some explanatory evidence, when Mr. Edwards objected to the filing of the paper; first, because it was proved *ex parte*, without opportunity of cross-examination, and, secondly, because it lays the basis of a new claim; whereupon the claimant consents that it be filed, to be used only in explanation of the claim as originally filed, and in no wise as an increase of the same—upon which condition the commission have allowed it to be filed.

Witness knows John Rumsey, who made the affidavit filed with the account; was one of the book-keepers in the United States Bank, employed as such during all the time the transactions stated in said account occurred, and that he is now and has always been one of the book-keepers of said bank. Knows his hand-writing, and the signature to the affidavit is his. The difference in the amount between this account and the one originally filed arises from the fact that in this account there is a charge made for coupons that is not in the first account, the bank having been made to pay them, on a garnishee process issued against the bank by one of the creditors of the state of Illinois.[11]

The undersigned further report, that all the other claims, upon which any evidence was offered, falling in classes, so that any evidence, applicable at all, was applicable to a whole class, we found it convenient, and even absolutely necessary, for the saving of time, to take a larger portion of the testimony under the head of "general evidence." Intermingled with this are occasional explanatory notes. The general evidence is as follows, to wit:

General evidence taken at Ottawa, Chicago and Springfield before Hon. N. Johnston and Hon. A. Lincoln, December, 1852.

William M. True, on behalf of the state, sworn, says—During the time the contractors were to work on the canal, he received canal scrip at par, as a merchant at Ottawa. Witness does not know that the hands received scrip of contractors at par; thinks merchants generally received it at par.

Cross-Examination.—Witness thinks he did not receive and pay out scrip as low as twenty-five cents on the dollar—thinks it was at one time received as low as twenty cents; there was a time when it rated at fifteen and twenty cents on the dollar, and business men generally refuse to deal in it at that time. Do not recollect whether the work on the canal was in progress or not. Cannot recollect that at any time after July, 1852, scrip was received by merchants at

[11] Footnote in source: "NOTE.—The testimony of this witness, so far as it may tend to lay the basis of a new claim, or to increase the original claim, is excluded, and is only received so far as it may tend to explain the original claim."

par. There was a time, while the canal was in progress, that scrip was received by the merchants as low as seventy-five cents on the dollar—no positive recollection of taking it lower than that.

Re-examination.—Cannot state that at any time from 1842 to 1845, it was received at par.

Continuation of general evidence taken at Chicago.

Alexander Brand, on behalf of claimants, sworn, says—That he has been engaged in the exchange business since 1839, in the city of Chicago. Has dealt in canal indebtedness. The first was the old 1840 interest scrip. Second class was certificates given for large balances due the contractors. Third class was what is now called indebtedness, and printed on the back of an engraved plate.

March 6, 1840. Exchange between here and New York on State Bank of Illinois, was 12 and 12½ per cent.

April 3, 1840. Some merchants in this city took scrip at par; George Smith, dealer in exchange and banker, bought it at 62½ and 68 cents.

April 16, 1840. Scrip was taken by many merchants at par, for most goods. The merchants contrived generally to increase the price of their goods. Some goods they would not sell for scrip, at par. Some had attempted to scale down scrip to 75 and 80 cents, selling goods at their cash prices; but that was not liked by purchasers. It was bought at 68 and 75 cents on the dollar, in Illinois money. When bought or sold for specie the price was different.

May 9, 1840. Scrip was getting more languid, at 70 cents. Many merchants were selling goods for it at par, adding something, I presume, to the prices. Exchange on New York 10 per cent.

May 13, 1840. Scrip, at this date was from 65 to 75 cents.

May 26, 1840. Witness sold five hundred dollars of scrip at 71 cents.

June 1, 1840. On this date, witness bought eleven hundred dollars at 73½ cents.

June 13, 1840. Scrip, at this date, from 70 to 72 cents.

June 28, 1840. Offered for a quantity of scrip 68 cents, but the nominal price was 65 cents.

July 9, 1840. Sold $1,052 for 70 cents, but purchasing at 65 cents. The above sale was on account of a St. Louis broker.

August 21, 1840. Sixty-five cents was as much as was given at this date. It had fallen suddenly, and was suspected that workmen would not take it any longer at par from the contractors. Exchange at this date on New York 8 per cent.

August 27, 1840. Witness bought at 65 cents; other brokers refused to give more than 62½ cents.

Sept. 3, 1840. Canal scrip is quoted at 62½ cents.

Sept. 26, 1840. Canal scrip is quoted at 65 cents, and exchange on New York 7 per cent.

Nov. 6, 1840. Exchange on New York 7 per cent., scrip 72 to 75 cents.

Nov. 18, 1840. Exchange on New York 3 per cent. This reduction of exchange was in consequence of the bank having bought part of the "contractors' loan."

December 1, 1840. Scrip was not selling for less than 70 cents upon and after the receipt of the governor's message.

Dec. 11, 1840. The "Branch Bank" at Chicago resumed specie payment on its own notes. Exchange on New York 3 per cent.

Dec. 17, 1840. Exchange on New York 3 per cent. Scrip, nominally, at 70 cents. The reduction of exchange spoken of was an important measure for the bank to facilitate the resumption of specie payments, in the opinion of the witness.

January 9, 1841. Scrip quoted at 63 to 68, dull, for State Bank bills. Exchange on New York 3 per cent premium.

Jan. 13, 1841. Scrip 62 to 68. Exchange on New York 3 per cent premium.

Jan. 15, 1841. Scrip dull—no fixed quotations—say 62 to 68.

February 15, 1841. Bank here ceased to draw to-day.

February 18, 1841. Exchange on New York from 8 to 10½ in State Bank paper. Specie was worth from 9 to 11 discount on State Bank paper. The value of specie here changed, owing to the greater or less demand for land sales. At this time, witness' impression is that the bank had again suspended specie payment.

Nov. 13, 1841. Exchange on New York 10½ per cent. About this date scrip sold for 45½ cents.

Nov. 20, 1841. Exchange on New York 11 per cent.

Dec. 2, 1841. Exchange on New York 12 to 13 per cent.

Dec. 4, 1841. Witness offered to sell scrip for 42½ cents—does not think he sold at that.

Dec. 17, 1841. Exchange on New York 15 per cent.

Dec. 28, 1841. Exchange on New York from 15 to 17 per cent.

Dec. 29, 1841. Sold over $2,000 of scrip at 40 cents.

January 19, 1842. Exchange on New York from 14 to 16 per cent.

Jan. 22, 1842. Witness offered twenty-five cents for five hundred dollars canal scrip, on the face, not counting interest.

Jan. 29, 1842. The price of canal certificates ranged from 20 to 25 and 30 cents.

In February the exchange on State Bank paper run up from 15 to 22 per cent. The bank soon after failed.

February 16, 1842. Canal office made a new issue on the back

of the blank checks on State Bank, afterwards known as canal indebtedness not bearing interest. Worth at this time about 25 cents.
Canal scrip worth from 28 to 33 cents, in currency.

March 5, 1842. Exchange for currency, (Indiana and Wisconsin money,) was 14 per cent. premium. Indebtedness selling at 20
and 25 cents, for currency.

May 26, 1842. Illinois State canal scrip, bearing interest, worth
30 to 25 cents, and indebtedness from 18 to 23 cents. Interest not
included in this scrip, but bought at the face. Next day, exchange
on New York 8 per cent.

June 11, 1842. Canal scrip sold on the face for 23 cents; indebtedness, with no interest, from 18 to 22 cents.

Aug. 5, 1842. Canal scrip and indebtedness might be bought for
15 cents, and sold at 20 cents.

Aug. 11, 1842. Scrip worth from 15 to 22 cents. Same price on
the 26th; and Sept. 5th same price.

Sept. 24, 1842. Scrip from 18 to 22 cents. This range of figures
includes canal scrip and indebtedness.

October 8 and 25, 1842. Quotations the same—18 to 22 cents.

Nov. 23, 1842. Scrip from 20 to 22 cents. Exchange on New
York, for Indiana and Ohio currency, 3 per cent.

Dec. 3, 1842. Price rising, temporarily, and worth from 18 to
25 cents.

Dec. 29, 1842. Scrip and indebtedness dull at from 17 to 22 cents.

Jan. 14, 1843. Scrip from 16 to 20 cents, and dull.

July 5, 1843. Scrip about 25 cents. July 17—worth 29 and 30
cents; and up to the 20th November did not range higher than 26
cents, but at the canal sale it was nominally as high as 30 cents.

All the above information was extracted from letters, and quotations of rates, written by witness to correspondents, and he believes the same to be as correct as he could write them at the time.
As a general thing, witness did not deal in scrip and indebtedness
for canal contractors. One of the canal contractors deposited with
witness canal indebtedness as security for borrowed money, and he
afterwards had to sell it to reimburse himself. The amount of indebtedness was twenty-five hundred dollars. It was sold in June,
July, and August, 1842, for about 20 cents on the dollar. The
indebtedness belonged to Mr. Bracken. Witness bought of E. W.
Herrick, one of the contractors, in the months of November and
December, 1845, nearly $1,500 of scrip and indebtedness, at from
32 to 33 cents on the dollar. May have bought from other contractors, but does not recollect the particulars of any purchase.

June 20, 1844. Witness bought in New York city $800 of scrip on the face, for $320; and bought, in Chicago, in the same month, indebtedness, for 32 cents. During July, August and September, that was about the rate it sold for here.

Oct. 3, 1844. Witness bought $130, on the face, for $44, being a little over 33 cents on the dollar.

Nov. 22, 1844. Bought $200 of indebtedness at 26 cents. In December bought again at the same rate.

May 22, 1845. Bought indebtedness at 30 cents. In July bought $1,000 at same rate.

Oct. 1845. Bought indebtedness at from 30 to 32 cents, and scrip, computing interest, about the same.

Feb. 20, 1846. Bought Scrip at 30 cents, computing interest. In the summer bought scrip at 28 and 30, and in September bought at 35 cents, on the face.

January, 1847. Bought, from January to March, for 26 and 28 cents.

In September, 1847, it run up to 35 cents. Governor's scrip was sold, during 1846 and 1847, generally at about the same rates.

Cross-Examination.—The legislature afterwards allowed interest to contractors on the indebtedness, from the time it was issued, but the contractors having parted with their indebtedness, in many instances, derived only a partial benefit from this provision.

For all canal lots and lands sold previous to and including the year 1843, scrip and indebtedness was taken at par; but persons buying paid much higher for the lots and lands, knowing that they could pay in scrip and indebtedness. My recollection is, that lots and lands brought three times as much as the appraisal.

Witness paid for S. ½ of lot 9 in block 5, fr. section 15, (sold in 1843,) $1,020—is now worth $3,000, cash—and paid for lot 5, block 12, same section, $620, in scrip. It has just been sold for $5,000. Lot 3, block 21, was sold for $225 in scrip, is now worth about $1,500. E. ½ lot 4, block 42, and lot 7, same block—one was sold for $3,580, and the other for $1,350—are now worth $4,000 each. Lot 7, block 1, sold for $2,170, is now worth $5,500.

(Counsel from claimants objects to the testimony in regard to the value of the property.)

Re-examination.—He cannot say that he remembers of any lots or land having been bought by contractors.

He does not know of any of the contractors having sold bonds for wheat, and lost the whole.

Edward J. Tinkham, on behalf of claimants, sworn, says. Has been in the banking and broker business in the city of Chicago since 1839. His impression that the per centage on State Bank of

Illinois between Chicago and New York, in 1840, was from 6 to 7 per cent. Cannot say what the per centage between New York and London was at that time.

Thinks that the exchange for State Bank of Illinois, in the fall of 1840 and spring of 1841, was gradually rising; that in the spring of 1841 it was 10 per cent.

He bought from 1840, and for a year or two afterwards, considerable scrip.

When the interest scrip was first issued, in March, 1840, the price varied in the market of Chicago, from 60 to 70 cents.

The canal indebtedness, when first issued, was worth, in this market, from 30 to 35 cents, but subsequently sold, and the house in which witness was engaged bought it, as low as 28 cents, and knows of sales at that rate; that the canal bonds were quoted at about the same rate; that at the time state indebtedness scrip had depreciated, and was worth about the same, including interest, to wit, 30 to 35 cents on the dollar. When witness speaks of scrip, he alludes to the scrip issued in 1840 bearing interest; and when he speaks of indebtedness, he alludes to an issue, made in '41 or '42, which did not bear interest. When witness speaks of the value of scrip and indebtedness being equal, he means the indebtedness on its face, and the scrip with the interest added in.

Cross-Examined.—From 1840 to 1845, the custom was, in sales of scrip at Chicago, that if he bought one hundred dollars of scrip with one year's interest upon it, at fifty cents on the dollar, he gave fifty-three dollars for it. When scrip was first issued I knew of instances where merchants received it at par for debts due them, depending on the character of the debt and the solvency of the debtor, and whether they could have got any thing else. Does know of indebtedness or canal bonds being taken in that way. Witness does not know as he ever sold at any rate.

Henry Smith, on behalf of the claimants, sworn. Says he has resided in Chicago since 1838. Prior to 1841 was engaged in carrying out a contract on the canal. Has no interest in any claim against the state. After 1841 was engaged in the mercantile business, and as a dealer in real estate. In 1842 William B. Ogden received some $18,000 or $20,000 in canal bonds from an association of contractors, to dispose of at New York city. Ogden exchanged some bonds for goods. Witness made the settlement between Ogden and the contractors. He knows of the goods having been received. These bonds were disposed of so as to net about twenty per cent. of their face; and witness believes that was the best disposition that could have been made of them, and was a higher rate than they could have been sold for cash. Witness knows that the same goods were paid out to hands at the Chicago market price in payment for their labor. Witness has heard the testimony of Alexander Brand. At the time referred to by him, I had more or less scrip and indebtedness passing through his hands. Concurs in his general statement in regard to their value at the times mentioned. Witness knows where scrip or indebtedness was taken by merchants for goods, or by laborers for labor, or for materials, or provisions for the canal, at par. A corresponding increase in the price was made to cover the depreciation so as to approximate to the cash value. Whenever payment was made to laborers par funds only were used in payment; and the price per day or month was always fixed on the intended payments of current par funds. No scrip or indebtedness was paid to laborers, except when at par, or discounted to par funds at the time. The same, also, in payment for materials or goods. There was but one price for labor by the day or month, and that was always understood to be for cash. From the first of May, 1838, to the stopping of the work on sections five and six, the witness speaks of all the cases which fell within his observation or knowledge. He was acquainted with many of the contractors, and their connection with the public works was generally disastrous, and in most cases ruinous to them.

George Steel, on behalf of claimants, sworn. Says witness was a contractor and one of the claimants. Has known of contractors buying cattle and provisions by paying half cash and half scrip; usually paid more than they could have bought the same for in cash. Scrip traded off in this way brought more than when sold to brokers. This was in the years of 1840 and 1841. Has known of cases where laborers were to receive part pay in scrip and part goods; but the men generally took their pay in goods, preferring to take goods to taking scrip at par, and they received very little scrip. Some of them were in debt for goods, and received no scrip. These are cases that fell under witness' observation. There may have been cases where the contractors had smaller stocks of goods and paid their men more scrip. I paid my men all cash, and Mr. Barnett paid his men in cash and goods at cash prices, and done a large amount of work after the indebtedness was issued. Witness knows of Mr. Barnett's borrowing fifteen thousand dollars, and kept his scrip. Thinks he now has from sixty to eighty thousand dollars. He, Mr. Barnett, told me about a year ago that he had from sixty to eighty thousand dollars. Witness knows from his own case and from information in regard to others that all the contractors, for some months, paid more or less cash. This was in the year 1841. The effect of Mr. Barnett and others paying cash to their hands was to render it difficult for other contractors to get hands without paying cash or a higher price in scrip. He does not know that other contractors paid a higher price in scrip. Heard them complain of the prejudicial effect of these cash payments. Witness knows of a dozen or more contractors who finished their contract in the years of 1841 and 1842. Mr. Matteson, Mr. Blanchard & Co., Steel & Aymer, among the number. Could name several other heavy contracts that were finished.

Cross-Examined.—In the winter of 1838 and 1839 provisions fell fifty percent from what it was in 1837, and labor from twenty to twenty-five per cent. Most of the contracts in 1838 and 1839, taken at lower rates, to correspond with the lower price of labor and provisions. The prices of provisions and labor was about the same in 1841 and 1842 as in 1839. Labor had fallen, and was very low in the winters of 1837 and 1838. He knew of contractors—Mr. Negus, Mr. Armstrong, Mr. Harvey, as well as himself—who bought a few lots at the sale of 1843. They had not the scrip to buy with, having hypothecated with the broker their scrip to raise funds to finish their contracts, and very few of the contractors bought.

D. L. Roberts, on behalf of the claimants, sworn. Says he was a contractor, and one of the claimants. Witness has heard the testimony of George Steel, and believes it to be, in the main, correct, and does not know it to be incorrect in any particular.

Cross-Examined.—Witness had a sub-contract as well as an original contract. As such sub-contractor he was to receive one-third cash, as the work progressed, and the balance when the state paid the contractor. The contractor failed, and witness made a compromise with him and received state indebtedness—a considerable larger amount than would have been due if taken at par. The contractor had received some of his pay from the state in indebtedness. Witness considers he is not yet paid according to his contract, but he took what he received by way of compromise, the contractor being insolvent. Mr. Bracken, the contractor referred to, paid the hands in his employ cash.

Re-examined.—Witness does not know of any other sub-contractor. Witness thinks the cause of Mr. Bracken's failure was the state not paying him in cash, according to contract. Does not know of any contractor, except Mr. Barnett, who yet holds state indebtedness. Witness knew many of the contractors and their circumstances at the time, and in his opinion most of them were broken down by losses on their contracts; and most of them parted with their indebtedness while it sold at a low figure.

James E. Bishop, on behalf of the state, sworn. Says, knows of but very few sub-contracts, and as far as his knowledge extends the sub-contractors were paid in cash. That was his practice with his sub-contractors.

Cross-Examined.—Witness, as a general thing, at first kept his indebtedness, hoping that the state would make it good. Witness sold a portion of his scrip at fifty cents on the dollar, for groceries and supplies for the men, about the year 1841, and paid the same out to other men at fair cash prices. The men received nearly all of their pay in goods, taking little, if any, scrip. What scrip I paid they took at par. After the bonds and scrip had fallen lower I sold two bonds in this city at eighteen cents on the dollar, which was the highest price in the market. Some contractors, before scrip had fallen so much, made an arrangement with their hands to take it at par. The hands, however, ceased to take it after a short time. While the arrangement existed the young men generally left the work, and the work was done by men of families, who received their pay principally in goods at the cash market rates.

Joel Manning, on behalf of claimants, sworn. Says, witness commenced as secretary of the canal board in 1836, and continued as such until the canal passed into the hands of the present trustees. Witness, as such secretary, some time since, gave certificates to various contractors upon the canal, to be used in presenting their claims to the legislature, which certificates are true in all matters of which they certify. These certificates are on file with the papers of the respective claims, and are now here in the hands and control of N. W. Edwards, counsel for the state. A list of the names of the claimants to whose claims these certificates apply, is on a sheet herewith filed, marked "General Evidence—A." Witness has examined the contract filed in the case of Stephens, Douglass and Norton, and all the other contracts were given in the same form, except the contracts made under the Morris letting. Witness has examined the originals of the documents reported on pages 17, 18, 19, 20, 21 and 23 of the Reports of the session of 1840 and 1841. To the best of his knowledge they are true copies of the originals.

Cross-Examined.—The papers, Nos. 2 and 3, pages 18 and 19, of the Reports of session of 1840 and 1841, were signed by all the contractors who received money under the Thornton loan. The other documents referred to were signed by the parties whose names are attached to the documents in said Reports. The contracts referred to in Mr. Steele's testimony were surrendered in 1837 and 1838. The following is a true copy of the instrument signed by the persons who availed themselves of the law named in the instrument:

"To Gholson Kercheval, James Mitchell and William M. Jackson, assessors of damages on the Illinois and Michigan canal:

"We, George Armour, Adam Lamb, and Richard McFadden, assignee of Thomas Williams, by Joel Manning, attorney in fact for said McFadden and Thomas Williams, contractors on the Illinois and Michigan canal, for the purpose of availing themselves of the privileges and benefits conferred upon them by an act entitled 'An act to provide for the completion of the Illinois and Michigan canal, and for the payment of the canal debt,' approved February 21, 1843, do hereby apply for an appraisal, according to the provisions of said act, of the actual damages which they will sustain in being deprived of their contracts on sections number twenty-five and twenty-six, on the summit division of the Illinois and Michigan canal; and we do hereby consent and agree that such appraisal and assessment of damages shall be made without allowing them any prospective damages, or any profits which they might have made had they finished said jobs or contracts. Dated at Lockport, Illinois, this twenty-sixth day of September, A. D. 1843.

ADAM LAMB,	THOMAS WILLIAMS,
GEO. ARMOUR,	RICHARD MCFADDEN,
By Geo. Steele, his attorney.	By J. Manning, his attorney."

The following is a list of sections and other work upon the Illinois and Michigan canal, let by the canal board from and after and including the lettings on the 20th and 22d days of September, 1841, during the presidency of Mr. Morris,[12] containing dates, jobs of work, and names of contractors:

Date of letting	Job of work	Names of contractors
1841, Sept. 22	Secs. 109, 112, 126, 151, 153, and stone culvert over Nettle creek,	John Lafferty, Thomas McKown, J. G. Patterson.
"	Secs. 110, 111, 131, and 132,	Walter D. McDonald, Michael Williams and Michael McDonald.
"	Secs. 113, 121, 122,	M. Benjamin
"	117	Titus H. Abbott
"	118,	M. Mott and F. L. Owens.
"	119, 120,	Jacob Francis.
"	123, 136, 137,	Thos. Galleher & Co.
"	124,	James Mullany.

[12] Isaac N. Morris succeeded William F. Thornton as president of the board of commissioners in 1842.

Date of letting	Job of work	Names of contractors
"	125,	John Darlin, Lot Whitcomb.
"	127,	James Cronan & Co.
"	128, 129,	Thomas Beale, Norton Twitchell.
"	130, 133, 134, 138,	H. L. Galleher & Co.
"	135, 142,	Wm. Reddick, Thomas O'Sullivan.
"	139,	Patrick Kenney & Co.
"	140,	Patrick & John Kelly.
"	141,	Thos. W. Hennessy, and J. Brennon & Co.
"	143, 144, 145, 146,	Timothy Kelly, and Jer. Crotty & Co.
"	Secs. 147, 149, 154, and stone culverts on sections 112, 149, 154,	Michael Kennedy, Patrick M. Kilduff, and B. Duffy & Co.
"	Secs. 148, 150,	George Armour and Adam Lamb.
"	Locks Nos. 9 and 10,	M. Kennedy, P. M. Kilduff, and B. Duffy & Co.
"	Sect. 152,	Dennis Kelley and Timothy Kelley.
"	Wood culverts: on secs. 119 and 121, 134, 141, 136, 142,	Thos. Campbell and John McGirr. Lafferty & Larkin. R. Johnson.
"	Stone culverts on secs 145 and 148,	Michael Killela.
"	Au Sable aqueduct, lock No. 8,	James Kinsley.
"	Secs, 114, 115, 116,	Buck Van Alstine.
24	161,	Hauley & Healy.
1842, Jan. 28	130,	Walter McDonald & Michael Williams.
"	123,	James Burk.
Feb. 18	143, 144, 145, 146,	Jeremiah Crotty.
	109, 112, 126, 151, 153, and Nettle creek aqueduct,	Declared abandoned.
"	125,	William E. Armstrong.
23	Culverts on secs. 134, 136 and 141,	A. D. Butterfield and C. L. Lukens.
Apr. 21	Sec. 118,	Andrew Kinsley.
June 7	141,	Rich'd Cody, Tho. Hennessy, Chas. Bannon.

Date of letting	Job of work	Names of contractors
June 7	125,	William E. Armstrong, Jas. Hart.
8	153,	Timothy Kelley.
Oct. 28	109, 112, 114, 116, 117, 123, 126, 133, 134, 136, 137, 138, 139, 140, 151, 153,	Declared abandoned.
"	Sec. 130,	Declared abandoned.
"	134,	Thos. Larkin.
"	138,	Maher & Castello.

At the "Morris lettings" the following order was made and posted up in a public place, and was so understood, in the opinion of the witness, by the contractors under that letting:

"*Ordered*, That the following be the conditions of letting the forty-six sections advertised for contract this day:

"1st. If no more acceptable arrangement can be made, the governor has promised to place in the hands of the commissioners state bonds, to be paid out to contractors at par, from time to time, as they are earned."—Made Sep. 20, 1841.

From the spring of 1841 to the winter following, we received orders from the contractors in favor of laborers and others, registered the orders, and, when requested, gave the bearer written acceptances; and during the winter of 1841 and 1842 we received what is called canal indebtedness, with which the orders and acceptances were redeemed when called for. Most of them were called for.

Re-examined.—Does not know what amount of these orders was presented by the laborers. Thinks considerable proportion was so presented. Does not know at what rate these orders were received from the contractors. They were drawn for so many dollars and cents. Knows that some contracts were completed after the work was generally abandoned in 1841. Among them were Steele and Aymer, Blanchard & Co., Roberts & Co., and others.

Mr. Edwards, attorney for the state, offered the journals of the legislature, messages of the governor, reports of the commissioners, engineers, and other officers under the canal laws, the report of Gen. Thornton on the "Thornton loan," printed correspondence between the governor and Gen. Thornton, and between Gen. Thornton and the contractors and others, relating to the disposition of bonds; also, the correspondence and agreement between

[184]

Gen. Thornton and the contractors, as evidence. The documents are referred to and considered as evidence, to save copying, and extracts of which are in the report of the counsel for the state.

The counsel for claimants objected to the reception, as evidence, of reports of "engineers and other officers" under the canal laws, not acting on behalf of the contractors.

Springfield.—Isaac N. Morris, on behalf of the state, sworn. Says, was canal commissioner in 1841 and 1842, about two years. When I assumed the control in part of the canal, I found the treasury exhausted of money, or there was but a small amount of funds in it, and no provision had been made by the legislature to supply it. The question was raised whether the board should suspend operations upon the work altogether, or proceed with it, and pay scrip and bonds, if the bonds could be obtained from Gov. Carlin. Many of the contractors and others urged a new letting, and we informed them of the kind of payments we could make, and that if they became bidders they would have to receive it at par. They expressed a willingness to do this, and the board accordingly instructed Mr. Gooding,[13] the chief engineer, to survey and make out a cash estimate of certain portions of the canal, which he did, and which was afterwards let out upon bids, the contractors, as I have stated, understanding they were to receive payment, as I have expressed it, in scrip and bonds at par. The board did not believe they were authorized to pay scrip and bonds in any other way. I cannot now remember the names of the particular contractors, but I am satisfied that those engaged upon the work, as well as those who proposed to take contracts, knew there were no funds in the canal office, and that they must receive scrip and bonds in payment, at par, if they went on with the work or took new contracts. I never heard any of the contractors object to receiving scrip or bonds, in compliance with the foregoing understanding. By the word *scrip* I do not mean regular six per cent. canal scrip, for that the board, as they understood the law, were not authorized to issue; but I refer to certificates or canal indebtedness such as the board had stricken off and issued.

In the case of the claim of Haven & Haven, the claimants and the counsel for the state agreed that no further evidence should be introduced on either side in that case.

The *old* evidence, filed with the several claims, was admitted in evidence, and the right of cross-examination waived by the counsel for the state.

The undersigned further report, that during their sitting at

[13] William Gooding.

Ottawa, C. L. Starbuck presented a claim for and on behalf of Andrew Kinsley, which claim the board refused to receive evidence upon, because of no sufficient evidence that it had been ever before presented.

That George Armour, Andrew Lamb and Thomas Williams, for the use of John and George Armour, presented a claim, founded on a decree of the Cook county circuit court, rendered June 5, 1852, and offered to prove the same, which was rejected by the board as a new claim.

That Alonzo Walbridge and Mary, his wife, William Johnson and Sarah, his wife, and Elias Keyes, for the use of Alonzo Walbridge, presented a claim for damages, arising out of the construction of the canal across sec. 14, township 33, range 4 east, part of the estate of Edward Keyes, deceased, and offered proof of the same, which was rejected by the board as a new claim.

The undersigned further report, that all the witnesses who testified before us were duly sworn, and gave their testimony under their oaths respectively.

All which is respectfully submitted.　　A. LINCOLN,
January 7, 1853.　　　　　　　　　　NOAH JOHNS[T]ON.

By way of supplement, we, the undersigned, submit, that while at Ottawa we engaged the use of the sheriff's office, with the expression of our belief that the state would make reasonable compensation for the same; that we so occupied said office three days; and that the sheriff's name is————Thorn.

We also state that on the 6th day of December, 1852, at Ottawa, we engaged Mr. R. E. Goodell, as clerk of our board; that he accompanied us to Chicago and thence to Springfield, and has been with us constantly up to the time of making this report.

We also state, that when we advertised the notice of our meeting, as mentioned in our report, we sent the same to the Ottawa Free Trader, Joliet Signal, and the Chicago Journal, with a note to the latter to request the other Chicago papers to copy; we mentioned that we supposed the state would foot the bills. None of the proprietors of the papers to whom we directly sent said notice, have presented a bill to us, but Alfred Dutch, proprietor of the Commercial Advertiser, who published under the request to copy, has presented us a bill of $3.00, which we suppose ought to be paid.

At the instance of the counsel for the state, Isaac N. Morris traveled from Quincy to Springfield, and appeared before us one day as a witness, for which we suppose he should be compensated.

As to ourselves, we state, that from the time we left our respective homes till we returned to Springfield, we were constantly engaged in this business; that we went to Chicago because we were satisfied we could save time by so doing. The bills below are correct in point of fact, and, as we suppose, are in accordance with the law:

State of Illinois to Noah Johnston, Dr.

To travel from Mount Vernon, by way of St. Louis, to Chicago, and back to Mount Vernon, by way of Naples, Springfield and St. Louis, 1,025 miles,	$102 50
To 44 days service,	176 00
	$278 50

State of Illinois to A. Lincoln, Dr.

To travel from Springfield, by way of Naples to Chicago, and back the same way, 650 miles,	$ 65 00
To 21 days service,	84 00
	$149 00

NOTE.—The difference in the number [of] days charged by one and the other of us, arises from the fact, that a large part of the time Mr. Lincoln was at home attending to his own business, while Mr. Johnston was necessarily away from his home, and was also engaged a good deal of the time in this business.

State of Illinois to R. E. Goodell, Dr.

To travel from Ottawa to Chicago, thence to Springfield and back to Ottawa, 650 miles,	$ 65 00
To 32 days service,	96 00
	$161 00

Respectfully submitted, this 7th of January, 1853.

A. LINCOLN,

N. JOHNSTON.

To Joel A. Matteson[1]

His Excellency, the Governor   Springfield,
    of the State of Illinois.   Jany. 10. 1853.

Sir: In July 1850, a man by the name of William D. Davis, was tried and convicted of the crime Manslaughter and sentenced to the Penetentiary for the term of three years, by the circuit court of Clark county, whither his case had been taken by a change of venue from Coles county.[2] I assisted in his defence, and thought his conviction was right, but that the term fixed was too long under the circumstances. I told him that if he should behave himself well for a considerable portion of the time, I would join in asking a pardon for the remainder. He has a young family, and has lost one of his arms. He has now served about five sixths of his time; and I understand, the Warden, who is now in Springfield, testifies that he has behaved well. Under these circumstances I hope he may be released from further confinement. Your Obt. Servt.

A. LINCOLN

1 ALS, I-Ar.
2 The Judge's Docket of the Clark County Circuit Court lists a "Special or called court . . . for the trial of William D. Davis . . . July 1st. A.D. 1850." The court files have disappeared.

To Ninian W. Edwards[1]

Mr. N. W. Edwards   Springfield, Jany 15, 1853
    Please pay N. W. Edwards & Co, eighty dollars, which will be in full of interest on your note till 1st May 1853.

A. LINCOLN.

1 Angle, p. 111. The inference is that Lincoln ran an account with Edwards' store, on which he wished his due interest to be applied.

To James Smith[1]

Rev. James Smith, D.D.:   Springfield, January 24, 1853.
    Sir:—The undersigned having listened with great satisfaction to the discourse, on the subject of temperance, delivered by you on last evening, and believing, that, if published and circulated among the people, it would be productive of good; would respectfully request a copy thereof for publication. Very Respectfully, Your friends:

Simeon Francis,	R. F. Ruth,	G. Jayne,
Thomas Lewis,	J. B. McCandless,	J. C. Planck,
John Irwin,	C. Birchall,	John E. Denny,
A. Camp,	J. B. Fosselman,	W. M. Cowgill,
E. G. Johns,	Henry M. Brown,	D. E. Ruckel,
John Williams,	Thomas Moffett,	Thomas M. Taylor,
John T. Stuart,	B. S. Edwards,	John A. Chesnut,
A. Maxwell,	Thomas Alsop,	Mat. Stacy,
H. Vanhoff,	W. B. Cowgill,	H. S. Thomas,
D. Spear,	M. Greenleaf,	B. B. Brown,
Reuben Coon,	James W. Barret,	William F. Aitkin,
Henry Yeakle,	P. Wright,	Allen Francis,
E. B. Pease,	S. Grubb, sr.,	A. Lincoln.

1 *A Discourse on the Bottle—Its Evils, and the Remedy; or, A Vindication of the Liquor-Seller, and the Liquor Drinker, from Certain Aspersions Cast upon Them by Many*, 1853, 1892. The letter is printed as a preface to the pamphlet. The Reverend James Smith was pastor of the First Presbyterian Church of Springfield.

Bill Introduced in Illinois Legislature
to Incorporate the Vermillion Coal and
Manufacturing Company[1]

February 5, 1853

A bill for an act to incorporate the "Vermillion Coal and Manufacturing Company"

Be it enacted by the People of the State of Illinois represented in the General Assembly: That John A. Rockwell,[2] his associates, successors and assigns, are hereby constituted a body politic and corporate, under the name and style of the "Vermillion Coal and Manufacturing Company" and under, and by that name, they may contract and be contracted with, sue and be sued, in all courts and places: they shall have the power to organize such company, by the appointment of a President and such other officers as they may deem necessary at such time and place as may be designated by notice previously given by them or a majority of them, and when thus organized, they may have a common seal, and alter the same; and shall have power to make such by-laws, rules, and regulations as they may deem necessary from time to time, for the government and management and prossecution of the business of the said company, not inconsistent with the constitution and laws of the United States or of this State.

Sec: 2. The said Company may engage in the business of the mining of coal, iron, clays, and other minerals; and of welling for salt, on lands now owned in whole, or in part by said John A. Rockwell near the Little Vermillion in the county of La Salle in the State of Illinois, and lands contiguous to the same, which may be hereafter purchased, and in the manufacture, sale, and transportation of the products of their mines, wells, and other commodities, as the company may think expedient. And the said company shall have power to construct a rail road from such point or points on said land as they may deem expedient to the nearest convenient point of the Illinois and Michigan canal or,[3] in lieu thereof, at their option to the nearest convenient point on the Illinois Central Railroad or on the Chicago and Rock Island Railroad; *provided* they shall not construct more than one such Railroad. And the right of way and occupancy may be acquired, and damages adjusted under the provisions of the law now in force in relation to the right of way; and when such damages are assessed and paid, or payment tendered, according to the provisions of said law, the

[189]

rights so acquired shall vest in said company for the uses and purposes thereof.

Sec: 3. Whenever any married woman, infant, or person *non compos mentis,* shall be entitled to damages on account of the passage of said railroad or it's branches over their land the guardian of such infant or person *non compos mentis* or the husband of such married woman, may release all damages for and in their behalf as fully as might be done by the parties when free from disability.

[1] AD, I-Ar. Lincoln had Asahel Gridley, state senator from McLean County, introduce the bill in the Senate on February 5. It was passed by the Senate on February 9, but died in the House upon adjournment. See Lincoln to Rockwell, February 15, *infra.*

[2] John A. Rockwell has not been identified beyond the circumstances indicated in this bill and Lincoln's letter of February 15, but a "John Rockwell" is listed in contemporary sources as a pioneer of LaSalle County.

[3] The original phrasing, deleted at this point, calls for all three connections rather than the choice of one. Lincoln explains the change in his letter to Rockwell, *infra.*

To Solon Cumins[1]

Solon Cumins Esq   Springfield, Ills.
Grand De tour Ills.   Feb. 14. 1853.

Dear Sir: Your letter in relation to Mr. Adams'[2] business is received. The time will possibly come when we shall need Bradshaw's testimony to the point you mention, but in the present attitude of the case we are not ready for it—it would not avail us *now* if we had it. Still, I shall be very glad if you will ascertain, and put down in writing, exactly what Bradshaw will swear, on the question of Denny having been paid for the land with Adams' money, & also, as to whether Adams, when he took the deed, had any knowledge of Kemper's judgment against Bradshaw. Ascertain these things & write me what they are. Very Respectfully

A. LINCOLN—

[1] ALS, IHi. See previous letters to Thomas J. Turner, *supra.*
[2] Adam Adams.

To John A. Rockwell[1]

Hon. John A. Rockwell.   Springfield, Ill., Feby. 15, 1853.

My dear Sir: I have failed to get your Coal Mining Charter.[2] Being very busy in the Courts when your letter reached me, I let a few days slip before attending to it A little more than a week before the close of the Session, I got a Bill for the Charter howsoever into the Senate, which Body it passed in about five days. It then went to the H.R. and was lost for want of time. No one was opposed to it, but every one was much more anxious about some other Bill, so it became evident a large proportion of all would be lost. With us there is no lengthening out the Session, over a day, to get through with business. The New Constitution, adopted in 1848, limits the pay of members to two dollars per day for the first six weeks, and to one dollar per day afterwards. The practical result is they never sit a day over the six weeks.

I have said there was no opposition to your bill. I should qualify this by saying that there was objection to allowing you to connect by railroads with the Canal and Rock Island roads, all three; and so I have to frame the bill to authorize you to make only *one* of such connections, with the option however, as to which one.

No objection was made about names; and accordingly the bill was to John A. Rockwell, his associates, successors & assigns.

If you continue to desire it, I will get it passed at the next Session—it being borne in mind that at a *called* Session the door may not be opened for such business. Your obt. Servant,

A. LINCOLN.

₁ Hertz, II, 613.   ₂ *Vide supra*, February 5.

To Usher F. Linder[1]

Dear Linder—   Springfield, March 8. 1853.

The change of circuits prevents my attending the Edgar court this Spring, and perhaps generally hereafter. There is a little Ejectment case from Bloomfield, in which the name of Davidson figures, but in which a couple of men by the name of Bailey are interested;[2] and for defending which I have been paid a little fee. Now I dislike to keep their money without doing the service; & I also hate to disgorge; and I therefore request of you to defend the case for me; & I will, in due time, do as much or more for you. Write me whether you can do it. Yours as ever,

A. LINCOLN

[1] ALS, IHi.

[2] Davidson *v.* Bailey was tried on April 29. Presumably Linder complied with Lincoln's request and defended the case, for Lincoln was attending court at Metamora in Woodford County on April 28 and could hardly have attended the trial at Paris on the next day. The Edgar County Circuit Court record, however, records that the case was tried on April 29 with Lincoln for the defendant.

To William D. Briggs[1]

W. D. Briggs, Esq.   Springfield,
Dear Sir.   March 19. 1853.

I suppose it will be necessary to take a deposition in the attachment case you mention.[2] It will have to be done under the act of March 1st. 1845—found in the Session acts of 1845, at page 27. The way will be to make out a notice with interrogatories, precisely as you do to take a deposition of a non-resident witness in an ordinary case, except that 4 weeks instead of 10 days time must be given; and as you can not serve the notice, post one copy on the court house door, & file the other in the clerks office 4 weeks before suing out the commission. If posted at the court-house I [sic] door I think it need not be published in a news-paper—*one* or the *other* will do.

As to the declaration, I suppose that a common count is all that is necessary, & accordingly I send a draft of that sort. Yours truly
                                                    A. LINCOLN—

P.S. When you send on for evidence, better also get an authenticated copy of the Charter. Also look over the declaration I send, fill in blanks, correct mistakes, if any, in names, amounts &c.
                                                    A LINCOLN.

[1] ALS, owned by A. V. D. Rousseau, Los Angeles, California. Briggs was a Tazewell County attorney.
[2] The only case on which Briggs at this time seems to have been associated with Lincoln was Harris Lime Rock Company *v.* Harris, tried at Pekin on May 3, Lincoln and Briggs for plaintiff. According to the record, the court fixed the plaintiff's damages at $5,000, on May 12.

To Henry E. Dummer[1]

Dear Dummer.   Springfield, March 28. 1853.

Inclosed please find three dollars—the smallest sum I could send by mail for the $2.50 you kindly advanced for me; which please accept, together with my thanks, and offer to reciprocate when occasion presents. Your friend as ever   A. LINCOLN—

[1] ALS, IHi.

To Lewis W. Ross and George W. Stipp[1]

                                                   [c. April, 1853]

I have to beg your pardon for not having wrote you before on the subject of the within. The rule to plead had expired months before you wrote me &, I presume, months before you were employed.

Mr. Lawrence,[2] who was for the plff. said if he did not believe it was the deft.'s own default, he would not hold on to it; but as it was, he would.   A. LINCOLN

[1] ALS, Public Library, Galesburg, Illinois. Ross and Stipp, attorneys at Lewistown, Illinois, had written to Lincoln on March 25, 1853, for information concerning an ejectment suit, Northrup v. Reynolds et al., which they had asked him to attend to months before in the U.S. District Court. Lincoln's undated reply is written on the verso of this letter. In view of Lincoln's very heavy court schedule in Springfield prior to April 2, and on the circuit from April 10 to June 5, it seems likely that he answered between April 3 and 9.

[2] Charles B. Lawrence, attorney of Prairie City, Illinois.

Deed to William M. Dorman[1]

April 8, 1853

This Indenture made this eighth day of April in the year of our lord, one thousand eight hundred and fifty three by and between Abraham Lincoln and Mary Lincoln his wife of the county of Sangamon and State of Illinois party of the first part and William M. Dorman of the county of Gallatin and State aforesaid party of the Second part. Witnesseth

That the said party of the first part for and in consideration of the sum of One hundred Dollars to them in hand paid by the said party of the second part the receipt whereof is hereby acknowledged have remised, released, and quit claimed and by these present do remise release and forever quit claim to the said party of the second part and his heirs and assigns forever, all the right title and interest of the said party of the first part in and to the South East quarter of Section twenty two in Township nine South of Range nine East[.] Situate[d] in the county of Gallatin aforesaid[.] To have & to hold to the said party of the second part and to his heirs and assigns forever, the above described tract of land, together with all and singular the privileges and appurtenances thereunto belonging.

In testimony whereof, the said party of the first part have hereunto set their hands and seals the day and year first above written

A. LINCOLN (SEAL)

MARY LINCOLN (SEAL)

[1] Copy, ISLA, from Gallatin County Record. Lincoln had taken a mortgage from Dorman on the property described in the deed to guarantee his fee in the case of Dorman v. Lane, begun in 1842. See Lincoln to Samuel D. Marshall, November 11, 1842, supra.

To Mason Brayman[1]

To M. Brayman,   Pekin, May 4th 1853.
I cannot go to Jonesboro.   A. LINCOLN

[1] Copy, ICHi. This is the copy of the telegram which was received by Brayman at Springfield. Lincoln was attending court at Pekin. Brayman was the principal attorney for the Illinois Central Railroad, and it may have been in this connection that he wished Lincoln to go to Jonesboro. Lincoln's first recorded Illinois Central case (Illinois Central Rail Road *v.* McGinnis) was tried in the Champaign County Circuit Court May 25, 1853.

To Joshua R. Stanford[1]

Mr. Joshua R. Stanford: Pekin,
Sir   May 12, 1853.

I hope the subject-matter of this letter will appear a sufficient apology to you for the liberty I, a total stranger, take in addressing you. The persons here, holding two lots under a conveyance made by you, as the attorney of Daniel M Baily,[2] now nearly twenty-two years ago, are in great danger of losing the lots; and very much—perhaps all—is to depend on the testimony you give as to whether you did, or did not account to Baily for the proceeds received by you on the sale of the lots. I therefore, as one of their counsel, beg of you to fully refresh your recollection, by every means in your power, before the time you may be called on to testify. If persons should come about you and show a disposition to pump you on this subject; it may be no more than prudent to remember that it may be possible they design to misrepresent you, and to embarrass the real testimony you may ultimately give. It may be six months or a year before you are called on to testify.
Respectfully   A. LINCOLN

[1] ALS, IHi. Joshua R. Stanford was an attorney of Griggsville, Illinois.
[2] Probably Daniel M. Bailey, one of the incorporators of the Tazewell County Farmers and Mechanics Company in 1843.

To George B. Kinkead[1]

George B. Kinkead, Esq   Danville, Ills—
Lexington, Ky—   May 27. 1853

I am here attending court a hundred and thirty miles from home; and where a copy of your letter of this month, to Mr. Edwards, reached me from him, last evening. I find it difficult to suppress my indignation towards those who have got up this claim against me. I would really be glad to hear Mr. Hemingway explain how he was induced to *swear* he *believed* the claim to be just! I

[194]

herewith inclose my answer.[2] If it is insufficient either in substance, or in the authentication of the oath, return it to me at at [*sic*] Springfield (where I shall be after about ten days) stating the defective points. You will perceive in my answer, that I ask the Petitioners to be ruled to file a bill of particulars, stating *names & residences* &c. I do this to enable me to absolutely disprove the claim. I can really prove by independent evidence, every material statement of my answer; and if they will name any living accessable man, as one of whom I have received their money, I will, *by that man* disprove the charge. I know it is for *them* to prove their claim, rather than for *me* to disprove it; but I am unwilling to trust the oath of any man, who either *made* or *prompted* the oath to the Petition.

Write me soon. Very Respectfully—   A. LINCOLN—

[1] ALS, owned by William H. Townsend, Lexington, Kentucky. For a full account of the case of Edward Oldham and Thomas Hemingway *v.* Abraham Lincoln, Ninian W. Edwards, and George B. Kinkead, see Townsend, *Abraham Lincoln Defendant* (1923). Kinkead was attorney for Lincoln and Edwards at Lexington, Kentucky, in the settlement of the estate of Robert S. Todd. Edwards was named with Lincoln in the petition of Oldham and Hemingway to the Fayette County (Kentucky) Circuit Court for an attachment of funds in the hands of Kinkead. The petition alleged that Lincoln had collected $472.54 for the firm of Oldham, Todd & Company, but had never paid it, and that Edwards owed the firm nine dollars for freight paid by the firm for him. Edwards' deposition (May 23, 1853) denied that the firm had paid freight for him, but quoted a letter from Robert S. Todd to Edwards (August 15, 1840) to the effect that Todd was sending five bales of cotton yarn in Edwards' care for the benefit of Todd's daughters Frances (Mrs. William S. Wallace) and Mary, who was then residing at the home of a third daughter, Mrs. Ninian W. Edwards. Todd's letter mentioned having paid the freight as far as Louisville, Kentucky. Todd was at the time a partner of Oldham and Hemingway in the firm Oldham, Todd & Company.

[2] *Vide infra.*

Answer to Petition of Edward Oldham and Thomas Hemingway[1]

May 27, 1853

The separate answer of Abraham Lincoln to a Petition exhibited in the Fayette circuit court in the Commonwealth of Kentucky, against said Lincoln, Ninian W. Edwards, and George B. Kinkead,

[1] ADS, Fayette County (Kentucky) Circuit Court files, Petition of Edward Oldham and Thomas Hemingway, May 11, 1853. In Lincoln's hand except for the signature of Samuel G. Craig and the attestation: "Filed & Noted June 13th 1853. Att Tho. S. Read clk." Although this document is part of a law case, it is not properly speaking one of attorney Lincoln's cases and therefore has been included with the letter to Kinkead (*supra*). See also the notice to Hemingway and Oldham, September 22, 1853, and further correspondence with Kinkead, July 6, September 13 and 30, 1853, March 31 and June 16, 1854, *infra*.

by Edward Oldham and Thomas Hemingway, senr. surviving partners of Oldham, Todd & Co.

This Respondent, saving, reserving &c, for answer to said Petition says he believes it is true, and therefore he admits that said Petitioner's are the surviving partners of said firm of Oldham Todd & Co; that said firm did consist of the persons named as the members thereof in said Petition; and that said Robert S. Todd did depart this life about the time stated in said Petition. But this Respondent utterly denies that he is, or ever was, indebted to said firm, or to said Petitioners as surviving partners thereof, or in any way howsoever; he denies that he ever collected $472.54/100 or any other sum whatever, for said firm, or of money belonging to said firm, or to said Petitioners, in any capaci[ty] whatever; he denies that he ever had placed in his charge for collection, any debt or claim for said firm, or for said Petitioners, of any sort whatever; and he denies that he ever was employed as the attorney or in any other capacity, of said firm, or of said Petitioners, in any matter whatever, so far as he remembers or believes. Respondent can not conceive on what the charge of said Petitioner's against him is founded, unless it be the following facts. In the autumn of 1843, and after Respondent had intermarried with said Robert S. Todd's daughter; said Robert S. Todd visited Springfield, Illinois, when and where, Respondent, for the first time in his life, met him. During that visit, said Todd remarked to this Respondent that there were two desperate or doubtful debts due Oldham Todd & Co—*one* at, or near Beardstown, Illinois, in charge of an attorney by the name of Henry E. Dummer, and the other at Shelbyville, Illinois, in charge of whom Respondent does not remember, and that if any thing could be collected on said debts he desired Respondent to take and retain it as his own. Afterwards, and, as Respondent remembers, in 1846, said Dummer paid over to this Respondent, the sum of fifty dollars, representing that sum to be all, beyond charges, that could be collected on the said claim in his hands. And as to the said debt at Shelbyville, nothing whatever has come to the hands of this Respondent directly or indirectly; and Respondent supposes said debt has not been paid to any one else, but remains wholly unpaid. If Respondent ever knew, he has forgotten the name of the debtor at Beardstown; but he believes one Marshall Basye was the debtor, or one of the debtors, at Shelbyville. Respondent was not desired to take, and did not take charge of said claims as an attorney, or in any otherwise than as herein stated; so far as he remembers or believes he never spoke or wrote to either of the debtors on the subject; nor ever in any way attempted to supersede the attornies in whose hands the claims were originally placed; and, with the exception of the fifty dollars afore-said, received by Respondent under the circumstances aforesaid, Respondent denies that he ever received any thing whatever, to which said firm, or said Petitioners could have a pretence of a claim. Respondent further states that when he visited Lexington in the autumn of 1849, as he remembers, he stated this whole matter to said Hemingway and to L. O. Todd,[2] as he now states it; and that, more recently, in the spring of 1852, he again fully stated it, in his sworn answer to a Bill filed for the adjustment of the estate of said Robert S. Todd, which answer doubtless is on file in the said Fayette circuit court, and Respondent supposes said court, in that case decided and adjusted the rights of the parties arising upon said state of facts. Respondent cares but little for said fifty dollars; if it is his legal right he prefers retaining it; but he objects to repay-ing it *once* to the estate of said Robert S. Todd, and *again* to said firm, or to said Petitioners; and he particularly objects to being compelled to pay money to said firm or said Petitioner's which he never received at all. Respondent prays that said Petitioners may be ruled to file a Bill of particulars, stating the *names* and *resi-dences* of the persons of whom, they claim that Respondent has collected money belonging to them. Respondent admits that he resides in Illinois; that said George B. Kinkead is his attorney; and that he had means in his hands belonging to Respondent, substan-tially as is in said Petition stated; and now having fully answered &c.   A. LINCOLN—

State of Illinois ⎫ ss
Vermilion County ⎰
Before me, Samuel G. Craig, clerk of the circuit court of the county aforesaid, this day personally appeared Abraham Lincoln, whose name is subscribed to the answer written on this sheet, and who being by me first duly sworn, states on oath that all the state-ments in said answer are true in substance and in fact. In witness whereof I have hereunto subscribed my name and affixed the seal of said court on this 27th. day of May AD. 1853.

SAML. G. CRAIG, Clk

2 Levi O. Todd, son of Robert S. Todd.

To David A. Smith[1]

D. A. Smith Esq.   Springfield,
Dear Sir: June 10. 1853.

We have had Dr. Higgins'[2] [ca]se under consideration; and, inasmuch as, by the [law] "he shall be subject to removal only for infi[delity to] the trust reposed in him, or incompetency [in] the discharge thereof"—we think the resolution [o]f removal, not placing the removal on either [of] these grounds, is, on it's face void; and we further think, that any removal, without giving the Dr. a chance to be heard in his defence, on the questions, of infidelity and incompetency, one or both, will be void. *Quo warranto*, we think, is the way; [an]d we think it some better that he should [h]old on, and leave his adversaries to proceed; but if his holding on would embarrass the institution, he might, without much disadvantage, leave, and commence the proceedings himself. Yours &c.

A LINCOLN

S T LOGAN

[1] ALS, owned by David A. Lansden, Cairo, Illinois. In Lincoln's hand except for Logan's signature, the letter is burned on one edge. Missing words have been restored by the editors.

[2] James M. Higgins, superintendent of the Illinois State Hospital for the Insane at Jacksonville, was removed by the board of trustees, June 6, 1853. The Morgan County Circuit Court in the fall term held that Higgins' removal was illegal, but the Illinois Supreme Court in January, 1854, reversed the decision. Lincoln was one of Higgins' attorneys before the Supreme Court.

To David A. Smith[1]

D. A. Smith, Esq   Springfield,
Dear Sir: June 17. 1853.

The depositions from New-York arrived this morning.[2] I have not had time to read them; but they are very long & are made by the [n]ine persons whose names follow, towit Jasper Corning, Thomas Denny, Guy Richards, James Boorman, John C. Brigham, John Marsh, Nathaniel Richards, George D. Phelps & William M. Halstead.

I have written to Carlinville,[3] as I promised you. Yours truly

A. LINCOLN—

[1] ALS, owned by Thomas W. Smith, San Carlos, California.

[2] Probably depositions in the case of Gilman *et al. v.* Hamilton *et al.* On this date the court sustained Lincoln & Smith's motion to open depositions.

[3] See endorsement: Nathaniel Coffin to Lincoln, June 21, *infra*.

Endorsement: Nathaniel Coffin to Lincoln[1]

[c. June 21, 1853]

You remember, I told you, I had written to Weer & Dubois.[2] I have received no answer from them. This afternoon when the cause was called, it was, on my motion, continued to the November term. Yours &c

A. LINCOLN

1 AES, IHi. Nathaniel Coffin, treasurer and trustee of Illinois College at Jacksonville was interested in a case involving the college trustees, Gilman *et al. v.* Hamilton *et al.*, and had written Lincoln June 21, 1853, for information. Lincoln's note appears on the bottom of Coffin's letter.

2 William Weer, Jr., attorney, and A. McKim Dubois, clerk of the Macoupin County Circuit Court, both of Carlinville.

To Adam Adams[1]

Adam Adams, Esq.   Springfield,
Dear Sir: June 23. 1853.

The summer term of the U.S. court is close upon us, and I wish to be ready to put your case before the court in the best possible shape. I suppose you and your witness will be down; and I wish you to call at the Land Office at Dixon, and procure & bring with you the *Register's* certificate, showing *who* entered the land, and the *date* of the entry. Mind, the *Register's* certificate—*not* the Receiver's receipt. The *Patent*, which I have, shows *who* entered the land, but does not show the *date* of the entry. I am trying to be prepared before-hand to get the case in the best shape I can. Yours truly   A. LINCOLN—

P.S. Since I wrote the above, Logan came in & proposed to continue the cause over this summer term. If you prefer doing this, Telegraph me at once & it shall be done   A. L.

1 ALS, IHi. Adams was a farmer residing in Ogle County whose post office was Grand DeTour. For comment on this case see the note from Lincoln to Turner, February 8, 1850, *supra*.

To Thomas J. Turner[1]

Hon. T. J. Turner: Springfield,
Dear Sir: June 27. 1853.

Your letter of the 20th. reached me, day-before yesterday. I had, the day before, written to Adams[2] to be on hand with his witnesses—but, at the request of Judge Logan,[3] who is Kemper's attorney, I put in a Post-script, saying to Adams, if he was agreed, the cause should be continued over the summer term. On subsequent reflection, I rather wish Adams may not agree. I have the case fresh in my mind, and therefore wish to keep it going till it is finished. I have already drafted a Bill of Exceptions, and my plan is to put the common law suit through the forms of a second trial, up to a verdict (which must be against us, under Judge D's view of the law) except, & save all the points, and then, *before judgment*, file our Bill and get an injunction. I shall begin preparing a Bill this afternoon, which I

[199]

wish to file during the ensuing term; and I believe I will do this, even should the ejectment suit be continued—and in order to [do] this, Mr. Adams must come down to swear to the Bill. In no event can we be ready for proof in the chancery suit at this time, so that we will need no other witness than the one that was here last summer. I wrote Mr. Adams about a Register's certificate & if he can find one or two missing tax receipts, let him bring them. I should be glad to see you & shake you by the hand; but as there is no contested jury question, I scarcely think you need be at the trouble & expense of coming. All the law questions which can arise at this term, the Judge has already decided. Very truly yours,

A. LINCOLN

[1] ALS, owned by George A. Ball, Muncie, Indiana. [2] *Vide supra.*
[3] Stephen T. Logan.

To George B. Kinkead[1]

Geo. B. Kinkead, Esq   Springfield, Ills.
Lexington, Ky.   July 6. 1853.

Dear Sir: I feel some anxiety about the suit which has been gotten up against me in your court; and I therefore hope you will pardon my requesting you to write me when your court sits— whether it is probable I shall have to take proof here &c. &c. In the autumn of 1849 I was at Lexington several days, during which time I was almost constantly with L. O. Todd; and if he shall, when this case comes on to be tried, *think* he *remembers* that I told him I had collected money for Oldham Todd & Co, the story would be plausable enough to require an answer. Such recollection would be an utter mistake; yet if something of the sort is not relied on, I can not not [*sic*] conceive how Mr. Hemingway[2] was induced to swear to the truth of the Bill; for they can not, in any other way, make the slightest show of proof. I therefore think it safest to look to their making this proof, as, at least, possible, and to be prepared for it. I have said before, and now repeat, that if they will name the man or men of whom, they say, I have collected money for them, I will *disprove* it. I hope you will write me at once. I conclude with the remark that I expect you to be compensated for your services in this case, in addition, to your compensation for your attention to our business, in common, there. Respectfully

A. LINCOLN—

[1] ALS, owned by William H. Townsend, Lexington, Kentucky.
[2] Thomas Hemingway.

Release of Mortgage Taken from
Daniel E. Ruckel[1]

July 7, 1853

In consideration of Daniel E. Ruckel having perfected the title to the other parcel of ground included in this mortgage[2] I do hereby release from said mortgage the lots therein described as Lots Nine, ten, eleven, and twelve, in Block Three, in Allen's addition to Springfield. Witness my hand and seal this 7th. day of July 1853.   A. LINCOLN

1 ADS, Sangamon County Deed Record, Book GG, 440-41. The release is written in the margins of the record book. See the promissory note drawn by Lincoln and signed by Ruckel, August 15, 1851, *supra*.
2 Part of lot 8 in block 10.

To Thomas J. Turner[1]

To Hon. Thomas J. Turner,   Springfield,
Freeport, Illinois.   August 15, 1853.

. . . When I served notice on Logan[2] I promised him that if he would name any attorney in the vicinity whom he would wish to be present at the taking of the depositions, I would request you to notify him of the time and place, but he is gone off to the "World's Fair" (without having named any. You will perceive Logan filed cross-interrogations; and which I hope may be as fully and fairly answered as our own. . . . Very truly your friend,

A. LINCOLN.

1 Hertz, II, 619. This partial text is the only source available. The letter seems to refer to the case of Adam Adams, for which see Lincoln to Adams, June 23, 1853, and previous letters to Turner, *supra*.   2 Stephen T. Logan.

To Lewis M. Hays[1]

Mount Pulaski, Logan Co. Ills
Mr. L. M. Hays,   Sept. 8, 1853.

Dear Sir: Court is in session here now, and on yesterday I got a judgment against G. W. Turley[2] for $116,90 cents. The reason the amount was no larger was that the defendant proved by two witnesses—a Wm. Dodd, and a Dr. Mershow[3]—that T. P. Taylor, in his lifetime, told them that Turley, in 1837, had offered to pay him the money on the note, and that he refused to take it, saying he never intended to collect it, and would give up, or destroy, the note; on which proof the court decided, and I think correctly, that interest could not be allowed between the *offer to pay* and the *bringing of the suit*. This cut off all the interest but the $16.90 as a fee, and will send you the $100 in any way you may direct. I am following the Circuit and shall be at Bloomington, Ills., two weeks, ending on the 24th of this month, from which place I will send you the money, if you will have a letter to reach me there on or before the last named day. I can buy an Eastern draft at Bloomington, or at Springfield after my return there, which I suppose will be the best way of remitting the money. Yours etc.

A. LINCOLN.

¹ Tracy, p. 46.

² Tracy gives this name as "Tenley," but other letters to Hays (April 23, 1851, October 27, 1852, *supra*) establish George W. Turley as the man.

³ Mershon? Efforts to identify the three men named have been unsuccessful, but the name "Mershon" occurs in contemporary sources while "Mershow" has not been found.

To Thompson R. Webber¹

T. R. Webber, Esq–   Bloomington,
My dear Sir: Sept. 12. 1853.

On my arrival here to court, I find that McLean county has assessed the land and other property of the Central Railroad, for the purpose of county taxation. An effort is about to be made to get the question of the right to so tax the Co. before the court, & ultimately before the Supreme Court, and the Co. are offering to engage me for them.² As this will be the same question I have had under consideration for you, I am somewhat trammelled by what has passed between you and me; feeling that you have the prior right to my services; if you choose to secure me a fee something near such as I can get from the other side. The question, in its magnitude, to the Co. on the one hand, and the counties in which the Co. has land, on the other, is the largest law question that can now be got up in the State; and therefore, in justice to myself, I can not afford, if I can help it, to miss a fee altogether. If you choose to release me; say so by return mail, and there an end. If you wish to retain me, you better get authority from your court, come directly over in the Stage, and make common cause with this county. Very truly your friend   A. LINCOLN—

¹ ALS, owned by Charles M. Webber, Urbana, Illinois. Thompson R. Webber was clerk of the Champaign County Circuit Court.

² Lincoln was retained by the Illinois Central rather than by the counties, accepting $250 as a fee on October 7, 1853.

To George B. Kinkead[1]

Geo. B. Kinkead, Esq   Bloomington, Ills.
Lexington, Ky.   Sept. 13. 1853.

Dear Sir: Your letter of the 2nd. Inst. to Mr. Edwards, has been forwarded by him to me here where I am attending court. When, in your letter to me, of the 12th. July, you gave the opinion that O. T. & Co. would abandon their suit, it was plain to my mind they intended no such thing, else they would have told you so plainly. The matter now takes me at great disadvantage, in this, that it will cost me more to leave the Circuit (which has just commenced) and attend to taking proof, than it would to give up the claim; and your letter does not mention the *time* of your next term.

But the great difficulty of all is the want of something definite, to take proof about. Without a bill of particulars stating the names of the persons of whom, O. T. & Co claim that I have collected money for them, any proof I can possibly take, will be wide of the mark—can not meet Levi's[2] statement, (which I now suppose he is determined to make) that "I told him I owed the amount attached." I can prove by John T. Stuart, of Springfield Illinois, that he & I were partners in the law from the Spring of 1837—to the Spring of 1841, and that, so far as he knows, we never had any business for O. T. & Co. By Stephen T. Logan of Springfield, Ills, that he & I were partners from the Spring of 1841 to the autumn of 1844, and that so far as he knows, he & I never had any business for O. T. & Co. By William H. Herndon of Springfield, Ills, that he & I have been partners from the autumn of 1844 up to the present time; and that so far as he knows, he & I never had any business for O. T. & Co—and by all three, that they never knew of me, individually, having any business for O. T. & Co. Also, by Ninian W. Edwards of Springfield, Ills, that so far as he knows or believes the whole of the business of O. T. & Co in Illinois passed through his hands, and that so far as he knows or believes, none of it ever went into my hands—that the claims at Beardstown & Shelbyville both passed through his hands, and were, in the fall of 1843, given to me, as desparate debts, by Mr. Todd, in manner as I have stated in my answer; and that less than three years ago, the father-in-law of one of the debtors, called on him to try to compound the debt. As I understand, both these claims went into judgments; and as to that at Beardstown, I can prove the truth of the answer, by the record, and by Henry E. Dummer of Beardstown, Cass Co. Ills. As to that at Shelbyville, I can prove the truth

[203]

of the answer, by the record that it was taken, not by me, but by a different attorney; and that it remains apparantly unsatisfied. By William F. Thornton of Shelbyville, Illinois, that he is the father-in-law of the debtor—that the debtor has gone to California; and that he left this, among others, as an unpaid debt, which he desired the witness to compound for him if he could.

All this I can prove; but without a Bill of particulars, it seems to me, it will not meet the case.

Can they not be ruled to give a Bill of particulars?

This matter harrasses my feelings a good deal; and I shall be greatly obliged if you will write me immediately, *under cover to Mr. Edwards at Springfield* Ills—telling me first, *when* is the next term of your court; and second, whether I *can* or can *not* have a bill of particulars. Yours truly   A. LINCOLN—

[1] ALS, IHi.   [2] Levi O. Todd.

Notice to Thomas Hemingway and Edward Oldham[1]

September 22, 1853

"Messrs Oldham & Hemingway, survivors of Oldham, Todd & Co. Gentlemen

Take notice that I will take depositions to be read by me in the suit now pending in the Fayette Circuit Court, wherein you are plaintiffs & I am Defendant with others, at the following times and places towit: At the office of the Clerk of the circuit court of Sangamon County, Illinois, in Springfield, on the 12 day of Novr. next, at which place I will take the deposition of J. T. Stewart & others.

At the office of the Clerk of the Cass Circuit Court in the town of Beardstown, County of Cass, State of Illinois, on the 15th. of Novr. 1853, at which place I will take the deposition of H. E. Dummer & others.

At the office of the Clerk of the circuit court of Shelby county, in the town of Shelbyville in said county, State of Illinois, on the 8th. of Novr. 1853, at which place I will take the deposition of William F. Thornton & others.

Sept. 22. 1853. ABRM. LINCOLN"

[1] ADS copy, Fayette County (Kentucky) Circuit Court files. There are two autograph copies of the notice in the court files, accompanying the depositions of Anthony Thornton and of Ninian W. Edwards and Eliphalet B. Hawley, respectively. On January 16, 1854, Oldham and Hemingway filed a motion to dismiss the suit, which was done at the next term of court beginning February 20.

To George B. Kinkead[1]

Geo. B. Kinkead, Esq.   Peoria, Ills.
Lexington, Ky.   Sept. 30. 1853.

Dear Sir   Your letter of the 22nd. has just reached me through Mr. Edwards; and for which I thank you heartily. I now feel that the case is entirely manage[a]ble. I well know who Hawley and Edwards are. The "Hawley" of that firm is Eliphalet B. Hawley; and the "Edwards" is no other than Ninian W. Edwards, whom you know nearly as well as I do, & being the same who, on behalf of himself, and the rest of us here, has conducted all the business with you, in relation to Mr. Todd's estate. Mr. Hawley still lives at Springfield; and I will thank you to give a notice to take his deposition at the same time and place named in my former letter[2] for the taking of that of Mr. Edwards & others at Springfield. Very truly Yours &c.   A. LINCOLN—

P.S. Still write me, under cover to Mr. Edwards at Springfield, who will forward to me.   A. L.

[1] ALS, IHi.
[2] This original letter has not been located, but it was probably written between September 13 and September 22. The notices which Lincoln copied for the court record (*vide supra*) bear the latter date, and presumably the notices were sent by Kinkead shortly after receiving Lincoln's missing letter of instructions.

To Mason Brayman[1]

M. Brayman, Esq   Pekin, Ills.
Dear Sir: Oct. 3, 1853.

Neither the county of McLean nor any one on it's behalf, has yet made any engagement with me in relation to it's suit with the Illinois Central Railroad, on the subject of taxation. I am now free to make an engagement for the Road; and if you think fit you may "count me in" Please write me, on receipt of this. I shall be here at least ten days. Yours truly   A. LINCOLN—

[1] ALS, PHi, Brayman replied from Springfield on October 7 enclosing his personal check for $250 as a general retainer fee. The so-called "receipt" for this fee, preserved in Brayman's papers, is merely the record kept by Brayman of the transaction and does not bear Lincoln's signature.

To Peter Doty[1]

Peter Doty Esq.   Pekin,
Dear Sir: Oct. 3, 1853.

Herein is the writ in the case of Hall against Wilson which I brought off to get the Sheriff's return amended. Please place it with the papers again. Yours truly   A. LINCOLN.

[1] ALS-F, Bloomington *Pantagraph*, February 12, 1915. Doty was clerk of the Woodford County Circuit Court.

To John Connelley[1]

Mr. John Connolly.   Pekin, Ills.
Dear Sir: Oct. 4. 1853.
     Inclosed is a certificate,[2] lacking only the date & your name. I
took the facts from the tax books here & suppose they are correct.
If you will fill the date and sign your name, and return the certificate, by the first mail, to me at this place, I shall be obliged, and
will pay your fee, when I return home. Yours truly
                                                  A. LINCOLN—

[1] ALS, Herbert Wells Fay Collection. John Connelley, whose name Lincoln
misspells, was appointed register of the Land Office at Springfield in March, 1853.
[2] This certificate and other documents drawn by Lincoln were filed in the case
of Joseph Gingerich v. Isaac W. Evans, et al., Woodford County Circuit Court.

To Lewis M. Hays[1]

                                              Springfield, Illinois,
L. M. Hays, Esq.   Nov. 11, 1853.
     Dear Sir: Inclosed is the draft for one hundred dollars. Absence
from home prevented my receiving your letter of the 12th October
until yesterday. Yours truly,   A. LINCOLN.

[1] Tracy, p. 48. The money was for the judgment collected against G. W. Turley. See Lincoln to Hays, September 8, supra.

To Thomas J. Turner[1]

                                        Springfield, Novr. 11. 1853–
Dear Sir: Judge Logan, Kemper's attorney, authorizes me [to]
say he consents to the within named clerk, taking the deposition,
in lieu of the man named in the commission, on condition that, if
you can, you will notify Kemper's lawyer there, of the time &
place. Mr. Adams[2] perhaps will know who the lawyer is. Dont
neglect, or fail for your life.   A. LINCOLN

[1] ALS-P, ISLA.   [2] Adam Adams.

To Henry E. Dummer[1]

Dear Dummer: Springfield, Novr. 17. 1853.
     While I was at Beardstown, I forgot to tell you that Wm. Butler
says if you will give him charge, and full discretion, of a claim in
your hands, against George G. Grubb,[2] late of Springfield, now of

[206]

Chicago, he knows how, and can, and will make something out of it for you. Please write him. Yours truly   A. LINCOLN—

1 ALS, IHi.
2 George G. Grubb had been for more than a decade in the general merchandise business in Springfield.

To James F. Joy[1]

James F. Joy. Esq   Springfield, Ills–
Dear Sir: Dec: 2. 1853.

Yours of Nov. 28. is received, and I am really pleased to learn that you are engaged in the case you mention. The case could not be transferred to Ottawa, other than by agreement of parties, and, as yet, there is no counsel here representing the party adverse to the Road. Besides this, though it might not be impossible, it would be inconvenient for me to go to Ottawa. The Court does not meet here, this ensuing term, till the first monday of January; and I think I can get the hearing of the case postponed to the beginning of February. Can you not be here by that time? Please write me. Yours truly   A. LINCOLN—

1 ALS, MiD. James F. Joy was an agent and attorney for the Illinois Central who worked with Lincoln in numerous cases involving the railroad.

To Thomas J. Turner[1]

Hon. T. J. Turner   Springfield,
Dear Sir,   Dec 14, 1853.

Your letter and the depositions both reached here yesterday; and, by agreement, Logan and I have opened the depositions and read them. By my agreement with Logan, made when I filed the Bill last summer, he has the option to continue the cause over this ensuing term, and he now elects to do so. This dispenses with your coming *now*, even if you should attend the trial when it does come off, which I think you need not do at any sacrifice. The depositions, in the main, are very good; yet there are two or three points, which I will mention, that I would prefer to have differently. First, and least, it does not appear that *Bovey*[2] advanced any of the money to pay Denny. Secondly, that Rollins sold to Adams,[3] that Adams advanced the money, and that the deed was to be made to Adams, *only appears by Bradshaws declarations and admissions —and quare*, are his declarations & admissions competent evidence? I hope they are, and will examine.

[207]

Thirdly—There is an obvious question unanswered—"Why was Bradshaw interfering in the matter at all? It is easy to argue against us, that he had some sort of interest, and took & held the legal title, till something beyond the money going to Denny should be paid to him, Bradshaw. The consideration mentioned in Bradshaws deed to Adams & Bovey, being greater than $1400 favors this argument.

Lastly, and what I dislike more than all, is that Jacob Adams proves that Adam Adams was *with* Bradshaw when he took the deed from Denny to himself. Is this really the fact? I had always understood that Adams & Bovey were totally ignorant of the reason of Bradshaw's taking the deed to himself, and also ignorant of the fact till Bs return to Rock river.

I have the right, at the term, of amending the Bill, without excluding the evidence already taken; and consequently I must be informed at once, whether Adams *was* with Bradshaw when he took the deed from Denny.

I shall write to Adams on the subject.

I understand Denny & Rollins are both dead; and I now wish we had proved the fact, as an excuse for not making them witnesses. Yours truly   A. LINCOLN.

[1] Hertz, II, 621-22.   [2] John Bovey.   [3] Adam Adams.

To Thomas J. Turner[1]

Hon: T. J. Turner: Springfield,
Dear Sir: Decr. 21. 1853

Yours of the 16th. is received. You say Adams[2] did go to Peoria with Bradshaw, but was not actually present when Bradshaw took the deed. But by whom can we *prove* that he was not actually with him? This is the point. We *can* use Bradshaw as a witness, and we ought, by all means, to do it, if we can have any assurance that he will testify fairly. What he told Phelps recently, is clearly hearsay, & we can not be allowed to prove it by Phelps; but Bradshaw would probably swear the same he told Phelps. It is now a great question with me whether we shall take Bradshaw's deposition; and I wish to know, at once, what you and our clients think of trusting him. He can make the matter entirely plain, on all the points, and no one else can. If you conclude to trust him, write me, and I will, at this term, get an order of court to examine him. Yours truly   A. LINCOLN

[1] ALS, owned by Alfred W. Stern, Chicago, Illinois.   [2] Adam Adams.

To Henry E. Dummer[1]

H. E. Dummer Esq   Springfield.
My dear Sir: Decr. 26. 1853.

Butler[2] has just shown me your letter to him concerning the Grubb[3] debt; and, in relation to your intimation that you might be induced to sell it, he desires me to say to you that, in a few days over three months he is *sure* to get the principal of the debt (without interest) and that after you shall have received this information, he will entertain any proposition you may make, to sell. Please write him again. Yours as ever   A. LINCOLN—

1 ALS, IHi.   2 William Butler.   3 George G. Grubb.

Opinion on the Two-Mill Tax[1]

[1854?]

Under these circumstances it remains with the General Assembly to determine, in their wisdom, whether any means can and shall be devised, to relieve the people from the payment of the two mill tax, while, at least as now, the collection of that tax is but a useless burthen upon them.

1 AD, IHi. The above date has been assigned this manuscript by the Illinois State Historical Library. The editors have been unable to confirm its accuracy. The two-mill tax had been provided for in Article XV of the State Constitution of 1848, which specified that "The fund so created shall be kept separate, and shall annually . . . be apportioned and paid over *pro rata* upon all such state indebtedness, other than the canal and school indebtedness. . . ."

To James F. Joy[1]

J. F. Joy, Esq   Springfield,
Dear Sir—   Jany. 25– 1854.

Yours of the 20th. is just received, and I suppose, ere this, you have received my answer to your despatch on the same subject. It is my impression the case will not be brought up for trial before the meeting of the Legislature, but I can not get the *promise* of the court to that effect. I can only venture to say the *first of February;*[2] but as this day draws nearer, I can see farther ahead, and will try to notify you again.

Allow me to suggest that it is not safe to regard the case too lightly. A great stake is involved, and it will be fiercely contended for. I think we shall carry it; but I have a suspicion that the *feeling* of some of the Judges is against us.

I suppose you are aware that the point to be made against us, that the Constitution *secures* to the counties the right to tax all

property, *beyond* the *power* of the Legislature to take it away.
Yours truly   A. LINCOLN—

¹ ALS-P, ISLA.
² Lincoln and Joy orally argued the case of the Illinois Central Railroad *v.* the
County of McLean before the State Supreme Court, February 28, 1854.

To W. W. R. Woodbury and William Fithian[1]

W. W. R. Woodbury &   Springfield,
Wm. Fithian   Jany. 26– 1854

Gentlemen—Your letter is received. You say Mrs. Sconce will
relinquish her rights under the Will. This she must do, in order
to get her legal rights. My opinion on all the questions asked is as
follows.

She will have Dower (that is one third for life) in the lands, for
which the Dr. assigned the certificates, and she will have nothing
more in those lands. (I suppose the lands lie in this State).

If the Dr. was in his right mind, he could *give away* the notes
and money; and if he did so, it will stand; so that this part of the
case depends upon how the *fact* may prove to be. Whoever admin-
isters must claim the notes and money, and contest with them, for
them. She need give no notice to the Genl. Land-office. I infer that
when Dr. Sconce died neither he nor his wife had any living child;
and if I am right in this, then Mrs. Sconce will hold th[r]ee
quarters of the land deeded to the child—thus—the child dying
without brother or sister the land went in halves, or equal parts to
the father and mother, and the father afterwards dying without a
living child, one half of his half went to his wife—making up the
three quarters. Their having the deed to the child will do no harm.

Better mention this to W. H. Lamon,[2] lest he should, unawares,
commit me to the other side. Yours &c.   A. LINCOLN—

¹ ALS-P, ISLA. Both Woodbury and Fithian were physicians at Danville,
Illinois, and friends of the late Dr. J. A. D. Sconce, whose widow had apparently
consulted them in regard to her husband's estate. Dr. Woodbury had been in
partnership with Dr. Sconce in the drug business, and had commenced the study
of medicine under the guidance of Dr. Fithian.
² In 1852 Ward H. Lamon and Lincoln had established an office together in
Danville and were in partnership to some extent in their practice in the Circuit
Court and Illinois Supreme Court.

To John Marshall[1]

Hon: John Marshall   Springfield,
Shawneetown, Ills.   Feby. 8. 1854.

My dear Sir: Your letter of the 1st. Inst. was received yesterday. I went at once to the Express office, got the books, placed

twenty three of them at one Book-Store; & twenty four at another, for sale, at a commission of ten per cent, and took their receipts. Of the other three books, I took one to the Register, one to the Journal, and took one home with me. I found that the editors and booksellers had all previously seen favorable notices of the work; and one of the booksellers had sent an order to Cincinnati for some copies of it. I am not much of a reader of this sort of literature; but my wife got hold of the volume I took home, read it half through last night, and is greatly interested in it. When the papers here shall have noticed it, I will send you copies. The charge at the Express office was only $1.50; I return herewith one dollar, & hold fifty cents subject to your order.

My attention to this matter has been rather a pleasure than a trouble. Yours truly—   A. LINCOLN—

1 ALS, ICHi. John Marshall was an attorney at Shawneetown, Illinois, who had represented Gallatin County in the state's First General Assembly. His daughter, Sarah Marshall Hayden, published a book of fiction in 1854 entitled *Early Engagements: and Florence, (a Sequel.)*. This must be the book referred to in this letter, since there is record of Lincoln's delivering twenty-three copies of *Early Engagements* to Birchall & Owen of Springfield on February 7 (IIIi).

To Joseph Gillespie[1]

Springfield, Feb. 11– 1854

To-day a petition was circulated in Springfield, and signed by some of the citizens, instructing the Sangamon members to vote for Brough's road.[2] Whether this is a movement to force the members to desert us, or to *excuse* them, being already so inclined, we do not certainly know; but either way, it behoves us, who have been their fast friends, in all things, for the last seventeen years, to have our eyes open. We sincerely hope the movement is too limited to amount to any thing, for we much prefer standing with old friends, to being driven to form new ones. But if Springfield, and Sangamon county, are determined to try their fortunes in other company, we have no power to hinder it; and all we can do is to take care of ourselves as we best may. They, of course, will not complain of us. It probably would *help* us more than Brough's road would *hurt* us, to be enabled to tap the East & West line of road running through Springfield, by forming a connection between La Fayette, Indiana and Paris in this state; and we have no doubt that Brough himself would be glad to help us to the connection, in consideration that we should withdraw our opposition to his road. It thus is plain, that if Springfield must sell us to Brough, she may find herself sold in the same market before the end of the session. Being released from Springfield, there are some other matters, of which she is not wholly indifferent, in relation to which we possibly could gain as many votes, even against Brough's road, as it is in the power of Springfield to take from us. It is our interest to be looking about for the means of [indemnity in case she is really][3] preparing to stab us.

[1] AL, owned by Charles S. Gillespie, Edwardsville, Illinois. Lincoln pencilled this note in the Senate chamber of the State Capitol, in Gillespie's absence. Gillespie came in as Lincoln was finishing, and hence the note is unsigned.

[2] John Brough's road, against which Lincoln seems to have been lobbying, was the Atlantic and Mississippi, which had failed for five years to obtain legislation authorizing construction, largely because of the opposition of a "State policy" group opposed to any project calculated to benefit a city of another state, in this case St. Louis, since the Atlantic and Mississippi proposed not to build to Alton but to Illinoistown (the present city of East St. Louis). Brough was at this time president of the Madison and Indianapolis Railroad.

[3] A partially illegible line, restored following Angle, p. 122.

To Robert Smith[1]

Dear Sir: Springfield, (Ills.) March 1, 1854.

We herewith send you our answer to the questions propounded in your letter of the 24th February, 1854. Yours, Respectfully,

JOHN T. STUART,

A. LINCOLN,

Hon. Robert Smith, Alton, Illinois.   B. S. EDWARDS.

First. Is the corporation legally formed?

The articles of association filed in the office of the Secretary of State, establish the length of the road at one hundred and sixty miles or thereabouts. They also show subscriptions to an amount in the aggregate less than forty thousand dollars. With the articles and endorsed thereon or annexed thereto, is filed the affidavit of three persons, named in said articles as Directors, stating that the "amount of stock necessary for the incorporation of said company has been subscribed, viz; *one hundred and sixty thousand dollars*, and that ten per cent. on the amount, viz: sixteen thousand dollars, has been actually paid in as required by law." The date of this certificate is August 7, 1850.

It is, we think, undoubted law, that such associations are con-

[1] Angle, pp. 123-28, taken from St. Louis, Missouri, *Intelligencer*, March 9, 1854. Robert Smith of Alton represented the "State policy" group opposed to the Atlantic and Mississippi Railroad. (See Lincoln to Gillespie, February 11, *supra*.) On February 23, the legislature granted the Atlantic and Mississippi authority to begin construction, but as Lincoln's opinion indicates there were flaws in the railroad's organization. The State Supreme Court upheld the act of February 23 as remedying any supposed defects in the original organization.

fined to the provisions of the act authorizing them, and cannot be organized until all its substantial enactments on the subject are complied with. See the case of "Valk vs. Crandall and others"—1st Sanford's Ch. Rep. p. 179. The substantial provisions of the act of Nov. 5, 1849, preliminary to the incorporation of the company, are contained in the first and second sections of the act. The language is explicit, "That any number of persons not less than twenty-five, being *subscribers* to the stock of any contemplated railroad may be formed into a *corporation* for the purpose of constructing, owning and maintaining such railroad *by complying with the following requirements.*" When stock to the amount of at least one thousand dollars for every mile of said road so intended to be built, shall be in good faith subscribed, and ten per cent. paid thereon as herein required, *then the said subscribers* may elect Directors for the said company, *thereupon* they shall severally subscribe articles of association, &c. "Each subscriber to such articles of association shall subscribe thereto his name, place of residence, and the number of shares of stock taken by him in such company. The *said* articles of association may, on complying with the next section, be filed in the office of Secretary of State, and thereupon the persons who have subscribed, and all persons who shall from time to time become stockholders in such company, shall be a body corporate by the names specified in such articles."

"*Sec.* 3. Such articles of association shall not be filed in the office of the Secretary of State, until ten per cent. on the amount of stock subscribed thereto, shall have been actually and in good faith paid in cash to the Directors named in such articles, nor until there is endorsed thereon, or annexed thereto, an affidavit made by at least three of the Directors named in such articles, that the amount of stock required by the first section has been subscribed, and that ten per cent. on the amount has actually been paid in."

We cannot doubt that the obvious intention of the Legislature was to require that all the preliminary steps to the incorporation of the company must appear on the face of the papers filed in the Secretary's office. The manifest propriety of such a requisition as security to the public against the formation of fictitious and irresponsible corporations, would of itself constitute a sufficient reason for this construction. The minuteness of detail contained in these sections is inconsistent with any other. Why such precision in these requirements, and the further requisition that these articles should be filed in the office of the Secretary, if not for the very purpose of manifesting the compliance with the provisions of the act? We think that the subscription of the amount prescribed by the first section must be antecedent to the formation either of a company or the corporation. Until this amount has been subscribed and the ten per cent. paid, the *articles of association* cannot be legally entered into. The language is: *When* stock to the amount required shall be in good faith subscribed and the ten per cent. paid, *"then* the *said subscribers* may elect directors for said company; *thereupon* they shall severally subscribe articles of association." Now, who are to subscribe these articles? Clearly, those who have subscribed the amount previously ascertained by the act, and have paid the per centage. These, and these only, are the *said subscribers* who *may elect directors*, the names of whom are to appear in the articles. Until the amount required is subscribed, no election of directors is authorized. Any persons elected directors by any number of subscribers prior to that event, would be illegally elected, and their certificate or affidavit would, so far as compliance with this act is concerned, be of no more legal validity than the statement of persons nowise connected with the company.

This view is corroborated by the 3d section of the act, which makes a certified copy of "any articles of association filed in pursuance of this act with a copy of the affidavit aforesaid endorsed thereon presumptive evidence of the incorporation of said company." Being only *presumptive* evidence, even if every thing required appeared on the face of the papers, the truthfulness of the statements contained in them might be controverted. Surely it was not intended that a copy of articles showing only a subscription of a part of the amount required, should be presumptive evidence of the subscription of the whole. And here we can see no reason for requiring an affidavit. The law requires the subscription to be made in *good faith*. The names of subscribers, if genuine, with the amount of their subscription, would show the liability of each, and afford the means of ascertaining the aggregate amount. The affidavit would make the *prima facie* evidence of the genuineness of the signatures, the *good faith* of the subscriptions, and the payment of the ten per cent. Two essential guaranties are thus afforded for the construction or honestly attempted construction of the contemplated road, viz; The personal responsibility of the subscribers, as provided in the 14th section of the act, and the affidavit of three directors to the good faith of the subscription and the payment of the instalment; and these, the articles subscribed as required, and the affidavit, constitute the presumptive evidence of incorporation. The one was not intended as a substitute for the other. The company could no more be organized without the subscriptions appearing on the articles than without the affidavit, and vice versa.

We think that the only subscriptions which would in any event be obligatory, are those which appear on the articles, or are subscribed on the books opened by the Commissioners. Now by reference to the 5th section it will be seen, that the commissioners are only authorized to open books, "from time to time *after the company shall be incorporated.*" Such subscriptions cannot supply the place of those which by the terms of the law are required to be made anterior, and as a condition precedent to the incorporation of the company. Without further extending the argument, we are clearly of opinion that the association called "The Atlantic and Mississippi Railroad Company" is not a corporation legally formed, "under the act to provide for a general system of railroad incorporations," approved November 5, 1849.

Second. Have they such an organization as entitles them to come before the present session of the Legislature? We think not. By the tenth section of the fourth article of the constitution the Governor "may on extraordinary occasions convene the general assembly by proclamation, and shall state in said proclamation the purpose for which they are to convene, and the general assembly shall enter on no legislative business except that for which they were specially called together."

The proclamation which is thus made the exclusive grant of legislative power at this session—which cannot constitutionally be transcended—is, so far as relates to this subject, in these words: "To pass laws recognizing the *existence of,* and conferring additional powers upon *corporations formed,* or which may be formed prior to the action of the legislature thereon, under the act to provide for a general system of railroad incorporation"—approved Nov. 5, 1849—"declare the public utility of their works, sanction the routes and termini thereof, and authorize the construction of the same." This language is plain and the meaning apparent. It is, not to recognize the existence of, and confer additional powers on *associations,* but *corporations formed* under the act—not companies whose organization had not been completed, but those who, by complying with the requirements of the general law have perfected their organization thereunder, so far as that could be done anterior to the legislation which is required by that law. It is apparent that the Governor had in contemplation the twenty-second section of the act containing provisions for those acts of the Legislature necessary to clothe the corporation with all the powers conferred by the act; and particularly to the last clause of that section, "And the Legislature reserve [the right] to itself to indicate the routes and termini of said roads, and the same shall not be constructed and commenced without the express sanction of the Legislature of this state by a law to be passed thereafter." It was intended that the assembly might sit *under* the law of '49, but not that they might legislate in direct conflict with its provisions.

The answers to the remaining questions, are we think, necessarily involved in what we have already stated. If we are correct in these opinions, then it follows, that *the Atlantic and Mississippi Railroad Company has no legal existence as a corporation—that the law of this session being beyond the power of the Legislature at a called session to pass, is a nullity; that no bonds could be issued, nor collections of subscriptions be enforced by a so called corporation which had no legal existence.* As all subscriptions must be supposed to have been made with reference to an organization under the general law, they would only be payable to a *corporation* legally formed under that law—while all who subscribed to the articles of association, may be presumed to have known that action of the Legislature according to the general law of Nov. 5, 1849, would be applied, for they will not we think, be presumed to have understood that such application would be made until all the prerequisites of that law had been complied with. All subscriptions, prior to the filing of the articles must, in our opinion, have been made with the implied or express understanding that the full amount required by the law would be bona fide subscribed, and the per centage paid, and until that event, they would not be bound. We do not think that by the mere act of subscription they assented to the filing of the articles before the one hundred and sixty thousand dollars had been legally subscribed. Those who subscribed after the alleged formation of the Company by the filing of the articles, will be presumed to have so subscribed with the understanding, that all the requisitions of the act had been complied with, and the articles of association had been legally filed in the office of the Secretary, and if this has not been done they would not be bound to pay their subscriptions.   JOHN T. STUART,

A. LINCOLN,

B. S. EDWARDS.

To George B. Kinkead[1]

Geo. B. Kinkead, Esq   Springfield, Ills.
Dear Sir: March 31– 1854
Your note of January last, informing me that Messrs Oldham & Hemingway[2] had dismissed their suit against me, was duly received. I write this now merely to say that I expect and desire you

to be paid a separate fee for your attention to that suit; and to authorize you to retain what you shall deem reasonable on that account, out of any money of mine which is, or may come into your hands. If nothing further for me, is, or is likely to be in your hands, write me and I will forward you the amount. Very truly Yours &c.   A. LINCOLN

1 ALS, IHi.
2 See Lincoln to Kinkead, May 27, 1853, and succeeding letters.

To Jesse Lincoln[1]

Springfield, Illinois, April 1, 1854.

My Dear Sir: On yesterday I had the pleasure of receiving your letter of the 16th of March. From what you say there can be no doubt that you and I are of the same family. The history of your family, as you give it, is precisely what I have always heard, and partly know, of my own. As you have supposed, I am the grandson of your uncle Abraham; and the story of his death by the Indians, and of Uncle Mordecai, then fourteen years old, killing one of the Indians, is the legend more strongly than [most prominent of] all others imprinted upon my mind and memory. I am the son of grandfather's youngest son, Thomas. I have often heard my father speak of his uncle Isaac residing at [on the] Watauga (I think), near where the then States of Virginia, North Carolina, and Tennessee join,—you seem now to be some hundred miles or so west of that [there]. I often saw Uncle Mordecai, and Uncle Josiah but once in my life; but I never resided near either of them. Uncle Mordecai died in 1831 or 2, in Hancock County, Illinois [Ill.], where he had then recently removed from Kentucky, and where his children had also removed, and still reside [live], as I understand. Whether Uncle Josiah is dead or living, I cannot tell, not having heard from him for more than twenty years. When I last heard of [from] him he was living on Big Blue River, in [Hancock County] Indiana (Harrison Co., I think), and where he had [has] resided ever since before ["before" not in sentence] the beginning of my recollection. My father (Thomas) died the 17th of January, 1851, in Coles County, Illinois [Ill.], where he had resided twenty [20] years. I am his only child. I have resided here, and hereabouts, twenty-three [23] years. I am forty-five[45] years of age, and have a wife and three children, the oldest eleven [11] years. My wife was born and raised at Lexington, Kentucky [Ky.]; and my connection with her has sometimes taken me there, where I have heard the older [old] people of her relations [relatives] speak of your uncle Thomas and his family. He is dead long ago, and his descendants have gone to some part of Missouri, as I recollect what I was told. When I was at Washington in 1848, I got up a correspondence with David Lincoln, residing at Sparta, Rockingham County, Virginia[V], who, like yourself, was a first cousin of my father; but I forget, if he informed me, which of my grandfather's brothers was his father. With Col. [Colonel] Crozier,[2] of whom you speak, I formed quite an intimate acquaintance, for a short one, while at Washington ["while at Washington" not in sentence]; and when you meet him again I will thank you to present him my respects. Your present governor, Andrew Johnson, was also at Washington while I was; and he told me of there being people of the name of Lincoln in Carter County, I think ["I think" not in sentence]. I can no longer claim to be a young man myself; but I infer that, as you are of the same generation as my father, you are some older. I shall be very glad to hear from you again. Very truly your relative,   A. LINCOLN.

[1] NH, 180-82, and *Illinois State Journal*, October 30, 1883, copying the Chattanooga *Times*. The newspaper text is not identical with that in the *Works*. Major variations in the *Journal* are inserted in brackets in the *Works* text. The original letter has not been located.
[2] John H. Crozier, congressman from Tennessee.

Certificate of Examination for
Hiram W. Beckwith and George W. Lawrence[1]

May 27, 1854

We have examined Hiram W Beckwith and George W. Lawrence touching their qualifications to practice law; and find them sufficiently qualified to commence the practice, and therefore recommend that Licenses be allowed them.   A. LINCOLN

Danville May 27, 1854.   L. SWETT

[1] ADS, owned by David Davis, Bloomington, Illinois. Beckwith had studied in the Danville office of Lincoln and Ward H. Lamon. After his admission to the bar he remained in the office until 1859, when he succeeded to the practice. George W. Lawrence has not been positively identified, but a George W. Lawrence, age 28, Macoupin County, Illinois, is listed in the U.S. Census of 1850.

To Milton K. Alexander[1]

[June 13, 1854]

It pains me to have to say that I forgot to attend to your business when I was in Clinton, at Court in May last. Your best way would be to address me a letter at Clinton, about the time I go there to court in the fall (Oct. 16th. I think) and then it will be fresh, & I will not forget or neglect it. Yours truly A. LINCOLN

1 ALS, owned by Judson A. Lamon, Chicago, Illinois. This note, postmarked Springfield, June 13, is written on the back of Alexander's letter of June 6, 1854, relative to a lot in Clinton, Illinois, which had been sold for taxes and which Alexander wished to recover. General Milton K. Alexander was a prominent citizen of Paris, Illinois, who had commanded the Second Brigade of Volunteers in the Black Hawk War.

To John D. Swallow[1]

[c. June 15, 1854]

Both your questions are the same. After you sold and deeded your property to Edmons, for a consideration which is worthless and fraudulent, any person who buys or takes a mortgage from Edmons, without *Notice* of the fraud, will hold the property against you; but whoever buys or takes a mortgage *after* your Bill is filed, is conclusively presumed to have had *notice* of the fraud, and therefore can have no better right against you than Edmonds himself had. This is the whole law of the case. Yours truly

A. LINCOLN.

1 Copy, ISLA, furnished by Frank E. Blane, Petersburg, Illinois. John D. Swallow was a resident of Postville in Logan County. Lincoln's note was written on the back of Swallow's letter of June 15, which reads in part as follows:

"I sold to A. Edmons my mill for two states Ioway and Wisconsin gave a warety deed for the mill—there seems to be, a spurias title as to the pattent with others I instituted a suit in chancery. Now if Edmons should want money and a stranger to the suit should loan him money and take a mortgage on the property (some three days after the record of the suit or bill was filed and notice served on Edmons—) will that mortgage be valid in and sustained at law—and if a piece of land was given for a pattent right and that right proves void and four months after a person comes and makes a purchas of said land in good faith an entire stranger to Edmons and the suit—can the purchaser hold the land at law[.] please write by return mail. yours Respectfully J. D. SWALLOW"

To George B. Kinkead[1]

Geo. B. Kinkead, Esq.   Springfield, Ills.
Lexington, Ky.   June 16. 1854.

Dear Sir: Your letter of the 8th. Inst. to N. W. Edwards, enclosing a draft of between two and three hundred dollars (I write from memory only as to the amount) reached here a day or two since, and was, in Mr. Edwards' absence, taken from the P. office and opened by his brother. It was shown to me this morning, and will be kept at the store of which Mr. Edwards is a partner until his return, which will be about six weeks hence & when, doubtless, he will write you.

I ran my eye over the contents of your letter, & only have to say you do not seem disposed to compensate yourself very liberally for the separate service you did for me. Yours truly

A. LINCOLN—

1 ALS, IHi.

To Oliver L. Davis[1]

O. L. Davis, Esq.   Springfield, June 22– 1854.

Dear Sir: You, no doubt, remember the enclosed memorandum being handed me in your office. I have just made the desired search, and find that no such deed has ever been here. Campbell,[2] the Auditor, says that if it were here, it would be in his office, and that he has hunted for it a dozen times, & could never find it. He says that one time and another, he has heard much about the matter—that it was not a deed for Right o Way, but a deed, outright, for Depot-ground—at least, a *sale* for Depot-ground, and there may never have been a deed. He says, if there is a deed, it is most probable Genl. Alexander,[3] of Paris, has it. Yours truly.

A. LINCOLN

[Memorandum]

A Deed from Joseph Patterson to the State of Illinois for the right of way one [*sic*] Lots 7 & 8 in Block 8 in McRoberts & Walkers Addition to Danville[4]

I am to examine for the record of this deed at Springfield and write the result to James G. Miles[5] or O. L. Davis at Danville.

1 ALS, CSmH. Oliver L. Davis was an attorney at Danville, Illinois.
2 Thomas H. Campbell, state auditor.   3 Milton K. Alexander.
4 This sentence is not in Lincoln's hand. Joseph Patterson was for many years justice of peace at Danville.
5 Lincoln first wrote "Myers," then deleted it and substituted "Miles." James G. Miles has not been identified.

Fragment on Government[1]

[July 1, 1854?]

The legitimate object of government, is to do for a community of people, whatever they need to have done, but can not do, *at all*, or can not, *so well do*, for themselves—in their separate, and individual capacities.

In all that the people can individually do as well for themselves, government ought not to interfere.

The desirable things which the individuals of a people can not do, or can not well do, for themselves, fall into two classes: those which have relation to *wrongs*, and those which have not. Each of these branch off into an infinite variety of subdivisions.

The first—that in relation to wrongs—embraces all crimes, misdemesnors, and non-performance of contracts. The other embraces all which, in its nature, and without wrong, requires combined action, as public roads and highways, public schools, charities, pauperism, orphanage, estates of the deceased, and the machinery of government itself.

From this it appears that if all men were just, there still would be *some*, though not *so much*, need of government.

1 AD, DLC-RTL. The date assigned to this fragment by Nicolay and Hay has been retained for want of satisfactory evidence to the contrary. It seems, however, to be an entirely arbitrary date, without supporting evidence. Together with the companion version (*infra*), which seems to be a revision, this fragment may have been used in, or at least intended for, a lecture, but if Lincoln delivered such a lecture no reference to it has been found.

Fragment on Government[1]

[July 1, 1854?]

Government is a combination of the people of a country to effect certain objects by joint effort. The best framed and best administered governments are necessarily expensive; while by errors in frame and maladministration most of them are more onerous than they need be, and some of them very oppressive. Why, then, should we have government? Why not each individual take to himself the whole fruit of his labor, without having any of it taxed away, in services, corn, or money? Why not take just so much land as he can cultivate with his own hands, without buying it of any one?

The legitimate object of government is "to do for the people what needs to be done, but which they can not, by individual effort, do at all, or do so well, for themselves." There are many such things—some of them exist independently of the injustice in the world. Making and maintaining roads, bridges, and the like; providing for the helpless young and afflicted; common schools; and disposing of deceased men's property, are instances.

But a far larger class of objects springs from the injustice of men. If one people will make war upon another, it is a necessity with that other to unite and coöperate for defense. Hence the military department. If some men will kill, or beat, or constrain others, or despoil them of property, by force, fraud, or noncompliance

[221]

with contracts, it is a common object with peaceful and just men
to prevent it. Hence the criminal and civil departments.

[1] NH, II, 182-83. This fragment is obviously related to the companion piece
supra. No trace of the original document or a copy remains in the Lincoln papers.

Fragment on Slavery[1]

[July 1, 1854?]

dent truth. Made so plain by our good Father in Heaven, that all
feel and *understand* it, even down to brutes and creeping insects.
The ant, who has toiled and dragged a crumb to his nest, will
furiously defend the fruit of his labor, against whatever robber as-
sails him. So plain, that the most dumb and stupid slave that ever
toiled for a master, does constantly *know* that he is wronged. So
plain that no one, high or low, ever does mistake it, except in a
plainly *selfish* way; for although volume upon volume is written
to prove slavery a very good thing, we never hear of the man who
wishes to take the good of it, *by being a slave himself.*

Most governments have been based, practically, on the denial
of equal rights of men, as I have, in part, stated them; *ours* began,
by *affirming* those rights. *They* said, some men are too *ignorant,*
and *vicious,* to share in government. Possibly so, said we; and, by
your system, you would always keep them ignorant, and vicious.
We proposed to give *all* a chance; and we expected the weak to
grow stronger, the ignorant, wiser; and all better, and happier together.

We made the experiment; and the fruit is before us. Look at it
—think of it. Look at it, in it's aggregate grandeur, of extent of
country, and numbers of population—of ship, and steamboat, and
rail-

[1] AD, ORB. The arbitrary date assigned to this fragment by Nicolay and Hay
has been retained for want of conclusive evidence to the contrary. It seems to
the editors probable that this single page is part of a speech composed in 1858-
1859. It may possibly have been part of the omitted portion in the speech at
Cincinnati, September 17, 1859 (*vide infra*), or a portion of some one of several
speeches in 1858 for which no report or manuscript has been found.

Fragment on Slavery[1]

[July 1, 1854?]

If A. can prove, however conclusively, that he may, of right, enslave B.—why may not B. snatch the same argument, and prove
equally, that he may enslave A?—

You say A. is white, and B. is black. It is *color,* then; the lighter, having the right to enslave the darker? Take care. By this rule, you are to be slave to the first man you meet, with a fairer skin than your own.

You do not mean *color* exactly?—You mean the whites are *intellectually* the superiors of the blacks, and, therefore have the right to enslave them? Take care again. By this rule, you are to be slave to the first man you meet, with an intellect superior to your own.

But, say you, it is a question of *interest;* and, if you can make it your *interest,* you have the right to enslave another. Very well. And if he can make it his interest, he has the right to enslave you.

[1] AD, ORB. The date assigned to this single page by Nicolay and Hay has been retained. Although probably not a part of the same document as the companion fragment, *supra,* it seems just as likely to belong to a later period.

Affidavit on Land Warrant[1]

State of Illinois
County of Sangamon } ss   July 15, 1854

Be it known that on this day appeared before the undersigned an acting justice of the peace for said county Abraham Lincoln to me known to be the identical person he represents himself to be & who after being by me duly sworn deposes and says that he is the identical Abraham Lincoln who was captain of the 4th Illinois volunteers in the Blackhawk War and the Identical Abraham Lincoln to whom the within Land Warrant for 40 acres was issued and that he desires to locate the same in his own name.

Witnesses   A. LINCOLN—

A. M. WATSON[2]

CHARLES ARNOLD[3]

Subscribed & Sworn to before me this 15th day of July 1854

WM. F. ELKIN Justice peace

[1] DS, DNA RG 49, Records of the General Land Office. The document appears on the verso of Military Bounty Land Warrant No. 52076, April 16, 1852.
[2] Abner M. Watson was constable of Sangamon County.
[3] Sheriff of Sangamon County.

Power of Attorney to John P. Davies[1]

July 15, 1854

Know all men by these presents that I Abraham Lincoln of the County of Sangamon in the State of Illinois reposing special trust and confidence in the skill and ability of John P. Davies in the

County of Dubuque State of Iowa do appoint him my true & lawful attorney in fact for me & in my name to Locate the Land Warrant no. 52076 for 40 acres issued to me on the North West ¼ of South West [quarter] of section no 20 in Township 84 north in range no 15 west of the Land subject to private entry at the Land office at Dubuque Iowa & for me & in my name to Execute all instruments in writing that may be necessary or legal in order fully to Execute the power herein granted & for your so doing this shall be your sufficient warrant.

Given under my hand & seal this 15th. day of July AD 1854

A. LINCOLN—(LS)

[1] DS, DNA RG 49, Records of the General Land Office. The document also carries the certification of William F. Elkin, J. P. On July 21, 1854, John P. Davies entered the forty acres which Lincoln had designated. For details concerning these land holdings, see Pratt, *Personal Finances of Abraham Lincoln*, p. 67 ff.

To Edward Seymour[1]

E. Seymour, Esqr.   Springfield,
Kaskaskia, Ills.   July 17. 1854.

Dear Sir: Your letter of the 13th. inclosing copy declaration & notice; in case of Morrison vs. Briggs,[2] came duly to hand. On examination I found the case had been docketted at this July term, with rule to plead in twenty days. To prevent a default, it was necessary to file a plea before the expiration of the twenty days; and accordingly I filed it on the 15th. Inst. Court has adjourned; and nothing but preparation is necessary on the case, till the 3rd. monday of Decr. when court sits again. In the mean time if you wish me to do any thing further on the case you would better get up your evidence of title and send it to me. Yours &c

A. LINCOLN—

[1] ALS, owned by Mrs. Arthur Seymour, Fort Gage, Illinois.
[2] An ejectment suit which Lincoln and Logan lost in the U.S. Circuit Court, December 20, 1854. The jury found for the plaintiff, awarding damages of one cent and ordering the defendant to restore the property.

Mortgage from Ritta A. da Silva[1]

August 11, 1854

This Indenture made this eleventh day of August in the year of our Lord one thousand, eight hundred and fiftyfour, by and between Ritta D. Sylva, of the City of Springfield, County of Sangamon, and State of Illinois, of the one part; and Abraham Lincoln, of the City, County and State aforesaid of the other part, Witnesseth:

That the said Ritta D. Sylva, for, and in consideration of, the sum of one hundred and twentyfive dollars, to her in hand paid, the receipt whereof is hereby acknowledged, has granted, bargained, and sold; and by these presents does grant, bargain and sell unto the said Abraham Lincoln, his heirs and assigns forever, the following described lot of ground, towit: Lot Five, in Block Six, in Wells & Peck's addition to the late town, now City, of Springfield, Illinois.

To have and to hold to the said Abraham Lincoln, his heirs and assigns forever, the above described lot of ground, together with all and singular the previleges and appurtenances thereunto belonging, or to belong.

Yet upon condition that whereas the said Ritta D. Sylva has executed her promissory note of even date herewith, for the sum of one hundred and twentyfive dollars, with interest at the rate of ten per cent per annum, payable to the said Abraham Lincoln, Four year after date—interest payable annually. Now, if said note shall be paid according to it's tenor and effect, the above conveyance is to be null and void, otherwise to remain in full force and effect.

In testimony whereof the said Ritta D. Sylva, has hereunto set her hand and seal the day and year above written.

RITTA ANGELICA DA SILVA [SEAL]

Satisfied in full. Nov. 26, 1858.

A. LINCOLN[2]

[1] AD, ORB. In Lincoln's handwriting, excepting the signature. The verso bears an attestation of the same date by N. W. Matheny. Ritta Angelica da Silva was a member of a group of Portuguese settlers who came to Springfield in 1849. [2] Lincoln's release is written across the left-hand margin.

Promissory Note Drawn for Ritta A. da Silva[1]

$125–   Springfield, August 11– 1854.

Four year after date I promise to pay Abraham Lincoln, one hundred and twenty-five dollars, with ten per cent interest per annum from date until paid, interest payable annually, for value received.   RITTA ANGELICA DA SILVA.

This note paid in full this Novr. 26, 1858. Receipt given yesterday for $125– of the money.   A. LINCOLN.[2]

[1] Hertz, II, 626.   [2] Lincoln's receipt is written across the face of the note.

To Richard Yates[1]

Hon. R. Yates,   Springfield,
Jacksonville, Ill.   August 18, 1854.

My dear Sir: I am disappointed at not having seen or heard from you since I met you more than a week ago at the railroad depot here. I wish to have the matter we spoke of settled and working to its consummation. I understand that our friend B. S. Edwards is entirely satisfied now, and when I can assure myself of this perfectly I would like, by your leave, to get an additional paragraph into the Journal, about as follows:

"To-day we place the name of Hon. Richard Yates at the head of our columns for reelection as the Whig candidate for this congressional district. We do this without consultation with him and subject to the decision of a Whig convention, should the holding of one be deemed necessary; hoping, however, there may be unanimous acquiescence without a convention."

May I do this? Answer by return mail.[2] Yours, as ever,

A. LINCOLN.

[1] Printed in "Lincoln," a speech of Honorable Richard Yates of Illinois in the House of Representatives, February 12, 1921.

[2] Yates came to Springfield for consultation, and on August 22, the *Illinois Journal* announced his candidacy in approximately the manner of Lincoln's suggestion. No convention was held.

To Richard S. Thomas[1]

Hon. R. S. Thomas.   Springfield, Aug 24, 1854–

Dear Sir: Your letter of the 19th. was received day before yesterday. The payee of the note did write me that he had written Allard[2] on the subject of the note in your hands; so that when Allard shows you the letter, you need not doubt its genuineness. If the letter does, unconditionally, or only with the condition of my consent, agree to take $110 and my fee, settle the matter that way. As to the amount of my fee, take ten dollars, which you and I will divide equally. Yours as ever   A. LINCOLN—

[1] Copy, DLC-HW.   [2] Probably Dr. Luther S. Allard of Virginia, Illinois.

Speech at Winchester, Illinois[1]

August 26, 1854

After the transaction of the regular business of the convention— adoption of resolutions, &c.,—the Hon. A. Lincoln of your city,[2]

[226]

who was present, was loudly called for to address the meeting. He responded to the call ably and eloquently, doing complete justice to his reputation as a clear, forcible and convincing public speaker. His subject was the one which is uppermost in the minds of the people—the Nebraska-Kansas bill; and the ingenious, logical, and at the same time fair and candid manner, in which he exhibited the great wrong and injustice of the repeal of the Missouri Compromise, and the extension of slavery into free territory, deserves and has received the warmest commendation of every friend of freedom who listened to him. His was masterly effort—said to be equal to any upon the same subject in Congress,—was replete with unanswerable arguments, which must and will effectually *tell* at the coming election.

1 *Illinois Journal*, September 2, 1854.
2 This report appears in a letter to the *Journal* signed "FINALITY," which describes the Scott County Whig meeting called for the purpose of appointing delegates to the state convention.

Speech at Carrollton, Illinois[1]

August 28, 1854

. . . . While Maj. HARRIS was speaking, Mr. LINCOLN of Springfield, arrived in the stage, and by request he addressed the crowd assembled in defense of the Missouri Compromise, and in opposition to so much of the Nebraska bill as repeals it—speaking more than two hours. . . .

1 Alton *Daily Telegraph*, August 31, 1854. A report in the *Illinois State Register*, September 1, adds to the indicated content of Lincoln's speech the fact that Lincoln spoke also "against the repeal of the fugitive slave law." Both reports are chiefly concerned with the campaign speech of Major Thomas L. Harris, Democratic candidate for congress.

To Alexander B. Morean[1]

A. B. Morean, Esq.   Springfield,
Sir: Sept. 7– 1854

Stranger tho' I am, personally, being a brother in the faith, I venture to write you. Yates[2] can not come to your court next week. He is obliged to be at Pike court where he has a case, with a fee of $500, $200 already paid. To neglect it would be unjust to himself, and *dishonest* to his client. Harris[3] will be with you, head up and tail up, for Nebraska. You must have some one to make an anti-Nebraska speech. Palmer[4] is the best, if you can get him, I think—Jo. Gillespie, if you can not get Palmer—and *somebody* anyhow, if you can get neither. But press Palmer hard. It is in his Senatorial District I believe. Yours &c   A. LINCOLN—

[1] ALS, ORB. Alexander B. Morean was a druggist and Whig politician of Jerseyville, Illinois.   [2] Richard Yates.   [3] Thomas L. Harris.
[4] John M. Palmer of Carlinville, *vide infra.*

To John M. Palmer[1]

(CONFIDENTIAL)

Hon. J. M. Palmer.   Springfield,
Dear Sir.   Sept. 7. 1854

You know how anxious I am that this Nebraska measure shall be rebuked and condemned every where. Of course I hope something from your position; yet I do not expect you to do any thing which may be wrong in your own judgment; nor would I have you do anything personally injurious to yourself. You are, and always have been, *honestly*, and *sincerely* a democrat; and I know how painful it must be to an honest sincere man, to be urged by his party to the support of a measure, which on his conscience he believes to be wrong. You have had a severe struggle with yourself, and you have determined *not* to swallow the *wrong*. Is it not just to yourself that you should, in a few public speeches, state your reasons, and thus justify yourself? I wish you would; and yet I say "dont do it, if you think it will injure you." You may have given your word to vote for Major Harris, and if so, of course you will stick to it. But allow me to suggest that you should avoid speaking of this; for it probably would induce some of your friends, in like manner, to cast their votes. You understand. And now let me beg your pardon for obtruding this letter upon you, to whom I have ever been opposed in politics. Had your party omitted to make Nebraska a test of party fidelity; you probably would have been the Democratic candidate for congress in the district. You deserved it, and I believe it would have been given you. In that case I should have been quit, happy that Nebraska was to be rebuked at all events. I still should have voted for the whig candidate; but I should have made no speeches, written no letters; and you would have been elected by at least a thousand majority. Yours truly   A. LINCOLN—

[1] ALS-F, ISLA. John McAuley Palmer was at this time state senator from Macoupin County. A strong anti-Nebraska Democrat, he became a Republican and ran for congress on the Republican ticket in 1859.

Speech at Springfield, Illinois[1]

September 9, 1854

Mr. Lincoln replied to Mr. C.,[2] and, with his usual ability, made the best of a bad position. We have never heard him when more at fault in covering up the heresies which he habitually takes to. The whole tenor of his discussion was to satisfy the whig portion of his audience that affiliation with abolitionism was the only salvation of their party, and (Heaven save the mark!) of the country! He knew nothing of the secret institution of which Mr. Calhoun spoke, and, like the Journal, even "doubted its existence." Of course he did. He "Knows Nothing" about it.

[1] *Illinois State Register*, September 11, 1854.
[2] John Calhoun, whom Richard Yates had defeated for congress in 1852.

Editorial on the Kansas-Nebraska Act[1]

September 11, 1854

THE 14TH SECTION.

The following is the 14th section of the Kansas-Nebraska law. It repeals the Missouri Compromise; and then puts in a declaration that it is not intended by this repeal to legislate slavery in or exclude it therefrom, the territory.

SEC. 14. That the constitution, and all the laws of the United States which are not locally inapplicable, shall have the same force and effect within said territory of Nebraska as elsewhere in the United States, except the 8th section of the act preparatory to the admission of Missouri into the Union, approved March sixth, eighteen hundred and twenty, which being inconsistent with the principles of non-intervention by congress with slavery in the States and Territories as recognized by the legislation of eighteen hundred and fifty, commonly called the compromise measures, is hereby declared inoperative and void; it being the true intent and meaning of this act not to legislate slavery into any territory or State, nor to exclude it therefrom, but to leave the people thereof perfectly free to form and regulate their domestic institutions in their own way, subject only to the constitution of the United States: Provided, that nothing herein contained shall be construed to revive or put in force any law or regulation which may have existed prior to the act of sixth of March, eighteen hundred and twenty, either protecting, establishing, prohibiting, or abolishing slavery.

The state of the case in a few words, is this: The Missouri Compromise excluded slavery from the Kansas-Nebraska territory. The repeal opened the territories to slavery. If there is any meaning to the declaration in the 14th section, that it does not mean to legislate slavery into the territories, [it] is this: that it does not require slaves to be sent there. The Kansas and Nebraska territories are now as open to slavery as Mississippi or Arkansas were when they were territories.

To illustrate the case—Abraham Lincoln has a fine meadow, containing beautiful springs of water, and well fenced, which John Calhoun had agreed with Abraham (originally owning the land in common) should be his, and the agreement had been consummated in the most solemn manner, regarded by both as sacred. John Calhoun, however, in the course of time, had become owner of an extensive herd of cattle—the prairie grass had become dried up and there was no convenient water to be had. John Calhoun then looks with a longing eye on Lincoln's meadow, and goes to it and throws down the fences, and exposes it to the ravages of his starving and famishing cattle. "You rascal," says Lincoln, "what have you done? what do you do this for?" "Oh," replies Calhoun, "everything is right. I have taken down your fence; but nothing more. It is my true intent and meaning not to drive my cattle into your meadow, nor to exclude them therefrom, but to leave them perfectly free to form their own notions of the feed, and to direct their movements in their own way!"

Now would not the man who committed this outrage be deemed both a knave and a fool,—a knave in removing the restrictive fence, which he had solemnly pledged himself to sustain;—and a fool in supposing that there could be one man found in the country to believe that he had not pulled down the fence for the purpose of opening the meadow for his cattle?

¹ *Illinois Journal*, September 11, 1854. Lincoln continued his debate with John Calhoun (*vide supra*, September 9) on the editorial page of the *Journal*. Although the editors have eschewed unsigned articles which have been attributed to Lincoln, the contents of this article seem to establish Lincoln's authorship beyond reasonable doubt.

Speech at Bloomington, Illinois¹

September 12, 1854

He first declared that the Southern slaveholders were neither better, nor worse than we of the North, and that we of the North were no better than they. If we were situated as they are, we should act and feel as they do; and if they were situated as we are, they should act and feel as we do; and we never ought to lose sight of this fact in discussing the subject. With slavery as existing in the slave States at the time of the formation of the Union, he had nothing to do. There was a vast difference between toler-

¹ Bloomington *Weekly Pantagraph*, September 20, 1854.

ating it there, and protecting the slaveholder in the rights granted him by the Constitution, and extending slavery over a territory already free, and uncontaminated with the institution. When our federal compact was made, almost all of the valley of the Mississippi belonged to the French, not us; and what little territory we had belonged to different States; Virginia owning almost all of what now constitutes the State of Ohio, Indiana, Illinois, Michigan, and Wisconsin. Thomas Jefferson, being a Virginian, proposed the cession of this territory to the general government, and in carrying out the measure, had the clause especially inserted, that slavery should never be introduced into it. Kentucky belonged also to Virginia, but was settled as a part of the State of Virginia, so that slavery was carried there by the first settlers from Virginia, and was admitted into the Union with the institution as existing there. Tennessee belonged to North Carolina, and was settled by emigrants from that State, and was afterwards admitted into the Union as Kentucky was. Alabama was settled from South Carolina and admitted in a similar manner. Thus three slave States were made from territories that belonged to individual slaveholding States.

Jefferson saw the necessity of our government possessing the whole valley of the Mississippi; and though he acknowledged that our Constitution made no provision for the purchasing of territory, yet he thought that the exigency of the case would justify the measure, and the purchase was made. When the lower part of this territory comprising the State of Louisiana, wished to be admitted, the institution of slavery having existed there long before the territory was bought, she was admitted with the institution without any opposition, as a right that belonged to her citizens.

There was an old French settlement in St. Louis and vicinity, with slaves; and that territory comprising what is now the State of Missouri, was settled in part by Slaveholders. And when that territory, according to the law, gave notice that they should apply for admission into the Union, the North voted that she should not be admitted unless she framed a State Constitution excluding involuntary servitude, and they were the majority. Neither the North nor the South would yield, and the discussion became angry and endangered the peace of the Union. A compromise was made by agreeing that all territory bought of the French, north of 36° 30', should be free, which secured the whole of Nebraska, Iowa and Minnesota to freedom, and left the balance of the French purchase south of the line to come in as free or not, as they might choose to frame their state Constitution.

Missouri chose to come in a slave-state, and was so admitted, as was afterwards Arkansas, according to the compromise. And afterwards, when first the Democrats and afterwards the Whigs held their Conventions at Baltimore, in forming their platforms they both declared that compromise to be a "finality," as to the subject of slavery, and the question of slave territory was by agreement settled forever.

There was no more agitation of the subject till near the close of our war with Mexico, when three millions were appropriated with the design that the President might purchase territory of Mexico, which resulted in our obtaining possession of California, New Mexico, and Utah. This was new territory, with which Jefferson's provision and the Missouri Compromise had nothing to do. The gold in California led to such a rush of immigration that that territory soon became filled with the requisite number of inhabitants, and they formed a constitution, and requested an admission into the Union. But the South objected because her constitution excluded slavery. This gave rise to the "Wilmot proviso," no more slave territory; next the "Omnibus bill," and finally what are called the "compromise measures of 1850," which comprised among other things the following:

1st. The "fugitive slave law," which was a concession on the part of the North to the South.

2d. California was admitted as a free State, called a concession of the South to the North.

3d. It was left with New Mexico, and Utah to decide when they became States, whether they would be free or not. This was supposed by the North to settle the question of slavery in this new territory, as the question with regard to the former territories had been settled forever.

The matter with regard to slavery was now settled, and no disturbance could be raised except by tearing up some of the Compromises with regard to the territory where it was already settled. The South had got all they claimed, and all the territory south of the compromise line had been appropriated to slavery; they had gotten and eaten their half of the loaf of bread; but all the other half had not been eaten yet; there was the extensive territory of Nebraska secured to freedom, that had not been settled yet. And the slaveholding power attempted to snatch that away. So on Jan. 4, 1854, Douglas introduced the famous Nebraska Bill, which was so constructed before its passage as to repeal the Missouri Compromise, and open all of the territory to the introduction of slavery. It was done without the consent of the people, and against their wishes, for if the matter had been put to vote before the people directly, whether that should be made a slave territory, they would have indignantly voted it down. But it was got up unexpectedly by the people, hurried through, and now they were called upon to sanction it.

They ought to make a strong expression against the imposition; that would prevent the consummation of the scheme. The people were the sovereigns, and the representatives their servants, and it was time to make them sensible of this truly democratic principle. They could get the Compromise restored. They were told that they could not because the Senate was Nebraska, and would be for years. Then fill the lower House with true Anti-Nebraska members, and that would be an expression of the sentiment of the people. And furthermore that expression would be heeded by the Senate. If this State should instruct Douglas to vote for the repeal of the Nebraska Bill, he must do it, for "the doctrine of instructions" was a part of his political creed. And he was not certain he would not be glad to vote its repeal anyhow, if it would help him fairly out of the scrape. It was so with other Senators; they will be sure to improve the first opportunity to vote its repeal. The people could get it repealed, if they resolved to do it.[2]

[2] An additional paragraph notes that lack of space prevents the *Pantagraph* from giving "the Speaker's lucid arguments against the bill." In another column a communication from "A Hearer" takes exception to a portion of Lincoln's speech which is not covered by the report, observing, "He recommends that the people should unite energetically for the restoration of the Missouri Compromise, but enjoined upon them not to oppose the Fugitive Slave Law, which would be repelling wrong with wrong. It was a compromise, and as citizens we were bound to stand up to it, and enforce it. Afterwards he added: 'I own, if I were called upon by a Marshal, to assist in catching a fugitive slave, I should suggest to him that others could run a great deal faster than I could.' . . .

"He said he would go in for sustaining any Fugitive Slave Law, that did not expose a free negro to any more danger of being carried into slavery, than our present criminal laws do an innocent person to the danger of being hung. But can this be said of the present Fugitive Slave Law . . . ? The fact is it does not. . . ."

To Mason Brayman[1]

M. Brayman, Esq   Bloomington
Dear Sir: Sept. 23, 1854

This is the last day of court here, and being about to leave, I have drawn on the I.C. R R Co or rather on you on their account, for $100, which the McLean County Bank have negociated for me. I have directed them to have the draft presented to you. Will you please see that it shall be honored?

The reason I have taken this liberty is, that since last fall, by your request I have declined all new business against the road, and out of which I suppose I could have realized several hundred dollars; have attended, both at DeWitt and here to a great variety of little business for the Co, most of which, however, remains unfinished, and have received nothing. I wish now to be charged with this sum, to be taken into account on settlement. Truly Yours &c   A. LINCOLN

P.S. The draft is in favor of Mr. Pardee,[2] who is Cashier of the Bank.

[1] ALS-F, ISLA.   [2] Theron Pardee.

Speech at Bloomington, Illinois[1]

September 26, 1854

Mr. LINCOLN said:

He would begin by noticing that part of the Judge's speech with which he closed—(the homily upon the Know-Nothings). And he would say on the start, that, like many others he *Knew Nothing* in regard to the Know-Nothings, and he had serious doubts whether such an organization existed—if such was the case, he had been slighted, for no intimation thereof had been vouchsafed to him. But he would say in all seriousness, that if such an organization, secret or public, as Judge Douglas had described, really existed, and had for its object interference with the rights of foreigners, the Judge could not deprecate it more severely than himself. If there was an order styled the Know-Nothings, and there was any thing bad in it, he was unqualifiedly against it; and if there was anything good in it, why, he said God speed it! [Laughter and applause.][2] But he would like to be informed on one point: if such a society existed, and the members were bound by such horrid oaths as Judge Douglas told about, he would really like to know how the Judge found out his secrets? [Renewed laughter.]

He would, before proceeding to the main argument, touch upon another subject. The Judge had called the new party *Black Republicans*. He might call names, and thereby pander to prejudice, as much as he chose: he [Mr. L.] would not bandy such language with him; but inasmuch as the Judge said there had been a swallowing up of the whigs by the Black Republicans or Abolitionists, he would like to have him look at his own case. Where now were

[1] Peoria *Weekly Republican*, October 6, 1854.
[2] Brackets are in the source unless otherwise indicated.

the Democratic majorities that were received by Mr. Pierce in 1852? Where are the 15,000 in New Hampshire and the 5,000 in Maine? Where are the former majorities of the democracy in Connecticut [and][3] in Iowa? Are they not swallowed up? and by what element? What right had Judge Douglas to intimate that none but abolitionists and tender-footed whigs were embraced in the "fusion," and that whigs were the only ones "swallowed up"? The abolitionists had swallowed up a great many of the Judge's friends, and more of them, if any thing, than of whigs. But he didn't think there was a very serious or alarming swallowing-up on either side—nothing in the least dangerous save to the Judge and his allies.

Mr. LINCOLN then proceeded to meet the main position of Mr. Douglas:

What was the Missouri Compromise? shortly after the organization of the Government we acquired the Northwest Territory. Under the auspices of Jefferson an Ordinance was enacted in 1787 prohibiting slavery forever in that territory. Ohio, Indiana, Illinois, Michigan and Wisconsin came into the Union as free States, under what is *now* called an infraction of the sarced right of self-government. By that infraction a section of country whose career in prosperity has no parallel, has been thus secured to freedom. In 1803 Mr. Jefferson purchased for $15,000,000 the territory of Louisiana, which was afterwards divided and two territories formed therefrom—New Orleans and St. Louis. New Orleans came into the Union as a State, under the title of Louisiana, in 1812, and met with no opposition on account of her slavery, because it already existed there. In 1818 Missouri manifested a desire to come into the Union. A portion of the States set up against authorizing her to form a State constitution. A bill might have been passed through the House admitting Missouri without the slavery restriction, but it could not have passed the Senate. Finally the matter was settled by the Northern members consenting to the admission of Missouri, with the understanding that in consideration thereof the South consented that slavery should forever be prohibited from entering any territory north of 36 degrees 30 minutes. A new contest then sprung up in regard to the clause which the bill contained excluding free negroes from the State, and another compromise was tacked on to the old one—altogether forming the Missouri Compromise. The question which caused the whole controversy was in reference to slavery in the territory that we purchased of France—including the present States of Louisiana, Arkansas, Missouri and

[3] Editors' insertion.

[235]

Iowa, and the territories of Minnesota, Kansas and Nebraska— *and over that only.*

After this Compromise had stood a good long time, a gentleman, in language much finer and more eloquent than he [Mr. L.] was capable of constructing, expressed himself in reference to it as follows:

All the evidences of public opinion at that day seemed to indicate that this Compromise had become canonized in the hearts of the American people as a sacred thing, which no ruthless hand should attempt to disturb.

This was certainly very strong, and it was spoken after the Missouri Compromise had been in existence twenty-nine years? Who was it that uttered this sentiment? What "Black Republican"?—[Immense laughter. A voice "Douglas."] No other than Judge Douglas himself. A more beautiful or more forcible expression was not to be found in the English language.

Who, then, was or had been opposed to the Missouri Compromise? [Sensation and applause.]

The manner in which Judge Douglas proved that the Democracy were formerly opposed to the Missouri Compromise was by asserting that they united upon Gen. Cass's Nicholson letter, which embodied a doctrine contrary to the principle of the Restrictive Line. One year previous to the writing of that letter the Wilmot Proviso was introduced, and Gen. Cass had on several occasions expressed himself in favor of it. Those expressions had cut him off from Southern votes, and he found he must do something to regain the good opinion of the South: so, on sober-second thought, he concluded to write that famous letter, which secured his nomination for the Presidency in 1848—and also secured his defeat. [Laughter.] But Judge Douglas said that the Democracy united on the Nicholson letter, and consequently repudiated the Missouri Compromise, as all the other parties had previously done. He tells us, however, that he introduced a proposition to extend the Missouri Compromise to the Pacific. *This was several months* AFTER *the Nicholson letter was written,* and thus the Judge was in favor of the Compromise after his whole party had united upon a doctrine which he now says is inconsistent with it! We must all have our mouths stopped by Judge Douglas, and receive his assertion that we have all been opposed to the Missouri Compromise, but he himself could have voted to extend it clear through to the Pacific. *He* was the only person ever in favor of the Compromise— who, then, passed it in the Senate in 1848? These (said Mr. Lincoln, in his earnest style) are *all afterthoughts*—ALL, ALL.

[236]

The Whigs voted against the extension of the Missouri Compromise to the Pacific. Now could that pass as a reasonable argument in favor of the Judge's proposition that they were against the Compromise itself? If, said Mr. Lincoln, I and my partner erect a house together, and he proposes to build an addition to it, do I, by my opposition to his plan, intimate a desire to have the whole house burned or torn down? It might just as well be asserted that a horse was not a horse, or that black was white, as that the refusal to enlarge or extend anything was the same as an expression of opinion against it. Yet this was the same kind of sophistry used by Judge Douglas; and if you take away this foundation, all his arguments on this point fall to the ground. It is hard, said Mr. LIN-COLN, to argue against such nonsense. The Judge puts words in the mouths of his audience with which to call them fools. Because no one interrupts him with a denial of his assertions, he takes them as admitted by the people, and builds upon them his monstrous and ridiculous propositions. He knows very well that the people have NOT always been opposed to the Missouri Compromise, [Many cries of No! No! Never!] although *no one answered his question to-day in the affirmative.* [Mr. Douglas had said in his speech "Is there a man here, except myself, who ever wa? in favor of the Missouri Compromise?" and a blank silence followed.—*Ed. Rep.*]

Mr. LINCOLN then reviewed the New Mexican question, in its bearings upon the present issue. President Polk concluded that he could acquire more territory if he had more money, and asked Congress for $2,000,000 with which to purchase New Mexico. To the bill granting this sum Mr. Wilmot moved an amendment, providing that slavery should be prohibited from entering the territory under consideration. This defeated the bill at that time. The Wilmot Proviso had nothing to do with the Northwest Territory or the Louisiana purchase, and the Missouri Compromise had nothing to do with New Mexico or Oregon, or with any other territory save that to which it was originally applied. By the treaty of Peace with Mexico in 1848 we acquired California, and in two years she applied for admission as a State. She came with a constitution prohibiting slavery, but there was a sufficient majority in the Senate to prevent her entering free. Then the question of boundary between Texas and New Mexico arose, and added to the agitation. The old fugitive slave law was then found to be inefficient. And finally the famous Georgia Pen, in Washington, where negroes were bought and sold within sight of the National Capitol, began to grow offensive in the nostrils of all good men,

Southerners as well as Northerners. All these subjects got into the Omnibus Bill, which was intended as a compromise between the North and the South, and the measures in which, although defeated in the aggregate, were all passed separately. The measures which the North gained by the passage of the Adjustment of 1850 were, the admission of California with a free Constitution and the discontinuance of the Georgia Pen; and those which the South gained were, the passage of the Fugitive Slave Law and the territorial bills of Utah and New Mexico, and the settlement of the Texas boundary. The North gained two measures and the South three. Such was the Compromise of 1850—a measure for the benefit of the South as well as of the North, and acquiesced in by the Whig and Democratic parties of the country.

Now what was there in the Compromise Measures of '50 that repudiated the Missouri Compromise? The North secured that portion of the Louisiana purchase north of 36.30 to freedom, by giving the South what they demanded as an equivalent therefor, namely, Missouri. We got it fairly and honestly, by paying for it: then what reason was there in endeavoring to make the stipulation upon which we purchased it apply as a principle to other and all future territories? The Missouri Compromise was a contract made between the North and the South, by which the former got all the Louisiana purchase north, and the latter all south, of the line of 36.30 *within that territory*. There was no show of sense in endeavoring to make this bargain apply to any future territory acquired by the United States.

Mr. L. reviewed with much keenness the sophistry, upon which great dependence is placed by the advocates of the Nebraska scheme, that the principle of allowing States to settle their own domestic institutions was applicable to the territories. He traced the relation that existed between them and the Government, showed them to be dependencies of it, and held up in a proper light the absurd proposition that Government could lay no restriction upon soil which it had bought and paid for, and over which it exercised a parental care.

He contended that the only way slavery could get a foothold anywhere was by going in by slow degrees, little by little, before there were people enough to form a territorial government. Then, when the government is to be organized, slavery is already on the ground—a "local institution"—and has an equal chance with freedom. Said Mr. L, if you will keep slavery out of any territory until there are 50,000 inhabitants, I will risk the chances of its ever being established there. He would venture on the good sense of fifty thousand people—that number could keep slavery out of South Carolina, were it not for the fact that [it][4] is already there. The strong argument that Kansas will be a slave State is that slavery *now exists* there, by recognition of Congress. It has already obtained a foothold, and is an institution of the territory— one of their "domestic institutions."

The sacred right of self-government, rightly understood, no one appreciated more than himself. But the Nebraska measure, so far from carrying out that right, was the grossest violation of it. The principle that men or States have the right of regulating their own affairs, is morally right and politically wise. Individuals held the sacred right to regulate their own family affairs; communities might arrange their own internal matter to suit themselves; States might make their own statutes, subject only to the Constituion of the whole country;—no one disagreed with this doctrine. It had, however, no application to the question at present at issue namely, whether slavery, a moral, social and political evil, should or should not exist in territory owned by the Government, over which the Government had control, and which looked to the Government for protection—unless it be true that a negro is not a man; if not, then it is no business of ours whether or not he is enslaved upon soil which belongs to us, any more than it is our business to trouble ourselves about the oyster-trade, cranberry-trade, or any other legitimate traffic carried on by the people in territory owned by the Government. If we admit that a negro is not a man, then it is right for the Government to own him and trade in the race, and it is right to allow the South to take their peculiar institution with them and plant it upon the virgin soil of Kansas and Nebraska. If the negro is not a man, it is consistent to apply the sacred right of popular sovereignty to the question as to whether the people of the territories shall or shall not have slavery; but if the negro, upon soil where slavery is not legalized by law and sanctioned by custom, *is* a man, then there is not even the shadow of popular sovereignty in allowing the first settlers upon such soil to decide whether it shall be right in all future time to hold men in bondage there.

Judge Douglas had said that the Illinois Legislation passed resolutions instructing him to repeal the Missouri Compromise. But said Mr. L., the Judge, when he refers to resolutions of instruction, always gets those which never passed both houses of the Legislature. The Legislature [passed][5] a resolution, upon this subject which the Judge either forgot or didn't choose to read. No man

[4] Editors' insertion.　　　[5] Editors' insertion.

who voted to pull down the Missouri Compromise represented the people, and [the Legislature]⁶ of this State never instructed Douglas or any one else to commit that act. And yet the Judge had told the people that they *were* in favor of repealing the Missouri Compromise, and all must acquiesce in his assumption or be denounced as abolitionists. What sophistry is this, said Mr. L., to contend and insist that you did instruct him to effect the repeal of the Missouri Compromise, when you know you never thought of such a thought of it [Cries of "No! No!!"]—that all the people of Illinois have always been opposed to that Compromise, when no man will say that he ever thought of its repeal previous to the introduction of the Nebraska bill.

⁶ Editors' insertion.

Speech at Springfield, Illinois¹

October 4, 1854

Taking up the anti-slavery ordinance of 1787, that had been applied to all the North-west Territory, Mr. Lincoln presented that act of the fathers of our republic, the vindicators of our liberty, and the framers of our government, as the *best* exposition of their views of slavery as an institution. It was also a most striking commentary of their political faith, and showed how the views of those political sages, to whom we owe liberty, government, and all, comported with the new-fangled doctrines of popular rights, invented in these degenerate latter days to cloak the spread of slavery.

Did not the ordinance of '87 declare that slavery or involuntary servitude, (except as a punishment for crime,) *should never exist* in the territory north and west of the Ohio river—the territory out of which have been successively carved the States of Ohio, Indiana, Illinois, Michigan and Wisconsin? Were not the people who were to settle that territory and form those States, capable of managing

¹ *Illinois Journal*, October 5, 1854. This summary indicates that Lincoln made much the same speech which he delivered at Peoria on October 15 (*vide infra*), and which has come to be associated primarily with that city rather than Springfield. The speech at Springfield according to the *Journal* "commenced at 2 o'clock" and continued "above three hours," which is approximately the length of the Peoria speech. It may be noted also that Lincoln had covered some of the same ground in his speeches at Bloomington, September 12 and 26, and in preceding speeches. At Springfield, Stephen A. Douglas had spoken on the preceding day, remaining to hear Lincoln's reply and to give a rebuttal. According to the *Journal*, Douglas followed Lincoln with a speech of two hours, which "was adroit and plausible, but had not the marble of logic in it." According to the Democratic *Illinois State Register* (October 6, 1854), however, Douglas "pounded him to pumice with his terrible war club of retort and argument."

their own affairs—of deciding all questions of domestic concern—
slavery included—for themselves? Why, then, did the founders of
liberty and republicanism on this continent tie their hands—rob
them of popular sovereignty—deny them the right of self-government in all things? Mr. Lincoln clearly showed that the ordinance
was recognized, lived up to, and obeyed. And observe its fruits,
said the orator—tyrannical and oppressive as its principle, in these
evil days, has come to be considered. No States in the world have
ever advanced as rapidly in population, wealth, the arts and ap-
pliances of life, and now have such promise of prospective greatness, as the very States that were born under the ordinance of '87,
and were deprived of the blessings of "popular sovereignty," as
contained in the Nebraska bill, and without which the people of
Kansas and Nebraska cannot get along at all! I fear, said the
speaker, that we of the north western States, never knew the depth
of our political misfortunes imposed by the ordinance of '87—we
never knew how miserable we were!

Mr. Lincoln next took up the Missouri Compromise, and
showed that it was a real Compromise between two parties—the
north and south—in which each had yielded something it had contended for, and obtained something it desired, and with which both
became satisfied and grew to reverence and uphold. Under the
Missouri Compromise the South had got Missouri and Arkansas,
slave States; the north got Iowa and would have had Nebraska. But
at this time one party having exhausted its share of the bargain,
demands an abrogation of the Compromise and a re-division of the
property.

Coming along down with history Mr. Lincoln recited the question that sprung up when we obtained territory from Mexico after
the late war. Mr. Wilmot, a political friend of Judge Douglas, had
proposed to make *all* that territory free. Judge Douglas had proposed to extend the Missouri Compromise line westward and make
the northern half of it free. Mr. Lincoln said that he had favored
the former and opposed the latter proposition. But because he and
others had done this, it had been falsely inferred that he and they
had *abandoned* the Missouri Compromise line and authorised its
destruction. If a man comes to me, said Mr. Lincoln, and advises
me to build an addition to my house and I decline to do so, shall
that man burn my house down, and say I have decided against
any house at all, because I am unwilling to spread it out and extend it? Not more absurd is such a case then to suppose that those
who fought against the extension of slavery into any territory at
the time free, were really manifesting hostility to the Missouri

Compromise line—a barrier which preserved a large territory to freedom. In connexion with the history of the Missouri Compromise and its pacification of the agitation that brought it forth, Mr. Lincoln took occasion to read from Judge Douglas' speech delivered in 1849 from the same stand from which Mr. Lincoln was speaking, in which Judge Douglas had declared that Compromise was "sacred;" having an "origin a[kin]² to that of the constitution" and [that] no "ruthless hand" would ever be found to disturb it. The reading of this extract brought down repeated and enthusiastic applause; which Judge Douglas didn't enjoy.

Mr. Lincoln put it home, direct to Judge Douglas, that after such extravagant encomiums on the Missouri Compromise—declaring it "akin" to the Constitution in its origin—it illy became *him* or others to apply unseemly names and epithets to himself (Lincoln) or other American citizens, who still retained a reverence and respect for the honored measure.

Having given thus the history of *Slavery prohibition*, in this government, showing that it was originated by the founders of the government, applied in '87, enforced ever since, ingrafted in all the great North West States, recognized in the Missouri Compromise, endorsed and approved by all Statesmen up to the present day, and so rapturously lauded by Judge Douglas himself in 1849, in the extract read from his speech, Mr. Lincoln bewailed it as a descending from the high republican faith of our ancestors, to repudiate that principle and to declare by the highest act of our government that we have no longer a choice between freedom and slavery—that both are equal with us—that we yield our territories as readily to one as the other! This was ignoble teaching. We were proclaiming ourselves political hypocrites before the world, by thus fostering Human Slavery and proclaiming ourselves, at the same time, the sole friends of Human Freedom.

It is vain, said Mr. Lincoln, for any advocate of the repeal of the Missouri Compromise to contend that it gives no sanction or encouragement to slavery. If I have a field, said the speaker, around which the cattle or the hogs linger and crave to pass the fence, and I go and tear down the fence, will it be supposed that I do not by that act encourage them to enter? *Even the hogs would know better*—Much more *men*, who are a higher order of the animal world.

The Missouri Compromise forbade Slavery to go north of 36.30. Our government breaks down that restriction and opens the door for slavery to enter where before it could not go. This is practically

² The paper is torn. Restorations are the editors'.

legislating for slavery, recognising it, endorsing it, propagating it, extending it. And this, said the speaker, is a woful coming down from the early faith of the republic.

Mr. Lincoln next proceeded to consider some of the excuses—or, lest that term should be offensive—some of the arguments of those who justify the destruction of the Missouri Compromise line. Beginning with Mr. Douglas, he remarked that that gentleman's defence of the repeal rested on two points: first, the popular will in favor of the repeal as manifested in previous legislation of Congress, and the instructions of the Illinois legislature to himself; and secondly, the soundness of the principle of the repeal—which make it right in itself. Mr. Lincoln took these up in order.

It was contended by Mr. Douglas that the Compromise of 1850 sanctioned principles that annulled the Missouri Compromise and required its formal repeal. This Mr. Lincoln denied—and denying, appealed to all the rules of legal interpretation. It was not intended by the legislators who adopted the Compromises of 1850, to repeal the Mo. Compromise, and the intention of the lawmaker, if it could be got at, was fully conclusive on that point. Mr. Lincoln recited and examined the Compromise-Measures of 1850. They consisted of five acts. 1. The admission of California as a free State. 2. The organization of Utah and New Mexico Territories, without a slavery prohibition. 3. The payment of $10,-000,000 to Texas and provision for new States to be formed from her territory. 4. The Fugitive Slave Law. 5. The prohibition of the Slave trade in the district of Columbia.

Mr. Lincoln maintained that a law could only be construed to operate on the *subject matter* of it; and that it was a sufficient reply to the argument he was answering, to say that not one of the Compromises of 1850 alluded to, or could, by indirection even, be understood to apply to Kansas and Nebraska. Those territories had already been legislated for—that legislation had become "canonized in the hearts of the people"—it was supposed that "no ruthless hand" would ever be reckless enough to disturb it—and it could not therefore, in any reasonable mind, be understood that the Compromises of 1850 were meant and intended to disturb it. Those Compromises were good for what they covered—no more.

Mr. Lincoln might have made his argument on this point doubly strong, (if indeed it had needed strength,) by calling attention to the fact that the Compromises of 1850, (in the bill relating to Texas) in direct and explicit terms recognised and re-reaffirmed [*sic*] the validity of the Missouri Compromise. This branch of Mr. Douglas's justification fails.

With regard to the instructions by the Illinois legislature, which Mr. Douglas quoted as his further justification in going for the repeal of the Missouri Compromise, Mr. Lincoln said he had looked in vain to find those instructions, where they should be. He did not say that no such resolutions had passed—he only averred that he had not been able to find them. Mr. Douglas here rose and proffered Mr. L. the reading of a copy of the resolutions. Mr. L. declined. "I know," said he "what resolutions Mr. Douglas is in the habit of reading, but they only passed one branch of the legislature." Mr. Douglas was greatly annoyed by this exposure, and interrupted Mr. Lincoln again; but Mr. L. left the subject by kindly requesting Mr. Douglas, if it was all the same to him, to read hereafter, in his public speeches, those resolutions which did pass the legislature, and not those that didn't.

In passing to the other excuses of the Douglas men for the repeal of the Missouri Compromise, Mr. Lincoln adverted to their usual assertion, that slavery will not go into Kansas and Nebraska, and that therefore there is no need of any bother about it. Mr. Lincoln pointed out on a small map he had before him, the old north-western boundary of Missouri. Slavery, said Mr. L., lost no time going up to the last limits of that boundary: In the course of time a "considerable scope of country adjoining north-west Missouri, but still lying east of the Missouri river" called the Platte country, was desired by Missouri, and to give the State a natural boundary" it was determined to extend the Missouri boundary line over that Platte country. It was done. And slavery lost no time in marching right in and going to the utmost verge of that boundary. Now, said Mr. Lincoln, it is said that there are more slaves in that extreme north-west portion of Missouri, jutting broadside against Kansas and Nebraska than in any other equal area in Missouri! Will it not go, then, into Kansas and Nebraska, if permitted? Why not? What will hinder? Do cattle nibble a pasture right up to a division fence, crop all close under the fence, and even put their necks through and gather what they can reach, over the line, and still refuse to pass over into that next green pasture, even if the fence shall be thrown down?

Mr. Lincoln now came to the arguments in favor of the Missouri Compromise repeal, or on the ground that the repeal is just and right in itself. He demanded what kind of "right" was meant in the proposition. He denied that there was any "constitutional" right to the repeal. He had already shown that the Mo. Compromise had received every sanction that any law could have to establish its constitutionality. It has been originated in principle, in the ordinance of '87, concurrently almost with our Constitution, and by the founders of it, who certainly understood its principles. It has been sustained by all courts and almost every great Statesman down to this day. What constitutional right existed for its repeal? Or what *legal* right? Can any one point to a law, in any of the past legislation of the country that creates the right named? The Compromises of 1850 are the only measures relied on, and it is already shown that they re-affirm instead of annul the right of Freedom under the Compromise.

What *natural* right requires Kansas and Nebraska to be opened to Slavery? Is not slavery universally granted to be, in the abstract, a gross outrage on the law of nature? Have not all civilized nations, our own among them, made the Slave trade capital, and classed it with piracy and murder? Is it not held to be the great wrong of the world? Do not the Southern people, the Slaveholders themselves, spurn the domestic slave dealer, refuse to associate with him, or let their families associate with his family, as long as the taint of his infamous calling is known?

Shall that institution, which carries a rot and a murrain in it, claim any right, by the law of nature, to stand by the side of Freedom, on a Soil that is free?

What *social or political* right, had slavery to demand the repeal of the Missouri Compromise, and claim entrance into States where it has never before existed? The theory of our government is Universal Freedom. "All men are created free and equal," says the Declaration of Independence. The word "Slavery" is not found in the Constitution. The clause that covers the institution is one that sends it *back* where it exists, not *abroad* where it does not. All legislation that has recognized or tolerated its extension, has been associated with a compensation—a Compromise—showing that it was something that moved forward, not by its own right, but by its own wrong.

It is said that the slaveholder has the same [political][3] right to take his negroes to Kansas that a freeman has to take his hogs or his horses. This would be true if negroes were property in the same sense that hogs and horses are. But is this the case? It is notoriously not so. Southern men do not treat their negroes as they do their horses. There are 400,000 free negroes in the United States. All the race came to this country as slaves. How came these negroes free? At $500 each, their value is $2,000,000. Can you find *two million dollars worth* of any other kind of property running about without an owner? These negroes are free, because

[3] Brackets in the source.

their owners, in some way and at some time, felt satisfied that the creatures had mind, feeling, souls, family affections, hopes, joys, sorrows—something that made them more than *hogs or horses*. Shall the Slaveholders require us to be more heartless and mean than they, and treat those beings as *property* which they themselves have never been able to treat so?

But there is another view of this branch of the subject, more unanswerable still. The citizens of Slave States, have a political power in the general government beyond their single votes and this violates the equality between American Citizens. Mr. Lincoln instanced Maine & South Carolina. Both these states have the same number of members of Congress, of Presidential electors, the same control therefore in National affairs. But Maine has more than twice as many free white citizens as South Carolina. The citizen of South Carolina is therefore twice as good or influential [and a fraction over,]⁴ as a free white citizen in a Free State. The State in which the number of negroes is the smallest, in proportion, still makes a voter in that State equal to one man and a tenth in a free State.

The basis of representation as fixed in the U.S. Constitution, making five negroes equal to three whites, had fixed this inequality. This Mr. Lincoln did not object to. It was "in the bond" and he would live faithfully by it. But certainly the Free States have the "right" to say whether or not more partners should be taken in on such terms. For himself he was unwilling that his neighbor, living on an equality by his side in Illinois, should by moving over into Kansas be elevated into a state of superiority over himself and become a man and a tenth, whereas before he was formerly only one man, like himself!

If this is "equal rights" for the Kansas settler, he would be glad to know what became of his own rights, and the rights of the people of the Free States; while they were thus made into only *fractions of men*, by the creation of *new* Slave States. It is said that the adoption or rejection of slavery in Kansas and Nebraska, concerns the people of those Territories alone—it is no business of ours. This is false, said Mr. Lincoln, it concerns our dearest rights, our equality with the citizens of those territories—which we are entitled to by every consideration of justice and constitutional guarantees.

The right of the people of Kansas and Nebraska to make themselves *superior* in political power and privilege to the individual citizens of the Free States, was thus effectually riddled, exposed

⁴ Brackets in the source.

and exploded by Mr. Lincoln, and the hearty and long continued plaudits of his great audience of freemen, showed how truly he had touched chords of their hearts.

Thus perished every vestige of excuse, offered by Mr. Douglas for the repeal of the Missouri Compromise. The act remained before Mr. L., Judge Douglas, and the audience, a naked humbug, a foul wrong, perpetrated under false pretences, sustained by weak inventions and afterthoughts, justified by the most miserable sophistries, and under the cloak of the right of the people of the territories to decide the slavery question for themselves, seeking to degrade the citizens of the Free States into mere atoms or fractions of American citizens, whose "rights" in the premises are, to be lorded over by a population outvoting them (through their negroes,) and to kiss the hand that thus humiliated them.

We cannot follow Mr. Lincoln further to-day. His remarks about Union saving were sound and patriotic, and his appeal to the Southern States for moderation and forbearance, fraternal and eloquent. He did not set so much store on the restoration of the Missouri Compromise by act of legislation, as he did on the immediate and effectual restoration of it by popular sentiment. This last was possible. Let the decided demonstration of the Free States secure it. That being done, the Union would again be safe and the people happy.

Speech at Peoria, Illinois[1]

October 16, 1854

MR. LINCOLN'S SPEECH.

On Monday, October 16, Senator DOUGLAS, by appointment, addressed a large audience at Peoria. When he closed he was greeted with six hearty cheers; and the band in attendance played a stirring air. The crowd then began to call for LINCOLN, who, as Judge Douglas had announced was, by agreement, to answer him. Mr. Lincoln then took the stand, and said—

"I do not arise to speak now, if I can stipulate with the audience to meet me here at half past 6 or at 7 o'clock. It is now several minutes past five, and Judge Douglas has spoken over three hours. If you hear me at all, I wish you to hear me thro'. It will take me as long as it has taken him. That will carry us beyond eight o'clock at night. Now every one of you who can remain that long, can just as well get his supper, meet me at seven, and remain one hour or

1 *Illinois Journal,* October 21, 23, 24, 25, 26, 27, 28, 1854.

two later. The Judge has already informed you that he is to have an hour to reply to me. I doubt not but you have been a little surprised to learn that I have consented to give one of his high reputation and known ability, this advantage of me. Indeed, my consenting to it, though reluctant, was not wholly unselfish; for I suspected if it were understood, that the Judge was entirely done, you democrats would leave, and not hear me; but by giving him the close, I felt confident you would stay for the fun of hearing him skin me."

The audience signified their assent to the arrangement, and adjourned to 7 o'clock P.M., at which time they re-assembled, and Mr. LINCOLN spoke substantially as follows:

The repeal of the Missouri Compromise, and the propriety of its restoration, constitute the subject of what I am about to say.

As I desire to present my own connected view of this subject, my remarks will not be, specifically, an answer to Judge Douglas; yet, as I proceed, the main points he has presented will arise, and will receive such respectful attention as I may be able to give them.

I wish further to say, that I do not propose to question the patriotism, or to assail the motives of any man, or class of men; but rather to strictly confine myself to the naked merits of the question.

I also wish to be no less than National in all the positions I may take; and whenever I take ground which others have thought, or may think, narrow, sectional and dangerous to the Union, I hope to give a reason, which will appear sufficient, at least to some, why I think differently.

And, as this subject is no other, than part and parcel of the larger general question of domestic-slavery, I wish to MAKE and to KEEP the distinction between the EXISTING institution, and the EXTENSION of it, so broad, and so clear, that no honest man can misunderstand me, and no dishonest one, successfully misrepresent me.

In order to [get?] a clear understanding of what the Missouri Compromise is, a short history of the preceding kindred subjects will perhaps be proper. When we established our independence, we did not own, or claim, the country to which this compromise applies. Indeed, strictly speaking, the confederacy then owned no country at all; the States respectively owned the country within their limits; and some of them owned territory beyond their strict State limits. Virginia thus owned the North-Western territory— the country out of which the principal part of Ohio, all Indiana, all

Illinois, all Michigan and all Wisconsin, have since been formed. She also owned (perhaps within her then limits) what has since been formed into the State of Kentucky. North Carolina thus owned what is now the State of Tennessee; and South Carolina and Georgia, in separate parts, owned what are now Mississippi and Alabama. Connecticut, I think, owned the little remaining part of Ohio—being the same where they now send Giddings to Congress, and beat all creation at making cheese. These territories, together with the States themselves, constituted all the country over which the confederacy then claimed any sort of jurisdiction. We were then living under the Articles of Confederation, which were superceded by the Constitution several years afterwards. The question of ceding these territories to the general government was set on foot. Mr. Jefferson, the author of the Declaration of Independence, and otherwise a chief actor in the revolution; then a delegate in Congress; afterwards twice President; who was, is, and perhaps will continue to be, the most distinguished politician of our history; a Virginian by birth and continued residence, and withal, a slave-holder; conceived the idea of taking that occasion, to prevent slavery ever going into the north-western territory. He prevailed on the Virginia Legislature to adopt his views, and to cede the territory, making the prohibition of slavery therein, a condition of the deed.[2] Congress accepted the cession, with the condition; and in the first Ordinance (which the acts of Congress were then called) for the government of the territory, provided that slavery should never be permitted therein. This is the famed ordinance of '87 so often spoken of. Thenceforward, for sixty-one years, and until in 1848, the last scrap of this territory came into the Union as the State of Wisconsin, all parties acted in quiet obedience to this ordinance. It is now what Jefferson foresaw and intended—the happy home of teeming millions of free, white, prosperous people, and no slave amongst them.

Thus, with the author of the declaration of Independence, the policy of prohibiting slavery in new territory originated. Thus, away back of the constitution, in the pure fresh, free breath of the revolution, the State of Virginia, and the National congress put that policy in practice. Thus through sixty odd of the best years of the republic did that policy steadily work to its great and beneficent end. And thus, in those five states, and five millions of free, enterprising people, we have before us the rich fruits of this pol-

[2] Lincoln later authorized correction of this statement; it was not a condition of the deed. See Lincoln to John L. Scripps, June 16, 1860, and to James O. Putnam, September 13, 1860, *infra*.

icy. But *now* new light breaks upon us. Now congress declares this ought never to have been; and the like of it, must never be again. The sacred right of self government is grossly violated by it! We even find some men, who drew their first breath, and every other breath of their lives, under this very restriction, now live in dread of absolute suffocation, if they should be restricted in the "sacred right" of taking slaves to Nebraska. That *perfect* liberty they sigh for—the liberty of making slaves of other people—Jefferson never thought of; their own father never thought of; they never thought of themselves, a year ago. How fortunate for them, they did not sooner become sensible of their great misery! Oh, how difficult it is to treat with respect, such assaults upon all we have ever really held sacred.

But to return to history. In 1803 we purchased what was then called Louisiana, of France. It included the now states of Louisiana, Arkansas, Missouri, and Iowa; also the territory of Minnesota, and the present bone of contention, Kansas and Nebraska. Slavery already existed among the French at New Orleans; and, to some extent, at St. Louis. In 1812 Louisiana came into the Union as a slave state, without controversy. In 1818 or '19, Missouri showed signs of a wish to come in with slavery. This was resisted by northern members of Congress; and thus began the first great slavery agitation in the nation. This controversy lasted several months, and became very angry and exciting; the House of Representatives voting steadily for the prohibition of slavery in Missouri, and the Senate voting as steadily against it. Threats of breaking up the Union were freely made; and the ablest public men of the day became seriously alarmed. At length a compromise was made, in which, like all compromises, both sides yielded something. It was a law passed on the 6th day of March, 1820, providing that Missouri might come into the Union *with* slavery, but that in all the remaining part of the territory purchased of France, which lies north of 36 degrees and 30 minutes north latitude, slavery should never be permitted. This provision of law, *is the Missouri Compromise.* In excluding slavery North of the line, the same language is employed as in the Ordinance of '87. It directly applied to Iowa, Minnesota, and to the present bone of contention, Kansas and Nebraska. Whether there should or should not, be slavery south of that line, nothing was said in the law; but Arkansas constituted the principal remaining part, south of the line; and it has since been admitted as a slave state without serious controversy. More recently, Iowa, north of the line, came in as a free state without controversy. Still later, Minnesota, north of the line, had a territorial organization without controversy. Texas principally south of the line, and West of Arkansas; though originally within the purchase from France, had, in 1819, been traded off to Spain, in our treaty for the acquisition of Florida. It had thus become a part of Mexico. Mexico revolutionized and became independent of Spain. American citizens began settling rapidly, with their slaves in the southern part of Texas. Soon they revolutionized against Mexico, and established an independent government of their own, adopting a constitution, with slavery, strongly resembling the constitutions of our slave states. By still another rapid move, Texas, claiming a boundary much further West, than when we parted with her in 1819, was brought back to the United States, and admitted into the Union as a slave state. There then was little or no settlement in the northern part of Texas, a considerable portion of which lay north of the Missouri line; and in the resolutions admitting her into the Union, the Missouri restriction was expressly extended westward across her territory. This was in 1845, only nine years ago.

Thus originated the Missouri Compromise; and thus has it been respected down to 1845. And even four years later, in 1849, our distinguished Senator, in a public address, held the following language in relation to it:

"The Missouri Compromise had been in practical operation for about a quarter of a century, and had received the sanction and approbation of men of all parties in every section of the Union. It had allayed all sectional jealousies and irritations growing out of this vexed question, and harmonized and tranquilized the whole country. It had given to Henry Clay, as its prominent champion, the proud sobriquet of the *"Great Pacificator"* and by that title and for that service, his political friends had repeatedly appealed to the people to rally under his standard, as a presidential candidate, as the man who had exhibited the patriotism and the power to suppress, an unholy and treasonable agitation, and preserve the Union. He was not aware that any man or any party from any section of the Union, had ever urged as an objection to Mr. Clay, that he was the great champion of the Missouri Compromise. On the contrary, the effort was made by the opponents of Mr. Clay, to prove that he was not entitled to the exclusive merit of that great patriotic measure, and that the honor was equally due to others as well as to him, for securing its adoption—that it had its origin in the hearts of all patriotic men, who desired to preserve and perpetuate the blessings of our glorious Union—an origin akin that of the constitution of the United States, conceived in the same spirit of fraternal affection, and calculated to remove forever, the only danger, which seemed to threaten, at some distant day, to sever the social bond of union. All the evidences of public opinion at that day, seemed to indicate that this Compromise had been canonized in the hearts of the American people, as a sacred thing which no ruthless hand would ever be reckless enough to disturb."

I do not read this extract to involve Judge Douglas in an inconsistency. If he afterwards thought he had been wrong, it was right for him to change. I bring this forward merely to show the high estimate placed on the Missouri Compromise by all parties up to so late as the year 1849.

But, going back a little, in point of time, our war with Mexico broke out in 1846. When Congress was about adjourning that session, President Polk asked them to place two millions of dollars under his control, to be used by him in the recess, if found practicable and expedient, in negociating a treaty of peace with Mexico, and acquiring some part of her territory. A bill was duly got up, for the purpose, and was progressing swimmingly, in the House of Representatives, when a member by the name of David Wilmot, a democrat from Pennsylvania, moved as an amendment "Provided that in any territory thus acquired, there shall never be slavery."

This is the origin of the far-famed "Wilmot Proviso." It created a great flutter; but it stuck like wax, was voted into the bill, and the bill passed with it through the House. The Senate, however, adjourned without final action on it and so both appropriation and proviso were lost, for the time. The war continued, and at the next session, the president renewed his request for the appropriation, enlarging the amount, I think, to three million. Again came the proviso; and defeated the measure. Congress adjourned again, and the war went on. In Dec., 1847, the new congress assembled. I was in the lower House that term. The "Wilmot Proviso" or the principle of it, was constantly coming up in some shape or other, and I think I may venture to say I voted for it at least forty times; during the short term I was there. The Senate, however, held it in check, and it never became law. In the spring of 1848 a treaty of peace was made with Mexico; by which we obtained that portion of her country which now constitutes the territories of New Mexico and Utah, and the now state of California. By this treaty the Wilmot Proviso was defeated, as so far as it was intended to be, a condition of the acquisition of territory. Its friends however, were still determined to find some way to restrain slavery from getting into the new country. This new acquisition lay directly West of our old purchase from France, and extended west to the Pacific ocean—and was so situated that if the Missouri line should be extended straight West, the new country would be divided by such extended line, leaving some North and some South of it. On Judge Douglas' motion a bill, or provision of a bill, passed the Senate to so extend the Missouri line. The Proviso men in the House, including myself, voted it down, because by implication, it gave up the Southern part to slavery, while we were bent on having it *all* free.

In the fall of 1848 the gold mines were discovered in California. This attracted people to it with unprecedented rapidity, so that on, or soon after, the meeting of the new congress in Dec., 1849, she already had a population of nearly a hundred thousand, had called a convention, formed a state constitution, excluding slavery, and was knocking for admission into the Union. The Proviso men, of course were for letting her in, but the Senate, always true to the other side would not consent to her admission. And there California stood, kept *out* of the Union, because she would not let slavery *into* her borders. Under all the circumstances perhaps this was not wrong. There were other points of dispute, connected with the general question of slavery, which equally needed adjustment. The South clamored for a more efficient fugitive slave law. The North clamored for the abolition of a peculiar species of slave trade in the District of Columbia, in connection with which, in view from the windows of the capitol, a sort of negro-livery stable, where droves of negroes were collected, temporarily kept, and finally taken to Southern markets, precisely like droves of horses, had been openly maintained for fifty years. Utah and New Mexico needed territorial governments; and whether slavery should or should not be prohibited within them, was another question. The indefinite Western boundary of Texas was to be settled. She was received a slave state; and consequently the farther West the slavery men could push her boundary, the more slave country they secured. And the farther East the slavery opponents could thrust the boundary back, the less slave ground was secured. Thus this was just as clearly a slavery question as any of the others.

These points all needed adjustment; and they were all held up, perhaps wisely to make them help to adjust one another. The Union, now, as in 1820, was thought to be in danger; and devotion to the Union rightfully inclined men to yield somewhat, in points where nothing else could have so inclined them. A compromise was finally effected. The south got their new fugitive-slave law;

and the North got California, (the far best part of our acquisition from Mexico,) as a free State. The south got a provision that New Mexico and Utah, *when admitted as States,* may come in *with* or *without* slavery as they may then choose; and the north got the slave-trade abolished in the District of Columbia. The north got the western boundary of Texas, thence further back eastward than the south desired; but, in turn, they gave Texas ten millions of dollars, with which to pay her old debts. This is the Compromise of 1850.

Preceding the Presidential election of 1852, each of the great political parties, democrats and whigs, met in convention, and adopted resolutions endorsing the compromise of '50; as a "finality," a final settlement, so far as these parties could make it so, of all slavery agitation. Previous to this, in 1851, the Illinois Legislature had indorsed it.

During this long period of time Nebraska had remained, substantially an uninhabited country, but now emigration to, and settlement within it began to take place. It is about one third as large as the present United States, and its importance so long overlooked, begins to come into view. The restriction of slavery by the Missouri Compromise directly applies to it; in fact, was first made, and has since been maintained, expressly for it. In 1853, a bill to give it a territorial government passed the House of Representatives, and, in the hands of Judge Douglas, failed of passing the Senate only for want of time. This bill contained no repeal of the Missouri Compromise. Indeed, when it was assailed because it did not contain such repeal, Judge Douglas defended it in its existing form. On January 4th, 1854, Judge Douglas introduces a new bill to give Nebraska territorial government. He accompanies this bill with a report, in which last, he expressly recommends that the Missouri Compromise shall neither be affirmed nor repealed.

Before long the bill is so modified as to make two territories instead of one; calling the Southern one Kansas.

Also, about a month after the introduction of the bill, on the judge's own motion, it is so amended as to declare the Missouri Compromise inoperative and void; and, substantially, that the People who go and settle there may establish slavery, or exclude it, as they may see fit. In this shape the bill passed both branches of congress, and became a law.

This is the *repeal* of the Missouri Compromise. The foregoing history may not be precisely accurate in every particular; but I am sure it is sufficiently so, for all the uses I shall attempt to make of it, and in it, we have before us, the chief material enabling us to correctly judge whether the repeal of the Missouri Compromise is right or wrong.

I think, and shall try to show, that it is wrong; wrong in its direct effect, letting slavery into Kansas and Nebraska—and wrong in its prospective principle, allowing it to spread to every other part of the wide world, where men can be found inclined to take it.

This *declared* indifference, but as I must think, covert *real* zeal for the spread of slavery, I can not but hate. I hate it because of the monstrous injustice of slavery itself. I hate it because it deprives our republican example of its just influence in the world—enables the enemies of free institutions, with plausibility, to taunt us as hypocrites—causes the real friends of freedom to doubt our sincerity, and especially because it forces so many really good men amongst ourselves into an open war with the very fundamental principles of civil liberty—criticising the Declaration of Independence, and insisting that there is no right principle of action but *self-interest*.

Before proceeding, let me say I think I have no prejudice against the Southern people. They are just what we would be in their situation. If slavery did not now exist amongst them, they would not introduce it. If it did now exist amongst us, we should not instantly give it up. This I believe of the masses north and south. Doubtless there are individuals, on both sides, who would not hold slaves under any circumstances; and others who would gladly introduce slavery anew, if it were out of existence. We know that some southern men do free their slaves, go north, and become tip-top abolitionists; while some northern ones go south, and become most cruel slave-masters.

When southern people tell us they are no more responsible for the origin of slavery, than we; I acknowledge the fact. When it is said that the institution exists; and that it is very difficult to get rid of it, in any satisfactory way, I can understand and appreciate the saying. I surely will not blame them for not doing what I should not know how to do myself. If all earthly power were given me, I should not know what to do, as to the existing institution. My first impulse would be to free all the slaves, and send them to Liberia,—to their own native land. But a moment's reflection would convince me, that whatever of high hope, (as I think there is) there may be in this, in the long run, its sudden execution is impossible. If they were all landed there in a day, they would all perish in the next ten days; and there are not surplus shipping and surplus money enough in the world to carry them there in many times ten days. What then? Free them all, and keep them among us as underlings? Is it quite certain that this betters their condition? I think I would not hold one in slavery, at any rate; yet the point is not clear enough for me to denounce people upon. What next? Free them, and make them politically and socially, our equals? My own feelings will not admit of this; and if mine would, we well know that those of the great mass of white people will not. Whether this feeling accords with justice and sound judgment, is not the sole question, if indeed, it is any part of it. A universal feeling, whether well or ill-founded, can not be safely disregarded. We can not, then, make them equals. It does seem to me that systems of gradual emancipation might be adopted; but for their tardiness in this, I will not undertake to judge our brethren of the south.

When they remind us of their constitutional rights, I acknowledge them, not grudgingly, but fully, and fairly; and I would give them any legislation for the reclaiming of their fugitives, which should not, in its stringency, be more likely to carry a free man into slavery, than our ordinary criminal laws are to hang an innocent one.

But all this; to my judgment, furnishes no more excuse for permitting slavery to go into our own free territory, than it would for reviving the African slave trade by law. The law which forbids the bringing of slaves *from* Africa; and that which has so long forbid the taking them *to* Nebraska, can hardly be distinguished on any moral principle; and the repeal of the former could find quite as plausible excuses as that of the latter.

The arguments by which the repeal of the Missouri Compromise is sought to be justified, are these:

First, that the Nebraska country needed a territorial government.

Second, that in various ways, the public had repudiated it, and demanded the repeal; and therefore should not now complain of it.

And lastly, that the repeal establishes a principle, which is intrinsically right.

I will attempt an answer to each of them in its turn.

First, then, if that country was in need of a territorial organization, could it not have had it as well without as with the repeal? Iowa and Minnesota, to both of which the Missouri restriction applied, had, without its repeal, each in succession, territorial organizations. And even, the year before, a bill for Nebraska itself, was within an ace of passing, without the repealing clause; and this in the hands of the same men who are now the champions of repeal. Why no necessity then for the repeal? But still later, when this very bill was first brought in, it contained no repeal. But, say they, because the public had demanded, or rather commanded the repeal, the repeal was to accompany the organization, whenever that should occur.

Now I deny that the public ever demanded any such thing— ever repudiated the Missouri Compromise—ever commanded its repeal. I deny it, and call for the proof. It is not contended, I believe, that any such command has ever been given in express terms. It is only said that it was done *in principle*. The support of the Wilmot Proviso, is the first fact mentioned, to prove that the Missouri restriction was repudiated in *principle*, and the second is, the refusal to extend the Missouri line over the country acquired from Mexico. These are near enough alike to be treated together. The one was to exclude the chances of slavery from the *whole* new acquisition by the lump; and the other was to reject a division of it, by which one *half* was to be given up to those chances. Now whether this was a repudiation of the Missouri line, in *principle*, depends upon whether the Missouri law contained any *principle* requiring the line to be extended over the country acquired from Mexico. I contend it did not. I insist that it contained no general principle, but that it was, in every sense, specific. That its terms limit it to the country purchased from France, is undenied and undeniable. It could have no principle beyond the intention of those who made it. They did not intend to extend the line to country which they did not own. If they intended to extend it, in the event of acquiring additional territory, why did they not say so? It was just as easy to say, that "in all the country west of the Mississippi, which we now own, *or may hereafter acquire* there shall never be slavery," as to say, what they did say; and they would have said it if they had meant it. An intention to extend the law is not only not mentioned in the law, but is not mentioned in any contemporaneous history. Both the law itself, and the history of the times are a blank as to any *principle* of extension; and by neither the known rules for construing statutes and contracts, nor by common sense, can any such *principle* be inferred.

Another fact showing the *specific* character of the Missouri law —showing that it intended no more than it expressed—showing that the line was not intended as a universal dividing line between free and slave territory, present and prospective—north of which slavery could never go—is the fact that by that very law, Missouri came in as a slave state, *north* of the line. If that law contained any prospective *principle*, the whole law must be looked to in order to ascertain what the *principle* was. And by this rule, the south could fairly contend that inasmuch as they got one slave state north of the line at the inception of the law, they have the right to have another given them *north* of it occasionally—now and then in the indefinite westward extension of the line. This demonstrates the absurdity of attempting to deduce a prospective *principle* from the Missouri Compromise line.

When we voted for the Wilmot Proviso, we were voting to keep slavery *out* of the whole Missouri [Mexican?] acquisition; and little did we think we were thereby voting, to let it *into* Nebraska, laying several hundred miles distant. When we voted against extending the Missouri line, little did we think we were voting to destroy the old line, then of near thirty years standing. To argue that we thus repudiated the Missouri Compromise is no less absurd than it would be to argue that because we have, so far, forborne to acquire Cuba, we have thereby, *in principle*, repudiated our former acquisitions, and determined to throw them out of the Union! No less absurd than it would be to say that because I may have refused to build an addition to my house, I thereby have decided to destroy the existing house! And if I catch you setting fire to my house, you will turn upon me and say I INSTRUCTED you to do it! The most conclusive argument, however, that, while voting for the Wilmot Proviso, and while voting against the EXTENSION of the Missouri line, we never thought of disturbing the original Missouri Compromise, is found in the facts, that there was then, and still is, an unorganized tract of fine country, nearly as large as the state of Missouri, lying immediately west of Arkansas, and south of the Missouri Compromise line; and that we never attempted to prohibit slavery as to it. I wish particular attention to this. It adjoins the original Missouri Compromise line, by its northern boundary; and consequently is part of the country, into which, by implication, slavery was permitted to go, by that compromise. There it has lain open ever since, and there it still lies. And yet no effort has been made at any time to wrest it from the south. In all our struggles to prohibit slavery within our Mexican acquisitions, we never so much as lifted a finger to prohibit it, as to this tract. Is not this entirely conclusive that at all times, we have held the Missouri Compromise as a sacred thing; even when against ourselves, as well as when for us?

Senator Douglas sometimes says the Missouri line itself was, *in principle*, only an extension of the line of the ordinance of '87— that is to say, an extension of the Ohio river. I think this is weak enough on its face. I will remark, however that, as a glance at the map will show, the Missouri line is a long way farther South than the Ohio; and that if our Senator, in proposing his extension, had stuck to the *principle* of jogging southward, perhaps it might not have been voted down so readily.

But next it is said that the compromises of '50 and the ratification of them by both political parties, in '52, established a *new principle*, which required the repeal of the Missouri Compromise. This again I deny. I deny it, and demand the proof. I have already stated fully what the compromises of '50 are. The particular part of those measures, for which the virtual repeal of the Missouri compromise is sought to be inferred (for it is admitted they contain nothing about it, in express terms) is the provision in the Utah and New Mexico laws, which permits them when they seek admission into the Union as States, to come in with or without slavery as they shall then see fit. Now I insist this provision was made for Utah and New Mexico, and for no other place whatever. It had no more direct reference to Nebraska than it had to the territories of the moon. But, say they, it had reference to Nebraska, *in principle*. Let us see. The North consented to this provision, not because they considered it right in itself; but because they were compensated—paid for it. They, at the same time, got California into the Union as a free State. This was far the best part of all they had struggled for by the Wilmot Proviso. They also got the area of slavery somewhat narrowed in the settlement of the boundary of Texas. Also, they got the slave trade abolished in the District of Columbia. For all these desirable objects the North could afford to yield something; and they did yield to the South the Utah and New Mexico provision. I do not mean that the whole North, or even a majority, yielded, when the law passed; but enough yielded, when added to the vote of the South, to carry the measure. Now can it be pretended that the *principle* of this arrangement requires us to permit the same provision to be applied to Nebraska, *without any equivalent at all?* Give us another free State; press the boundary of Texas still further back, give us another step toward the destruction of slavery in the District, and you present us a similar case. But ask us not to repeat, for nothing, what you paid for in the first instance. If you wish the thing again, pay again. That is the *principle* of the compromises of '50, if indeed they had any principles beyond their specific terms—it was the system of equivalents.

Again, if Congress, at that time, intended that all future territories should, when admitted as States, come in with or without slavery, at their own option, why did it not say so? With such an universal provision, all know the bills could not have passed. Did they, then—could they—establish a *principle* contrary to their own intention? Still further, if they intended to establish the principle that wherever Congress had control, it should be left to the people to do as they thought fit with slavery why did they not authorize the people of the District of Columbia at their adoption to abolish slavery within these limits? I personally know that this has not been left undone, because it was unthought of. It was frequently spoken of by members of Congress and by citizens of Washington six years ago; and I heard no one express a doubt that a system of gradual emancipation, with compensation to owners, would meet the approbation of a large majority of the white people of the District. But without the action of Congress they could say nothing; and Congress said "no." In the measures of 1850 Congress had the subject of slavery in the District expressly in hand. If they were then establishing the *principle* of allowing the people to do as they please with slavery, why did they not apply the *principle* to that people?

Again, it is claimed that by the Resolutions of the Illinois Legislature, passed in 1851, the repeal of the Missouri compromise was demanded. This I deny also. Whatever may be worked out by a criticism of the language of those resolutions, the people have never understood them as being any more than an endorsement of the compromises of 1850; and a release of our Senators from voting for the Wilmot Proviso. The whole people are living witnesses, that this only, was their view. Finally, it is asked "If we did not mean to apply the Utah and New Mexico provision, to all future territories, what did we mean, when we, in 1852, endorsed the compromises of '50?"

For myself, I can answer this question most easily. I meant not to ask a repeal, or modification of the fugitive slave law. I meant not to ask for the abolition of slavery in the District of Columbia. I meant not to resist the admission of Utah and New Mexico, even should they ask to come in as slave States. I meant nothing about additional territories, because, as I understood, we then had no territory whose character as to slavery was not already settled. As to Nebraska, I regarded its character as being fixed, by the Missouri compromise, for thirty years—as unalterably fixed as that of my own home in Illinois. As to new acquisitions I said "sufficient unto the day is the evil thereof." When we make new acquaintances, [acquisitions?] we will, as heretofore, try to manage them some how. That is my answer. That is what I meant and said; and I appeal to the people to say, each for himself, whether that was not also the universal meaning of the free States.

And now, in turn, let me ask a few questions. If by any, or all these matters, the repeal of the Missouri Compromise was commanded, why was not the command sooner obeyed? Why was the repeal omitted in the Nebraska bill of 1853? Why was it omitted in the original bill of 1854? Why, in the accompanying report, was such a repeal characterized as a *departure* from the course pursued in 1850? and its continued omission recommended?

I am aware Judge Douglas now argues that the subsequent express repeal is no substantial alteration of the bill. This argument seems wonderful to me. It is as if one should argue that white and black are not different. He admits, however, that there is a literal change in the bill; and that he made the change in deference to other Senators, who would not support the bill without. This proves that those other Senators thought the change a substantial one; and that the Judge thought their opinions worth deferring to. His own opinions, therefore, seem not to rest on a very firm basis even in his own mind—and I suppose the world believes, and will continue to believe, that precisely on the substance of that change this whole agitation has arisen.

I conclude then, that the public never demanded the repeal of the Missouri compromise.

I now come to consider whether the repeal, with its avowed principle, is intrinsically right. I insist that it is not. Take the particular case. A controversy had arisen between the advocates and opponents of slavery, in relation to its establishment within the country we had purchased of France. The southern, and then best part of the purchase, was already in as a slave State. The controversy was settled by also letting Missouri in as a slave State; but with the agreement that within all the remaining part of the purchase, North of a certain line, there should never be slavery. As to what was to be done with the remaining part south of the line, nothing was said; but perhaps the fair implication was, that it should come in with slavery if it should so choose. The southern part, except a portion heretofore mentioned, afterwards did come in with slavery, as the State of Arkansas. All these many years since 1820, the Northern part had remained a wilderness. At length settlements began in it also. In due course, Iowa, came in as a free State, and Minnesota was given a territorial government, without removing the slavery restriction. Finally the sole remaining part, North of the line, Kansas and Nebraska, was to be organized; and it is proposed, and carried, to blot out the old dividing line of thirty-four years standing, and to open the whole of that country to the introduction of slavery. Now, this, to my mind, is manifestly unjust. After an angry and dangerous controversy, the parties made friends by dividing the bone of contention. The one party first appropriates her own share, beyond all power to be disturbed in the possession of it; and then seizes the share of the other party. It is as if two starving men had divided their only loaf; the one had hastily swallowed his half, and then grabbed the other half just as he was putting it to his mouth!

Let me here drop the main argument, to notice what I consider rather an inferior matter. It is argued that slavery will not go to Kansas and Nebraska, *in any event*. This is a *palliation*—a *lullaby*. I have some hope that it will not; but let us not be too confident. As to climate, a glance at the map shows that there are five slave States—Delaware, Maryland, Virginia, Kentucky, and Missouri— and also the District of Columbia, all north of the Missouri compromise line. The census returns of 1850 show that, within these, there are 867,276 slaves—being more than one-fourth of all the slaves in the nation.

It is not climate, then, that will keep slavery out of these territories. Is there any thing in the peculiar nature of the country? Missouri adjoins these territories, by her entire western boundary, and slavery is already within every one of her western counties. I have even heard it said that there are more slaves, in proportion to whites, in the north western county of Missouri, than within any county of the State. Slavery pressed entirely up to the old western boundary of the State, and when, rather recently, a part of that boundary, at the north-west was moved out a little farther west, slavery followed on quite up to the new line. Now, when the restriction is removed, what is to prevent it from going still further? Climate will not. No peculiarity of the country will—nothing in *nature* will. Will the disposition of the people prevent it? Those nearest the scene, are all in favor of the extension. The yankees, who are opposed to it may be more numerous; but in military phrase, the battle-field is too far from *their* base of operations.

But it is said, there now is *no* law in Nebraska on the subject of slavery; and that, in such case, taking a slave there, operates his freedom. That *is* good book-law; but is not the rule of actual practice. Wherever slavery is, it has been first introduced without law. The oldest laws we find concerning it, are not laws introducing it; but *regulating* it, as an already existing thing. A white man takes his slave to Nebraska now; who will inform the negro that he is free? Who will take him before court to test the question of his freedom? In ignorance of his legal emancipation, he is kept chopping, splitting and plowing. Others are brought, and move on in the same track. At last, if ever the time for voting comes, on the question of slavery, the institution already in fact exists in the country, and cannot well be removed. The facts of its presence, and the difficulty of its removal will carry the vote in its favor. Keep it out until a vote is taken, and a vote in favor of it, can not be got in any population of forty thousand, on earth, who have been drawn together by the ordinary motives of emigration and settlement. To get slaves into the country simultaneously with the whites, in the incipient stages of settlement, is the precise stake played for, and won in this Nebraska measure.

The question is asked us, "If slaves will go in, notwithstanding the general principle of law liberates them, why would they not equally go in against positive statute law?—go in, even if the Missouri restriction were maintained?" I answer, because it takes a much bolder man to venture in, with his property, in the latter case, than in the former—because the positive congressional enactment is known to, and respected by all, or nearly all; whereas the negative principle that *no* law is free law, is not much known except among lawyers. We have some experience of this practical difference. In spite of the Ordinance of '87, a few negroes were brought into Illinois, and held in a state of quasi slavery; not enough, however to carry a vote of the people in favor of the institution when they came to form a constitution. But in the adjoining Missouri country, where there was no ordinance of '87— was no restriction—they were carried ten times, nay a hundred times, as fast, and actually made a slave State. This is fact—naked fact.

Another LULLABY argument is, that taking slaves to new countries does not increase their number—does not make any one slave who otherwise would be free. There is some truth in this, and I am glad of it, but it [is] not WHOLLY true. The African slave trade is not yet effectually suppressed; and if we make a reasonable deduction for the white people amongst us, who are foreigners, and the descendants of foreigners, arriving here since 1808, we shall find the increase of the black population out-running that of the white, to an extent unaccountable, except by supposing that some of them too, have been coming from Africa. If this be so, the opening of new countries to the institution, increases the demand for, and augments the price of slaves, and so does, in fact, make slaves of freemen by causing them to be brought from Africa, and sold into bondage.

But, however this may be, we know the opening of new countries to slavery, tends to the perpetuation of the institution, and so does KEEP men in slavery who otherwise would be free. This result we do not FEEL like favoring, and we are under no legal obligation to suppress our feelings in this respect.

Equal justice to the south, it is said, requires us to consent to the extending of slavery to new countries. That is to say, inasmuch as you do not object to my taking my hog to Nebraska, therefore I must not object to you taking your slave. Now, I admit this is perfectly logical, if there is no difference between hogs and negroes. But while you thus require me to deny the humanity of the negro, I wish to ask whether you of the south yourselves, have ever been willing to do as much? It is kindly provided that of all those who come into the world, only a small percentage are natural tyrants. That percentage is no larger in the slave States than in the free. The great majority, south as well as north, have human sympathies, of which they can no more divest themselves than they can of their sensibility to physical pain. These sympathies in the bosoms of the southern people, manifest in many ways, their sense of the wrong of slavery, and their consciousness that, after all, there is humanity in the negro. If they deny this, let me address them a few plain questions. In 1820 you joined the north, almost unanimously, in declaring the African slave trade piracy, and in annexing to it the punishment of death. Why did you do this? If you did not feel that it was wrong, why did you join in providing that men should be hung for it? The practice was no more than bringing wild negroes from Africa, to sell to such as would buy them. But you never thought of hanging men for catching and selling wild horses, wild buffaloes or wild bears.

Again, you have amongst you, a sneaking individual, of the class of native tyrants, known as the "SLAVE-DEALER." He watches your necessities, and crawls up to buy your slave, at a speculating price. If you cannot help it, you sell to him; but if you can help it, you drive him from your door. You despise him utterly. You do not recognize him as a friend, or even as an honest man. Your children must not play with his; they may rollick freely with the little negroes, but not with the "slave-dealers" children. If you are obliged to deal with him, you try to get through the job without so much as touching him. It is common with you to join hands with the men you meet; but with the slave dealer you avoid the ceremony—instinctively shrinking from the snaky contact. If he grows rich and retires from business, you still remember him, and still keep up the ban of non-intercourse upon him and his family. Now why is this? You do not so treat the man who deals in corn, cattle or tobacco.

And yet again; there are in the United States and territories, including the District of Columbia, 433,643 free blacks. At $500 per head they are worth over two hundred millions of dollars. How comes this vast amount of property to be running about without owners? We do not see free horses or free cattle running at large. How is this? All these free blacks are the descendants of slaves, or have been slaves themselves, and they would be slaves now, but for SOMETHING which has operated on their white owners, inducing them, at vast pecuniary sacrifices, to liberate them. What is that SOMETHING? Is there any mistaking it? In all these cases it is your sense of justice, and human sympathy, continually telling you, that the poor negro has some natural right to himself—that those who deny it, and make mere merchandise of him, deserve kickings, contempt and death.

And now, why will you ask us to deny the humanity of the slave? and estimate him only as the equal of the hog? Why ask us to do what you will not do yourselves? Why ask us to do for *nothing*, what two hundred million of dollars could not induce you to do?

But one great argument in the support of the repeal of the Missouri Compromise, is still to come. That argument is "the sacred right of self government." It seems our distinguished Senator has found great difficulty in getting his antagonists, even in the Senate to meet him fairly on this argument—some poet has said

"Fools rush in where angels fear to tread."

At the hazzard of being thought one of the fools of this quotation, I meet that argument—I rush in, I take that bull by the horns.

I trust I understand, and truly estimate the right of self-government. My faith in the proposition that each man should do precisely as he pleases with all which is exclusively his own, lies at the foundation of the sense of justice there is in me. I extend the principles to communities of men, as well as to individuals. I so extend it, because it is politically wise, as well as naturally just: politically wise, in saving us from broils about matters which do not concern us. Here, or at Washington, I would not trouble myself with the oyster laws of Virginia, or the cranberry laws of Indiana.

The doctrine of self government is right—absolutely and eternally right—but it has no just application, as here attempted. Or perhaps I should rather say that whether it has such just application depends upon whether a negro is *not* or *is* a man. If he is *not* a man, why in that case, he who *is* a man may, as a matter of self-government, do just as he pleases with him. But if the negro *is* a man, is it not to that extent, a total destruction of self-government, to say that he too shall not govern *himself?* When the white man governs himself that is self-government; but when he governs himself, and also governs *another* man, that is *more* than self-government—that is despotism. If the negro is a *man,* why then my ancient faith teaches me that "all men are created equal;" and that there can be no moral right in connection with one man's making a slave of another.

Judge Douglas frequently, with bitter irony and sarcasm, paraphrases our argument by saying "The white people of Nebraska are good enough to govern themselves, *but they are not good enough to govern a few miserable negroes!!*"

Well I doubt not that the people of Nebraska are, and will continue to be as good as the average of people elsewhere. I do not say the contrary. What I do say is, that no man is good enough to govern another man, *without that other's consent.* I say this is the leading principle—the sheet anchor of American republicanism. Our Declaration of Independence says:

"We hold these truths to be self evident: that all men are created equal; that they are endowed by their Creator with certain inalienable rights; that among these are life, liberty and the pursuit of happiness. That to secure these rights, governments are instituted among men, DERIVING THEIR JUST POWERS FROM THE CONSENT OF THE GOVERNED."

I have quoted so much at this time merely to show that according to our ancient faith, the just powers of governments are derived from the consent of the governed. Now the relation of masters and slaves is, PRO TANTO, a total violation of this principle. The master not only governs the slave without his consent; but he governs him by a set of rules altogether different from those which he prescribes for himself. Allow ALL the governed an equal voice in the government, and that, and that only is self government.

Let it not be said I am contending for the establishment of political and social equality between the whites and blacks. I have already said the contrary. I am not now combating the argument of NECESSITY, arising from the fact that the blacks are already amongst us; but I am combating what is set up as MORAL argument for allowing them to be taken where they have never yet been—arguing against the EXTENSION of a bad thing, which where it already exists, we must of necessity, manage as we best can.

In support of his application of the doctrine of self-government,

Senator Douglas has sought to bring to his aid the opinions and examples of our revolutionary fathers. I am glad he has done this. I love the sentiments of those old-time men; and shall be most happy to abide by their opinions. He shows us that when it was in contemplation for the colonies to break off from Great Britain, and set up a new government for themselves, several of the states instructed their delegates to go for the measure PROVIDED EACH STATE SHOULD BE ALLOWED TO REGULATE ITS DOMESTIC CONCERNS IN ITS OWN WAY. I do not quote; but this in substance. This was right. I see nothing objectionable in it. I also think it probable that it had some reference to the existence of slavery amongst them. I will not deny that it had. But had it, in any reference to the carrying of slavery into NEW COUNTRIES? That is the question; and we will let the fathers themselves answer it.

This same generation of men, and mostly the same individuals of the generation, who declared this principle—who declared independence—who fought the war of the revolution through—who afterwards made the constitution under which we still live—these same men passed the ordinance of '87, declaring that slavery should never go to the north-west territory. I have no doubt Judge Douglas thinks they were very inconsistent in this. It is a question of discrimination between them and him. But there is not an inch of ground left for his claiming that their opinions—their example—their authority—are on his side in this controversy.

Again, is not Nebraska, while a territory, a part of us? Do we not own the country? And if we surrender the control of it, do we not surrender the right of self-government? It is part of ourselves. If you say we shall not control it because it is ONLY part, the same is true of every other part; and when all the parts are gone, what has become of the whole? What is then left of us? What use for the general government, when there is nothing left for it [to] govern?

But you say this question should be left to the people of Nebraska, because they are more particularly interested. If this be the rule, you must leave it to each individual to say for himself whether he will have slaves. What better moral right have thirty-one citizens of Nebraska to say, that the thirty-second shall not hold slaves, than the people of the thirty-one States have to say that slavery shall not go into the thirty-second State at all?

But if it is a sacred right for the people of Nebraska to take and hold slaves there, it is equally their sacred right to buy them where they can buy them cheapest; and that undoubtedly will be on the coast of Africa; provided you will consent to not hang them for going there to buy them. You must remove this restriction too, from the sacred right of self-government. I am aware you say that taking slaves from the States to Nebraska, does not make slaves of freemen; but the African slave-trader can say just as much. He does not catch free negroes and bring them here. He finds them already slaves in the hands of their black captors, and he honestly buys them at the rate of about a red cotton handkerchief a head. This is very cheap, and it is a great abridgement of the sacred right of self-government to hang men for engaging in this profitable trade!

Another important objection to this application of the right of self-government, is that it enables the first FEW, to deprive the succeeding MANY, of a free exercise of the right of self-government. The first few may get slavery IN, and the subsequent many cannot easily get it OUT. How common is the remark now in the slave States—"If we were only clear of our slaves, how much better it would be for us." They are actually deprived of the privilege of governing themselves as they would, by the action of a very few, in the beginning. The same thing was true of the whole nation at the time our constitution was formed.

Whether slavery shall go into Nebraska, or other new territories, is not a matter of exclusive concern to the people who may go there. The whole nation is interested that the best use shall be made of these territories. We want them for the homes of free white people. This they cannot be, to any considerable extent, if slavery shall be planted within them. Slave States are places for poor white people to remove FROM; not to remove TO. New free States are the places for poor people to go to and better their condition. For this use, the nation needs these territories.

Still further; there are constitutional relations between the slave and free States, which are degrading to the latter. We are under legal obligations to catch and return their runaway slaves to them —a sort of dirty, disagreeable job, which I believe, as a general rule the slave-holders will not perform for one another. Then again, in the control of the government—the management of the partnership affairs—they have greatly the advantage of us. By the constitution, each State has two Senators—each has a number of Representatives; in proportion to the number of its people—and each has a number of presidential electors, equal to the whole number of its Senators and Representatives together. But in ascertaining the number of the people, for this purpose, five slaves are counted as being equal to three whites. The slaves do not vote; they are only counted and so used, as to swell the influence of the white people's votes. The practical effect of this is more aptly shown by a comparison of the States of South Carolina and Maine. South Carolina has six representatives, and so has Maine; South Carolina has eight presidential electors, and so has Maine. This is precise equality so far; and, of course they are equal in Senators, each having two. Thus in the control of the government, the two States are equals precisely. But how are they in the number of their white people? Maine has 581,813—while South Carolina has 274,567. Maine has twice as many as South Carolina, and 32,679 over. Thus each white man in South Carolina is more than the double of any man in Maine. This is all because South Carolina, besides her free people, has 384,984 slaves. The South Carolinian has precisely the same advantage over the white man in every other free State, as well as in Maine. He is more than the double of any one of us in this crowd. The same advantage, but not to the same extent, is held by all the citizens of the slave States, over those of the free; and it is an absolute truth, without an exception, that there is no voter in any slave State, but who has more legal power in the government, than any voter in any free State. There is no instance of exact equality; and the disadvantage is against us the whole chapter through. This principle, in the aggregate, gives the slave States, in the present Congress, twenty additional representatives—being seven more than the whole majority by which they passed the Nebraska bill.

Now all this is manifestly unfair; yet I do not mention it to complain of it, in so far as it is already settled. It is in the constitution; and I do not, for that cause, or any other cause, propose to destroy, or alter, or disregard the constitution. I stand to it, fairly, fully, and firmly.

But when I am told I must leave it altogether to OTHER PEOPLE to say whether new partners are to be bred up and brought into the firm, on the same degrading terms against me, I respectfully demur. I insist, that whether I shall be a whole man, or only, the half of one, in comparison with others, is a question in which I am somewhat concerned; and one which no other man can have a sacred right of deciding for me. If I am wrong in this—if it really be a sacred right of self-government, in the man who shall go to Nebraska, to decide whether he will be the EQUAL of me or the DOUBLE of me, then after he shall have exercised that right, and thereby shall have reduced me to a still smaller fraction of a man than I already am, I should like for some gentleman deeply skilled in the mysteries of sacred rights, to provide himself with a microscope, and peep about, and find out, if he can, what has become of my sacred rights! They will surely be too small for detection with the naked eye.

Finally, I insist, that if there is ANY THING which it is the duty of the WHOLE PEOPLE to never entrust to any hands but their own, that thing is the preservation and perpetuity, of their own liberties, and institutions. And if they shall think, as I do, that the extension of slavery endangers them, more than any, or all other causes, how recreant to themselves, if they submit the question, and with it, the fate of their country, to a mere hand-full of men, bent only on temporary self-interest. If this question of slavery extension were an insignificant one—one having no power to do harm—it might be shuffled aside in this way. But being, as it is, the great Behemoth of danger, shall the strong gripe of the nation be loosened upon him, to entrust him to the hands of such feeble keepers?

I have done with this mighty argument, of self-government. Go, sacred thing! Go in peace.

But Nebraska is urged as a great Union-saving measure. Well I too, go for saving the Union. Much as I hate slavery, I would consent to the extension of it rather than see the Union dissolved, just as I would consent to any GREAT evil, to avoid a GREATER one. But when I go to Union saving, I must believe, at least, that the means I employ has some adaptation to the end. To my mind, Nebraska has no such adaptation.

"It hath no relish of salvation in it."

It is an aggravation, rather, of the only one thing which ever endangers the Union. When it came upon us, all was peace and quiet. The nation was looking to the forming of new bonds of Union; and a long course of peace and prosperity seemed to lie before us. In the whole range of possibility, there scarcely appears to me to have been any thing, out of which the slavery agitation could have been revived, except the very project of repealing the Missouri compromise. Every inch of territory we owned, already had a definite settlement of the slavery question, and by which, all parties were pledged to abide. Indeed, there was no uninhabited country on the continent, which we could acquire; if we except some extreme northern regions, which are wholly out of the question. In this state of case, the genius of Discord himself, could scarcely have invented a way of again getting [setting?] us by the ears, but by turning back and destroying the peace measures of the past. The councils of that genius seem to have prevailed, the Missouri compromise was repealed; and here we are, in the midst of a new slavery agitation, such, I think, as we have never seen before. Who is responsible for this? Is it those who resist the measure; or those who, causelessly, brought it forward, and pressed it through, having reason to know, and, in fact, knowing it must and would be so resisted? It could not but be expected by its author, that it would be looked upon as a measure for the extension of slavery, aggravated by a gross breach of faith. Argue as you will, and long as you will, this is the naked FRONT and ASPECT, of the measure. And in this aspect, it could not but produce agitation. Slavery is founded in the selfishness of man's nature—opposition to it, is [in?] his love of justice. These principles are an eternal antagonism; and when brought into collision so fiercely, as slavery extension brings them, shocks, and throes, and convulsions must ceaselessly follow. Repeal the Missouri compromise—repeal all compromises—repeal the declaration of independence—repeal all past history, you still can not repeal human nature. It still will be the abundance of man's heart, that slavery extension is wrong; and out of the abundance of his heart, his mouth will continue to speak.

The structure, too, of the Nebraska bill is very peculiar. The people are to decide the question of slavery for themselves; but WHEN they are to decide; or HOW they are to decide; or whether, when the question is once decided, it is to remain so, or is it to be subject to an indefinite succession of new trials, the law does not say, Is it to be decided by the first dozen settlers who arrive there? or is it to await the arrival of a hundred? Is it to be decided by a vote of the people? or a vote of the legislature? or, indeed by a vote of any sort? To these questions, the law gives no answer. There is a mystery about this; for when a member proposed to give the legislature express authority to exclude slavery, it was hooted down by the friends of the bill. This fact is worth remembering. Some yankees, in the east, are sending emigrants to Nebraska, to exclude slavery from it; and, so far as I can judge, they expect the question to be decided by voting, in some way or other. But the Missourians are awake too. They are within a stone's throw of the contested ground. They hold meetings, and pass resolutions, in which not the slightest allusion to voting is made. They resolve that slavery already exists in the territory; that more shall go there; that they, remaining in Missouri will protect it; and that abolitionists shall be hung, or driven away. Through all this, bowie-knives and six-shooters are seen plainly enough; but never a glimpse of the ballot-box. And, really, what is to be the result of this? Each party WITHIN, having numerous and determined backers WITHOUT, is it not probable that the contest will come to blows, and bloodshed? Could there be a more apt invention to bring about collision and violence, on the slavery question, than this Nebraska project is? I do not charge, or believe, that such was intended by Congress; but if they had literally formed a ring, and placed champions within it to fight out the controversy, the fight could be no more likely to come off, than it is. And if this fight should begin, is it likely to take a very peaceful, Union-saving turn? Will not the first drop of blood so shed, be the real knell of the Union?

The Missouri Compromise ought to be restored. For the sake of the Union, it ought to be restored. We ought to elect a House of Representatives which will vote its restoration. If by any means, we omit to do this, what follows? Slavery may or may not be established in Nebraska. But whether it be or not, we shall have repudiated—discarded from the councils of the Nation—the SPIRIT of COMPROMISE; for who after this will ever trust in a national compromise? The spirit of mutual concession—that spirit which first gave us the constitution, and which has thrice saved the Union —we shall have strangled and cast from us forever. And what shall we have in lieu of it? The South flushed with triumph and tempted to excesses; the North, betrayed, as they believe, brooding on wrong and burning for revenge. One side will provoke; the other resent. The one will taunt, the other defy; one agrees [aggresses?], the other retaliates. Already a few in the North, defy all constitutional restraints, resist the execution of the fugitive slave law, and even menace the institution of slavery in the states where it exists.

Already a few in the South, claim the constitutional right to take to and hold slaves in the free states—demand the revival of the slave trade; and demand a treaty with Great Britain by which fugitive slaves may be reclaimed from Canada. As yet they are but few on either side. It is a grave question for the lovers of the Union, whether the final destruction of the Missouri Compromise, and with it the spirit of all compromise will or will not embolden and embitter each of these, and fatally increase the numbers of both.

But restore the compromise, and what then? We thereby restore the national faith, the national confidence, the national feeling of brotherhood. We thereby reinstate the spirit of concession and compromise—that spirit which has never failed us in past perils, and which may be safely trusted for all the future. The south ought to join in doing this. The peace of the nation is as dear to them as to us. In memories of the past and hopes of the future, they share as largely as we. It would be on their part, a great act—

great in its spirit, and great in its effect. It would be worth to the nation a hundred years' purchase of peace and prosperity. And what of sacrifice would they make? They only surrender to us, what they gave us for a consideration long, long ago; what they have not now, asked for, struggled or cared for; what has been thrust upon them, not less to their own astonishment than to ours.

But it is said we cannot restore it; that though we elect every member of the lower house, the Senate is still against us. It is quite true, that of the Senators who passed the Nebraska bill, a majority of the whole Senate will retain their seats in spite of the elections of this and the next year. But if at these elections, their several constituencies shall clearly express their will against Nebraska, will these senators disregard their will? Will they neither obey, nor make room for those who will?

But even if we fail to technically restore the compromise, it is still a great point to carry a popular vote in favor of the restoration. The moral weight of such a vote can not be estimated too highly. The authors of Nebraska are not at all satisfied with the destruction of the compromise—an endorsement of this PRINCIPLE, they proclaim to be the great object. With them, Nebraska alone is a small matter—to establish a principle, for FUTURE USE, is what they particularly desire.

That future use is to be the planting of slavery wherever in the wide world, local and unorganized opposition can not prevent it. Now if you wish to give them this endorsement—if you wish to establish this principle—do so. I shall regret it; but it is your right. On the contrary if you are opposed to the principle—intend to give it no such endorsement—let no wheedling, no sophistry, divert you from throwing a direct vote against it.

Some men, mostly whigs, who condemn the repeal of the Missouri Compromise, nevertheless hesitate to go for its restoration, lest they be thrown in company with the abolitionist. Will they allow me as an old whig to tell them good humoredly, that I think this is very silly? Stand with anybody that stands RIGHT. Stand with him while he is right and PART with him when he goes wrong. Stand WITH the abolitionist in restoring the Missouri Compromise; and stand AGAINST him when he attempts to repeal the fugitive slave law. In the latter case you stand with the southern disunionist. What of that? you are still right. In both cases you are right. In both cases you oppose [expose?] the dangerous extremes. In both you stand on middle ground and hold the ship level and steady. In both you are national and nothing less than national. This is good old whig ground. To desert such ground, because of any company, is to be less than a whig—less than a man—less than an American.

I particularly object to the NEW position which the avowed principle of this Nebraska law gives to slavery in the body politic. I object to it because it assumes that there CAN be MORAL RIGHT in the enslaving of one man by another. I object to it as a dangerous dalliance for a few [free?] people—a sad evidence that, feeling prosperity we forget right—that liberty, as a principle, we have ceased to revere. I object to it because the fathers of the republic eschewed, and rejected it. The argument of "Necessity" was the only argument they ever admitted in favor of slavery; and so far, and so far only as it carried them, did they ever go. They found the institution existing among us, which they could not help; and they cast blame upon the British King for having permitted its introduction. BEFORE the constitution, they prohibited its introduction into the north-western Territory—the only country we owned, then free from it. AT the framing and adoption of the constitution, they forbore to so much as mention the word "slave" or "slavery" in the whole instrument. In the provision for the recovery of fugitives, the slave is spoken of as a "PERSON HELD TO SERVICE OR LABOR." In that prohibiting the abolition of the African slave trade for twenty years, that trade is spoken of as "The migration or importation of such persons as any of the States NOW EXISTING, shall think proper to admit," &c. These are the only provisions alluding to slavery. Thus, the thing is hid away, in the constitution, just as an afflicted man hides away a wen or a cancer, which he dares not cut out at once, lest he bleed to death; with the promise, nevertheless, that the cutting may begin at the end of a given time. Less than this our fathers COULD not do; and NOW [MORE?] they WOULD not do. Necessity drove them so far, and farther, they would not go. But this is not all. The earliest Congress, under the constitution, took the same view of slavery. They hedged and hemmed it in to the narrowest limits of necessity.

In 1794, they prohibited an out-going slave-trade—that is, the taking of slaves FROM the United States to sell.

In 1798, they prohibited the bringing of slaves from Africa, INTO the Mississippi Territory—this territory then comprising what are now the States of Mississippi and Alabama. This was TEN YEARS before they had the authority to do the same thing as to the States existing at the adoption of the constitution.

In 1800 they prohibited AMERICAN CITIZENS from trading in slaves between foreign countries—as, for instance, from Africa to Brazil.

In 1803 they passed a law in aid of one or two State laws, in restraint of the internal slave trade.

In 1807, in apparent hot haste, they passed the law, nearly a year in advance, to take effect the first day of 1808—the very first day the constitution would permit—prohibiting the African slave trade by heavy pecuniary and corporal penalties.

In 1820, finding these provisions ineffectual, they declared the trade piracy, and annexed to it, the extreme penalty of death. While all this was passing in the general government, five or six of the original slave States had adopted systems of gradual emancipation; and by which the institution was rapidly becoming extinct within these limits.

Thus we see, the plain unmistakable spirit of that age, towards slavery, was hostility to the PRINCIPLE, and toleration, ONLY BY NECESSITY.

But NOW it is to be transformed into a "sacred right." Nebraska brings it forth, places it on the high road to extension and perpetuity; and, with a pat on its back, says to it, "Go, and God speed you." Henceforth it is to be the chief jewel of the nation—the very figure-head of the ship of State. Little by little, but steadily as man's march to the grave, we have been giving up the OLD for the NEW faith. Near eighty years ago we began by declaring that all men are created equal; but now from that beginning we have run down to the other declaration, that for SOME men to enslave OTHERS is a "sacred right of self-government." These principles can not stand together. They are as opposite as God and mammon; and whoever holds to the one, must despise the other. When Pettit, in connection with his support of the Nebraska bill, called the Declaration of Independence "a self-evident lie" he only did what consistency and candor require all other Nebraska men to do. Of the forty odd Nebraska Senators who sat present and heard him, no one rebuked him. Nor am I apprized that any Nebraska newspaper, or any Nebraska orator, in the whole nation, has ever yet rebuked him. If this had been said among Marion's men, Southerners though they were, what would have become of the man who said it? If this had been said to the men who captured André, the man who said it, would probably have been hung sooner than André was. If it had been said in old Independence Hall, seventy-eight years ago, the very door-keeper would have throttled the man, and thrust him into the street.

Let no one be deceived. The spirit of seventy-six and the spirit of Nebraska, are utter antagonisms; and the former is being rapidly displaced by the latter.

[275]

Fellow countrymen—Americans south, as well as north, shall we make no effort to arrest this? Already the liberal party throughout the world, express the apprehension "that the one retrograde institution in America, is undermining the principles of progress, and fatally violating the noblest political system the world ever saw." This is not the taunt of enemies, but the warning of friends. Is it quite safe to disregard it—to despise it? Is there no danger to liberty itself, in discarding the earliest practice, and first precept of our ancient faith? In our greedy chase to make profit of the negro, let us beware, lest we "cancel and tear to pieces" even the white man's charter of freedom.

Our republican robe is soiled, and trailed in the dust. Let us re-purify it. Let us turn and wash it white, in the spirit, if not the blood, of the Revolution. Let us turn slavery from its claims of "moral right," back upon its existing legal rights, and its arguments of "necessity." Let us return it to the position our fathers gave it; and there let it rest in peace. Let us re-adopt the Declaration of Independence, and with it, the practices, and policy, which harmonize with it. Let north and south—let all Americans—let all lovers of liberty everywhere—join in the great and good work. If we do this, we shall not only have saved the Union; but we shall have so saved it, as to make, and to keep it, forever worthy of the saving. We shall have so saved it, that the succeeding millions of free happy people, the world over, shall rise up, and call us blessed, to the latest generations.

At Springfield, twelve days ago, where I had spoken substantially as I have here, Judge Douglas replied to me—and as he is to reply to me here, I shall attempt to anticipate him, by noticing some of the points he made there.

He commenced by stating I had assumed all the way through, that the principle of the Nebraska bill, would have the effect of extending slavery. He denied that this was INTENDED, or that this EFFECT would follow.

I will not re-open the argument upon this point. That such was the intention, the world believed at the start, and will continue to believe. This was the COUNTENANCE of the thing; and, both friends and enemies, instantly recognized it as such. That countenance can not now be changed by argument. You can as easily argue the color out of the negroes' skin. Like the "bloody hand" you may wash it, and wash it, the red witness of guilt still sticks, and stares horribly at you.

Next he says, congressional intervention never prevented slavery, any where—that it did not prevent it in the north west territory, now [nor?] in Illinois—that in fact, Illinois came into the Union as a slave State—that the principle of the Nebraska bill expelled it from Illinois, from several old States, from every where.

Now this is mere quibbling all the way through. If the ordinance of '87 did not keep slavery out of the north west territory, how happens it that the north west shore of the Ohio river is entirely free from it; while the south east shore, less than a mile distant, along nearly the whole length of the river, is entirely covered with it?

If that ordinance did not keep it out of Illinois, what was it that made the difference between Illinois and Missouri? They lie side by side, the Mississippi river only dividing them; while their early settlements were within the same latitude. Between 1810 and 1820 the number of slaves in Missouri INCREASED 7,211; while in Illinois, in the same ten years, they DECREASED 51. This appears by the census returns. During nearly all of that ten years, both were territories—not States. During this time, the ordinance forbid slavery to go into Illinois; and NOTHING forbid it to go into Missouri. It DID go into Missouri, and did NOT go into Illinois. That is the fact. Can any one doubt as to the reason of it?

But, he says, Illinois came into the Union as a slave State. Silence, perhaps, would be the best answer to this flat contradiction of the known history of the country. What are the facts upon which this bold assertion is based? When we first acquired the country, as far back as 1787, there were some slaves within it, held by the French inhabitants at Kaskaskia. The territorial legislation, admitted a few negroes, from the slave States, as indentured servants. One year after the adoption of the first State constitution the whole number of them was—what do you think? just 117—while the aggregate free population was 55,094—about 470 to one. Upon this state of facts, the people framed their constitution prohibiting the further introduction of slavery, with a sort of guaranty to the owners of the few indentured servants, giving freedom to their children to be born thereafter, and making no mention whatever, of any supposed slave for life. Out of this small matter, the Judge manufactures his argument that Illinois came into the Union as a slave State. Let the facts be the answer to the argument.

The principles of the Nebraska bill, he says, expelled slavery from Illinois? The principle of that bill first planted it here—that is, it first came, because there was no law to prevent it—first came before we owned the country; and finding it here, and having the ordinance of '87 to prevent its increasing, our people struggled along, and finally got rid of it as best they could.

But the principle of the Nebraska bill abolished slavery in several of the old States. Well, it is true that several of the old States, in the last quarter of the last century, did adopt systems of gradual emancipation, by which the institution has finally become extinct within their limits; but it MAY or MAY NOT be true that the principle of the Nebraska bill was the cause that led to the adoption of these measures. It is now more than fifty years, since the last of these States adopted its system of emancipation. If Nebraska bill[3] is the real author of these benevolent works, it is rather deplorable, that he has, for so long a time, ceased working all together. Is there not some reason to suspect that it was the principle of the REVOLUTION, and not the principle of Nebraska bill, that led to emancipation in these old States? Leave it to the people of those old emancipating States, and I am quite sure they will decide, that neither that, nor any other good thing, ever did, or ever will come of Nebraska bill.

In the course of my main argument, Judge Douglas interrupted me to say, that the principle [of] the Nebraska bill was very old; that it originated when God made man and placed good and evil before him, allowing him to choose for himself, being responsible for the choice he should make. At the time I thought this was merely playful; and I answered it accordingly. But in his reply to me he renewed it, as a serious argument. In seriousness then, the facts of this proposition are not true as stated. God did not place good and evil before man, telling him to make his choice. On the contrary, he did tell him there was one tree, of the fruit of which, he should not eat, upon pain of certain death. I should scarcely wish so strong a prohibition against slavery in Nebraska.

But this argument strikes me as not a little remarkable in another particular—in its strong resemblance to the old argument for the "Divine right of Kings." By the latter, the King is to do just as he pleases with his white subjects, being responsible to God alone. By the former the white man is to do just as he pleases with his black slaves, being responsible to God alone. The two things are precisely alike; and it is but natural that they should find similar arguments to sustain them.

I had argued, that the application of the principle of self-government, as contended for, would require the revival of the African slave trade—that no argument could be made in favor of a man's right to take slaves to Nebraska, which could not be equally well

---

[3] Lincoln seems to be personifying here; otherwise, omission of "the" would not have been consistent in this and succeeding references in this paragraph. Editorials in Illinois newspapers prior to this speech refer to the villain "Nebraska Bill" as a person, indicating a common usage during the campaign.

made in favor of his right to bring them from the coast of Africa. The Judge replied, that the constitution requires the suppression of the foreign slave trade; but does not require the prohibition of slavery in the territories. That is a mistake, in point of fact. The constitution does NOT require the action of Congress in either case; and it does AUTHORIZE it in both. And so, there is still no difference between the cases.

In regard to what I had said, the advantage the slave States have over the free, in the matter of representation, the Judge replied that we, in the free States, count five free negroes as five white people, while in the slave States, they count five slaves as three whites only; and that the advantage, at last, was on the side of the free States.

Now, in the slave States, they count free negroes just as we do; and it so happens that besides their slaves, they have as many free negroes as we have, and thirty-three thousand over. Thus their free negroes more than balance ours; and their advantage over us, in consequence of their slaves, still remains as I stated it.

In reply to my argument, that the compromise measures of 1850, were a system of equivalents; and that the provisions of no one of them could fairly be carried to other subjects, without its corresponding equivalent being carried with it, the Judge denied out-right, that these measures had any connection with, or dependence upon, each other. This is mere desperation. If they have no connection, why are they always spoken of in connection? Why has he so spoken of them, a thousand times? Why has he constantly called them a SERIES of measures? Why does everybody call them a compromise? Why was California kept out of the Union, six or seven months, if it was not because of its connection with the other measures? Webster's leading definition of the verb "to compromise" is "to adjust and settle a difference, by mutual agreement with concessions of claims by the parties." This conveys precisely the popular understanding of the word compromise. We knew, before the Judge told us, that these measures passed separately, and in distinct bills; and that no two of them were passed by the votes of precisely the same members. But we also know, and so does he know, that no one of them could have passed both branches of Congress but for the understanding that the others were to pass also. Upon this understanding each got votes, which it could have got in no other way. It is this fact, that gives to the measures their true character; and it is the universal knowledge of this fact, that has given them the name of compromise so expressive of that true character.

I had asked "If in carrying the provisions of the Utah and New

Mexico laws to Nebraska, you could clear away other objection, how can you leave Nebraska "perfectly free" to introduce slavery BEFORE she forms a constitution—during her territorial government?—while the Utah and New Mexico laws only authorize it WHEN they form constitutions, and are admitted into the Union?" To this Judge Douglas answered that the Utah and New Mexico laws, also authorized it BEFORE; and to prove this, he read from one of their laws, as follows: "That the legislative power of said territory shall extend to all rightful subjects of legislation consistent with the constitution of the United States and the provisions of this act."

Now it is perceived from the reading of this, that there is nothing express upon the subject; but that the authority is sought to be implied merely, for the general provision of "all rightful subjects of legislation." In reply to this, I insist, as a legal rule of construction, as well as the plain popular view of the matter, that the EXPRESS provision for Utah and New Mexico coming in with slavery if they choose, when they shall form constitutions, is an EXCLUSION of all implied authority on the same subject—that Congress, having the subject distinctly in their minds, when they made the express provision, they therein expressed their WHOLE meaning on that subject.

The Judge rather insinuated that I had found it convenient to forget the Washington territorial law passed in 1853. This was a division of Oregon, organizing the northern part, as the territory of Washington. He asserted that, by this act, the ordinance of '87 theretofore existing in Oregon, was repealed; that nearly all the members of Congress voted for it, beginning in the H.R., with Charles Allen of Massachusetts, and ending with Richard Yates, of Illinois; and that he could not understand how those who now oppose the Nebraska bill, so voted then, unless it was because it was then too soon after both the great political parties had ratified the compromises of 1850, and the ratification therefore too fresh, to be then repudiated.

Now I had seen the Washington act before; and I have carefully examined it since; and I aver that there is no repeal of the ordinance of '87, or of any prohibition of slavery, in it. In express terms, there is absolutely nothing in the whole law upon the subject—in fact, nothing to lead a reader to THINK of the subject. To my judgment, it is equally free from every thing from which such repeal can be legally implied; but however this may be, are men now to be entrapped by a legal implication, extracted from covert language, introduced perhaps, for the very purpose of entrapping them? I sincerely wish every man could read this law quite through, carefully watching every sentence, and every line, for a repeal of the ordinance of '87 or any thing equivalent to it.

Another point on the Washington act. If it was intended to be modelled after the Utah and New Mexico acts, as Judge Douglas, insists, why was it not inserted in it, as in them, that Washington was to come in with or without slavery as she may choose at the adoption of her constitution? It has no such provision in it; and I defy the ingenuity of man to give a reason for the omission, other than that it was not intended to follow the Utah and New Mexico laws in regard to the question of slavery.

The Washington act not only differs vitally from the Utah and New Mexico acts; but the Nebraska act differs vitally from both. By the latter act the people are left "perfectly free" to regulate their own domestic concerns, &c.; but in all the former, all their laws are to be submitted to Congress, and if disapproved are to be null. The Washington act goes even further; it absolutely prohibits the territorial legislation [legislature?], by very strong and guarded language, from establishing banks, or borrowing money on the faith of the territory. Is this the sacred right of self-government we hear vaunted so much? No sir, the Nebraska bill finds no model in the acts of '50 or the Washington act. It finds no model in any law from Adam till today. As Phillips[4] says of Napoleon, the Nebraska act is grand, gloomy, and peculiar; wrapped in the solitude of its own originality; without a model, and without a shadow upon the earth.

In the course of his reply, Senator Douglas remarked, in substance, that he had always considered this government was made for the white people and not for the negroes. Why, in point of mere fact, I think so too. But in this remark of the Judge, there is a significance, which I think is the key to the great mistake (if there is any such mistake) which he has made in this Nebraska measure. It shows that the Judge has no very vivid impression that the negro is a human; and consequently has no idea that there can be any moral question in legislating about him. In his view, the question of whether a new country shall be slave or free, is a matter of as utter indifference, as it is whether his neighbor shall plant his farm with tobacco, or stock it with horned cattle. Now, whether this view is right or wrong, it is very certain that the great mass of mankind take a totally different view. They consider slavery a great moral wrong; and their feelings against it, is not evanescent,

[4] Charles Phillips, famed British orator, to whose oration *The Character of Napoleon*. . . . (1817) Lincoln probably refers.

but eternal. It lies at the very foundation of their sense of justice; and it cannot be trifled with. It is a great and durable element of popular action, and, I think, no statesman can safely disregard it.

Our Senator also objects that those who oppose him in this measure do not entirely agree with one another. He reminds me that in my firm adherence to the constitutional rights of the slave States, I differ widely from others who are co-operating with me in opposing the Nebraska bill; and he says it is not quite fair to oppose him in this variety of ways. He should remember that he took us by surprise—astounded us—by this measure. We were thunderstruck and stunned; and we reeled and fell in utter confusion. But we rose each fighting, grasping whatever he could first reach—a scythe—a pitchfork—a chopping axe, or a butcher's cleaver. We struck in the direction of the sound; and we are rapidly closing in upon him. He must not think to divert us from our purpose, by showing us that our drill, our dress, and our weapons, are not entirely perfect and uniform. When the storm shall be past, he shall find us still Americans; no less devoted to the continued Union and prosperity of the country than heretofore.

Finally, the Judge invokes against me, the memory of Clay and of Webster. They were great men; and men of great deeds. But where have I assailed them? For what is it, that their life-long enemy, shall now make profit, by assuming to defend them against me, their life-long friend? I go against the repeal of the Missouri compromise; did they ever go for it? They went for the compromise of 1850; did I ever go against them? They were greatly devoted to the Union; to the small measure of my ability, was I ever less so? Clay and Webster were dead before this question arose; by what authority shall our Senator say they would espouse his side of it, if alive? Mr. Clay was the leading spirit in making the Missouri compromise; is it very credible that if now alive, he would take the lead in the breaking of it? The truth is that some support from whigs is now a necessity with the Judge, and for thus it is, that the names of Clay and Webster are now invoked. His old friends have deserted him in such numbers as to leave too few to live by. He came to his own, and his own received him not, and Lo! he turns unto the Gentiles.

A word now as to the Judge's desperate assumption that the compromises of '50 had no connection with one another; that Illinois came into the Union as a slave state, and some other similar ones. This is no other than a bold denial of the history of the country. If we do not know that the Compromises of '50 were dependent on each other; if we do not know that Illinois came into the Union as a free state—we do not know any thing. If we do not know these things, we do not know that we ever had a revolutionary war, or such a chief as Washington. To deny these things is to deny our national axioms, or dogmas, at least; and it puts an end to all argument. If a man will stand up and assert, and repeat, and re-assert, that two and two do not make four, I know nothing in the power of argument that can stop him. I think I can answer the Judge so long as he sticks to the premises; but when he flies from them, I can not work an argument into the consistency of a maternal gag, and actually close his mouth with it. In such a case I can only commend him to the seventy thousand answers just in from Pennsylvania, Ohio and Indiana.

Speech at Chicago, Illinois[1]

October 27, 1854

. . . . His speech of last evening was as thorough an exposition of the Nebraska iniquity as has ever been made, and his eloquence greatly impressed all his hearers, but it was manifest, as he frequently remarked that "he could not help feeling foolish in answering arguments which were no arguments at all." He could not help feeling silly in beating the air before an intelligent audience. It is a fruitless job to pound dry sand, under the delusion that it is a rock. The laborer may get his eyes full, but the sand is just as sandy as it was before.

. . . . He said that he had heard Mr. Douglas argue half an hour to show that there was a necessity of territorial organization in Nebraska and Kansas, as though it was the main point of all his efforts, and as though somebody was actually going to dispute him. It was a great trick among some public speakers to hurl a naked absurdity at his audience, with such confidence that they should be puzzled to know if the speaker didn't see some point of great magnitude in it which entirely escaped their observation. A neatly varnished sophism would be readily penetrated, but a great, rough *non sequitur* was sometimes twice as dangerous as a well polished fallacy.

In reference to a certain beast who inhabits a neighboring State, the democracy of which State sends him to the Senate, of course, Mr. L. said "there was one man in Congress, John Pettit,[2] who had no difficulty in seeing that our Declaration of Independence was a 'self-evident lie.' More than this, he had no hesitation in saying so in a public debate in Washington. The Declaration of Independence was a 'self-evident lie.' What would have happened if

[283]

he had said it in old Independence Hall? The door-keeper would have taken him by the throat and stopped his rascally breath awhile, and then have hurled him into the street."

¹ Chicago *Daily Journal*, October 30, 1854. The report deals at length with Lincoln's character and rise to prominence, but only the passages which report his speech are here reproduced. This is the only report located which tells much of the contents of the speech.   ² Senator from Indiana.

To Richard Yates¹

Naples, Oct. 30. 1854

Dear Yates: I am here now going to Quincy, to try to give Mr. Williams² a little life. I expect to be back in time to speak at Carlinville on Saturday, if thought expedient. What induces me to write now is that at Jacksonville as I came down to-day, I learned that the English in Morgan county have become dissatisfied about No-Nothingism.³ Our friends, however, think they have got the difficulty arrested. Nevertheless, it would be safer, I think, to do something on the subject, which you alone can do. The inclosed letter,⁴ or draft of a letter, I have drawn up, of which I think it would be well to make several copies, and have one placed in the hands of a safe friend, at each precinct where any considerable number of the foreign citizens, german as well as english—vote. Not knowing exactly where a letter will reach you soonest I fear this can not be very promptly attended to; but if the copies get into the proper hands the day before the election, it will be time enough. The whole of this is, of course, subject to your own judgment.   LINCOLN

¹ ALS-P, ISLA.
² Archibald Williams, who was also a candidate for congress and like Yates was to be defeated in spite of Lincoln's efforts.
³ Yates sent Lincoln's letter to Isaac N. Arnold on June 17, 1869, with the following comment: "The matter suggested within was not attended to and it so happened that I lost my elec. . . . I was beaten only two hundred votes over one half of which would have voted for me but for a false and sworn to statement that I had been seen in a Know Nothing Lodge."
⁴ The enclosure has not been located.

To Richard Yates¹

Dear Yates: Naples, Ill., November 1 [October 31], 1854.

I am on my way to Quincy to speak for our old friend Archie Williams. On my way down I heard at Jacksonville a story which may harm you if not averted—namely, that you have been a Know-Nothing. I suggest that you get a denial—something like the inclosed draft[2] which I have made—into the hands of a safe man in each precinct.

The day before election will do. Yours, as ever,

A. LINCOLN.

[1] Printed in "Lincoln," speech of the Honorable Richard Yates of Illinois in the House of Representatives, February 12, 1921. Richard Yates the second, son of Lincoln's friend, may have misdated this letter, or Lincoln may have done so, which seems less probable, but which, in the absence of the original, cannot be determined. At any rate, Lincoln was not in Naples but in Quincy on November 1 (Orville H. Browning, *Diary*). As will be seen from Lincoln's letter to Yates on October 30, Lincoln did not know where Yates could be reached by letter, and presumably wrote this additional note on the same subject. The latest date at which it could have been written was October 31.

[2] See note 4, Lincoln to Yates, October 30, *supra*.

To Adam Adams[1]

[November, 1854]

I have talked with Peters;[2] and he is not certain; but inclines to re[me]mber that you *were* present when the deed was made. That wont do. Turner writes me that he has found out where Bradshaw is. Do you know *what* he will swear? Better go right to Turner, & takes [*sic*] measures to get Bradshaw's deposition. I write to Turner by this mail. Yours truly   A. LINCOLN—

[1] ALS, owned by Miss Paula Angle, Chicago, Illinois. Lincoln's note is written on the back of Adams' letter to Lincoln, November 1, 1854. For further information on this case, see previous letters to Adams and to Thomas J. Turner.

[2] Judge Onslow Peters, before whom the deed in question had been executed, according to Adams. Adams maintained he was not present himself, and suggested that Peters could verify the fact.

Speech at Quincy, Illinois[1]

November 1, 1854

Hon. A. Lincoln, of Springfield addressed a large audience at Kendall's Hall on Wednesday evening. We regret that we cannot give a full sketch of his address. The large company present listened with unwearied attention and an approbation emphasised by repeated outbursts of enthusiastic applause. The address was one of the clearest, most logical, argumentative and convincing discourses on the Nebraska question to which we have listened. Commencing with the history of its earliest events which led to the Compromise of 1820, he traced that Compromise up to the present time, showing that it had ever remained in the hearts of the people a sacred thing which no ruthless hand should have dared to destroy.

[285]

Mr. Lincoln left a most favorable impression upon those who heard him. He is one of the "truly great men" of Illinois.

1 Quincy *Whig*, November 3, 1854.

To Charles Hoyt[1]

Mr. Charles Hoyt   Clinton, DeWitt Co.
Dear Sir: Nov. 10. 1854

You used to express a good deal of partiality for me; and if you are still so, now is the time. Some friends here are really for me, for the U.S. Senate; and I should be very grateful if you could make a mark for me among your members. Please write me at all events, giving me the names, post-offices, and *"political position"* of members round about you. Direct to Springfield.

Let this be confidential. Yours truly   A. LINCOLN—

1 ALS-P, ISLA. Charles Hoyt was a prominent merchant and mill owner at Aurora, Illinois. In July 1850, Lincoln had represented Hoyt in an important lawsuit involving a patent on a water wheel. Hoyt replied on November 20 and 27 giving the information Lincoln requested (DLC-RTL).

To Jacob Harding[1]

Harding, Esq   Clinton, DeWitt Co.
My dear Sir   Nov. 11. 1854

I have a suspicion that a whig has been elected to the Legislature from Edgar. If this is not so, why then *"nix cum arous"* but if it is so, then could you not make a mark with him for me, for U.S. Senator?—I really have some chance. Please write me at Springfield, giving me the names, post-offices, and political positions, of your representative and senator, whoever they may be.

Let this be confidential. Yours truly   A. LINCOLN

1 ALS, MnHi. Jacob Harding was a resident of Paris, Illinois.

To Orville H. Browning[1]

Springfield, Nov. 12, 1854

Dear Browning: At daylight the morning after the election, I had to go to court at DeWitt county, and I then had nothing of any account to write you. On my return last night I found your letter. Yates is beaten from 100 to 150. The whole thing was done in Morgan & Scott counties; in all the rest of the District we did better than we expected. The quarrel over the Insane Asylum[2] & the turning of about 200 english whigs in the two counties against him, because of Know-Nothingism, was what did the work for him. He now has in the two counties only about 100 majority; whereas two years ago, he had 521.

We now understand here that Mr. Williams is beaten also. Schuyler and Brown[3] are said to have played thunder.

It looks as if Anti Nebraska will have the H.R—the Senate doubtful.

By the returns in, Miller appears to have beaten Moore for Treasurer.[4] The only thing that throws doubt upon this is, that there is not much in from the South yet; and among the little that is in, there are some favorable signs to Moore. For instance, in Greene, Harris beats Yates over 400 while Moore beats Miller over 900.

Also, in St. Clair Moore has over 900 majority while, on the contrary, Trumbull, and Anti Nebraska generally, have about 900 majority. In all other places heard from Moore is getting along about like Nebraska. From what I see I think he must be beaten an average of 2500 in each of the four Northern Congressional Districts. Washburne, Woodworth, Norton and Knox are certainly elected.[5] It is believed Norton has a majority in every county of his District— in Vermillion alone 1120. Trumbull's election is sure by a very large majority. The Democrats here claim that Allen[6] is re-elected; and I fear it is so; though it is not quite certain. In the four Northern counties, old Col. Archer[7] gains over 400 on him; and I can hear nothing from any other county, though it is probable the dems. have something. I believe this is all I know. Yours truly

A. LINCOLN—

1 ALS, IHi.   2 See Lincoln to David A. Smith, June 10, 1853, *supra.*
3 Counties in Archibald Williams' district.
4 On the contrary, Democrat John Moore had defeated James Miller.
5 Elihu B. Washburne of Galena; James H. Woodworth, prominent merchant and former mayor of Chicago; Jesse O. Norton, attorney of Joliet; and James Knox, attorney of Knoxville.
6 James C. Allen, attorney of Palestine, a former member of the state House of Representatives.
7 William B. Archer, who had for years represented Clark County in the legislature.

To Noah W. Matheny[1]

N. W. Matheny: Springfield,
Clerk of the county court   Novr. 25– 1854
   of Sangamon County, Illinois

Sir: I hereby decline to accept the office of Representative in the General Assembly, for the said county of Sangamon, to which office I am reported to have been elected on the 7th. of Novr. Inst. I therefore desire that you notify the Governor of this vacancy, in order that legal steps be taken to fill the same. Your Obt. Servt.

A. LINCOLN—

[1] ALS, IHi.

To Ichabod Codding[1]
(COPY)

I. Codding, Esq   Springfield,
Dear Sir   Novr. 27. 1854

Your note of the 13th. requesting my attendance of the Republican State Central Committee, on the 17th. Inst. at Chicago, was, owing to my absence from home, received on the evening of that day (17th) only. While I have pen in hand allow me to say I have been perplexed some to understand why my name was placed on that committee. I was not consulted on the subject; nor was I apprized of the appointment, until I discovered it by accident two or three weeks afterwards. I suppose my opposition to the principle of slavery is as strong as that of any member of the Republican party; but I had also supposed that the *extent* to which I feel authorized to carry that opposition, practically; was not at all satisfactory to that party. The leading men who organized that party, were present, on the 4th. of Oct. at the discussion between Douglas and myself at Springfield,[2] and had full oppertunity to not misunderstand my position. Do I misunderstand theirs? Please write, and inform me. Yours truly   A. LINCOLN—

[1] ALS copy, DLC-RTL. Ichabod Codding was a noted abolition and temperance lecturer who was one of the most active leaders in the new Republican party movement in Illinois, often referred to contemporaneously as "fusionists." The predominance of abolitionists among the fusionists gave Lincoln some uncertainty as to his willingness to join forces with them. At this point Lincoln was willing to co-operate with them, but refused to join them.

[2] An anti-Nebraska Republican convention had been held at Springfield on October 4-5; Lincoln did not attend.

To Thomas J. Henderson[1]

T. J. Henderson, Esq   Springfield,
My dear Sir—   Novr. 27, 1854

It has come round that a whig may, by possibility, be elected to the U.S. Senate; and I want the chance of being the man. You are a member of the Legislature, and have a vote to give. Think it over, and see whether you can do better than to go for me.

Write me, at all events; and let this be confidential. Yours truly

A. LINCOLN—

[1] ALS, owned by Fred H. Dunbar, Princeton, Illinois. Thomas J. Henderson was an anti-Nebraska member of the state House of Representatives.

To Elihu N. Powell[1]

E. N. Powell, Esq   Springfield,
My dear Sir: Nov. 27– 1854

Acting on your advice, and my own judgment, I have declined accepting the office of Representative of this county. I only allowed myself to be elected, because it was supposed my doing so would help Yates.

Things look reasonably well; but I fear some will insist on a platform, which I can not stand upon.

Please write me again when you discover any thing worth writing about. Yours as ever   A. LINCOLN—
P.S. Can I venture to write directly to Dr. Arnold?[2]   A– L–

[1] ALS, owned by Wayne C. Townley, Bloomington, Illinois. Elihu N. Powell was an attorney at Peoria, partner of William F. Bryan.
[2] Dr. John D. Arnold of Peoria, an anti-Nebraska Whig who had been elected recently to the state Senate.

To Hugh Lemaster[1]

Hugh LeMaster, Esq.   Springfield,
My dear Sir: Nov. 29, 1854.

I have got it into my head to try to be U.S. Senator, and I wish somehow to get at your Whig member, Mr. Babcock. I am not acquainted with him—could you not make or cause to be made, a mark with him for me? Would not Judge Kellogg lend a helping hand? J. P. Boris,[2] I venture to hope, would be willing to give a lift. Please write me at all events; and let this be confidential, so far as practicable. Yours as ever,   A. LINCOLN.

[1] Lewiston, Maine, *Journal*, February 19, 1949. Hugh Lemaster, editor of the Fulton County *Republican* at Lewistown, Illinois, answered on December 11 that he had "conversed with some of our most prominent (working) Whigs and they all say elect Lincoln. I have not seen Judge [William] Kellogg nor Rep. [Amos C.] Babcock. . . . I am satisfied that Judge will favor your election. . . . A. C. Babcock is a man of small stature . . . but a true Whig . . . & . . . will soon learn his duty." (DLC-RTL).
[2] No person by this name has been identified, and the editors suspect that the source is in error.

Resolutions on the Death of Charles R. Welles[1]

November 29, 1854

Whereas, since the last term of our circuit court Charles R. Welles suddenly terminated his mortal career under an attack of that fearful scourge, the cholera, which has desolated the hearts and homes of unnumbered thousands—

Resolved, That by his death the bar of Springfield has lost a highly esteemed, upright and honorable member of the legal profession.

Resolved, That his strict integrity, his social character and christian virtues endeared him to his friends, secured the confidence of his acquaintances, and rendered him a useful member of society.

Resolved, That we deeply sympathise with his family and friends in their bereavement, but in the midst of their affliction we doubt not they experience consolation in the assurance that their loss is his eternal gain.

Resolved, That a copy of these proceedings be presented to the widow and family of the deceased, and to his honor, Judge Davis, of the circuit court, with a request that they may be entered at full upon the records of the court, and that the city papers be requested to publish the same.

[1] *Illinois Journal,* December 9, 1854. Lincoln, John T. Stuart and James C. Conkling were appointed to draw up the resolutions for adoption by the Sangamon County Bar. How much Lincoln contributed to the composition is uncertain.

To Joseph Gillespie[1]

J. Gillespie, Esq
My dear Sir

Springfield,
Dec: 1– 1854

I have really got it into my head to try to be United States Senator; and if I could have your support my chances would be reasonably good. But I know, and acknowledge, that you have as just claims to the place as I have; and therefore I do not ask you to yield to me, if you are thinking of becoming a candidate yourself. If, however, you are not, then I should like to be remembered affectionately by you; and also, to have you make a mark for me with the Anti-Nebraska members, down your way. If you know, and have no objection to tell, let me know whether Trumbull[2] intends to make a push. If he does, I suppose the two men in St. Clair, and one or both in Madison will be for him.

We have the Legislature clearly enough on joint ballot; but the Senate is very close; and Calhoun[3] told me to-day that the Nebraska men will stave off the election if they can. Even if we get into joint vote, we shall have difficulty to unite our forces.

Please write me, and let this be confidential   Your friend as ever

A. LINCOLN—

[1] ALS, MoSHi.
[2] Lyman Trumbull had just been elected to congress as an anti-Nebraska man.
[3] John Calhoun of Sangamon County.

To John McLean[1]

Hon. Justice McLean—   Springfield, Ills.
Sir: Decr. 6. 1854

I understand it is in contemplation to displace the present Clerk, and appoint a new one for the Circuit and District courts of Illinois. I am very friendly to the present incumbent, and both for his own sake and that of his family, I wish him to be retained so long as it is possible for the court to do so.

In the contingency of his removal, however, I have recommended William Butler as his successor; and I do not wish what I write now, to be taken as any abatement of that recommendation.

William J. Black, is also an applicant for the appointment; and I write this, at the solicitation of his friends, to say that he is every way worthy of the office; and that, I doubt not, the conferring it upon him, will give great satisfaction. Your Obt. Servt.

                                        A. LINCOLN—

[1] ALS, ORB.

Bond for John T. Stuart[1]

                                        December 6, 1854

Know all men by these presents that I, John T. Stuart Stephen T. Logan, Abraham Lincoln Benjamin S. Edwards and John Cook & Wm. J. Black are held and firmly bound unto The People of the State of Illinois for the use and benefit of any and all persons interrested in the penal sum of One hundred thousand Dollars lawful money &c for the true payment of which We bind ourselves, our Heirs Executors & Administrators firmly by these presents. Dated this sixth Day of December AD 1854.

The condition of this obligation is such that whereas the said John T. Stuart has been this day appointed Receiver of the assetts and property of "The Mechanics and Farmers Bank" located at the city of Springfield in said State of Illinois by the Honorable David Davis Judge of the Circuit Court within and for the County of Sangamon and State aforesaid,—Now if the said John T. Stuart shall well and truly do and perform all such things as shall be required of him by Law as such Receiver and shall well and truly pay over all such sums of money as shall come into his hands as such Receiver to the persons respectively entitled thereto then this Bond to be void otherwise to be and remain in full force and virtue.

In testimony whereof said Obligors have hereunto set their hands and seals the day and year above written

John T. Stuart (Seal)	Benjamin S. Edwards (Seal)
S T. Logan (Seal)	John Cook[2] (Seal)
A. Lincoln— (Seal)	W. J. Black. (Seal)

Approved Dec. 6, 1854
D Davis.
—Judge &c—

[1] DS, IHi.   [2] John Cook was one of Springfield's leading businessmen.

To Herbert W. Fay[1]

H. W. Fay.   Springfield, December 11, 1854.

My Dear Sir: When you were in the legislature you helped to pass some bills of mutual interest, at that time either in jest or earnest you suggested me for Senator. My friends are now asking me to make the race. See the representatives and senator of your district and let me know what indorsement I may expect in that locality. Your friend as ever,   A. LINCOLN.

[1] *Week by Week in Springfield*, November 19, 1932. Herbert W. Fay was state representative from DeKalb County 1850-1852.

To Elihu B. Washburne[1]

Hon: E. B. Washburne.   Springfield, Ills.
My dear Sir: Dec: 11, 1854

Your note of the 5th. is just received. It is too true that by the official returns Allen beats Col Archer one vote.[2] There is a report to-day that there is a mistake in the returns from Clay county, giving Allen sixty votes more than he really has; but this, I fear is itself a mistake. I have just examined the returns from that county at the Secretarie's office, and find that the agregate vote for Sheriff only falls short, by three votes, of the agregate as reported, of Allen & Archer's vote. Our friends, however, are hot on the track; and will probe the matter to the bottom.

As to my own matter, things continue to look reasonably well. I wrote your friend, George Gage;[3] and, three days ago, had an answer from him, in which he talks out plainly, as your letter taught me to expect. To-day I had a letter from Turner.[4] He says he is not committed, & will not be until he sees how most effectually to oppose slavery extension.

I have not ventured to write all the members in your district, lest some of them should be offended by the indelicacy of the thing —that is, coming from a total stranger. Could you not drop some of them a line? Very truly your friend, A. LINCOLN—

1 ALS, IHi.
2 James C. Allen was declared elected to congress over William B. Archer and served until July 18, 1856, when the House of Representatives decided he was not entitled to his seat. He won the election to fill the vacancy thus caused and served out the term.
3 George Gage was a Whig state senator from McHenry County.
4 Thomas J. Turner, state representative from Stephenson County, who was elected speaker of the House.

To Elihu B. Washburne[1]

Hon: E. B. Washburne   Springfield,
My dear Sir: Dec: 14, 1854

So far as I am concerned, there must be something wrong about U.S. Senator, at Chicago. My most intimate friends there do not answer my letters; and I can not get a word from them. Wentworth[2] has a knack of knowing things better than most men. I wish you would pump him, and write me what you get from him. Please do this as soon as you can, as the time is growing short. Dont let *any one* know I have written you this; for there may be those opposed to me, nearer about you than you think. Very truly Yours &c   A. LINCOLN

1 ALS, IHi.
2 John Wentworth, Chicago Democrat, who was completing his fifth term in congress.

To Thomas J. Henderson[1]

Hon. T. J. Henderson: Springfield
Dear Sir: Decr. 15. 1854

Yours of the 11th. was received last night, and for which I thank you.[2] Of course I prefer myself to all others; yet it is neither in my heart nor my conscience to say I am any better man than Mr. Williams.[3] We shall have a terrible struggle with our adversaries. They are desperate, and bent on desperate deeds. I accidentally learned of one of the leaders here writing to a member South of here, in about the following language. "We are beaten. They have a clear majority of at least nine, on joint ballot. They *outnumber* us, but we must *outmanage* them. Douglas must be sustained. We must elect the Speaker; and we must elect a Nebraska U S. Senator, or elect none at all." Similar letters, no doubt, are written to every Nebraska member. Be considering how we can best meet, and foil, and beat them.

I send you, by this mail, a copy of my Peoria speech. You may have seen it before; or you may not think it worth seeing now.

Do not speak of the Nebraska letter mentioned above; I do not wish it to become public, that I received such information. Yours truly
A. LINCOLN—

¹ ALS, owned by Fred H. Dunbar, Princeton, Illinois.
² Henderson had replied to Lincoln's previous letter of November 27 (*supra*) that he was not committed.   ³ Archibald Williams.

To Leonard Swett¹

L. Swett, Esq   Springfield,
Dear Sir: Dec: 17. 1854.
I can not learn of a single copy of the Revised Code being here for sale. Sorry; but it seems to be so.

Does the Rev. John S. Barger² occasi[o]nally cross your path?—
Yours truly
A. LINCOLN—

¹ ALS-P, ISLA. Leonard Swett began the practice of law at Clinton and later removed to Bloomington, where he was at this time. He had become recognized as one of the leading attorneys of the Eighth Judicial Circuit and was more or less closely associated with Lincoln from this time forward.
² The Reverend John S. Barger was a prominent Methodist and one of the founders of Illinois Wesleyan University at Bloomington.

Opinion Concerning John Fitzgerald¹

December 18, 1854
John Fitzgerald, eighteen years of age, able-bodied, but without pecuniary means, came directly from Ireland to Springfield Illinois, and there stopped, and sought employment, with no present intention of returning to Ireland, or going elsewhere. After remaining in the city some three weeks, part of the time employed, and part not, he fell sick, and became a public charge. It has been submitted to me, whether the city of Springfield, or the County of Sangamon is, by law, to bear the charge.

It is my opinion, and decision, that the City is to bear it. I base this upon the construction I give the 4th. Section of the 13th. Article of the new city charter (Approved March 2, 1854)   I think the Legislature intended that all public charges, arising from the indigence of persons, *resident* within the City, were to be borne by the City—and not by the County. I think it was not the intention that this class of charges was to be parcelled out between the city and county, by critical discussions on the words "citizen" "pauper" and the like.

Dec: 18– 1854.   A. LINCOLN—

[1] ADS, IHi.

To Elihu B. Washburne[1]

Hon: E. B. Washburne   Springfield, Dec: 19. 1854

My dear Sir: Yours of the 12th. just received. The objection of your friend at Winnebago rather astonishes me. For a Senator to be the impartial representative of his whole State, is so plain a duty, that I pledge myself to the observance of it without hesitation; but not without some mortification that any one should suspect me of an inclination to the contrary. I was eight years a representative of Sangamon county in the Legislature; and, although, in a conflict of interests between that and other counties, it perhaps would have been my duty to stick to Old Sangamon; yet it is not within my recollection that the Northern members ever wanted my vote for any interest of theirs, without getting it. My distinct recollection is, that the Northern members, and Sangamon members, were always on good terms, and always co-operating on measures of policy. The canal was then the great Northern measure, and it, from first to last, had our votes as readily as the votes of the North itself. Indeed, I shall be surprized if it can be pointed out that in any instance, the North sought our aid, and failed to get it.

Again, I was a member of Congress one term—the term when Mr. Turner[2] was the legal member, and you were a lobby member from your then District. Now I think I might appeal to Mr. Turner and yourself, whether you did not always have my feeble service for the asking. In the case of conflict, I might without blame, have prefered my own District. As a Senator, I should claim no right, as I should feel no inclination, to give the central portion of the state any preference over the North, or any other portion of it. Very truly your friend   A. LINCOLN

[1] ALS, owned by North Shore Country Day School, Winnetka, Illinois.
[2] Thomas G. Turner, representative 1847-1849.

List of Members of the Illinois Legislature in 1855[1]

[January 1, 1855?]

Senate

Adams, Augustus	W.	Kane
Adams, John H.	W.	Stephenson
Arnold, Dr. J. D.	W.	Peoria
Bryan, Silas	D.	Wayne
Campbell, James M.	A.N.D.	McDonough
Carlin, William	D.	Adams
Cook, Burton C.	A.N.D.	LaSalle
Corder, A. P.	D.	Williamson
Davis, Jacob C.	D.	Hancock
Detrich, J. E.	D.	Randolph
Gage, George	W.	McHenry
Graham, Benjamin	D.	Henry
Gillespie, Joseph	W.	Madison
Jernigan, G. R.	D.	Christian
Judd, Norman B.	A.N.D.	Cook
Kuykendoll [Kuykendall], A. J.	D.	Gal[l]atin
Morrison, J. L. D.	W.	St. Clair
Morton, Joseph	D.	Morgan
O'Kean, Mortimer	D.	Jasper
Osgood, Uri	A.N.D.	Will
Palmer, John M.	A.N.D.	Macoupin
Ruggles, James M.	W.	Mason
Sutphen [Sutphin], H. L.	D.	Pike
Talcott, Wait	W.	Winnebago
Watson, William [D.]	W.	Coles

Democrats, 11— Of these, Mr. Graham did not vote last winter, [and his district A.N.D. over 2000][2] and Mr. Detrich has since written a letter against the repeal of the Mo. Comp.

Whigs 9 A.N.D. 5— Of these two classes, a great many[3] have gone into the Republican organization.

H.R.

Allen, George T.	A.N.D.	Madison
Allen, William J.	D.	Williamson

[1] AD, ORB; AD, owned by H. T. Morgan, Peoria, Illinois. The two copies of this list, both in Lincoln's hand and on seven pages of identical small notebooks, are possibly the only survivors of several prepared by Lincoln for the use of his supporters in his bid for the United States senatorship. One prepared for Samuel C. Parks, representative from Logan County, is now in the Barrett Collection and has provided the present text. The other was prepared for Robert Boal, representative from Marshall County. The minor variations in the Boal copy are indicated in footnotes. Each copy carries an endorsement written and signed by its original recipient stating the circumstances under which he received the notebook.

[2] In Parks copy but not in Boal copy.

[3] Boal copy reads "several" for "a great many."

[296]

Baker, Henry S.	A.N.D.	Madison
Babcock, A. C.	W.	Fulton
Bennett, Isaac R.	D.	Morgan
Bradford, James M.	D.	Clinton
Boal, Robert	W.	Marshall
Brown, H. A.	D.	Scott
Brown, Saml. W.	W.	Knox
Cline, W. N. [William M.]	D.	Fulton
Courtney, [James]	W.	Vermilion
Dearborn, Jonathan	D.	Brown
Day, Frederick S.	A.N.D.	LaSalle
Diggins, Wesley	W.	McHenry
Dunlap, M. L.	W.	Cook
Funkhouser, Presley	D.	Fayette
Foss, Robert H.	A.N.D.	Cook
Foster, George F.	A.N.D.	Cook
Gray, G. M[W].	N.W.	Massac
Gregg, Hugh	D.	Jefferson
Grove, Henry A.	W.	Peoria
Holbrook, James C.	W.	Randolph
Hosmer, P. E.	D.	Perry
Hopkins, C. C.	D.	Wayne
Heath, Randolph	D.	Lawrence
Holliday, G. H.	D.	Macoupin
Higbee, C. L.	D.	Pike
Henderson, T. J.	W.	Stark
Hills, E. O.	A.N.D.	DuPage
Hackney, Benjamin	W.	Kane
Henry, Miles S.	W.	Lee[4]
Hinch [Benjamin P.][5]	D.	Gal[l]atin
Jones, Albert G.	W.	Coles
Johns, Henry C.	W.	Piatt
Kinney, Wm. C.	A.N.D.	St. Clair
Logan, Stephen T.	W.	Sangamon
Lovejoy, Owen	Abn.	Bureau
Lee, William M.	W.	R. [Rock] Island
Little, W. A.	W.	Jo Daviess
Lyman, William	A.N.D.	Winnebago
Lawrence, L. W.	W.	Boone
Martin, Saml. H.	D.	White
Masters, S. D.	D.	Menard
McClain [McLain], Dudley	D.	Edgar
McClure, Thos. B[R].	W.	Clark
McClun, John E.	W.	McLean
McCri[e]llis, L. F.	D.	Jersey
McDaniel, Jonathan	D.	Sangamon
Morrison, W. R.	D.	Monroe
Moulton, Saml. W.	D.	Shelby

4 Boal copy reads "Whiteside." Henry represented both counties.
5 Hinch's first name and initial are omitted in both copies.

Preston, F. D.	D.	Richland
Pursley, James M.	D.	Greene
Parks, Saml. C.	W.	Logan
Parks, G. D. A.	A.N.D.	Will
Patten [Patton], William	A.N.D.	DeKalb
Pinckney, D. J.	W.	Ogle
Rawlings, F. M.	D.	Alexander
Richmond, Henry	D.	Montg[ome]ry
Richmond, John P.	D.	Schuyler
Richmond, Thomas	A.N.D.	Cook
Riblett, Henry	W.	Tazewell
Rice, Wm. C.	W.	Henderson
Sams, Thomas M.	D.	Franklin
Seehorn, Eli	D.	Adams
Sullivan, H. V.	W.	Adams
Strawn, David	A.N.D.	LaSalle
Strunk, John	W.	Kankakee
Sargent, Porter	W.	Carroll
Swan, Hurlbut	W.	Lake
Tanner, T. B.	D.	Marion
Trapp, A. H	A.N.D.	St. Clair
Turner, T. J.	A.N.D.	Stephenson
Walker, George	D.	Hancock
Wheeler, Alanson	W.	Kendall

Democrats	30	
Whigs.	28	
A.N.D.	14	—Of these two[6] last classes

many have gone into the Republican organization.

Nebraska Whig	1
Abolitionist	1
Vacancy	1

[6] Boal copy lists "Abn. 1" before this sentence and reads "Of the three last classes, a great many. . . ."

Outline for Speech to the Colonization Society[1]

[January 4, 1855?]

1434–   A portaguse [sic] captain, on the coast of Guinea, seizes a few Affrican lads, and sells them in the South of Spain.

1501–2–3.   Slaves are carried from Africa to the Spanish colonies in America.

1516–17   Charles 5th. of Spain gives encouragement to the African Slave trade.

1562–   John Hawkins carries slaves to the British West Indies.

[298]

1620   A dut[c]h ship carries a cargo of African slaves to Virginia.
1626–   Slaves introduced into New-York.
1630 to 41. Slaves introduced into Massachusetts.
1776.   The period of our revolution, there were about 600-000 slaves in the colonies; and there are now in the U.S. about 3¼ millions.

Soto, the catholic confessor of Charles 5. opposed Slavery and the Slave trade from the beginning; and, in 1543, procured from the King some amelioration of its rigors.

The American colonies, from the beginning, appealed to the British crown, against the Slave trade; but without success.

1727–   Quakers begin to agitate for the abolition of Slavery within their own denomination
1751–   Quakers succeed in abolishing Slavery within their own denomination.
1787–   Congress, under the confederation, passes an Ordinance forbidding Slavery to go to the North Western Territory.
1808–   Congress, under the constitution, abolishes the Slave trade, and declares it piracy.
1776. to 1800–Slavery abolished in all the States North of Maryland and Virginia.
All the while– Individual conscience at work.

1816–   Colonization Society is organized—it's direct object—history—and present prospects of success.
          Its colateral objects—Suppression of Slave trade—commerce—civilization and religion.

Objects of this meeting.[2]

1 AD, DLC-RTL. The date of this manuscript is derived from the fact that Lincoln addressed the Colonization Society on January 4, 1855. He had been announced as speaker the year before, on January 12, 1854, but was prevented by illness in his family (*Journal*, January 14, 1854). Also, on August 30, 1853, he had spoken to the society. Although the outline might conceivably have been prepared for one of the earlier occasions, it seems in appearance to belong to the period of the Resolutions Recommending Amendment of the Kansas-Nebraska Act (*infra*). The date [1849] assigned to the manuscript in the RTL collection cannot be supported. There is no published report of the meeting so far as can be determined.

2 The fact that the outline appears in the RTL collection between draft one and draft two of the resolutions (*infra*), suggests that the purpose of the meeting may have been to adopt the resolutions and recommend their adoption by the General Assembly.

Drafts of Resolutions Recommending Amendment of the Kansas-Nebraska Act[1]

[January 4, 1855?]

[First Draft?]

Whereas the African Slave-trade ought not to be revived by law.

And whereas the principle of non-intervention by congress, as laid down in those parts of Sections fourteen and thirtytwo of the act of congress entitled "An act to organize the Territories of Nebraska and Kansas" Approved [blank] which reads as follows, towit

[middle of page blank for insertion]

requires the repeal of all laws of congress abolishing, or hindering said African Slave-trade; and requires that all persons wishing to own slaves should be left "perfectly free" to purchase them on the coast of Africa, and take them to, and hold them within, the Terrtories of the United States, if they choose to do so, therefore

Resolved by the General Assembly of the State of Illinois, that our Senators in Congress be instructed and, our Representatives requested, to use their best endeavors to procure the repeal of the above recited parts of said Act to organize the Territories of Nebraska and Kansas.

Resolved further, that our said Senators be instructed, and our said Representatives requested; to procure the revival and re-enactment, of the eighth section of the act preparatory to the admission of Missouri into the Union, approved March sixth, eighteen hundred and twenty.

Resolved further, that they use their utmost endeavors to prevent the said Terrtories of Nebraska and Kansas, or either of them, or any part of either of them, ever coming into this Union as a Slave-state or states.

Resolved further, that they use their utmost constitutional endeavors to prevent Slavery ever being established in any county or place, where it does not now legally exist.

Resolved further, that our said Senators and Representatives, resist to their utmost, the now threatened attempt to divide California, in order to erect one portion thereof into a slave state—

[Second Draft?]

Resolved by the People of the State of Illinois represented in the General Assembly:

[300]

That our Senators in Congress be instructed, and our Representatives requested, as follows, towit—

1. To use their utmost endeavors to repeal so much of the fourteenth, and thirtysecond Sections of the act of congress, entitled "an act to organize the Territories of Nebraska and Kansas" approved [blank] as is found in the words following, towit

[half page blank for insertion]

2. To use their utmost endeavors to procure the revival, and reenactment, of the eighth Section of the act preparatory to the admission of Missouri into the Union, approved, March sixth eighteen hundred and twenty.

3. To use their utmost endeavors to prevent the said Territories of Nebraska and Kansas, or either of them, or any part of either of them, ever coming into the Union as a Slave-state, or states.

4 To use their utmost endeavors to prevent domestic slavery ever being established in any country, or place, where it does not now legally exist.

5. To resist, to their utmost, the now threatened attempt to divide California, in order to erect one portion thereof into a slave-state.

6. To resist, to their utmost, the now threatened attempt to revive the African slave-trade.

1 ADf, DLC-RTL. Presumably these resolutions were drawn by Lincoln in January 1855, for the purpose of having them introduced in the legislature. The Journals of House and Senate record other resolutions concerning the Kansas-Nebraska Bill, but Lincoln's resolutions do not appear. Which of Lincoln's two drafts represent his revision is difficult to determine, but the order in which they appear seems the probable order of composition.

Opinion Concerning the Estates of Joseph Smith and James M. Bradford[1]

January 6, 1855

Joseph Smith and James M. Bradford, were partners in trade. Bradford died, and there was, and is, an administration of his estate. Smith, as surviving partner, proceeded to settle the firm business; but without finishing it, died also, and there is an administration of his estate.

1st. Who, according to law, is to finish the adjustment of the firm business.

2nd. If any firm debt has been lost, which Smith could have saved during his surveyorship, is Smith's estate liable for Bradford's share of such lost debt?

3rd. If it be held that Smith's administrator, is to settle up the firm business, and any firm debt he lost, which such administrator could have saved, is Smith's estate liable for Bradford's share of that debt?

4 In the absence of any agreement, is the partner who advanced more cash than the other, entitled to interest on the excess?

5 If the surviving partner, make advances, to pay debts, is he entitled to interest?

6 While the firm was in active business, the estate of Micajah Smith loaned certain money to the firm, which is still unpaid.

At what *rate*, and in what *manner*, is interest to be allowed on this?

The foregoing questions having been submitted the following are our answers.

To the 1st. We say the Administrators of the estate of Joseph Smith deceased.

To the 2nd. & 3rd. We reply—in our opinion Joseph Smith the surviving partner, and after his death—his administrators, are chargeable with all the debts that at the time, of, and after the death of James M. Bradford, were good, and could have been collected by the use of ordinary diligence—that is, such diligence as a prudent business man would exercise in the management of his own affairs of a similar character—and that in settling the accounts the estate of Joseph Smith deceased is to be charged with all the debts due to the partnership that were good at the time of the death of Bradford, except such as they can show satisfactorily, could not have been collected by said Joseph Smith in his life time, or by them since his death, by the use of the diligence aforesaid.

The 4 & 5th. questions we answer with a negative ·

To the 6th. The firm of Bradford & Smith is liable to repay money borrowed with simple interest upon the amounts loaned from *the times* they were so severally loaned. The interest cannot be compounded. If no agreement as to interest was made, with the creditor—the rate of interest would be six per cent. As between the estates of Bradford, & Smith—from the time (if such be the case) sufficient money was received from the assets of the firm, by Smith or his administrators, or might by the use of ordinary diligence as aforesaid have been collected to pay *all* the debts due by the partnership—the estate of Bradford would be chargeable with no part of that interest. A. LINCOLN—

Jany 6. 1855. B. S. EDWARDS

¹ ADS, owned by Morton D. Hull, Chicago, Illinois. The questions are in Lincoln's handwriting and the answers in that of Edwards.

To Elihu B. Washburne¹

(CONFIDENTIAL)

Hon: E. B. Washburne. Springfield,

My dear Sir: Dec: [January] 6– 1855

I telegraphed you as to the organization of the two houses. T. J. Turner, elected Speaker 40 to 24. House not full. Dr. Richmond of Schuyler was his opponent. Anti-Nebraska also elected all the other officers of the H.R. In the Senate, Anti-Nebraska elected George T. Brown, of the Alton Courier, Secretary; and Dr. Ray² of the Galena Jeffersonian, one of the clerks. In fact they elected all the officers; but some of them were Nebraska men elected over the regular Nebraska nominees. It is said that by this, they get one or two Nebraska Senators to go for bringing on the Senatorial election. I can not vouch for this. As to the Senatorial election I think very little more is known than was before the meeting of the Legislature. Besides the ten or a dozen, on our side, who are willing to be known as candidates, I think there are fifty secretly watching for a chance. I do not know that it is much advantage to have the largest number of votes at the start. If I did know this to be an advantage I should feel better; for I can not doubt but I have more committals than any other one man. Your District comes up tolerably well for me; but not unanamously by any means—George Gage is for me, as you know. J. H. Adams is not committed to me but I think will be for me. Mr. Talcott will not be for me as a first choice. Dr. Little and Mr. Sargent are openly for me. Prof— Pinckney is for me, but wishes to be quiet. Dr. Whitney³ writes me that Rev: Mr. Lawrence will be for me; and his manner to me so indicates; but he has not spoken it out. Mr. Swan, I have some slight hopes of. Turner says he is not committed; and I shall get him whenever I can make it appear to be his interest to go for me. Dr. Lyman and old Mr. Diggins will never go for me as a first choice. M. P. Sweet is here as a candidate; and I understand he claims that he has 22 members committed to him. I think some part of his estimate must be based on insufficient evidence; as I can not well see where they are to be found; and as I can learn the name of one only—Day of La Salle. Still, it may be so. There are more than 22 Anti-Nebraska members who are not committed to me. Tell Norton that Mr. Strunk and Mr. Wheeler come out plump for me; and for which I thank him. Judge Parks I have decided hopes for; but he says he is not committed. I understand myself as having 26 committals; and I do not think any other one man has ten—may be mistaken though. The whole Legislature stands,

		A.N.		N.	
Senate	—	13		12—	
H.R.	"	44	"	31—	
		57		43	
		43			

14 maj. All here, but Kinney, of St. Clair.

Our special election[4] here is plain enough when understood. Our adversaries pretended to be running no candidate, secretly notified all their men to [be] on hand; and, favored by a very rainy day got a complete snap judgment on us. In Novr. Sangamon gave Yates 2166 votes. On the rainy day she gave our man only 984— leaving him 82 votes behind. After all, the result is not of the least consequence. The Locos kept up a great chattering over it till the organization of the HR. since which they all seem to have forgotten it.

G's letter to L. I think has not been received. Ask him if he sent it. Yours as ever   A. LINCOLN—

[1] ALS, IHi. Writing shortly after the first of the year, Lincoln misdated the month.

[2] Charles H. Ray, who later became editor of the Chicago *Tribune*.

[3] Dr. Daniel H. Whitney of Boone County, Illinois.

[4] A special election held to fill the vacancy in the legislature caused by Lincoln's resignation (see letter to Matheny, November 25, 1854, *supra*). Norman M. Broadwell was the defeated candidate.

To Elihu B. Washburne[1]

Hon: E. B. Washburne—   Springfield,
My dear Sir: Feby. 9– 1855

The agony is over at last; and the result you doubtless know. I write this only to give you some particulars to explain what might appear difficult of understanding. I began with 44 votes,[2] Shields 41, and Trumbull 5—yet Trumbull was elected. In fact 47 different members voted for me—getting three new ones on the second ballot, and losing four old ones. How came my 47 to yield to T's 5?. It was Govr. Matteson's work. He has been secretly a candidate every since (before even) the fall election. All the members round about the canal were Anti-Nebraska; but were, nevertheless nearly all democrats, and old personal friends of his. His plan was to privately impress them with the belief that he was as good Anti-Nebraska as any one else—at least could be secured to be so by instructions, which could be easily passed. In this way he got from four to six of that sort of men to really prefer his election to that of any other man—all "sub rosa" of course. One notable instance of this sort was with Mr. Strunk of Kankakee. At the beginning of the session he came a volunteer to tell me he was for me & would walk a hundred miles to elect me; but lo, it was not long before he leaked it out that he was going for me the first few ballots & then for Govr. Matteson.

The Nebraska men, of course, were not for Matteson; but when they found they could elect no avowed Nebraska man they tardily determined, to let him get whomever of our men he could by whatever means he could and ask him no questions. In the mean time Osgood, Don. Morrison & Trapp of St. Clair had openly gone over from us. With the united Nebraska force, and their recruits, open & covert, it gave Matteson more than enough to elect him. We saw into it plainly ten days ago; but with every possible effort, could not head it off. All that remained of the Anti Nebraska force, excepting Judd, Cook, Palmer[,] Baker & Allen of Madison, & two or three of the secret Matteson men, would go into caucus, & I could get the nomination of that caucus. But the three Senators & one of the two representatives above named "could never vote for a whig" and this incensed some twenty whigs to "think" they would never vote for the man of the five. So we stood, and so we went into the fight yesterday; the Nebraska men very confident of the election of Matteson, though denying that he was a candidate; and we very much believing also, that they would elect him. But they wanted first to make a show of good faith to Shields by voting for him a few times, and our secret Matteson men also wanted to make a show of good faith by voting with us a few times. So we led off. On the seventh ballot, I think, the signal was given to the Neb. men, to turn on to Matteson, which they acted on to a man, with one exception; my old friend Strunk going with them giving him 44 votes. Next ballot the remaining Neb. man, & one pretended Anti- went on to him, giving him 46. The next still another giving him 47, wanting only three of an election. In the mean time, our friends with a view of detaining our expected bolters had been turning from me to Trumbull till he he [sic] had risen to 35 & I had been reduced to 15. These would never desert me except by my direction; but I became satisfied that if we could prevent Matteson's election one or two ballots more, we could not possibly do so a single ballot after my friends should begin to return to me from Trumbull. So I determined to strike at once; and accordingly advised my remaining friends to go for him, which they did & elected him on that the 10th. ballot.

Such is the way the thing was done. I think you would have done the same under the circumstances; though Judge Davis, who came down this morning, declares he never would have consented to the 47 men being controlled by the 5. I regret my defeat moderately, but I am not nervous about it. I could have headed off every combination and been elected, had it not been for Matteson's double game—and his defeat now gives me more pleasure than my own gives me pain. On the whole, it is perhaps as well for our general cause that Trumbull is elected. The Neb. men confess that they hate it worse than any thing that could have happened. It is a great consolation to see them worse whipped than I am. I tell them it is their own fault—that they had abundant opertunity [*sic*] to choose between him & me, which they declined, and instead forced it on me to decide between him & Matteson.

With my grateful acknowledgments for the kind, active, and continued interest you have taken for me in this matter, allow me to subscribe myself   Yours forever   A. LINCOLN—

1 ALS, IHi.
2 Including the speaker of the House, Lincoln polled 45 votes.

To William H. Henderson[1]

Hon: W. H. Henderson: Springfield, Ills.
My dear Sir: Feby. 21– 1855

Your letter of the 4th. covering a lot of old deeds was received only two days ago. Wilton[2] says he has the order but can not lay his hand upon it easily, and can not take time to make a thorough search, until he shall have gone to & returned from Chicago. So I lay the papers by, and wait.

The election is over, the Session is ended, and I am *not* Senator. I have to content myself with the honor of having been the first choice of a large majority of the fiftyone members who finally made the election. My larger number of friends had to surrender to Trumbull's smaller number, in order to prevent the election of Matteson, which would have been a Douglas victory. I started with 44 votes & T. with 5.[3] It was rather hard for the 44 to have to surrender to the 5—and a less good humored man than I, perhaps would not have consented to it—and it would not have been done without my consent. I could not, however, let the whole political result go to ruin, on a point merely personal to myself.

Your son,[4] kindly and firmly stood by me from first to last; and for which he has my everlasting gratitude. Your friend as ever

A. LINCOLN

[1] ALS-P, ISLA.   [2] Harry Wilton, U.S. Marshall.
[3] Including the speaker of the House, Lincoln polled 45 votes.
[4] Thomas J. Henderson.

Notes Drawn for Nathaniel Hay[1]

Springfield, March 2. 1855.

Due A Lincoln sixteen dollars and eighty cents for value received.   N HAY

$200.   Springfield, March 2. 1855

On the ninth day of April next I promise to pay A. Lincoln two hundred dollars, with ten per cent interest after due until paid, for value received.   N HAY

[1] AD, owned by Mrs. Logan Hay, Springfield, Illinois. Both notes are in Lincoln's handwriting and signed by Nathaniel Hay. See Lincoln's "explanation," June 9, 1856, *infra*.

To William Fithian[1]

Dear Doctor: Springfield, March 8. 1855

Your letter duly received. I guess you brought your suit wrong. No other than an action of *Covenant*—not *debt*—will lie on the lease a copy of which you sent me. With this is a set of papers complete, for a new suit in the right form. If, however, the only responsable man is dead, there is no use of bringing a new suit, or in prossecuting the old one. You can get no judgment against his estate in that way. You must file the claim in the Probate court; or wait the year & then sue his administrator. Yours as ever

A. LINCOLN

[1] ALS, owned by Mrs. Stephen Abbot, Randlett, Utah.

To Henry E. Dummer[1]

H. E. Dummer, Esq.   Springfield,
My dear Sir: March 10– 1855

A firm of lawyers in New-York have sent me a money bond, of $2000 for collection. Both the parties to the bond reside in New-

York, but the obligor has a farm of 330 acres, within about a mile of Rushville in Schuyler county, out of which, by an attachment suit, the obligee wishes collection to be made. As I do not practice in Rushville, I have concluded to send you the job, if you will write me, saying you will take it. What say you? The attorneys who send me the claim, say their client is a good responsible man. Yours as ever A. Lincoln—

[1] ALS, IHi.

To James S. Sandford, Mortimer Porter, and Ambrose K. Striker[1]

Messrs. Sandford, Porter & Striker New York

Springfield, March 10– 1855

Gentlemen: Yours of the 5th. is received; as also was that of 15th. Decr. last, inclosing bond of Clift to Pray. When I received the bond, I was dabbling in politics; and, of course, neglecting business. Having since been beaten out, I have gone to work again.

As I do not practice at Rushville, I to-day open a correspondence, with Henry E. Dummer, Esq, of Beardstown, Ills, with the view of getting the job into his hands. He is a good man if he will undertake it. Write me whether I shall do this, or return the bond to you. Very Respectfully A. Lincoln

[1] ALS, NSk.

To Anson L. Brewer[1]

A. L. Brewer, Esq Dear Sir

Springfield, Ills. March 16, 1855.

Your letter of the 8th. is just received. It has all the while been understood that the estate of Blackledge[2] is solvent, & that the Kelly[3] claim is good. After I sent back to you & got the authentication of record corrected, I commenced a suit in the circuit court; and about this time Blackledge died. The case is not in the county of my residence; so that I am only there at the terms of the circuit court. At the first term after B's death, my partner, who was attending court in that county that term, dismissed the suit and filed the record in the Probate court as a claim against the estate. This we both thought was the best way of doing. Last fall I turned out of my way to come by that county to see after the claim; and was surprized to be told that the claim had not been allowed, or acted on.

On the 2nd. of April court takes me there again, when I shall give special attention to the matter. Yours &c.   A. LINCOLN

¹ ALS, owned by Robert Wisden, St. Joseph, Michigan. The case referred to was Kelly *v.* estate of Blackledge in the Logan County Circuit Court.
² Jesse D. Blackledge had died since the beginning of the suit. See Lincoln's note of November 17, 1852.   ³ James Kelly of New Lisbon, Ohio.

To Henry E. Dummer¹

Dear Dummer.   Springfield: March 19. 1855

Yours of the 16th. is just received. Herewith are the bond, and both the letters of my correspondents, in relation to it. The letters contain all the information I have on the subject. I wrote them the same day I wrote you, that I was going to send you the claim, if you would take it.

Logan is willing to take the vacant seat on the Supreme Bench; but he is very anxious to not be beaten, if he is put on the track as a candidate. Our friends here, and everywhere, so far as I have heard, are for him; but it behooves us to be wide awake. At the last congressional elections there was a small majority against us in the Middle Division. I am quite anxious for Logan's election, first, because he will make the best Judge, & second because it would hurt his feelings to be beaten worse than it would almost any one else. Your friend as ever   A. Lincoln—

¹ ALS, IHi. See Lincoln's letters of March 10, *supra.*

To Orville H. Browning¹

Hon: O. H. Browning.   Springfield, March 23, 1855

My dear Sir   Your letter to Judge Logan² has been shown to us by him; and, with his consent, we answer it. When it became probable that there would be a vacancy on the Supreme Bench, public opinion, on this side of the river,³ seemed to be universally directed to Logan as the proper man to fill it. I mean public opinion on *our* side in politics, with very small manifestation in any different direction by the other side. The result is, that he has been a good deal pressed to allow his name to be used, and he has consented to it, provided it can be done with perfect cordiality and good feeling on the part of all our own friends. We, the undersigned, are very anxious for it; and the more so now that he has been urged, until his mind is turned upon the matter. We, therefore are very glad of your letter, with the information it brings us, mixed only with a regret that we can not elect Logan and Walker⁴ both. We shall be glad, if you will hoist Logan's name, in your Quincy papers. Very truly Your friends,   A. LINCOLN.

B. S. EDWARDS.

JOHN T STUART

¹ ALS, ORB. The letter carries in addition the following endorsement: "I concur in the propriety of running Judge Logan—as he has consented. He would I think be elected easier than Mr Walker. This side of the river. Mr Walker is almost wholly out of public notice. Personally I esteem Mr Walker highly & would be glad to see him elected   D DAVIS"   ² Stephen T. Logan.
³ The Illinois River.
⁴ Pinkney H. Walker of McDonough County is probably referred to. He was appointed to the Supreme Court of Illinois in February, 1858 and elected to the same office in June following.

To David Davis¹

Hon. David Davis: Springfield, Ills., March 30, 1855.

Dear Sir—The undersigned members of the bar in Springfield, would respectfully request your assent to an announcement of yourself as a candidate for re-election to the office of Judge of the Circuit Court, in, and for this judicial circuit.

Satisfied with the ability and impartiality with which the duties of the office have been discharged by you for the past six years,— they are confident that your acceptance of the office for another term would give general satisfaction to the people, and meet with the approbation of the members of the bar in the circuit.

With the hope that you will return an affirmative answer to this request, we are—Your friends.

Thomas Moffett,	D. B. Campbell,	E. B. Herndon,
Jas. H. Matheny, Aty & Cl'k,	A. Campbell,	James C. Conkling,
Silas W. Robbins,	W. J. Black,	A. McWilliams,
James B. White,	D. A. Brown,	W. H. Herndon,
T. G. Taylor,	Stephen T. Logan,	S. M. Cullom,
Geo. W. Shutt,	John T. Stuart,	G. Rucker,
Wm. B. Baird,	A. Lincoln,	N. M. Broadwell,
Wm. J. Conkling,	B. S. Edwards,	Geo. W. Shaw.

¹ *Illinois Journal*, April 13, 1855. Davis' letter of assent, April 10, 1855, is printed immediately following.

Resolutions on the Death of David B. Campbell¹

April [17] 1855

WHEREAS, it has pleased Almighty God in the dispensations of his Providence, to cut down at meridian of life, and in the vigor of his usefulness, a most esteemed member of this bar, David B. Campbell, for many years attorney general of the state, who departed this life on Saturday the 1st inst., at Springfield, after a lingering illness, which had confined him to his room for several months—therefore,

Resolved, That we, the members of this bar, feel with deep sensibility the loss which the profession and society have sustained in the loss of your departed brother.

Resolved, That we cherish the highest respect for the professional learning of the deceased, for the integrity and uprightness of his professional and private life and for the estimable qualities which characterized him as a man a friend and a companion.

Resolved, That we deeply sympathize with the afflicted relatives of the deceased, in the melancholy bereavement which they have sustained.

Resolved, That the chairman of this meeting transmit to the relatives of the deceased, a copy of the proceedings of this meeting, as a testimonial of the high estimation in which we, the members of this bar held our departed brother, and in token of our unaffected sorrow for his loss.

Resolved, That the chairman present the proceedings of this meeting to the circuit court of M'Lean county, now in session, and move that the same be entered on the records thereof.

Resolved, That the proceedings of this meeting be furnished to the papers of this circuit for publications.

[1] *Illinois Journal*, April 27, 1855. The McLean County Common Law Record, VI, 196-97, dates the adoption of Lincoln's resolutions on April 17.

Endorsement of Stephen A. Corneau[1]

April 26, 1855

The undersigned, from knowledge of S. A. CORNEAU, and having confidence in his ability to perform the duties of clerk of the supreme court, of the second grand division of Illinois, do recommend him, to the members of the bar and public, as a competent person to fill said office.

[1] *Illinois Journal*, April 26, 1855. The endorsement carries names of thirty-one attorneys, including Lincoln's. A similar endorsement appeared in other papers over the state. Corneau, a resident of Springfield prominent in civic affairs, had previously been bailiff of the U.S. District Court.

To W. F. Boggs[1]

W. F. Boggs, Esq. Springfield, Ills,
Kingston, Mo. May 14– 1855

Although my christian name is *Abraham*, and not *Edward*, the within letter is evidently intended for me. Whether I ever gave Mr. Barnett a discharge I can not remember; nor do I know whether it would now be proper for me [to] give him one, not having, or knowing where to find, any of the old rolls or papers of my company. I do very well remember, however, that Clardy Barnett, a small man, with a scar on his face, and not far from my own age, which is now 46, did serve more than fourteen days (near forty I think) in the company of which I had the command as Captain, in Col. —— Thompson's[2] Regiment of Mounted Volunteers, in the Black-Hawk War of 1832—and that he was entitled to an honorable discharge. We went from Sangamon county, Illinois; and Samuel Whiteside of Madison Co, Ills, was our Brigadier General. Yours &c.   A. LINCOLN—

1 ALS, IHi. Lincoln wrote on the back of a letter from Boggs, who was trying to obtain for Barnett the land bounty voted by congress to volunteers who had served in the Black Hawk War.   2 Samuel M. Thompson.

To Jacob Harding[1]

Danville, May 25. 1855

Friend Harding: I have been reading your paper[2] three or four years, and have paid you nothing for it. Herewith is a receipt of Sylvanus Sandford[3] for two claims amounting to ten dollars. If he has collected the money, get it from him, and put it into your pocket, saying nothing further about it.

And now, if you please, I should be glad for you to put in your paper of this week, the names of *Stephen T. Logan,* as a candidate for Judge of the Supreme court; and of *Stephen A. Corneau,* for Clerk of the Supreme Court.

Please also print, and distribute a suitable number of tickets for them; and we, at Springfield will pay the reasonable charge.

As the Sir-name [*sic*] of our candidate for clerk is rather an uncommon one I try to write it very plainly—"Corneau" the last letter being, not an "N" but an "U" Very truly yours

A. LINCOLN—

1 ALS, MnHi.
2 The *Prairie Beacon* published at Paris, Illinois, by Harding.
3 Attorney at Paris. See Lincoln's letter of June 1, *infra.*

To D. R. and S. Sandford[1]

[c. June 1 ? 1855]

The five dollars within named, received. From Paris[2] I sent Harding an order for both claims. One of them he wont get; the other, I wish you and he would try to get   Yours truly

A LINCOLN

1 ALS, owned by Robert S. Lamon, Chicago, Illinois. This undated letter was written on the back of a letter from the Sandfords, dated at Paris, Illinois, May 16, 1855, enclosing five dollars collected on one of two notes which Lincoln had left with them for collection. The date of receipt at Paris endorsed on Lincoln's letter is June 3, 1855.

2 Lincoln sent the order from Danville to Paris. See letter to Harding, May 25, *supra*.

To Henry C. Whitney[1]

H. C. Whitney, Esq   Springfield,
My dear Sir: June 7. 1855

Your note containing election news is received; and for which I thank you. It is all of no use, however. Logan is worse beaten than any other man ever was since elections were invented—beaten more than 1200 in this county.

It is conceded on all hands that the Prohibitory law is also beaten.[2] Yours truly   A. LINCOLN—

1 ALS, owned by Mrs. Logan Hay, Springfield, Illinois. Whitney was a young attorney at Urbana, Illinois, whose association with Lincoln became elaborated in his book *Life on the Circuit with Lincoln* (1892), which contained some valuable and much questionable material.

2 The so-called "Maine Law" prohibiting the sale of intoxicants.

Notes Drawn for Nathaniel and John Hay[1]

$453.57   Springfield, June 25– 1855
One year after date we or either of us promise to pay Mrs. Maria L. Bullock four hundred and fiftythree dollars and fiftyseven cents, with interest from date, at the rate of six per cent per annum, until paid, for value received.   NATHANIEL HAY
         JOHN HAY

$453.57   Springfield, June 25– 1855
Two years after date we or either of us promise to pay Mrs. Maria L. Bullock four hundred and fiftythree dollars and fiftyseven cents, with interest from date at the rate of six per cent per annum until paid, for value received.   NATHANIEL HAY
         JOHN HAY

1 AD, RPB. Both notes are in Lincoln's handwriting, except the signatures. They represent the purchase of land owned by Lincoln's client Maria L. Bullock, an aunt of Mrs. Lincoln's at Lexington, Kentucky. See receipts, November 13, 1856, and letter of August 31, 1855, *infra*.

To Aaron L. Chapin[1]

Rev. A. L. Chapin: Chicago,
Sir: July 5. 1855.

On the evening of the 3rd., after Banking hours, Judge D. Davis left with me $480 in currency, with the request that I would deposite it, to your credit, in the Banking house of Geo. Smith & Co, and send you the certificate of deposite. Yesterday, being *the 4th,* the Bank was closed. This morning I made the deposite, and herewith is the certificate. Yours &c.   A. LINCOLN—

[1] ALS, IHi. Aaron L. Chapin was a clergyman and educator, president of Beloit College at Beloit, Wisconsin.

To Charles Hoyt[1]

Mr. Charles Hoyt   Chicago,
My dear Sir: July 10– 1855

The U.S. Court is in session here now; and we have succeeded, by agreement with Edwards,[2] in getting your case, and the three Rock-Island cases,[3] dismissed, with leave to the plaintiff to reinstate them by the next term, if he desires. Edwards says he has heared nothing from Parker, or Cushman, or any of their men, since their case was disposed of in the Supreme court, now more than a year ago. Judge McLean says Parker is broken up, and seems to be doing nothing further about his cases. From all this, I suppose the cases are not very likely to be reinstated. Your friend, as ever   A. LINCOLN—

P.S. It would perhaps be best to make no movement about costs till after next term, lest this should stir them up to re-instate the cases.   A. L.

[1] ALS, Aurora Historical Society, Aurora, Illinois. See Lincoln's letter of November 10, 1854, and note, *supra.*   [2] Benjamin S. Edwards.
[3] The Rock Island cases, concerned with patent infringement, were related to the case of Z. Parker *v.* Charles Hoyt, alleged infringement of patent on a water wheel, in which Lincoln had represented Hoyt before the U.S. District Court, July 9-24, 1850. Cushman and the several other persons involved in the suits have not been identified.

To Peter H. Watson[1]

P. H. Watson, Esq.,   Springfield, Ill.,
Washington, D.C.,   July 23, 1855.

My dear Sir: At our interview here in June, I understood you to say you would send me copies of the Bill and Answer in the case of McCormick vs. Manny and Co. and also of depositions, as fast as they could be taken and printed. I have had nothing from you since. However, I attended the U.S. Court at Chicago, and while there, got copies of the Bill and Answer. I write this particularly to urge you to forward on to me the additional evidence as fast as you can. During August, and the remainder of this month, I can devote some time to the case, and, of course, I want all the material that can be had.

During my stay at Chicago, I went out to Rockford, and spent half a day, examining and studying Manny's Machine.

I think you ought to be sworn before the evidence closes: of this however I leave you and others to judge. Very truly Yours,

A. LINCOLN.

1 Tracy, pp. 58-59. Peter H. Watson was a patent attorney representing John H. Manny and associates, manufacturers of a mechanical reaper, who were being sued for alleged patent infringement by Cyrus H. McCormick, inventor of the McCormick reaper. Other attorneys associated with Watson on the case, in addition to Lincoln, were George Harding, a patent attorney of Philadelphia, and Edwin M. Stanton of Pittsburgh, later Lincoln's secretary of war. The trial took place in Cincinnati in September, but although Lincoln attended he took no part in the case. The story of how he was snubbed by his associates, Stanton in particular, has been told many times; a brief factual account may be found in Pratt, *Personal Finances of Abraham Lincoln*, pp. 54-56.

To Charles Ballance[1]

C. Ballance, Esq   Springfield,
Dear Sir: July 27, 1855

Your letters of the 23rd. & 24th., the first having nothing, and the other $20 in it, are both received. Money is always acceptable to me; but when I left Chicago, I was not in *"extremis"* on that subject.

Browning had written me that the court was hung in our Hall case.[2] Yours as ever   A. LINCOLN—

1 ALS, owned by Mrs. Charles M. Booth, Los Angeles, California. Ballance was an attorney at Peoria, Illinois.

2 Orville H. Browning and Lincoln represented William A. Hall in Joseph L. Papin *v.* William A. Hall, a Peoria French claim case in the U.S. Court, on July 17. In another French claim case, Robert Forsyth *v.* City of Peoria, Lincoln and Archibald Williams represented Forsyth on July 11, losing the case. These cases involved land titles dating back to the old French settlement at Peoria.

To Anson L. Brewer[1]

A. L. Brewer Esq.   Springfield, Ill.,
Dear Sir:—   July 27, 1855

Yours of the 21st is received. When I wrote you in March I explained to you the sources of the delay so far. When I went to that

County in April, I did give the case my special attention. I commenced a suit in Probate Court; and, as the executor would waive nothing, the time for trial extended beyond the term of the Circuit Court and of course came on when I had to be elsewhere. However my partner went up especially to attend to it and when the trial (if it could be called a trial) was over the Judge declined deciding then, but took the case under advisement. There was really nothing to decide, only the *grave* question whether the record with the certificates (which last, you remember we got up ourselves) proves the debt—and yet the Judge finally decided that against us!!! When the decision was made, we notified by letter, and we sent up an appeal bond, to take the case to Circuit Court, which sits again in September. Thus stands the case now. Yours &c

A. LINCOLN

¹ Printed in Henry C. Friend, "Abraham Lincoln as a Receiving Attorney: Kelly *vs*. Blackledge," *Commercial Law Journal*, Vol. 54, No. 2, February, 1949.

To Owen Lovejoy¹

Hon: Owen Lovejoy: Springfield,
My dear Sir: August 11– 1855

Yours of the 7th. was received the day before yesterday. Not even *you* are more anxious to prevent the extension of slavery than I; and yet the political atmosphere is such, just now, that I fear to do any thing, lest I do wrong. Know-nothingism has not yet entirely tumbled to pieces—nay, it is even a little encouraged by the late elections in Tennessee, Kentucky & Alabama. Until we can get the elements of this organization, there is not sufficient materials to successfully combat the Nebraska democracy with. We can not get them so long as they cling to a hope of success under their own organization; and I fear an open push by us now, may offend them, and tend to prevent our ever getting them. About us here, they are mostly my old political and personal friends; and I have hoped their organization would die out without the painful necessity of my taking an open stand against them. Of their principles I think little better than I do of those of the slavery extensionists. Indeed I do not perceive how any one professing to be sensitive to the wrongs of the negroes, can join in a league to degrade a class of white men.

I have no objection to "fuse" with any body provided I can fuse on ground which I think is right; and I believe the opponents of slavery extension could now do this, if it were not for this K.N.ism. In many speeches last summer I advised those who did me the

honor of a hearing to "stand with any body who stands right"—
and I am still quite willing to follow my own advice. I lately saw,
in the Quincy Whig, the report of a preamble and resolutions,
made by Mr. Williams, as chairman of a committee, to a public
meeting and adopted by the meeting. I saw them but once, and
have them not now at command; but so far as I can remember
them, they occupy about the ground I should be willing to "fuse"
upon.

As to my personal movements this summer, and fall, I am quite
busy trying to pick up my lost crumbs of last year. I shall be here
till September; then to the circuit till the 20th. then to Cincinnati,
awhile, after a Patent right case; and back to the circuit to the end
of November. I can be seen here any time this month; and at
Bloomington at any time from the 10th. to the 17th. of September.
As to an extra session of the Legislature, I should know no better
how to bring that about, than to lift myself over a fence by the
straps of my boots. Your truly   A. Lincoln—

1 ALS, CSmH.

Advertisement[1]

August 13, 1855

SALE OF TOWN LOTS.

THAT PARCEL OF LAND LYING BEtween Washington and
Adams Streets, and immediately west of the late residence of Dr.
Todd,[2] has been surveyed into Town Lots; and, ON SATURDAY
the 18th of AUGUST, inst., at 2 o'clock, p.m., upon the premises,
a portion of said Lots will be offered at public auction.

TERMS favorable, to be made known at the time and place of
sale.   A. LINCOLN,
                                                  for Proprietor.

1 *Illinois State Journal*, August 13, 1855. The land advertised belonged to
Maria L. Bullock. See Lincoln's letter of August 31, *infra*.
2 Dr. John Todd.

To George Robertson[1]

Hon: Geo. Robertson   Springfield, Ills.
Lexington, Ky.   Aug. 15. 1855

My dear Sir: The volume you left for me has been received.
I am really grateful for the honor of your kind remembrance, as
well as for the book. The partial reading I have already given it,
has afforded me much of both pleasure and instruction. It was new

[317]

to me that the exact question which led to the Missouri compromise,[2] had arisen before it arose in regard to Missouri; and that you had taken so prominent a part in it. Your short, but able and patriotic speech upon that occasion, has not been improved upon since, by those holding the same views; and, with all the lights you then had, the views you took appear to me as very reasonable.

You are not a friend of slavery in the abstract. In that speech you spoke of *"the peaceful extinction of slavery"* and used other expressions indicating your belief that the thing was, at some time, to have an end[.] Since then we have had thirty six years of experience; and this experience has demonstrated, I think, that there is no peaceful extinction of slavery in prospect for us. The signal failure of Henry Clay, and other good and great men, in 1849, to effect any thing in favor of gradual emancipation in Kentucky, together with a thousand other signs, extinguishes that hope utterly. On the question of liberty, as a principle, we are not what we have been. When we were the political slaves of King George, and wanted to be free, we called the maxim that "all men are created equal" a self evident truth; but now when we have grown fat, and have lost all dread of being slaves ourselves, we have become so greedy to be *masters* that we call the same maxim "a self-evident lie" The fourth of July has not quite dwindled away; it is still a great day—*for burning fire-crackers!!!*

That spirit which desired the peaceful extinction of slavery, has itself become extinct, with the *occasion*, and the *men* of the Revolution. Under the impulse of that occasion, nearly half the states adopted systems of emancipation at once; and it is a significant fact, that not a single state has done the like since. So far as peaceful, voluntary emancipation is concerned, the condition of the negro slave in America, scarcely less terrible to the contemplation of a free mind, is now as fixed, and hopeless of change for the better, as that of the lost souls of the finally impenitent. The Autocrat of all the Russias will resign his crown, and proclaim his subjects free republicans sooner than will our American masters voluntarily give up their slaves.

Our political problem now is "Can we, as a nation, continue together *permanently—forever*—half slave, and half free?" The problem is too mighty for me. May God, in his mercy, superintend the solution. Your much obliged friend, and humble servant

A. LINCOLN—

[1] ALS, DLC. Judge George Robertson of Lexington, Kentucky, had acted as counsel for Lincoln and the other Illinois heirs of Robert S. Todd in the suit against Robert Wickliffe in 1849. A member of congress 1817-1821, he had

served with distinction also in various judicial and state offices in Kentucky and was professor of law in Transylvania College from 1834 to 1857. Visiting Springfield in Lincoln's absence, on July 9 he left an inscribed copy of his collection of speeches and papers entitled *Scrap Book on Law and Politics, Men and Times.* This identical volume, with Lincoln's letter laid in, is now in the Rare Book Collection of The Library of Congress.

2 In regard to the Arkansas Territory in 1819.

Deposition Made for Additional Bounty Land[1]

State of Illinois, } SS.
Sangamon County.   August 21, 1855

On this 21st day of August A. D. one thousand eight hundred and fifty-five, personally appeared before me, a justice of the peace, within and for the county and State aforesaid, Abraham Lincoln, aged 46 years, a resident of Sangamon County in the State of Illinois, who being duly sworn according to law, declares that he is the identical Abraham Lincoln, who was Captain of a company, in the regiment of Illinois Mounted Volunteers, commanded by Col. Saml. M. Thompson, in the war with the British band of Sacs and other Tribes of Indians on our Northwestern Frontier in A.D. 1832 known as the "Black Hawk War"—That he Volunteered at the state and county aforesaid on or about the 21st. day of April 1832 for no definite time, and continued in actual service in said war for about 40 days, that he has heretofore made application for bounty land, under the act of September 28, 1850, and received a land warrant, No. 52,076, for forty (40) acres, which he has since Located and cannot now return.

He makes this declaration for the purpose of obtaining the additional bounty land to which he may be entitled under the act approved the 3d day of March, 1855. He also declares, that he has never applied for nor received, under this or any other act of Congress, any bounty land warrant except the one above mentioned.

ABRAHAM LINCOLN

1 DS, DNA RG 15 A. The document bears also attestations of Simeon Francis and Edward Clark and certifications by Josiah Francis and N. W. Matheny.

To John L. Miller[1]

August 21, 1855

Herewith is the Bill. Fill in the names of the arbitrators in the blank left for that purpose. Also, get copies of your deed and bond, as indicated in the bill, mark them (A) & (B.) and file them with the Bill. Aug 21. 1855   A. LINCOLN

[1] ALS, owned by Edward Riley, Eureka, Illinois. John L. Miller of Metamora, Illinois, was suing for divorce from his wife Susan F. Miller. The bill drawn by Lincoln and with blanks filled in by Miller was filed in Woodford County, August 27.

To Joshua F. Speed[1]

Dear Speed: Springfield, Aug: 24, 1855

You know what a poor correspondent I am. Ever since I received your very agreeable letter of the 22nd. of May I have been intending to write you in answer to it. You suggest that in political action now, you and I would differ. I suppose we would; not quite as much, however, as you may think. You know I dislike slavery; and you fully admit the abstract wrong of it. So far there is no cause of difference. But you say that sooner than yield your legal right to the slave—especially at the bidding of those who are not themselves interested, you would see the Union dissolved. I am not aware that *any one* is bidding you to yield that right; very certainly *I* am not. I leave that matter entirely to yourself. I also acknowledge *your* rights and *my* obligations, under the constitution, in regard to your slaves. I confess I hate to see the poor creatures hunted down, and caught, and carried back to their stripes, and unrewarded toils; but I bite my lip and keep quiet. In 1841 you and I had together a tedious low-water trip, on a Steam Boat from Louisville to St. Louis. You may remember, as I well do, that from Louisville to the mouth of the Ohio there were, on board, ten or a dozen slaves, shackled together with irons.[2] That sight was a continual torment to me; and I see something like it every time I touch the Ohio, or any other slave-border. It is hardly fair for you to assume, that I have no interest in a thing which has, and continually exercises, the power of making me miserable. You ought rather to appreciate how much the great body of the Northern people do crucify their feelings, in order to maintain their loyalty to the constitution and the Union.

I do oppose the extension of slavery, because my judgment and feelings so prompt me; and I am under no obligation to the contrary. If for this you and I must differ, differ we must. You say if you were President, you would send an army and hang the leaders of the Missouri outrages upon the Kansas elections; still, if Kansas fairly votes herself a slave state, she must be admitted, or the Union must be dissolved. But how if she votes herself a slave state *unfairly*—that is, by the very means for which you say you

[1] ALS, MHi.   [2] See Lincoln to Mary Speed, September 27, 1841, *supra*.

would hang men? Must she still be admitted, or the Union be dissolved? That will be the phase of the question when it first becomes a practical one. In your assumption that there may be a *fair* decision of the slavery question in Kansas, I plainly see you and I would differ about the Nebraska-law. I look upon that enactment not as a *law*, but as *violence* from the beginning. It was conceived in violence, passed in violence, is maintained in violence, and is being executed in violence. I say it was *conceived* in violence, because the destruction of the Missouri Compromise, under the circumstances, was nothing less than violence. It was *passed* in violence, because it could not have passed at all but for the votes of many members, in violent disregard of the known will of their constituents. It is *maintained* in violence because the elections since, clearly demand it's repeal, and this demand is openly disregarded. *You* say men ought to be hung for the way they are executing that law; and *I* say the way it is being executed is quite as good as any of its antecedents. It is being executed in the precise way which was intended from the first; else why does no Nebraska man express astonishment or condemnation? Poor Reeder[3] is the only public man who has been silly enough to believe that any thing like fairness was ever intended; and he has been bravely undeceived.

That Kansas will form a Slave constitution, and, with it, will ask to be admitted into the Union, I take to be an already settled question; and so settled by the very means you so pointedly condemn. By every principle of law, ever held by any court, North or South, every negro taken to Kansas is free; yet in utter disregard of this —in the spirit of violence merely—that beautiful Legislature gravely passes a law to hang men who shall venture to inform a negro of his legal rights. This is the substance, and real object of the law. If, like Haman, they should hang upon the gallows of their own building, I shall not be among the mourners for their fate.

In my humble sphere, I shall advocate the restoration of the Missouri Compromise, so long as Kansas remains a territory; and when, by all these foul means, it seeks to come into the Union as a Slave-state, I shall oppose it. I am very loth, in any case, to withhold my assent to the enjoyment of property *acquired*, or *located*, in good faith; but I do not admit that *good faith*, in taking a negro to Kansas, to be held in slavery, is a *possibility* with any man. Any man who has sense enough to be the controller of his own prop-

[3] Andrew H. Reeder, appointed governor of Kansas Territory by President Pierce in June, 1854.

erty, has too much sense to misunderstand the outrageous character of this whole Nebraska business. But I digress. In my opposition to the admission of Kansas I shall have some company; but we may be beaten. If we are, I shall not, on that account, attempt to dissolve the Union. On the contrary, if we succeed, there will be enough of us to take care of the Union. I think it probable, however, we shall be beaten. Standing as a unit among yourselves, you can, directly, and indirectly, bribe enough of our men to carry the day—as you could on an open proposition to establish monarchy. Get hold of some man in the North, whose position and ability is such, that he can make the support of your measure—whatever it may be—a *democratic party necessity*, and the thing is done. *Apropos* of this, let me tell you an anecdote. Douglas introduced the Nebraska bill in January. In February afterwards, there was a call session of the Illinois Legislature. Of the one hundred members composing the two branches of that body, about seventy were democrats. These latter held a caucus, in which the Nebraska bill was talked of, if not formally discussed. It was thereby discovered that just three, and no more, were in favor of the measure. In a day or two Douglas' orders came on to have resolutions passed approving the bill; and they were passed by large majorities!!! The truth of this is vouched for by a bolting democratic member. The masses too, democratic as well as whig, were even, nearer unanamous against it; but as soon as the party necessity of supporting it, became apparent, the way the democracy began to see the *wisdom* and *justice* of it, was perfectly astonishing.

You say if Kansas fairly votes herself a free state, as a christian you will rather rejoice at it. All decent slave-holders *talk* that way; and I do not doubt their candor. But they never *vote* that way. Although in a private letter, or conversation, you will express your preference that Kansas shall be free, you would vote for no man for Congress who would say the same thing publicly. No such man could be elected from any district in any slave-state. You think Stringfellow & Co[4] ought to be hung; and yet, at the next presidential election you will vote for the exact type and representative of Stringfellow. The slave-breeders and slave-traders, are a small, odious and detested class, among you; and yet in politics, they dictate the course of all of you, and are as completely your masters, as you are the masters of your own negroes.

You enquire where I now stand. That is a disputed point. I think

[4] Benjamin F. Stringfellow was a leader of the pro-slavery armed forces in the Kansas struggle; his brother John H. Stringfellow edited the *Squatter Sovereign* at Atchison and was speaker of the territorial House of Representatives.

I am a whig; but others say there are no whigs, and that I am an abolitionist. When I was at Washington I voted for the Wilmot Proviso as good as forty times, and I never heard of any one attempting to unwhig me for that. I now do no more than oppose the *extension* of slavery.

I am not a Know-Nothing. That is certain. How could I be? How can any one who abhors the oppression of negroes, be in favor of degrading classes of white people? Our progress in degeneracy appears to me to be pretty rapid. As a nation, we began by declaring that *"all men are created equal."* We now practically read it "all men are created equal, *except negroes.*" When the Know-Nothings get control, it will read "all men are created equal, except negroes, *and foreigners, and catholics.*" When it comes to this I should prefer emigrating to some country where they make no pretence of loving liberty—to Russia, for instance, where despotism can be taken pure, and without the base alloy of hypocracy.

Mary will probably pass a day or two in Louisville in October. My kindest regards to Mrs. Speed. On the leading subject of this letter, I have more of her sympathy than I have of yours.

And yet let [me] say I am   Your friend forever

A. LINCOLN—

To Mrs. Maria L. Bullock[1]

Mrs. Maria L. Bullock: Springfield,

Dear Aunt: August 31– 1855

The following is a correct statement of your business, so far as I have transacted it for you.

The land out of town I had surveyed into separate parcels; and on June 23, 1855 had it sold at public auction for sums amounting in the aggregate to $1427-92¼ cents.

On the 25th. of June, I received of the purchasers in cash, two sums, together amounting to $143.68. On the same day you deeded to one of the purchasers, John Connelly, senr. one parcel of the land; and I took from him his two notes with personal security, together amounting to $377—payable in one and two years, with six per cent interest from date; and also his mortgage on the parcel of land.

On the same day you deeded to Nathaniel Hay the other three parcels of the land; and I took from him his two notes,[2] with personal security, together amounting to $907-14 cents; payable in one and two years, with interest from date, at six per cent; and also took his mortgage on the premises.

Of the $143.68, cash received by me, I paid out for taking acknowledgements of deeds & mortgages, for advertising notice of sale in newspaper, printing notice bills thereof; to auctioneers; for recording mortgages, and to Surveyor & hands, the aggregate sum of $42.70. And on the 27th. of June 1855, I delivered to you a certificate of deposite made at Clark's Exchange Bank for $101-00.

The land in town, in connection with some land owned by Elijah Iles, he and I had surveyed into town lots; and a Plat made and filed for record as Bullock's addition to the City of Springfield. On the 18th. of August 1855, I had your part of the lots sold at public auction, for various sums,[3] amounting in the agregate to $990. Soon after, I received of the purchasers various sums in cash, amounting in the aggregate to $197. On the 20th. day of August 1855, I took from John Cook his two notes, together amounting to $468—payable in one and two years, with six per cent interest from date; and I took no mortgage from him—& you, on the same day deeded him his lots. On the same day you deeded Patrick Keiley[4] his lots; and I took of him his two notes, together amounting to $153, payable in one and two years, with six per cent interest from date, and also his mortgage on his lots.

On the same day you deeded to William S. Viney[5] his lots; and I took his two notes for the aggregate sum of $162, payable in one and two years, with six per cent interest from date; and also his mortgage on his lots.

On the same day you deeded to Elijah Iles, & to the City for him, the lots bid off by him; and I took neither notes or mortgage of him, I deducting ten dollars, and he paying the remainder of his bids, cash down. Of the $197—cash received by me, I paid out for taking acknowledgements of Plat, deeds & mortgages; for recording same; for advertising & Bills for Sale; to Surveyor & hands; and to auctioneer, the aggregate sum of $38-10. Also to Matheny's[6] heirs for quit claim deed, to remove cloud from title $50. On the 27th. of August I handed you the certificate of deposite at Clark's Exchange Bank for $106-90 cents; and I now hand you $2-08 cents

Aggregate of Sales		$2417-92.
Amount of notes	$2067-14	
Deduction to Iles.	10-00	
Expenses	80-80	
Paid Mathenys heirs	50-00	
Paid you	209-98	
	2417-92.	

[324]

The notes are in my hands, & the mortgages are at the Record-
ers office subject to my control. They are all in your name. The
taxes of this year I suppose you will have to pay. Very truly
yours   A. LINCOLN

1 ALS-P, ISLA.   2 *Vide supra*, June 25.
3 See advertisement, August 13, *supra*.
4 Patrick Keiley has not been further identified.
5 William S. Viney, a Sangamon County farmer.   6 Charles R. Matheny.

To John H. Manny and Company[1]

Messrs. Manny and Co.   Springfield,
Rockford, Ill.   Sept. 1, 1855.
    Since I left Chicago about the 18th of July, I have heard nothing
concerning the Reaper suit. I addressed a letter to Mr. Watson,[2]
at Washington, requesting him to forward me the evidence, from
time to time, as it should be taken, but I have received no answer
from him.
    Is it still the understanding that the case is to be heard at Cin-
cinnati on the 20th inst.?
    Please write me on the receipt of this. Yours truly,
                                                A. LINCOLN.

1 Tracy, p. 61.   2 Peter H. Watson, July 23, *supra*.

To James F. Joy[1]

J. F. Joy, Esq.   Bloomington,
Chicago, Ills.   Sept. 14. 1855
    Dear Sir   I have to day drawn on you in favor of the McLean
County Bank, or rather it's cashier, for one hundred and fifty dollars. This is intended as a fee for all services done by me for the
Illinois Central Railroad, since last September, within the counties
of McLean and DeWitt. Within that term, and in the two counties, I have assisted, for the Road, in at least fifteen cases (I believe, one or two more) and I have concluded to lump them off at
ten dollars a case. With this explanation, I shall be obliged if you
will honor the draft   Yours truly   A. LINCOLN

1 ALS-P, ISLA. On the bottom of the page appears the following:
    The above facts are true, and I think the charges very reasonable.
    Bloomington   D DAVIS
    Septr 14. 1855.   Judge of DeWitt
                                       & McLean Cir Courts

To James F. Joy[1]

J. F. Joy, Esq   Cincinnati,
Chicago, Ills   Sept. 19, 1855

Dear Sir: On monday, after I had reached the Depot, to come
on here, your despach was brought me. I ran to the Telegraph
office and answered briefly, and was near being left by the cars.
This is the first moment I have since had to write you. When I
drew the draft at Bloomington, I wrote you, in explanation, and
mailed the letter within thirty minutes after I signed the draft.
The draft and letter should have gone by the same mail, and I can
not understand why they did not. I hope the latter has reached
you before this. The explanation was, and is, that for one year—
that is, two terms of court in each county—I have attended to
from fifteen to seventeen, cases for the I. C. Co, in the counties of
McLean & DeWitt for which I have not been paid. The exact
number of the cases, and the names of the parties I could only
have given, when I drew, by going down to DeWitt, which I
thought scarcely necessary, particularly, as the presiding Judge
added a note to my letter, stating I had performed the services, and
that the charge I made was very reasonable.

I will add now, what I did not state in my former letter, that it
was at Mr. Brayman's request, made two years ago, I declined taking any new case against the company, and attended to these
cases as they came up from time to time, and that he paid me for
this class of business up to some time in September 1854. I hope
this is satisfactory. Yours truly   A. LINCOLN—

1 ALS-P, ISLA. Lincoln was in Cincinnati for the McCormick *v.* Manny trial.

To John Loughborough[1]

Surveyor General: Springfield, Ills–
St. Louis, Mo.   Oct. 10– 1855

Sir: Will you please send me a statement of each quarter Section, and fractional quarter Section, upon which, by Brown's survey, any Peoria French claim is laid? Your reasonable charge for
the same shall be promptly paid. Your Obt. Servt.

                                                      A. LINCOLN—

1 ALS, I-Ar. Lincoln's request was answered October 12, fee $4.00, which was
paid October 15. Lincoln probably wanted the data in connection with the suit
of Papin *v.* Hall. See Lincoln to Charles Ballance, July 27, 1855, and note, *supra.*

To Anson L. Brewer[1]

A. L. Brewer, Esq.   Springfield, Ills. Nov. 5. 1855.

Would have answered sooner, but was absent. At the September Term, the defendant made fight, with apparant confidence, but the court decided for us, and we got judgment for the amount of the old judgment and interest. The main point taken, in defence was, that a bar, or a short Act of Limitations, we have here, had been completed after the claim was filed, in the Probate court, but before a formal suit was brought. The court held that the filing of the claim saved the Statutes bar. They took Exceptions & talk of going to the Supreme court. That court sits in Jany. and I have thought it best to wait till after the first term before I begin to press for payment.   A. LINCOLN

[1] ALS, RPB. See Lincoln to Brewer, March 16, *supra*.

To Isham Reavis[1]

Isham Reavis, Esq.   Springfield,
My dear Sir: Novr. 5– 1855

I have just reached home, and found your letter of the 23rd. ult. I am from home too much of my time, for a young man to read law with me advantageously. If you are resolutely determined to make a lawyer of yourself, the thing is more than half done already. It is but a small matter whether you read *with* any body or not. I did not read with any one. Get the books, and read and study them till, you understand them in their principal features; and that is the main thing. It is of no consequence to be in a large town while you are reading. I read at New-Salem, which never had three hundred people living in it. The *books*, and your *capacity* for understanding them, are just the same in all places. Mr. Dummer is a very clever man and an excellent lawyer (much better than I, in law-learning); and I have no doubt he will cheerfully tell you what books to read, and also loan you the books.

Always bear in mind that your own resolution to succeed, is more important than any other one thing. Very truly Your friend
                                                A. LINCOLN

[1] ALS, owned by C. Frank Reavis, New York City. Isham Reavis, Jr., resided near Chandlerville, Illinois, and had been a student at Illinois College. Following his father's death, he decided to study law.

To James M. Loughborough[1]

James M. Loughborough, Esq.   Springfield,
Dear Sir   Dec: 12. 1855

To-day I received from Louisville, an unrecorded deed from your uncle P. S. L. to Lawrence Young, of date March 10–1845, for

		S. E.	27–	T 21.	N. R.	7 E.	160	acres
E	½	S W	27	"	"		80	"
S	½	N. E.	27	"	"		80	"
W	½	S. W.	26	"	"		80	"
W	½	N E.	15	"	"		80	"
							480	"

It was sent me with the request that I should have it recorded, and make some search for tax-titles. I have written back declining to do either; & saying I hold the deed subject to order.

I have thought proper to notify you of this at once. Yours truly
                                               A. LINCOLN—

[1] ALS, ICHi. James M. Loughborough was at this time clerk in the office of his father John Loughborough, surveyor general for Illinois and Missouri, at St. Louis. See Lincoln to Speed, *infra.*

To Joshua F. Speed[1]

Dear Speed   Springfield, Dec: 12. 1855

Yours of the 7th. accompanied by the deed of P. S. Loughborough, to Lawrence Young, is this day received; and I answer in haste to say, that I am engaged for James M. Loughborough, and it might not be consistent with my duty to him, for me to to [*sic*] attend to the business for Mr. Young. I shall therefore hold the deed subject to your order; suggesting that the land is in Champaign county, and that I think H. C. Whitney, of Urbana, would be a very proper person to entrust the business to.

All well. Kindest regards to Mrs. S. Your friend as ever
                                               A. Lincoln—

[1] ALS, IHi. See Lincoln to James M. Loughborough, *supra.* On the bottom of the page appears Speed's note as follows: "Wrote Lincoln to send deed to H C Whitney 17 Decr 1855."

To Charles Hoyt[1]

C. Hoyt, Esq   Springfield,
My dear Sir   Jany 16. 1856

Our case[2] is decided against us. The decision was announced this morning. Very sorry; but there is no help. The history of the case, since it came here, is this. On friday morning last, Mr. Joy[3] filed his papers, and entered his motion for a mandamus, and urged me to take up the motion as soon as possible. I already had the points and authorities sent me by you, and by Mr. Goodrich,[4] but had not studied them. I began preparing as fast as possible. The evening of the same day I was again urged to take up the case. I refused, one [*sic*] the ground that I was not ready; and on which plea I also got off over saturday. But on monday (the 14th.) I had to go into it. We occupied the whole day, I using the larger part. I made every point, and used every authority sent me by yourself & by Mr. Goodrich; and, in addition, all the points I could think of, and all the authorities I could find myself. I had 6 Barr—70. and made all out of it that I could. When I closed the argument on my part, a large package was handed me, which proved to [be] the Plat you sent me. The court received it of me; but it was not different from the Plat already in the record. I do not think I could ever have argued the case better than I did. I did nothing else, but prepare *to* argue, and *argue,* this case, from friday morning till monday evening.

Very sorry for the result; but I do not think it could have been prevented. Your friend as ever   A. LINCOLN—

1 ALS, IHi.
2 In the Illinois Supreme Court, Chicago, Burlington & Quincy *v.* Isaac G. Wilson, judge of the Thirteenth Circuit, a mandamus case to require the judge to appoint commissioners to appraise certain property in Aurora, Illinois, which the railroad wanted for shops, station, etc.   3 James F. Joy.
4 Grant Goodrich, a Chicago attorney.

Petition for Pardon of James H. Lee[1]

State of Illinois ⎫ Jan 21st. A.D. 1856.
City of Springfield⎭

To his Excellency The Governor[2] of the state of Illinois.

The undersigned your petitioners, humbly present to your honor the following statement of facts which are submitted for your just consideration. On or about the 15th of May last one James H. Lee was committed by Justice Adams of this City upon a charge of larceny—he remained in the Jail of Sangamon county until the last Term of the circuit court at which time he was sentenced by his Honor, Judge Davis to one year's imprisonment in the penitentiary. Your petitioners respectfully represent that although the said Lee may have been guilty of taking the sum of money alledged towit—$26.00, yet we believe that it was the first time he was ever guilty of a crime & we sincerely think he has determined &

will be an honest & upright man in future. Your petitioners humbly pray that your Excellency will exercise in this case, your reprieving power that the said Lee may again be restored to his freedom & to his grieved & distressed relationship and your petitioners will ever pray &c. &c

[1] DS, I-Ar. Lincoln's and forty-eight other signatures appear on the document.   [2] Joel A. Matteson.

To Levi Davis[1]

Dear Levi: Springfield, Feby. 11. 1856
    Here is the abstract. The case was decided on the Statute of Limitations. Also you find the certified order of the Court, herewith. Yours as ever   A. LINCOLN

[1] ALS, IHi. Lincoln's note is written on the back of a copy of the printed "Abstract. Charles Manning and Henry R. Glover, *versus* Henry A. Warren, Hiram Bridges and Asa Snell, *et al.* Appeal from Jersey Co.," in the Illinois Supreme Court. Davis was solicitor for Manning and Glover in the lower court. The case was argued and lost by Lincoln on February 11.

To Richard P. Morgan[1]

R. P. Morgan, Esq   Springfield, Feby. 13, 1856
    Dear Sir: Says Tom to John "Heres your old rotten wheelbarrow" "Ive broke it, usin on it" "I wish *you* would mend it, case I shall want to borrow it this arter-noon."
    Acting on this as a precedent, I say "Heres your old "chalked hat" "I wish you would take it, and send me a new one, case I shall want to use it the first of March"   Yours truly
                                                      A. LINCOLN—

[1] ALS-F, ISLA. Morgan was superintendent of the Chicago & Alton at Bloomington, Illinois. The term "chalked hat," applied to a pass, has been explained by way of the white check placed in the hatband of a passenger riding on a pass.

To George U. Miles[1]

G. U. Miles, Esq.   Springfield,
Petersburg, Ills.   Feb. 14. 1856
    Dear Sir: Major Harris[2] left a letter with me, in order that I might do something for you, in regard to your Goodman, or McAtee[3] land. I understand the facts of the case to be as follows—
    Dec. 25, 1840— Christian Goodman gave his note, and a mortgage on this land (S.E. frt. 1/4 of Sec: 22-17-6) to William W. Vigal, to secure $112– with twelve per cent.

[330]

Jany. 7, 1842— Note credited $50

Jany. 7, 1842— Note assigned by Vigal to Thomas Lewis.

Aug. 20, 1842. Note assigned by Lewis to F. T. King.

Jany. 2, 1843. Note assigned by King to Webster & Hickox.

In 1850 or 1851, I commenced a foreclosure suit on the note & mortgage, in the Circuit court of Sangamon county, for Webster & Hickox.

While this suit was pending, Goodman sold the *land* to McAtee, and Webster & Hickox also sold the note and mortgage to McAtee; and Mr. Hickox directed me to do no more with the suit for him & Webster; but to hold it up subject to the direction of McAtee. So the suit has stood ever since, and still stands.

I now learn from Major Harris' letter that McAtee died, and that the land has since been sold (by the administrator of McAtee, to pay debts) to John Baker; and that Baker has since sold to you. The reason I write you is, that I can not understand, from the Major's letter, precisely what your difficulty is. He tells me that McAtee bought the land of Goodman; and if this is so, and he paid for the land, and Goodman deeded it to him, I do not perceive that you are in any difficulty at all.

Did McAtee pay Goodman for the land?

Did Goodman deed it to McAtee?

If either of these is true, Goodman's heirs have no right to the land, though his widow would have dower, if she did not join in the deed. Please write me; and return me this letter, as it will save me hunting up the facts again. Yours &c   A. LINCOLN—

1 ALS, DLC-HW.   2 Thomas L. Harris.
3 Probably Smith McAtee, a farmer.

To Elihu N. Powell[1]

Dear Powell: Springfield, Feb. 15. 1856

When you wrote me from Chicago about our Aspinall case,[2] I had done nothing with it. But being thereby stirred up, I looked into it, and took fright, lest the Statute of Limitations had matured against it, since the papers were in my hands. To make sure, if it had not, that it should not, I brought the suit at once in our Sangamon Circuit Court,—not knowing where Aspinall lives, so as to sue in the Federal court.

The transcript of record which you gave me, showed the judgment to have been rendered in Nov. 1850; but something about it made me suspect that to be a mistake. I sent the transcript to Mr. Gantt,[3] who returned it to me day-before yesterday, amended,

showing the date of the judgment to be Nov. 1852. So, we are on
our feet again as to the Statute of Limitations. This morning I finished, and filed the declaration Q.E.D. Yours as ever

A. LINCOLN—

¹ ALS, IHi.
² Thomas Aspinall *v.* Thomas Lewis, Willis H. Johnson, and John B. Moffett.
³ Unidentified.

To George U. Miles¹

[Springfield Ills. Feby 17th 1856]

But, my dear Sir, I understand the land is worth $1200 or $1500.
Now deduct credit, and count interest on the note, and you will
find that $203.41 cents is the utmost a decree could be rendered
for up to Jany. 7. 1856.

Suppose I foreclose, you will bid the same; if nobody bids more,
all will be well; but somebody will bid more; and then how will
you stand? You will have to let the land go for that sum; or bid
higher, and advance the cash for all above that sum. Dont you
see?   A. LINCOLN

¹ ALS, DLC-HW. This note is dated "Springfield, Ills, Feby 17th 1856," but
not in Lincoln's handwriting. See Lincoln to Miles, February 14, *supra.*

To Gustave P. Koerner¹

Hon: G. P. Koerner.   Springfield, Feb. 18. 1856

My dear Sir: You left here sooner than I expected; else I should
have asked you on what terms you settled your fee in the case, in
connection with which we met at Carlinville last fall. I think you
said you had no objection to tell me. If you have not, please write
me at once, as I wish to regulate my claim somewhat by yours.
Very truly Yours,   A. LINCOLN—

¹ ALS, MoSHi. Gustave P. Koerner was an attorney at Belleville, Illinois,
associated with Lincoln in trying the case of Clark & Morrison *v.* Page & Bacon
on September 6, 1855. Lyman Trumbull and Koerner represented the complain-
ants, Lincoln and William H. Underwood of Belleville the defendants.

To George P. Floyd¹

Mr. George P. Floyd,   Springfield, Illinois,
Quincy, Illinois.   February 21, 1856.

Dear Sir: I have just received yours of 16th, with check on
Flagg & Savage for twenty-five dollars. You must think I am a
high-priced man. You are too liberal with your money.

Fifteen dollars is enough for the job. I send you a receipt for fifteen dollars, and return to you a ten-dollar bill. Yours truly,

A. LINCOLN.

¹ Tracy, p. 66. Lincoln had drawn papers for Floyd in connection with the leasing of a hotel at Quincy.

Speech at Decatur, Illinois¹

February 22, 1856

Mr. Oglesby² was then loudly called for. Mr. O. made a number of witty remarks and concluded by toasting Mr. Abram Lincoln as the warm and consistent friend of Illinois, and our next candidate for the U. S. Senate. (Prolonged applause.)

Mr. Lincoln arose and said the latter part of that sentiment I am in favor of. (Laughter) Mr. L. said, that he was very much in the position of the man who was attacked by a robber, demanding his money, when he answered, "my dear fellow, I have no money, but if you will go with me to the light, I will give you my note;" and, resumed Mr. L., if you will let me off, I will give you my note. (Laughter, and loud cries of go on.) Mr. Lincoln then proceeded to address the assemblage for some half hour, in his usual masterly manner, frequently interrupted by the cheers of his hearers.

In reply to a complimentary toast, Mr. L. addressed the assembled guests for half an hour in his happiest vein. In the course of his remarks he expressed his hearty concurrence in the resolutions adopted by the Convention,³ and his willingness to buckle on his armor for the approaching contest with the Pierce party.

¹ Decatur *State Chronicle*, February 28, 1856, and Peoria *Weekly Republican*, February 29, 1856. The occasion was a dinner concluding the Anti-Nebraska Editors' Convention at Decatur.   ² Richard J. Oglesby of Decatur.

³ Among other things, the resolutions adopted by the convention called for securing "to Kansas and Nebraska the legal guaranty against slavery of which they were deprived at the cost of the violation of the plighted faith of the nation," and declared against Know-Nothingism, and in favor of "liberty of conscience as well as political freedom."

Opinion on Pre-emption of Public Land¹

March 6, 1856

"Can there be any valid pre-emption on sections of land, *alternate* to the Sections granted to the Illinois Central Railroad?"

My opinion is asked on the above question.

[333]

MARCH 6, 1856

"An Act to appropriate the proceeds of the sales of the public lands, and to grant pre-emption rights" Approved Sep. 4. 1841, contains the first *permanent,* or *prospective* pre-emption law.

5 U.S. Stat. at Large 453.

Sections ten, eleven, twelve, thirteen, fourteen, and fifteen, of this act, relate exclusively to pre-emptions. In Section ten it is provided that "no sections of land reserved to the United States *alternate* to other sections granted to any of the States for the construction of any canal, railroad, or other public improvement, shall be liable to entry under and by virtue of the provisions of this act."

This act continues to be our general pre-emption law, up to the present time—and, although some supplementary provisions had afterwards been enacted, the above provision, in section ten, remained untouched up to Sep. 20. 1850, when the Central Railroad grant was made.

The latter act, preserved existing pre-emptions, on the even sections, granted generally, for the Road; but made no mention of pre-emptions, as to the odd sections reserved to the United States.

9 Stat. at Large 466.

August 2. 1852 "An Act to protect actual Settlers upon the Land on the Line of the Central Railroad and Branches, by granting Pre-emption Rights thereto," was passed. By this act, pre-emptions were given on these reserved Sections, to *such* persons as were settlers on them, on Sep. 20. 1850, in such way as to be entitled to the benefit of the act of Sep. 4. 1841.

10 Stat. at Large—27.

This, it is perceived, limits the right to those who had made actual settlements upon the lands, on the 20th. of Sep. 1850—the date of the Central Railroad grant.

March 3. 1853 "An Act to extend Pre-emption Rights to certain lands therein mentioned" was enacted.

By this act the general pre-emption laws are extended to these reserved Sections, with a proviso "That no person shall be entitled to the benefit of this act who has not settled and improved, or shall not settle and improve such lands prior to the final allotment of the alternate sections, to such Railroads by the General Land Office" 10 Stat. at Large—244.

I have examined all the subsequent acts of Congress up to the close of the Session, on March 3. 1855; and I do not discover that the above quoted proviso has even been disturbed—"An Act for the Relief of Settlers on Lands reserved for Railroad purposes" Approved, March 27. 1854—does not affect the act last aforesaid. 10 Stat. at Large 269.

The final allotment of the alternate sections to the Illinois Central Railroad Company, by the General Land-Office, was made on the 13th. day of March. 1852.

It is my opinion that persons who settled on those reserved sections *prior* to the date of said "final allotment" might have valid pre-emptions; and that those who settled thereon *after* the date of said allotment, can not.

As to the *mode* of redress, in cases of pre-emptions having been *improperly* allowed by the Register and Receiver, it is more difficult to answer, owing to that matter depending upon the regulations, or special action, of the Departments, and not upon express statutory provisions.

I understand that if a pre-emption be *illegally* allowed by the Register and Receiver, or, even *legally* allowed, but upon *false* or *fraudulent* proof, and forwarded to the General Land Office; the party interested to contest the pre-emption, may address a letter, or petition, to the Commissioner of the General Land-Office, describing the land, stating the facts, and pointing out wherein the illegality or fraud consists, and asking for a re-hearing; and that, thereupon, the Commissioner will direct the Register and Receiver to give a re-hearing, upon notice to both pre-emptor, and contestant.

I, therefore, would advise that wherever, on these reserved sections, a settlement and improvement have been made *before* the "allotment" of the General Land Office, towit before, March 13. 1852– and a claim is now set up the claim should be contested, on the ground that the right has been lost, by not being followed up with claim, proof, and payment, in *due time*—See Section 15 of the Act of Sep. 4. 1841.

In cases where settlements were made *after* the allotment, contest them on the ground that there never was a right.

The contest to be made in the mode above pointed out. The letter, or petition, to the Commissioner, should, in this class of cases, contain a reference to the aforesaid Acts of Sep. 4. 1841—Sep. 20. 1850. August 2. 1852—March 3. 1853 & March 27. 1854—and particularly to that of March 3. 1853.

Also, if it be intended to assail the proof which the pre-emptor has made, as being *false* or *fraudulent*, it would be better to verify the Petition by affidavit.

March 6. 1856   A. LINCOLN

[1] ADS, owned by Mrs. Edna Orendorff Macpherson, Springfield, Illinois. The opinion was written for the Illinois Central Railroad.

To John D. Caton[1]

Hon: J. D. Caton   Springfield,
Dear Sir: March 21. 1856

Mr. C. H. Moore,[2] of DeWitt county, sends you a record asking an order for a supersedeas. If you allow it, Mr. Moore himself is abundantly good for surety, and we desire that you name him as such in the order. Very truly Your friend—   A. LINCOLN

[1] ALS, DLC-Caton Papers. John D. Caton was a judge on the Illinois Supreme Court.

[2] Clifton H. Moore, an attorney at Clinton, Illinois, wrote Judge Caton on March 24 enclosing the record and asking a writ of error and supersedeas. Moore and Lincoln were associated in a number of cases as attorneys for the Illinois Central.

Opinion on Land Titles in Beloit, Wisconsin[1]

March 24, 1856

On the foregoing statement of facts, I should arrange the inhabitants of Beloit, in their contest with Dillingham,—into two classes—those who claim under conveyances from Crane *before* his Patent issued, forming one class; and those claiming under conveyances from him, *after* his Patent, forming another.

In the contest with the latter class, both parties claiming under Crane, neither can dispute his title.

                    2. Greenl. Ev. Sec. 307 & cases cited
                    2. Carter (Ia).   123

And the title of the inhabitants being the *elder* is unquestionably the better, unless the deeds are void for *vagueness* of description.

But a deed for land is never void for vagueness of description, when the land can be identified by anything and every thing referred to on the face of the deed.

    McIver vs Walker. 9 Cranch 173 (in
    3 Cond. 338 & note at the end of the on)
    3 Ark. 18
    11 Illinois 318—279
    13. Illinois 308—16 Mis. 124.

In this case I have not seen the deeds; but doubtless they mention the town of Beloit, and refer to the recorded Plat. Geography fixes the general locality of Beloit; and living witnesses will prove its

[1] ADS, CSmH. Apparently this seven-page manuscript is only the latter portion of the opinion. The preceding portion has not been located. The only reference to the opinion which has been found is in a letter from David Davis to Lincoln, February 20, 1856 (original owned by Mrs. Edna Orendorff Macpherson, Springfield, Illinois), which requests Lincoln to give an opinion for Lucius G. Fisher of Beloit, Wisconsin, who had sent Davis a statement of the case with the request that he select a lawyer to submit the question to.

more precise location from the first. Also the Plat, to which the deeds refer, connects itself with the known State line on the South, and with the natural boundary of Rock-River on the West. By this unmistakeable boundaries [*sic*], apply the Plat to the face of the ground and it identifies each lot where the inhabitants claim it to be—locates the lots on the land owned by Crane when he made the deeds, and so passes the titles under and by the deeds.

There being no difficulty in identifying or locating the several lots, the deeds are not void.

I assume that the deeds from Crane to the inhabitants were duly recorded, before the execution of Cranes deed to Cooper, under which latter, Dillingham claims. If so, Dillingham can not set up want of notice to Cooper, first, because the recorded deeds notified him of the Plat, and the Plat notified him of the locality of the ground,—and it is nothing to the point, that the Plat was wanting in legal sufficiency to pass the title of a boat-landing, or other ease-ment, to the public. And secondly, because the actual possession was notice to him as to all the lots actually occupied.

I have no doubt this class can successfully defend against eject-ment brought by any one claiming through the deed from Crane to Cooper.

The class who claim under conveyances from Crane *before* his Patent issued, have to meet some additional questions.

The titles of this class, I think, are also good, in *Equity*, if not at law, as against the Cooper title. Any one claiming under that title can not, in equity, question the validity of Cranes pre-emption entry—because his own title, equally with ours, stands on that entry. In equal right better is the condition of him in possession. The validity of the pre-emption entry being thus out of question, Crane's quit claim deeds to us, gave us the equitable title at least, even granting that the strict legal title did not devolve upon Crane before his Patent issued, and did not inure to us when the Patent did issue.

This, however subject to the question whether our deeds from Crane are or not absolutely void, as being in the teeth of the pre-emption law under which Crane made the entry.

That they were so void, our adversary can urge against us, with-out, at all, assailing his own title.

The pre-emption Act of Congress, May 29, 1830 was for one year's duration only, and contained a provision that "all assignments and transfers of the right of pre-emption given by this act, prior to the issuance of patents, shall be null and void" 1. Land Laws—473.

On the 23. Jany. 1832, and after the above act had expired by its own limitation, but while many patents remained unissued upon entries made under the act, congress passed another act, supplementary to the former, providing that persons who had purchased under the former act, might assign and transfer their certificates of purchase, or final receipts, and that patents might issue in the name of such assignee, anything in the former act to the contrary notwithstanding. 1 Land Laws, 492.

July 14—1832. Congress revived the act of May 29, 1830 for a special class of cases. 1 Land Laws, 510.

June 19, 1834. Congress passed another act reviving the act of May 29, 1830 to continue in force for two years from its passage, but being silent as to the supplementary act of Jan. 23, 1832. 1 Land Laws, 525

March 6, 1835. Mr. Attorney General Butler gave an official opinion that the revival of the original law of 1830, by the act of 1834, was to be considered as embracing the provisions ingrafted thereon by the supplementary act of 1832. Land Oppinions 196

June 22, 1838 congress again revived the act of 1830, for two years longer. 1 Land Laws, 574

Under this latter act the pre-emption entry now in question, was made.
If, as decided by the Attorney General, the act of 1834, revived the Supplementary act of 1832, as well as the original of 1830, so did the act of 1838. As to that question there is no difference between the Acts of 1834 and 1838. That the act of 1838 revived the Supplementary act of 1832, has the additional argument in it's favor, of being passed by congress with the supposed knowledge of the constructions the Attorney General had put upon the act of 1834. It is a rule of law that when a statute has been enacted, and has been construed by the courts, and another Legislature, even of a different state, re-enacts, or adopts the old statute, it also adopts the courts construction of it. And this is reasonable. If a Legislature approve a statute, but disapprove a construction which the courts have given it, they will not re-enact the law, without, in some way, protesting against the construction.
So in this case—From 1835, to 1838, pre-emption entries, before patents issued, had constantly been assigned and transferred, under the decision of the Attorney General, and with the approbation of the Land Departments, and congress, when in 1838 it again had the subject in hand, had it not approved the practice, would have expressed its disapproval.

This being so, Crane's conveyances before his patent, were not void, but valid, at least in equity. And, of this equity, as in the other class of cases, Cooper had full notice.

But in addition to this, the Circuit Court of the United States for the District of Illinois, in the case of Morgan vs. Curtenius *et al*, 4 McLean 366, fully decided, against the very objection made in this case, that the deed of a pre-emptioner, under the act of 1830, made *before* his patent issued, was after the patent issued to the pre-emptioner, a valid legal title, against a title derived from the pre-emptioner subsequently to his patent. This is our case precisely—and it is worthy of note that, the decision being made by a court of the U.S. upon laws of the U.S. is of superior authority to decisions made by the State courts, if indeed there were any such to the contrary. The decision is also important, in holding that the title is a legal one; and there is no doubt this is the law in Illinois, and also in Wisconsin, unless, in this particular, the law of Wisconsin is different from ours,—which is not probable.

I therefore think both classes of the inhabitants of Beloit, have a full legal legal [*sic*] defence against the Cooper title.

The case of Gardner vs Brown *et al* 2. Wisconsin R. 153, is nothing against this. In that case, the defendants had no deed from Crane or any one else—had never purchased of Crane or any one else. The public had no deed from Crane or any one else. The Plat was legally insufficient to pass the title of the "Landing" to the public. The landing was not a necessary easement to the lots afterwards sold by Crane; and the public had never *used* it as a landing so as to get a right in that way. And if they had, that would have given the defendants no right to squat upon it for private use.

The Streets certainly, and perhaps the public square, stand on different ground. The inhabitants are doubly protected as to them. First, because they are necessary and convenient easements to the lots sold by Crane, and so designated by him at the time of selling. Secondly, because the public had used them, with Crane's knowledge and approbation, long enough before his deed to Cooper, to establish a dedication.   8 Wend. 85.   11 do. 487.   11 B. Mon. 155. 12. Ills. 35-60.   13 Ills. 312 [.]   15. Ills. 236.   6 Peters 431. Upon the whole case, as to both classes of the inhabitants of Beloit, I should advise that they pay nothing for the Cooper title; bring no suit of their own; but quietly await the attack of the adversary. If the attack shall ever be made, it will be made at law, and should be defended at law; and if, finally, the interposition of a court of Equity shall become necessary, there will still be time and oppertunity of resorting to it.   A. LINCOLN

March 24, 1856

To Nicholas H. Ridgely[1]

N. H. Ridgely, Esq   Pekin,
Dear Sir: May 1. 1856
I have just examined the papers and record of the partition case
mentioned in your letter, and found them all right, except the
Sheriff's return of the service of process on the child; and as the old
Sheriff, who made the service, was here, I got leave of the court, &
had him to amend the return. It is all right now, I think. Yours truly
                                                          A LINCOLN—

[1] ALS, IHi. Nicholas H. Ridgely had written Lincoln to clear a flaw in the
title of the land on which the Springfield Gas Works stood.

Call for Republican Convention[1]

May 10, 1856
TO THE CITIZENS OF SANGAMON COUNTY.
    The undersigned, citizens of Sangamon county, who are opposed
to the Repeal of the Missouri Compromise, and who are opposed to
the present Administration, and who are in favor of restoring the
administration of the General Government to the Policy of Washington and Jefferson, would suggest the propriety of a County
Convention, to be held in the City of Springfield, on SATURDAY, the
TWENTY-FOURTH day of MAY, 1856, to appoint Delegates to the
Bloomington Convention.

[1] *Illinois State Journal,* May 10, 1856. Of one hundred and twenty-nine signers,
the names of Lincoln and Herndon head the list. Herndon had signed for Lincoln,
who was attending court at Pekin, Illinois. When Lincoln's conservative friends
protested, Herndon wrote Lincoln and received a telegram sanctioning his act
(Herndon, II, 382).

Speech at Bloomington, Illinois[1]

May 28, 1856
    In the evening a meeting was held in front of Pike House, and
several speeches were made. The speakers were Lincoln, Washburne, Palmer, Swett, Lovejoy and Wentworth.
    Lincoln led off; said he didn't expect to make a speech then; that
he had prepared himself for one, but 'twas not suitable at that time;
but that after awhile he would make them a most excellent one.
Notwithstanding, he kept on speaking, told his old story about the
fence (meaning Missouri restriction) being torn down and the cattle
eating up the crops, then talked about the outrages in Kansas; said
a man couldn't think, dream or breathe of a free state there, but

[340]

what he was kicked, cuffed, shot down and hung; he then got very pathetic over *poor* Delahay and Tom Shoemaker.[2] By the way, Mr. Register, I wonder if any one in this community knows Delahay and Shoemaker; if so we pass them and also Lincoln's speech, and come next to that of Washburne, which was celebrated only for the vehement and uproarious manner with which it was delivered.

[1] *Illinois State Register*, May 31, 1856.
[2] Mark W. Delahay's newspaper office at Leavenworth, Kansas, had been destroyed by pro-slavery men in October 1855. Thomas C. Shoemaker, a free-soiler formerly of Springfield, Illinois, had been appointed receiver of the Land Office for Kansas in 1855 and was removed from office in October, 1856. He was killed at Leavenworth in a barroom brawl growing out of a political argument in April, 1857.

Speech at Bloomington, Illinois[1]

May 29, 1856

Abraham Lincoln, of Sangamon, came upon the platform amid deafening applause. He enumerated the pressing reasons of the present movement. He was here ready to fuse with anyone who would unite with him to oppose slave power; spoke of the bugbear disunion which was so vaguely threatened. It was to be remembered that the *Union must be preserved in the purity of its principles as well as in the integrity of its territorial parts.* It must be "Liberty and Union, now and forever, one and inseparable." The sentiment in favor of white slavery now prevailed in all the slave state papers, except those of Kentucky, Tennessee and Missouri and Maryland. Such was the progress of the National Democracy. Douglas once claimed against him that Democracy favored more than his principles, the individual rights of man. Was it not strange that he must stand there now to defend those rights against their former eulogist? The Black Democracy were endeavoring to cite Henry Clay to reconcile old Whigs to their doctrine, and repaid them with the very cheap compliment of National Whigs.

[1] Alton *Weekly Courier*, June 5, 1856. This brief report is the only contemporary account of the so-called "Lost Speech" delivered at the Bloomington convention. The lengthy reconstruction made by Henry C. Whitney in 1896, which has appeared in other collections of Lincoln's writings and speeches, is not, in the opinion of the editors, worthy of serious consideration.

To Daniel D. Page and Henry D. Bacon[1]

Messrs Page & Bacon:
Gentlemen

Springfield,
May 31. 1856

The letter of Mr. Parsons,[2] of the 22nd. accompanied, by one to Mr. Dickson, and also by one from Mr. Dickson[3] to your Mr. Bacon, owing to my absence, was received on yesterday only. I went to Mr. Dickson at once, and had a conference with him. I do not think he is acting in bad faith. He is a new Marshal, and when he made the agreement with Mr. Parsons, he did not know of the law and regulations out of which the difficulty grows. The sum of the difficulty is that the Government is entitled to a contingent residuum of his fees and emoluments, and he fears and believes he can not lawfully lessen, or destroy that residuum. He says the Judge is of that opinion; and really I have fears of it myself, though it did not occur to me, when the stipulation was made.

Mr. Dickson instructs me to say to you that he wishes nothing for himself beyond what he stipulated for; but that he can not make a false oath to conceal the real truth of the transaction; and he can not subject himself to pay a large sum, or any sum, to the government, out of his own pocket. He says if you give him perfect security that he shall lose nothing, he is still willing to stand to his agreement. Herewith I send you a statement of the matter handed me by Mr. Dickson, containing references to the laws & instructions. Your counsel at St. Louis can examine the question; and if they conclude you can not safely give the security, so much the more certain is it that Mr. Dickson can not safely proceed without it.

In the mean time I shall try to examine the question more fully myself. Yours truly   A. LINCOLN—

[1] ALS, owned by H. D. B. Soulé, San Francisco, California. Page & Bacon were merchants and leading bankers of St. Louis, Missouri.

[2] Lewis B. Parsons, St. Louis attorney, who was legal adviser to Page & Bacon.

[3] Archimedes C. Dickson, marshal of the U.S. Circuit Court for Southern Illinois.

To Lyman Trumbull[1]

Hon: Lyman Trumbull   Springfield, June 7, 1856

My dear Sir: The news of Buchanan's[2] nomination came yesterday; and a good many whigs, of conservative feelings, and slight pro-slavery proclivities, withal, are inclining to go for him, and will do it, unless the Anti-Nebraska nomination shall be such as to divert them. The man to effect that object is Judge McLean;[3] and his nomination would save every whig, except such as have already gone over hook and line, as Singleton,[4] Morrison,[5] Constable,[6] & others. J. T. Stuart, Anthony Thornton, James M. Davis (the old settler) and others like them, will heartily go for McLean, but will every one go for Buchanan, as against Chase, Banks, Seward, Blair or Fremont.[7] I think they would stand Blair or Fremont for Vice-President—but not more.

Now there is a grave question to be considered. Nine tenths of the Anti-Nebraska votes have to come from old whigs. In setting stakes, is it safe to totally disregard them? Can we possibly win, if we do so? So far they have been disregarded. I need not point out the instances.

I think I may trust you to believe I do not say this on my own personal account. I am *in*, and shall go for any one nominated unless he be *"platformed"* expressly, or impliedly, on some ground which I may think wrong.

Since the nomination of Bissell we are in good trim in Illinois, save at the point I have indicated. If we can save pretty nearly all the whigs, we shall elect him, I think, by a very large majority.

I address this to you, because your influence in the Anti-Nebraska nomination will be greater than that of any other Illinoi[s]an.

Let this be confidential. Yours very truly   A. LINCOLN

1 ALS, CSmH.
2 James Buchanan had been nominated at Cincinnati following Douglas' withdrawal on the night of June 5.
3 Justice John McLean had come recently into sharp political focus with the unauthorized announcement in the press of his avowed intention to dissent in the event the Supreme Court decided against Dred Scott, and with publication of his letter of May 13 to Lewis Cass, in which he stated "I never doubted that Congress had this power [to prohibit slavery in a territory], and I could never have expressed doubt on the subject."   4 James W. Singleton.
5 James L. D. Morrison.   6 Charles H. Constable.
7 Salmon P. Chase, Nathaniel P. Banks, William H. Seward, and Francis P. Blair were not really available. Both Blair and Banks were promoting John C. Frémont, Seward was not interested, and Chase was too radical.

Explanation Written for Joshua F. Amos[1]

June 9, 1856

Explanation

In April 1849 I loaned Nathaniel Hay two hundred dollars, for which I took his note at six per cent for first six months and ten per cent afterwards. At the time, he owed me some trifle for fees. Afterwards from time to time I had bricks of him, and once he paid me ten dollars in money. In January or February 1855 we made a turn by which he paid the First Presbyterian Church twelve or fourteen dollars for me. On the 2nd. of March 1855, we had a settlement including all these things; and as the old note was already nearly covered with former settlements and credits, he took it up, and gave me the note and due-bill herewith filed, the note being for the original principal loaned, and the due-bill for a ballance of interest due. After this, in June 1855, he furnished me bricks for the founda-

tion of a fence, amounting to fifteen or sixteen dollars, which I have always considered as having substantially paid the due-bill. In August 1855 he furnished me bricks for the pit of a privy, for which he or his estate is entitled to a credit on the note. The exact amount of this last lot of bricks, I never knew; but I suppose the administrator can find it on Mr. Hay's books.   A. LINCOLN—
June 9. 1856.

[1] ADS, owned by the heirs of Stuart Brown, Springfield, Illinois. Joshua F. Amos was administrator of the estate of Nathaniel Hay. See notes, March 2, 1855, *supra*, and receipt, May 16, 1857, *infra*.

Speech at Springfield, Illinois[1]

June 10, 1856

Mr. Lincoln opened his speech, and for more than an hour he bored his audience with one of the weakest speeches that he ever perpetrated. He was evidently laboring under much restraint, conscious that he was doling out new doctrine to the old whigs about him, and fearful that in keeping within moderate bounds, he would so filter his discourse that it would not in any degree reach the end he desired. He would occasionally launch out and lead his hearers to think that the most ultra abolitionism would follow, when, under the old whig eyes we have mentioned, he would soften his remarks to a supposed palatable texture. In this way, backing and filling, he frittered away anything of argument that he might have presented, convincing his audience, however, that his niggerism has as dark a hue as that of Garrison or Fred Douglass[2] but that his timidity before the peculiar audience he addressed prevented its earnest advocacy with the power and ability he is known to possess.

The gist of his remarks were intended to show that the democratic party favors the extension of slavery, that black republicanism aims to prevent it; by what process we did not learn from him, nor did he furnish any evidence of the truth of his allegation against the democracy. He was opposed to the extension of slavery. So are we. But we desire to see it done in a constitutional manner—by the act of the people interested. For leaving the decision of the question there, by the adjustment of '50, and by the Nebraska act, black republicanism has raised another furor in the country, and until very lately, they have claimed for congress the power to refuse the admission of any new state recognizing slavery by its constitution. Latterly, this plank of their platform has been suppressed. We heard nothing of it on Tuesday evening from Mr. Lincoln. The same caving in as to the restoration of the Missouri restriction, marks the latter day policy of the sectional party, and he as cautiously avoided it. They seek power, Mr. Lincoln naively told us, by the agglomeration of all the discordant elements of faction, and if obtained, the now suppressed platform of ultra abolitionism will be avowed and acted upon. He boldly avowed, in one of his many escapings, that there could be no Union with slavery. That agitation would be ceaseless until it shall be swept away, but the mode of its eradication he left to inference from his own antecedents and those of the ruling spirits of black-republicanism—Garrison, Greeley, Seward, Sumner, and others of that genus.

To attain power, by whatever means, was the burden of his song, and he pointed to the complexion of the Bloomington ticket as evidence of the desire of the factions to attain it by any process. Bissell, a renegade democrat, headed it.[3] Hoffman, a German nondescript, followed; Miller, ex-whig and probable know-nothing, followed next, while Hatch, Dubois and Powell, avowed knownothings, brought up the rear. With such a medley—such a fusion of opposites, none can doubt that the end and aim of the Bloomington organization is "power"—and *place*, and that its managers would sink any principle, trample upon right, law and constitution to attain their object.

Mr. Lincoln's allusion to Bissell's services as a warrior was singularly malapropos, in him, at least; Bissell's laurels having been won in a war, the "identical spot" on which it commenced never could be learned by Mr. L., and consequently had his inveterate opposition during its entire progress, by his congressional action in hampering the democratic administration in its prosecution. In this connection, Bissell may well exclaim—"Save me from such backing!"

Except from the squad of claquers we have mentioned, Mr. Lincoln's remarks were received with coldness. He convinced nobody of his own sincerity, of the justness of his cause, nor did he elicit any applause except from the drilled few who occupied the front benches.

[1] *Illinois State Register*, June 12, 1856. This is the only report available. In spite of the political obfuscation of the *Register*, it is possible to trace dimly the thread of Lincoln's argument.

[2] William L. Garrison and Frederick Douglass, celebrated Negro orator and abolitionist who had escaped from slavery.

[3] The Republican state ticket was as follows: William H. Bissell, for governor; Francis A. Hoffman, for lieutenant governor (a native of Germany lacking the requisite fourteen years of citizenship, he was later replaced by John Wood of Adams County); James Miller, for treasurer; Ozias M. Hatch, for secretary of state; Jesse K. Dubois, for auditor; William H. Powell, for superintendent of public instruction.

To John Van Dyke[1]

Springfield, Illinois, June 27, 1856.

My Dear Sir: Allow me to thank you for your kind notice of me in the Philadelphia Convention.

When you meet Judge Dayton present my respects, and tell him I think him a far better man than I for the position he is in, and that I shall support both him and Colonel Frémont most cordially. Present my best respects to Mrs. Van Dyke, and believe me. Yours truly,

A. LINCOLN.

[1] NH, II, 289-90. John Van Dyke of New Brunswick, New Jersey, was a Whig representative in the Thirtieth and Thirty-first Congresses. In his speech before the Republican National Convention on June 19, he paid tribute to Lincoln as follows: ". . . I knew Abraham Lincoln in Congress well, and for months I sat by his side. I knew him all through, and knew him to be a first-rate man in every respect; and if it had not been the will and pleasure of the Convention to have selected William L. Dayton, I know with what perfect alacrity I would have gone for him. . . ." Lincoln received 110 votes for the vice-presidential nomination on the first ballot. Senator Dayton of New Jersey received the nomination. *Proceedings of the First Three Republican National Conventions*, Minneapolis, 1893, p. 59 ff.

Speech at Princeton, Illinois[1]

July 4, 1856

After the company had secured their refreshments, and had walked around and enjoyed themselves for near an hour, the chairman again called the meeting to order and introduced to them Hon. A. Lincoln, of Springfield, who then proceeded to address the assembled multitude. Mr. Lincoln commenced back at the formation of the American government, and made a hasty review of our history, glancing at all the most important features in our legislation. He spoke in the first place of that Declaration made to the world, by our Fore Fathers, "That all men are born free and equal," and from that time he moved on down to the famous ordinance of 1787, the ordinance that was passed and under which Virginia, [if our memory serves us aright][2] granted the five states of Ohio, Indiana, Illinois, Michigan and Wisconsin, to the general government, and in that vast territory, slavery and involuntary servitude, except for crime was forever prohibited. He then came to speak of the Missouri Compromise, and on this point he dwelt at full length, as the repeal of this act is the measure that is now causing so much excitement throughout our country. He said the people had lived in comparative peace and quiet, with only an occasional brush. During Gen. Jackson's administration, the Calhoun Nullifying doctrine sprang up, but Gen. Jackson, with that decision of character that ever characterized him, put an end to it. Then again in 1845, when Texas

[346]

knocked at the door and requested admission there sprang up another excitement on the slavery question. That finally passed off until the excitement in regard to the territories of Washington and Utah, came up which was the cause of the passage of the Compromise measures of 1850. It then ran on until 1854, when Douglas, in announcing his bill for the organization of the territories of Kansas and Nebraska, recommended Congress to repeal the Missouri Compromise, which move raised such an excitement around the White House and throughout the country as never before was heard of in this Union. Mr. Lincoln took his seat amid loud and enthusiastic cheers.

[1] Tiskilwa, Illinois, *Independent*, July 11, 1856. Lincoln was preceded by Burton C. Cook of Ottawa and Joseph Knox of Rock Island, and followed by Owen Lovejoy. According to the *Independent* "from 8,000 to 10,000 people" attended the celebration.   [2] Brackets are in the source.

To Henry C. Whitney[1]

Dear Whitney: Springfield, July 9. 1856
    I now expect to go to Chicago on the 15th., and I probably shall remain there, and thereabouts, for about two weeks.
    It turned me blind when I first heard Swett was beaten, and Lovejoy nominated;[2] but after much anxious reflection, I really believe it is best to let it stand. This, of course, I wish to be confidential.
    Lamon did get your Deeds. I went with him to the office, got them, and put them in his hand myself. Yours very truly
                                                        A. LINCOLN—

[1] ALS, owned by heirs of Charles S. Lewis, Indianapolis, Indiana.
[2] Owen Lovejoy received the Republican nomination for congress over Leonard Swett in the third congressional district.

To James Berdan[1]

James Berdan, Esq.   Springfield,
My dear Sir: July 10. 1856
    I have just received your letter of yesterday; and I shall take the plan you suggest into serious consideration. I expect to go to Chicago about the 15th., and I will then confer with other friends upon the subject. A union of our strength, to be effected in some way, is indispensable to our carrying the State against Buchanan. The inherent obstacle to any plan of union, lies in the fact that of those germans which we now have with us, large numbers will fall away, so soon as it is seen that their votes, cast with us, may *possibly* be used to elevate Mr. Fil[l]more.
    If this inherent difficulty were out of the way, one small improve-

ment on your plan occurs to me. It is this. Let Fremont and Fillmore men unite on one entire ticket, with the understanding that that ticket, if elected, shall cast the vote of the State, for whichever of the two shall be known to have received the larger number of electoral votes, in the other states.

This plan has two advantages. It carries the electoral vote of the State where it will do most good; and it also saves the waste vote, which, according to your plan would be lost, and would be equal to two in the general result. But there may be disadvantages also, which I have not thought of. Your friend, as ever

A. LINCOLN—

1 ALS, IaDaM.

To James W. Grimes[1]

Hon. J. W. Grimes   Springfield, Ills.
My dear Sir: July 12, 1856

Yours of the 29th. of June was duly received. I did not answer it, because it plagued me. This morning I received another, from Judd and Peck,[2] written by consultation with you.

Now let me tell you why I am plagued.

First I can hardly spare the time.

Secondly, I am superstitious. I have scarcely known a party, preceding an election, to call in help from the neighboring states, but they lost the state. Last fall our friends had Wade of Ohio, & others in Maine; and they lost the state. Last Spring, our adversaries had New-Hampshire full of South Carolinians, and *they* lost the State. And so generally. It seems to stir up more enemies than friends.

Have the enemy called in any foreign help. If they have a foreign champion there, I should have no objection to drive a nail in his track. I shall reach Chicago on the night of the 15th. to attend a little business in court. Consider the things I have suggested, and write me at Chicago. Especially write me whether Browning[3] consents to visit you. Your Obt. Servt.   A. LINCOLN—

1 ALS-P, ISLA. Governor James W. Grimes of Iowa had invited Lincoln to speak. Lincoln did not go.   2 Norman B. Judd and Ebenezer Peck of Chicago.
3 Orville H. Browning.

Speech at Chicago, Illinois[1]

July 19, 1856

A large meeting was held in Dearborn Park on Saturday evening to hear the speech of Mr. Lincoln, and we have never seen an audience held for so long a time in the open air to listen to an argumentative speech. The speaker was calm, clear and forcible, constantly referring to indisputable facts in our political history, and drawing conclusions from them in favor of supporting the Anti-Nebraska platform and nominees, that were unanswerable. He showed how the South does not put up her own men for the Presidency, but holds up the prize that the ambition of Northern men may make bids for it. He demonstrated in the strongest manner, that the only issue now before us, is freedom or slavery, that the perpetuity of our institutions is dependent upon maintaining the former against the aggressions of the latter, and held up the bug bear of disunion, threatened by the slavery extensionists, to the scorn and contempt it deserves.

He spoke in Dearborn Park, and was listened to by a very large audience. The speech was one that did him eminent credit, and which cannot fail to produce a telling effect upon the political sentiment of Chicago. The exposure of the fallaciousness of the position taken by Mr. Fillmore in his Albany speech[2] was timely and effective; and his refutation of the charge of sectionalism, so flippantly made by the slavery-extensionists against the Republican party, was full and able. Every point he touched upon was elucidated by the clearness of his logic, and with his keen blade of satire he laid bare the revolting features of policy of the pseudo-Democracy.

[1] Chicago *Democratic Press*, July 21, 1856, and Peoria *Weekly Republican*, July 25, 1856.
[2] Millard Fillmore had been nominated for president by the Know-Nothing or American Party on February 26 while he was abroad. Upon his arrival at New York on June 22, he made numerous speeches in and around New York City and en route to his home at Buffalo. The most notable of these speeches was his "Union Speech" at Albany on June 26, in which he charged the Republican party with being sectional.

Fragment on Sectionalism[1]

[c. July 23, 1856]

SECTIONALISM.

It is constantly objected to Fremont & Dayton, that they are supported by a *sectional* party, who, by their *sectionalism*, endanger the National Union. This objection, more than all others, causes

[1] AD, John Scheide Library, Titusville, Pennsylvania. The similarity between the argument of this fragment and the speech at Galena, Illinois, July 23, *infra*, suggests that Lincoln wrote the fragment near this date. Reports of other speeches throughout the campaign indicate that Lincoln repeated his argument many times, but no other report is so closely identified with the language of the manuscript.

men, really opposed to slavery extension, to hesitate. Practically, it is the most difficult objection we have to meet.

For this reason, I now propose to examine it, a little more carefully than I have heretofore done, or seen it done by others.

First, then, what is the question between the parties, respectively represented by Buchanan and Fremomont?

Simply this: "*Shall slavery be allowed to extend into U.S. teritories, now legally free?*" Buchanan says it *shall;* and Fremont says it shall *not*.

That is the *naked* issue, and the *whole* of it. Lay the respective platforms side by side; and the difference between them, will be found to amount to precisely that.

True, each party charges upon the other, *designs* much beyond what is involved in the issue, as stated; but as these charges can not be fully proved either way, it is probably better to reject them on both sides, and stick to the naked issue, as it is clearly made up on the record.

And now, to restate the question "*Shall slavery be allowed to extend into U.S. teritories, now legally free?*" I beg to know *how one* side of that question is more sectional than the other? Of course I expect to effect nothing with the man who makes this charge of sectionalism, without caring whether it is just or not. But of the *candid, fair,* man who has been puzzled with this charge, I do ask how is *one* side of this question, more *sectional*, than the other? I beg of him to consider well, and answer calmly.

If one side be as sectional as the other, nothing is gained, as to sectionalism, by changing sides; so that each must choose sides of the question on some other ground—as I should think, according, as the one side or the other, shall appear nearest right.

If he shall really think slavery *ought* to be extended, let him go to Buchanan; if he think it ought *not* let [him] go to Fremont.

But, Fremont and Dayton, are both residents of the free-states; and this fact has been vaunted, in high places, as excessive *sectionalism*.

While interested individuals become *indignant* and *excited*, against this manifestation of *sectionalism*, I am very happy to know, that the Constitution remains calm—keeps cool—upon the subject. It does say that President and Vice President shall be resident of different states; but it does not say one must live in a *slave*, and the other in a *free* state.

It has been a *custom* to take one from a slave, and the other from a free state; but the custom has not, at all been uniform. In 1828 Gen. Jackson and Mr. Calhoun, both from slave-states, were placed on the same ticket; and Mr. Adams and Dr. Rush both from the free-states, were pitted against them. Gen: Jackson and Mr. Calhoun were elected; and qualified and served under the election; yet the whole thing never suggested the idea of sectionalism.

In 1841, the president, Gen. Harrison, died, by which Mr. Tyler, the Vice-President & a slave state man, became president. Mr. Mangum,[2] another slave-state man, was placed in the Vice Presidential chair, served out the term, and no fuss about it—no sectionalism thought of.

In 1853 the present president came into office. He is a free-state man. Mr. King, the new Vice President elect, was a slave state man; but he died without entering on the duties of his office.[3] At first, his vacancy was filled by Atchison,[4] another slave-state man; but he soon resigned, and the place was supplied by Bright,[5] a free-state man. So that right now, and for the year and a half last past, our president and vice-president are both actually free-state men.

But, it is said, the friends of Fremont, avow the purpose of electing him exclusively by free-state votes, and that this is unendurable *sectionalism*.

This statement of fact, is not exactly true. With the friends of Fremont, it is an *expected necessity*, but it is not an *"avowed purpose,"* to elect him, if at all, principally, by free state votes; but it is, with equal intensity, true that Buchanan's friends expect to elect him, if at all, chiefly by slave-state votes.

Here, again, the sectionalism, is just as much on one side as the other.

The thing which gives most color to the charge of Sectionalism, made against those who oppose the spread of slavery into free territory, is the fact that *they* can get no votes in the slave-states, while their opponents get all, or nearly so, in the slave-states, and also, a large number in the free States. To state it in another way, the Extensionists, can get votes all over the Nation, while the Restrictionists can get them only in the free states.

This being the fact, *why* is it so? It is not because one *side* of the question dividing them, is more sectional than the *other;* nor because of any difference in the mental or moral structure of the people North and South. It is because, in that question, the people of the South have an immediate palpable and immensely great pecuniary interest; while, with the people of the North, it is merely an

---

[2] Willie P. Mangum.　　　[3] William R. King died on April 18, 1853.
[4] David R. Atchison of Missouri, elected March 4, 1853.
[5] Jesse D. Bright of Indiana, elected December 5, 1854; Lewis Cass of Michigan had been elected on December 4 for one day only.

abstract question of moral right, with only *slight*, and *remote* pecuniary interest added.

The slaves of the South, at a moderate estimate, are worth a
thousand millions of dollars. Let it be permanently settled that this
property may extend to new teritory, without restraint, and it
greatly *enhances*, perhaps quite *doubles*, its value at once. This immense, palpable pecuniary interest, on the question of extending
slavery, unites the Southern people, as one man. But it can not be
demonstrated that the *North* will gain a dollar by restricting it.

Moral principle is all, or nearly all, that unites us of the North.
Pity 'tis, it is so, but this is a looser bond, than pecuniary interest.
Right here is the plain cause of *their perfect* union and *our want*
of it. And see how it works. If a Southern man aspires to be president, they choke him down instantly, in order that the glittering
prize of the presidency, may be held up, on Southern terms, to the
greedy eyes of Northern ambition. With this they tempt us, and
break in upon us.

The democratic party, in 1844, elected a Southern president.
Since then, they have neither had a Southern candidate for *election*,
or *nomination*. Their Conventions of 1848—1852 and 1856, have
been struggles exclusively among *Northern* men, each vieing to out-
bid the other for the Southern vote—the South standing calmly by
to finally cry going, going, gone, to the highest bidder; and, at the
same time, to make its power more distinctly seen, and thereby to
secure a still higher bid at the next succeeding struggle.

"Actions speak louder than words" is the maxim; and, if true, the
South now distinctly says to the North "Give us the *measures*, and
you take the *men*"

The total withdrawal of Southern aspirants, for the presidency,
multiplies the number of Northern ones. These last, in competing
with each other, commit themselves to the utmost verge that,
through their own greediness, they have the least hope their Northern supporters will bear. Having got committed, in a race of com-
petetion, necessity drives them into union to sustain themselves.
Each, at first secures all he can, on personal attachments to him,
and through *hopes* resting on him personally. Next, they unite with
one another, and with the perfectly banded South, to make the
offensive position they have got into, "a party measure." This done,
large additional numbers are secured.

When the repeal of the Missouri compromise was first proposed,
at the North there was litterally *"nobody"* in favor of it. In February 1854 our Legislature met in call, or extra, session. From them
Douglas sought an indorsement of his then pending measure of

Repeal. In our Legislature were about 70 democrats to 30 whigs. The former held a caucus, in which it was resolved to give Douglas the desired indorsement. Some of the members of that caucus bolted —would not stand it—and they now divulge the secrets. They say that the caucus fairly confessed that the Repeal was wrong; and they placed their determination to indorse it, solely on the ground that it was *necessary* to sustain Douglas. Here we have the direct evidence of how the Nebraska-bill obtained it's strength in Illinois. It was given, not in a sense of right, but in the teeth of a sense of wrong, to *sustain Douglas*. So Illinois was divided. So New England, for Pierce; Michigan for Cass, Pensylvania for Buchan[an], and all for the Democratic party.

And when, by such means, they have got a large portion of the Northern people into a position contrary to their own honest impulses, and sense of right; they have the impudence to turn upon those who do stand firm, and call them *sectional*.

Were it not too serious a matter, this cool impudence would be laughable, to say the least.

Recurring to the question *"Shall slavery be allowed to extend into U.S. teritory now legally free?["]*

This *is* a sectional question—that is to say, it is a question, in its nature calculated to divide the American people geographically. Who is to *blame* for that? *who* can help it? Either side *can* help it; but how? Simply by *yielding* to the other side. There is no other way. In the whole range of *possibility*, there is no other way. Then, which side shall yield? To this again, there can be but one answer— the side which is in the *wrong*. True, we differ, as to which side *is* wrong; and we boldly say, let all who really think slavery ought to spread into free teritory, openly go over against us. There is where they rightfully belong.

But why should any go, who really think slavery ought not to spread? Do they really think the *right* ought to yield to the *wrong*? Are they afraid to stand by the *right*? Do they fear that the constitution is too weak to sustain them in the right? Do they really think that by right surrendering to wrong, the hopes of our constitution, our Union, and our liberties, can possibly be bettered?

Speech at Galena, Illinois[1]

July 23, 1856

LINCOLN ON DISUNION.

Hon. ABRAHAM LINCOLN hits the nail on the head every time, and in this instance it will be seen, he has driven it entirely out of sight,—if we succeed as well as we anticipate in re-producing from memory his argument in relation to "Disunion."

Mr. LINCOLN was addressing himself to the opponents of FRE-MONT and the Republican party, and had referred to the charge of "sectionalism," and then spoke something as follows in relation to another charge, and said:

"You further charge us with being Disunionists. If you mean that it is our aim to dissolve the Union, for myself I answer, that is untrue; for those who act with me I answer, that it is untrue. Have you heard us assert that as our aim? Do you really believe that such is our aim? Do you find it in our platform, our speeches, our conversation, or anywhere? If not, withdraw the charge.

"But, you may say, that though it is not your *aim*, it will be the result, if we succeed, and that we are therefore Disunionists in fact. This is a grave charge you make against us, and we certainly have a right to demand that you specify in what way we are to dissolve the Union. How are we to effect this?

"The only specification offered is volunteered by Mr. Fillmore, in his Albany speech.[2] His charge is, that if we elect a President and Vice President both from the Free States, it will dissolve the Union. This is open folly. The Constitution provides, that the President and Vice President of the United States shall be of different States; but says nothing as to the latitude and longitude of those States. In 1828, Andrew Jackson of Tennessee, and John C. Calhoun of South Carolina, were elected President and Vice President, both from slave States; but no one thought of dissolving the Union then, on that account. In 1840, Harrison of Ohio, and Tyler of Virginia, were elected. In 1841, Harrison died, and John Tyler succeeded to the Presidency, and William R. King, of Alabama,[3] was elected Acting Vice-President by the Senate; but no one supposed that the Union was in danger. In fact, at the very time Mr. Fillmore uttered this idle charge, the state of things in the United States disproved it. Mr. Pierce of New Hampshire, and Mr. Bright of Indiana,—both from free States,—are President and Vice President; and the Union stands, and *will* stand. You do not contend that it ought to dissolve the Union, and the facts show that it *won't*; therefore, the charge may be dismissed without further consideration.

"No other specification is made, and the only one that could be made is, that the restoration of the restriction of '87, making the United States territory free territory, would dissolve the Union. Gentlemen, it will require a decided majority to pass such an act. We, the majority, being able constitutionally to do all that we purpose, would have no desire to dissolve the Union. Do you say that such restriction of slavery would be unconstitutional and that some of the States would not submit to its enforcement? I grant you that an unconstitutional act is not a law; but I do not ask, and will not take your construction of the Constitution. The Supreme Court of the United States is the tribunal to decide such questions, and we will submit to its decisions; and if you do also, there will be an end of the matter. Will you? If not, who are the disunionists, you or we? We, the majority, would not strive to dissolve the Union; and if any attempt is made it must be by you, who so loudly stigmatize us as disunionists. But the Union, in any event, won't be dissolved. We don't want to dissolve it, and if you attempt it, *we won't let you.* With the purse and sword, the army and navy and treasury in our hands and at our command, you *couldn't do it.* This Government would be very weak, indeed, if a majority, with a disciplined army and navy, and a well-filled treasury, could not preserve itself, when attacked by an unarmed, undisciplined, unorganized minority.

"All this talk about the dissolution of the Union is humbug— nothing but folly. *We* won't dissolve the Union, and *you* shan't."

1 Galena *Weekly North-Western Gazette,* July 29, 1856, and *Illinois State Journal,* August 8, 1856. See also, the fragment on Sectionalism, *supra.*

2 On June 26, 1856. See note 2, speech at Chicago, July 19, *supra.*

3 The *Gazette* reads "W.P. Mangum, of N. Carolina," but this supposed error is corrected in the *Journal.* Actually both men served as "president pro tempore of the Senate" following Tyler's elevation: King, March 4-11, 1841, and Mangum, May 31, 1842–March 3, 1845. Samuel L. Southard of New Jersey served between the two.

Editorial on the Right of Foreigners to Vote[1]

July 23, 1856

What's in the Wind?

In the Buchanan paper[2] of this city, we saw yesterday morning, a labored communication, to prove that foreigners, who have not been naturalized, according to the laws of the United States, even though they resided here previous to the adoption of our new Constitution, cannot legally vote for Presidential electors.

This is a grave error, and we presume the writer was led into it by assuming, that none but a citizen of the United States can vote for Electors: whereas, the U.S. Constitution expressly provides, that "Each State may appoint, *in such manner as the Legislature thereof may direct,* a number of Electors equal to the whole number of Senators and Representatives to which the State may be entitled in the Congress;" . . Art. Sec 2.

Our Legislature *has* directed, that unnaturalized foreigners, who were here before the adoption of our late State Constitution, shall, in common with others, vote for and appoint Presidential Electors. There is no room for cavil in this: The whole is left to the State Legislature. The Legislature needs not to use voters at all as instruments in the appointment of Electors. So well is this understood everywhere, that several of the States heretofore appointed their Electors directly by the Legislatures; and we believe South Carolina does so yet.

Let not this class of foreigners be alarmed. Our Legislature has directed that they may vote for Electors; and the U.S. Constitution has expressly authorized the Legislature to make that direction.

But, what's in the wind? Why are Mr. Buchanan's friends anxious to deprive foreigners of their votes? We pause for an answer.

[1] Galena *Weekly North-Western Gazette*, July 29, 1856. Across the top of the first page of this issue in the files of the *Gazette* is written in pencil, "The editorial headed 'What's in the Wind,' was written by Abraham Lincoln. H. H. Houghton." Houghton was editor and proprietor of the *Gazette*, and this signed statement is the basis for inclusion of the editorial. The editorial appeared first in the Galena *Daily Advertiser*, July 23, which was the daily published by Houghton.   [2] The Galena *Courier*.

To Artemas Hale[1]

Hon. Artemas Hale   Springfield,
Bridgewater—Mass.   July 28. 1856

My dear Sir: Yours of the 24th. Inst. is just received. I very cheerfully give you my opinion as to the prospects of the Presidential election in this state & Indiana; premising that I am a Fremont man, so that you can make due allowance for my partiality.

I have no doubt, then, that the opposition to Buchanan, are the majority in both these states; but, that opposition being divided between Fremont & Fil[l]more, places both states in some danger. I think the danger is not great in Indiana; but some greater here. The Fil[l]more men have no power in either state, beyond dividing strength, and thereby bettering the chances of Buchanan. They know this; and I still hope the bulk of them will think better than to throw away their votes for such an object. Your Obt. Servant

A. LINCOLN

[1] ALS, NNP. Artemas Hale had been a Whig representative with Lincoln in the Thirtieth Congress.

To B. Clarke Lundy and Others[1]

B. Clarke Lundy & Others: Springfield, July 28, 1856.

On reaching home day before yesterday, I found your letter of the 15th. I regret to say I can not be with you on the 4th of Sept. I am under prior obligation to attend a meeting of our friends at Galesburg on that day, if I can possibly leave our courts, which will then be in session.

Stand by the *cause*, and the cause will carry you through. Yours truly,   A. LINCOLN.

¹ Tracy, p 68. Dr. B. Clarke Lundy, a son of the famous abolitionist Benjamin Lundy, resided in Putnam County, Illinois.

To John M. Palmer[1]

Hon: J. M. Palmer.   Springfield,

Dear Sir: Aug: 1, 1856

It is our judgment that whether you do or do not finally stand as a candidate for Congress, it is better for you to not to publicly decline for a while.

It is a long time till the election; and what may turn up no one can tell. Yours truly   A. LINCOLN—   W. H. HERNDON

                         RICHD. YATES   WM JAYNE[2]

¹ ALS, The Rosenbach Company, Philadelphia and New York.
² Dr. William Jayne, son of Dr. Gershom Jayne, followed his father's medical practice in Springfield and became also a leading Republican.

To Joseph Gillespie[1]

Dear Gillespie—   Springfield, Aug: 2, 1856

About nine years ago, it seems that "Lincoln & Herndon" obtained a judgment here in the Federal court, for Rockhill & Co vs Bradford & Brother, or Bradford & Son or some firm name having Bradford in it.² The last named firm, it seems, lived, or did business at Lebanon, or Greenville or somewhere there. You now know who I mean. Are they now, or have they since 1847, been good for a debt of $1400.00?

Another matter—I am to attend a political meeting at Paris, Edgar Co. on the 6th. My plan is to leave here on the morning train on the 5th. reaching Alton at 12 or 1 o clock, & then taking the first train towards Terre Haute. I am very anxious to see you personally. Can you not meet me at Alton? or fall in with me some where on the train? Do, if you can. Yours as ever   A. LINCOLN—

¹ ALS, MoSHi. Across the top of the page is written Gillespie's presentation of the letter to E. C. Rice, January 23, 1874.
² Rockwell *et al. v.* Bradford.

To John Bennett[1]

John Bennett, Esq   Springfield,
Dear Sir: Aug: 4, 1856

I understand you are a Fillmore man. If, as between Fremont and Buchanan, you *really* prefer the election of Buchanan, then burn this without reading a line further.

But if you would like to defeat Buchanan, and his gang, allow me a word with you. Does any one pretend that Fillmore can carry the vote of this State? I have not heared a single man pretend so. Every vote taken from Fremont and given to Fillmore, is just so much in favor of Buchanan. The Buchanan men see this; and hence their great anxiety in favor of the Fillmore movement. They know where the shoe pinches. They now greatly prefer having a man of your character go for Fillmore than for Buchanan, because they expect several to go with you, who would go for Fremont, if you were to go directly for Buchanan.

I think I now understand the relative strength of the three parties in this state, as well as any other one man does; and my opinion is that to-day, Buchanan has about 85,000—Fremont 78,000, and Fillmore 21,000. This gives B. the State by 7000; and leaves him in the minority of the whole 14,000.

Fremont and Fillmore men being united on Bissell, as they already are, he can not be beaten.

This is not a long letter, but it contains the whole story. Yours as ever   A. Lincoln—

[1] ALS-F, ISLA. Compare the lithographed letter of September 8, *infra*.

To Hezekiah G. Wells[1]

Hon: H. G. Wells: Springfield, Ills.
Dr. Sir   Aug. 4. 1856

Yours of July 24th. inviting me to be present at a Fremont mass meeting, to be held on the 27th. of August, at Kalamazoo, has been forwarded to me by Mr. Mechem[2] of Kankakee. It would afford me great pleasure to be with you, and I will do so if possible; but I can not promise positively.

We are having trouble here that needs the attention of all of us. I mean the Fillmore movement. With the Fremont and Fillmore men united, here in Illinois, we have Mr. Buchanan in the hollow of our hand; but with us divided, as we now are, he has us. This is the short and simple truth, as I believe. Very Respectfully

A. Lincoln—

1 ALS, MiK-M. Hezekiah G. Wells, a prominent Michigan state and county office holder, was chairman of the executive committee in charge of the Republican rally to be held at Kalamazoo on August 27.

2 Lincoln's spelling of this name may have been "Machin." The two "*e's*" have been written in over Lincoln's letters by another hand. Neither name has led to an identification of the person involved.

Speech at Paris, Illinois[1]

August 6, 1856

We shall not undertake to tell what he said to the people, but we do not hesitate to say that his arguments on the leading issue between the parties were unanswerable; and we wish every man in the State could hear the same. He showed very clearly that so far as parties have become sectional, the fault is not with those who are advocating the principles of the founders of the Government—not with the Republican party, who are opposing those waging war against those principles—but that the blame must fall upon those who have resolved to jeopard the Union for the extension of an institution which the Statesmen of the Revolution thought an evil in the country, and hoped would ultimately be altogether eradicated from the land.

1 Paris *Prairie Beacon*, August 8, 1856.

Speech at Shelbyville, Illinois[1]

August 9, 1856

Lincoln then took the stand and made a three hours speech. It was prosy and dull in the extreme—all about "freedom," "liberty" and niggers. He answered nothing that had been said by Mr. Moulton, and dodged every issue in the present canvass, and attempted to make small side issues of no importance. He ridiculed the idea of disunion, and used a great many sophisms to divert the public mind from the true issue of the day.

1 *Illinois State Register*, August 19, 1856. Although other papers mention the meeting and Lincoln's speech, no other report has been located which gives any indication of the content. The occasion was a Democratic rally addressed by Samuel W. Moulton, Shelbyville attorney and leading Democrat.

To Lyman Trumbull[1]

Hon: L. Trumbull: Springfield,
My dear Sir   Aug: 11. 1856
    I have just returned from speaking at Paris and Grandview in Edgar county—& Charleston and Shelbyville, in Coles and Shelby

counties. Our whole trouble along there has been & is Fillmoreism. It loosened considerably during the week, not under my preaching, but under the election returns from Mo. Ky. Ark. & N.C. I think we shall ultimately get all the Fillmore men, who are realy anti-slavery extension—the rest will probably go to Buchanan where they rightfully belong; if they do not, so much the better for us. The great difficulty with anti-slavery extension Fillmore men, is that they suppose Fillmore as good as Fremont on that question; and it is a delicate point to argue them out of it, they are so ready to think you are *abusing* Mr. Fillmore.

Mr. Conkling[2] showed me a letter of yours, from which I infer you will not be in Ills. till 11th. Sept. But for that I was going to write you to make appointments at Paris, Charleston, Shelbyville, Hillsboro, &c. immediately after the adjournment. They were tolerably well satisfied with my work along there; but they believe with me, that you can touch some points that I can not; and they are very anxious to have you do it. Yours as ever   A. LINCOLN

[1] ALS, CSmH.   [2] James C. Conkling.

To Jesse K. Dubois[1]

Springfield, Aug. 19, 1856.

Dear Dubois: Your letter on the same sheet with Mr. Miller's[2] is just received. I have been absent four days. I do not know when your court sits.

Trumbull has written the Committee here to have a set of appointments made for him commencing here in Springfield, on the 11th of Sept., and to extend throughout the south half of the State. When he goes to Lawrenceville, as he will, I will strain every nerve to be with you and him. More than that I cannot promise now. Yours as truly as ever,   A. LINCOLN.

[1] Tarbell (Appendix), p. 322.
[2] Probably James Miller, candidate for state treasurer.

To Hezekiah G. Wells[1]

Hon: H. G. Wells.   Springfield, Ills.
Dear Sir: Augt. 21. 1856

At last I am able to say, no accident preventing, I will be with you on the 27th. I suppose I can reach in time, leaving Chicago the same morning. I shall go to the Matteson House, Chicago, on the evening of the 26th. Yours truly   A. LINCOLN

[1] ALS, MiU-C.

[360]

Speech at Kalamazoo, Michigan[1]

August 27, 1856

Fellow countrymen:—Under the Constitution of the U.S. another Presidential contest approaches us. All over this land—that portion at least, of which I know much—the people are assembling to consider the proper course to be adopted by them. One of the first considerations is to learn what the people differ about. If we ascertain what we differ about, we shall be better able to decide. The question of slavery, at the present day, should be not only the greatest question, but very nearly the sole question. Our opponents, however, prefer that this should not be the case. To get at this question, I will occupy your attention but a single moment. The question is simply this:—Shall slavery be spread into the new Territories, or not? This is the naked question. If we should support Fremont successfully in this, it may be charged that we will not be content with restricting slavery in the new territories. If we should charge that James Buchanan, by his platform, is bound to extend slavery into the territories, and that he is in favor of its being thus spread, we should be puzzled to prove it. We believe it, nevertheless. By taking the issue as I present it, whether it shall be permitted as an issue, is made up between the parties. Each takes his own stand. This is the question: Shall the Government of the United States prohibit slavery in the United States.

We have been in the habit of deploring the fact that slavery exists amongst us. We have ever deplored it. Our forefathers did, and they declared, as we have done in later years, the blame rested on the mother Government of Great Britain. We constantly condemn Great Britain for not preventing slavery from coming amongst us. She would not interfere to prevent it, and so individuals were enabled to introduce the institution without opposition. I have alluded to this, to ask you if this is not exactly the policy of Buchanan and his friends, to place this government in the attitude then occupied by the government of Great Britain—placing the nation in the position to authorize the territories to reproach it, for refusing to allow them to hold slaves. I would like to ask your attention, any gentleman to tell me when the people of Kansas are

---

[1] Detroit *Daily Advertiser*, August 29, 1856. The occasion was a giant Republican "concourse" with a "free public table," parades, eight bands, and the Battle Creek Glee Club providing entertainment. Four speakers stands were going simultaneously during the afternoon, so that the *Advertiser* lamented its single stenographic reporter assigned to report the speeches and added, "Our reporter stuck to the main stand. . . ." Lincoln was preceded by Zachariah Chandler of Detroit and introduced by Hezekiah G. Wells of the Republican executive committee.

going to decide. When are they to do it? How are they to do it? I asked that question two years ago—when, and how are [they] to do it? Not many weeks ago, our new Senator from Illinois, (Mr. Trumbull) asked Douglas how it could be done. Douglas is a great man—at keeping from answering questions he don't want to answer. He would not answer. He said it was a question for the Supreme Court to decide. In the North, his friends argue that the people can decide it at any time. The Southerners say there is no power in the people, whatever. We know that from the time that white people have been allowed in the territory, they have brought slaves with them. Suppose the people come up to vote as freely, and with as perfect protection as we could do it here. Will they be at liberty to vote their sentiments? If they can, then all that has ever been said about our provincial ancestors is untrue, and they could have done so, also. We know our Southern friends say that the General Government cannot interfere. The people, say they, have no right to interfere. They could as truly say,—"It is amongst us—we cannot get rid of it."

But I am afraid I waste too much time on this point. I take it as an illustration of the principle, that slaves are admitted into the territories. And, while I am speaking of Kansas, how will that operate? Can men vote truly? We will suppose that there are ten men who go into Kansas to settle. Nine of these are opposed to slavery. One has ten slaves. The slaveholder is a good man in other respects; he is a good neighbor, and being a wealthy man, he is enabled to do the others many neighborly kindnesses. They like the man, though they don't like the system by which he holds his fellow-men in bondage. And here let me say, that in intellectual and physical structure, our Southern brethren do not differ from us. They are, like us, subject to passions, and it is only their odious institution of slavery, that makes the breach between us. These ten men of whom I was speaking, live together three or four years; they intermarry; their family ties are strengthened. And who wonders that in time, the people learn to look upon slavery with complacency? This is the way in which slavery is planted, and gains so firm a foothold. I think this is a strong card that the Nebraska party have played, and won upon, in this game.

I suppose that this crowd are opposed to the admission of slavery into Kansas, yet it is true that in all crowds there are some who differ from the majority. I want to ask the Buchanan men, who are against the spread of slavery, if there be any present, why not vote for the man who is against it? I understand that Mr. Fillmore's position is precisely like Buchanan's. I understand that, by

the Nebraska bill, a door has been opened for the spread of slavery
in the Territories. Examine, if you please, and see if they have
ever done any such thing as try to shut the door. It is true that
Fillmore tickles a few of his friends with the notion that he is not
the cause of the door being opened. Well; it brings him into this
position: he tries to get both sides, one by denouncing those who
opened the door, and the other by hinting that he doesn't care a
fig for its being open. If he were President, he would have one side
or the other—he would either restrict slavery or not. Of course it
would be so. There could be no middle way. You who hate slavery
and love freedom, why not, as Fillmore and Buchanan are on the
same ground, vote for Fremont? Why not vote for the man who
takes your side of the question? "Well," says Buchanier, "it is
none of our business." But is it not *our* business? There are several
reasons why I think it is our business. But let us see how it is.
Others have urged these reasons before, but they are still of use. By
our Constitution we are represented in Congress in proportion to
numbers, and in counting the numbers that give us our representatives, three slaves are counted as two people. The State of Maine
has six representatives in the lower house of Congress. In strength
South Carolina is equal to her. But stop! Maine has *twice as many*
white people, and 32,000 to boot! And is that fair? I don't complain of it. This regulation was put in force when the exigencies
of the times demanded it, and could not have been avoided. Now,
one man in South Carolina is the same as two men here. Maine
should have twice as many men in Congress as South Carolina. It
is a fact that any man in South Carolina has more influence and
power in Congress today than any two now before me. The same
thing is true of all slave States, though it may not be in the same
proportion. It is a truth that cannot be denied, that in all the free
States no white man is the equal of the white man of the slave
States. But this is in the Constitution, and we must stand up to it.
The question, then is, "Have we no interest as to whether the
white man of the North shall be the equal of the white man of the
South?" Once when I used this argument in the presence of Douglas, he answered that in the North the black man was counted as
a full man, and had an equal vote with the white, while at the
South they were counted at but three-fifths. And Douglas, when
he had made this reply, doubtless thought he had forever silenced
the objection.

Have we no interest in the free Territories of the United States—
that they should be kept open for the homes of free white people?
As our Northern States are growing more and more in wealth and

population, we are continually in want of an outlet, through which it may pass out to enrich our country. In this we have an interest —a deep and abiding interest. There is another thing, and that is the mature knowledge we have—the greatest interest of all. It is the doctrine, that the people are to be driven from the maxims of our free Government, that despises the spirit which for eighty years has celebrated the anniversary of our national independence.

We are a great empire. We are eighty years old. We stand at once the wonder and admiration of the whole world, and we must en-quire what it is that has given us so much prosperity, and we shall understand that to give up that one thing, would be to give up all future prosperity. This cause is that every man can make himself. It has been said that such a race of prosperity has been run no-where else. We find a people on the North-east, who have a dif-ferent government from ours, being ruled by a Queen. Turning to the South, we see a people who, while they boast of being free, keep their fellow beings in bondage. Compare our Free States with either, shall we say here that we have no interest in keeping that principle alive? Shall we say—"Let it be." No—we have an in-terest in the maintenance of the principles of the Government, and without this interest, it is worth nothing. I have noticed in Southern newspapers, particularly the Richmond *Enquirer,* the Southern view of the Free States. They insist that slavery has a right to spread. They defend it upon principle. They insist that their slaves are far better off than Northern freemen. What a mis-taken view do these men have of Northern laborers! They think that men are always to remain laborers here—but there is no such class. The man who labored for another last year, this year labors for himself, and next year he will hire others to labor for him. These men don't understand when they think in this manner of Northern free labor. When these reasons can be introduced, tell me not that we have no interest in keeping the Territories free for the settlement of free laborers.

I pass, then, from this question. I think we have an ever grow-ing interest in maintaining the free institutions of our country.

It is said that our party is a sectional party. It has been said in high quarters that if Fremont and Dayton were elected the Union would be dissolved. The South do not think so. I believe it! I be-lieve it! It is a shameful thing that the subject is talked of so much. Did we not have a Southern President and Vice-President at one time? And yet the Union has not yet been dissolved. Why, at this very moment, there is a Northern President and Vice-President. Pierce and King were elected, and King died without ever taking his seat. The Senate elected a Northern man from their own numbers, to perform the duties of the Vice-President. He resigned his seat, however, as soon as he got the job of making a slave State out of Kansas.[2] Was not that a great mistake?

(A voice.—"He didn't mean that!")

Then why didn't he speak what he did mean? Why did not he speak what he ought to have spoken? That was the very thing. He should have spoken manly, and we should then have known where to have found him. It is said we expect to elect Fremont by Northern votes. Certainly we do not think the South will elect him. But let us ask the question differently. Does not Buchanan expect to be elected by Southern votes? Fillmore, however, will go out of this contest the most national man we have. He has no prospect of having a single vote on either side of Mason and Dixon's line, to trouble his poor soul about. (Laughter and cheers.)

We believe that it is right that slavery should not be tolerated in the new territories, yet we cannot get support for this doctrine, except in one part of the country. Slavery is looked upon by men in the light of dollars and cents. The estimated worth of the slaves at the South is $1,000,000,000, and in a very few years, if the institution shall be admitted into the territories, they will have increased fifty per cent in value.

Our adversaries charge Fremont with being an abolitionist. When pressed to show proof, they frankly confess that they can show no such thing. They then run off upon the assertion that his supporters are abolitionists. But this they have never attempted to prove. I know of no word in the language that has been used so much as that one "abolitionist," having no definition. It has no meaning unless taken as designating a person who is abolishing something. If that be its signification, the supporters of Fremont are not abolitionists. In Kansas all who come there are perfectly free to regulate their own social relations. There has never been a man there who was an abolitionist—for what was there to be abolished? People there had perfect freedom to express what they wished on the subject, when the Nebraska bill was first passed. Our friends in the South, who support Buchanan, have five disunion men to one at the North. This disunion is a sectional question. Who is to blame for it? Are we? I don't care how you express it. This government is sought to be put on a new track. Slavery is to be made a ruling element in our government. The question can be avoided in but two ways. By the one, we must submit, and al-

2 David R. Atchison of Missouri, who was elected president pro tempore of the Senate, March 3, 1853, but resigned the following December to sponsor legislation for organizing the Kansas and Nebraska territories in the interest of the pro-slavery faction.

low slavery to triumph, or, by the other, we must triumph over the black demon. We have chosen the latter manner. If you of the North wish to get rid of this question, you must decide between these two ways—submit and vote for Buchanan, submit and vote that slavery is a just and good thing and immediately get rid of the question; or unite with us, and help us to triumph. We would all like to have the question done away with, but we cannot submit.

They tell us that we are in company with men who have long been known as abolitionists. What care we how many may feel disposed to labor for our cause? Why do not you, Buchanan men, come in and use your influence to make our party respectable? (Laughter.) How is the dissolution of the Union to be consummated? They tell us that the Union is in danger. Who will divide it? Is it those who make the charge? Are they themselves the persons who wish to see this result? A majority will never dissolve the Union. Can a minority do it? When this Nebraska bill was first introduced into Congress, the sense of the Democratic party was outraged. That party has ever prided itself, that it was the friend of individual, universal freedom. It was that principle upon which they carried their measures. When the Kansas scheme was conceived, it was natural that this respect and sense should have been outraged. Now I make this appeal to the Democratic citizens here. Don't you find yourself making arguments in support of these measures, which you never would have made before? Did you ever do it before this Nebraska bill compelled you to do it? If you answer this in the affirmative, see how a whole party have been turned away from their love of liberty! And now, my Democratic friends, come forward. Throw off these things, and come to the rescue of this great principle of equality. Don't interfere with anything in the Constitution. That must be maintained, for it is the only safeguard of our liberties. And not to Democrats alone do I make this appeal, but to all who love these great and true principles. Come, and keep coming! Strike, and strike again! So sure as God lives, the victory shall be yours. (Great cheering.)

Speech at Petersburg, Illinois[1]

August 30, 1856

Petersburg, September 1st.

Editors Register: On Saturday last our town was honored by the presence of that great high-priest of abolitionism, Abram

Lincoln. His mission had been foretold by hand-bills, stating that he would "address the people of Menard upon the important issues of the day." The curiosity of many of our citizens was naturally aroused, as such a thing as a Fremont speech (which this promised to be) had never been heard in Menard county. A considerable number, therefore, turned out to hear him, among whom was your correspondent. I arrived there rather late, for the gentleman had commenced speaking. As I entered I heard him pronouncing, with thundering emphasis, a beautiful passage from Webster's compromise speech, and that, too, *without the quotations*. This was a promising commencement; but it was soon evident that he had read Webster for the *letter* rather than the *spirit*. He then branched off by condemning "the representative system of the south," and displayed its alleged evils in every possible, and we may say impossible, manner. He then fell back, by spasmodic convulsions, to pronouncing eulogies upon the constitution, hardly remembering that this same "damning representative system of the south" was one of the essential compromises of that constitution, and that this same thing had been the rant and cant of all northern fanatics against the constitution ever since its adoption. He wished all to read the black republican platform; and, after reading that platform, he wished any man to point out the sectionalism in it. There was none. (Let him look at the flag of his country raised upon that platform, with fifteen glorious stars erased from its national constellation, and ask the same question.) "It was a slander," he said, "upon the good sense of the southern people to say that if Fremont is elected that the Union will be divided; that it matters not if both candidates be from free states," and here he repeats that which you have satisfactorily answered—that both president and vice president of the United States now are from the free states. He cited David Wilmot as one of his "democratic" authorities; gave a history of a bargain between Long John Wentworth and President Pierce, stating that when the Nebraska bill was first proposed, the president had called him (Wentworth) to his councils in order to find out what he had better do, and which side he should take, promising, in the meanwhile, that [he] would abide his (W'.s) decision; that he had broken his word, and taken the other side. All of this Lincoln knew to be true, for Long John had told him so! He said that when the Nebraska bill was first proposed, that there was *not a man* in Illinois in favor of it. Wonder how they came to be, and who brought about the mighty change, and how was it, if Mr. Lincoln speaks truth, that all the democrats, and with four exceptions only, all their opponents, including Mr. O. M. Hatch, Mr. Lincoln's candidate for secretary of state, voted directly for a resolution in the house of representatives of Illinois in 1851 which indorsed the principles of the Nebraska bill, and how was it that all the democrats, and all their opponents but *four*, in the house of representatives of Illinois, in 1851, instructed our members of congress to organize all *future* territories on those principles, as a continuance of the adjustment of 1850? He said the democrats "pronounced the declaration of independence a self-evident lie."

After continuing in this strain for some time, a "change came over the spirit of his dreams," while he directed his attention to the Fillmoreites present, advising them to fuse with abolitionism, for it was "anything to beat the democrats." Ever and anon he raised his voice, and, with terrible "shrieks for freedom," told them to "come to the rescue," for the little mustang is in danger. For all this, receiving no signs of sympathy, he became disgusted at his own impudence.

And here quietly vanished away the *post mortem* candidate for the vice presidency of the abolition political cock-boat, the depot master of the underground railroad, the great Abram Lincoln. He left no traces of his appearance, and has now "gone to be seen no more," leaving behind him, in Menard, half a dozen poor souls, to mourn the political death-knell of John C. Fremont in next November. Yours,   MANLIUS.

[1] *Illinois State Register*, September 4, 1856. This is the only report available which gives any indication of the contents of the speech.

Speech at Jacksonville, Illinois[1]

September 6, 1856

The meeting was addressed during the afternoon by Hon. Abe Lincoln, in a speech which occupied some two hours. We reached the ground soon after he commenced speaking and found him discussing the subject of Kansas affairs. He referred to the principle of the Kansas law; it permitted the people to settle the question of slavery for themselves, yet the territorial legislature, elected by a Missouri constituency, had passed, together with good wholesome laws, a law in direct conflict with this principle, making it a penal

[1] *The Illinois Sentinel* (Jacksonville), September 12, 1856. Although heavily loaded with Democratic strictures, this report of Lincoln's speech is the only one available which gives an account of his argument. Lincoln spoke in the early afternoon and returned to Springfield on the 4 o'clock train in order to speak that night at another meeting. No report of the Springfield speech of the same date is available.

offense to declare that slavery was not legal in Kansas, or that Kansas should become a free State, and punishing the individual so offending by attaching to his leg a chain and ball. He omitted, however, to inform the audience that this very law was annulled by the Kansas bill which recently passed the democratic U. S. Senate; that every black republican in the Senate voted against thus annulling this obnoxious law; that the black republicans in the House also refused to pass the bill which annulled the law; and that, therefore, the black republicans are alone responsible for the present existence of such a law in Kansas. In connection with the charge that the legislature of Kansas was elected by a Missouri constituency, he overlooked the fact that the evidence adduced by the investigations upon this subject, embraced in the several reports, goes to prove that if every Missouri vote had been thrown out, (and they were thrown out at some of the precincts, and new elections had,) it would not have changed the majority in the body, nor changed the character of its legislation. The law above referred to by Mr. Lincoln, has been denounced by the most prominent democrats of the country, and by the more prominent of the democratic press. The democracy have proven the sincerity of their disapprobation of this obnoxious law by voting for its repeal, while the black republicans have voted against its repeal, and thus continued it on the statute book. Who, then, are the friends of this law, the democracy, or Mr. Lincoln and his party?

After quoting an article from the Richmond Enquirer to prove that the democracy, to be consistent, should indorse slavery as morally right, that the constitution would afford no protection to slavery in the States unless this ground was assumed—he proceeded to state the gist of the issue in the present canvass. That issue was the intervention of congress to prohibit the extension of slavery— shall slavery be extended, or shall its extension be prohibited by a law of congress. To render Mr. Lincoln's position more fully understood it should be stated thus:—shall the people of each territory be permitted to decide the question of slavery for themselves, in accordance with the compromise of 1850, and the Kansas-Nebraska law, or shall the extension of slavery be prohibited by a sectional majority in congress. This is the true meaning of the statement of the issue made by Mr. Lincoln. The free States comprise a large majority of the nation; Mr. Lincoln and the black republican party seek to unite the numerical strength of the north on this sectional question, and thus, by a majority vote in congress, nullify the popular sovereignty principle of the compromise of 1850, and the Kansas organic law.

Without advancing any constitutional arguments to prove the power of congress to prohibit slavery in the territories, Mr. Lincoln assumed that it should be prohibited by congress, and should not be left discretionary with the people of the territory, who, he imagined, were incompetent to prevent its introduction even if so disposed; that if once introduced it would be harder to eradicate than to keep out at the start. He referred to the original introduction of slavery into the colonies by the mother country, and stated that the new territories occupy now exactly the same relation to the States of the Union that the colonies did to the mother country then; that England has been censured for permitting the introduction of slavery into the colonies then, and the States of the Union will hereafter be censured for suffering its introduction (by the will of the people of the territories themselves) into the new territories now. He also read an extract from a speech made by Henry Clay in reference to the territories acquired from Mexico, in which Mr. Clay expressed himself as opposed to legislating slavery into those territories; but Mr. Lincoln forgot to inform the audience that Mr. Clay was also opposed to *prohibiting* slavery in the territories; that the distinguished sage of Ashland was one of the leaders that established the doctrine of non-intervention by congress in reference to those very territories—the very principle Mr. Lincoln and his party are now assailing. Mr. Clay and Mr. Webster informed the country, in their speeches upon this subject, that they advocated the adjustment of the question of slavery in the territories upon this principle, because the doctrine of leaving the question with the people of the territories was a right principle, and because they believed it to be the only means of preserving the Union. We have then the high authority of Mr. Clay and Mr. Webster to strengthen the inference that, in assailing the principle of non-intervention, Mr. Lincoln and the woolly party are working to endanger if not dissolve the Union.

We think the assertion made by Mr. Lincoln, that the Territories occupy the same relative position to the States as did the Colonies to the mother country, an unfortunate one for himself, his principles and his party. If this parallel be a true one, then do the black republicans seek to enforce the very doctrines which caused the American revolution and a separation from the mother country. The mother country imposed upon the colonies local laws against their consent, and denied them the privilege of regulating their own domestic affairs—hence the revolution. The black republicans would impose upon the people of the territories a law in reference to their local affairs whether they (the people of the territories) desire it or not, thus imitating the tyranny of the mother country, and denying the great principle of self government. If the relations of the territories to the States be parallel to those which existed between the colonies and the mother country, then the people of the territories have the right to resist, even by revolution, the imposition of such a law—as did the people of the colonies. If Mr. Lincoln denies the right of the people of the territories to so resist, then he condemns the act of the American revolution, and sustains the tyranny of George the Third against our revolutionary sires.

England introduced slavery into the colonies against the wishes of the people of the colonies. England may therefore justly be censured for the evil she has imposed. The doctrine of non-intervention does not legislate slavery, nor necessarily introduce it, into the territories. If the people of the territories themselves introduce and establish slavery, they alone are responsible for the evil—not the States of the Union.

Mr. Lincoln then defined Fremont's position. He was in favor of congressional intervention, as warranted both by the constitution and expediency. He (Lincoln) would go for Fremont on that account—would go for the woolly horse itself, if necessary to secure congressional prohibition of slavery in the territories. (Meaning the woolly horse which Fremont certified had been taken by him in the Rocky Mountains, and with which, on the faith of Fremont's certificate, Barnum humbugged the public). He referred to the charge that the black republicans were a sectional party; he presumed this charge was based upon the fact that the republican candidates were from the free States; that if this made them a sectional party, so was the democratic party a sectional party—the present executive and vice-president were both citizens of the north. He denied that the black republicans were a sectional party, *although he admitted they expected to elect their ticket by the exclusive votes of the free states;* and charged, as an offset, that the democrats rested their hopes for the success of Buchanan on the southern States alone.

The attempt of Mr. Lincoln to evade the conclusion that the black republicans are a sectional party, by referring to the fact that Mr. Pierce is also a northern man, is a dodge we have seen attempted by some of the country fusion papers, but were surprised to see such a weak and silly subterfuge advanced to an intelligent audience by a gentleman of ability and standing like Mr. Lincoln.

It is well known that Mr. Pierce was nominated by a national convention, composed of delegates from every State in the Union, that thus he was the candidate of a national party, and as such he has been sustained in his administration by all sections of the country. Mr. Buchanan was nominated in the same way. He is thus a national candidate. Fremont was nominated by a convention composed only of delegates from the northern States. He has no party, no supporters, in one half of the Union; therefore he is the sectional candidate of a sectional party. The flattering illusion that Buchanan does not expect a support in the free States, will be dissipated in a few weeks, if such an illusion really exists in the mind of Mr. Lincoln.

Towards the close of the speech the distinguished speaker referred to the charge that the principles and issue of the black republican party tended to a dissolution of the Union. He denied that it was so—asked who was going to dissolve the Union. The black republicans would not do it in the event of success; they would then be in the majority; would have the power; would have the army, the navy and the treasury under their control, and could compel obedience to the laws enacted. A majority would never want to dissolve the Union. Then it would be done, if done at all, by the minority—by the south. In that event the minority would alone be responsible—not the black republican party.

When this same question of congressional prohibition of slavery in the territories was agitated in congress in 1850, threatening to cause a disruption of the government, the North constituted, as now, the majority. Mr. Fillmore, a northern man, occupied the executive chair; they had a northern majority in congress, and through the executive and that majority held the power; they had the army, the navy, and the treasury under their control; yet they did not undertake to subdue the South to submission on this question of intervention. Mr. Webster, a northern man, and the acknowledged leader of the whig party in the north, did not press an act of prohibition upon the South, and say to them, a majority has done this; if you refuse to submit, upon you alone will rest the responsibility of disunion. Mr. Webster acknowledged the minority rights of the South, and he appreciated too highly the inestimable value of the Union to endanger it by infringing upon those rights. His capacious mind grasped the great principle of popular sovereignty as the only safe and just rule for the adjustment of the question. That adjustment was made and sanctioned by the country. Mr. Lincoln tells us that the black republican party are striving to unite the votes of the north on Fremont for the express purpose of annulling that adjustment principle—to secure by the majority of northern votes a prohibition of slavery in the territories by congress. If, as Mr. Webster foresaw, disunion follow the act, the South are to bear the responsibility of resisting the majority; the black republicans will be no disunionists; they will have merely introduced a civil war, in which they will have the army, navy and treasury, to back them.

Mr. Lincoln referred briefly to Mr. Fillmore. He considered that Fillmore stood upon the same platform with Buchanan. Scolded at Douglas for opening the door, (permitting the people of the territory to decide the question for themselves,) but refusing to shut it; there could be no middle ground on this question; there could be no third party. Mr. Fillmore had taken position with Buchanan (and he might have added with Clay and Webster,) in favor of non-intervention. He could not go for Fillmore for another reason. He (Lincoln) did not like the Know Nothings. They were, however, an ephemeral party, and would soon pass away.

He closed by giving a glowing and prophetic picture of the exultation and joy that would animate the country should Buchanan be elected. Rockets would go up in all directions; guns would be fired, and a general shout would go up all over the country. Could a stranger witness these rejoicings from the region of the clouds, he would naturally imagine that [a] new era of freedom had dawned upon the country; but, said Mr. L., it would only be the extension of slavery; and he urged upon his friends to prevent; if possible, these rejoicings, which seemed to loom prophetically upon his mental vision. He then made a farfetched appeal to the democrats, as the longtime advocates of individual liberty as against the whig party, to support Fremont—after which he left the stand.

We must say that we regard Mr. Lincoln as a fine speaker. He is certainly the ablest black republican that has taken the stump at this place during the canvass; yet he utterly failed to sustain by satisfactory arguments the black republican issue of intervention. We have given the leading points of his speech. In the evening a small crowd, the tail end of the meeting, was addressed by Mr. Knapp,[2] of Winchester. We did not attend.

[2] Nathan M. Knapp.

To J. B. McFarland[1]

J. B. M'Farland   Springfield,
LaFayette, Ia. [Indiana]   Sept. 7. 1856

Dear Sir   Your invitation to me to be with you on the 1–2–& 3rd. of Oct. at the Tippecanoe Battle Ground, is received. I fear I can not attend; but I will if I can. Yours &c   A. LINCOLN

[1] ALS, IHi. McFarland was evidently a Republican of LaFayette, Indiana, but he has not been further identified.

Form Letter to Fillmore Men[1]

Dear Sir,   Springfield, Sept. 8, 1856

I understand you are a Fillmore man. Let me prove to you that every vote withheld from Fremont, and given to Fillmore, *in this state*, actually lessens Fillmore's chance of being President.

Suppose Buchanan gets *all* the slave states, and Pennsylvania, and *any other* one state besides; *then he is elected*, no matter who gets all the rest.

But suppose Fillmore gets the two slave states of Maryland and Kentucky; *then* Buchanan *is not* elected; Fillmore goes into the House of Representatives, and may be made President by a compromise.

But suppose again Fillmore's friends throw away a few thousand votes on him, in *Indiana* and *Illinois*, it will inevitably give these states to Buchanan, which will more than compensate him for the loss of Maryland and Kentucky; will elect him, and leave Fillmore no chance in the H.R. or out of it.

This is as plain as the adding up of the weights of three small hogs. As Mr. Fillmore has no possible chance to carry Illinois *for himself*, it is plainly his interest to let Fremont take it, and thus keep it out of the hands of Buchanan. Be not deceived. *Buchanan* is the hard horse to beat in this race. Let him have Illinois, and nothing can beat him; *and he will get Illinois*, if men persist in throwing away votes upon Mr. Fillmore.

Does some one persuade, you that Mr. Fillmore can carry Illinois? Nonsense! There are over seventy newspapers in Illinois opposing Buchanan, only three or four of which support Mr. Fillmore, *all* the rest going for Fremont. Are not these newspapers a fair index of the proportion of the voters. If not, tell me why.

Again, of these three or four Fillmore newspapers, *two* at least, are supported, in part, by the Buchanan men, as I understand. Do not they know where the shoe pinches? They know the Fillmore movement helps *them*, and therefore they help *it*.

Do think these things over, and then act according to your judgment. Yours very truly,   A. LINCOLN

(Confidential)

---

[1] Copies of this letter were lithographed and mailed out by Lincoln with date line and salutation added to suit. Copies dated September 8 are extant as follows: to Ed. Lawrence (owned by D. F. Nichols, Lincoln, Illinois); to Harrison Maltby (DLC-HW); to Rev. E. Roberts (owned by Arch W. Roberts, North Hollywood, California); to Thomas Hull (owned by Lewis O. Williams, Clinton, Illinois); to Luther Hill (location unknown). One of the many others who received copies

was John Kirkpatrick of Logan County, who published the letter together with his reply of September 26 in the Logan County *Democrat*, whence it was widely copied in the opposition press. Numerous other copies bearing later dates indicate that Lincoln continued to send the letter throughout September and October.

Speech at Bloomington, Illinois[1]

September 12, 1856

Hon. A. LINCOLN addressed the audience in a speech of great eloquence and power. He showed up the position of the Fillmore party in fine style, both as to its prospects of success, and as to the propriety of supporting a candidate whose greatest recommendation, as urged by his supporters themselves, is that he is *neutral* upon the one only great political question of the times. He pointed out in regular succession, the several steps taken by the Administration in regard to slavery in the Territories, from the repeal of the Missouri Compromise down to the latest Border Ruffian invasion of Kansas, and the inevitable tendency of each and all of them to effect the spread of slavery over that country; showed the official endorsement of the Administration by the Democratic party in the Cincinnati Convention, and the openly avowed position of the Southern wing of the party on the subject of slavery-extension; contrasting all this with the assertion of our Northern Democratic speakers, that they are not in favor of the extension of slavery, with a clearness and force we have never heard excelled, and which must have made the *honest* Democrats, if any such there were present, feel as if they had received an eye-opener.

[1] Bloomington *Weekly Pantagraph*, September 17, 1856.

To Robert S. Boal[1]

Dr. R. Boal.   Springfield,
My dear Sir: Sept. 14. 1856

Yours of the 8th. inviting me to be with [you] at Lacon on the 30th. Inst. is received. I feel that I owe you, and our friends of Marshall, a good deal; and I will come if I can; and if I do not get there, it will be because I shall think my efforts are more needed further South.

Present my respects to Mrs. Boal, and believe [me], as ever Your friend   A. LINCOLN

[1] ALS, owned by H. T. Morgan, Peoria, Illinois.

To Friedrich K. F. Hecker[1]

Frederick Hecker, Esq.   Springfield,
My dear Sir,   Sept. 14, 1856

Your much valued letter of the 7th is received. Could you not be with us here on the 25th of this month, when we expect to have a large mass-meeting? We cannot dispense with your services in this contest; and we ought, in a pecuniary way, to give you some relief in the difficulty of having your house burnt.[2] I have started a proposition for this, among our friends, with a prospect of some degree of success. It is but fair and just; and I hope you will not decline to accept what we may be able to do.

Please write me whether you can be here on the 25th. Very truly yours,   A. LINCOLN.

[1] Hertz, II, 690. Friedrich Karl Franz Hecker was an exiled German revolutionist, citizen of St. Clair County, Illinois, and a leader among the German Republicans of the state.

[2] Hecker's home burned August 12, 1856, while he was addressing a Frémont meeting.

To Henry O'Conner[1]

Henry O'Conner,   Springfield,
Muscatine Iowa.   Sept. 14, 1856

Dear Sir   Yours, inviting me to attend a mass meeting on the 23rd. Inst. is received. It would be very pleasant to strike hands with the Fremonters of Iowa, who have led the van so splendidly, in this grand charge which we hope and believe will end in a most glorious victory. All thanks, all honor to Iowa!!

But Iowa is out of all danger, and it is no time for us, when the battle still rages, to pay holy-day visits to Iowa. I am sure you will excuse me for remaining in Illinois, where much hard work is still to be done. Yours very truly   A. LINCOLN

[1] ALS-F, ISLA.

Speech at Olney, Illinois[1]

September 20, 1856

ABE LINCOLN tried his best to get up steam, but with all his tact in that line, it was a dead failure. But about thirty listened. Said he, "I am an old one; if twelve of you will sit down and look at me, I will talk to you, if not, I will desist." The twelve sat down, he spoke a few minutes, and throwing up his hands in disgust and despair, said—"Oh, I can't interest this crowd," and left the stand.

[1] St. Louis, *Missouri Republican*, September 24, 1856. This brief comment occurs in a letter from an Olney correspondent (signed "Q.") describing a political meeting at which both Lincoln and Douglas, as well as other notables, spoke.

[376]

Speech at Vandalia, Illinois[1]

September 23, 1856

Hon. Ab. Lincoln, the veteran Whig orator of Illinois, having now arrived, was next called out. He began by saying that a few days previously, passing through Vandalia to an appointment of his own, he learned that a Democratic meeting was in progress in the square and came up. The speaker on the stand was one of his earliest political and personal friends, Mr. Davis, known in these parts as "Long Jim Davis."[2] Long Jim at the meeting referred to paid him (Mr. L.) particular attention, and Mr. L., a gentleman of the old school, now proceeded to pay his respects to his long friend. Mr. D. had abused him because he voted while in Congress in favor of the Wilmot Proviso. But *after* that wicked vote, this same gentleman, believing that he (Mr. L.) the only Whig from Illinois, had some influence with Gen. Taylor, requested his influence to procure for him (Davis) a certain *Land Office*, and he got it![3] [laughter.]

One of Mr. D.'s arguments to prove the Republican a disunion party was, that they made their flag with only thirteen stars on it! At the close of Mr. D.'s speech, Mr. L. took him to the corner of the State House and pointing to the Democratic flag (still flying there), requested him to count the stars. He did so, and in there were just thirteen! [Old liner in the crowd—"That's for the thirteen original States."] Lincoln—"Then you don't *care* anything about the *new States*. That leaves Illinois out of the Union!["]

Mr. Davis admitted in his speech (in order to hedge against it) that he made the first Anti-Nebraska speech *printed* in Illinois— and added, "if any of these little men (Republicans) want a speech on the subject I will send them one of mine." Mr. L. thought it must be a *very* little man who could learn anything from that speech. [Laughter.] Having thus disposed of his friend "Long Jim," in a manner so genial and mirthful that the victim himself, had he been present, could not have taken umbrage at it, Mr. L. addressed himself to the general topics of the day. He adverted to the attempt to stigmatize the Republican party as fanatical and disunion on account of the sentiments of particular supporters of that party, and showed, by quoting from the disunion speeches of Toombs, Slidell, Wise and Brooks,[4] that this argument was a two-edged sword.

A medical gentleman launched another democratic argument at the speaker by saying, as he shrugged his shoulders, "I must be a woolly head!" L.—"Very well, shave *off* the wool then." This repartee told with the more effect, as there was an unlucky twist in the doctor's hair and whiskers, and was evidently enjoyed by the audience more than by himself.

He demonstrated that the Republicans are walking in the "old paths"—read the recorded sentiments of Washington, Jefferson and others, and dwelt at length upon the position of Henry Clay, (now quoted against him,) the Nestor of the old Whig party. After quoting the declarations of these canonized leaders of both the great parties, he pointed to the doctor who had before interrupted him, and inquired, "What more than this has Fremont said, that you call him a woolly head? I ask you, sir?"

The Doctor seemed suddenly to have lost the organs of speech. L.—"You can make this charge, and yet, when called upon to justify it, your lips are *sealed*." One or two lawyers put their heads together with the Doctor's. Mr. L. (smiling)—"That's right, gentlemen, take counsel together, and give me your answer." Doctor (trying to look cheerful)—"He found the woolly horse and ate dogs." L.—*That* aint true—but if it was, how does it prove that Fremont is a *woolly head*—how?" The Doctor, wearing the expression of a man standing on a bed of live coals, did not get off any answer. Mr. L. (after a long pause)—You're *treed*, my friend." [Loud laughter.]

Both the speakers were frequently interrupted by certain Buchanan men, whose zeal was without knowledge, and we are confident that all who adventured upon this undertaking went away with a lively recollection of the adage about handling edged tools. Although much of the speaking was a hand-to-hand fight, owing to the discourtesy of certain opposers, yet the self-possession, wit, and unflagging good nature of the speakers, made the discussion *tell* on the sober, honest men who listened. . . .

1 Chicago *Democratic Press*, September 27, 1856. Brackets are in the source.
2 James M. Davis.
3 See Lincoln to Josiah B. Herrick, January 19, 1849, *supra*.
4 Senator Robert Toombs of Georgia, Senator John Slidell of Louisiana, Governor Henry A. Wise of Virginia, and Representative Preston S. Brooks of South Carolina.

To Julian M. Sturtevant[1]

Rev. J. M. Sturtevant   Springfield,
Jacksonville, Ills   Sept. 27. 1856

My dear Sir: Owing to absence yours of the 16th. was not received till the day-before yesterday. I thank you for your good opinion of me personally, and still more for the deep interest you take in the cause of our common country. It pains me a little that you have deemed it necessary to point out to me how I may be compensated for throwing myself in the breach now. This assumes that I am merely calculating the chances of personal advancement. Let me assure you that I decline to be a candidate for congress, on my clear conviction, that my running would *hurt*, & not *help* the cause. I am willing to make any personal sacrafice, but I am not willing to do, what in my own judgment, is, a sacrafice of the cause itself. Very truly Yours   A. LINCOLN

1 ALS-P, ISLA. Julian M. Sturtevant was president of Illinois College at Jacksonville and a pronounced anti-slavery man.

Speech at Peoria, Illinois[1]

October 9, 1856

. . . . On this occasion he went over the whole battle field of the two great contending armies, one *for* and the other *against* slavery and slave labor, and showed, most triumphantly, that our young, gallant and world-renowned commander was the man for the day —the man to right the ship of State, and, like the stripling of Israel, to slay the boasting Goliaths of slaveocracy that have beset the national capitol and defiled the sanctums of liberty, erected and consecrated by the old prophets and fathers of this republic.

1 Peoria *Weekly Republican*, October 17, 1856.

Speech at Belleville, Illinois[1]

October 18, 1856

. . . . He [Lincoln] showed that there are only two parties and only two questions now before the voters. A Kentuckian, as he is, familiar with Slavery and its evils, he vindicated the cause of free labor, "that national capital," in the language of Col. FREMONT, "which constitutes the real wealth of this great country, and creates that intelligent power in the masses alone to be relied on as the bulwark of free institutions." He showed the tendency and aim of the Sham Democracy to degrade labor to subvert the true ends of Government and build up Aristocracy, Despotism and Slavery. The platforms of BUCHANAN and FREMONT were contrasted, and the opposite tendency of each to the other was shown with the clearness of light. The rights of man were eloquently vindicated. The only object of government, the good of the governed, not the interests of Slaveholders—the securing of life, liberty and the pursuit of happiness; this true end of all Government was well enforced. The Kentuckian, LINCOLN, defended the Declaration of American Independence against the attacks of the degenerate Vermonter, DOUGLAS, and against BRECKENRIDGE and the whole ruling class of the South. Here was a Southerner, with eloquence that would bear a comparison with HENRY CLAY's, defending Liberty and the North against the leaders of the Border Ruffians and Doughfaces of Illinois. STEPHEN A. DOUGLAS, the traitor to Freedom, was exposed, and his arguments refuted by LINCOLN. This associate of HECKER[2] referred to the Germans and the noble position taken by them in just and dignified terms. When he called down the blessings of the Almighty on their heads, a thrill of sympathy and pleasure ran through his whole audience. They all rejoiced that clap-traps, false issues and humbugs are powerless with the great heart of Germany in America. LINCOLN and HECKER were inscribed on many banners. . . .

[1] Belleville *Weekly Advocate*, October 22, 1856.
[2] Friedrich K. F. Hecker. See letter to Hecker, September 14, *supra*.

To Abraham Jonas[1]

A. Jonas, Esq   Urbana,
My dear Sir: Oct. 21. 1856
   I am here at court, and find myself so "hobbled" with a particular case, that I can not leave, & consequently, can not be with you on the 23rd., I regret this exceedingly, but there is no help for it. Please make the best appology, for me, in your power. Your friend as ever   A. LINCOLN—

[1] ALS, ORB. An English Jew and prominent Mason, Jonas practiced law in partnership with Henry Asbury at Quincy, Illinois.

To James M. Ruggles[1]

J. M. Ruggles, Esq.   Springfield,
Dear Sir: Oct. 28. 1856
   I write this to appologise for not being with you to-day. I was forced off to Pike county, where I spoke yesterday, and I have just returned. *Be assured I could not help it.* Yours truly
                                                    A. LINCOLN—

[1] ALS, IHi. James M. Ruggles of Havana, Illinois, was state senator from Mason County.

To Robert M. Ewing[1]

R. M. Ewing, Esq.   Springfield,
Petersburg, Ills.   Novr. 12. 1856

Dear Sir   Yours of the 8th. inclosing the forged article "From the New-York Tribune" published in the Menard Index, was received yesterday. Although the getting up of the thing was intended to deceive, and was very malicious and wicked, I do not think much could be made by exposing it. When you shall have exposed it, they will then say they merely meant it as a "take off" and never intended it to be understood as genuine. If you had a local paper there to simply denounce it as a forgery, that would be well enough; but I doubt whether anything else can be done with it, to advantage.

I am truly glad you are determined to fight on. In the next struggle I hope we shall be able to pull together. Let us all try to make it so. Yours Respectfully   A. LINCOLN—

[1] ALS, IHi. At this time Robert M. Ewing was a schoolteacher living at Petersburg. In later years he edited the *Public Reaper* and the *DeWitt County Republican* at Farmer City and Clinton, Illinois.

Receipts to Joshua F. Amos[1]

Received, Novr. 13 1856, of J. F. Amos, one of the Admrs. of Nathaniel Hay, decd. four hundred and ninety dollars and fifty two cents, in full of principal & interest of the within note to date

MARIA L. BULLOCK
Pr. A. LINCOLN—

Received, Novr. 13. 1856 of J. F. Amos, one of the Admrs. of Nathaniel Hay decd. four hundred and seventy nine dollars, and seventynine cents, in full of principal & interest, to date, a deduction of $10.73 being made because paid before due.

MARIA L. BULLOCK
Pr. A. LINCOLN

[1] ADS, RPB. The receipts appear on the back of the notes given by Nathaniel and John Hay, June 25, 1855, *supra*.

To Richard Thorne[1]

R. Thorne, Esq   Springfield,
My dear Sir: Nov. 13. 1856

It is now fully settled that Bissell & our State ticket are elected by 6000 or 7000 majority. Buchanan gets the state by a majority not quite so large.

Some little expense bills are on me; and I have concluded to draw on you for $20. more, which is still ten dollars within the authority you kindly gave me. Your much obliged friend

A. LINCOLN

¹ ALS-P, ISLA. Former sheriff Richard Thorne was a merchant of Ottawa, Illinois, who apparently had subscribed to the Republican campaign expenses.

To Jonathan Haines¹

Jonathan Haines Esq.   Springfield
Dear Sir: Nov. 24– 1856.

Your letter asking instructions as to taking depositions of witnesses at a distance is received. You know I think our case is not yet ready for taking depositions, but as you wish to take them notwithstanding I give you such instructions as I can. There are two ways, First notify the opposite party or his lawyer, in writing that on such a day (more than ten days after you give the notice) you will send out from the Clerk's office a commission to take the deposition. The notice must contain a copy of the interrogations intended to put to each witness. Then notice will have to be drawn up by a lawyer and I cannot do it unless you were with me to give names places of residence and questions to be asked.

Second, go to some lawyer near where the witnesses live who is in the habit of practicing in the U.S. Courts and get him to superintend the taking of the deposition *de bene esse* as the lawyers call it. He will know how to do it. The lat[t]er is the mode I would advise in the present case.

I really do not know when the next term of court begins but as you pass Chicago you can learn in a moment. Yours Truly

A. LINCOLN.

¹ Hertz, II, 692-93. Jonathan Haines was a manufacturer of reapers at Pekin, Illinois. See Lincoln to Haines, November 25, 1857, *infra*. The case referred to was probably one involving patent priority. George H. Rugg *v*. Jonathan Haines, appealing from a decision of the commissioner of patents awarding priority to Haines in respect to an invention relating to harvesting machines, was decided in favor of Haines by the Circuit Court of the District of Columbia in October, 1855. George H. Rugg was a manufacturer of reapers at Ottawa, Illinois.

Fragment on Stephen A. Douglas¹

[December, 1856?]

Twenty-two years ago Judge Douglas and I first became acquainted. We were both young then; he a trifle younger than I. Even then, we were both ambitious; I, perhaps, quite as much so as he. With *me*, the race of ambition has been a failure—a flat failure; with *him* it has been one of splendid success. His name fills the nation; and is not unknown, even, in foreign lands. I affect no contempt for the high eminence he has reached. So reached, that the oppressed of my species, might have shared with me in the elevation, I would rather stand on that eminence, than wear the richest crown that ever pressed a monarch's brow.

1 AD-P, ISLA. This single page of manuscript is dated on the basis of the fact that, according to Lincoln's own statement written in the margin of Samuel C. Parks' copy of Howells' *Life of Abraham Lincoln* (1860), p. 41, Lincoln first saw Douglas "at Vandalia, Decr. 1834."

Speech at a Republican Banquet, Chicago, Illinois[1]

December 10, 1856

. . . . The President[2] then read the first regular toast: "1st THE UNION—The North will maintain it—the South will not depart therefrom"

Hon. Abram Lincoln of Springfield, amid most deafening cheers, arose to reply to this toast. He said he could most heartily indorse the sentiment expressed in the toast. During the whole canvass we had been assailed as the enemies of the Union, and he often had occasion to repudiate the sentiments attributed to us. He said that the Republican party was the friend of the Union. [Cheers.] It was the friend of the Union now; and if it had been entirely successful, it would have been the friend of the Union more than ever, [Loud and long continued cheers]. He maintained that the Liberty for which we contended could best be obtained by a firm, a steady adherence to the Union. As Webster said, "Not Union without liberty, nor liberty without Union; but Union and liberty, now and forever, one and inseparable." [Loud Cheers.] The speaker said we had selected and elected a Republican State ticket. We have done what we supposed to be our duty. It is now the duty of those elected to give us a good Republican Administration. In regard to the

1 Chicago *Democratic Press*, December 11, 1856; *Illinois State Journal*, December 16, 1856. The entire speech was summarized in the *Press*, but only the conclusion of the speech was printed in the *Journal* as furnished to the *Journal* in manuscript by Lincoln. Our text follows the *Press* for the first part and the *Journal* for the conclusion.

2 Jonathan Y. Scammon, prominent Chicago attorney and businessman, whose political activity led to his election as representative to the legislature in 1860.

Governor-elect, Col. Bissell,—[Loud and long-continued cheers and waving of handkerchiefs]—he referred to the opposite party saying that "he couldn't take the oath." Well, they said "he couldn't be elected," and as they were mistaken once, he thought they were not unlikely to be mistaken again. *"They* wouldn't take such an oath!" Oh, no! [Laughter.] "They would cut off their right arm first." He would like to know one of them who would not part with his right arm to have the privilege of taking the oath. Their conduct reminded him of the darky who, when a bear had put its head into the hole and shut out the daylight, cried out, "What was darkening de hole?" "Ah," cried the other darky, who was on to the tail of the animal, "if de tail breaks you'll find out." [Laughter and cheers.] Those darkies at Springfield see something darkening the hole, but wait till the tail breaks on the 1st of January, and they will see. [Cheers.] The speaker referred to the anecdote of the boy who was talking to another as to whether Gen. Jackson could ever get to Heaven. Said the boy "He'd get there if he had a mind to." [Cheers and laughter.] So was it with Col. Bissell,—he'd do whatever he had a mind to. [Cheers.]

We have another annual Presidential Message. Like a rejected lover, making merry at the wedding of his rival, the President felicitates hugely over the late Presidential election. He considers the result a signal triumph of good principles and good men, and a very pointed rebuke of bad ones. He says the people did it. He forgets that the "people," as he complacently calls only those who voted for Buchanan, are in a minority of the whole people, by about four hundred thousand voters—one full tenth of all the voters. Remembering this, he might perceive that the "Rebuke" may not be quite as durable as he seems to think—that the majority may not choose to remain permanently rebuked by that minority.

The President thinks the great body of us Fremonters, being ardently attached to liberty, in the abstract, were duped by a few wicked and designing men. There is a slight difference of opinion on this. We think *he*, being ardently attached to the hope of a second term, *in the concrete,* was duped by men who had liberty every way. He is in the cat's paw. By much dragging of chestnuts from the fire for others to eat, his claws are burnt off to the gristle, and he is thrown aside as unfit for further use. As the fool said to King Lear, when his daughters had turned him out of doors, "He's a shelled pea's cod."

So far as the President charges us "with a desire to change the domestic institutions of existing States;" and of "doing every thing in our power to deprive the Constitution and the laws of moral authority," for the whole party, on *belief*, and for myself, on *knowledge* I pronounce the charge an unmixed, and unmitigated falsehood.

Our government rests in public opinion. Whoever can change public opinion, can change the government, practically just so much. Public opinion, or [on?] any subject, always has a *"central idea,"* from which all its minor thoughts radiate. That "central idea" in our political public opinion, at the beginning was, and until recently has continued to be, "the equality of men." And although it was always submitted patiently to whatever of inequality there seemed to be as matter of actual necessity, its constant working has been a steady progress towards the practical equality of all men. The late Presidential election was a struggle, by one party, to discard that central idea, and to substitute for it the opposite idea that slavery is right, in the abstract, the workings of which, as a central idea, may be the perpetuity of human slavery, and its extension to all countries and colors. Less than a year ago, the Richmond *Enquirer*, an avowed advocate of slavery, regardless of color, in order to favor his views, invented the phrase, "State equality," and now the President, in his Message, adopts the *Enquirer's* catch-phrase, telling us the people "have asserted the constitutional equality of each and all of the States of the Union as States." The President flatters himself that the new central idea is completely inaugurated; and so, indeed, it is, so far as the mere fact of a Presidential election can inaugurate it. To us it is left to know that the majority of the people have not yet declared for it, and to hope that they never will.

All of us who did not vote for Mr. Buchanan, taken together, are a majority of four hundred thousand. But, in the late contest we were divided between Fremont and Fillmore. Can we not come together, for the future. Let every one who really believes, and is resolved, that free society is not, *and shall not be*, a failure, and who can conscientiously declare that in the past contest he has done only what he thought best—let every such one have charity to believe that every other one can say as much. Thus let bygones be bygones. Let past differences, as nothing be; and with steady eye on the real issue, let us reinaugurate the good old "central ideas" of the Republic. We *can* do it. The human heart *is* with us—God is with us. We shall again be able not to declare, that "all States as States, are equal," nor yet that "all citizens as citizens are equal," but to renew the broader, better declaration, including both these and much more, that "all *men* are created equal."

To Orville H. Browning[1]

Springfield, Dec. 15– 1856

Dear Browning: Your letter, requesting me to send you a document of John M. Walker,[2] is received. I received it saturday; and I took a long hunt for the paper yesterday; but could not find it. In fact I have no recollection of ever having had it.

When I tried the case[3] once with Mr. Williams at Chicago in July 1855, I wrote Mr. Walker a very full statement of the condition of the case, as I then understood it. If he still has the statement, it might be of some service.

It has been suggested by some of our friends that during the session of the Legislature here this winter, the Republicans, ought to get up a sort of party State address; and again it has been suggested that you could draw up such a thing as well if not better than any of us. Think about it. Yours as ever   A. LINCOLN.

[1] ALS, CSmH.   [2] Unidentified.
[3] Probably Forsyth *v.* Peoria, which Lincoln and Archibald Williams for the plaintiff lost to Browning, July 11-13, 1855.

Remarks to the Springfield Bar
on the Retirement of James H. Matheny[1]

December 20, 1856

This is the first intimation I have had that any such meeting as this was intended. It takes me considerably by surprise, particularly as it might be expected that I am to say something. Much could be said of the man named in the resolutions, and of his public services. Indeed, much could be said, which, if said of other men, would be sheer flattery, whilst in respect to him it falls far short of the whole truth. That I have long esteemed Mr. Matheny as a man and a friend, is known to you all. But that I should mete out to you the full measure of his worth, I shall not now attempt to do. Besides, much of this has already been beautifully and graphically done by my friend Mr. Herndon.[2] Mr. Chairman, allow me in conclusion to say that I fully concur in all that has been said and done on this occasion.

[1] *Illinois State Journal*, December 24, 1856.
[2] Elliott B. Herndon presented resolutions which were adopted commending Matheny's services as clerk of the Sangamon County Circuit Court.

To Robert S. Boal[1]

Dr. R. Boal   Springfield,
Dear Sir: Decr. 25. 1856

Yours of the 22nd. is just received.

I suppose the "Chenery House" is likely to be the Republican Head Quarters. I find the best that can be done there is to give you the room you had two years ago, or one like it, at $21 per week, with fire and light, for the two persons. I do not believe you can do better, at any of the Hotels. If you conclude to take it, Mr. Chenery wishes you to write him immediately.

When I was at Chicago two weeks ago I saw Mr. Arnold;[2] and from a remark of his, I inferred he was thinking of the Speakership, though I think he was not anxious about it. He seemed most anxious for harmony generally, and particularly that the contested seats from Peoria and McDonough might be rightly determined.

Since I came home I had a talk with Cullom,[3] one of our American representatives here; and he says he is for you for Speaker, and also that he thinks, all the Americans will be for you, unless it be Gorin[4] of Macon, of whom he can not speak.

If you would like to be Speaker go right up and see Arnold. He is talented, a practiced debater; and, I think, would do himself more credit on the floor, than in the Speaker's seat. Go and see him; and if you think fit, show him this letter. Your friend as ever

A. LINCOLN—

1 ALS, owned by H. T. Morgan, Peoria, Illinois.
2 Isaac N. Arnold, representative from Cook County.
3 Shelby M. Cullom.   4 Jerome R. Gorin.

Fragment on the Dred Scott Case[1]

[January, 1857?]

What would be the effect of this, if it should ever be the creed of a dominant party in the nation? Let us analyse, and consider it.

It affirms that, whatever the Supreme Court may decide as to the constitutional restriction on the power of a teritorial Legislature, in regard to slavery in the teritory, must be obeyed, and enforced by all the departments of the federal government.

Now, if this is sound, as to this particular constitutional question, it is equally sound of *all* constitutional questions; so that the proposition substantially, is "Whatever decision the Supreme court makes on *any* constitutional question, must be obeyed, and enforced by all the departments of the federal government."

Again, it is not the full scope of this creed, that if the Supreme court, having the particular question before them, shall decide that Dred Scott is a slave, the executive department must enforce the decision against Dred Scott. If this were it's full scope, it is presumed, no one would controvert it's correctness. But in this narrow scope, there is no room for the Legislative department to enforce the decision; while the creed affirms that *all* the departments must enforce it. The creed, then, has a broader scope; and what is it? It is this; that so soon as the Supreme court decides that Dred Scott is a slave, the whole community must decide that not only Dred Scott, but that *all* persons in like condition, are rightfully slaves

¹ AD, DLC-RTL. This two-page document has been given the date [1856?] in the Lincoln Papers, probably by Nicolay and Hay. The content indicates that composition antedated the Dred Scott decision, and also that Lincoln was exploring the position taken by Douglas and his followers at the time when the Supreme Court was known to be actively considering the case—December, 1856–March, 1857.

Endorsement of the *American Statesman*¹

Springfield Ills. Jany. 6. 1857

I have very briefly glanced over a new work, in the hands of Mr. T. U. Webb,² called the American Statesman; and I think it may be safely said that the volume is invaluable to those desirous of accurate and full references to the political history of our country.

A. LINCOLN

¹ ADS, IHi. Mounted on the end papers of the prospectus of the *American Statesman: A Political History* by Andrew W. Young (Derby & Miller, Publishers, New York) which contains a list of subscribers including "Lincoln & Herndon."   ² Timothy U. Webb, canvasser for the publishers.

Invitation¹

February 5, [1857]

Mr. & Mrs. Lincoln will be pleased to see you Thursday evening Feb. 5. at 8. o'clock

¹ AL-P, ISLA. Several of these invitations in Lincoln's handwriting are extant, photostats of two being in the files: one addressed to Adolph F. C. Mueller, representative in the legislature from Cook County, and another to Edward R. Thayer, Springfield businessman. Orville H. Browning's *Diary* records under date of "[1857]—Thursday Feby 5 . . . At night attended a large & pleasant party at Lincoln's."

To William A. Jennings and James R. Oatman[1]

February 11, 1857

The within notice was handed me to-day by Mr. Moore; and I did not notice at the time that your first names are not in it. You see what the object is; and you better attend at the time and place of taking the depositions.

I direct to Jennings and Oatman because I can not remember your christian names; and to *Eureka,* because I rather think that is your nearest office.

Keep this.   A. LINCOLN.

Springfield Feb. 11. 1857

[1] ALS-P, ISLA. Written on the back of a notice of taking depositions in Allen W. Phares *v.* Jennings & Oatman, DeWitt County Circuit Court, a case involving the defendants' failure to pay for several thousand bushels of shelled corn.

To James Steele and Charles Summers[1]

Messrs Steele & Summers   Springfield,
Gentlemen   Feb. 12th. 1857

Yours of the 10th. covering a claim of Mr. D. A. Morrison against the Illinois Central Railroad Company is received. I have been in the regular retainer of the Co. for two or three years; but I expect they do not wish to retain me any longer.[2] The road not passing this point, there is no one here for me to present the claim to.

I have concluded to say to you, that I am going to Chicago, if nothing prevents, on the 21st. Inst. and I will then ascertain whether they discharge me; & if they do, as I expect, I will attend to your business & write you. If this is satisfactory, let it so stand —if not write me at once. Yours truly   A. LINCOLN

[1] ALS, IHi. James Steele and Charles Summers were law partners at Paris, Illinois.

[2] Lincoln was bringing suit against the Illinois Central for his $5,000 fee for defending the railroad in the McLean County tax case. His services were not, however, discontinued, and when the case of Morrison *v.* the Illinois Central, involving the right of the railroad to restrict its liability as a common carrier, reached the Supreme Court, Lincoln and Orlando B. Ficklin won the case for the Illinois Central.

To John E. Rosette[1]

(Private.)

John E. Rosette, Esq.   Springfield, Ill., February 20, 1857.

Dear Sir:—Your note about the little paragraph in the Republican was received yesterday, since which time I have been too unwell to

[389]

notice it. I had not supposed you wrote or approved it. The whole originated in mistake. You know by the conversation with me that I thought the establishment of the paper unfortunate, but I always expected to throw no obstacle in its way, and to patronize it to the extent of taking and paying for one copy. When the paper was brought to my house, my wife said to me, "Now are you going to take another worthless little paper?" I said to her *evasively*, "I have not directed the paper to be left." From this, in my absence, she sent the message to the carrier. This is the whole story. Yours truly,   A. LINCOLN.

[1] Herndon, III, 429. Herndon did not profess to know about the incident which gave rise to the letter. Rosette was an attorney at Springfield who edited the *Republican* beginning with its first issue, February 9, 1857, until some time in April of the same year. Since files are not available, one can only guess that the "little paragraph" made caustic comment on Mrs. Lincoln's "message to the carrier."

Notes for Speech at Chicago, Illinois[1]

February 28, 1857

With the future of this party, the approaching city election will have something to do—not, indeed, to the extent of making or breaking it, but still to help or to hurt it.

Last year the city election here was lost by our friends; and none can safely say, but that fact lost us the electoral ticket at the State election.

Although Chicago recovered herself in the fall, there was no general confidence that she could do so; and the Spring election encouraged our enemies, and haunted and depressed our friends to the last.

Let it not be so again.

Let minor differences, and personal preferences, if there be such; go to the winds.

Let it be seen by the result, that the cause of free-men and free-labor is stronger in Chicago that day, than ever before.

Let the news go forth to our thirteen hundred thousand brethren, to gladden, and to multiply them; and to insure and accelerate that consumation, upon which the happy destiny of all men, everywhere, depends.

We[2] were without party history, party pride, or party idols.

We were a collection of individuals, but recently in political hostility, one to another; and thus subject to all that distrust, and suspicion, and jealousy could do.

Every where in the ranks of the common enemy, were old party and personal friends, jibing, and jeering, and framing deceitful arguments against us.

We were scarcely met at all on the real issue.

Thousands avowed our principles, but turned from us, professing to believe we *meant* more than we *said*.

No argument, which was true in fact, made any head-way against us. This we know.

We were constantly charged with seeking an amalgamation of the white and black races; and thousands turned from us, not believing the charge (no one believed it) but *fearing* to face it themselves.

1 AD, first page owned by Miss Elsie Logan, Springfield, Illinois. AD, second page, owned by William H. Diller, Springfield, Illinois. Two pages of notes in Lincoln's handwriting are identified by their contents as being those used on the occasion of the ratification meeting for Republican nominations for municipal officers of Chicago, held in Metropolitan Hall on Saturday evening, February 28, 1857.

2 Beginning of the second page as numbered by Lincoln. The continuity is tenuous, however, and the assumption that the unnumbered page printed preceding this one is the first page of one set of notes may not be justified. The contents of page two, however, reflect a similar retrospective view of the formation of the Republican party for its first major campaign in 1856, and each page is written on the same kind of paper. For these reasons the fragments have been linked as they are printed here for the first time.

Fragment on Formation of the Republican Party[1]

[c. February 28, 1857]

Upon those men who are, in sentiment, opposed to the spread, and nationalization of slavery, rests the task of preventing it. The Republican organization is the embodyment of that sentiment; though, as yet, it by no means embraces all the individuals holding that sentiment. The party is newly formed; and in forming, old party ties had to be broken, and the attractions of party pride, and influential leaders were wholly wanting. In spite of old differences, prejudices, and animosities, it's members were drawn together by a paramount common danger. They formed and manouvered in the face of the deciplined enemy, and in the teeth of all his persistent misrepresentations. Of course, they fell far short of gathering in all of their own. And yet, a year ago, they stood up, an army over thirteen hundred thousand strong. That army is, to-day, the best hope of the nation, and of the world. Their work is before them; and from which they may not guiltlessly turn away.

1 AD, The Rosenbach Company, Philadelphia and New York. This single page is associated with the preceding notes for the Chicago speech solely on grounds of similar reference and content. Although it seems obvious in its references to the election of 1856, the specific occasion of composition has not been determined.

Declaration:

Abraham Lincoln *vs*. Illinois Central Railroad[1]

State of Illinois ⎱ SS.
McLean County ⎰

In the Circuit Court of
McLean County.
April Term. A.D. 1857.

Abraham Lincoln, plaintiff, complains of the Illinois Central Railroad Company, defendants, being in custody &c. of a plea of trespass on the case, on promises:

For that whereas heretofore, towit, on the first day of January in the year of our Lord one thousand eight hundred and fiftyseven, at the county aforesaid, in consideration that the said plaintiff, at the special interest and request of the said defendants, had before that time, done, performed, bestowed, and given his work and labor, care, diligence, attendance and skill, as an attorney and solicitor of and for the said defendants, and upon their retainer, in and about the prosecuting, defending, and soliciting of divers causes, suits, and business for the said defendants, they, the said defendants, undertook, and then and there faithfully promised the said plaintiff to pay him so much money as he therefor reasonably deserved to have of the said defendants, when they, the said defendants should be thereunto afterwards requested. And the said plaintiff avers, that he therefore reasonably deserved to have, of the said defendants, the sum of five thousand dollars, towit, at the county aforesaid, whereof the said defendants, afterwards, towit, on the day and year aforesaid, had notice.

Yet the said defendants (although often requested so to do) have not as yet paid the said sum of money, or any part thereof; but so to do have hitherto wholly neglected and refused, and still do neglect and refuse. To the damage of the said plaintiff of Six thousand dollars; and therefore he brings his suit &c.

LINCOLN, *per se*.

(Copy of account sued on)
The Illinois Central Railroad Company
                    To A. Lincoln   Dr.
To professional services in the case of the Illinois Central Railroad Company, against the County of McLean, twice argued in the Supreme Court of the State of Illinois, and finally decided at the December Term 1855. $5000.00

[1] AD, owned by Mrs. Edna Orendorff Macpherson, Springfield, Illinois. An exception to inclusion of Lincoln's law cases is made in the instance of this declaration and the brief of Lincoln's argument (June 23, *infra*) because of their biographical interest.

To Jesse K. Dubois[1]

Hon: J. K. Dubois.   Springfield,
Auditor &c.   April 6 1857.

Dear Sir: In answer to your querries in relation to the 4th. 8th. and 9th. sections of the bank law of Feb. 14, 1857– and the other provisions of law therein refered to, I give as my opinion

First: That *no stocks whatever* can be received by you at any greater rate of valuation than ten per cent less than the market price of said stocks, such market price to be ascertained, according to the old law.

Second: That no *non-interest* paying bonds can, in any event, be received by you at any greater rate than fifty cents to the dollar and not even for that much, unless their market price shall be as high as sixty, the old law not being altered by the new, in this respect.

Third— That in relation to the banks already in existence no new duty is imposed on you by the 8th. section of the new law, *unless such banks apply for the issuing of new circulating notes,* in which case, it is your duty to be satisfied that they have the fifty thousand dollars actual cash capital, before you issue such new notes. Note. As to the old law, I would abide the constructions of the old Auditor, till further advised.

Fourth: That in relation, both to old and new banks, in the very language of the 9th. section section [*sic*] of the new law "No more circulating notes shall be issued, under any circumstances to any bank or association organized under said act until the Auditor shall be satisfied that such bank or association has such actual capital as is required in the first" (8th. really meant) "section of this act."

This opinion is given as to your duty under the new law *after* it takes effect, and is not intended to apply to the time of between passage, and its taking effect. Yours truly   A. LINCOLN

[1] ALS, ORB.

To Thomas Meharry[1]

Thomas Meharry, Esq   Urbana Ills.
Dear Sir.   April 21. 1857

Owing to absence from home your letter of the 6th. was received only two days ago. The land in question, as I suppose, is the two dollar and a half land, and my opinion is that there can be no lawful preemptions on those lands, based on a settlement made *after,* the allotment of those lands, in 1852 or 3 I think. If I am right in this opinion, your entry is valid, and you can recover the land. I suppose yours, and your brother's adversary, are in possession; and if so, I would advise suits in Ejectment to be brought in the U. S. court, at Springfield. I can not tell in advance what fee I would charge, because I can not know the amount of trouble I may have. If the pre-emptioners have had patents issued to them, the cases, as I think, can still be managed, but they will be a good deal more troublesome.

If you conclude to have suits brought, & to engage me to bring them, call and see me at Springfield, from the 5th. to 10th. of May, at which time you will probably find me at home. I mention this, because I am absent a good deal. Yours, truly   A. LINCOLN—

¹ ALS, owned by Vinton Meharry, Lebanon, Indiana. A draft of his letter to Lincoln, April 6, 1857, preserved along with Lincoln's reply, indicates that Thomas Meharry, a resident of Pleasant Hill, Indiana, had "boug[h]t or entered a qu[a]rter Section of land at the sale of public lands at Danville Illanois on November the 24th. 1855 . . . in Champaign County Illanoise." On August 17, 1855, two pre-emptions had been made on the same piece of land and "one of them has proven up and entered the land again. . . ." Meharry wished to know whether Lincoln would take his case, and possibly a similar case for his brother James Meharry, and for what fee.

Petition to William H. Bissell¹

[May 8, 1857]

To His Excellency, the Governor of the State of Illinois

We, the undersigned citizens of Logan county, respectfully represent, that at the March term 1856 of the Sangamon circuit court, John Hibbs was found guilty of manslaughter, and sentenced to the Penitentiary for the term of two years; that the deceased came to his death in Logan county, and the case was taken to Sangamon by change of venue; that it was never certain that he came to his death by the hand of Hibbs; and yet it is certain that if he did, it was without any premeditation or malice whatever. He has now served in the Penitentiary one year; his family are in great need of the support he should give them; and we would be much gratified, if he should be pardoned for the remainder of his term.

¹ AD, I-Ar. The petition written by Lincoln is signed by forty citizens of Logan County, Illinois. See Lincoln's endorsement *infra*.

Endorsement: David Davis to William H. Bissell¹

[c. May 8, 1857]

We defended John Hibbs, mentioned in Judge Davis' letter above; and we concur with the Judge, that a pardon now, after his having served about fourteen months of his two years, would not be improper.   A. LINCOLN

                                                                    JOHN T. STUART

¹ AES, I-Ar. Judge Davis' letter to Governor Bissell, May 8, 1857, states "There was no motive for the killing *proved*, and none that was even reasonable suggested. . . ."

To Charles D. Gilfillan¹

C. D. Gilfillan, Chairman &c.   Springfield,
Dear Sir: May 9. 1857.
    Your letter of the 1st. Inst. inviting me to visit your Teritory, and to give such assistance as I might be able, to the Republican cause, during your approaching political struggles, is received. I have no great faith in the success of my efforts; still it is with some regret I have to say I can not visit you before the June election; and I can not, as yet, say I will be able to do so in the summer or fall. Having devoted the most of last year to politics, it is a *necessity* with me to devote this, to my private affairs.
    I have learned that our Republican Senator, Judge Trumbull, will be with you. You will find him a *true* and an *able* man.
    May the God of the right, give you the victory *now*, as He surely will in the end. Your Obt. Servt.   A. LINCOLN—

¹ ALS, owned by Mrs. Edward C. Dugan, St. Paul, Minnesota. Charles D. Gilfillan was a prominent Republican of St. Paul, Minnesota.

Receipt to Joshua F. Amos¹

Received, May 16. 1857, of Joshua F. Amos, administrator of the estate of Nathaniel Hay deceased, two hundred and twentyfive dollars, in full of all my demands against said estate.
                                                        A. LINCOLN—

¹ ADS, owned by Mrs. Logan Hay, Springfield, Illinois.

To Joseph W. Brackett¹

Joseph W. Brackett, Esq   Springfield, May 18, 1857
    Dear Sir   Your three letters, two dated April 28th. and the other May 1st. were received by me on the 9th. of May, when I returned home after an absence of two weeks. I went immediately to the Land-Office to file the Declarations of Jacob Warner and Cyrus Conkling, and failed to get the thing consummated, in consequence of there being nothing in the Office showing the quantity of land

in the tracts, sought to be pre-empted. I think the Register's intentions were correct, but he was perplexed as to what he ought to do, because of the peculiarity of the case, and consequently he put me off from time to time till now. Herewith I send you the certificates, bearing date May 9th. being the day I first presented the declarations.

I shall be ready to assist further in the cases, when occasion arises. One of your letters had one dollar in it, and another, ten. I paid two to the Register, and pocketed the other nine. Yours &c.

A. Lincoln.

[1] ALS-P, ISLA. Joseph W. Brackett, attorney of the pre-emptors to the island of Rock Island, Illinois, had retained Lincoln as counsel. Brackett resided at Rock Island, as did Warner and Conkling.

To Jonathan K. Cooper and Hugh W. Reynolds[1]

Messrs Cooper & Reynolds   Springfield,
Gentlemen   May 28. 1857
Your letter of the 25th. to G. W. Lowry,[2] has been handed me to answer. I brought the suit of Eshrick, Black & Co. vs Tobias [,] Hittle & Co.[3] the clerk tells me the process has been served in time, and I suppose a judgment will be had at the ensuing June Term, unless the defendants appear and make a case for a continuance, of the probability of which last, I know nothing. Yours truly

A. Lincoln—

[1] ALS, InFtwL. Jonathan K. Cooper and Hugh W. Reynolds were law partners at Peoria, Illinois.   [2] George W. Lowry, clerk of the U.S. Circuit Court.
[3] Filed May 16, judgment obtained June 3, in the U.S. Circuit Court. Joseph Eshrick, John S. Black, and Robert T. Black were merchants at Philadelphia, Pennsylvania; James Tobias, William Hittle, and Jonathan Myers were the Illinois defendants.

To Paul Cornell, Charles B. Waite, and John A. Jameson[1]

Messrs. Cornell, Waite & Jameson   Springfield
Chicago, Ills.   June 2. 1857.
Gentlemen: Yours of the 29th. was duly received. This morning I went to the Register with four hundred dollars in gold in my hand and tendered to the Register of the Land Office a written application to enter the land, as you requested, all which the Register declined. I have made a written memorandum of the facts, deposited the gold with J. Bunn[2] (who furnished it to me on the draft

you sent) and took his Certificate of deposite, which certificate and memorandum I hold subject to your order.

Now, if you please, send me ten dollars, as a fee. Yours Truly

A. LINCOLN

[1] Copy, DLC-HW. Cornell, Waite & Jameson was a leading law firm in Chicago.   [2] Jacob Bunn.

To Charles A. Purdy[1]

Charles A. Purdy, Esq   Springfield,
Dear Sir: June 9. 1857.

Yours of the 5th. was duly received. The Register of the Land-Office here tells me that no patents come to this office on entries made at the other offices, before they were all concentred here. He says the way for you to get your Patents, is to send these Receipts or Certificates to the General Land Office, with your address, and the Patents will be forwarded directly to your address. Accordingly, I inclose the Receipts to you.

I also inclose the other documents, with the Certificate of our Secretary of State attached, as you desired.

I am glad the Sniffin & Harris suit is likely to be settled. Yours truly   A. LINCOLN—

[1] ALS, owned by R. E. Burdick, New York City. Efforts to identify Charles A. Purdy have been unsuccessful.

Brief of Argument
in Abraham Lincoln *vs.* Illinois Central Railroad[1]

[June 23, 1857]

Proof

Retainer.

Brayman & Joy's[2] letters, with proof of their signatures, and that they were the active agents of the Company.

That I did the service, arguing the case twice.

Logan & Stuart.[3]

What was the question. How decided—& on what point.

The record—the final order—& the opinion. That *I*, and not Joy, made the point & argument on which the case turned.

Logan & Stuart.

The Company own near two million acres; & their road runs through twentysix counties.

That half a million, put at interest, would scarcely pay the tax.

Are, or not the *amount* of *labor*, the *doubtfulness* and *difficulty* of the *question*, the *degree* of *success* in the *result;* and the *amount* of pecuniary interest *involved*, not merely in the particular case, but covered by the principle decided, and thereby *secured* to the client, all proper elements, by the custom of the profession to consider in determining what is a reasonable fee in a given case.

That $5000 is not an unreasonable fee in this case.

[1] AD, owned by Mrs. Edna Orendorff Macpherson, Springfield, Illinois. See Declaration, April, 1857, *supra*. The case was called June 18. No one appearing for the railroad, the jury assessed damages a^ $5,000. On June 23, on motion of the defendant's attorney, John M. Douglas, the verdict was set aside, and another jury called. This jury found for Lincoln in the amount of $4,800, Lincoln having forgot a $200 retainer paid to him by the railroad.

[2] Mason Brayman and James F. Joy.

[3] Stephen T. Logan and John T. Stuart.

Speech at Springfield, Illinois[1]

June 26, 1857

FELLOW CITIZENS:—I am here to-night, partly by the invitation of some of you, and partly by my own inclination. Two weeks ago Judge Douglas spoke here on the several subjects of Kansas, the Dred Scott decision, and Utah. I listened to the speech at the time, and have read the report of it since. It was intended to controvert opinions which I think just, and to assail (politically, not personally,) those men who, in common with me, entertain those opinions. For this reason I wished then, and still wish, to make some answer to it, which I now take the opportunity of doing.

I begin with Utah.[2] If it prove to be true, as is probable, that the people of Utah are in open rebellion to the United States, then Judge Douglas is in favor of repealing their territorial organization, and attaching them to the adjoining States for judicial purposes. I say, too, if they are in rebellion, they ought to be somehow

[1] *Illinois State Journal*, June 29, 1857. Copies of this speech were advertised by the *Journal* for sale. It was copied and commented on widely throughout the state, at least two papers copying it in full (Decatur, *Illinois State Chronicle*, July 2; Clinton *Central Transcript*, July 9).

[2] The Mormon State of Deseret, established with the capital at Salt Lake City, and with a constitution adopted March 4, 1849, had been refused admission to the Union in 1850 prior to the passage of the act creating the Territory of Utah. The Mormons never accepted the territorial government as more than temporary, and maintained the form of the Deseret organization until admission was granted in 1883. Conflict between the two authorities was frequent and sometimes violent, as in the present instance when Brigham Young as Deseret governor led the Mormons in refusal to obey federal laws. Federal troops were sent into the territory to maintain federal authority, but Mormon resistance delayed the march into Salt Lake City until June 26, 1858.

coerced to obedience; and I am not now prepared to admit or deny that the Judge's mode of coercing them is not as good as any. The Republicans can fall in with it without taking back anything they have ever said. To be sure, it would be a considerable backing down by Judge Douglas from his much vaunted doctrine of self-government for the territories; but this is only additional proof of what was very plain from the beginning, that that doctrine was a mere deceitful pretense for the benefit of slavery. Those who could not see that much in the Nebraska act itself, which forced Governors, and Secretaries, and Judges on the people of the territories, without their choice or consent, could not be made to see, though one should rise from the dead to testify.

But in all this, it is very plain the Judge evades the only question the Republicans have ever pressed upon the Democracy in regard to Utah. That question the Judge well knows to be this: "If the people of Utah shall peacefully form a State Constitution tolerating polygamy, will the Democracy admit them into the Union?" There is nothing in the United States Constitution or law against polygamy; and why is it not a part of the Judge's "sacred right of self-government" for that people to have it, or rather to *keep* it, if they choose? These questions, so far as I know, the Judge never answers. It might involve the Democracy to answer them either way, and they go unanswered.

As to Kansas. The substance of the Judge's speech on Kansas is an effort to put the free State men in the wrong for not voting at the election of delegates to the Constitutional Convention. He says: *"There is every reason to hope and believe that the law will be fairly interpreted and impartially executed, so as to insure to every bona fide inhabitant the free and quiet exercise of the elective franchise."*

It appears extraordinary that Judge Douglas should make such a statement. He knows that, by the law, no one can vote who has not been registered; and he knows that the free State men place their refusal to vote on the ground that but few of them have been registered. It is *possible* this is not true, but Judge Douglas knows it is asserted to be true in letters, newspapers and public speeches, and borne by every mail, and blown by every breeze to the eyes and ears of the world. He knows it is boldly declared that the people of many whole counties, and many whole neighborhoods in others, are left unregistered; yet, he does not venture to contradict the declaration, nor to point out how they *can* vote without being registered; but he just slips along, not seeming to know there is any such question of fact, and complacently declares: "There is every reason to hope and believe that the law will be fairly and impartially executed, so as to insure to every *bona fide* inhabitant the free and quiet exercise of the elective franchise."

I readily agree that if all had a chance to vote, they ought to have voted. If, on the contrary, as they allege, and Judge Douglas ventures not to particularly contradict, few only of the free State men had a chance to vote, they were perfectly right in staying from the polls in a body.

By the way since the Judge spoke, the Kansas election has come off. The Judge expressed his confidence that all the Democrats in Kansas would do their duty—including "free state Democrats" of course. The returns received here as yet are very incomplete; but so far as they go, they indicate that only about one sixth of the registered voters, have really voted; and this too, when not more, perhaps, than one half of the rightful voters have been registered, thus showing the thing to have been altogether the most exquisite farce ever enacted. I am watching with considerable interest, to ascertain what figure "the free state Democrats" cut in the concern. Of course they voted—all democrats do their duty—and of course they did not vote for slave-state candidates. We soon shall know how many delegates *they* elected, how many candidates they had, pledged for a free state; and how many votes were cast for them.

Allow me to barely whisper my suspicion that there were no such things in Kansas "as free state Democrats"—that they were altogether mythical, good only to figure in newspapers and speeches in the free states. If there should prove to be one real living free state Democrat in Kansas, I suggest that it might be well to catch him, and stuff and preserve his skin, as an interesting specimen of that soon to be extinct variety of the genus, Democrat.

And now as to the Dred Scott decision. That decision declares two propositions—first, that a negro cannot sue in the U.S. Courts; and secondly, that Congress cannot prohibit slavery in the Territories. It was made by a divided court—dividing differently on the different points. Judge Douglas does not discuss the merits of the decision; and, in that respect, I shall follow his example, believing I could no more improve on McLean and Curtis, than he could on Taney.

He denounces all who question the correctness of that decision, as offering violent resistance to it. But who resists it? Who has, in spite of the decision, declared Dred Scott free, and resisted the authority of his master over him?

Judicial decisions have two uses—first, to absolutely determine the case decided, and secondly, to indicate to the public how other similar cases will be decided when they arise. For the latter use, they are called "precedents" and "authorities."

We believe, as much as Judge Douglas, (perhaps more) in obedience to, and respect for the judicial department of government. We think its decisions on Constitutional questions, when fully settled, should control, not only the particular cases decided, but the general policy of the country, subject to be disturbed only by amendments of the Constitution as provided in that instrument itself. More than this would be revolution. But we think the Dred Scott decision is erroneous. We know the court that made it, has often over-ruled its own decisions, and we shall do what we can to have it to over-rule this. We offer no *resistance* to it.

Judicial decisions are of greater or less authority as precedents, according to circumstances. That this should be so, accords both with common sense, and the customary understanding of the legal profession.

If this important decision had been made by the unanimous concurrence of the judges, and without any apparent partisan bias, and in accordance with legal public expectation, and with the steady practice of the departments throughout our history, and had been in no part, based on assumed historical facts which are not really true; or, if wanting in some of these, it had been before the court more than once, and had there been affirmed and re-affirmed through a course of years, it then might be, perhaps would be, factious, nay, even revolutionary, to not acquiesce in it as a precedent.

But when, as it is true we find it wanting in all these claims to the public confidence, it is not resistance, it is not factious, it is not even disrespectful, to treat it as not having yet quite established a settled doctrine for the country—But Judge Douglas considers this view awful. Hear him:

"The courts are the tribunals prescribed by the Constitution and created by the authority of the people to determine, expound and enforce the law. Hence, whoever resists the final decision of the highest judicial tribunal, aims a deadly blow to our whole Republican system of government—a blow, which if successful would place all our rights and liberties at the mercy of passion, anarchy and violence. I repeat, therefore, that if resistance to the decisions of the Supreme Court of the United States, in a matter like the points decided in the Dred Scott case, clearly within their jurisdiction as defined by the Constitution, shall be forced upon the country as a political issue, it will become a distinct and naked issue between the friends and the enemies of the Constitution—the friends and the enemies of the supremacy of the laws."

Why this same Supreme court once decided a national bank to be constitutional; but Gen. Jackson, as President of the United States, disregarded the decision, and vetoed a bill for a re-charter, partly on constitutional ground, declaring that each public functionary must support the Constitution, *"as he understands it."* But hear the General's own words. Here they are, taken from his veto message:

"It is maintained by the advocates of the bank, that its constitutionality, in all its features, ought to be considered as settled by precedent, and by the decision of the Supreme Court. To this conclusion I cannot assent. Mere precedent is a dangerous source of authority, and should not be regarded as deciding questions of constitutional power, except where the acquiescence of the people and the States can be considered as well settled. So far from this being the case on this subject, an argument against the bank might be based on precedent. One Congress in 1791, decided in favor of a bank; another in 1811, decided against it. One Congress in 1815 decided against a bank; another in 1816 decided in its favor. Prior to the present Congress, therefore the precedents drawn from that source were equal. If we resort to the States, the expressions of legislative, judicial and executive opinions against the bank have been probably to those in its favor as four to one. There is nothing in precedent, therefore, which if its authority were admitted, ought to weigh in favor of the act before me."

I drop the quotations merely to remark that all there ever was, in the way of precedent up to the Dred Scott decision, on the points therein decided, had been against that decision. But hear Gen. Jackson further—

"If the opinion of the Supreme court covered the whole ground of this act, it ought not to control the co-ordinate authorities of this Government. The Congress, the executive and the court, must each for itself be guided by its own opinion of the Constitution. Each public officer, who takes an oath to support the Constitution, swears that he will support it as he understands it, and not as it is understood by others."

Again and again have I heard Judge Douglas denounce that bank decision, and applaud Gen. Jackson for disregarding it. It would be interesting for him to look over his recent speech, and see how exactly his fierce philippics against us for resisting Supreme Court decisions, fall upon his own head. It will call to his mind a long and fierce political war in this country, upon an issue which, in his own language, and, of course, in his own changeless estimation, was "a distinct and naked issue between the friends and the enemies of the Constitution," and in which war he fought in the ranks of the enemies of the Constitution.

I have said, in substance, that the Dred Scott decision was, in part; based on assumed historical facts which were not really true; and I ought not to leave the subject without giving some reasons for saying this; I therefore give an instance or two, which I think fully sustain me. Chief Justice Taney, in delivering the opinion of the majority of the Court, insists at great length that negroes were no part of the people who made, or for whom was made, the Declaration of Independence, or the Constitution of the United States.

On the contrary, Judge Curtis, in his dissenting opinion, shows that in five of the then thirteen states, to wit, New Hampshire, Massachusetts, New York, New Jersey and North Carolina, free negroes were voters, and, in proportion to their numbers, had the same part in making the Constitution that the white people had. He shows this with so much particularity as to leave no doubt of its truth; and, as a sort of conclusion on that point, holds the following language:

"The Constitution was ordained and established by the people of the United States, through the action, in each State, of those persons who were qualified by its laws to act thereon in behalf of themselves and all other citizens of the State. In some of the States, as we have seen, colored persons were among those qualified by law to act on the subject. These colored persons were not only included in the body of 'the people of the United States,' by whom the Constitution was ordained and established; but in at least five of the States they had the power to act, and, doubtless, did act, by their suffrages, upon the question of its adoption."

Again, Chief Justice Taney says: "It is difficult, at this day to realize the state of public opinion in relation to that unfortunate race, which prevailed in the civilized and enlightened portions of the world at the time of the Declaration of Independence, and when the Constitution of the United States was framed and adopted." And again, after quoting from the Declaration, he says: "The general words above quoted would seem to include the whole human family, and if they were used in a similar instrument at this day, would be so understood."

In these the Chief Justice does not directly assert, but plainly assumes, as a fact, that the public estimate of the black man is more favorable *now* than it was in the days of the Revolution. This assumption is a mistake. In some trifling particulars, the condition of that race has been ameliorated; but, as a whole, in this country, the change between then and now is decidedly the other way; and their ultimate destiny has never appeared so hopeless as in the last three or four years. In two of the five States—New Jersey and North Carolina—that then gave the free negro the right of voting, the right has since been taken away; and in a third—New York— it has been greatly abridged; while it has not been extended, so far as I know, to a single additional State, though the number of the States has more than doubled. In those days, as I understand, masters could, at their own pleasure, emancipate their slaves; but since then, such legal restraints have been made upon emancipation, as to amount almost to prohibition. In those days, Legislatures held the unquestioned power to abolish slavery in their respective States; but now it is becoming quite fashionable for State Constitutions to withhold that power from the Legislatures. In those days, by common consent, the spread of the black man's bondage to new countries was prohibited; but now, Congress decides that it *will* not continue the prohibition, and the Supreme Court decides that it *could* not if it would. In those days, our Declaration of Independence was held sacred by all, and thought to include all; but now, to aid in making the bondage of the negro universal and eternal, it is assailed, and sneered at, and construed, and hawked at, and torn, till, if its framers could rise from their graves, they could not at all recognize it. All the powers of earth seem rapidly combining against him. Mammon is after him; ambition follows, and philosophy follows, and the Theology of the day is fast joining the cry. They have him in his prison house; they have searched his person, and left no prying instrument with him. One after another they have closed the heavy iron doors upon him, and now they have him, as it were, bolted in with a lock of a hundred keys, which can never be unlocked without the concurrence of every key; the keys in the hands of a hundred different men, and they scattered to a hundred different and distant places; and they stand musing as to what invention, in all the dominions of mind and matter, can be produced to make the impossibility of his escape more complete than it is.

It is grossly incorrect to say or assume, that the public estimate of the negro is more favorable now than it was at the origin of the government.

Three years and a half ago, Judge Douglas brought forward his famous Nebraska bill. The country was at once in a blaze. He scorned all opposition, and carried it through Congress. Since then he has seen himself superseded in a Presidential nomination, by one indorsing the general doctrine of his measure, but at the same time standing clear of the odium of its untimely agitation, and its gross breach of national faith; and he has seen that successful rival Constitutionally elected, not by the strength of friends, but by the division of adversaries, being in a popular minority of nearly four hundred thousand votes. He has seen his chief aids in his own State, Shields and Richardson, politically speaking, successively tried, convicted, and executed, for an offense not their own, but his. And now he sees his own case, standing next on the docket for trial.

There is a natural disgust in the minds of nearly all white people, to the idea of an indiscriminate amalgamation of the white and black races; and Judge Douglas evidently is basing his chief hope, upon the chances of being able to appropriate the benefit of this disgust to himself. If he can, by much drumming and repeating, fasten the odium of that idea upon his adversaries, he thinks he can struggle through the storm. He therefore clings to this hope, as a drowning man to the last plank. He makes an occasion for lugging it in from the opposition to the Dred Scott decision. He finds the Republicans insisting that the Declaration of Independence includes ALL men, black as well as white; and forthwith he boldly denies that it includes negroes at all, and proceeds to argue gravely that all who contend it does, do so only because they want to vote, and eat, and sleep, and marry with negroes! He will have it that they cannot be consistent else. Now I protest against that counterfeit logic which concludes that, because I do not want a black woman for a *slave* I must necessarily want her for a *wife*. I need not have her for either, I can just leave her alone. In some respects she certainly is not my equal; but in her natural right to eat the bread she earns with her own hands without asking leave of any one else, she is my equal, and the equal of all others.

Chief Justice Taney, in his opinion in the Dred Scott case, admits that the language of the Declaration is broad enough to include the whole human family, but he and Judge Douglas argue that the authors of that instrument did not intend to include negroes, by the fact that they did not at once, actually place them on an equality with the whites. Now this grave argument comes to just nothing at all, by the other fact, that they did not at once, *or ever afterwards,* actually place all white people on an equality with one or another. And this is the staple argument of both the Chief Justice and the Senator, for doing this obvious violence to the plain unmistakable language of the Declaration. I think the authors of that notable instrument intended to include *all* men, but they did not intend to declare all men equal *in all respects.* They did not mean to say all were equal in color, size, intellect, moral developments, or social capacity. They defined with tolerable distinctness, in what respects they did consider all men created equal—equal in "certain inalienable rights, among which are life, liberty, and the pursuit of happiness." This they said, and this meant. They did not mean to assert the obvious untruth, that all were then actually enjoying that equality, nor yet, that they were about to confer it immediately upon them. In fact they had no power to confer such a boon. They meant simply to declare the *right*, so that the *enforcement* of it might follow as fast as circumstances should permit. They meant to set up a standard maxim for free society, which should be familiar to all, and revered by all; constantly looked to, constantly labored for, and even though never perfectly attained, constantly approximated, and thereby constantly spreading and deepening its influence, and augmenting the happiness and value of life to all people of all colors everywhere. The assertion that "all men are created equal" was of no practical use in effecting our separation from Great Britain; and it was placed in the Declaration, not for that, but for future use. Its authors meant it to be, thank God, it is now proving itself, a stumbling block to those who in after times might seek to turn a free people back into the hateful paths of despotism. They knew the proneness of prosperity to breed tyrants, and they meant when such should re-appear in this fair land and commence their vocation they should find left for them at least one hard nut to crack.

I have now briefly expressed my view of the *meaning* and *objects* of that part of the Declaration of Independence which declares that "all men are created equal."

Now let us hear Judge Douglas' view of the same subject, as I find it in the printed report of his late speech. Here it is:

"No man can vindicate the character, motives and conduct of the signers of the Declaration of Independence, except upon the hypothesis that they referred to the white race alone, and not to the African, when they declared all men to have been created equal—that they were speaking of British subjects on this continent being equal to British subjects born and residing in Great Britain—that they were entitled to the same inalienable rights, and among them were enumerated life, liberty and the pursuit of happiness. The Declaration was adopted for the purpose of justifying the colonists in the eyes of the civilized world in withdrawing their allegiance from the British crown, and dissolving their connection with the mother country."

My good friends, read that carefully over some leisure hour, and ponder well upon it—see what a mere wreck—mangled ruin —it makes of our once glorious Declaration.

"They were speaking of British subjects on this continent being equal to British subjects born and residing in Great Britain!" Why, according to this, not only negroes but white people outside of Great Britain and America are not spoken of in that instrument. The English, Irish and Scotch, along with white Americans, were included to be sure, but the French, Germans and other white people of the world are all gone to pot along with the Judge's inferior races.

I had thought the Declaration promised something better than the condition of British subjects; but no, it only meant that we should be *equal* to them in their own oppressed and *unequal* condition. According to that, it gave no promise that having kicked off the King and Lords of Great Britain, we should not at once be saddled with a King and Lords of our own.

I had thought the Declaration contemplated the progressive improvement in the condition of all men everywhere; but no, it merely "was adopted for the purpose of justifying the colonists in the eyes of the civilized world in withdrawing their allegiance from the British crown, and dissolving their connection with the mother country." Why, that object having been effected some eighty years ago, the Declaration is of no practical use now—mere rubbish—old wadding left to rot on the battle-field after the victory is won.

I understand you are preparing to celebrate the "Fourth," tomorrow week. What for? The doings of that day had no reference to the present; and quite half of you are not even descendants of those who were referred to at that day. But I suppose you will celebrate; and will even go so far as to read the Declaration. Suppose after you read it once in the old fashioned way, you read it once more with Judge Douglas' version. It will then run thus: "We hold these truths to be self-evident that all British subjects who were on this continent eighty-one years ago, were created equal to all British subjects born and *then* residing in Great Britain."

And now I appeal to all—to Democrats as well as others,—are you really willing that the Declaration shall be thus' frittered away?—thus left no more at most, than an interesting memorial of the dead past? thus shorn of its vitality, and practical value; and left without the *germ* or even the *suggestion* of the individual rights of man in it?

But Judge Douglas is especially horrified at the thought of the mixing blood by the white and black races: agreed for once—a thousand times agreed. There are white men enough to marry all the white women, and black men enough to marry all the black women; and so let them be married. On this point we fully agree with the Judge; and when he shall show that his policy is better adapted to prevent amalgamation than ours we shall drop ours, and adopt his. Let us see. In 1850 there were in the United States, 405,751, mulattoes. Very few of these are the offspring of whites and *free* blacks; nearly all have sprung from black *slaves* and white masters. A separation of the races is the only perfect preventive of amalgamation but as an immediate separation is impossible the next best thing is to *keep* them apart *where* they are not already together. If white and black people never get together in Kansas, they will never mix blood in Kansas. That is at least one self-evident truth. A few free colored persons may get into the free States, in any event; but their number is too insignificant to amount to much in the way of mixing blood. In 1850 there were in the free states, 56,649 mulattoes; but for the most part they were not born there—they came from the slave States, ready made up. In the same year the slave States had 348,874 mulattoes all of home production. The proportion of free mulattoes to free blacks— the only colored classes in the free states—is much greater in the slave than in the free states. It is worthy of note too, that among the free states those which make the colored man the nearest to equal the white, have, proportionably the fewest mulattoes the least of amalgamation. In New Hampshire, the State which goes farthest towards equality between the races, there are just 184 Mulattoes while there are in Virginia—how many do you think? 79,775, being 23,126 more than in all the free States together.

These statistics show that slavery is the greatest source of amalgamation; and next to it, not the elevation, but the degeneration of the free blacks. Yet Judge Douglas dreads the slightest restraints on the spread of slavery, and the slightest human recognition of the negro, as tending horribly to amalgamation.

This very Dred Scott case affords a strong test as to which party most favors amalgamation, the Republicans or the dear Unionsaving Democracy. Dred Scott, his wife and two daughters were all involved in the suit. We desired the court to have held that they were citizens so far at least as to entitle them to a hearing as to whether they were free or not; and then, also, that they were in fact and in law really free. Could we have had our way, the chances of these black girls, ever mixing their blood with that of white people, would have been diminished at least to the extent that it could not have been without their consent. But Judge Douglas is delighted to have them decided to be slaves, and not human enough to have a hearing, even if they were free, and thus left subject to the forced concubinage of their masters, and liable to become the mothers of mulattoes in spite of themselves—the very state of case that produces nine tenths of all the mulattoes—all the mixing of blood in the nation.

Of course, I state this case as an illustration only, not meaning to say or intimate that the master of Dred Scott and his family, or any more than a per centage of masters generally, are inclined to exercise this particular power which they hold over their female slaves.

I have said that the separation of the races is the only perfect preventive of amalgamation. I have no right to say all the members of the Republican party are in favor of this, nor to say that as a party they are in favor of it. There is nothing in their platform directly on the subject. But I can say a very large proportion of its members are for it, and that the chief plank in their platform —opposition to the spread of slavery—is most favorable to that separation.

Such separation, if ever effected at all, must be effected by colonization; and no political party, as such, is now doing anything directly for colonization. Party operations at present only favor or retard colonization incidentally. The enterprise is a difficult one; but "when there is a will there is a way;" and what colonization needs most is a hearty will. Will springs from the two elements of moral sense and self-interest. Let us be brought to believe it is morally right, and, at the same time, favorable to, or, at least, not against, our interest, to transfer the African to his native clime, and we shall find a way to do it, however great the task may be. The children of Israel, to such numbers as to include four hundred thousand fighting men, went out of Egyptian bondage in a body.

How differently the respective courses of the Democratic and Republican parties incidentally bear on the question of forming a will—a public sentiment—for colonization, is easy to see. The Republicans inculcate, with whatever of ability they can, that the negro is a man; that his bondage is cruelly wrong, and that the field of his oppression ought not to be enlarged. The Democrats deny his manhood; deny, or dwarf to insignificance, the wrong of his bondage; so far as possible, crush all sympathy for him, and cultivate and excite hatred and disgust against him; compliment themselves as Union-savers for doing so; and call the indefinite outspreading of his bondage "a sacred right of self-government."

The plainest print cannot be read through a gold eagle; and it will be ever hard to find many men who will send a slave to Liberia, and pay his passage while they can send him to a new country, Kansas for instance, and sell him for fifteen hundred dollars, and the rise.

To Orville H. Browning[1]

Dear Browning.   Springfield, June 29th, 1857.
When I went to Bloomington. . . I saw Mr. Price[2] and learned from him that this note was a sort of "insolvent fix-up" with his creditors—a fact in his history I have not before learned of.

[1] Hertz, II, 704. This fragmentary text is all that is available. The original has not been located.
[2] Although there were several Prices in Bloomington, the particular man meeting Lincoln's qualification has not been identified.

Agreement Regarding the Missouri *Democrat*[1]

July 3, 1857

We, the undersigned, each agree to be one of ten persons to furnish five hundred dollars, to be used in giving circulation, in Southern and Middle Illinois, to the newspaper published at St. Louis, Missouri, and called "The Missouri Democrat"—said sum of five hundred dollars to be paid over to John G. Nicolay, so soon as he shall furnish evidence that he has made arrangements with the proprietors of that paper, giving promise of a reasonable degree of success in the enterprize.

July 3. 1857.   A. Lincoln   L. Trumbull
                     O. M. Hatch   John Wood
                     Jesse K Dubois   William Ross[3] pr O. M. H.
                     John Williams[2]

[1] ADS-P, ISLA. John G. Nicolay had edited the Pike County *Free Press* in 1856, and in 1857 was active as agent for the Chicago *Tribune*. The agreement drawn by Lincoln to promote the circulation of the *Democrat*, a staunch Republican paper, in the part of Illinois where Republican support would be badly needed the following year, seems to fit in with Nicolay's similar soliciting for the *Tribune*, and suggests that Nicolay was in the employ of Republican party leaders even before he became a clerk in the office of Ozias M. Hatch, secretary of state, a few months later. The verso of the agreement bears two endorsements by Nicolay, recording receipt of twenty-five dollars on the within from Hatch and the same amount from Dubois.   [2] John Williams, Springfield merchant.
[3] William Ross, prominent Republican of Pike County, Nicolay's home.

To Gustave P. Koerner[1]

Hon: G. Koerner.   Springfield,
Dear Sir: July 19. 1857
    Your letter of the 8th. to Lincoln & Herndon was received & opened by Mr. Herndon in my absence; but finding it relating to

business with which I was more familiar he laid it by till my return, which was only yesterday.

The judgment of Page & Bacon against the Ohio & Mississippi
Railroad Company, in the U.S. court here, was taken, by confession
on a cognovit, at the March term 1856 for the sum of $312,413,74
—including costs. Execution issued April 16th. 1856, which was,
by order of the plaintiffs returned unsatisfied, sale having been
postponed, June 6. 1856. While it was in the hands of the Marshal,
it was levied on the entire property of the Road (as I suppose, a
large amount at any rate) which levy remains undisposed of.

Will you please remember that our Sangamon Circuit Court
commences Augt. 10– when I suppose our Quo Warranto case[2] will
come up, and when I shall be glad to have the benefit of your legal
assistance. Yours very truly   A. LINCOLN—

[1] ALS, CSmH.
[2] The People *ex rel.* Koerner *et al. v.* N. H. Ridgely *et al.*, which involved the
appointment of Koerner and others as trustees of the State Bank of Illinois.

To Lyman Porter and Company[1]

Messrs Porter & Co.   Springfield,
Mackinaw   Tazewell Co. Ills.   July 19. 1857.

Gentlemen   Owing to my absence, yours of the 6th. Inst. with
inclosures, were not received till yesterday. The circuits are so
divided now that I can not attend the Tazewell court, regularly, if
at all, any more. I therefore think you better have a lawyer that
can certainly attend to it. If Prettyman[2] can not give his attention
to carry it through, I think Mr. Roberts,[3] at Pekin, is getting to be
a quite safe lawyer.

I return you the inclosures. Yours truly   A. LINCOLN—

[1] ALS, owned by C. L. Porter, Lafayette, Indiana. Lyman Porter was engaged
in a general merchandising business.   [2] Benjamin S. Prettyman.
[3] James Roberts.

To William H. Young[1]

W. H. Young, Esq   Springfield,
Dear Sir.   July 19. 1857

Mr. Herndon received yours of the 14th. addressed to him and
me, and kept it for me to answer when I should return, which
was only yesterday.

We are willing to be with you in the case or cases of Alies &
Morrison,[2] subject to the condition, however, that I shall have to

be at Chicago during part—perhaps all—of your next term. Mr. Herndon will be on hand; and if this will do, send on the full statement of facts. Yours truly   A. LINCOLN—

1 ALS, IHi.
2 There is no further record of Lincoln's connection with this case.

To B. Clarke Lundy[1]

B. C. Lundy, Esq.   Springfield,
Dear Sir: July 20, 1857
    Owing to my absence, yours of the 10th was not received till a day or so ago. Senator Trumbull's speech and my own have both been published in pamphlet form, at the Illinois Journal offices,[2] but the copies printed off have been exhausted. They will have a new supply printed by the time this reaches you, and you can write them. Their price is a dollar per hundred. Mine is much larger and better print than it was in the Journal paper. Send directly to the Journal for the number of each you want, directing them how and where to send them.
    What you say about our party doing something this year is perfectly right; on that subject open a correspondence with N. B. Judd, of Chicago, telling him I suggested it to you. I believe you are in the Peoria Senatorial district—a district that has to be very thoroughly cultivated—outside of it, up your way does not need much.
    I have another matter in contemplation, which I will not mention now, but concerning which I may write you in a month or so.
Yours truly,   A. LINCOLN.

1 Hertz, II, 704.
2 *Vide supra,* June 26. Senator Lyman Trumbull spoke at Springfield on June 29, the speech being printed in the *Illinois State Journal,* July 1 and 2.

To B. Clarke Lundy[1]

Dear Sir: Springfield, Aug. 5. 1857
    Some time ago you wrote me expressing the opinion that something should be done *now,* to secure the next Legislature. You were perfectly right; and I now suggest that, from the poll-books in the county clerk's office, you have made alphabetical lists of all the voters in each precinct, or Township (I believe you have Township organization) the lists to be in separate letter books, and to be corrected, by striking off such as may have died or removed, and adding such as will be entitled to vote at the next elec-

tion. This will not be a heavy job, and you see how, like a map, it lays the whole field before you. You know, at once, *how*, and with *whom* to work.

You will have no trouble to carry your county of Putnam; but you are (as I remember) part of the Peoria Senatorial District, and that is close and questionable, so that you need every vote you can get in Putnam[.] Let all be so quiet that the adve[r]sary shall not be notified. Yours truly　　　　　　　A. LINCOLN

1 ALS, RPB.

To Robert E. Williams[1]

R. E. Williams, Esq.　　　　　　　　　　Springfield,
Dear Sir　　　　　　　　　　　　　　Aug: 15. 1857.

Yours of the 12th. in relation to a suit of Bakewell vs Allin,[2] was received a day or two ago. I well remember the transaction; but as Bakewell will need no lawyer but you, and as there is likely to be some feeling, and both the parties are old friends of mine, I prefer, if I can, to keep out of the case. Of course I will not engage against Mr. Bakewell. Yours truly　　　　　　　A. LINCOLN

1 ALS-P, ISLA. Robert E. Williams was a lawyer at Bloomington, Illinois.

2 The case has not been positively identified, and of the several residents of Bloomington and vicinity bearing the names given, there are too many possibilities to warrant listing.

To James W. Grimes[1]

His Excellency,　　　　　　　　　　Springfield, Ills.
James W. Grimes　　　　　　　　　Aug: [c.17] 1857.

Dear Sir　Yours of the 14th. is received and I am much obliged for the legal information you give.

You can scarcely be more anxious than I, that the next election in Iowa shall result in favor of the Republicans. I lost nearly all the working part of last year, giving my time to the canvass; and I am altogether too poor to lose two years together. I am engaged in a suit in the U.S. Court at Chicago, in which the Rock-Island Bridge Co. is a party[.] The trial is to commence the 8th. of September, and probably will last two or three weeks. During the trial it is not improbable that all hands may come over and take a look at the Bridge, & if it were possible to make it hit right, I could then speak at Davenport.[2] My courts go right on without cessation till late in November. Write me again, pointing out the most striking points of difference between your old, and new constitutions; and also whether Democratic and Republican party lines were drawn in the adoption of it; & which were for, and which against it. If by possibility I could get over amongst you, it might be of some advantage to know these things in advance. Yours very truly

A. LINCOLN—

1 ALS, IaCrM.

2 The trial was held September 8-24, but Lincoln did not visit Davenport. The question of whether he visited the site of the bridge has been and is a matter of controversy. The evidence that he did is contained in a copy of a letter purportedly written by N. B. Judd to Lincoln, September 4, 1857, in which he mentions Lincoln's trip to Rock Island "last Tuesday," which would have been September 1. This purported copy of Judd's letter is of questionable authenticity.

Endorsement on Petition for Pardon of Moses Loe[1]

[August 18, 1857]

I defended Moses Loe in the case mentioned, and, with the exception of the assistance of a younger man at the trial, who volunteered merely to try his hand, the whole defence rested on me. I know Loe to have been a very young man at the time of the offence, and that more than half his time, (originally eight years) has elapsed since his conviction. As to his previous character, or his conduct in the State prison I know nothing; but willing to trust the numerous and very respectable gentlemen who speak to these points, I cheerfully join the request that he be pardoned for the remainder of his term.

A. LINCOLN—

1 AES, I-Ar. The certification appearing on the petition is dated August 18, 1857. Lincoln had defended Loe on the charge of manslaughter in the DeWitt County Circuit Court, May 19, 1853.

To Jesse K. Dubois[1]

Dear Jesse K.   Chicago, Sept. 13. 1857

Several persons here keep teasing me about you and the Bank commissioners not enforcing the banking laws. In my stupidity, I do not believe I quite understand what the ground of complaint is; but it appears to me to be this; that the stocks which the banks have on deposite have depreciated; that in such case, it is your duty to make the banks deposite additional stocks, or, in default, wind them up; and that you do not perform this duty. Now how is this? Write me plainly enough to make me understand; and write soon too, for I am annoyed about it a good deal. Your friend as ever

A. LINCOLN

1 ALS-P, ISLA. Jesse K. Dubois had been elected auditor of public accounts in 1856.

Speech to the Jury
in the Rock Island Bridge Case, Chicago, Illinois[1]

Tuesday, September 22d, 1857.

Mr. A. Lincoln addressed the jury: He said he did not purpose to assail anybody, that he expected to grow earnest as he proceeded, but not ill-natured. There is some conflict of testimony in the case, but one quarter of such a number of witnesses, seldom agree, and even if all had been on one side some discrepancy might have been expected. We are to try and reconcile them, and to believe that they are not intentionally erroneous, as long as we can. He had no prejudice against steamboats or steamboatmen, nor any against St. Louis, for he supposed they went about as other people would do in their situation. St. Louis as a commercial place, may desire that this bridge should not stand, as it is adverse to her commerce, diverting a portion of it from the river; and it might be that she supposed that the additional cost of railroad transportation upon the productions of Iowa, would force them to go to St. Louis if this bridge was removed. The meetings in St. Louis[2] were connected with this case, only as some witnesses were in it and thus had some prejudice [to] add color to their testimony.

The last thing that would be pleasing to him would be, to have one of these great channels, extending almost from where it never freezes to where it never thaws, blocked up. But there is a travel from East to West, whose demands are not less important than that of the river. It is growing larger and larger, building up new countries with a rapidity never before seen in the history of the world. He alluded to the astonishing growth of Illinois, having grown within his memory to a population of a million and a half, to Iowa and the other young and rising communities of the Northwest.

[1] Chicago *Daily Democratic Press*, September 24, 1857. Because of its unusual interest, this case received complete reporting by Robert Hitt, which appeared daily in the *Press*, September 9-25. The Rock Island bridge was the first across the Mississippi and became the center of a fight between steamboat and railroad interests when on May 6, 1856, about two weeks after its completion, the steamboat *Effie Afton* crashed into one of the bridge piers and burned to the water's edge, destroying a span of the bridge. Jacob S. Hurd and associates, owners of the *Afton*, bringing suit against the bridge company for damages, were backed by steamboat interests up and down the river, and the St. Louis Chamber of Commerce, foreseeing the effect of railroad bridges on St. Louis as the center of steamboat transportation, promoted the cause. Lincoln, Norman B. Judd, and Joseph Knox represented the owners of the bridge. Hezekiah M. Wead, Corydon Beckwith of Chicago, and Timothy D. Lincoln of Cincinnati represented Hurd *et al.*

[2] Meetings of the Chamber of Commerce of St. Louis at which the steamboat owners and pilots were exhorted to make the case a *cause célèbre.*

This current of travel has its rights, as well as that north and south. If the river had not the advantage in priority and legislation, we could enter into free competition with it and we would surpass it. This particular line has a great importance, and the statement of its business during little less than a year shows this importance. It is in evidence that from September 8, 1856, to August 8, 1857, 12,586 freight cars and 74,179 passengers passed over this bridge. Navigation was closed four days short of four months last year, and during this time, while the river was of no use, this road and bridge were equally valuable. There is, too, a considerable portion of time, when floating or thin ice makes the river useless, while the bridge is as useful as ever. This shows that this bridge must be treated with respect in this court and is not to be kicked about with contempt.

The other day Judge Wead[3] alluded to the stripe [strife?] of the contending interests, and even a dissolution of the Union. Mr. Lincoln thought the proper mood for all parties in this affair, is to "live and let live," and then we will find a cessation of this trouble about the bridge. What mood were the steamboat men in when this bridge was burned? Why there was a shouting, a ringing of bells and whistling on all the boats as it fell. It was a jubilee, a greater celebration than follows an excited election.

The first thing I will proceed to is the record of Mr. Gurney[4] and the complaint of Judge Wead, that it did not extend back over all the time from the completion of the bridge. The principal part of the navigation after the bridge was burned passed through the span. When the bridge was repaired and the boats were a second time confined to the draw, it was provided that this record should be kept. That is the simple history of that book.

From April 19, 1856, to May 6—17 days—there were 20 accidents, and all the time since then, there has been but 20 hits, including 7 accidents; so that the dangers of this place are tapering off, and, as the boatmen get cool, the accidents get less. We may soon expect, if this ratio is kept up, that there will be no accidents at all.

Judge Wead said, while admitting that the floats went straight through, there was a difference between a float and a boat, but I do not remember that he indulged us with an argument in support of this statement. Is it because there is a difference in size? Will not a small body and a large one, float the same way, under the

---

[3] Wead addressed the jury on the preceding day, making the most of the sectional strife which the bridge was causing.

[4] Seth Gurney, keeper of the bridge.

same influence? True, a flat boat would float faster than an egg-shell, and the egg-shell might be blown away by the wind, but if under the *same influence* they would go the same way. Logs, floats, boards, various things, the witnesses say all show the same current. Then is not this test reliable? At all depths too, the direction of the current is the same. A series of these floats would make a line as long as a boat, and would show any influence upon any part, and all parts of the boat.

I will now speak of the angular position of the piers. What is the amount of the angle? The course of the river is a curve and the pier is straight. If a line is produced from the upper end of the long pier straight with the pier to a distance of 350 feet, and a line is drawn from a point in the channel opposite this point to the head of the pier, Col. Mason[5] says they will form an angle of 20 degrees; but the angle if measured at the pier, is 7 degrees—that is, we would have to move the pier 7 degrees, and then it would be exactly straight with the current. Would that make the navigation better or worse? The witnesses of the plaintiffs seemed to think it was only necessary to say that the pier was angling to the current, and that settled the matter. Our more careful and accurate witnesses say, that though they have been accustomed to seeing the piers placed straight with the current, yet, they could see that here the current has been made straight by us, in having made this slight angle—that the water now runs just right now—that it is straight and cannot be improved. They think that if the pier was changed the eddy would be divided, and the navigation improved; and that as it is, the bridge is placed in the best manner possible.

I am not now going to discuss the question what is a material obstruction? We do not very greatly differ about the law. The cases produced here, are, I suppose, proper to be taken into consideration by the Court in instructing the jury. Some of them I think are not exactly in point, but still I am willing to trust his honor, Judge McLean, and take his instructions as law.

What is *reasonable* skill and care? This is a thing of which the jury are to judge. I differ from them in saying that they are found to exercise no more care than they took before the building of the bridge. If we are allowed by the Legislature to build a bridge, which will require them to do more than before, when a pilot comes along, it is unreasonable for him to dash on, heedless of this structure, which has been *legally put there*. The Afton came there

5 R. B. Mason, a civil engineer residing at Dubuque, Iowa, and a contractor on the construction of the Dubuque and Pacific Railroad, who testified for the defense as to the river current in relation to the bridge piers.

on the 5th, and lay at Rock Island until next morning. When the boat lies up, the pilot has a holiday, and would not any of these jurors have then gone around there, and got acquainted with the place? Parker[6] has shown here that he does not understand the draw. I heard him say that the fall from the head to the foot of that pier was four feet! He needs information. He could have gone there that day and have seen there was no such fall. He should have discarded passion, and the chances are that he would have had no disaster at all. He was bound to make himself acquainted with it.

McCammon[7] says that "the current and the swell coming from the long pier, drove her against the long pier." Drove her towards the very pier from which the current came! It is an absurdity, an impossibility. The only reconciliation I can find for this contradiction, is in a current which White says strikes out from the long pier, and then, like a ram's horn, turns back, and this might have acted somehow in this manner.

It is agreed by all that the plaintiffs' boat was destroyed; that it was destroyed upon the head of the short pier; that she moved from the channel, where she was, with her bow above the head of the long pier, till she struck the short one, swung around under the bridge, and there was crowded under the bridge and destroyed.

I shall try to prove that the average velocity of the current through the draw with the boat in it, should be five and a half miles an hour; that it is slowest at the head of the pier,—swiftest at the foot of the pier. Their lowest estimate, in evidence, is six miles an hour, their highest twelve miles. This was the testimony of men who had made no experiment—only conjecture. We have adopted the most exact means. The water runs swiftest in high water, and we have taken the point of nine feet above low water. The water, when the Afton was lost, was seven feet above low water, or at least a foot lower than our time. Brayton[8] and his assistants timed the instruments—the best known instruments for measuring currents. They timed them under various circumstances, and they found the current five miles an hour, and no more. They found that the water, at the upper end, ran slower than five miles; that below it was swifter than five miles, but that the average was five miles. Shall men, who have taken no care, who conjecture, some of whom speak of twenty miles an hour be

6 Nathaniel W. Parker, pilot of the *Afton*, who testified for the plaintiffs.

7 Joseph McCammon, a pilot who was in the wheelhouse but not acting pilot at the time of the crash.

8 Benjamin B. Brayton, engineer in charge of construction of the bridge.

believed, against those who have had such a favorable and well-improved opportunity? They should not even *qualify* the result. Several men have given their opinions as to the distance of the Carson,[9] and I suppose if *one* should go and *measure* that distance, you would believe him in preference to all of them.

These measurements were made when the boat was not in the draw. It has been ascertained what is the area of the cross-section of the stream, and the area of the face of the piers, and the engineers say, that the piers being put there will increase the current proportionably as the space is decreased. So with the boat in the draw. The depth of the channel was 22 feet, the width 116 feet—multiply these and you have the square feet across the water of the draw, viz.: 2,552 feet. The Afton was 35 feet wide and drew five feet, making a fourteenth of the sum. Now one-fourteenth of five miles is five-fourteenths of one mile—about one-third of a mile—the increase of the current. We will call the current $5\frac{1}{2}$ miles per hour.

The next thing I will try to prove is that the plaintiffs' boat had power to run six miles an hour in that current. It has been testified that she was a strong, swift boat, able to run eight miles an hour up stream in a current of four miles an hour, and fifteen miles down stream. Strike the average and you will find what is her average—about $11\frac{1}{2}$ miles. Take the $5\frac{1}{2}$, miles which is the speed of the current in the draw, and it leaves the power of the boat in that draw at six miles an hour, 528 feet per minute, and $8\frac{4}{5}$ feet to the second.

Next I propose to show that there are no cross currents. I know their witnesses say that there are cross currents—that, as one witness says, there are three cross currents and two eddies. So far as mere statement without experiment, and mingled with mistakes can go, they have proved. But can these men's testimony be compared with the nice, exact, thorough experiments of our witnesses. Can you believe that these floats go across the currents? It is inconceiveable that they could not have discovered every possible current. How do boats find currents that floats cannot discover? We assume the position then that those cross currents are not there. My next proposition is that the Afton passed between the S. B. Carson and Iowa shore. That is undisputed.

Next I shall show that she struck first the short pier, then the long pier, then the short one again and there she stopped. Mr. Lincoln cited the testimony of eighteen witnesses on this point. How did the boat strike Baker[10] when she went in! Here is an endless variety of opinion. But ten of them say what pier she struck;

[9] The steamboat *S. B. Carson*.   [10] John A. Baker, mate on the *Afton*.

three of them testify that she struck first the short, then the long, then the short pier for the last time. None of the rest substantially contradict this. I assume that these men have got the truth, because I believe it an established fact.

My next proposition is that after she struck the short and long pier and before she got back to the short pier the boat got right with her bow out. So says the Pilot Parker—that he "got her through until her starboard wheel passed the short pier." This would make her head about even with the head of the long pier. He says her head was as high or higher than the head of the long pier. Other witnesses confirm this one. The final stroke was in the splash door, aft the wheel. Witnesses differ but the majority say that she struck thus.

Court adjourned.

FOURTEENTH DAY

WEDNESDAY, September 23, 1857.

Mr. A. Lincoln resumed. He said he should conclude as soon as possible. He said the colored map of the plaintiffs, which was brought in during the advanced stages of the trial, showed itself that the cross currents alleged did not exist; that the current as represented would drive an ascending boat to the long pier, but not to the short pier as they urged. He explained from a model of a boat where the splash door is, just behind the wheel. The boat struck on the lower shoulder of the short pier, as she swung round, in the splash door, then as she went on round she struck the point or end of the pier, where she rested. Her engineers say the starboard wheel then was rushing round rapidly. Then the boat must have struck the upper point of the pier so far back as not to disturb the wheel. It is forty feet from the stern of the Afton to the splash door, and thus it appears that she had but forty feet to go to clear the pier.

How was it that the Afton, with all her power, flanked over from the channel to the short pier without moving one inch ahead? Suppose she was in the middle of the draw, her wheel would have been 31 feet from the short pier. The reason she went over thus is, her starboard wheel was not working. I shall try to establish the fact that that wheel was not running, and, that after she struck, she went ahead strong on this same wheel. Upon the last point the witnesses agree—that the starboard wheel was running after she struck—and no witnesses say that it was running while she was out in the draw flanking over. Mr. Lincoln read from the testimony of various witnesses to prove that the starboard wheel was not working while she was out in the stream. Other witnesses show that the captain said something of the machinery of the wheel, and the inference is that he knew the wheel was not working. The fact is undisputed, that she did not move one inch ahead, while she was moving this 31 feet sideways. There is evidence proving that the current there is only five miles an hour, and the only explanation is that her power was not all used—that only one wheel was working. The pilot says he ordered the engineers to back her out. The engineers differ from him and say that they kept one going ahead. The bow was so swung that the current pressed it over; the pilot pressed the stern over with the rudder, though not so fast but that the bow gained on it, and, only one wheel being in motion, the boat merely stood still so far as motion up and down is concerned, and thus she was thrown upon this pier.

The Afton came into the draw after she had just passed the Carson, and, as the Carson no doubt kept the true course, the Afton going around her, got out of the proper way, got across the current, into the eddy which is west of a straight line drawn down from the long pier, was compelled to resort to these changes of wheels, which she did not do with sufficient adroitness to save her. Was it not her own fault that she entered wrong? so far, wrong that she never got right. Is the defence to blame for that?

For several days we were entertained with depositions about boats "smelling a bar." Why did the Afton then, after she had come up smelling so close to the long pier sheer off so strangely? When she got to the centre of the very nose she was smelling, she seems suddenly to have lost her sense of smell and flanks over to the short pier.

Mr. Lincoln said there was no practicability in the project of building a tunnel under the river, for there is not a tunnel that is a successful project, in the world. A suspension bridge cannot be built so high, but that the chimneys of the boats will grow up till they cannot pass. The steamboatmen will take pains to make them grow. The cars of a railroad, cannot, without immense expense, rise high enough to get even with a suspension bridge, or go low enough to get down through a tunnel. Such expense is unreasonable.

The plaintiffs have to establish that the bridge is a material obstruction, and that they managed their boat with reasonable care and skill. As to the last point, high winds have nothing to do with it, for it was not a windy day. They must show "due skill and care." Difficulties going down stream, will not do, for they were going up stream. Difficulties with barges in tow, have nothing to do with it, for they had no barge. He said he had much more to say, many things he could suggest to the jury, but he would close to save time.[11]

[11] Unable to agree on a verdict (nine for the bridge, three against), the jury was discharged. Further litigation against the bridge was not settled until December, 1862, when the U.S. Supreme Court set aside a District Court order to remove a part of the bridge.

Receipt to Jacob Ruckel[1]

September 28, 1857

Received, Sept. 28. 1857 of Jacob Ruckel three hundred dollars, which is in full of the principal of a note and mortgage I held on the late Daniel E. Ruckel; Mr. Beach[2] to settle the interest due from last christmas.

I have entered satisfaction on the record of the mortgage, and am to hand over the original mortgage and note.

A LINCOLN.

[1] ADS, IHi. Jacob Ruckel was in the general merchandise business in Springfield. Daniel E. Ruckel was an older brother. See the note drawn for Daniel E. Ruckel, August 15, 1851.

[2] Richard H. Beach, Springfield merchant, administrator of the estate of Daniel E. Ruckel.

Mortgage and Note Drawn for Jacob Ruckel[1]

September 28, 1857

This Indenture made this twentyeighth day of September in the year of our Lord one thousand eight hundred and fiftyseven by and between Jacob Ruckel, and Laura A. Ruckel, his wife, of the City of Springfield in the State of Illinois, party of the first part; and Abraham Lincoln, of the City and State aforesaid, party of the second part, Witnesseth:

That the said party of the first part, for and in consideration of the sum of five hundred dollars to them in hand paid, the receipt whereof is hereby acknowledged, have granted, bargained, and sold; and by these presents do grant, bargain, and sell unto the said party of the second part, his heirs and assign's forever, the following described real estate, towit:

One hundred and two feet from East to West, of the East parts of Lots Thirteen, Fourteen, Fifteen, and Sixteen, in Block Four, in E. Iles' Addition to the late town, now City of Springfield

To have and to hold to the said party of the second part, his heirs and assigns forever, the above described real estate, together with all and singular the privileges and appurtenances thereunto belonging.

[422]

Yet upon the condition that whereas the above named Jacob Ruckel has executed his promissory note of even date herewith, for the sum of five hundred dollars, payable to the said Abraham Lincoln, one year after date, with interest thereon at the rate of ten per cent per annum, from date until paid, for value received. Now if said note and interest shall be fully paid according to the tenor and effect of said note, the above conveyance is to be void; otherwise to remain in full force and effect.

In testimony whereof the said party of the first part have hereunto set their hands and seals, the day and year first above written.

J. RUCKEL (SEAL)
L. A. RUCKEL (SEAL)

$500–   Springfield, September 28. 1857–

One year after date I promise to pay Abraham Lincoln five hundred dollars, together with interest thereon at the rate of ten per cent per annum from date until paid, for value received.

J. RUCKEL.

Nov. 27. 1858. Received on the within fifty dollars, being first year's interest.

Secnd years Int. also paid.

Nov. 17. 1860. Received fifty dollars third year's interest.[2]

1 AD-P, ISLA. The note and receipts appear on the mortgage document, and for this reason all are taken together. The attestation on the mortgage is by N. W. Matheny.

2 The final receipt, January 29, 1864, for principal and interest in full, $667.05, is by Lincoln's agent, Robert Irwin.

To Samuel Briggs[1]

Saml Briggs, Esq   Springfield,
Dear Sir   Sept. 29. 1857

Your letter in regard to organizing the town of Delevan, and also inclosing five dollars, has been received.

I have examined the statute, and considered your questions; and am of opinion that the original election having gone beyond the Town-plat, to the extent of a square mile, is lawful and valid.

I think the Trustees can not exceed a mile square, as boundaries of the town, but may lessen them, within the mile square.

The five dollars is a sufficient fee. Yours truly

A. LINCOLN

1 ALS, RPB. Samuel Briggs was a resident of Delavan (current spelling), Illinois, which was incorporated in 1858 over the protest of many citizens.

To Richard Yates[1]

Hon: R. Yates—   Springfield,
Dear Sir: Sept. 30. 1857–

Your letter, called out by the letter of J. O. Johnson,[2] was received by me on my return from Chicago.

Mr. Johnson wrote the letter by concert with me; and is entirely reliable. He is a new-comer; but he can devote more time to getting up an organization, than any one I know, who knows as well as he, how to do it.

And now, let me say, I wish you could make up your mind to come to the Legislature from Morgan next term. You can be elected, and I doubt some whether any other friend can. It will be something of a sacrafice to you; but can you not make it?[3] Yours as ever   A. LINCOLN.

[1] ALO D. IOLA.
[2] John O. Johnson resided at Springfield, 1857-1859, but little else can be learned concerning him. Apparently Lincoln had employed him as a party organizer.   [3] Yates did not run, and a Democrat was elected.

Call for Sangamon County Convention[1]

October 8, 1857

To the VOTERS of SANGAMON COUNTY.

All those who are opposed to the policy of the present National Administration are requested to meet in the various precincts in Sangamon county, and nominate or appoint Delegates to meet in MASS CONVENTION, in the city of Springfield, on

Monday, October 19th, 1857,

To nominate candidates for the various County offices at the November Election.

Each Precinct is requested to send five Delegates.

Abraham Lincoln	E B Hawley,	A M Watson
S M Cullom	James M Garland	W Jayne
S T Logan	O H Abel	J W Smith
Archibald Vanderin	Isaac A Hawley	C Fessenden
Pascal P Enos	Thomas S Mather	E H Emery Jameson
W H Bailhache	John Williams	Richard Latham
P L Earnest	Wm H Herndon	J B Broadwell
J D Bail	J. H Matheny	D P Broadwell
C W Matheny	Wm Lavely	J E Denny
C M Smith	J M Allen	

[424]

1 *Illinois State Journal*, October 8, 1857. Signers of the call not previously identified are as follows: Archibald J. Van Deren, drygoods merchant; Pascal P. Enos, clerk of the U.S. Circuit Court; William H. Bailhache, who was in partnership with Edward L. Baker as proprietor and editor of the *Illinois State Journal;* Peter L. Earnest, politician and minor officeholder; John D. Bail, attorney and poet; Clark M. Smith, merchant; James M. Garland, bookkeeper at E. B. Hawley & Company; Oramel H. Abel, salesman for E. B. Hawley & Company; Thomas S. Mather, real estate and insurance agent; John W. Smith, state representative from Sangamon County in 1848, census commissioner, 1845, 1855; Cortes Fessenden, civil engineer and surveyor; E. H. Emery Jameson, editor (Springfield *Republican*), contractor and builder; John B. Broadwell (father) and Daniel P. Broadwell (son), merchants; John E. Denny, carpenter.

To Gustave P. Koerner[1]

(Confidential)

Hon. G. Koerner   Springfield, Oct. 25. 1857.

My dear Sir: Our Sangamon Circuit Court is now in session, and will continue in session for two or three weeks yet. By agreement with Logan, I can fix up your *Quo Warranto* case,[2] at any time, during the term, for the Supreme Court this ensuing winter. Now, for the object of this note. I want your authority, *at my discretion,* to pass the case over the next term of the Supreme Court. I can not mention the reason now; but there is a reason which I believe you will appreciate, when you come to know it. The reason is precisely the same to you and to me, not being of any pecuniary interest to either. I write like letters to Brown and Yates.[3] Please answer at once. Yours very truly   A. LINCOLN

1 ALS, MoSHi.
2 Stephen T. Logan was attorney for Nicolas H. Ridgely in the case. See letter of July 19, *supra.* The case had been called and continued on August 11.
3 William Brown and Richard Yates, law partners, of Jacksonville, Illinois, who were also involved in the case.

To Salmon A. Phelps[1]

[November, 1857]

If the case is as stated within, I will attend to the case in the Supreme court for ten dollars.   A. LINCOLN.

1 ALS, owned by Mrs. Dana Mendenhall, Indianapolis, Indiana. The note was written on the last page of Phelps' letter and returned to Phelps, Lincoln keeping the portion which described the case. Salmon A. Phelps, of Greenville, Illinois, as attorney for John A. Smith, had lost the case in the Bond County Circuit Court. Isaac Smith had sued his uncle John A. Smith, both of Greenville, Illinois, for a buggy which Isaac had won on an election bet from one George Moffett, but which Moffett had sold to John A. Smith before Isaac could get possession.

Petition to William H. Bissell
for Pardon of George High[1]

[November 7, 1857]

To his Excellency, the Governor of the State of Illinois.

We, the undersigned citizens of Vermilion County respectfully represent that George High was, at the fall term of the Champaign county circuit court, 1855, convicted of the crime of horse-stealing, and sentenced to the penitentiary for the term of three years; that the offence was committed in this county, and the trial was in Champaign by change of venue; that he has now been in the penitentiary more than two years, and was confined in jail about fourteen months previous to his conviction; that most of us took an active interest in procuring his conviction; that we now think public justice has been satisfied in his case; and as he is yet quite a young man, we hope and believe some lenity towards him, would be favorable to his reformation for the future. We therefore respectfully ask that he be pardoned for the remainder of his term.

I have been acquainted with the circumstances of George High's case from the time of his arrest; and I cheerfully join in the request that he may be pardoned. Novr– 10– 1857.   A. LINCOLN—

[1] AD, I-Ar. This petition in Lincoln's handwriting bears twenty-seven signatures of citizens of Vermilion County, including the prosecuting attorneys O. L. Davis and Ward H. Lamon. Judge David Davis as well as Lincoln wrote out an endorsement. Davis' endorsement is dated November 7, at Danville. Lincoln apparently carried the petition to Springfield personally, and then added his own endorsement on November 10.

To Ozias Bailey[1]

O. Bailey, Esq.   Springfield,
Dear Sir: Nov. 14. 1857

Your letter in relation to Railroad suits was duly received. I regret to say it is impossible for me to attend to courts in Coles or Edgar, or any of the counties in Judge Harlan's[2] circuit. I should be pleased to oblige you if I could. Yours truly   A. LINCOLN—

[1] ALS, IHi. Ozias Bailey was representative from Edgar County, 1850-1852.
[2] Justin Harlan, judge of the Fourth Circuit.

To Jonathan Haines[1]

Jonathan Haines, Esq.   Springfield
Dear Sir: Nov. 25. 1857.

I have now determined to go to Chicago on saturday the 28th. Inst. to remain about a week, and if you and Rugg[2] can be on hand

I suppose we can find a chance to get your case in. I can not name a certain day, because I am going up for a case which is to begin the 1st Dec; and if I could, the court might not agree. Yours truly

A LINCOLN—

1 ALS-P, ISLA. Jonathan Haines of Pekin, Illinois, inventor of the Buckeye Mower and the Haines Illinois Header. The case referred to has not been certainly identified but probably had to do with patent infringements. Haines & Haines *v.* Talcott *et al.* may be the case. See Lincoln to Peter H. Watson, March 2, 1859, *infra,* and Lincoln to Haines, November 24, 1856, *supra.*

2 George H. Rugg.

To Joseph W. Brackett[1]

J. W. Brackett, Esq.   Springfield,
Dear Sir: Novr. 27– 1857

Yours of the 7th. was received in due course. I have been to the Land Office two or three times about it, and, for the last time, this morning. The Register will not receive and file the pre emption proofs as you desire. He conceives it to be his duty to refuse.

Yours &c   A. LINCOLN

1 ALS-P, ISLA. See Lincoln to Brackett, May 18, 1857, *supra.*

To Lyman Trumbull[1]

Hon: Lyman Trumbull.   Chicago, Nov. 30. 1857.

Dear Sir: Herewith you find duplicates of a notice which I wish to be served upon the Miss French, or now Mrs. Gray, who married the late Franklin C. Gray.[2] You understand what person I mean.

Please hand her one copy, and note on the other that you have done so, the date of service, and your signature & return it to me at Springfield.

What think you of the probable *"rumpus"* among the democracy over the Kansas constitution?[3] I think the Republicans should stand clear of it. In their view both the President and Douglas are wrong; and they should not espouse the cause of either, because they may consider the other a little the farther wrong of the two.

From what I am told here, Douglas tried, before leaving, to draw off some Republicans on this dodge, and even succeeded in making some impression on one or two. Yours very truly

A. LINCOLN—

1 ALS, CSmH.

2 Mary A. Gray was divorced by Franklin C. Gray in 1851. He married Matilda C. French. Mary A. Gray *v.* Matilda C. French, *et al.,* in the Illinois Supreme Court, was a suit to have the divorce decree reversed.

3 In a famous interview between President Buchanan and Stephen A. Douglas

prior to the opening of Congress in December, Buchanan was reported to have threatened political reprisal if Douglas fought the admission of Kansas under the Lecompton Constitution, an administration measure. Douglas refused because of the Constitution's slavery clause, and proceeded to fight the administration with the support of a handful of Democratic senators, but with considerable Republican support. Lincoln's view of party strategy was not generally followed, most Republican leaders supporting Douglas.

To Lyman Trumbull[1]

Hon: L. Trumbull: Springfield, Decr. 18. 1857

Dear Sir: Yours of the 7th. telling me that Mrs. Gray *is* in Washington, reached [me] last night. Herewith I return the notices which I will thank you to serve and return as before requested. This notice is not required by *law;* and I am giving it merely because I think *fairness* requires it.

Nearly all the democrats here stick to Douglas; but they are hobbling along with the idea that there is no split between him and Buchanan. Accordingly they indulge the most extravagant eulogies on B., & his message; and insist that he has not indorsed the Lecompton Constitution.

I wish not to tax your time; but when you return the notice, I shall be glad to have your general view of the then present aspect of affairs. Yours very truly A. LINCOLN

[1] ALS, CSmH. See letter of November 30, *supra.*

To Henry C. Whitney[1]

Henry C. Whitney, Esq Springfield,
My dear Sir: Dec 18. 1857.

Coming home from Bloomington last night I found your letter of the 15th.

I know of no express statute or decisions as to what a J. P. upon the expiration of his term shall do with his docket books, papers, unfinished business &c. but so far as I know, the *practice* has been to hand over to the successor, and to cease to do anything further whatever, in perfect analoge to Sec's 110 & 112—and I have supposed & do suppose this is the law. I think the successor may forthwith do, whatever the retiring J.P. might have done. As to the proviso to Sec. 114 I think it was put in to cover possible cases, by way of caution, and not to authorize the J.P. to go forward and finish up whatever might have been begun by him.

The view I take I believe is the common law principle, as to retiring officers and their successors, to which I remember but one exception, which is the case of Sheriffs and ministerial officers of that class.

I have not had time to examine this subject fully, but I have great confidence I am right.

You must not think of offering me pay for this.

Mr. John O. Johnson[2] is my friend; I gave your name to him. He is doing the work of trying to get up a republican organization. I do not suppose Long John[3] ever saw or heard of him. Let me say to you confidentially, that I do not entirely appreciate what the republican papers of Chicago are so constantly saying against Long John. I consider those papers truly devoted to the republican cause, and not unfriendly to me; but I *do* think that more of what they say against "Long John" is dictated by personal malice than [they] themselves are conscious of. We can not afford to lose the services of "Long John" and I do believe the unrelenting warfare made upon him, is injuring our cause. I mean this to be confidential.

If you quietly co-operate with Mr. J. O. Johnson, in getting up an organization I think it will be right. Your friend as ever

A. LINCOLN

[1] ALS-P, ISLA.   [2] See letter to Yates, September 30, *supra.*
[3] "Long" John Wentworth, editor of the Chicago *Democrat.*

To Jesse K. Dubois[1]

Dear Dubois   Bloomington Dec: 21, 1857

J. M. Douglas, of the I.C.R.R. Co is here, and will carry this letter. He says they have a large sum (near $90,000) which they will pay into the Treasury now, if they have an assurance that they shall not be sued before Jany. 1859— otherwise not. I really wish you could consent to this. Douglas says they *can not* pay more, & I believe him.

I do not write this as a lawyer seeking an advantage for a client; but only as a friend, only urging you to do, what I think I would do if I were in your situation. I mean this as private and confidential only, but I feel a good deal of anxiety about it. Yours as ever

A. LINCOLN—

[1] ALS, owned by A. H. Greenly, Hoboken, New Jersey. John M. Douglas, attorney for the Illinois Central, was attempting to make temporary settlement of a disputed claim for taxes due the state. Dubois was state auditor.

To William H. Davenport[1]

W. H. Davenport,   Springfield,
Dear Sir: Dec. 28. 1857

When I went to Danville in the fall I found that Don Carlos had not yet been served with process. I was greatly vexed, and made an affidavit to have a publication made for him, as one who was evading process. Before the end of the term Drake & Moses[2] (lawyers) concluded to, and did enter his appearance, upon which they were ruled to file answers by some day this winter. I think Jany. 1, but not quite certain. That was all I could do. When the answers shall be filed, I ought to have copies of them & I have not yet provided for getting them. Yours very truly   A. LINCOLN—

[1] ALS, owned by J. E. Davenport, South Pasadena, California. William H. Davenport *v.* Lafayette H. Sconce and William C. Don Carlos concerned a fraudulent land registration made by Don Carlos while a clerk in the Land Office at Danville, Illinois. All were residents of Danville.
[2] John V. Drake and John(?) Moses.

To Lyman Trumbull[1]

Hon. Lyman Trumbull,   Bloomington, Ill. Dec.—

Dear Sir: What does the New-York Tribune mean by it's constant eulogising, and admiring, and magnifying [of][2] Douglas? Does it, in this, speak the sentiments of the republicans at Washington? Have they concluded that the republican cause, generally, can be best promoted by sacraficing us here in Illinois? If so we would like to know it soon; it will save us a great deal of labor to surrender at once.

As yet I have heared of no republican here going over to Douglas; but if the Tribune continues to din his praises into the ears of it's five or ten thousand republican readers in Illinois, it is more than can be hoped that all will stand firm.

I am not complaining. I only wish a fair understanding. Please write me at Springfield. Your Obt. Servt.   A. LINCOLN—

[1] ALS, CSmH. See Lincoln to Trumbull, November 30, *supra,* note 3.
[2] Lincoln had written "of" but deleted it.

To Robert A. Kinzie[1]

Robert A. Kinzie, Esq   Springfield, Illinois,
Dear Sir: Jany. 5 1858.

I suppose you are aware that Johnson and Jones[2] are at law about a portion of the made land attached to your addition to Chicago & and [*sic*] on the North side of the Harbor. I have been engaged, as an attorney on Jones' side; and if you have no objection to do so, I shall be obliged if you will answer the following questions—

1. Could you now certainly designate the point where the North side of the North pier, and the Lake shore met, before the new land began to form?

2. How long was it after the pier had reached that point, and continued Eastward, into the Lake, before the made land had formed, and filled in Eastward, on the North side of the pier, as much as sixty feet?

3. Do you remember whether any new land had formed at the time you sold and gave a bond to Hubbard?[3] and if any had then formed, how much?

4. Do you remember whether any new land had formed at the time you deeded to Johnson & if any, how much?

5. At the time you laid out the addition, how far was it from where the South side of Water-Street struck the Lake Shore, down Southward along the Lake shore to where the East line of Lot 35 struck it?

I shall be greatly obliged, if you will answer these questions. Your friend   A. LINCOLN—

[1] ALS-P, ISLA. The famous but inaccurately named "Sandbar Case" for which Lincoln was preparing was Johnston v. Jones and Marsh, which had been in the courts since 1855 and which was not finally settled until April 4, 1860, when Lincoln and associated attorneys won a verdict in the U.S. Court for the defendants. The case involved land made by sand washed in by Lake Michigan along the north side of the North Pier, built by the U.S. Government in 1833 along a new channel entrance for the Chicago River into the lake. The most accurate brief discussion of the facts may be found in John M. Zane, "Lincoln, the Constitutional Lawyer," *Abraham Lincoln Association Papers* (1933), pp. 41-42, n. 18.

[2] William S. Johnston (Lincoln misspelled the name) and William Jones. Sylvester Marsh was also one of the defendants.

[3] Gurdon S. Hubbard, prominent Chicago businessman.

To Usher F. Linder and Henry P. H. Bromwell[1]

Messrs Linder & Bromwell   Springfield,
Gentlemen—   Jany. 13. 1858

Your letter & declaration received. I have just made some little corrections in the declaration and commenced the suit—to next June Term—it could not be earlier.

Herewith is a blank bond for cost which you will please sign and return. Sign your individual names. Need not fill up the bond, but understand that the clerk will do that. Yours truly

A. LINCOLN.

[1] ALS, DLC-Bromwell Papers. Linder and Bromwell were law partners at Charleston, Illinois. The case has not been identified.

To Joseph Gillespie[1]

Hon: Joseph Gillespie   Springfield,
My dear Sir: Jany. 19. 1858

   This morning Col. McClernand showed me a Petition for a man-
— damus[2] against the Secretary of State to compel him to certify the
apportionment act of last session; and he says it will be presented
to the Court to-morrow morning. We shall be allowed three or four
days to get up a return; and I, for one, want the benefit of consultation with you. Please come right up. Yours as ever

                                                       A. LINCOLN—

   [1] ALS, owned by Charles S. Gillespie, Edwardsville, Illinois. Lincoln apparently wrote Gillespie, Republican leader in the state senate, and fearing that the
letter might not be promptly delivered if Gillespie were away, then telegraphed
George T. Brown (*infra*) on the same day.
   [2] The mandamus case. People *ex rel.* Lanphier and Walker *v.* Hatch, involved
Governor Bissell's veto of the apportionment act passed by the last session of the
legislature which had gerrymandered the state to Republican disadvantage. Bissell had mistakenly signed the act and then awkwardly his hope in deference to
the protest from his party leaders in the legislature, after the signed act had been
returned to the secretary of state, Ozias M. Hatch. His veto message, under the
circumstances, was refused by the Democratic House, and upon adjournment the
Democrats carried the act up to the state Supreme Court by mandamus. On February 2, John A. McClernand argued the case for the Democrats; Lincoln and
Jackson Grimshaw appeared for Hatch. The court's decision upholding the governor's right to change his mind so long as the act was still in his control was
handed down on February 6. See Lincoln's letters to Gillespie and Koerner, February 7, 1858, *infra*.

To George T. Brown[1]

                                         Alton January 19th 1858
The following dispatch has just been received,
   Dated, Springfield 19th 1858
To Hon Geo T Brown
   Send Jo Gillespie up here at once. Don't fail   A LINCOLN

   [1] D, owned by Charles S. Gillespie, Edwardsville, Illinois. This is the copy
received at the Alton office of the Illinois and Mississippi Telegraph Company,
George T. Brown was publisher of the Alton *Courier*.

To Henry E. Dummer[1]

H. E. Dummer, Esq   Springfield,
My dear Sir   Feb. 7. 1858

   The Court *affirmed* our county-bond & Railroad case.[2] I presented your brief, but pointed a[r]gument to the court; to which
I subjoined as good a one of my own as I could; but, as it has resulted, all to no purpose. As yet no opinion is filed; so that we do

not know whether it is decided on the merits, or on some colateral point. Yours as ever   A. LINCOLN

1 ALS, owned by R. E. Burdick, New York City. The original has been "doctored" in the name "Dummer" to the extent of adding a *t* and a final *s*, making the name read "Duntmers."

2 In Sprague *v.* the Illinois River Railroad Company, Lincoln and Dummer appeared for the complainant in the Cass County Circuit Court on November 21, 1857. The court ordered the injunction in the case dissolved and the bill dismissed. On February 6, 1858, the Illinois Supreme Court affirmed the lower court.

To Joseph Gillespie[1]

Hon: J. Gillespie   Springfield,
My dear Sir   Feb. 7, 1858

Yesterday morning the Court overruled the Demurrer to Hatch's Return in the Mandamus case. McClernand was present, said nothing about pleading over; and so I suppose the matter is ended.

The court gave no reason for the decision; but Peck tells me confidentially, that they were unanamous in the opinion that even if the Govr. had signed the Bill purposely, he had the right to strike his name off so long as the bill remained in his custody & control Yours as ever   A. LINCOLN—

1 ALS, owned by Charles S. Gillespie, Edwardsville, Illinois. See Lincoln to Gillespie, January 19, *supra,* for circumstances and persons involved in this case.

To Gustave P. Koerner[1]

Hon: G. Koerner   Springfield,
My dear Sir: Feb. 7, 1857 [1858]

The Court, on yesterday, over-ruled, the Demurrer to Hatch's Return in the Mandamus case. They merely announced that they over-ruled the demurrer, stating no ground, or reason for doing so. Let this be confidential, but Peck told me that in the consultation room, they unanamously declared in his presence, that if the Gov. had signed the Bill purposely he had the right to change his mind and strike his name off, so long as the Bill remained in his control.

McClernand was present when the decision was announced, said nothing about pleading over; & I presume the matter is ended Yours as ever   A. LINCOLN

1 ALS, owned by William K. Koerner, St. Louis, Missouri. Lincoln's date, 1857, is an obvious error. See the preceding letters to Gillespie, January 19, and February 7, 1858, *supra.*

To Edward G. Miner[1]

Edward G. Miner, Esq.   Springfield,
My dear Sir: Feby. 19, 1858–
    Mr. G. A. Sutton[2] is an applicant for Superintendent of the ad-
dition to the Insane Asylum; and I understand it partly depends
on you whether he gets it. Mr. Sutton is my fellow-townsman, and
friend; and I therefore wish to say for him, that he is a man of
sterling integrity; and, as a master mechanic, or builder, not surpassed by any in our city, or any I have known anywhere, so far
as I can judge. I hope you will consider me as being really interested for Mr. Sutton, and not as writing this merely to relieve myself of importunity. Please show this to Col. Wm. Ross,[3] and let
him consider it as intended as much for him as yourself. Your
friend as ever   A. LINCOLN

    [1] ALS, owned by Edward G. Miner (grandson), Rochester, New York. Ed-
ward G. Miner was a Whig representative in the legislature from Scott County,
1846.
    [2] Goyn A. Sutton, architect and builder, and mayor of Springfield (1860).
    [3] William Ross of Pike County was a trustee of the Insane Asylum.

To Samuel C. Davis and Company[1]

Messrs S. C. Davis & Co.   Springfield, Ills. Feb. 23. 1858
    Yours of the 20th. received yesterday. We have just now paid
the costs in the cases as per statement sent you. It took $330.90 to
pay them. Currency answered the purpose. We used the $300 of
yours we had here on deposite—and we drew on you, in favor of
Mr. Ridgely[2] for the remaining $30.90.[3] The draft to Mr. Ridgely
on you is signed "A Lincoln" and not "Lincoln & Herndon.["]
This was done inadvertantly, and we mention it in order that you
may not misunderstand the draft when you see it.
    All this cost the defendants have, eventually, to pay. By the law
of the U. S. court, there is a docket fee of ten dollars in each such
case as these, taxed as costs, & when collected, paid to the plaintiff's
attorney. There being ten of these cases of yours, we, as your
attorneys, received one hundred dollars of this cost. You ultimately recover these docket fees back from the defendants, the same as
the other costs.
    We are in some perplexity about the collection of these debts.
The Marshal now has the executions and will soon call on the defendants. Any that may pay in money, or turn out sufficient of
personal property, will be easy cases; but in cases where real estate is turned out, we see no way to be safe, as to *titles* and *value*,

but to visit the several localities, and examine carefully. If, as with you in Missouri, third persons would buy real estate at execution sales, we might leave them to take care of themselves on *titles* and *values;* but here with us, under our redemption laws, third persons never bid & consequently plaintiffs have to buy in themselves & if not posted on *titles* & values, they get badly bit. The same is applicable to the foreclosure cases; and if you know any thing as to titles & values of the mortgaged premises in the cases of Thomas J. Kinney & Campbell & Hundl[e]y, we wish you would write us.

We have instructed the marshal to report to us accurately in all cases when he can find nothing but real estate. Yours very truly LINCOLN & HERNDON.

1 ALS, ORB. A note at the top of the letter reads as follows: "This letter is not to be published. W. H. Herndon." S. C. Davis and Company were wholesale merchants in St. Louis, Missouri. 2 Nicholas H. Ridgely.

3 Written over this figure in a different handwriting is the following notation: "Paid 24th."

Inscription in the Autograph Album
of Henry B. Rankin[1]

To-day, Feb. 23 1858, the owner honored me with the privilege of writing the first name in this book. A. LINCOLN—

1 ADS, owned by Mrs. Clayton Barber, Springfield, Illinois. Following Lincoln's inscription appears one by Herndon. Henry B. Rankin studied for a brief period in the Lincoln & Herndon office.

To Owen Lovejoy[1]

Hon: O. Lovejoy. Springfield,
Dear Sir March 8. 1858.

I have just returned from court in one of the counties of your District,[2] where I had an inside view that few will have who correspond with you; and I feel it rather a duty to say a word to you about it.

Your danger *has been* that democracy would wheedle some republican to run against you without a nomination, relying mainly on democratic votes. I have seen the strong men who could make the most trouble in that way, and find that they view the thing in the proper light, and will not consent to be so used. But they have been urgently tempted by the enemy; and I think it is still the point for you to guard most vigilantly. I think it is not expected that you can be beaten for a nomination; but do not let what I say, as to that, lull you.

Now, let this be strictly confidential; not that there is anything wrong in it; but that I have some highly valued friends who would not like me any the better for writing it. Yours very truly

A. LINCOLN

P.S. Be glad to hear from you.

1 ALS, CSmH.
2 Lincoln attended the DeWitt County Circuit Court from March 1 to March 6.

To Solon Cumins[1]

Solon Cumins, Esq   Chicago,
My dear Sir: March 11, 1858
    This morning the court decided our case *in our favor*. Very glad of it. Yours truly   A. LINCOLN—

1 ALS, ICHi. See Lincoln to Thomas J. Turner, February 8, 1850, *supra*. Although this case was in the U.S. courts from 1850 to 1858, there are no records of it except in Lincoln's correspondence.

To William H. Bissell[1]

His Excellency   Lincoln,
W. H. Bissell   March 22– 1858
    Dear Sir   Samuel Jones and James Jones, at court here last week, were found guilty of stealing five shoats, or small hogs. I have been appealed to, to say something in favor of their being pardoned. They are father and son. I know nothing to say, except that he is an old citizen (I mean the father) and his neighbors appear more anxious that he and his son should be pardoned, than I have known in any other case. This is really all [I] can say. I was not concerned in the trial; and consequently did not listen to the evidence. Your Obt. Servt.   A. LINCOLN—

1 ALS, I-Ar. Lincoln's letter is accompanied by letters from Judge David Davis before whom the case was tried, and Ward H. Lamon, state's attorney who prosecuted, and a petition signed by members of the bar—all unanimous in believing the pardon should be granted.

To Jonathan Haines[1]

Jonathan Haines, Esq   Springfield,
Dear Sir: March 27. 1858
    This morning, on coming home, I found your letter of the 22nd.
    As to Rugg,[2] I would do nothing now till the suit we have tried, is disposed of fully, or, at least, more fully than it is.

[436]

As to a suit against Many,[3] I really can not find time to prepare such a suit, until the Spring courts are over. Yours truly

A. LINCOLN—

[1] ALS, IHi.

[2] George H. Rugg. See letter of November 24, 1856, *supra*.

[3] Although the spelling is clearly "Many," Lincoln may refer to John H. Manny (see letter of July 23, 1855).

First Lecture on Discoveries and Inventions[1]

[April 6, 1858]

All creation is a mine, and every man, a miner.

The whole earth, and all *within* it, *upon* it, and *round about* it, including *himself*, in his physical, moral, and intellectual nature, and his susceptabilities, are the infinitely various "leads" from which, man, from the first, was to dig out his destiny.

In the beginning, the mine was unopened, and the miner stood *naked*, and *knowledgeless*, upon it.

Fishes, birds, beasts, and creeping things, are not miners, but *feeders* and *lodgers*, merely. Beavers build houses; but they build them in nowise differently, or better now, than they did, five thousand years ago. Ants, and honey-bees, provide food for winter; but just in the *same way* they did, when Solomon refered the sluggard to them as patterns of prudence.[2]

Man is not the only animal who labors; but he is the only one who *improves* his workmanship. This improvement, he effects by *Discoveries*, and *Inventions*. His first important discovery was the fact that he was naked; and his first invention was the fig-leaf-apron. This simple article—the apron—made of leaves, seems to have been the origin of *clothing*—the one thing for which nearly

[1] AD, owned by Bradford M. Melvin, San Francisco, California. In 1865, Dr. Samuel H. Melvin, at the time a resident of Springfield, received the manuscript along with the manuscript of the second lecture on the same subject (*vide infra*, February 11, 1859) from "aunt Lizzie" Grimsley (widow of Harrison J. Grimsley and daughter of Dr. John Todd), from the collection of papers which Lincoln had left with her before departing from Springfield in 1861. The manuscript of the second lecture was sold by Dr. Melvin to Charles Gunther,·Chicago, Illinois; the first was kept in his own possession. This first lecture was delivered at Bloomington before the Young Men's Association on April 6, 1858, and was reported in the Bloomington *Pantagraph*, April 9, 1858, sufficiently to establish the precedence of this version over that of the second lecture as revised and delivered on February 11, 1859.

[2] Lincoln deletes "examples," inserts "patterns," and deletes the following sentence which stood first in the next paragraph: "Beavers, and musk-rats, build houses, but they build no better ones *now*, than they did five thousand years ago. Ants, and honey-bees, lay up their winter stocks of provisions; but they do so, no wise better, or less laboriously, than they did at the dawn of creation."

half of the toil and care of the human race has ever since been expended. The most important improvement ever made in connection with clothing, was the invention of *spinning* and *weaving.* The spinning jenny, and power-loom, invented in modern times, though great *improvements,* do not, *as inventions,* rank with the ancient arts of spinning and weaving. Spinning and weaving brought into the department of clothing such abundance and variety of material. Wool, the hair of several species of animals, hemp, flax, cotten, silk, and perhaps other articles, were all suited to it, affording garments not only adapted to wet and dry, heat and cold, but also susceptible of high degrees of ornamental finish. Exactly *when,* or *where,* spinning and weaving originated is not known. At the first interview of the Almighty with Adam and Eve, after the fall, He made "coats of skins, and clothed them" Gen: 3-21.

The Bible makes no other alusion to clothing, *before* the flood. Soon *after* the deluge Noah's two sons covered him with a *garment;* but of what material the garment was made is not mentioned. Gen. 9-23.

Abraham mentions *"thread"* in such connection as to indicate that spinning and weaving were in use in his day—Gen. 14.23— and soon after, reference to the art is frequently made. *"Linen breeches,* ["] are mentioned,—Exod. 28.42—and it is said "all the women that were wise hearted, did *spin* with their hands" (35-25) and, "all the women whose hearts stirred them up in wisdom, *spun* goat's hair" (35-26). The work of the *"weaver"* is mentioned— (35-35). In the book of Job, a very old book, date not exactly known, the *"weavers shuttle"* is mentioned.

The above mention of *"thread"* by Abraham is the oldest recorded alusion to spinning and weaving; and *it* was made about two thousand years after the creation of man, and now, near four thousand years ago. Profane authors think these arts originated in Egypt; and this is not contradicted, or made improbable, by any thing in the Bible; for the alusion of Abraham, mentioned, was not made until after he had sojourned in Egypt.

The discovery of the properties of *iron,* and the making of *iron tools,* must have been among the earliest of important discoveries and inventions. We can scarcely conceive the possibility of making much of anything else, without the use of iron tools. Indeed, an iron *hammer* must have been very much needed to make the *first* iron hammer with. A *stone* probably served as a substitute. How could the *"gopher wood"* for the Ark, have been gotten out without an axe? It seems to me an axe, or a miracle, was indispensable. Corresponding with the prime necessity for iron, we find at least one very early notice of it. Tubal-cain was "an instructer of every artificer in *brass* and *iron*["]—Gen: 4-22. Tubal-cain was the seventh in decent from Adam; and his birth was about one thousand years before the flood. *After* the flood, frequent mention is made of *iron,* and *instruments* made of iron. Thus "instrument of iron" at Num: 35-16; "bed-stead of iron" at Deut. 3-11—; "the iron furnace ["] at 4-20— and "iron tool" at 27-5. At 19-5— very distinct mention of "the ax to cut down the tree" is made; and also at 8-9, the promised land is described as "a land whose stones are iron, and out of whose hills thou mayest dig brass." From the somewhat frequent mention of brass in connection with iron, it is not improbable that brass—perhaps what we now call copper—was used by the ancients for some of the same purposes as iron.

Transportation—the removal of person, and goods—from place to place—would be an early *object,* if not a *necessity,* with man. By his natural powers of locomotion, and without much assistance from Discovery and invention, he could move himself about with considerable facility, and even, could carry small burthens with him. But very soon he would wish to lessen the labor, while he might, at the same time, extend, and expedite the business. For this object, wheel-carriages, and water-crafts—wagons and boats—are the most important inventions. The use of the wheel & axle, has been so long known, that it is difficult, without reflection, to estimate it at it's true value.[3]

The oldest recorded allusion to the wheel and axle is the mention of a "chariot" Gen: 41-43. This was in Egypt, upon the occasion of Joseph being made Governor by Pharaoh. It was about twentyfive hundred years after the creation of Adam. That the chariot then mentioned was a wheel-carriage drawn by animals, is sufficiently evidenced by the mention of chariot-*wheels,* at Exod. 14-25, and the mention of chariots in connection with *horses,* in the same chapter, verses 9 & 23. So much, at present, for land-transportation.

Now, as to transportation by *water,* I have concluded, without sufficient authority perhaps, to use the term "boat" as a general

[3] The following passage has been deleted by Lincoln at this point: "But let us immagine, for a moment, that all the wheels are locked forever; and we shall at once conclude that the world is num[b]ed. A common jumper, made of hickory poles, with fifty cents worth of labor, would then be worth more than the President's carriage, and even the largest train of Railroad cars in existence. Indeed the Railroad itself would be utterly worthless. That wagon load of wheat which was to have gone to the river to-morrow, can not go; and the barrel of salt which was to have been brought by the return trip, can not come. Aunt Lizzie's pleasure trip to New-York, Boston, and Niagara Falls, is entirely '*done for*[.]' More particular alusion will hereafter be made to the wheel & axle."

name for all water-craft. The boat is indispensable to navigation. It is not probable that the philosophical principle upon which the use of the boat primarily depends—towit, the *principle*, that any thing will float, which can not sink without displacing more than it's own *weight* of water—was known, or even thought of, before the first boats were made. The sight of a crow standing on a piece of drift-wood floating down the swolen current of a creek or river, might well enough suggest the specific idea to a savage, that he could himself get upon a log, or on two logs tied together, and somehow work his way to the opposite shore of the same stream. Such a suggestion, so taken, would be the birth of navigation; and such, not improbably, it really was. The leading idea was thus caught; and whatever came afterwards, were but improvements upon, and auxiliaries to, it.

As man is a land animal, it might be expected he would learn to travel by land somewhat earlier than he would by water. Still the crossing of streams, somewhat less deep for wading, would be an early necessity with him. If we pass by the Ark, which may be regarded as belonging rather to the *miraculous*, than to *human* invention, the first notice we have of water-craft, is the mention of "ships" by Jacob—Gen: 49-13. It is not till we reach the book of Isaiah that we meet with the mention of "oars" and "sails."

As mans *food*—his first necessity—was to be derived from the vegitation of the earth, it was natural that his first care should be directed to the assistance of that vegitation. And accordingly we find that, even before the fall, the man was put into the garden of Eden "to dress it, and to keep it." And when afterwards, in consequence of the first transgression, *labor* was imposed on the race, as a *penalty*—a *curse*—we find the first born man—the first heir of the curse—was "a tiller of the ground." This was the beginning of agriculture; and although, both in point of time, and of importance, it stands at the head of all branches of human industry, it has derived less direct advantage from Discovery and Invention, than almost any other. The plow, of very early origin; and reaping, and threshing, machines, of modern invention are, at this day, the principle improvements in agriculture. And even the oldest of these, the plow, could not have been conceived of, until a precedent conception had been caught, and put into practice—I mean the conception, or idea, of substituting other forces in nature, for man's own muscular power. These other forces, as now used, are principally, the *strength* of animals, and the *power* of the wind, of running streams, and of steam.

Climbing upon the back of an animal, and making it carry us, might not, occur very readily. I think the back of the camel would never have suggested it. It was, however, a matter of vast importance.

The earliest instance of it mentioned, is when "Abraham rose up early in the morning, and saddled his ass,["] Gen. 22-3 preparatory to sacraficing Isaac as a burnt-offering; but the allusion to the *saddle* indicates that riding had been in use some time; for it is quite probable they rode bare-backed awhile, at least, before they invented saddles.

The *idea*, being once conceived, of riding *one* species of animals, would soon be extended to others. Accordingly we find that when the servant of Abraham went in search of a wife for Isaac, he took ten *camels* with him; and, on his return trip, "Rebekah arose, and her damsels, and they rode upon the camels, and followed the man" Gen 24-61[.]

The *horse*, too, as a riding animal, is mentioned early. The Red-sea being safely passed, Moses and the children of Israel sang to the Lord "the *horse*, and his *rider* hath he thrown into the sea." Exo. 15-1.

Seeing that animals could bear *man* upon their backs, it would soon occur that they could also bear other burthens. Accordingly we find that Joseph's bretheren, on their first visit to Egypt, "laded their asses with the corn, and departed thence" Gen. 42-26.

Also it would occur that animals could be made to *draw* burthens *after* them, as well as to bear them upon their backs; and hence plows and chariots came into use early enough to be often mentioned in the books of Moses—Deut. 22-10. Gen. 41-43. Gen. 46-29. Exo. 14-25[.]

Of all the forces of nature, I should think the *wind* contains the largest amount of *motive power*—that is, power to move things. Take any given space of the earth's surface—for instance, Illinois —; and all the power exerted by all the men, and beasts, and running-water, and steam, over and upon it, shall not equal the one hundredth part of what is exerted by the blowing of the wind over and upon the same space. And yet it has not, so far in the world's history, become proportionably *valuable* as a motive power. It is applied extensively, and advantageously, to sail-vessels in navigation. Add to this a few wind-mills, and pumps, and you have about all. That, as yet, no very successful mode of *controlling*, and *directing* the wind, has been discovered; and that, naturally, it moves by fits and starts—now so gently as to scarcely stir a leaf, and now so roughly as to level a forest—doubtless have been the insurmountable difficulties. As yet, the wind is an *untamed*, and *unharnessed* force; and quite possibly one of the greatest discoveries hereafter to be made, will be the taming, and harnessing of the wind. That the difficulties of controlling this power are very great is quite evident by the fact that they have already been perceived, and struggled with more than three thousand years; for that power was applied to sail-vessels, at least as early as the time of the prophet Isaiah.

In speaking of *running streams,* as a motive power, I mean it's application to mills and other machinery by means of the *"water wheel"*—a thing now well known, and extensively used; but, of which, no mention is made in the bible, though it is thought to have been in use among the romans—(Am. Ency. tit—Mill) [.] The language of the Saviour "Two women shall be grinding at the mill &c" indicates that, even in the populous city of Jerusalem, at that day, mills were operated by hand—having, as yet had no other than human power applied to them.

The advantageous use of *steam power* is, unquestionably, a modern discovery.

And yet, as much as two thousand years ago the power of steam was not only observed, but an ingenius toy was actually made and put in motion by it, at Alexandria in Egypt.

What appears strange is, that neither the inventor of the toy, nor any one else, for so long a time afterwards, should perceive that steam would move *useful* machinery as well as a toy.[4]

[4] The manuscript ends abruptly at the top of a page. Probably there was more to the lecture which Lincoln utilized in his revised version (*q.v.*, February 11, 1859, *infra*).

Endorsement: J. S. Copes to Lincoln[1]

[c. April 8, 1858]

See Jesse A. Pickrell about this letter.

[1] AE, DLC-RTL. Written on the envelope containing Copes' letter written from New Orleans, Louisiana, April 8, 1858, the endorsement has been added to by another hand, "I must" written above and "that is so" written below. Copes inquired about a tract of land in Sangamon County. Jesse A. Pickrell was a farmer living in the vicinity of the land in question.

Endorsement: Petition to William H. Bissell for Pardon of David Thompson[1]

April 12, 1858

I was appointed by the court to defend in part the above named David Thompson. I thought at the time his conviction was wrong, and I am now clearly of opinion he ought to be pardoned. I have recently been at Woodford; and the universal sentiment there seems to be in favor of his pardon. April 12, 1858.   A. LINCOLN

1 AES, I-Ar. David Thompson was a resident of Woodford County, Illinois.

To Thomas A. Marshall[1]

Hon: T. A. Marshall   Urbana, Ills.
Charleston, Ills.   April 23. 1858

My dear Sir   I wish you, G. W. Rives of Edgar, and O. L. Davis, of Vermilion, to co-operate in getting a Senatorial candidate on the track, in your District.[2] Davis is here, and agrees to do his part. The adversary has his eye upon that district, and will beat us, unless we also are wide awake. Under the circumstances, a District convention *may*, or may *not* be the best way—you three to judge of that. I think you better take some good reliable Fillmore men into conference with you, and also some proper person or persons from Cumberland. Indeed, it may appear expedient to select a Fillmore man as the candidate. I also write to Rives. I am most anxious to know that you will not neglect the matter, not doubting that you will do it rightly, if you only take hold of it.

I was in Springfield during the sittings of the two democratic conventions day-before-yesterday. Say what they will, they are having an abundance of trouble. Our own friends were also there, in considerable numbers from different parts of the State. They are all in high spirits, and think, if we do not win, it will be our own fault. So I really think. Your friend as ever,   A. LINCOLN

1 ALS, DLC. Thomas A. Marshall was a prominent Coles County Republican.
2 George W. Rives, state representative from Edgar County, 1849-1850, and Oliver L. Davis, state representative from Vermilion County, 1851-1852 and 1857-1858, were both possible candidates. On the same date Lincoln wrote to Rives. Rives' reply of May 15, 1858 (DLC-RTL), specified that Davis was the strongest candidate and that the principal objection to Marshall was the fact that he was a banker. Marshall became the candidate, however, and was elected.

To Elihu B. Washburne[1]

Hon. E. B. Washburne,   Urbana, Ills.
My dear Sir: April 26. 1858.

I am rather a poor correspondent, but I think perhaps I ought to write you a letter just now. I am here at this time; but I was at home during the sitting of the two democratic conventions.[2] The day before the[3] conventions I received a letter from Chicago having, among other things, on other subjects, the following in it:

"A reliable republican, but an old line whig lawyer, in this city told me to-day that *he himself had seen* a letter from one of our republican congressmen, advising us all to go for the re-election of

Judge Douglass. He said he was injoined to keep the author a secret & he was going to do so. From him I learnt that he was not an old line democrat, or abolitionist. This narrows the contest down to the congressmen from the Galena and Fulton Dists."

The above is a litteral copy of all the letter contained on that subject. The morning of the conventions Mr. Herndon showed me your letter of the 15th. to him, which convinced me that the story in the letter from Chicago was based upon some mistake, misconstruction of language, or the like. Several of our friends were down from Chicago, and they had something of the same story amongst them, some half suspecting that you were inclined to favor Douglas, and others thinking there was an effort to wrong you.

I thought neither was exactly the case; that the whole had originated in some misconstruction, coupled with a high degree of sensitiveness on the point, and that the whole matter was not worth another moment's consideration.

Such is my opinion now, and I hope you will have no concern about it. I have written this because Charley Wilson[4] told me he was writing you, and because I expect Dr. Ray,[5] (who was a little excited about the matter) has also written you; and because I think, I perhaps, have taken a calmer view of the thing than they may have done. I am satisfied you have done no wrong, and nobody has intended any wrong to you.

A word about the conventions. The democracy parted in not a very encouraged state of mind.

On the contrary, our friends, a good many of whom were present, parted in high spirits. They think if we do not triumph the fault will be our own, and so I really think. Your friend as ever

A LINCOLN

[1] ALS, IHi.
[2] Both the Douglas Democrats and the Buchanan Democrats held conventions at Springfield on April 21.
[3] Lincoln wrote "the." Another hand has changed the word to "these."
[4] Charles L. Wilson, publisher of the Chicago *Daily Journal.*
[5] Charles H. Ray, editor of the Chicago *Tribune* and Republican state chairman, wrote to Washburne, May 2, 1858, explaining that the trouble came out of Wilson's showing a letter of Washburne's to Samuel L. Baker of Chicago, ". . . a d——d stupid ass, who went to Wentworth who then wrote to Lincoln." (DLC-Washburne Papers)

Endorsement: Julius Lehmann to Lincoln[1]

[c. May 4, 1858]

Mark me down on your side.   A. LINCOLN

[1] AES, IHi. Dr. Julius Lehmann of Bloomington, Illinois, wrote May 4, 1858, to engage Lincoln in the case of Julius Lehmann *v.* Herman Schroeder. Lehmann got judgment in the amount of $5,000, January 8, 1859.

Endorsement: Jonathan K. Cooper to Lincoln[1]

[c. May 7, 1858]

I do not know Mr. Phelps; but I do know Mr. Cooper to be a
good and true man.   A. LINCOLN

[1] AES, DLC-RTL. Jonathan K. Cooper of Peoria wrote Lincoln on May 7,
1858, asking his influence with Governor William H. Bissell to obtain for George
Phelps of Lewistown, Illinois, appointment to the post of prosecuting attorney,
recently vacated by resignation of John S. Bailey of McDonough County.

To Josiah M. Lucas[1]

Springfield, May 10, 1858.

My Dear Sir: Your long and kind letter was received to-day. It
came upon me as an agreeable old acquaintance. Politically speaking, there is a curious state of things here. The impulse of almost
every Democrat is to stick to Douglas; but it horrifies them to have
to follow him out of the Democratic party. A good many are annoyed that he did not go for the English contrivance,[2] and thus
heal the breach. They begin to think there is a "negro in the
fence,"—that Douglas really wants to have a fuss with the President;—that sticks in their throats. Yours truly,   A. LINCOLN.

[1] NH, II, 358. Josiah M. Lucas had written from Washington where he held
a federal job dating from Lincoln's term in congress. See earlier letters to Lucas.

[2] William H. English, representative from Indiana, who had offered the "English Bill" providing for the admission of Kansas under the Lecompton Constitution after acceptance by plebiscite of the citizens of the territory. The bill
became law, but the Kansas voters rejected the proposal in August, 1858.

To Elihu B. Washburne[1]

Hon. E. B. Washburne   Springfield, Ills.,
My dear Sir: May 10, 1858

I have just reached home from the circuit, and found your letter
of the 2nd. and for which I thank you. My other letter to you was
meant for nothing but to hedge against bad feeling being gotten up,
between those who ought to be friends, out of the incident mentioned in that letter. I sent you an extract from the Chicago letter
in order to let you see that the writer did not profess to know anything himself; and I now add, that his informant told me that he
did tell him exactly what he wrote me—at least I distinctly so understood him. The informant[2] is an exceedingly clever fellow; and
I think he, having had a hasty glance at your letter to Charley Wilson, misconstrued it, and consequently, misreported it to the writer
of the letter to me. I must repeat that I think the thing did not originate in malice to you, or to any one; and that the best way all

round is to now forget it entirely. Will you not adjourn in time to be here at our State convention in June? Your friend as ever

A. LINCOLN

¹ ALS, Hill School, Pottstown, Pennsylvania.
² See Lincoln to Washburne, April 26, *supra*, and note.

To Joseph Means¹

Joseph Means   Springfield,
Dear Sir   May 11. 1858

The statements made within, if true are evidence of *fraud* on the part of the executor in selling the land. Fraud by the principles of law, invalidates everything. To get rid of this sale, a bill in chancery is to be filed, charging the fraud, and then, if the fraud can be *proved*, the sale will be set aside. This is all that can be said. Any lawyer will know how—to do it. Yours &c   A. LINCOLN

¹ ALS-F, ISLA. Joseph Means was a farmer near Eureka, Illinois, who had written Lincoln about some property that had belonged to his widowed daughter.

To Jediah F. Alexander¹

J. F. Alexander, Esq   Springfield,
Greenville, Ills.   May 15. 1858

My dear Sir   I reached home a week ago and found yours of the 1st. inviting me to name a time to meet and address a political meeting in Bond county. It is too early, considering that when I once begin making political speeches I shall have no respite till November. The *labor* of that I might endure, but I really can not spare the time from my business.

Nearer the time I will try to meet the people of Bond, if they desire.

I will only say now that, as I understand, there remains all the difference there ever was between Judge Douglas & the Republicans—*they* insisting that Congress *shall*, and *he* insisting that congress *shall not*, keep slavery out of the Teritories *before* & *up to the time* they form State constitutions. No republican has ever contended that, *when* a constitution is to be formed, any but the *people* of the teritory shall form it. Republican's have never contended that congress should *dictate* a constitution to any state or teritory; but they have contended that the people should be *perfectly* free to form their constitution in their own way—as *perfectly* free from the *presence* of *slavery* amongst them, as from every other improper influence.

In voting together in opposition to a constitution being forced upon the people of Kansas, neither Judge Douglas nor the Republicans, has conceded anything which was ever in dispute between them. Yours very truly   A. LINCOLN

¹ ALS, owned by Mrs. Paul F. Alexander, New Rochelle, New York. Jediah F. Alexander was founder and editor of the Greenville *Advocate* at Greenville, Illinois.

To Elihu B. Washburne[1]

Hon. E. B. Washburne   Springfield,
My dear Sir   May 15. 1858.

Yours of the 6th. accompanied by yours of April 12th. to C. L. Wilson was received day-before-yesterday.

There certainly is nothing in the letter to Wilson, which I, in particular, or republicans in general, could complain of. Of that, I was quite satisfied before I saw the letter. I believe there has been no malicious intent to misrepresent you; I hope there is no longer any misunderstanding, and that the matter may drop.

Eight or ten days ago I wrote Kellogg from Beardstown. Get him to show you the letter. It gave my view of the *field*, as it appeared then. Nothing has occurred since, except that it grows more, and more quiet since the passage of the English contrivance.

The State Register, here, is evidently laboring to bring it's old friends into what the doctors call the *"comatose state"*—that is, a sort of drowsy, dreamy condition, in which they may not perceive or remember that there has ever been, or is, any difference between Douglas & the President. This could be done, *if* the Buchanan men would allow it—which, however, the latter seem determined not to do.

I think our prospects gradually, and steadily, grow better; though we are not yet clear out of the woods by a great deal. There is still some effort to make trouble out of "Americanism." If that were out of the way, for all the rest, I believe we should be "out of the woods." Yours very truly   A. LINCOLN

¹ ALS, IHi.

Speech at Edwardsville, Illinois[1]

May 18, 1858

The speeches of Hon. A. LINCOLN, Hon. JOHN M. PALMER, Col. DELAHAY² and Hon. J. GILLESPIE were both able and eloquent, and listened to with an attention seldom witnessed. The present position and prospects of the Republican party were truthfully set forth, and although no two of the speakers perfectly agreed upon the details of political action, all were unanimous in declaring their opposition to the fraudulent attempts of the administration and the slave power to force institutions upon a free people against their consent.

¹ Alton *Weekly Courier*, May 20, 1858. Lincoln spoke at a Madison County Republican meeting.   ² Mark W. Delahay.

Fragment of a Speech[1]

[c. May 18, 1858]

From time to time, ever since the Chicago "Times" and "Illinois State Register" declared their opposition to the Lecompton constitution,[2] and it began to be understood that Judge Douglas was also opposed to it, I have been accosted by friends of his with the question, "What do you think now?" Since the delivery of his speech in the Senate,[3] the question has been varied a little. "Have you read Douglas's speech?" "Yes." "Well, what do you think of it?" In every instance the question is accompanied with an anxious inquiring stare, which asks, quite as plainly as words could, "Can't you go for Douglas now?" Like boys who have set a bird-trap, they are watching to see if the birds are picking at the bait and likely to go under.

I think, then, Judge Douglas knows that the Republicans wish Kansas to be a free State. He knows that they know, if the question be fairly submitted to a vote of the people of Kansas, it will be a free State; and he would not object at all if, by drawing their attention to this particular fact, and himself becoming vociferous for such fair vote, they should be induced to drop their own organization, fall into rank behind him, and form a great free-State Democratic party.

But before Republicans do this, I think they ought to require a few questions to be answered on the other side. If they so fall in with Judge Douglas, and Kansas shall be secured as a free State, there then remaining no cause of difference between him and the regular Democracy, will not the Republicans stand ready, haltered and harnessed, to be handed over by him to the regular Democracy,

[1] NH, IV, 225-36, and AD, NNP. Nicolay and Hay entitle this "Fragment: Notes for Speeches [October 1, 1858?]." The date is demonstrably several months too late by the references in the context. Obviously the piece was written prior to the House Divided Speech of June 16, 1858. The fact that Lincoln prepared and delivered a speech to the Republican County Convention at Edwardsville, Illinois, on May 18, 1858, suggests that this fragment may represent his survey of Republican political policy at that meeting, of which only a scanty newspaper report has been found (*infra*). It is possible, however, that the fragment was written several weeks earlier. It seems reasonably certain that the key reference and much of the argument in the identical language of the House Divided Speech was derived from this earlier speech fragment, or that the fragment was in part actually a preliminary draft of that speech. Although only one page representing the last two paragraphs of the manuscript has been located, Nicolay and Hay presumably had access to the document intact for the *Complete Works*.

[2] Both papers came out against the Lecompton Constitution in November, 1857.

[3] Douglas spoke in the Senate on December 9, 1857, the day following President Buchanan's message commending the Lecompton Constitution.

to filibuster indefinitely for additional slave territory,—to carry slavery into all the States, as well as Territories, under the Dred Scott decision, construed and enlarged from time to time, according to the demands of the regular slave Democracy,—and to assist in reviving the African slave-trade in order that all may buy negroes where they can be bought cheapest, as a clear incident of that "sacred right of property," now held in some quarters to be above all constitutions?

By so falling in, will we not be committed to or at least compromitted with, the Nebraska policy?

If so, we should remember that Kansas is saved, not by that policy or its authors, but in spite of both—by an effort that cannot be kept up in future cases.

Did Judge Douglas help any to get a free-State majority into Kansas? Not a bit of it—the exact contrary. Does he now express any wish that Kansas, or any other place, shall be free? Nothing like it. He tells us, in this very speech, expected to be so palatable to Republicans, that he cares not whether slavery is voted down or voted up.[4] His whole effort is devoted to clearing the ring, and giving slavery and freedom a fair fight. With one who considers slavery just as good as freedom, this is perfectly natural and consistent.

But have Republicans any sympathy with such a view? They think slavery is wrong; and that, like every other wrong which some men will commit if left alone, it ought to be prohibited by law. They consider it not only morally wrong, but a "deadly poison" in a government like ours, professedly based on the equality of men. Upon this radical difference of opinion with Judge Douglas, the Republican party was organized. There is all the difference between him and them now that there ever was. He will not say that he has changed; have you?

Again, we ought to be informed as to Judge Douglas's present opinion as to the inclination of Republicans to marry with negroes. By his Springfield speech we know what it was last June;[5] and by his resolution dropped at Jacksonville in September we know what it was then.[6] Perhaps we have something even later in a Chicago

4 In Douglas' speech of December 9, 1857.

5 Douglas' speech on June 12, 1857, which Lincoln answered on June 26, 1857, *supra*.

6 Douglas was reported in the Morgan *Journal* to have accidentally "dropped" at the railway station at Jacksonville, during his visit of September 9, a resolution intended for adoption by Democratic meetings in endorsement of the Dred Scott decision and in opposition to "Negro equality." The Democratic Jacksonville *Sentinel* (September 25) denounced the resolution as a hoax perpetrated by the *Journal*, but when the Morgan County Democratic Convention met, it

speech, in which the danger of being "stunk out of church" was descanted upon.[7] But what is his opinion on the point now? There is, or will be, a sure sign to judge by. If this charge shall be silently dropped by the judge and his friends, if no more resolutions on the subject shall be passed in Douglas Democratic meetings and conventions, it will be safe to swear that he is courting. Our "witching smile" has "caught his youthful fancy"; and henceforth Cuffy and he are rival beaux for our gushing affections.

We also ought to insist on knowing what the judge now thinks on "Sectionalism." Last year he thought it was a "clincher" against us on the question of Sectionalism, that we could get no support in the slave States, and could not be allowed to speak, or even breathe, south of the Ohio River.

In vain did we appeal to the justice of our principles. He would have it that the treatment we received was conclusive evidence that we deserved it. He and his friends would bring speakers from the slave States to their meetings and conventions in the free States, and parade about, arm in arm with them, breathing in every gesture and tone, "How we national apples do swim!" Let him cast about for this particular evidence of his own nationality now, Why, just now, he and Frémont would make the closest race imaginable in the Southern States.

In the present aspect of affairs what ought the Republicans to do? I think they ought not to oppose any measure merely because Judge Douglas proposes it. Whether the Lecompton constitution should be accepted or rejected is a question upon which, in the minds of men not committed to any of its antecedents, and controlled only by the Federal Constitution, by republican principles, and by a sound morality, it seems to me there could not be two opinions. It should be throttled and killed as hastily and as heartily as a rabid dog. What those should do who are committed to all its

---

adopted the resolution on October 10, as follows: "Whereas certain black Republican papers of this State have published a resolution, said to have been written by Hon. S. A. Douglas . . . we adopt the resolution . . . to-wit: Resolved, That we approve of the decision of the Supreme Court of the United States, in determining that negroes are not citizens, and are utterly opposed to placing negroes on an equality with white men, by allowing them to vote and hold office, and serve on juries, and testify in the courts against white men, *and marry white women*, as advocated by those who claim that the declaration of Independence asserts that white men and negroes were created equal by the Almighty. . . ." (Jacksonville *Sentinel*, October 16, 1857).

[7] Speaking at the dedication of a new Democratic Hall at Chicago, November 11, 1857, Douglas was reported as lamenting that "Black Republicans . . . will allow the blacks to push us from our sidewalk (Oh!) and elbow us out of car seats (Oh? Oh!) *and stink us out of our places of worship.* . . ." (Chicago *Daily Democratic Press*, November 12, 1857).

antecedents is their business, not ours. If, therefore, Judge Douglas's bill[8] secures a fair vote to the people of Kansas, without contrivance to commit any one farther, I think Republican members of Congress ought to support it. They can do so without any inconsistency. They believe Congress ought to prohibit slavery wherever it can be done without violation of the Constitution or of good faith. And having seen the noses counted, and actually knowing that a majority of the people of Kansas are against slavery, passing an act to secure them a fair vote is little else than prohibiting slavery in Kansas by act of Congress.

Congress cannot dictate a constitution to a new State. All it can do at that point is to secure the people a fair chance to form one for themselves, and then to accept or reject it when they ask admission into the Union. As I understand, Republicans claim no more than this. But they do claim that Congress can and ought to keep slavery out of a Territory, up to the time of its people forming a State constitution; and they should now be careful to not stultify themselves to any extent on that point.

I am glad Judge Douglas has, at last, distinctly told us that he cares not whether slavery be voted down or voted up. Not so much that this is any news to me; nor yet that it may be slightly new to some of that class of his friends who delight to say that they "are as much opposed to slavery as anybody."

I am glad because it affords such a true and excellent definition of the Nebraska policy itself. That policy, honestly administered, is exactly that. It seeks to bring the people of the nation to not care anything about slavery. This is Nebraskaism in its abstract purity —in its very best dress.

Now, I take it, nearly everybody does care something about slavery—is either for it or against it; and that the statesmanship of a measure which conforms to the sentiments of nobody might well be doubted in advance.

But Nebraskaism did not originate as a piece of statesmanship. General Cass, in 1848, invented it, as a political manoeuver, to secure himself the Democratic nomination for the presidency. It served its purpose then, and sunk out of sight. Six years later Judge Douglas fished it up, and glozed it over with what he called, and still persists in calling, "sacred rights of self-government."

Well, I, too, believe in self-government as I understand it; but I do not understand that the privilege one man takes of making a

---

[8] Douglas' bill to authorize the people of Kansas to form a constitution was reported December 18, 1857. Referred to the Committee on Territories, it was dropped in favor of the Administration bill, and later the English bill.

slave of another, or holding him as such, is any part of "self-government." To call it so is, to my mind, simply absurd and ridiculous. I am for the people of the whole nation doing just as they please in all matters which concern the whole nation; for those of each part doing just as they choose in all matters which concern no other part; and for each individual doing just as he chooses in all matters which concern nobody else. This is the principle. Of course I am content with any exception which the Constitution, or the actually existing state of things, makes a necessity. But neither the principle nor the exception will admit the indefinite spread and perpetuity of human slavery.

I think the true magnitude of the slavery element in this nation is scarcely appreciated by any one. Four years ago the Nebraska policy was adopted, professedly, to drive the agitation of the subject into the Territories, and out of every other place, and especially out of Congress.

When Mr. Buchanan accepted the presidential nomination, he felicitated himself with the belief that the whole thing would be quieted and forgotten in about six weeks. In his inaugural, and in his Silliman letter, at their respective dates, he was just not quite in reach of the same happy consummation. And now, in his first annual message, he urges the acceptance of the Lecompton constitution (not quite satisfactory to him) on the sole ground of getting this little unimportant matter out of the way.

Meanwhile, in those four years, there has really been more angry agitation of this subject, both in and out of Congress, than ever before. And just now it is perplexing the mighty ones as no subject ever did before. Nor is it confined to politics alone. Presbyterian assemblies, Methodist conferences, Unitarian gatherings, and single churches to an indefinite extent, are wrangling, and cracking, and going to pieces on the same question. Why, Kansas is neither the whole nor a tithe of the real question.

A house divided against itself cannot stand.

I believe the government cannot endure permanently half slave and half free. I expressed this belief a year ago;[9] and subsequent developments have but confirmed me. I do not expect the Union to be dissolved. I do not expect the house to fall; but I do expect it will cease to be divided. It will become all one thing or all the

[9] No speech or letter of 1857 records the specific language. Probably Lincoln expressed the belief numerous times after the Dred Scott Decision was announced. The belief is implicit in his speech at Springfield on June 26, 1857, *supra.*

other. Either the opponents of slavery will arrest the further spread of it, and put it in course of ultimate extinction; or its advocates will push it forward till it shall become alike lawful in all the States, old as well as new. Do you doubt it? Study the Dred Scott decision, and then see how little even now remains to be done. That decision may be reduced to three points.

The first is that a negro cannot be a citizen. That point is made in order to deprive the negro, in every possible event, of the benefit of that provision of the United States Constitution which declares that "the citizens of each State shall be entitled to all privileges and immunities of citizens in the several States."

The second point is that the United States Constitution protects slavery, as property, in all the United States territories, and that neither Congress, nor the people of the Territories, nor any other power, can prohibit it at any time prior to the formation of State constitutions.

This point is made in order that the Territories may safely be filled up with slaves, before the formation of State constitutions, thereby to embarrass the free-State sentiment, and enhance the chances of slave constitutions being adopted.

The third point decided is that the voluntary bringing of Dred Scott into Illinois by his master, and holding him here a long time as a slave, did not operate his emancipation—did not make him free.

This point is made, not to be pressed immediately; but if acquiesced in for a while, then to sustain the logical conclusion that what Dred Scott's master might lawfully do with Dred in the free State of Illinois, every other master may lawfully do with any other one or one hundred slaves in Illinois, or in any other free State. Auxiliary to all this, and working hand in hand with it, the Nebraska doctrine is to educate and mold public opinion to "not care whether slavery is voted up or voted down." At least Northern public opinion must cease to care anything about it. Southern public opinion may, without offense, continue to care as much as it pleases.

Welcome,[10] or unwelcome, agreeable, or disagreeable, whether this shall be an entire slave nation, *is* the issue before us. Every incident—every little shifting of scenes or of actors—only clears away the intervening trash, compacts and consolidates the opposing hosts, and brings them more and more distinctly face to face.

[10] The last two paragraphs have been edited from the single page of manuscript in the Pierpont Morgan Library. See further discussion of the two pages of another fragment (c. August 21, 1858, *infra*) associated with this page.

The conflict will be a severe one; and it will be fought through by those who *do* care for the result, and not by those who do not care—by those who are *for*, and those who are against a legalized national slavery. The combined charge of Nebraskaism, and Dred Scottism must be repulsed, and rolled back. The deceitful cloak of "self-government" wherewith "the sum of all villanies" seeks to protect and adorn itself, must be torn from it's hateful carcass. That burlesque upon judicial decisions, and slander and profanation upon the honored names, and sacred history of republican America, must be overruled, and expunged from the books of authority.

To give the victory to the right, not *bloody bullets,* but *peaceful ballots* only, are necessary. Thanks to our good old constitution, and organization under it, these alone are necessary. It only needs that every right thinking man, shall go to the polls, and without fear or prejudice, *vote* as he *thinks.*

Opinion Written for William B. Warren[1]

May 20, 1858

Understanding that Col. W. B. Warren, being owner in fee of the land described in the attached bond, contracted to sell it as per said bond; that under said contract Bennett[2] took possession, and made some improvements, including some plank fencing; that afterwards Bennet abandoned his contract, left the possession, and surrendered said bond to said Warren; and that some person or persons claiming that said Bennett was his or their debtor, knocked the planks of the fences off the posts [and] carried the planks away.

I think Warren can maintain trespass against such persons; or Replevin for the planks themselves if they can be found and identified.   A. LINCOLN

Springfield, May 20. 1858

[1] ADS, owned by Miss Virginia W. Baird, San Diego, California.
[2] Unidentified.

To William H. Davenport[1]

W. H. Davenport, Esq.   Springfield,
Dear Sir   May 22. 1858

Yours of the 14th. is just received. In your case at Danville, I got just so far, and no farther, than to be ready to take testimony for the next term. I guess we will have to take the deposition of the

man on the land. (I forget his name just now) We want to prove
by him that he was not notified of his entry being cancelled.

At this sitting I write Judge Harriott[2] about your father's[3] business. Yours truly   A. LINCOLN

[1] ALS, owned by Philip D. Neiswender, San Clemente, California. William
H. Davenport was a farmer near Eureka, Illinois.
[2] James Harriott, judge of the Twenty-first Circuit.
[3] Reverend William Davenport.

To Elihu B. Washburne[1]

Hon. E. B. Washburne   Springfield,
My dear Sir   May 27– 1858–

Yours requesting me to return you the now some what noted
"Charley Wilson letter"[2] is received; and I herewith return that
letter.

Political matters just now bear a very *mixed* and *incongruous*
aspect. For several days the signs have been that Douglas and the
President had probably burned [*sic*] the hatchet, Doug's friends
at Washington going over to the President's side, and his friends
here & South of here, talking as if there never had been any serious
difficulty, while the President himself does nothing for his own
peculiar friends here. But this morning my partner, Mr. Herndon,
receives a letter from Mr. Medill of the Chicago Tribune, showing
the writer to be in great alarm at the prospect North of Republicans going over to Douglas, on the idea that Douglas is going to
assume steep free-soil ground, and furiously assail the administration on the stump when he comes home. There certainly is a
double game being played some how. Possibly—even *probably*—
Douglas is temporarily deceiving the President in order to crush
out the 8th. of June convention here. Unless he plays his double
game more successfully than we have often seen done, he can not
carry many republicans North, without at the same time losing
a larger number of his old friends South.

Let this be confidential. Yours as ever   A. LINCOLN

[1] ALS, IHi.   [2] See letters of April 26, May 10 and 15, *supra*.

To I [srael?] S. Piper[1]

I. S. Piper, Esq   Springfield,
Dear Sir   May 28. 1858.

Yours of the 20th. inclosing copy of notice to send out a dedimus
&c. was received only yesterday. If, at the time of selling you the
Bill of iron the plaintiffs agreed to insure it, and did not insure it,

and you lost in consequence, you could set off the damage against their Bill, *if you could prove the facts*. But you can not be allowed to prove anything by Shoup.[2] He was a party to the contract—is now a party to the suit; and no arrangement between you and him can make him a competent witness. Yours Respectfully

A. LINCOLN.

[1] ALS-P, ISLA. The recipient of this letter has not been satisfactorily identified, but an Israel S. Piper is listed in the Illinois state census for 1855 as a resident of Fulton County.   [2] Unidentified.

To Stephen A. Hurlbut[1]

S. A. Hurlbut, Esq   Springfield,
My dear Sir   June 1. 1858.

Yours of the 29th. of May is just received. I suppose it is hardly necessary that any expression of preference for U.S. Senator, should be given at the county, or other local conventions and meetings.[2] When the Republicans of the whole State met together at the State convention, the thing will then be thought of, and something will or will not be done, according as the united judgment may dictate.

I do not find republicans from the old *democratic* ranks more inclined to Douglas than those from the old whig ranks—indeed I find very little of such inclination in either class; but of that little, the larger portion, falling under my observation, has been among old whigs. The republicans from the old democratic ranks, constantly say to me "Take care of your old whigs, and have no fears for us[.]" I am much obliged to you for your letter; and shall be pleased to see you at the convention. Yours very truly,

A. LINCOLN.

[1] ALS, RPB. Stephen A. Hurlbut of Belvidere, Illinois, was elected to the Illinois House of Representatives in 1858 and again in 1859, but entered the army as a brigadier general in May 1861.

[2] The unprecedented action of ninety-four county Republican conventions endorsing Lincoln as the choice of the party was the "remonstrance against outside intermeddling" on the part of Horace Greeley and other Eastern Republicans, who advocated that Douglas should receive Republican support in his fight with the administration forces (Chicago *Tribune*, June 14, 1858).

To Charles L. Wilson[1]

Charles L. Wilson, Esq.   Springfield,
My Dear Sir   June 1. 1858.

Yours of yesterday, with the inclosed newspaper slip, is received. I have never said, or thought more, as to the inclination of some of our Eastern republican friends to favor Douglas, than I expressed in your hearing on the evening of the 21st. April, at the State Library in this place. I have believed—do believe now—that Greely, for instance, would be rather pleased to see Douglas re-elected over me or any other republican; and yet I do not believe it is so, because of any secret arrangement with Douglas. It is be-cause he thinks Douglas' superior position, reputation, experience, and *ability*, if you please, would more than compensate for his lack of a pure republican position, and therefore, his re-election do the general cause of republicanism, more good, than would the election of any one of our better undistinguished pure republicans. I do not know how *you* estimate Greely, but *I* consider him incapable of corruption, or falsehood. He denies that he directly is taking part in favor of Douglas, and I believe him. Still his *feel-ing* constantly manifests itself in his paper, which, being so ex-tensively read in Illinois, is, and will continue to be, a drag upon us. I have also thought that Govr. Seward too, feels about as Greely does; but not being a newspaper editor, his feeling, in this respect, is not much manifested. I have no idea that he is, by conversations or by letters, urging Illinois republicans to vote for Douglas.

As to myself, let me pledge you my word that neither I, nor any friend of mine so far as I know, has been setting stake against Gov. Seward. No combination has been made *with* me, or *proposed* to me, in relation to the next Presidential candidate. The same thing is true in regard to [the] next Governor of our State. I am not directly or indirectly committed to any one; nor has any one made any advance to me upon the subject. I have had many free con-versations with John Wentworth; but he never dropped a remark that led me to suspect that he wishes to be Governor. Indeed, it is due to truth to say that while he has uniformly expressed him-self for me, he has never hinted at any condition.

The signs are that we shall have a good convention on the 16th. and I think our prospects generally, are improving some every day. I believe we need nothing so much as to get rid of unjust suspicions of one another. Yours very truly   A. LINCOLN.

[1] ALS copy, DLC-RTL.

To W. H. Gray[1]

W. H. Gray, Esq.   Springfield,
Dear Sir—   June 4, 1858.

Yours of the 31st of May, accompanied by a printed notice of your Clinton county meeting, is just received. The U.S. court commences its summer term here the day before your meeting, and morally speaking, it is impossible for me to leave. I hope and believe you will not be without able and interesting speakers. The delegates you appoint will meet a large and good convention here on the 11th. Our prospects appear cheering everywhere. I think it only needs that those who feel that our position is right should stand firm, and be active, when action is needed.

Thanking you for your kind invitation, allow me to subscribe myself, Your friend, A. LINCOLN.

[1] Hertz, II, 708-709. W. H. Gray wrote Lincoln from Carlyle, Illinois, May 31, 1858 (DLC-RTL). Further information about him is not available.

To Samuel Wilkinson[1]

Samuel Wilkinson Esq Springfield,
My dear Sir June 10, 1858

Yours of the 26th. May came to hand only last night. I know of no effort to unite the Reps. & Buc. men, and *believe* there is none. Of course the Republicans do not try to keep the common enemy from dividing; but, so far as I *know*, or *believe*, they will not unite with either branch of the division. Indeed it is difficult for me to see, on what ground they could unite; but it is useless to spend words, there is simply nothing of it. It is a trick of our enemies to try to excite all sorts of suspicions and jealosies amongst us. We hope that our Convention on the 16th. bringing us together, and letting us hear each other talk will put an end to most of this. Yours truly A. LINCOLN

[1] ALS, IHi. Samuel Wilkinson resided at Farmington, in Fulton County, Illinois.

To Ward H. Lamon[1]

W. H. Lamon, Esq Springfield,
My dear Sir: June 11th. 1858

Yours of the 9th. written at Joliet is just received. Two or three days ago I learned that McLean had appointed delegates in favor of Lovejoy,[2] and thenceforward I have considered his re-nomination a fixed fact. My *opinion*—if my opinion is of any consequence in this case, in which it is no business of mine to interfere—remains unchanged that running an independent candidate against Lovejoy, will not do—that it will result in nothing but disaster all round. In the first place whoever so runs will be beaten, and will be spotted for life; in the second place, while the race is in progress,

he will be under the strongest temptation to trade with the democrats, and to favor the election of certain of their friends to the
Legislature; thirdly, I shall be held responsible for it, and Republican members of the Legislature, who are partial to Lovejoy, will,
for that, oppose me; and lastly it will in the end lose us the District altogether. There is no safe way but a convention; and if, in
that convention upon a common platform, which all are willing to
stand upon, one who has been known as an abolitionist, but who
is now occupying none but common ground, can get the majority
of the votes to which *all* look for an election, there is no safe way
but to submit[.]

As to the inclination of some Republicans to favor Douglas, that
is one of the chances I have to run, and which I intend to run
with patience.

I write in the court room. Court has opened and I must close.
Yours as ever   A. LINCOLN.

¹ ALS, CSmII.
² Owen Lovejoy, representative from the Third District, which included Mc-
Lean County.

Brief Autobiography¹

June [15?] 1858

Born, February 12, 1809, in Hardin County, Kentucky.
Education defective.
Profession, a lawyer.
Have been a captain of volunteers in Black Hawk war.
Postmaster at a very small office.
Four times a member of the Illinois legislature, and was a mem-
    ber of the lower house of Congress. Yours, etc.,

A. LINCOLN.

¹ NH, II, 368. According to Nicolay and Hay, "The compiler of the 'Dictionary of Congress' states that while preparing the work for publication, in 1858,
he sent to Mr. Lincoln the usual request for a sketch of his life, and received
the following reply." The *Dictionary of Congress*, compiled by Charles Lanman,
was published in 1859. Lincoln's manuscript has not been located.

Notes of Argument in Law Case¹

[June 15, 1858?]

Legislation and *adjudication* must follow, and conform to, the
progress of society.

The progress of society now begins to produce cases of the transfer, for debts, of the entire property of Railroad corporations; and to enable transferees to use, and enjoy, the transfered property, *legislation*, and adjudication, begins to be necessary.

Shall this class of legislation, just now beginning with us, be *general* or *special*?

Section Ten, of our constitution, requires that it should be general, if possible. (Read the section)

Special legislation always trenches upon the judicial department; and, in so far, violates Section Two, of the constitution (Read it).

Just reasoning—policy—is in favor of general legislation—else the legislature will be *loaded down* with the investigation of special cases—a work which the courts *ought* to perform, and can perform much more perfectly. How can the Legislature rightly decide the facts in dispute between P. & B. and S. C. & Co.

It is said that, under a general law, whenever a R. R. Co. gets tired of it & doubts, it may transfer *fraudulently*, to get rid of them.

So they may—so may individuals; and which—the *legislature* or the *courts* is best suited to try the question of fraud in either case?

It is said, if a purchaser have acquired legal rights, let him not be robbed of them; but if he needs *legislation*, let him submit to just terms to obtain it.

Let him, say we, have general law in advance (guarded in every possible way against fraud) so that when he acquires a legal right, he will have no occasion to wait for additional legislation—and if he has practiced fraud, let the courts so decide.

[1] AD, ORB. An exception to the rule of excluding law cases has been made for this document because of its bearing on Lincoln's philosophy of law. The date assigned by Nicolay and Hay (II, 366-67) has been retained for want of evidence in the document or concerning the case involved. The identical document appears again in Nicolay and Hay (XI, 112) and in Hertz (II, 737) dated December (?) 1858. A note in Herndon's handwriting on the last page of the document specifies that it was written "about the year 1858." Another pencil notation in an unknown hand labels it a "Brief of a legal argument in a case of appeal to the Supreme Court of Illinois in a Rail Road Case," and a type-written notation on the same page reads "ARGUMENT BEFORE THE SUPREME COURT OF ILLINOIS BY MR. LINCOLN IN ILLINOIS CENTRAL CASE." No case which Lincoln argued for the Illinois Central has been discovered to which the argument seems fitting. Herndon's vagueness suggests that he did not know. Lincoln's reference in paragraph seven to "P.& B. and S.C. & Co." suggests that the case involved Page & Bacon, for whom Lincoln handled a few cases (see letter of May 31, 1856), but the identity of S.C. & Co. has not been determined. A case involving Henry D. Bacon of Page & Bacon, and the Ohio and Mississippi Railroad (see letter to Koerner, July 19, 1857) seems an excellent possibility except for the fact that none of the principals named in the suit can be identified with Lincoln's "S.C. & Co." Pending further discoveries, the identity of the case remains uncertain.

"A House Divided":
Speech at Springfield, Illinois[1]

June 16, 1858

The Speech, immediately succeeding, was delivered, June 16, 1858 at Springfield Illinois, at the close of the Republican State convention held at that time and place; and by which convention Mr. Lincoln had been named as their candidate for U. S. Senator. Senator Douglas was not present.[2]

Mr. PRESIDENT and Gentlemen of the Convention.[3]

If we could first know *where* we are, and *whither* we are tending, we could then better judge *what* to do, and *how* to do it.

We are now far into the *fifth* year, since a policy was initiated, with the *avowed* object, and *confident* promise, of putting an end to slavery agitation.

Under the operation of that policy, that agitation has not only, *not ceased*, but has *constantly augmented*.

In *my* opinion, it *will* not cease, until a *crisis* shall have been reached, and passed.

"A house divided against itself cannot stand."

I believe this government cannot endure, permanently half *slave* and half *free*.

I do not expect the Union to be *dissolved*—I do not expect the house to *fall*—but I *do* expect it will cease to be divided.

It will become *all* one thing, or *all* the other.

Either the *opponents* of slavery, will arrest the further spread of it, and place it where the public mind shall rest in the belief that it is in course of ultimate extinction; or its *advocates* will push

---

[1] *Illinois State Journal*, June 18, 1858, and Debates Scrapbook, ORB. The basic *Journal* text, which followed Lincoln's original manuscript in paragraphing and use of italics and received his passing attention at least in proof, has been collated with the Chicago *Daily Tribune* text (June 19, 1858) chosen by Lincoln for inclusion in the debates scrapbook which he sent to George M. Parsons of the Republican Central Executive Committee (see Lincoln to Parsons, December 19, 1859) for use in preparing the Follett, Foster and Company edition of the *Debates*. The debates scrapbook, in the Barrett Collection, is a large folio into which Lincoln pasted clippings of the several speeches made by himself and by Stephen A. Douglas which were to make up the *Debates*. Corrections appear in the margins in Lincoln's handwriting, and a prefatory statement, also in Lincoln's hand, precedes the text of the speech. Lincoln's corrections have been incorporated in the text and designated by a footnote. Variations in spelling between the two texts have been resolved in favor of common usage, with exceptions specifically annotated.

[2] Lincoln's preface written in the debates scrapbook.

[3] In *Tribune*, not in *Journal*.

it forward, till it shall become alike lawful in *all* the States, *old* as well as *new*—*North* as well as *South*.

Have we no *tendency* to the latter condition?

Let any one who doubts, carefully contemplate that now almost complete legal combination—piece of *machinery* so to speak—compounded of the Nebraska doctrine, and the Dred Scott decision. Let him consider not only *what work* the machinery is adapted to do, and *how well* adapted; but also, let him study the *history* of its construction, and trace, if he can, or rather *fail*, if he can, to trace the evidences of design, and concert of action, among its chief bosses, from the beginning.

But, so far, *Congress* only, had acted; and an *indorsement* by the people, *real* or apparent, was indispensable, to *save* the point already gained, and give chance for more.

The new year of 1854 found slavery excluded from more than half the States by State Constitutions, and from most of the national territory by Congressional prohibition.

Four days later, commenced the struggle, which ended in repealing that Congressional prohibition.

This opened all the national territory to slavery; and was the first point gained.

This necessity had not been overlooked; but had been provided for, as well as might be, in the notable argument of *"squatter sovereignty,"* otherwise called *"sacred right of self government,"* which latter phrase, though expressive of the only rightful basis of any government, was so perverted in this attempted use of it as to amount to just this: That if any *one* man, choose to enslave *another*, no *third* man shall be allowed to object.

That argument was incorporated into the Nebraska bill itself, in the language which follows: *"It being the true intent and meaning of this act not to legislate slavery into any Territory or state, not exclude it therefrom; but to leave the people thereof perfectly free to form and regulate their domestic institutions in their own way, subject only to the Constitution of the United States."*

Then opened the roar of loose declamation in favor of "Squatter Sovereignty," and "Sacred right of self government."

"But," said opposition members, "let us be more *specific*—let us *amend* the bill so as to expressly declare that the people of the territory *may* exclude slavery." "Not we," said the friends of the measure; and down they voted the amendment.

While the Nebraska bill was passing through congress, a *law case*, involving the question of a negroe's freedom, by reason of his owner having voluntarily taken him first into a free state and then a territory covered by the congressional prohibition, and held him as a slave, for a long time in each, was passing through the U.S. Circuit Court for the District of Missouri; and both Nebraska bill and law suit were brought to a decision in the same month of May, 1854. The negroe's name was "Dred Scott," which name now designates the decision finally made in the case.

Before the *then* next Presidential election, the law case came *to,* and was argued *in* the Supreme Court of the United States; but the *decision* of it was deferred until *after* the election. Still, *before* the election, Senator Trumbull, on the floor of the Senate, requests the leading advocate of the Nebraska bill to state *his opinion* whether the people of a territory can constitutionally exclude slavery from their limits; and the latter answers, "That is a question for the Supreme Court."

The election came. Mr. Buchanan was elected, and the *indorsement,* such as it was, secured. That was the *second* point gained. The indorsement, however, fell short of a clear popular majority by nearly four hundred thousand votes, and so, perhaps, was not overwhelmingly reliable and satisfactory.

The *outgoing* President, in his last annual message, as impressively as possible *echoed back* upon the people the *weight* and *authority* of the indorsement.

The Supreme Court met again; *did not* announce their decision, but ordered a re-argument.

The Presidential inauguration came, and still no decision of the court; but the *incoming* President, in his inaugural address, fervently exhorted the people to abide by the forthcoming decision, *whatever it might be.*

Then, in a few days, came the decision.

The reputed author of the Nebraska bill finds an early occasion to make a speech at this capitol indorsing the Dred Scott Decision, and vehemently denouncing all opposition to it.

The new President, too, seizes the early occasion of the Silliman letter to *indorse* and strongly *construe* that decision, and to express his *astonishment* that any different view had ever been entertained.

At length a squabble springs up between the President and the author of the Nebraska bill, on the *mere* question of *fact,* whether the Lecompton constitution was or was not, in any just sense, made by the people of Kansas; and in that squabble the latter declares that all he wants is a fair vote for the people, and that he *cares* not whether slavery be voted *down* or voted *up.* I do not understand his declaration that he cares not whether slavery be voted down or voted up, to be intended by him other than as an *apt definition* of the *policy* he would impress upon the public mind—the *principle* for which he declares he has suffered much, and is ready to suffer to the end.

And well may he cling to that principle. If he has any parental feeling, well may he cling to it. That principle, is the only *shred* left of his original Nebraska doctrine. Under the Dred Scott decision, "squatter sovereignty" squatted out of existence, tumbled down like temporary scaffolding—like the mould at the foundry served through one blast and fell back into loose sand—helped to carry an election, and then was kicked to the winds. His late *joint* struggle with the Republicans, against the Lecompton Constitution, involves nothing of the original Nebraska doctrine. That struggle was made on a point, the right of a people to make their own constitution, upon which he and the Republicans have never differed.

The several points of the Dred Scott decision, in connection with Senator Douglas' "care not" policy, constitute the piece of machinery, in its *present* state of advancement. This was the third point gained.[4]

The *working* points of that machinery are:

First, that no negro slave, imported as such from Africa, and no descendant of such slave can ever be a *citizen* of any State, in the sense of that term as used in the Constitution of the United States.

This point is made in order to deprive the negro, in every possible event, of the benefit of this provision of the United States Constitution, which declares that—

"The citizens of each State shall be entitled to all privileges and immunities of citizens in the several States."

Secondly, that "subject to the Constitution of the United States," neither *Congress* nor a *Territorial Legislature* can exclude slavery from any United States territory.

This point is made in order that individual men may *fill up* the territories with slaves, without danger of losing them as property, and thus to enhance the chances of *permanency* to the institution through all the future.

Thirdly, that whether the holding a negro in actual slavery in a free State, makes him free, as against the holder, the United States courts will not decide, but will leave to be decided by the courts of any slave State the negro may be forced into by the master.

This point is made, not to be pressed *immediately;* but, if acquiesced in for a while, and apparently *indorsed* by the people at an election, *then* to sustain the logical conclusion that what Dred

[4] Sentence inserted by Lincoln in debates scrapbook.

Scott's master might lawfully do with Dred Scott, in the free State of Illinois, every other master may lawfully do with any other *one*, or one *thousand* slaves, in Illinois, or in any other free State.

Auxiliary to all this, and working hand in hand with it, the Nebraska doctrine, or what is left of it, is to *educate* and *mould* public opinion, at least *Northern* public opinion, to not *care* whether slavery is voted *down* or voted *up*.

This shows exactly where we now *are;* and *partially* also, whither we are tending.

It will throw additional light on the latter, to go back, and run the mind over the string of historical facts already stated. Several things will *now* appear less *dark* and *mysterious* than they did *when* they were transpiring. The people were to be left "perfectly free" "subject only to the Constitution." What the *Constitution* had to do with it, outsiders could not *then* see. Plainly enough *now*, it was an exactly fitted *niche,* for the Dred Scott decision to afterwards come in, and declare the *perfect freedom* of the people, to be just no freedom at all.

Why was the amendment, expressly declaring the right of the people to exclude slavery, voted down? Plainly enough *now*, the adoption of it, would have spoiled the niche for the Dred Scott decision.

Why was the court decision held up? Why, even a Senator's individual opinion withheld, till *after* the Presidential election? Plainly enough *now*, the speaking out *then* would have damaged the *"perfectly free"* argument upon which the election was to be carried.

Why the *outgoing* President's felicitation on the indorsement? Why the delay of a reargument? Why the incoming President's *advance* exhortation in favor of the decision?

These things *look* like the cautious *patting* and *petting* a spirited horse, preparatory to mounting him, when it is dreaded that he may give the rider a fall.

And why the hasty after indorsements of the decision by the President and others?

We can not absolutely *know* that all these exact adaptations are the result of preconcert. But when we see a lot of framed timbers, different portions of which we know have been gotten out at different times and places and by different workmen—Stephen, Franklin, Roger and James,[5] for instance—and when we see these timbers joined together, and see they exactly make the frame of a house or a mill, all the tenons and mortices exactly fitting, and all

[5] Stephen A. Douglas, Franklin Pierce, Roger B. Taney, James Buchanan.

the lengths and proportions of the different pieces exactly adapted
to their respective places, and not a piece too many or too few—
not omitting even scaffolding—or, if a single piece be lacking, we
can see the place in the frame exactly fitted and prepared to yet
bring such piece in—in *such* a case, we find it impossible to not
believe that Stephen and Franklin and Roger and James all understood one another from the beginning, and all worked upon a common *plan* or *draft* drawn up before the first lick was struck.

It should not be overlooked that, by the Nebraska bill, the people
of a *State* as well as *Territory,* were to be left *"perfectly free"*
"subject only to the Constitution."

Why mention a *State?* They were legislating for *territories,* and
not *for* or *about* States. Certainly the people of a State *are* and
ought to be subject to the Constitution of the United States; but
why is mention of this *lugged* into this merely *territorial* law?
Why are the people of a *territory* and the people of a *state* therein
lumped together, and their relation to the Constitution therein
treated as being *precisely* the same?

While the opinion of *the Court,* by Chief Justice Taney, in the
Dred Scott case, and the separate opinions of all the concurring
Judges, expressly declare that the Constitution of the United
States neither permits Congress nor a Territorial legislature to exclude slavery from any United States territory, they all *omit* to
declare whether or not the same Constitution permits a *state,* or
the people of a State, to exclude it.

Possibly, this was a mere *omission;* but who can be *quite* sure, if
McLean or Curtis[6] had sought to get into the opinion a declaration
of unlimited power in the people of a *state* to exclude slavery from
their limits, just as Chase and Macy[7] sought to get such declaration, in behalf of the people of a territory, into the Nebraska bill—
I ask, who can be quite *sure* that it would not have been voted
down, in the one case, as it had been in the other.

The nearest approach to the point of declaring the power of a
State over slavery, is made by Judge Nelson.[8] He approaches it
more than once, using the precise idea, and *almost* the language
too, of the Nebraska act. On one occasion his exact language is,
"except in cases where the power is restrained by the Constitution
of the United States, the law of the State is supreme over the
subject of slavery within its jurisdiction."

In what *cases* the power of the *states is* so restrained by the U.S.

[6] Justices John McLean and Benjamin R. Curtis.
[7] Senator Salmon P. Chase of Ohio and Representative Daniel Macy of Indiana.　　[8] Justice Samuel Nelson.

Constitution, is left an *open* question, precisely as the same question, as to the restraint on the power of the *territories* was left open in the Nebraska act. Put *that* and *that* together, and we have another nice little niche, which we may, ere long, see filled with another Supreme Court decision, declaring that the Constitution of the United States does not permit a *state* to exclude slavery from its limits.

And this may especially be expected if the doctrine of "care not whether slavery be voted *down* or voted *up*," shall gain upon the public mind sufficiently to give promise that such a decision can be maintained when made.

Such a decision is all that slavery now lacks of being alike lawful in all the States.

Welcome or unwelcome, such decision *is* probably coming, and will soon be upon us, unless the power of the present political dynasty shall be met and overthrown.

We shall *lie down* pleasantly dreaming that the people of *Missouri* are on the verge of making their State *free;* and we shall *awake* to the *reality*, instead, that the *Supreme* Court has made *Illinois* a *slave* State.

To meet and overthrow the power of that dynasty, is the work now before all those who would prevent that consummation.

That is *what* we have to do.

But *how* can we best do it?

There are those who denounce us *openly* to their *own* friends, and yet whisper *us softly*, that *Senator Douglas* is the *aptest* instrument there is, with which to effect that object. *They* do *not* tell us, nor has *he* told us, that he *wishes* any such object to be effected. They wish us to *infer* all, from the facts, that he now has a little quarrel with the present head of the dynasty; and that he has regularly voted with us, on a single point, upon which, he and we, have never differed.

They remind us that *he* is a very *great man*, and that the largest of *us* are very small ones. Let this be granted. But "a *living dog* is better than a *dead lion*." Judge Douglas, if not a *dead* lion *for this work*, is at least a *caged* and *toothless* one. How can he oppose the advances of slavery? He don't *care* anything about it. His avowed *mission is impressing* the "public heart" to *care* nothing about it.

A leading Douglas Democratic newspaper thinks Douglas' superior talent will be needed to resist the revival of the African slave trade.

Does Douglas believe an effort to revive that trade is approaching? He has not said so. Does he *really* think so? But if it is, how can he resist it? For years he has labored to prove it a *sacred right* of white men to take negro slaves into the new territories. Can he possibly show that it is *less* a sacred right to *buy* them where they can be bought cheapest? And, unquestionably they can be bought *cheaper in Africa* than in *Virginia*.

He has done all in his power to reduce the whole question of slavery to one of a mere *right of property;* and as such, how can *he* oppose the foreign slave trade—how can he refuse that trade in that "property" shall be "perfectly free"—unless he does it as a *protection* to the home production? And as the home *producers* will probably not *ask* the protection, he will be wholly without a ground of opposition.

Senator Douglas holds, we know, that a man may rightfully be *wiser to-day* than he was *yesterday*—that he may rightfully *change* when he finds himself wrong.

But, can we for that reason, run ahead, and *infer* that he *will* make any particular change, of which he, himself, has given no intimation? Can we *safely* base *our* action upon any such *vague* inference?

Now, as ever, I wish to not *misrepresent* Judge Douglas' *position*, question his *motives*, or do ought that can be personally offensive to him.

Whenever, *if ever*, he and we can come together on *principle* so that *our great cause* may have assistance from *his great ability*, I hope to have interposed no adventitious obstacle.

But clearly, he is not *now* with us—he does not *pretend* to be— he does not *promise* to *ever* be.

Our cause, then, must be intrusted to, and conducted by its own undoubted friends—those whose hands are free, whose hearts are in the work—who *do care* for the result.

Two years ago the Republicans of the nation mustered over thirteen hundred thousand strong.

We did this under the single impulse of resistance to a common danger, with every external circumstance against us.

Of *strange, discordant,* and even, *hostile* elements, we gathered from the four winds, and *formed* and fought the battle through, under the constant hot fire of a disciplined, proud, and pampered enemy.

Did we brave all *then*,[9] to *falter* now?—*now*—when that same enemy is *wavering*, dissevered and belligerent?

The result is not doubtful. We shall not fail—if we stand firm, we shall not fail.

[9] "Then" in *Journal*; "them" in *Tribune*, corrected by Lincoln to "then."

Wise councils[10] may *accelerate* or *mistakes*[11] *delay* it, but, sooner or later the victory is *sure* to come.

[10] *Tribune* has "counsels."
[11] "Mistakes" in *Journal;* "mistake" in *Tribune,* corrected by Lincoln to "mistakes."

To Andrew McCallen[1]

Hon. A. McCallen   Springfield June 19, 1858
My dear Sir, Yours of the 12th. by the hand of Mr. Edwards[2] was duly received. I conversed several times quite freely with Mr. Olney.[3] I do not perceive that we here, or the general convention here could rightfully determine any thing between Messrs Olney & Wiley.[4] You in the District must fix that.

Let me make a remark not suggested by your letter. I think too much reliance is placed in noisy demonstrations—importing speakers from a distance and the like. They excite prejudice and close the avenues to sober reason. The "home production" principle in my judgement is the best. You and Sexton[5] and Olney and others whose hearts are in the work should quietly form your plans and carry them out energetically among your own neighbors. You perceive my idea; and I really think it the best. Yours very truly
A LINCOLN

[1] Copy, DLC-HW.
[2] John W. Edwards of Shawneetown, Illinois, publisher of the *Southern Illinoisan,* who came to Springfield as a delegate to the Republican convention.
[3] John Olney of Shawneetown, also a delegate.
[4] Benjamin L. Wiley of Jonesboro, a candidate for Congress until September, when he withdrew.
[5] Orville Sexton, state representative from Gallatin County 1844-1845 and 1851-1852.

To James W. Somers[1]

James W. Somers, Esq   Springfield,
Dear Sir   June 19. 1858.
Yours of the 10th. in relation to the suit of Thompson, White & Pryor vs Wilson & Park, was received some days ago. There was no ground upon which to stand the case off. Judgment is entered for $555.33, besides costs not yet made up. If you send me the $200 I will apply it on the judgment any day; but I think you need be in no great hurry about it.[2] I charge no fee in the case.

Please tell your Uncle William[3] that judgment also went against

Miller & Jaquith, there being no ground upon which to stand off. Why were you not here to the convention? We had a great time. Yours very truly   A. LINCOLN—

¹ ALS, IHi. James W. Somers was an attorney at Urbana, Illinois.
² See letter of June 25, *infra*.
³ William D. Somers, also an attorney at Urbana.

To Sydney Spring¹

Sydney Spring, Esq   Springfield
My dear Sir: June 19. 1858
    Your letter introducing Mr. Faree [*sic*]² was duly received. There was no opening to nominate him for Superintendent of Public Instruction but, through him, Egypt made a most valuable contribution to the convention. I think it may be fairly said, that he came off the lion of the day—or rather of the night. Can you not elect him to the Legislature? It seems to me he would be hard to beat. What objection could be made to him?
    What is your Senator Martin³ saying & doing? What is Webb⁴ about?
    Please write me. Yours truly   A. LINCOLN

¹ ALS, owned by Sydney T. Spring (grandson), Grayville, Illinois. Sydney Spring was a resident of White County.
² James J. Ferree of Carmi, Illinois.   ³ Samuel H. Martin, also of Carmi.
⁴ Edwin B. Webb, who had served with Lincoln in the legislature.

To Orville H. Browning¹

O. H. Browning, Esq   Springfield,
My dear Sir   June 22, 1858.
    Mrs. Macready² has appeared here again this morning; and it now occurs to me as strange that I did not think to ask you whether you can surely be on hand at the next term, if we continue the case till then. Can you? Answer as soon as possible, after receiving this. If you can possibly be here at this term say so, and about what day; but I understood you that probably you can not be here again at this term. Yours truly   A LINCOLN—

¹ ALS, IHi.
² Mrs. Mary Macready of New York City was suing the City of Alton for $5,000 damages for injuries incurred while she was appearing in Alton in a series of readings from Shakespeare. She had fallen into an excavation (cellar door) in the sidewalk at night seriously injuring her ankle, back, etc.

To John L. Scripps[1]

Jno. L. Scripps, Esq   Springfield,
My dear Sir   June 23, 1858

Your kind note of yesterday is duly received. I am much flattered by the estimate you place on my late speech; and yet I am much mortified that any part of it should be construed so differently from any thing intended by me. The language, "place it where the public mind shall rest in the belief that it is in course of ultimate extinction," I used deliberately, not dreaming then, nor believing now, that it asserts, or intimates, any power or purpose, to interfere with slavery in the States where it exists. But, to not cavil about language, I declare that whether the clause used by me, will bear such construction or not, I never so intended it. I have declared a thousand times, and now repeat that, in my opinion, neither the General Government, nor any other power outside of the slave states, can constitutionally or rightfully interfere with slaves or slavery where it already exists. I believe that whenever the effort to spread slavery into the new territories, by whatever means, and into the free states themselves, by Supreme court decisions, shall be fairly headed off, the institution will then be in course of ultimate extinction; and by the language used I meant only this.

I do not intend this for publication; but still you may show it to any one you think fit. I think I shall, as you suggest, take some early occasion to publicly repeat the declaration I have already so often made as before stated. Yours very truly   A. LINCOLN

---

[1] ALS, IHi. John L. Scripps was editor of the Chicago *Daily Democratic Press*, which within a few days after this letter was written, on July 1, was consolidated with the Chicago *Tribune*, Scripps remaining on the staff.

To Lyman Trumbull[1]

Hon. Lyman Trumbull   Springfield,
My dear Sir: June 23, 1858

Your letter of the 16th. reached me only yesterday. We had already seen, by Telegraph, a report of Douglas' general onslaught upon every body but himself.[2] I have this morning seen the Washington Union, in which I think the Judge is rather worsted in regard to that onslaught.

In relation to the charge of an alliance between the Republicans and Buchanan men in this state, if being rather pleased to see a

division in the ranks of the democracy, and not doing anything to prevent it, be such alliance, then there is such alliance—at least that is true of me. But if it be intended to charge that there is any alliance by which there is to be any concession of principle on either side, or furnishing of the sinews, or partition of offices, or swopping of votes, to any extent; or the doing of anything, great or small, on the one side, for a consideration, express or implied, on the other, no such thing is true so far as I know or believe.

Before this reaches you, you will have seen the proceedings of our Republican State Convention. It was really a grand affair, and was, in all respects, all that our friends could desire.

The resolution in effect nominating me for Senator I suppose was passed more for the object of closing down upon this everlasting croaking about Wentworth, than anything else.

The signs look reasonably well. Our State ticket, I think, will be elected without much difficulty. But, with the advantages they have of us, we shall be very hard run to carry the Legislature.

We shall greet your return home with great pleasure. Yours very truly   A. LINCOLN

[1] ALS, CSmH.
[2] Douglas' speech in the Senate, June 15, 1858, denounced a supposed plot between Republicans and Buchanan Democrats to divide the Democratic party in Illinois and elect Republicans to all offices, including that of United States Senator.

To Henry C. Whitney[1]

H. C. Whitney, Esq   Springfield,
My dear Sir   June 24. 1858

Your letter enclosing the attack of the Times[2] upon me was received this morning. Give yourself no concern about my voting against the supplies, unless you ar[e] without faith that a lie can be successfully contradicted. There is not a word of truth in the charge, and I am just considering a little as to the best shape to put a contradiction in. Show this to whomever you please, but do not publish it in the papers. Your friend as ever   A. LINCOLN

[1] ALS-P, ISLA.
[2] The Chicago Times, June 23, 1858, charged that Lincoln in Congress had voted against a bill appropriating money for purchase of medicine and employment of nurses for Mexican War veterans. See also Lincoln to Medill, June 25, infra.

To Alexander Campbell[1]

A. Campbell, Esq   Springfield,
My dear Sir   June 25– 1858

In 1856 you gave me authority to draw on you for any sum not exceeding five hundred dollars. I see clearly that such a privilege would be more available now than it was then. I am aware that times are tighter now than they were then. Please write me at all events; and whether you can now do anything or not, I shall continue grateful for the past. Yours very truly   A LINCOLN

[1] ALS, ICHi. This letter is incorrectly dated January 25, 1858, in Hertz, II, 707. Alexander Campbell, a leading Republican of LaSalle, Illinois, was elected state representative in 1858. Lincoln had drawn on Campbell in 1856 for "between $200 and $300." Campbell did not answer Lincoln's query until August 2, explaining that he had hoped to make some collections but had been unsuccessful and therefore could not advance any money at the time, though he hoped to be able to send $50 later on (DLC-RTL).

To Joseph Medill[1]

J Medill, Esq   Springfield,
My dear Sir   June 25 1858

Your note of the 23rd. did not reach me till last evening. The Times article I saw yesterday morning. I will give you a brief history of facts, upon which you may rely with entire confidence, and from which you can frame such articles or paragraphs as you see fit.

I was in Congress but a single term. I was a candidate when the Mexican war broke out—and I then took the ground, which I never varied from, that the Administration had done wrong in getting us into the war, but that the Officers and soldiers who went to the field must be supplied and sustained at all events. I was elected the first Monday of August 1846, but, in regular course, only took my seat December 6, 1847. In the interval all the battles had been fought, and the war was substantially ended, though our army was still in Mexico, and the treaty of peace was not finally concluded till May 30. 1848. Col. E. D. Baker had been elected to congress from the same district, for the regular term next preceding mine; but having gone to Mexico himself, and having resigned his seat in Congress, a man by the name of John Henry, was elected to fill Baker's vacancy, and so came into congress before I did. On the 23rd. day of February 1847 (the very day I believe, Col. John Hardin was killed at Buena Vista, and certainly more than nine months before I took a seat in congress) a bill corresponding with great accuracy to that mentioned by the Times, passed the House of Representatives, and *John Henry* voted against

[473]

it, as may be seen in the Journal of that session at pages 406-7. The bill became a law; and is found in the U.S. Statutes at Large—Vol. 9. page 149.

This I suppose is the real origin of the Times' attack upon me. In its' blind rage to assail me, it has seized on a vague recollection of Henry's vote, and appropriated it to me. I scarcely think any one is quite vile enough to make such a charge in such terms, without some slight belief in the truth of it.

Henry was my personal and political friend; and, as I thought, a very good man; and when I first learned of that vote, I well remember how astounded and mortified I was. This very bill, voted against by Henry, passed into a law, and made the appropriations for the year ending June 30. 1848—extending a full month beyond the actual and formal ending of the war. When I came into congress, money was needed to meet the appropriations made, and to be made; and accordingly on the 17th. day of Feb. 1848, a bill to borrow 18.500 000. passed the House of Representatives, for which I voted, as will appear by the Journal of that session page 426, 427. The act itself, reduced to 16.000 000 (I suppose in the Senate) is found in U.S. Statutes at Large Vol. 9- 217.

Again, on the 8th. of March 1848, a bill passed the House of Representatives, for which I voted, as may be seen by the Journal 520-521[.] It passed into a law, and is found in U.S. Statutes at Large Page 215 and forward. The last section of the act, on page 217—contains an appropriation of 800 000. for clothing the volunteers.

It is impossible to refer to all the votes I gave but the above I think are sufficient as specimens; and you may safely deny that I ever gave any vote for withholding any supplies whatever, from officers or soldiers of the Mexican war. I have examined the Journals a good deal; and besides I can not be mistaken; for I had my eye always upon it. I must close to get this into the mail. Yours very truly   A. LINCOLN

1 ALS, owned by the Chicago *Tribune.* Joseph Medill was associated with Dr. Charles H. Ray as publisher of the Chicago *Tribune.*

To James W. Somers[1]

James W. Somers, Esq   Springfield,
My dear Sir   June 25. 1858.
    Yours of the 22nd. enclosing a draft of $200 was duly received. I have paid it on the judgment,[2] and herewith you have the receipt.

I do not wish to say any thing as to who shall be the Republican candidate for the Legislature in your District, further than that I have full confidence in Dr. Hull.[3] Have you ever got in the way of consulting with McKinley,[4] in political matters? He is true as steel and his judgment is very good. The last I heard from him he rather thought Weldon[5] of DeWitt was our best timber for representative, all things considered. But you there, must settle it among yourselves.

It may well puzzle older heads than yours to understand *how*, as the Dred Scott decision holds, congress can authorize a teritorial Legislature to do every thing else, and can *not* authorize them to prohibit slavery. That is one of the things the court can *decide* but can never give an intelligible reason for. Yours very truly, A. LINCOLN

[1] ALS, IHi.   [2] See Lincoln to Somers, June 19, *supra.*
[3] Dr. Peter K. Hull of Piatt County.
[4] James B. McKinley, a lawyer at Urbana, Illinois.
[5] Lawrence Weldon, who was not elected state representative, however, until 1860.

To Anton C. Hesing, Henry Wendt, Alexander Fisher, Committee[1]

A. C. Hesing, H. Wendt, A. Fisher, Committee: Springfield,
Gents:— June 30, 1858.

Your kind letter, inviting me to be present at your celebration of the anniversary of American Independence, to be held on the fifth, and upon which occasion a Banner is to be presented to the German Republicans of the 7th Ward of your city, is received. I regret to say my engagements are such that I cannot be with you. I have several previous invitations, all of which I have been compelled to decline, except one, which will take but a single day of my time. To attend yours would require at least four. I send you a sentiment:

Our German Fellow-Citizens:—Ever true to *Liberty*, the *Union*, and the Constitution—true to Liberty, not *selfishly*, but upon *principle*—not for special *classes* of men, but for *all* men; true to the Union and the Constitution, as the best means to advance that liberty. Your ob't serv't, A. LINCOLN

[1] Chicago *Daily Press and Tribune*, July 7, 1858. Anton C. Hesing was the acknowledged leader responsible for swinging his Chicago German compatriots into the Republican party. Elected mayor of Chicago in 1860, he became established as one of the most powerful political bosses of the era following the Civil War. The Chicago directories list only two possible candidates for the other members of the committee, Henry Wendt and Alexander Fisher.

1858 Campaign Strategy[1]

[July ? 1858]

House of Representatives—Old districts.

Let all the districts go, as desparate, from one to five inclusive; seven and eight; ten and eleven; fifteen to twenty inclusive; twentythree; twentyeight, to thirty inclusive— Struggle for the following.

	Buc.	Fre.	Fill.	Moore.	Miller.
6th District 1 Randolph	1292	709	546	1399	996
		546			
	1255	1255		996	
	37 nett against us			403 nett against us.	

	Buc.	Fre.	Fill.	Moore.	Miller
9 District 1 Wabash	481	122	485	480	545
White	1062	27	845	1080	804
	1543	149	1330	1560	1349
			149		
	1479		1479	1349	
	64 nett against us.			111 [sic] nett against us.	

	Buc.	Fre.	Fill.	Moore.	Miller.
12 District 2 St. Clair	1728	1996	973	1731	2936
		973			
		2969			
		1728			1731
		1241 nett for us.		nett for us. 1205	

	Buc.	Free.	Fill	Moore.	Miller
13 District 1 Clinton	840	161	362	834	514
Bond	607	153	659	623	785
	1447	316 [sic]			
			1021	1457	1299
			311 [sic]		
	1332		1332	1299	
	115 nett against us.			158 nett against us.	

	Buc.	Free.	Fill	Moore.	Miller
14. District 2 Madison	1451.	1111	1658.	1489	2689
		1111			
		2769			
		1451			1489
		1318 nett for us.		nett for us. 1200	

[1] AD, owned by Mrs. Edna Orendorff Macpherson, Springfield, Illinois. The eight pages of manuscript were preserved among the papers in the Lincoln & Herndon office and came into the possession of Alfred Orendorff, Herndon's partner in later years. There is no certainty as to the precise date on which Lincoln calculated the possible results of the election and formulated his strategy, but the letter to Joseph Gillespie, July 16, *infra*, indicates that Lincoln's calculation was made by this time. The manuscript is accompanied by a newspaper clipping which tabulates the Illinois election returns of November 4, 1856, from which Lincoln took his figures.

22. District 1 Jersey
          Calhoun

702	387	530	705.	907
391	70	163	463	239
1093	457	693	1168	1146
		457		
		1150		
		1093	1146	
		57 nett	22 nett against us.	
		for us.		

24. District 1 Edgar

1342	952	308	1337	1250
	308			
1260	1260		1250	
82 nett against us.			87 nett against us.	

25. District 1 Coles
          Moultrie

1178	783	796	1303	1278
432	154	305	439	450
1610	937	1101	1742	1728
		937		
		2038		
		1610	1728	
		428 nett	14 nett against us.	
		for us.		

26. District. 2 Sangamon

2475	1174	1612	2597	2450
		1174		
		2786		
		2475	2450	
		311 nett	147 nett against us.	
		for us.		

27 District 2 Morgan
         Scott

1656	963	885	1664	1827
843	183	536	853	678
2499	1146	1421	2517	2505
		1146		
		2567		
		2499	2505	
		68 nett	12 nett against us.	
		for us.		

31. District 1 Hancock.

2011	1120	999	2011	2091
	999			
	2119			
	2011			2011
	108 nett for us.	nett for us. 80		

32 District 1 Mc.Donough

1370	590	864	1382	1406
		590		
		1454		
		1370		1382
		84 nett	nett for us. 24	
		for us.		

33. District 2 Fulton

2724	2021	898	2806	2642
	898			
	2919			
	2724		2642	
	195 nett for us—	164 nett against us.		

[477]

34	1 Cass.	914	303	438	923	898
	Menard	854	109	668	863	768
		1768	412	1106	1786	1466 [*sic*]
				412		
		1518		1518	1466	
		250 nett against us.			320 nett against us.	

35.	1 Mason	737	267	553	740	794
	Logan	823	655	484	840	1116
		1560	922	1037	1580	1910
				922		
				1959		
				1560		1580
				399 **nett**	**nett**	
				for us.	for us.	330

36	1 Macon	821	500	393	866	804
	DeWitt	679	623	378	691	973
	Piatt	310	85	350	362	380
	Champaign	550	732	236	553	887
		2160	1940	1357	2492 [*sic*]	
						3044
			1357			
			3297			
			2160			2492
			1137 nett for us.		**nett**	
					for us	552

38	1 McLean	1517	1937	560	1654	2299
			560			
			2497			
			1517			1654
			980 nett for us.		**nett**	
					for us.	**645**

39	1 Tazewell	1313.	1028.	757	1337	1418.
			757			
			1785			
			1313			1337
			472 nett for us.			41 [*sic*]
						nett for us

41	2 Peoria	2459	2082	391	2459	2380
	Stark.	353	718	152	357	870
		2812	2800	543	2816	3250
				543		
		3343	3343.			2816
	nett for us.	531			nett for us.	434

The 37th. 40th. 42nd. and all upward we take without question.

Recapitulation

Democrats certain—	19 districts with	22 representatives.
Republicans certain	19 districts with	27	do.
Questionable	20 districts with	26	do.

Taking the Moore & Miller[2] vote as a test, and 14 of the questionable go to the democrats, and 12 to the republicans, making the whole stand

Democrats 36
Republicans 39.

Taking the joint vote of Fremont and Fillmore against Buchanan, as a test, and the whole will stand

Democrats 27
Republicans 48.

By this, it is seen, we give up the districts numbered 1.2.3.4 5.7.8. 10.11.15.16.17.18.19.20.23.28.29.& 30, with 22 representatives—

We take to ourselves, without question 37.40.42.43.44.45.46.47. 48.49.50.51.52.53.54.55.56.57.& 58. with 27 representatives—

Put as doubtful, and to be struggled for, 6.9.12.13.14.21.22.24.25. 26.27.31.32.33.34.35.36.38.39 & 41. with 26 representatives

Of these put as doubtful, taking the Moore & Miller vote as a a [*sic*] test, the 6.9.13.21.22.24.25.26.27.33.& 34 with 14 representatives are against us, which added to the 22 certain against us makes 36— By the same test the 12.14.31.32.35.36.38.39.&41. with 12 representatives, and for us, which added to the 27 certain for us makes 39—

Taking the joint vote of Fremont & Fillmore against Buchanan as a test; and the 21.22.25.26.27.&33. with 9 representatives are brought over to our side—raising us to 48 & reducing our adversary to 27—

Recapitulation—[3]

37	1	6	1	
40	1	9	1	
42	1	13	1	
43	2	21	1	1
44	1	22	1	1
45	3	24	1	
46	2	25	1	1
47	1	26	2	2
48	1	27	2	2
49	1	33	2	2
50	1	34	1	
51.	2			

[2] John Moore and James Miller were the Democratic and Republican candidates for state treasurer, respectively.

[3] The next page of manuscript is merely the columns of figures as given.

52	1
53	1
54	2
55	1
56	2
57	2
58	1
	—

[Senate]

Fight on the old districts—and first, as to *Senators*.

We already have Judd, Parks, Cook[,] Henderson, and Vanderen.[4]   5

No trouble to re-elect Gage, Talcott, Adams & Addams.[5]   4

    So many certain   —

                            9.

We must struggle for, first:

Gillespie's district,

	Buc.	Fre.	Fill.	Moore.	Miller.
Bond	607	153	659	623	785
Madison	1451	1111	1658	1489	2689
Montgomery	992	162	686	1003	844
			3003		4318
		1426	1426		
			4429		
	3050		3050	3115	3115
			1379 nett for us.		1203 nett for us

Palmer's district.

	Buc.	Free.	Fill	Moore.	Miller.
Greene	1565	245	719	1620	825
Jersey	702	387	530	705	907
Macoupin	1778	823	1010	1813	1771
	4045		2259	4138	
		1455	1455	3503	3503
	3714		3714	635 nett against us.	
	331 nett against us				

Watson's district

	Buc.	Fre.	Fill	Moore.	Miller
Coles	1178	783	796	1303	1278
Cumberland	641	246	235	683	404
Edgar	1342	952	308	1337	1250
Vermilion	1111	1506	194	1112	1670
	4272	3487	1533	4435	4602
		1533			
		5020			
		4272			4435
		748 nett for us			167 nett for us.

[4] Norman B. Judd, G. D. A. Parks, Burton C. Cook, Thomas J. Henderson, and Cyrus W. Vanderen were re-elected according to Lincoln's expectation.

[5] George Gage, Wait Talcott, and Augustus Adams failed of re-election; John H. Addams was re-elected.

Fuller's district.

	Buc	Fre.	Fill	Moore.	Miller
Cass	914	303	438	923	698
Logan	823	655	484	840	1116
Mason	737	267	553	740	794
Menard	854	109	668	863	768
Tazewell	1313	1028	757	1337	1418
	4641	2362	2900	4703	4794
			2362		
			5262		
			4641		4703
			621 nett for us.		91 nett for us

Arnold's district

	Buc	Free	Fill	Moore	Miller.
Marshall	834	1008	115	839	1010
Putnam	307	532	115	329	637
Peoria	2459	2082	391	2459	2380
Woodford	747	596	189	794	731
	4347	4218	810	4421	4758
		810			
		5028			
		4347			4421
	681 nett for us.				337 nett for us

Rose's district.

	Buc	Fre.	Fill.	Moore	Miller.
Hancock	2011	1120	999	2011	2091
Henderson	610	757	153	616	904
Schuyler	1369	388	570	1379	946
	3990	2265	1722	4006	3941
		1722			
	3987	3987		3941	
	3 nett against us			65 nett against us.	

Desparate. Sutphen's district

	Buc	Fre.	Fill	Moore.	Miller
Calhoun	391	70	163	463	239
Pike	2163	1053	1010	2210	2012
Scott	843	183	536	853	678
	3397	1306	1709	3526	2929
			1306		
	3015		3015	2929	
	382 nett against us.			597 nett against us.	

Desparate. Carlin's district

	Buc	Fre.	Fill.	Moore.	Miller.
Adams	3311	2226	662	3318	2897
Brown	903	169	433	901	586
	4214	2395	1095	4219	3483
		1095			
	3490	3490		3483	
	724 nett against us.			736 nett against us.	

Kuykendoll's district.
  No use in trying.

Democrats hold over in all the remaining districts.

Fragment on the Struggle Against Slavery[1]

[c. July, 1858]

I have never professed an indifference to the honors of official station; and were I to do so now, I should only make myself ridiculous. Yet I have never failed—do not now fail—to remember that in the republican cause there is a higher aim than that of mere office. I have not allowed myself to forget that the abolition of the Slave-trade by Great Brittain, was agitated a hundred years before it was a final success; that the measure had it's open fire-eating opponents; it's stealthy "dont care" opponents; it's dollar and cent opponents; it's inferior race opponents; its negro equality opponents; and its religion and good order opponents; that all these opponents got offices, and their adversaries got none. But I have also remembered that though they blazed, like tallow-candles for a century, at last they flickered in the socket, died out, stank in the dark for a brief season, and were remembered no more, even by the smell. School-boys know that Wilbe[r]force, and Granville Sharpe [sic],[2] helped that cause forward; but who can now name a single man who labored to retard it? Remembering these things I can not but regard it as possible that the higher object of this contest may not be completely attained within the term of my natural life. But I can not doubt either that it will come in due time. Even in this view, I am proud, in my passing speck of time, to contribute an humble mite to that glorious consummation, which my own poor eyes may not last to see.

[1] AD-F, ISLA, and Hertz, II, 705-706. The last two sentences are not in the facsimile. Probably this fragment is a portion of a speech manuscript prepared during the campaign, but separated from associated pages by Robert Todd Lincoln, who in presenting the fragment to the Duchess of St. Albans wrote on September 17, 1892, that "The MS. is a note made in preparing for one of the speeches in the joint-debate Campaign between Mr. Douglas & my father in 1858." (Parke-Bernet Catalog No. 908, December 9, 1947, p. 126.)
[2] William Wilberforce and Granville Sharp.

To Richard Lloyd[1]

R. Lloyd, Esq.   [July, 1858?]

You see the purport of the within letter. I can do no more in the case. I think you better employ another—either Judge Logan[2] here, or Judge Purple[3] at Peoria, & let him correspond with Grimshaw[4] at once. Yours truly   A. LINCOLN

[1] ALS, owned by Charles W. Olsen, Chicago, Illinois. Richard Lloyd of Henry, Illinois, wrote Lincoln under date of July 10, 1858, "Can you form any opinion as to when my case will be called. Powell vs. Ament et al? Please keep me advised. . . ." (DLC-RTL).   [2] Stephen T. Logan.

3 Norman H. Purple.
4 Probably Jackson Grimshaw, an attorney of Pittsfield, Illinois, who moved to Quincy, and entered partnership with Archibald Williams in 1857.

To Robert Moseley[1]

Robert Mosely Esq   Springfield,
My dear Sir: July 2. 1858

Your letter of the 29th. is received, and for which I thank you. Herewith I send a little article which I wish you would have published in the "Pra[i]rie Beacon" next week.[2] Besides my own recollection, I have carefully examined the Journals since I saw you; and I know the editor will be entirely safe in publishing the article. Get it into the first paper. Yours very truly   A. LINCOLN—

1 ALS, IHi. Robert Moseley, whose name Lincoln misspells, was a Republican politician elected state representative from Edgar County in 1858.
2 The *Prairie Beacon*, edited by Jacob Harding, was published at Paris, Illinois. Files of the *Beacon* have been searched for the article sent by Lincoln, without success.

Toast to the Pioneer Fire Company of Springfield, Illinois[1]

July 5, 1858

"The Pioneer Fire Company." May they extinguish all the bad flames, but keep the flame of patriotism ever burning brightly in the hearts of the ladies.

1 *Illinois State Journal*, July 7, 1858. The occasion was a banquet given by the Pioneer Fire Company for the Union Fire Company of Jacksonville, Illinois.

To John J. Crittenden[1]

Springfield, July 7, 1858.

Dear Sir: I beg you will pardon me for the liberty in addressing you upon only so limited an acquaintance, and that acquaintance so long past. I am prompted to do so by a story being whispered about here that you are anxious for the reëlection of Mr. Douglas to the United States Senate, and also of Harris, of our district, to the House of Representatives, and that you are pledged to write letters to that effect to your friends here in Illinois, if requested. I do not believe the story, but still it gives me some uneasiness. If such was your inclination, I do not believe you would so express yourself. It is not in character with you as I have always estimated you.

[483]

You have no warmer friends than here in Illinois, and I assure you nine tenths—I believe ninety-nine hundredths—of them would be mortified exceedingly by anything of the sort from you. When I tell you this, make such allowance as you think just for my position, which, I doubt not, you understand. Nor am I fishing for a letter on the other side. Even if such could be had, my judgment is that you would better be hands off!

Please drop me a line; and if your purposes are as I hope they are not, please let me know. The confirmation would pain me much, but I should still continue your friend and admirer. Your obedient servant,   A. LINCOLN.

P.S. I purposely fold this sheet within itself instead of an envelop.

¹ NH, III, 17-18. Crittenden replied on July 29 (DLC-RTL) that he had "openly, ardently and frequently expressed" in conversation his belief that Douglas' re-election was a necessity, but that he had written no letters to Illinoisans, and only three or four elsewhere, in reply to letters received. He also stipulated that what he had said about Douglas applied as well to Representative Thomas L. Harris.

Speech at Chicago, Illinois¹

July 10, 1858

The succeeding speech was delivered by Mr. Lincoln, on Saturday Evening, July 10, 1858, at Chicago, Illinois.
Senator Douglas was not present.²

My Fellow Citizens:—On yesterday evening, upon the occasion of the reception given to Senator Douglas, I was furnished with a seat very convenient for hearing him, and was otherwise very courteously treated by him and his friends, and for which I thank him and them. During the course of his remarks my name was mentioned in such a way, as I suppose renders it at least not improper that I should make some sort of reply to him. I shall not attempt to follow him in the precise order in which he addressed the assembled multitude upon that occasion, though I shall perhaps do so in the main.

¹ Debates Scrapbook, ORB. The debates scrapbook which Lincoln prepared (see Speech at Springfield, Illinois, June 16, 1858, n. 1, *supra*) uses the text of the Chicago *Daily Democrat*, July 13, 1858. Lincoln's additions and corrections are indicated by footnotes. In addition the text of the Chicago *Daily Press and Tribune*, July 12, 1858, has been collated, with important variations indicated in footnotes. All brackets are in the source.

² Prefatory statement written by Lincoln in the debates scrapbook. Douglas had spoken the preceding day; Lincoln was present.

A QUESTION OF VERACITY—THE ALLIANCE.

There was one question to which he asked the attention of the crowd, which I deem of somewhat less importance—at least of propriety for me to dwell upon—than the others, which he brought in near the close of his speech, and which I think it would not be entirely proper for me to omit attending to,[3] and yet if I were not to give some attention to it now, I should probably forget it altogether. [Applause]. While I am upon this subject, allow me to say that I do not intend to indulge in that inconvenient mode sometimes adopted in public speaking, of reading from documents; but I shall depart from that rule so far as to read a little scrap from his speech, which notices this first topic of which I shall speak —that is, provided I can find it in the paper. (Examines the Press and Tribune of this morning). A voice—"Get out your specs."

I have made up my mind to appeal to the people against the combination that has been made against me!—the Republican leaders have formed an alliance, an unholy and unnatural alliance, with a portion of unscrupulous federal office-holders. I intend to fight that allied army wherever I meet them. I know they deny the alliance, but yet these men who are trying to divide the Democratic party for the purpose of electing a Republican Senator in my place, are just as much the agents and tools of the supporters of Mr. Lincoln. Hence I shall deal with this allied army just as the Russians dealt with the allies at Sebastopol—that is, the Russians did not stop to inquire, when they fired a broadside, whether it hit an Englishman, a Frenchman, or a Turk. Nor will I stop to inquire, nor shall I hesitate, whether my blows shall hit these Republican leaders or their allies who are holding the federal offices and yet acting in concert with them.

Well now, gentlemen, is not that very alarming? [Laughter.] Just to think of it! right at the outset of his canvass, I, a poor, kind, amiable, intelligent, [laughter] gentleman, [laughter and renewed cheers] I am to be slain in this way. Why, my friend, the Judge, is not only, as it turns out, not a dead lion, nor even a living one— he is the rugged Russian Bear! [Roars of laughter and loud applause.]

But if they will have it—for he says that we deny it—that there is any such alliance, as he says there is—and I don't propose hanging very much upon this question of veracity—but if he will have it that there is such an alliance—that the Administration men and we are allied, and we stand in the attitude of English, French and Turk, he occupying[4] the position of the Russian, in that case,[5]

3 "Altogether" deleted by Lincoln.
4 "Occupies" corrected by Lincoln to "occupying."
5 "That in case" corrected by Lincoln to "in that case."

I beg that he will indulge us while we barely suggest to him, that these allies took Sebastopol. [Long and tremendous applause.]

Gentlemen, only a few more words as to this alliance. For my part, I have to say, that whether there be such an alliance, depends, so far as I know, upon what may be a right definition of the term *alliance*. If for the Republican party to see the other great party to which they are opposed divided among themselves, and not try to stop the division and rather be glad of it—if that is an alliance I confess I am in; but if it is[6] meant to be said that the Republicans had formed an alliance going beyond that, by which there is[7] contribution of money or sacrifice of principle on the one side or the other, so far as the Republican party is concerned, if there be any such thing, I protest that I neither know anything of it, nor do I believe it. I will however say—as I think this branch of the argument is lugged in—I would before I leave it, state, for the benefit of those concerned, that one of those same Buchanan men did once tell me of an argument that he made for his opposition to Judge Douglas. He said that a friend of our Senator Douglas had been talking to him, and had among other things said to him: "Why, you don't want to beat Douglas?" "Yes," said he "I do want to beat him, and I will tell you why. I believe his original Nebraska bill was right in the abstract, but it was wrong in the time that it was brought forward. It was wrong in the application to a territory in regard to which the question had been settled; it was brought forward at a time when nobody asked him; it was tendered to the South when the South had not asked for it, but when they could not well refuse it; and for this same reason he forced that question upon our party: it has sunk the best men all over the nation, everywhere; and now when our President, struggling with the difficulties of this man's getting up, has reached the very hardest point to turn in the case, he deserts him, and I am for putting him where he will trouble us no more." [Applause.]

Now, gentlemen, that is not my argument—that is not my[8] argument at all. I have only been stating to you the argument of a Buchanan man. You will judge if there is any force in it. [Applause.]

WHAT IS POPULAR SOVEREIGNTY?

Popular sovereignty! everlasting popular sovereignty! [Laughter and continued cheers.] Let us for a moment inquire into this vast matter of popular sovereignty. What is popular sovereignty?

---

[6] "Is" inserted by Lincoln.   [7] "Is" inserted by Lincoln.
[8] "The" corrected by Lincoln to "my."

We recollect that at an early period in the history of this struggle, there was another name for this same thing—*Squatter Sovereignty*. It was not exactly Popular Sovereignty but Squatter Sovereignty. What do those terms mean? What do those terms mean when used now? And vast credit is taken by our friend, the Judge, in regard to his support of it, when he declares the last years of his life have been, and all the future years of his life shall be, devoted to this matter of popular sovereignty. What is it? Why, it is the sovereignty of the people! What was Squatter Sovereignty? I suppose if it had any significance at all it was the right of the people to govern themselves, to be sovereign of their own affairs while they were squatted down in a country not their own, while they had squatted on a territory that did not belong to them, in the sense that a State belongs to the people who inhabit it—when it belonged to the nation—such right to govern themselves was called "Squatter Sovereignty."

Now I wish you to mark. What has become of that Squatter Sovereignty? What has become of it? Can you get anybody to tell you now that the people of a territory have any authority to govern themselves, in regard to this mooted question of Slavery, before they form a State Constitution? No such thing at all, although there is a general running fire, and although there has been a hurrah made in every speech on that side, assuming that policy had given the people of a territory the right to govern themselves upon this question; yet the point is dodged. To-day it has been decided—no more than a year ago it was decided by the Supreme Court of the United States, and is insisted upon to-day, that the people of a territory have no right to exclude Slavery from a territory, that if any one man chooses to take slaves into a territory, all the rest of the people have no right to keep them out. This being so, and this decision being made one of the points that the Judge approved, and one in the approval of which he says he means to keep me down—put me down I should not say, for I have never been up. He says he is in favor of it, and sticks to it, and expects to win his battle on that decision, which says that there is no such thing as Squatter Sovereignty; but that any one man may take slaves into a territory, and all the other men in the territory may be opposed to it, and yet by reason of the constitution they cannot prohibit it. When that is so, how much is left of this vast matter of Squatter Sovereignty I should like to know?—(a voice) —"it has all gone."

When we get back, we get to the point of the right of the people to make a constitution. Kansas was settled, for example, in

1854. It was a territory yet, without having formed a Constitution, in a very regular way, for three years. All this time negro slavery could be taken in by any few individuals, and by that decision of the Supreme Court, which the Judge approves, all the rest of the people cannot keep it out; but when they come to make a Constitution they may say they will not have Slavery. But it is there; they are obliged to tolerate it in some way, and all experience shows that it will be so—for they will not take the negro slaves and absolutely deprive the owners of them. All experience shows this to be so. All that space of time that runs from the beginning of the settlement of the Territory until there is sufficiency of people to make a State Constitution—all that portion of time popular sovereignty is given up. The seal is absolutely put down upon it by the Court decision, and Judge Douglas puts his own upon the top of that, yet he is appealing to the people to give him vast credit for his devotion to popular sovereignty. (Applause.)

Again, when we get to the question of the right of the people to form a State Constitution as they please, to form it with Slavery or without Slavery—if that is anything new, I confess I don't know it. Has there ever been a time when anybody said that any other than the people of a Territory itself should form a Constitution? What is now[9] in it, that Judge Douglas should have fought several years of his life, and pledged himself to fight all the remaining years of his life for? Can Judge Douglas find anybody on earth that said that anybody else should form a constitution for a people? (A voice, "Yes.") Well, I should like you to name him; I should like to know who he was. (Same voice—"John Calhoun.")

Mr. Lincoln—No, sir, I never heard of even John Calhoun saying such a thing. He insisted on the same principle as Judge Douglas; but his mode of applying it in fact, was wrong. It is enough for my purpose to ask this crowd, when ever a Republican said anything against it? They never said anything against it, but they have constantly spoken for it; and whosoever will undertake to examine the platform, and the speeches of responsible men of the party, and of irresponsible men, too, if you please, will be unable to find one word from anybody in the Republican ranks, opposed to that Popular Sovereignty which Judge Douglas thinks that he has invented. [Applause.] I suppose that Judge Douglas will claim in a little while, that he is the inventor of the idea that the people should govern themselves: [cheers and laughter]; that nobody ever thought of such a thing until he brought it forward. We do remember, that in that old Declaration of Independence, it is said that

9 "New" is probably correct, as in *Tribune*.

"We hold these truths to be self-evident that all men are created equal; that they are endowed by their Creator with certain inalienable rights; that among these are life, liberty, and the pursuit of happiness; that to secure these rights, governments are instituted among men, deriving their just powers from the consent of the governed." There is the origin of Popular Sovereignty. [Loud applause]. Who, then, shall come in at this day and claim that he invented it. [Laughter and applause.]

LECOMPTON CONSTITUTION.

The Lecompton Constitution connects itself with this question, for it is in this matter of the Lecompton Constitution that our friend Judge Douglas claims such vast credit. I agree that in opposing the Lecompton Constitution so far as I can perceive, he was right. ["Good," "good."] I do not deny that at all; and gentlemen, you will readily see why I could not deny it, even if I wanted to. But I do not wish to; for all the Republicans in the nation opposed it, and they would have opposed it just as much without Judge Douglas' aid, as with it. They had all taken ground against it long before he did. Why, the reason that he urges against that Constitution, I urged against him a year before. I have the printed speech in my hand. The argument that he makes, why that Constitution should not be adopted, that the people were not fairly represented nor allowed to vote, I pointed out in a speech a year ago, which I hold in my hand now, that no fair chance was to be given to the people. ["Read it," "read it."] I shall not waste your time by trying to read it. ["Read it," "read it."] Gentlemen, reading from speeches is a very tedious business, particularly for an old man that has to put on spectacles, and the more so if the man be so tall that he has to bend over to the light. [Laughter.]

A little more, now, as to this matter of popular sovereignty and the Lecompton Constitution. The Lecompton Constitution, as the Judge tells us, was defeated. The defeat of it was a good thing or it was not. He thinks the defeat of it was a good thing, and so do I, and we agree in that. Who defeated it?

A voice—Judge Douglas.

Mr. Lincoln—Yes, he furnished himself, and if you suppose he controlled the other Democrats that went with him, he furnished *three* votes, while the Republicans furnished *twenty*. [Applause.]

That is what he did to defeat it. In the House of Representatives he and his friends furnished some twenty votes, and the Republicans furnished *ninety odd*. [Loud applause.] Now who was it that did the work?

A voice—Douglas.

Mr. Lincoln—Why, yes, Douglas did it! To be sure he did.

Let us, however, put that proposition another way. The Republicans could not have done it without Judge Douglas. Could he have done it without them. [Applause.] Which could have come the nearest to doing it without the other? [Renewed applause. "That's it," "that's it;" "good," "good."]

A voice—Who killed the bill?

Another voice—Douglas.

Mr. Lincoln—Ground was taken against it by the Republicans long before Douglas did it. The proportion of opposition to that measure is about five to one.

A Voice—"Why don't they come out on it?"

Mr. Lincoln—You don't know what you are talking about, my friend. I am quite willing to answer any gentleman in the crowd who asks an *intelligent* question. [Great applause.]

Now, who in all this country has ever found any of our friends of Judge Douglas' way of thinking, and who have acted upon this main question, that has ever thought of uttering a word in behalf of Judge Trumbull? A voice—"we have." I defy you to show a printed resolution passed in a Democratic meeting—I take it upon myself to defy any man to show a printed resolution of a Democratic meeting, large or small, in favor of Judge Trumbull, or any of the five to one Republicans who beat that bill. Every thing must be for the Democrats! They did every thing, and the five to one that really did the thing, they snub over, and they do not seem to remember that they have an existence upon the face of the earth. [Applause.]

LINCOLN AND DOUGLAS.

Gentlemen: I fear that I shall become tedious, (Go on, go on.) I leave this branch of the subject to take hold of another. I take up that part of Judge Douglas' speech in which he respectfully attended to me. [Laughter.]

Judge Douglas made two points upon my recent speech at Springfield. He says they are to be the issues of this campaign. The first one of these points he bases upon the language in a speech which I delivered at Springfield, which I believe I can quote correctly from memory. I said there that "we are now far into the fifth year since a policy was instituted for the avowed object and with the confident promise of putting an end to slavery agitation; under the operation of that policy, that agitation had only not ceased, but has constantly augmented."—(A voice)—

"That's the very language." "I believe it will not cease until a crisis shall have been reached and passed. A house divided against itself cannot stand. I believe this government cannot endure permanently half slave and half free." [Applause.] "I do not expect the Union to be dissolved,"—I am quoting from my speech—"I do not expect the house to fall, but I do expect it will cease to be divided. It will become all one thing or the other. Either the opponents of slavery will arrest the spread of it, and place it where the public mind shall rest in the belief that it is in the course of ultimate extinction, or its advocates will push it forward until it shall become alike lawful in all the States, North as well as South." [Good, good.]

What is the paragraph. In this paragraph which I have quoted in your hearing, and to which I ask the attention of all, Judge Douglas thinks he discovers great political heresy. I want your attention particularly to what he has inferred from it. He says I am in favor of making all the States of this Union uniform in all their internal regulations; that in all their domestic concerns I am in favor of making them entirely uniform. He draws this inference from the language I have quoted to you. He says that I am in favor of making war by the North upon the South for the extinction of slavery; that I am also in favor of inviting (as he expresses it) the South to a war upon the North, for the purpose of nationalizing slavery. Now, it is singular enough, if you will carefully read that passage over, that I did not say that I was in favor of anything in it. I only said what I expected would take place. I made a prediction only—it may have been a foolish one perhaps. I did not even say that I desired that slavery should be put in course of ultimate extinction. I do say so now, however, [great applause] so there need be no longer any difficulty about that. It may be written down in the great[10] speech. [Applause and laughter.]

Gentlemen, Judge Douglas informed you that this speech of mine was probably carefully prepared. I admit that it was. I am not master of language; I have not a fine education; I am not capable of entering into a disquisition upon dialectics, as I believe you call it; but I do not believe the language I employed bears any such construction as Judge Douglas put upon it. But I don't care about a quibble 'in regard to words. I know what I meant, and I will not leave this crowd in doubt, if I can explain it to them, what I really meant in the use of that paragraph.

I am not, in the first place, unaware that this Government has

10 "Next" is probably correct, as in *Tribune*.

endured eighty-two years, half slave and half free. I know that. I am tolerably well acquainted with the history of the country, and I know that it has endured eighty-two years, half slave and half free. I *believe*—and that is what I meant to allude to there—I *believe* it has endured because, during all that time, until the introduction of the Nebraska Bill, the public mind did rest, all the time, in the belief that slavery was in course of ultimate extinction. ["Good!" "Good!" and applause.] That was what gave us the rest that we had through that period of eighty-two years; at least, so I believe. I have always hated slavery, I think as much as any Abolitionist. [Applause.] I have been an Old Line Whig. I have always hated it, but I have always been quiet about it until this new era of the introduction of the Nebraska Bill began. I always believed that everybody was against it, and that it was in course of ultimate extinction. (Pointing to Mr. Browning, who stood near by.) Browning thought so; the great mass of the nation have rested in the belief that slavery was in course of ultimate extinction. They had reason so to believe.

The adoption of the Constitution and its attendant history led the people to believe so; and that such was the belief of the framers of the Constitution itself. Why did those old men, about the time of the adoption of the Constitution, decree that Slavery should not go into the new Territory, where it had not already gone? Why declare that within twenty years the African Slave Trade, by which slaves are supplied, might be cut off by Congress? Why were all these acts? I might enumerate more of these acts—but enough. What were they but a clear indication that the framers of the Constitution intended and expected the ultimate extinction of that institution. [Cheers.] And now, when I say, as I said in my speech that Judge Douglas has quoted from, when I say that I think the opponents of slavery will resist the farther spread of it, and place it where the public mind shall rest with the belief that it is in course of ultimate extinction, I only mean to say, that they will place it where the founders of this Government originally placed it.

I have said a hundred times, and I have now no inclination to take it back, that I believe there is no right, and ought to be no inclination in the people of the free States to enter into the slave States, and interfere with the question of slavery at all. I have said that always. Judge Douglas has heard me say it—if not quite a hundred times, at least as good as a hundred times; and when it is said that I am in favor of interfering with slavery where it exists, I know it is unwarranted by anything I have ever *intended*, and, as I believe, by anything I have ever *said*. If, by any means, I have ever used language which could fairly be so construed, (as, however, I believe I never have,) I now correct it.

[Here the shouts of the Seventh Ward Delegation announced that they were coming in procession. They were received with enthusiastic cheers.]

So much, then, for the inference that Judge Douglas draws, that I am in favor of setting the sections at war with one another. I know that I never meant any such thing, and I believe that no fair mind can infer any such thing from anything I have ever said. ["Good," "good."]

Now in relation to his inference that I am in favor of a general consolidation of all the local institutions of the various States. I will attend to that for a little while, and try to inquire, if I can, how on earth it could be that any man could draw such an inference from anything I said. I have said, very many times, in Judge Douglas' hearing, that no man believed more than I in the principle of self-government; that it lies at the bottom of all my ideas of just government, from beginning to end. I have denied that his use of that term applies properly. But for the thing itself, I deny that any man has ever gone ahead of me in his devotion to the principle, whatever he may have done in efficiency in advocating it. I think that I have said it in your hearing—that I believe each individual is naturally entitled to do as he pleases with himself and the fruit of his labor, so far as it in no wise interferes with any other man's rights—[applause]—that each community, as a State, has a right to do exactly as it pleases with all the concerns within that State that interfere with the rights of no other State, and that the general government, upon principle, has no right to interfere with anything other than that general class of things that does concern the whole. I have said that at all times. I have said, as illustrations, that I do not believe in the right of Illinois to interfere with the cranberry laws of Indiana, the oyster laws of Virginia, or the Liquor Laws of Maine. I have said these things over and over again, and I repeat them here as my sentiments.

How is it, then, that Judge Douglas infers, because I hope to see slavery put where the public mind shall rest in the belief that it is in the course of ultimate extinction, that I am in favor of Illinois going over and interfering with the cranberry laws of Indiana? What can authorize him to draw any such inference? I suppose there might be one thing that at least enabled *him* to draw such an inference that would not be true with me or with many others, that is, because he looks upon all this matter of slavery as an exceedingly little thing—this matter of keeping one-sixth of the population of the whole nation in a state of oppression and tyranny unequalled in the world. He looks upon it as being an exceedingly little thing—only equal to the question of the cranberry laws of Indiana—as something having no moral question in it—as something on a par with the question of whether a man shall pasture his land with cattle, or plant it with tobacco—so little and so small a thing, that he concludes, if I could desire that anything should be done to bring about the ultimate extinction of that little thing, I must be in favor of bringing about an amalgamation of all the other little things in the Union. Now, it so happens—and there, I presume, is the foundation of this mistake—that the Judge thinks thus; and it so happens that there is a vast portion of the American people that do *not* look upon that matter as being this very little thing. They look upon it as a vast moral evil; they can prove it is such by the writings of those who gave us the blessings of liberty which we enjoy, and that they so looked upon it, and not as an evil merely confining itself to the States where it is situated; and while we agree that, by the Constitution we assented to, in the States where it exists we have no right to interfere with it because it is in the Constitution and we are by both duty and inclination to stick by that Constitution in all its letter and spirit from beginning to end. [Great applause.]

So much then as to my disposition—my wish—to have all the State legislatures blotted out, and to have one general consolidated government, and a uniformity of domestic regulations in all the States, by which I suppose it is meant if we raise corn here, we must make sugar cane grow here too, and we must make those[11] which grow North, grow in the South. All this I suppose he[12] understands I am in favor of doing. Now, so much for all this nonsense—for I must call it so. The Judge can have no issue with me on a question of establishing uniformity in the domestic regulations of the States.

DRED SCOTT DECISION.

A little now on the other point—the Dred Scott Decision. Another one of the issues he says that is to be made with me, is upon his devotion to the Dred Scott Decision, and my opposition to it.

I have expressed heretofore, and I now repeat, my opposition to the Dred Scott Decision, but I should be allowed to state the nature of that opposition, and I ask your indulgence while I do so. What is fairly implied by the term Judge Douglas has used "re-

11 "Those things" in *Tribune*.   12 "The Judge" in *Tribune*.

sistance to the Decision?" I do not resist it. If I wanted to take Dred Scott from his master, I would be interfering with property, and that terrible difficulty that Judge Douglas speaks of, of interfering with property, would arise. But I am doing no such thing as that, but all that I am doing is refusing to obey it as a political rule. If I were in Congress, and a vote should come up on a question whether slavery should be prohibited in a new territory, in spite of that Dred Scott decision, I would vote that it should. [Applause; "good for you;" "we hope to see it;" "that's right."]

Mr. Lincoln—That is what I would do. ["You will have a chance soon."] Judge Douglas said last night, that before the decision he might advance his opinion, and it might be contrary to the decision when it was made; but after it was made he would abide by it until it was reversed. Just so! We let this property abide by the decision, but we will try to reverse that decision. [Loud applause—cries of "good."] We will try to put it where Judge Douglas would not object, for he says he will obey it until it is reversed. Somebody has to reverse that decision, since it is made, and we mean to reverse it, and we mean to do it peaceably.

What are the uses of decisions of courts? They have two uses. As rules of property they have two uses. First—they decide upon the question before the court. They decide in this case that Dred Scott is a slave. Nobody resists that. Not only that, but they say to everybody else, that persons standing just as Dred Scott stands is [*sic*] as he is. That is, they say that when a question comes up upon another person it will be so decided again, unless the court decides in another way, [cheers—cries of "good,"] unless the court overrules its decision. [Renewed applause]. Well, we mean to do what we can to have the court decide the other way. That is one thing we mean to try to do.

The sacredness that Judge Douglas throws around this decision, is a degree of sacredness that has never been before thrown around any other decision. I have never heard of such a thing. Why, decisions apparently contrary to that decision, or that good lawyers thought were contrary to that decision, have been made by that very court before. It is the first of its kind; it is an astonisher in legal history. [Laughter.] It is a new wonder of the world. [Laughter and applause.] It is based upon falsehood in the main as to the facts—allegations of facts upon which it stands are not facts at all in many instances, and no decision made on any question— the first instance of a decision made under so many unfavorable circumstances—thus placed has ever been held by the profession as law, and it has always needed confirmation before the lawyers regarded it as settled law. But Judge Douglas will have it that all hands must take this extraordinary decision, made under these extraordinary circumstances, and give their vote in Congress in accordance with it, yield to it and obey it in every possible sense. Circumstances alter cases. Do not gentlemen here remember the case of that same Supreme Court, some twenty-five or thirty years ago, deciding that a National Bank was constitutional? I ask, if somebody does not remember that a National Bank was declared to be constitutional? ["Yes," "yes"] Such is the truth, whether it be remembered or not. The Bank charter ran out, and a re-charter was granted by Congress. That re-charter was laid before General Jackson. It was urged upon him, when he denied the constitutionality of the bank, that the Supreme Court had decided that it was constitutional; and that[13] General Jackson then said that the Supreme Court had no right to lay down a rule to govern a co-ordinate branch of the government, the members of which had sworn to support the Constitution—that each member had sworn to support that Constitution as he understood it. I will venture here to say, that I have heard Judge Douglas say that he approved of General Jackson for that act. What has now become of all his tirade about "resistance to the Supreme Court?" ["Gone up," "Gone to the Theatre."]

My fellow citizens, getting back a little, for I pass from these points, when Judge Douglas makes his threat of annihilation upon the "alliance." He is cautious to say that that warfare of his is to fall upon the leaders of the Republican party. Almost every word he utters and every distinction he makes, has its significance. He means for the Republicans that do not count themselves as leaders, to be his friends; he makes no fuss over them; it is the leaders that he is making war upon. He wants it understood that the mass of the Republican party are really his friends. It is only the leaders that are doing something, that are intolerant, and that requires extermination at his hands. As this is clearly and unquestionably the light in which he presents that matter, I want to ask your attention, addressing myself to the Republicans here, that I may ask you some questions, as to where you, as the Republican party, would be placed if you sustained Judge Douglas in his present position by a re-election? I do not claim, gentlemen, to be unselfish, I do not pretend that I would not like to go to the United States Senate, (laughter), I make no such hypocritical pretense, but I do say to you that in this mighty issue, it is nothing to you—nothing to the mass of the people of the nation, whether or not Judge

13 "That" omitted in *Tribune*, probably correctly.

Douglas or myself shall ever be heard of after this night, it may be a trifle to either of us, but in connection with this mighty question, upon which hang the destinies of the nation, perhaps, it is absolutely nothing; but where will you be placed if you re-endorse Judge Douglas? Don't you know how apt he is—how exceedingly anxious he is at all times to seize upon anything and everything to persuade you that something *he* has done *you* did yourselves? Why, he tried to persuade you last night that our Illinois Legislature instructed him to introduce the Nebraska bill. There was nobody in that legislature ever thought of such a thing; and when he first introduced the bill, he never thought of it; but still he fights furiously for the proposition, and that he did it because there was a standing instruction to our Senators to be always introducing Nebraska bills. [Laughter and applause] He tells you he is for the Cincinnati platform, he tells you he is for the Dred Scott decision. He tells you, not in his speech last night, but substantially in a former speech, that he cares not if slavery is voted up or down—he tells you the struggle on Lecompton is past—it may come up again or not, and if it does he stands where he stood when in spite of him and his opposition you built up the Republican party. If you endorse him you tell him you do not care whether slavery be voted up or down, and he will close, or try to close your mouths with his declaration repeated by the day, the week, the month and the year. Is that what you mean? (cries of "no," one voice "yes.") Yes, I have no doubt you who have always been for him if you mean that. No doubt of that (a voice "hit him again") soberly I have said, and I repeat it I think in the position in which Judge Douglas stood in opposing the Lecompton Constitution he was right, he does not know that it will return, but if it does we may know where to find him, and if it does not we may know where to look for him and that is on the Cincinnati platform. Now I could ask the Republican party after all the hard names that Judge Douglas has called them by—all his repeated charges of their inclination to marry with and hug[14] negroes—all his declarations of Black Republicanism— by the way we are improving, the black has got rubbed off—but with all that, if he be endorsed by Republican votes where do you stand? Plainly you stand ready saddled, bridled and harnessed and waiting to be driven over to the slavery extension camp of the nation [a voice "we will hang ourselves first"]—just ready to be driven over tied together in a lot—to be driven over, every man with a rope around his neck, that halter being held by Judge Douglas. That is the question. If Republican men have

[14] "Buy" in *Tribune*, probably incorrect.

been in earnest in what they have done, I think they had better not do it, but I think that the Republican party is made up of those who, as far as they can peaceably, will oppose the extension of slavery, and who will hope for its ultimate extinction.[15] If they believe it is wrong in grasping up the new lands of the continent, and keeping them from the settlement of free white laborers, who want the land to bring up their families upon; if they are in earnest, although they may make a mistake, they will grow restless, and the time will come when they will come back again and re-organize, if not by the same name, at least upon the same principles as their party now has. It is better, then, to save the work while it is begun. You have done the labor; maintain it—keep it. If men choose to serve you, go with them; but as you have made up your organization upon principle, stand by it; for, as surely as God reigns over you, and has inspired your mind, and given you a sense of propriety, and continues to give you hope, so surely you will still cling to these ideas, and you will at last come back again after your wanderings, merely to do your work over again. [Loud applause.]

We were often—more than once at least—in the course of Judge Douglas' speech last night, reminded that this government was made for white men—that he believed it was made for white men. Well, that is putting it into a shape in which no one wants to deny it, but the Judge then goes into his passion for drawing inferences that are not warranted. I protest, now and forever, against that counterfeit logic which presumes that because I do not want a negro woman for a slave, I do necessarily want her for a wife. [Laughter and cheers.] My understanding is that I need not have her for either, but as God made us separate, we can leave one another alone and do one another much good thereby. There are white men enough to marry all the white women, and enough black men to marry all the black women, and in God's name let them be so married. The Judge regales us with the terrible enormities that take place by the mixture of races; that the inferior race bears the superior down. Why, Judge, if we do not let them get together in the Territories they won't mix there. [Immense applause.]

A voice—"Three cheers for Lincoln." [The cheers were given with a hearty good will.]

Mr. Lincoln—I should say at least that that is a self evident truth.

15 *Tribune* has an additional clause as follows: "—who will believe, if it ceases to spread, that it is in course of ultimate extinction."

Now, it happens that we meet together once every year, sometime about the 4th of July, for some reason or other. These 4th of July gatherings I suppose have their uses. If you will indulge me, I will state what I suppose to be some of them.

We are now a mighty nation, we are thirty—or about thirty millions of people, and we own and inhabit about one-fifteenth part of the dry land of the whole earth. We run our memory back over the pages of history for about eighty-two years and we discover that we were then a very small people in point of numbers, vastly inferior to what we are now, with a vastly less extent of country,—with vastly less of everything we deem desirable among men,—we look upon the change as exceedingly advantageous to us and to our posterity, and we fix upon something that happened away back, as in some way or other being connected with this rise of prosperity. We find a race of men living in that day whom we claim as our fathers and grandfathers; they were iron men, they fought for the principle that they were contending for; and we understood[16] that by what they then did it has followed that the degree of prosperity that we now enjoy has come to us. We hold this annual celebration to remind ourselves of all the good done in this process of time of how it was done and who did it, and how we are historically connected with it; and we go from these meetings in better humor with ourselves—we feel more attached the one to the other, and more firmly bound to the country we inhabit. In every way we are better men in the age, and race, and country in which we live for these celebrations. But after we have done all this we have not yet reached the whole. There is something else connected with it. We have besides these men—descended by blood from our ancestors—among us perhaps half our people who are not descendants at all of these men, they are men who have come from Europe—German, Irish, French and Scandinavian—men that have come from Europe themselves, or whose ancestors have come hither and settled here, finding themselves our equals in all things. If they look back through this history to trace their connection with those days by blood, they find they have none, they cannot carry themselves back into that glorious epoch and make themselves feel that they are part of us, but when they look through that old Declaration of Independence they find that those old men say that "We hold these truths to be self-evident, that all men are created equal," and then they feel that that moral sentiment taught in that day evidences their relation to those men, that it is the father of all moral principle in them, and that they have

16 *Tribune* has "understand."

[499]

a right to claim it as though they were blood of the blood, and flesh of the flesh of the men who wrote that Declaration, (loud and long continued applause) and so they are. That is the electric cord in that Declaration that links the hearts of patriotic and liberty-loving men together, that will link those patriotic hearts as long as the love of freedom exists in the minds of men throughout the world. [Applause.]

Now, sirs, for the purpose of squaring things with this idea of "don't care if slavery is voted up or voted down," for sustaining the Dred Scott decision [A voice—"Hit him again"], for holding that the Declaration of Independence did not mean anything at all, we have Judge Douglas giving his exposition of what the Declaration of Independence means, and we have him saying that the people of America are equal to the people of England. According to his construction, you Germans are not connected with it. Now I ask you in all soberness, if all these things, if indulged in, if ratified, if confirmed and endorsed, if taught to our children, and repeated to them, do not tend to rub out the sentiment of liberty in the country, and to transform this Government into a government of some other form. Those arguments that are made, that the inferior race are to be treated with as much allowance as they are capable of enjoying; that as much is to be done for them as their condition will allow. What are these arguments? They are the arguments that kings have made for enslaving the people in all ages of the world. You will find that all the arguments in favor of king-craft were of this class; they always bestrode the necks of the people, not that they wanted to do it, but because the people were better off for being ridden. That is their argument, and this argument of the Judge is the same old serpent that says you work and I eat, you toil and I will enjoy the fruits of it. Turn in[17] whatever way you will—whether it come from the mouth of a King, an excuse for enslaving the people of his country, or from the mouth of men of one race as a reason for enslaving the men of another race, it is all the same old serpent, and I hold if that course of argumentation that is made for the purpose of convincing the public mind that we should not care about this, should be granted, it does not stop with the negro. I should like to know if taking this old Declaration of Independence, which declares that all men are equal upon principle and making exceptions to it where will it stop. If one man says it does not mean a negro, why not[18] another say it does not mean some other man? If that declaration is not the truth, let us get the Statute book, in which we

17 "It" in *Tribune*.   18 "May not" in *Tribune*.

find it and tear it out! Who is so bold as to do it! [Voices—"me" "no one," &c.] If it is not true let us tear it out! [cries of "no, no,"] let us stick to it then, [cheers] let us stand firmly by it then. [Applause.]

It may be argued that there are certain conditions that make necessities and impose them upon us, and to the extent that a necessity is imposed upon a man he must submit to it. I think that was the condition in which we found ourselves when we established this government. We had slavery among us, we could not get our constitution unless we permitted them to remain in slavery, we could not secure the good we did secure if we grasped for more, and having by necessity submitted to that much, it does not destroy the principle that is the charter of our liberties. Let that charter stand as our standard.

My friend has said to me that I am a poor hand to quote Scripture. I will try it again, however. It is said in one of the admonitions of the Lord, "As your Father in Heaven is perfect, be ye also perfect." The Savior, I suppose, did not expect that any human creature could be perfect as the Father in Heaven; but He said, "As your Father in Heaven is perfect, be ye also perfect." He set that up as a standard, and he who did most towards reaching that standard, attained the highest degree of moral perfection. So I say in relation to the principle that all men are created equal, let it be as nearly reached as we can. If we cannot give freedom to every creature, let us do nothing that will impose slavery upon any other creature. [Applause.] Let us then turn this government back into the channel in which the framers of the Constitution originally placed it. Let us stand firmly by each other. If we do not do so we are turning in the contrary direction, that our friend Judge Douglas proposes—not intentionally—as working in the traces[19] tend to make this one universal slave nation. [A voice—"that is so."] He is one that runs in that direction, and as such I resist him.

My friends, I have detained you about as long as I desired to do, and I have only to say, let us discard all this quibbling about this man and the other man—this race and that race and the other race being inferior, and therefore they must be placed in an inferior position—discarding our standard that we have left us. Let us discard all these things, and unite as one people throughout this land, until we shall once more stand up declaring that all men are created equal.

My friends, I could not, without launching off upon some new topic, which would detain you too long, continue to-night. [Cries

19 "Traces that tend" in *Tribune.*

[501]

of "go on."] I thank you for this most extensive audience that you have furnished me to-night. I leave you, hoping that the lamp of liberty will burn in your bosoms until there shall no longer be a doubt that all men are created free and equal.

Mr. Lincoln retired amid a perfect torrent of applause and cheers.

To William H. Hanna[1]

W. H. Hanna, Esq.   Springfield,
My dear Sir: July 15, 1858
Reaching home yesterday evening I found your letter of the 13th. No accident preventing, I will be with you Friday afternoon and evening. I do not know that there will be any opening for me, but I shall try to be on the grounds to take the chances. Your friend, as ever   A. LINCOLN

[1] Typed copy, IHi. William H. Hanna was an attorney at Bloomington, Illinois.

To Gustave P. Koerner[1]

Hon. G. Koerner: Springfield,
My dear Sir   July 15. 1858
I have just been called on by one of our german republicans here, to ascertain if Mr. Hecker[2] could not be prevailed on to visit this region, and address the germans, at this place, and a few others at least. Please ascertain & write me. He would, of course, have to be paid something. Find out from him about how much.

I have just returned from Chicago. Douglas took nothing by his motion there. In fact, by his rampant indorsement of the Dred Scott decision he drove back a few republicans who were favorably inclined towards him. His tactics just now, in part is, to make it appear that he is having a triumphal entry into; and march through the country; but it is all as bombastic and hollow as Napoleon's bulletins sent back from his campaign in Russia. I was present at his reception in Chicago, and it certainly was very large and imposing; but judging from the opinions of others better acquainted with faces there, and by the strong call for me to speak. when he closed, I really believe we could have voted him down in that very crowd. Our meeting, twentyfour hours after, called only twelve hours before it came together and got up without trumpery, was nearly as large, and five times as enthusiastic.

I write this, for your private eye, to assure you that there is no solid shot, in these bombastic parades of his. Yours very truly

A. LINCOLN

1 ALS, owned by Miss Sophie Rombauer, Brickey's, Missouri.
2 Friedrich K. F. Hecker.

To Joseph Gillespie[1]

Hon. Joseph Gillespie
My dear Sir:

Springfield,
July 16. 1858.

I write this to say that from the specimens of Douglas democracy we occasionally see here from Madison, we learn that they are making very confident calculation of beating both you, and your friends for the lower House in that county. They offer to bet upon it. Billings and Job[2] respectively, have been up here, and were each, as I learn, talking largely about it. If they do so, it can only be done by carrying the Fillmore men of 1856, very differently from what they seem to be going in other parts. Below is the vote of 1856, in your District.

	Buc.	Fre.	Fill.
Bond	607	153	659
Madison	1451	1111	1658
Montgy.	992	162	686
	3050	1426	3003

By this you will see, if you go through the calculation, that if *they* get one quarter of the Fillmore votes and *you* three quarters, they will beat you 125 votes. If they get one *fifth* and you four fifths, you beat them 179. In Madison alone if our friends get 1000 of the Fillmore votes, and their opponents the remainder—658, we win by just two votes.

This shows the whole field, on the basis of the election of 1856. Whether, since then, any Buchanan men, or Fremonters have shifted ground, and how the majority of *new* voters will go, you can judge better than I.

Of course you, *on* the ground, can better determine your line of tactics, than any one off the ground; but it behooves you to be wide awake, and actively working. Dont neglect it; and write me at your first leisure. Yours as ever   A. LINCOLN—

1 ALS, owned by Charles S. Gillespie, Edwardsville, Illinois.
2 Henry W. Billings, lawyer and judge at Alton, Illinois, and Zephaniah B. Job, who was elected state representative from Madison County in 1858.

Remarks at Bloomington, Illinois[1]

July 16, 1858

As soon as Judge Douglas retired, loud calls were made for Hon. Abraham Lincoln. Mr. L. held back for a little while, but the crowd finally succeeded in inducing him to come upon the stand. He was received with three rousing cheers—much louder than those given to Judge Douglas. He remarked that he appeared before the audience for the purpose of saying that he would take an early opportunity to give his views to the citizens of this place regarding the matters spoken of in Judge Douglas' speech. "This meeting," said Mr. Lincoln, "was called by the friends of Judge Douglas, and it would be improper for me to address it." Mr. L. then retired amid loud cheering.

[1] Bloomington *Pantagraph*, July 17, 1858; *Illinois State Journal*, July 21, 1858.

Remarks at Atlanta, Illinois[1]

July 17, 1858

When the Judge retired from the stand, vociferous calls were made for "Lincoln!" "Lincoln!!" "Lincoln!!!" Mr. L. appeared before the audience, and remarked that feelings of delicacy prompted him to refrain from addressing them. He said he appreciated the kindness which induced his friends to call him out, but he hoped they would not insist on a speech from him on that occasion.

[1] Bloomington *Pantagraph*, July 17, 1858; *Illinois State Journal*, July 21, 1858.

Speech at Springfield, Illinois[1]

July 17, 1858

Delivered, as indicated by the heading.
Senator Douglas not present.[2]

FELLOW CITIZENS:—Another election, which is deemed an important one, is approaching, and, as I suppose, the Republican party will, without much difficulty elect their State ticket. But in regard

[1] Debates Scrapbook, ORB. Lincoln used the pamphlet reprint (Monaghan 12) in the debates scrapbook (see Speech at Springfield, June 16, 1858, n.1, *supra*), and made only one correction, as indicated in a footnote. Except for Lincoln's deletion of cheering throughout the speech, which has not been observed, the text follows the debates scrapbook, with important variations in the text of the *Illinois State Journal*, July 20, 21, 1858, given in the footnotes. Collation of punctuation with the *Journal* text has also provided a few marks not in the debates scrapbook text.

[2] Lincoln's prefatory note in the debates scrapbook. Douglas had spoken in the afternoon. Lincoln spoke at night.

to the Legislature, we, the Republicans, labor under some disadvantages. In the first place, we have a Legislature to elect upon an apportionment of the representation made several years ago, when the proportion of the population was far greater in the South (as compared with the North) than it now is; and inasmuch as our opponents hold almost entire sway in the South, and we a correspondingly large majority in the North, the fact that we are now to be represented as we were years ago, when the population was different, is to us a very great disadvantage. We had, in the year 1855, according to law, a census or enumeration of the inhabitants, taken for the purpose of a new apportionment of representation. We know what a fair apportionment of representation upon that census would give us. We know that it could not if fairly made, fail to give the Republican party from six to ten more members of the Legislature than they can probably get as the law now stands. It so happened at the last session of the Legislature, that our opponents, holding the control of both branches of the Legislature, steadily refused to give us such an apportionment as we were rightfully entitled to have upon the census already taken.[3] The Legislature steadily refused to give us such an apportionment as we were rightfully entitled to have upon the census taken of the population of the State. The Legislature would pass no bill upon that subject, except such as was at least as unfair to us as the old one, and in which, in some instances, two men in the Democratic regions were allowed to go as far towards sending a member to the Legislature as three were in the Republican regions. Comparison was made at the time as to representative and senatorial districts, which completely demonstrated that such was the fact. Such a bill was passed, and tendered to the Republican Governor for his signature; but principally for the reasons I have stated, he withheld his approval, and the bill fell without becoming a law.

Another disadvantage under which we labor is, that there are one or two Democratic Senators who will be members of the next Legislature, and will vote for[4] the election of Senator, who are holding over in districts in which we could, on all reasonable calculation, elect men of our own, if we only had the chance of an election. When we consider that there are but twenty five Senators in the Senate, taking two from the side where they rightfully be-

[3] The *Journal* has an additional digression at this point, as follows: "[A rocket goes up near the window.] I expect that we shall have as much of that as we can conveniently get along with. I was saying that the Legislature steadily refused to give us such an apportionment as we were rightfully entitled to have upon the census taken of the population of the State."

[4] *Journal* has "upon."

long and adding them to the other, is to us a disadvantage not to be lightly regarded. Still, so it is; we have this to contend with. Perhaps there is no ground of complaint on our part. In attending to the many things involved in the last general election for President, Governor, Auditor, Treasurer, Superintendent of Public Instruction, Members of Congress, of the Legislature, County officers, and so on, we allowed these things to happen by want of sufficient attention, and we have no cause to complain of our adversaries, so far as this matter is concerned. But we have some cause to complain of the refusal to give us a fair apportionment.

There is still another disadvantage under which we labor, and to which I will ask your attention. It arises out of the relative positions of the two persons who stand before the State as candidates for the Senate. Senator Douglas is of world wide renown. All the anxious politicians of his party, or who have been of his party for years past, have been looking upon him as certainly, at no distant[5] day, to be the President of the United States. They have seen in his round, jolly, fruitful face, postoffices, landoffices, marshalships, and cabinet appointments, chargeships and foreign missions, bursting and sprouting out in wonderful exuberance ready to be laid hold of by their greedy hands. [Great laughter.] And as they have been gazing upon this attractive picture so long, they cannot, in the little distraction that has taken place in the party, bring themselves to give[6] up the charming hope; but with greedier anxiety they rush about him, sustain him, and give him marches, triumphal entries, and receptions beyond what even in the days of his highest prosperity they could have brought about in his favor. On the contrary nobody has ever expected me to be President. In my poor, lean, lank, face, nobody has ever seen that any cabbages were sprouting out. [Tremendous cheering and laughter.] These are disadvantages all, taken together, that the Republicans labor under. *We* have to fight this battle upon principle, and upon principle alone. I am, in a certain sense, made the standard-bearer in behalf of the Republicans. I was made so merely because there had to be some one so placed—I being in no wise, preferable to any other one of the twenty-five—perhaps a hundred we have in the Republican ranks. Then I say I wish it to be distinctly understood and borne in mind, that we have to fight this battle without many—perhaps without any—of the external aids which are brought to bear against us. So I hope those with whom I am surrounded have principle enough to nerve themselves for the task and leave nothing undone, that can be fairly done, to bring about the right result.

[5] *Journal* has "very distant."   [6] *Journal* has "quite give."

After Senator Douglas left Washington, as his movements were made known by the public prints, he tarried a considerable time in the city of New York; and it was heralded that, like another Napoleon, he was lying by, and framing the plan of his campaign. It was telegraphed to Washington City, and published in the *Union*, that he was framing his plan for the purpose of going to Illinois to pounce upon and annihilate the treasonable and disunion speech which Lincoln had made here on the 16th of June. Now, I do suppose that the Judge really spent some time in New York maturing the plan of the campaign, as his friends heralded for him. I have been able, by noting his movements since his arrival in Illinois, to discover evidences confirmatory of that allegation. I think I have been able to see what are the material points of that plan. I will, for a little while, ask your attention to some of them. What I shall point out, though not showing the whole plan, are, nevertheless, the main points, as I suppose.

They are not very numerous. The first is Popular Sovereignty. The second and third are attacks upon my speech made on the 16th of June. Out of these three points—drawing within the range of Popular Sovereignty the question of the Lecompton Constitution— he makes his principal assault. Upon these his successive speeches are substantially one and the same. On this matter of Popular Sovereignty I wish to be a little careful. Auxiliary to these main points, to be sure, are their thunderings of cannon, their marching and music, their fizzlegigs and fireworks; but I will not waste time with them. They are but the little trappings of the campaign.

Coming to the substance—the first point—"Popular Sovereignty." It is to be labelled upon the cars in which he travels; put upon the hacks he rides in; to be flaunted upon the arches he passes under, and the banners which wave over him. It is to be dished up in as many varieties as a French cook can produce soups from potatoes. Now, as this is so great a staple of the plan of the campaign, it is worth while to examine it carefully; and if we examine only a very little, and do not allow ourselves to be misled, we shall be able to see that the whole thing is the most arrant Quixotism that was ever enacted before a community. What is the[7] matter of Popular Sovereignty? The first thing, in order to understand it, is to get a good definition of what it is, and after that to see how it is applied.

I suppose almost every one knows, that in this controversy, whatever has been said, has had reference to the question of negro slavery. We have not been in a controversy about the right of the

7 *Journal* has "this."

people to govern themselves in the *ordinary* matters of domestic concern in the States and Territories. Mr. Buchanan in one of his late messages, (I think when he sent up the Lecompton Constitution,) urged that the main points to which the public attention had been directed, was not in regard to the great variety of small domestic matters, but was directed to the question of negro slavery; and he asserts, that if the people had had a fair chance to vote on that question, there was no reasonable ground of objection in regard to minor questions. Now, while I think that the people had *not* had given, or offered them, a fair chance upon that slavery question; still, if there had been a fair submission to a vote upon that main question, the President's proposition would have been true to the uttermost. Hence, when hereafter, I speak of popular sovereignty, I wish to be understood as applying what I say to the question of slavery only, not[8] to other minor domestic matters of a Territory or a State.

Does Judge Douglas, when he says that several of the past years of his life have been devoted to the question of "popular sovereignty," and that all the remainder of his life shall be devoted to it, does he mean to say that he has been devoting his life to securing to the people of the territories the right to exclude slavery from the territories? If he means so to say, he means to deceive; because he and every one knows that the decision of the Supreme Court, which he approves and makes especial ground of attack upon me for disapproving, forbids the people of a territory to exclude slavery. This covers the whole ground, from the settlement of a territory till it reaches the degree of maturity entitling it to form a State Constitution. So far as all that ground is concerned, the Judge is not sustaining popular sovereignty, but absolutely opposing it. He sustains the decision which declares that the popular will of the territories has no constitutional power to exclude slavery during their territorial existence. [Cheers] This being so, the period of time from the first settlement of a territory till it reaches the point of forming a State Constitution, is not the thing that the Judge has fought for or is fighting for, but on the contrary, he has fought for, and is fighting for, the thing that annihilates and crushes out that same popular sovereignty.

Well, so much being disposed of, what is left? Why, he is contending for the right of the people, when they come to make a State Constitution, to make it for themselves, and precisely as best suits themselves. I say again, that is Quixotic. I defy contradiction when I declare that the Judge can find no one to oppose him on that

[8] *Journal* has "and not."

proposition. I repeat, there is nobody opposing that proposition on *principle*. Let me not be misunderstood. I know that, with reference to the Lecompton Constitution, I may be misunderstood; but when you understand me correctly, my proposition will be true and accurate. Nobody is opposing, or has opposed, the right of the people, when they form a Constitution, to form it for themselves. Mr. Buchanan and his friends have not done it; they, too, as well as the Republicans and the Anti-Lecompton Democrats, have not done it; but, on the contrary, they together have insisted on the right of the people to form a Constitution for themselves. The difference between the Buchanan men on the one hand, and the Douglas men and the Republicans on the other, has not been on a question of principle, but on a question of *fact*.

The dispute was upon the question of fact, whether the Lecompton Constitution had been fairly formed by the people or not. Mr. Buchanan and his friends have not contended for the contrary principle any more than the Douglas men or the Republicans. They have insisted that whatever of small irregularities existed in getting up the Lecompton Constitution, were such as happen in the settlement of all new Territories. The question was, was it a fair emanation of the people? It was a question of fact, and not of principle. As to the principle, all were agreed. Judge Douglas voted with the Republicans upon that matter of fact.

He and they, by their voices and votes, denied that it was a fair emanation of the people. The Administration affirmed that it was. With respect to the evidence bearing upon that question of fact, I readily agree that Judge Douglas and the Republicans had the right on their side, and that the Administration was wrong. But I state again that as a matter of principle there is no dispute upon the right of a people in a Territory, merging into a State to form a Constitution for themselves without outside interference from any quarter. This being so, what is Judge Douglas going to spend his life for? Is he going to spend his life in maintaining a principle that nobody on earth opposes? [Cheers.] Does he expect to stand up in majestic dignity, and go through his *apotheosis* and become a god, in the maintaining of a principle which neither a man nor a mouse in all God's creation is opposing? [Tremendous cheering.] Now something in regard to the Lecompton Constitution more specially;[9] for I pass from this other question of popular sovereignty as the most errant humbug that has ever been attempted on an intelligent community.

As to the Lecompton Constitution, I have already said that on

9 *Journal* has "specifically."

the question of fact as to whether it was a fair emanation of the people or not, Judge Douglas with the Republicans and some Americans had greatly the argument against the Administration; and while I repeat this, I wish to know what there is in the opposition of Judge Douglas to the Lecompton Constitution that entitles him to be considered the only opponent to it—as being *par excellence* the very *quintessence* of that opposition. I agree to the rightfulness of his opposition. He in the Senate and his class of men there formed the number *three* and no more. In the House of Representatives his class of men—the anti Lecompton Democrats—formed a number of about twenty. It took one hundred and twenty to defeat the measure against one hundred and twelve. Of the votes of that one hundred and twenty, Judge Douglas' friends furnished twenty, to add to which, there were six Americans and ninety-four Republicans. I do not say that I am precisely accurate in their numbers, but I am sufficiently so for any use I am making of it.

Why is it that twenty shall be entitled to all the credit of doing that work, and the hundred none of it? Why, if, as Judge Douglas says, the honor is to be divided and due credit is to be given to other parties, why is just so much given as is consonant with the wishes, the interests and advancement of the twenty? My understanding is, when a common job is done, or a common enterprise prosecuted, if I put in five dollars to your one, I have a right to take out five dollars to your one. But he does not so understand it. He declares the dividend of credit for defeating Lecompton upon a basis which seems unprecedented and incomprehensible.

Let us see. Lecompton in the raw was defeated. It afterwards took a sort of cooked up shape, and was passed in the English bill. It is said by the Judge that the defeat was a good and proper thing. If it was a good thing, why is he entitled to more credit than others, for the performance of that good act, unless there was something in the antecedents of the Republicans that might induce every one to expect them to join[10] in that good work, and at the same time, something leading them to doubt that he would? Does he place his superior claim to credit, on the ground that he performed a good act which was never expected of him? He says I have a proneness for quoting scripture. If I should do so now, it occurs that perhaps he places himself somewhat upon the ground of the parable of the lost sheep which went astray upon the mountains, and when the owner of the hundred sheep found the one that was lost, and threw it upon his shoulders, and came home rejoicing, it was said that there was more rejoicing over the one sheep that was lost and had

[10] *Journal* has "expect that they would join."

been found, than over the ninety and nine in the fold. [Great cheering, renewed cheering.] The application is made[11] by the Saviour in this parable, thus, "Verily, I say unto you, there is more rejoicing in heaven over one sinner that repenteth, than over ninety and nine just persons that need no repentance." [Cheering.]

And now, if the Judge claims the benefit of this parable, *let him repent.* [Vociferous applause.] Let him not come up here and say: I am the only just person; and you are the ninety-nine sinners! *Repentance,* before *forgiveness* is a provision of the Christian system, and on that condition alone will the Republicans grant his forgiveness. [Laughter and cheers.]

How will he prove that we have ever occupied a different position in regard to the Lecompton Constitution or any principle in it? He says he did not make his opposition on the ground as to whether it was a free or slave constitution, and he would have you understand that the Republicans made their opposition because it ultimately became a slave constitution. To make proof in favor of himself on this point, he reminds us that he opposed Lecompton before the vote was taken declaring whether the State was to be free or slave. But he forgets to say that our Republican Senator Trumbull, made a speech against Lecompton, even before he did.

Why did he oppose it? Partly, as he declares, because the members of the Convention who framed it were not fairly elected by the people; that the people were not allowed to vote unless they had been registered; and that the people of whole counties, in some instances, were not registered. For these reasons he declares the constitution was not an emanation, in any true sense, from the people. He also has an additional objection as to the mode of submitting the constitution back to the people. But bearing on the question of whether the delegates were fairly elected, a speech of his, made something more than twelve months ago, from this stand, becomes important. It was made a little while before the election of the delegates who made Lecompton. In that speech he declared there was every reason to hope and believe the election would be fair; and if any one failed to vote, it would be his own culpable fault.

I, a few days after, made a sort of answer to that speech. In that answer, I made, substantially, the very argument with which he combatted his Lecompton adversaries in the Senate last winter. I pointed to the facts that the people could not vote without being registered, and that the time for registering had gone by. I commented on it as wonderful that Judge Douglas could be ignorant

11 *Journal* has "the moral is applied."

of these facts, which every one else in the nation so well knew.

I now pass from popular sovereignty and Lecompton. I may have occasion to refer to one or both.

When he was preparing his plan of campaign, Napoleon like, in New York, as appears by two speeches I have heard him deliver since his arrival in Illinois, he gave special attention to a speech of mine, delivered here on the 16th of June last. He says that he carefully read that speech. He told us that at Chicago a week ago last night, and he repeated it at Bloomington last night. Doubtless, he repeated it again to-day, though I did not hear him. In the two first places—Chicago and Bloomington—I heard him; to-day I did not. [A voice—Yes; he said the same thing.] He said he had carefully examined that speech; *when*, he did not say; but there is no reasonable doubt it was when he was in New York preparing his plan of campaign. I am glad he did read it carefully. He says it was evidently prepared with great care. I freely admit it was prepared with care. I claim not to be more free from errors than others—perhaps scarcely so much; but I was very careful not to put anything in that speech as a matter of fact, or make any inferences which did not appear to me to be true, and fully warrantable. If I had made any mistake I was willing to be corrected; if I had drawn any inference in regard to Judge Douglas, or any one else, which was not warranted, I was fully prepared to modify it as soon as discovered. I planted myself upon the truth, and the truth only, so far as I knew it, or could be brought to know it.

Having made that speech with the most kindly feeling towards Judge Douglas, as manifested therein, I was gratified when I found that he had carefully examined it, and had detected no error of fact, nor any inference against him, nor any misrepresentations, of which he thought fit to complain. In neither of the two speeches I have mentioned, did he make any such complaint. I will thank any one who will inform me that he, in his speech to day, pointed out anything I had stated, respecting him, as being erroneous. I presume there is no such thing. I have reason to be gratified that the care and caution used in that speech, left it so that he, most of all others interested in discovering error, has not been able to point out one thing against him which he could say was wrong. He seizes upon the doctrines he supposes to be included in that speech, and declares that upon them will turn the issues of this campaign. He then quotes, or attempts to quote, from my speech. I will not say that he willfully misquotes, but he does fail to quote accurately. His attempt at quoting is from a passage which I believe I can quote accurately from memory. I shall make the quotation now, with some comments upon it, as I have already said, in order that the Judge shall be left entirely without excuse for misrepresenting me. I do so now, as I hope, for the last time. I do this in great caution, in order that if he repeats his misrepresentation, it shall be plain to all that he does so willfully. If, after all, he still persists, I shall be compelled to reconstruct[12] the course I have marked out for myself, and draw upon such humble resources as I have, for a new course, better suited to the real exigencies of the case. I set out in this campaign, with the intention of conducting it strictly as a gentleman, in substance at least, if not in the outside polish. The latter I shall never be, but that which constitutes the inside of a gentleman I hope I understand, and am not less inclined to practice than others. [Cheers.] It was my purpose and expectations that this canvass would be conducted upon principle, and with fairness on both sides; and it shall not be my fault, if this purpose and expectation shall be given up.

He charges, in substance, that I invite a war of sections; that I propose all the local institutions of the different States shall become consolidated and uniform. What is there in the language of that speech which expresses such purpose, or bears such construction? I have again and again said that I would not enter into any of the States to disturb the institution of slavery. Judge Douglas said, at Bloomington, that I used language most able and ingenious for concealing what I really meant; and that while I had protested against entering into the slave States, I nevertheless did mean to go on the banks of Ohio and throw missiles into Kentucky to disturb them in their domestic institutions.

I said, in that speech, and I meant no more, that the institution of slavery ought to be placed in the very attitude where the framers of this Government placed it, and left it. I do not understand that the framers of our Constitution left the people of the free States in the attitude of firing bombs or shells into the slave States. I was not using that passage for the purpose for which he infers I did use it. I said: "We are now far advanced into the fifth year since a policy was created for the avowed object and with the confident promise of putting an end to slavery agitation. Under the operation of that policy that agitation has not only not ceased, but has constantly augmented. In my opinion it will not cease till a crisis shall have been reached and passed. 'A house divided against itself can not stand.' I believe that this Government cannot endure permanently half slave and half free. It will become all

12 *Journal* has "reconsider."

one thing or all the other. Either the opponents of slavery will arrest the further spread of it, and place it where the public mind shall rest in the belief that it is in the course of ultimate extinction, or its advocates will push it forward till it shall become alike lawful in all the States, old as well as new, North as well as South."

Now you all see, from that quotation, I did not express my *wish* on anything. In that passage I indicated no wish or purpose of my own; I simply expressed my *expectation*. Cannot the Judge perceive the distinction between a *purpose* and an *expectation*. I have often expressed an expectation to die, but I have never expressed a *wish* to die. I said at Chicago, and now repeat, that I am quite aware this government has endured, half slave and half free, for eighty-two years. I understand that little bit of history. I expressed the opinion I did, because I perceived—or thought I perceived—a new set of causes introduced. I did say, at Chicago, in my speech there, that I do wish to see the spread of slavery arrested and to see it placed where the public mind shall rest in the belief that it is in course of ultimate extinction. I said that because I supposed, when the public mind shall rest in that belief, we shall have peace on the slavery question. I have believed—and now believe—the public mind did rest on that belief up to the introduction of the Nebraska bill.

Although I have ever been opposed to slavery, so far I rested in the hope and belief that it was in course of ultimate extinction. For that reason, it had been a minor question with me. I might have been mistaken; but I had believed, and now believe, that the whole public mind, that is the mind of the great majority, had rested in that belief up to the repeal of the Missouri Compromise. But upon that event, I became convinced that either I had been resting in a delusion, or the institution was being placed on a new basis—a basis for making it perpetual, national and universal. Subsequent events have greatly confirmed me in that belief. I believe that bill to be the beginning of a conspiracy for that pur-. pose. So believing, I have since then considered that question a paramount one. So believing, I have thought the public mind will never rest till the power of Congress to restrict the spread of it, shall again be acknowledged and exercised on the one hand, or on the other, all resistance be entirely crushed out. I have expressed that opinion, and I entertain it to-night. It is denied that there is any tendency to the nationalization of slavery in these States.

Mr. Brooks, of South Carolina, in one of his speeches, when they were presenting him with canes, silver plate, gold pitchers and the like, for assaulting Senator Sumner, distinctly affirmed his opinion that when this Constitution was formed, it was the belief of no man that slavery would last to the present day.

He said, what I think, that the framers of our Constitution placed the institution of slavery where the public mind rested in the hope that it was in course of ultimate extinction. But he went on to say that the men of the present age, by their experience, have become wiser than the framers of the Constitution; and the invention[13] of the cotton gin had made the perpetuity of slavery a necessity in this country.

As another piece of evidence tending to the same point:— Quite recently in Virginia, a man—the owner of slaves—made a will providing that after his death certain of his slaves should have their freedom if they should so choose, and go to Liberia, rather than remain in slavery. They chose to be liberated. But the persons to whom they would descend as property, claimed them as slaves. A suit was instituted, which finally came to the Supreme Court of Virginia, and[14] was therein decided against the slaves, upon the ground that a negro cannot make a choice—that they had no legal power to choose—could not perform the condition upon which their freedom depended.

I do not mention this with any purpose of criticising, but to connect it with the arguments as affording additional evidence of the change of sentiment upon this question of slavery in the direction of making it perpetual and national. I argue now as I did before, that there is such a tendency, and I am backed not merely by the facts, but by the open confession in the Slave States.

And now as to the Judge's inference, that because I wish to see slavery placed in the course of ultimate extinction—placed where our fathers originally placed it—I wish to annihilate the State Legislatures—to force cotton to grow upon the tops of the Green Mountains—to freeze ice in Florida—to cut lumber[15] on the broad Illinois prairies—that I am in favor of all these ridiculous and impossible things.

It seems to me it is a complete answer to all this, to ask, if, when Congress did have the fashion of restricting slavery from free territory; when courts did have the fashion of deciding that taking a slave into a free country made him free—I say it is a sufficient answer, to ask, if any of this ridiculous nonsense about consolidation, and uniformity, did actually follow. Who heard of any such thing, because of the Ordinance of '87? because of the Missouri Restric-

13 *Journal* has "inventor."
14 "And" inserted by Lincoln, as in the *Journal*.
15 *Journal* has "timber."

[515]

tion? because of the numerous court decisions of that character?

Now, as to the Dred Scott decision; for upon that he makes his last point at me. He boldly takes ground in favor of that decision.

This is one-half the onslaught, and one-third of the entire plan of the campaign. I am opposed to that decision in a certain sense, but not in the sense which he puts on it. I say that in so far as it decided in favor of Dred Scott's master and against Dred Scott and his family, I do not propose to disturb or resist the decision.

I never have proposed to do any such thing. I think, that in respect for judicial authority, my humble history would not suffer in a comparison with that of Judge Douglas. He would have the citizen conform his vote to that decision; the Member of Congress, his; the President, his use of the veto power. He would make it a rule of political action for the people and all the departments of the government. I would not. By resisting it as a political rule, I disturb no right of property, create no disorder, excite no mobs.

When he spoke at Chicago, on Friday evening of last week, he made this same point upon me. On Saturday evening I replied and reminded him of a Supreme Court decision which he opposed for at least several years. Last night, at Bloomington, he took some notice of that reply; but entirely forgot to remember that part of it.

He renews his onslaught upon me, forgetting to remember that I have turned the tables against himself on that very point. I renew the effort to draw his attention to it. I wish to stand erect before the country as well as[16] Judge Douglas, on this question of judicial authority; and therefore I add something to the authority in favor of my own position. I wish to show that I am sustained by authority, in addition to that heretofore presented. I do not expect to convince the Judge. It is part of the plan of his campaign, and he will cling to it with a desperate gripe. Even, turn it upon him—turn the sharp point against him, and gaff him through—he will still cling to it till he can invent some new dodge to take the place of it.

In public speaking it is tedious reading from documents; but I must beg to indulge the practice to a limited extent. I shall read from a letter written by Mr. Jefferson in 1820, and now to be found in the seventh volume of his correspondence, at page 177. It seems he had been presented by a gentleman of the name of Jarvis with a book, or essay, or periodical, called the "Republican," and he was writing in acknowledgement of the present, and noting some of its contents. After expressing the hope that the work will produce a favorable effect upon the minds of the young, he proceeds to say:

[16] *Journal* has "as well as before."

That it will have this tendency may be expected, and for that reason I feel an urgency to note what I deem an error in it, the more requiring notice as your opinion is strengthened by that of many others. You seem in pages 84 and 148, to consider the judges as the ultimate arbiters of all constitutional questions—a very dangerous doctrine indeed and one which would place us under the despotism of an oligarchy. Our judges are as honest as other men, and not more so. They have, with others, the same passions for party, for power, and the privilege of their corps. Their maxim is, "boni judicis est ampliare jurisdictionem"; and their power is the more dangerous as they are in office for life, and not responsible, as the other functionaries are, to the elective control. The Constitution has erected no such single tribunal, knowing that to whatever hands confided, with the corruptions of time and party, its members would become despots. It has more wisely made all the departments co-equal and co-sovereign within themselves.

Thus we see the power claimed for the Supreme Court by Judge Douglas, Mr. Jefferson holds, would reduce us to the despotism of an oligarchy.

Now, I have said no more than this—in fact, never quite so much as this—at least I am sustained by Mr. Jefferson.

Let us go a little further. You remember we once had a national bank. Some one owed the bank a debt; he was sued and sought to avoid payment, on the ground that the bank was unconstitutional. The case went to the Supreme Court, and therein it was decided that the bank was constitutional. The whole Democratic party revolted against that decision. General Jackson himself asserted that he, as President, would not be bound to hold a national bank to be constitutional, even though the Court had decided it to be so. He fell in precisely with the view of Mr. Jefferson, and acted upon it under his official oath, in vetoing a charter for a national bank. The declaration that Congress does not possess this constitutional power to charter a bank, has gone into the Democratic platform, at their national conventions, and was brought forward and reaffirmed in their last convention at Cincinnati. They have contended for that declaration, in the very teeth of the Supreme Court, for more than a quarter of a century. In fact, they have reduced the decision to an absolute nullity. That decision, I repeat, is repudiated in the Cincinnati platform; and still, as if to show that effrontery can go no farther, Judge Douglas vaunts in the very speeches in which he denounces me for opposing the Dred Scott decision, that he stands on the Cincinnati platform.

Now, I wish to know what the Judge can charge upon me, with respect to decisions of the Supreme Court which does not lie in all its length, breadth, and proportions at his own door. The plain truth is simply this: Judge Douglas is *for* Supreme Court decisions when he likes[17] and against them when he does not like them. He is for the Dred Scott decision because it tends to nationalize slavery —because it is part of the original combination for that object. It so happens, singularly enough, that I never stood opposed to a decision of the Supreme Court till this. On the contrary, I have no recollection that he was ever particularly in favor of one till this. He never was in favor of any, nor opposed to any,[18] till the present one, which helps to nationalize slavery.

Free men of Sangamon—free men of Illinois—free men everywhere—judge ye between him and me, upon this issue.

He says this Dred Scott case is a very small matter at most—that it has no practical effect; that at best, or rather, I suppose, at worst, it is but an abstraction. I submit that the proposition that the thing which determines whether a man is free or a slave, is rather *concrete* than *abstract*. I think you would conclude that it was, if your liberty depended upon it, and so would Judge Douglas if his liberty depended upon it. But suppose it was on the question of spreading slavery over the new territories that he considers it as being merely[19] an abstract matter, and one of no practical importance. How has the planting of slavery in new countries always been effected? It has now been decided that slavery cannot be kept out of our new territories by any legal means. In what does our new territories now differ in this respect, from the old colonies when slavery was first planted within them? It was planted as Mr. Clay once declared, and as history proves true, by individual men[20] in spite of the wishes of the people; the mother government refusing to prohibit it, and withholding from the people of the colonies the authority to prohibit it for themselves. Mr. Clay says this was one of the great and just causes of complaint against Great Britain by the colonies, and the best apology we can now make for having the institution amongst us. In that precise condition our Nebraska politicians have at last succeeded in placing our own new territories; the government will not prohibit slavery within them, nor allow the people to prohibit it.

I defy any man to find any difference between the policy which originally planted slavery in these colonies and that policy which now prevails in our own new Territories. If it does not go into them, it is only because no individual wishes it to go. The Judge indulged himself, doubtless, to-day, with the question as to what I am going to do with or about the Dred Scott decision. Well,

---

[17] *Journal* has "likes them; and."
[18] *Journal* has "He never was in favor of any; nor I opposed to any."
[19] *Journal* has "nearly."   [20] *Journal* has "industrious men."

Judge, will you please tell me what you did about the Bank decision? Will you not graciously allow us to do with the Dred Scott decision precisely as you did with the Bank decision? You succeeded in breaking down the moral effect of that decision; did you find it necessary to amend the Constitution? or to set up a court of negroes in order to do it?

There is one other point. Judge Douglas has a very affectionate leaning towards the Americans and old Whigs. Last evening, in a sort of weeping tone, he described to us a death bed scene. He had been called to the side of Mr. Clay, in his last moments, in order that the genius of "popular sovereignty" might duly descend from the dying man and settle upon him, the living[21] and most worthy successor. He could do no less than promise that he would devote the remainder of his life to "popular sovereignty;" and then the great statesman departs in peace. By this part of the "plan of the campaign," the Judge has evidently promised himself that tears shall be drawn down the cheeks of all old Whigs, as large as half grown apples.

Mr. Webster, too, was mentioned; but it did not quite come to a death-bed scene, as to him. It would be amusing, if it were not disgusting, to see how quick these compromise-breakers administer on the political effects of their dead adversaries, trumping up claims never before heard of, and dividing the assets among themselves. If I should be found dead tomorrow morning, nothing but my insignificance could prevent a speech being made on my authority, before the end of next week. It so happens that in that "popular sovereignty" with which Mr. Clay was identified, the Missouri Compromise was expressly reserved; and it was a little singular if Mr. Clay cast his mantle upon Judge Douglas on purpose to have that compromise repealed.

Again, the Judge did not keep faith with Mr. Clay when he first brought in his Nebraska bill. He left the Missouri Compromise unrepealed, and in his report accompanying the bill, he told the world he did it on purpose. The manes of Mr. Clay must have been in great agony, till thirty days later, when "popular sovereignty" stood forth in all its glory.

One more thing. Last night Judge Douglas tormented himself with horrors about my disposition to make negroes perfectly equal with white men in social and political relations. He did not stop to show that I have said any such thing, or that it legitimately follows from any thing I have said, but he rushes on with his assertions. I adhere to the Declaration of Independence. If Judge Douglas and

21 *Journal* has "this loving and most worthy."

his friends are not willing to stand by it, let them come up and amend it. Let them make it read that all men are created equal except negroes. Let us have it decided, whether the Declaration of Independence, in this blessed year of 1858, shall be thus amended. In his construction of the Declaration last year he said it only meant that Americans in America were equal to Englishmen in England. Then, when I pointed out to him that by that rule he excludes the Germans, the Irish, the Portuguese, and all the other people who have come amongst us since the Revolution, he reconstructs his construction. In his last speech he tells us it meant Europeans.

I press him a little further, and ask if it meant to include the Russians in Asia? or does he mean to exclude that vast population from the principles of our Declaration of Independence? I expect ere long he will introduce another amendment to his definition. He is not at all particular. He is satisfied with any thing which does not endanger the nationalizing of negro slavery. It may draw white men down, but it must not lift negroes up. Who shall say, "I am the superior, and you are the inferior?"

My declarations upon this subject of negro slavery may be misrepresented, but can not be misunderstood. I have said that I do not understand the Declaration to mean that all men were created equal in all respects. They are not our equal in color; but I suppose that it does mean to declare that all men are equal in some respects; they are equal in their right to "life, liberty, and the pursuit of happiness." Certainly the negro is not our equal in color— perhaps not in many other respects; still, in the right to put into his mouth the bread that his own hands have earned, he is the equal of every other man, white or black. In pointing out that more has been given you, you can not be justified in taking away the little which has been given him. All I ask for the negro is that if you do not like him, let him alone. If God gave him but little, that little let him enjoy.

When our Government was established, we had the institution of slavery among us. We were in a certain sense compelled to tolerate its existence. It was a sort of necessity. We had gone through our struggle and secured our own independence. The framers of the Constitution found the institution of slavery amongst their other institutions at the time. They found that by an effort to eradicate it, they might lose much of what they had already gained. They were obliged to bow to the necessity. They gave power to Congress to abolish the slave trade at the end of twenty years. They also prohibited it in the Territories where it did not exist. They did what they could and yielded to the necessity for the rest. I also yield to all which follows from that necessity. What I would most desire would be the separation of the white and black races.

One more point on this Springfield speech which Judge Douglas says he has read so carefully. I expressed my belief in the existence of a conspiracy to perpetuate and nationalize slavery. I did not profess to know it, nor do I now. I showed the part Judge Douglas had played in the string of facts, constituting to my mind, the proof of that conspiracy. I showed the parts played by others.

I charged that the people had been deceived into carrying the last Presidential election, by the impression that the people of the Territories might exclude slavery if they chose, when it was known in advance by the conspirators, that the Court was to decide that neither Congress nor the people could so exclude slavery. These charges are more distinctly made than any thing else in the speech.

Judge Douglas has carefully read and re-read that speech. He has not, so far as I know, contradicted those charges. In the two speeches which I heard he certainly did not. On his own tacit admission I renew that charge. I charge him with having been a party to that conspiracy and to that deception for the sole purpose of nationalizing slavery.

Mr. Lincoln sat down amidst loud and continued cheering.

To Henry E. Dummer[1]

Henry E. Dummer, Esq   Springfield,
My dear Sir: July 20. 1858.

When I was in Beardstown last Spring, Dr. Sprague said if I would leave a bill, he would pay it before long.[2] I do not now remember that I spoke to you about it. I am now in need of money. Suppose we say the amount shall be $50–? If the Dr. is satisfied with that, please get the money and send it to me.

And while you have pen in hand, tell me what you may know about politics, down your way. Yours as ever   A. LINCOLN—

[1] ALS, IHi.
[2] The bill was undoubtedly Lincoln's fee in Charles Sprague *v.* Illinois River Railroad Company, tried by Lincoln and Dummer in the Cass County Circuit Court, November 21, 1857, and reviewed by the Illinois Supreme Court, February 4, 1858. The case concerned the effect of amendments to the railroad company's charter on the liability of subscribers to the company's stock. Sprague was president of the Rock Island and Alton Railroad Company.

To John Mathers[1]

Jno. Mathers, Esq.   Springfield,
My dear Sir: July 20 1858

Your kind and interesting letter of the 19th. was duly received. Your suggestions as to placing one's self on the offensive, rather than the *defensive*, are certainly correct. That is a point which I shall not disregard. I spoke here on Saturday-night. The speech, not very well reported, appears in the State Journal of this morning. You, doubtless, will see it; and I hope you will perceive in it, that I am already improving. I would mail you a copy now, but I have not one at hand.

I thank you for your letter; and shall be pleased to hear from you again. Yours very truly   A. LINCOLN—

[1] ALS-F, Jacksonville *Daily Journal*, February 13, 1909. John Mathers, brick manufacturer, was a prominent citizen of Jacksonville, Illinois, who became the first mayor when the city was incorporated in 1867.

To Stephen A. Douglas[1]

Hon. S. A. Douglas   Chicago, Ills.
My Dear Sir   July 24, 1858.

Will it be agreeable to you to make an arrangement for you and myself to divide time, and address the same audiences during[2] the present canvass? Mr. Judd, who will hand you this, is authorized to receive your answer; and, if agreeable to you, to enter into the terms of such arrangement. Your Obt. Servt   A. LINCOLN

[1] Debates Scrapbook, ORB, and copy by Norman B. Judd, DLC-RTL. The Judd copy carries the following note by Judd: "Delivered the original of which the above is a true copy to the Hon. S. A. Douglass at Chicago on the 24 July 1858 and received for answer that he would send me down an answer when he sent down his mail on Monday morning. N. B. Judd." Lincoln did not receive Douglas' reply till July 29 (*vide infra*).
[2] "During" appears in the Judd copy.

To Daniel A. Cheever[1]

D. A. Cheever, Esq   Springfield,
My dear Sir.   July 25– 1858

On reaching home last evening I found yours of the 20th. It is my purpose to visit Tazewell before long; but I can not yet tell when. When I can determine, I will write you again. In the mean time let the friends be fixing things up as well as they can. Yours very truly   A. LINCOLN

[1] ALS, owned by William Beck, Sayre, Pennsylvania. The top of the page bears Cheever's notation: "Ansd. Aug. 3d. 1858." The bottom of the page bears a note by Cheever's son, Washington Irving Cheever, that "The above letter was written to Dr. D. A. Cheever at the time he figured in politics in Tazewell Co. . . ."

To Joseph T. Eccles[1]

J. T. Eccles, Esq   Springfield,
My dear Sir   July 25– 1858

Your two letters are received. I shall try to visit Hillsboro' this canvass; but I can not yet say when.

As I have made two speeches at Springfield—one June 16 & one July 17—I am not sure which it is you want. I shall go to the Journal office to-morrow, and see what can be done for you. Yours very truly   A. LINCOLN

[1] ALS, IHi.

To Joseph Gillespie[1]

Hon. J. Gillespie.   Springfield,
My dear Sir   July 25. 1858.

Your doleful letter of the 18th. was received on my return from Chicago last night. I do hope you are worse scared than hurt, though you ought to know best. We must not lose that district. We must make a job of it, and save it. Lay hold of the proper agencies and secure all the Americans you can, at once. I do hope, on closer inspection, you will find they are not half gone. Make a little test. Run down one of the poll-books of the Edwardsville precinct, and take the first hundred known American names. Then quietly ascertain how many of them are actually going for Douglas. I think you will find less than fifty. But even if you find find [*sic*] fifty, make sure of the other fifty—that is, make sure of all you can at all events. We will set other agencies to work, which shall compensate for the loss of a good many Americans. Dont fail to check the stampede at once. Trumbull, I think will be with you before long. There is much he can not do, and *some* he can. I have reason to hope there will be other help of an appropriate kind. Write me again. Yours as ever   A. LINCOLN—

[1] ALS-P, ISLA. See Lincoln to Gillespie, July 16, *supra*. Gillespie had replied on July 18 (DLC-RTL) that Douglas would carry at least half of the American (Know-Nothing) votes in the district for the Democratic candidate for the state senate, not because they were in favor of Douglas' politics, but because they felt Gillespie had been in the state senate long enough. The German Republicans

could not be counted on outside of Highland, Illinois. Samuel A. Buckmaster could beat him, but that he would do all he could. Gillespie's prediction that Buckmaster could defeat him was confirmed at the polls.

To Gustave P. Koerner[1]

Hon. G. Koerner
My dear Sir,

Springfield,
July 25. 1858.

Yours of late date was duly received. Many germans here are anxious to have Mr. Hecker[2] come; but I suppose your judgement is best. I write this mostly because I learn we are in great danger in Madison. It is said half the Americans are going for Douglas; and that slam will ruin us if not counteracted. It appears to me this fact of itself, would make it, at least no harder for us to get accessions from the Germans. We must make a special job of Madison. Every edge must be made to cut. Can not you, Canisius,[3] and some other influential Germans set a plan on foot that shall gain us accession from the Germans, and see that, at the election, none are cheated in their ballots? Gillespie thinks that thing is sometimes practiced on the German in Madison. Others of us must find the way to save as many Americans as possible. Still others must do other things. Nothing must be left undone. Elsewhere things look reasonably well. Please write me. Yours as ever

A. LINCOLN.

[1] Copy, ISLA. The copy from which the text is derived was supplied some years ago by M. Welte & Söhne, Freiburg, Germany.
[2] Friedrich K. F. Hecker.
[3] Dr. Theodore Canisius edited the Alton *Freie Presse*. He moved to Springfield in March, 1859, and became editor of the *Illinois Staats Anzeiger* under Lincoln's ownership, May 30, 1859.

To George W. Woods[1]

Geo. W. Woods, Pres. &c.
Dear Sir:

Springfield,
July 25. 1858

Owing to my absence yours of the 19th. was not sooner received and answered. A proposal of mine is before Judge Douglas to divide time, and both address the same audiences. Till I know the result, I can not say when I can visit Carlinville, being inclined to do so at the earliest day possible. I will write again, when I shall be informed on the point.

Please show this to Hon. J. M. Palmer, for whom I partly intend it. Yours truly
A. LINCOLN—

[1] ALS, IHi. George W. Woods was president of the Abolition Club of Macoupin County.

Speech at Clinton, Illinois[1]

July 27, 1858

In the evening, in compliance with the earnest wishes of his many friends here, Mr. Lincoln addressed the people at the Court House yard. At the commencement of his speech the people were scattered over the town, but they soon began to pour in, and in a short time the yard north of the Court House was crowded with an attentive audience of ladies and gentlemen. Mr. Lincoln began in his own plain, straight-forward manner, by calling attention to Mr. Douglas' plan of the campaign, and his ready observance of the Mormon precept: "Sound your own horn, for behold if you sound not your own horn, your horn shall not be sounded." He then alluded to the immense credit which Douglas claimed for his *discovery* and advocacy of "squatter sovereignty." He said that Mr. Douglas claimed the confidence of the people on the ground that *he* had initiated the policy of giving the people the right of governing themselves, and he enquired whether in the practice of that much boasted Douglas policy, the people of Kansas had not really less control of their own affairs than the people of any state or Territory in the whole history of the world! To this pointed enquiry the people responded with hearty cheers and cries of "good." He then showed that so far as experience can afford evidence, squatter sovereignty is a failure. After a withering allusion to the angelic temper, which Douglas had displayed in his speech, Mr. Lincoln congratulated the people on the fact that the little giant had at last been forced to quote his words correctly. "This," said Mr. Lincoln, "is all I want, and I only ask my friends and all who are eager for the truth, that when they hear me represented as saying or meaning anything strange, they will turn to my own words and examine for themselves. I do not wish Douglas to put words into my mouth. I do not wish him to construe my words as he pleases, and then represent me as meaning what he wishes me to mean, but I do wish the people to read and judge for themselves." Mr. Lincoln then proceeded to treat the conspiracy charge which Douglas had so furiously denied in the afternoon. He said that he had made the charge deliberately and calmly, believing when he did so that the evidence of a thousand corroborating circumstances fully bore him out. When he saw a number of men engaged in pursuing a similar work, when he saw that their efforts all tended in the same direction, that each was performing a necessary part, and

[1] Clinton *Central Transcript*, July 30, 1858. Douglas spoke in the afternoon, and Lincoln was in the audience.

that the combined labors of all had the effect of building an edifice, he did not believe that the coincidence occurred by chance, but that there was a preconceived plan, a common design running through the whole of it. He had never made the charge nor pretended to make it upon any knowledge that he had personally, apart from the evidence before the public; nay, he had told the public repeatedly why, and on what grounds he brought the charge. Douglas might pretend honesty and try to impress upon the minds of his hearers by the affected indignation with which he denied the charge, but when he, (Lincoln) saw Mr. Douglas filling so prominent a part in the movement towards the nationalization of slavery—when he saw the important sphere which he had performed in the common design, he could not resist the conclusion "that Douglas either was a conspirator or the dupe of conspirators." At this point the audience testified its approval by tremendous cheering. Mr. Lincoln then referred to the charge that Douglas brought against him of being *sectional* in his policy and associates. "Now," said Mr. Lincoln, "I have merely to say, that inasmuch as the party to which I belong extends at least over all the free states, and commands a majority of them, and even extends into the South; and inasmuch as Mr. Douglas cannot command one Congressional District, north or south, east or west, outside of Illinois, which, I ask, best deserves to be termed sectional, he or I?" (Cheers) Mr. Lincoln then addressed himself to the matter of the Dred Scott decision, and came down with crushing force, upon the decision and those who maintained it. In reply to the allegation of Douglas that a man who would give an opinion on a case before his election to a judgeship, which case he would afterwards be called upon to decide, must be a man utterly unworthy of respect; he declared that on that point Douglas was the best possible authority, inasmuch as he was elected upon the merits of a pre-judged case to the Supreme bench of Illinois. And Mr. Lincoln was prepared to prove by the declarations of hundreds of living men that Douglas himself had often publicly approved of the action of the Democratic party, and General Jackson in over-riding the decision of the Supreme Court in the affair of the United States Bank. Mr. Lincoln then proceeded to consider the question of slavery extension; he declared that he hated slavery, but that he did not consider that the public had any right to interfere with the institution where it existed under state laws. He did not believe that the white man held a right to deprive the negro of the little which God had given him; but he did not consider that therefore, the distinct races must be socially and politically equal. But for the sake of millions of the free laborers of the north,—for the sake of the poor white man of the South, and, for the sake of the eternal prosperity of the Union, he was opposed to slavery extending one inch beyond its present limits.

He then referred to the lies which had been circulated concerning his vote in Congress concerning the supplies to the soldiers in the Mexican War. He said that he was opposed to that war on principle, but that on every motion to grant extra pay, votes of thanks, land warrants, or supplies, he had invariably voted "yes." We hope that every one who listened to the gross falsehoods of Mr. Lincoln's enemies will examine the records for themselves, and there find the truth of what Mr. Lincoln says. At the conclusion of his speech he was greeted by tremendous cheers.

Speech at Monticello, Illinois[1]

July 29, 1858

LINCOLN proceeded on his way to Monticello, some of us bearing him company, the Judge returning on his proper route. A meeting was at once organized to hear him speak. He mounted in the court house square and thence spoke for about half an hour. He would not speak then, he would, however, read the correspondence with the Judge, together with the reply he was going to send the Judge, all of which he did. Then he went on to answer the Judge; he commenced his Springfield speech, and thereupon he asserted that he did not desire *negro equality* in all things, *he only wanted that the words* of the Declaration of Independence should be applied, to wit: "That all men are created free and equal," which latter remark, taken in connection with the two closing paragraphs of his Chicago speech, according to my understanding, gave the lie direct to his first assertion. He then very abruptly came to a close by remarking that he would bring his friend Judge TRUMBULL to answer Mr. DOUGLAS.

[1] *Missouri Republican*, August 1, 1858. This fragmentary and politically biased report is the only one available which indicates the content of the speech. According to the correspondent of the *Republican*, Lincoln met Douglas on the way to the railway station as Douglas was leaving following his speech earlier in the afternoon. Having a draft and a final copy of his reply to Douglas' letter of July 24 in his pocket, Lincoln offered to compare them and hand Douglas his .reply at once. Upon Douglas' declining to wait, Lincoln retained the letter until he returned to Springfield later that night.

To Stephen A. Douglas[1]

Hon. S. A. Douglas   Springfield,
Dear Sir   July 29. 1858

Yours of the 24th. in relation to an arrangement to divide time
and address the same audiences, is received; and, in appology for
not sooner replying, allow me to say that when I sat by you at
dinner yesterday[2] I was not aware that you had answered my note,
nor certainly, that my own note had been presented to you. An
hour after I saw a copy of your answer in the Chicago Times; and,
reaching home, I found the original awaiting me. Protesting that
your insinuations of attempted unfairness on my part are unjust;
and with the hope that you did not very considerately make them,
I proceed to reply. To your statement that "It has been suggested
recently that an arrangement had been made to bring out a third
candidate for the U. S. Senate[3] who, with yourself, should canvass
the state in opposition to me &c." I can only say that such suggestion must have been made by yourself; for certainly none such
has been made by, or to me; or otherwise, to my knowledge. Surely you did not *deliberately* conclude, as you insinuate, that I was
expecting to draw you into an arrangement, of terms to be agreed
on by yourself, by which a third candidate, and my self, "in concert, might be able to take the opening and closing speech in every
case."

---

[1] ALS copy, DLC-RTL, and Debates Scrapbook, ORB. Douglas' letter of the
24th (DLC-RTL) is as follows:
To Hon. A. Lincoln   Chicago,
Dear Sir: July 24th, 1858
    Your note of this date, in which you inquire if it would be agreeable to me
to make an arrangement to divide the time and address the same audiences
during the present canvass was handed me by Mr Judd.
    Recent events have interposed difficulties in the way of such an arrangement.
I went to Springfield last week for the purpose of conferring with the Democratic State Central committee upon the mode of conducting the canvass and
with them and under their advice, made a list of appointments covering the
entire period until late in October. The people of the several localities have been
notified of the time and places of the meetings. These appointments have all
been made for Democratic meetings and arrangements have been made by
which the Democratic candidates for congress, for the Legislature and other
offices will be present and address the people. It is evident, therefore, that these
various candidates, in connection with myself, will occupy the whole time of the
day and evening and leave no opportunity for other speeches.
    Besides, there is another consideration which should be kept in mind. It has
been suggested recently that an arrangement had been made to bring out a third
candidate for the U. S. Senate, who, with yourself, should canvass the state in
opposition to me, and with no other purpose than to insure my defeat by dividing the Democratic party for your benefit. If I should make this arrangement
with you, it is more than probable that this other candidate, who has a common
object with you, would desire to become a party to it and claim the right to

As to your surprise that I did not sooner make the proposal to divide time with you, I can only say I made it as soon as I resolved to make it. I did not know but that such proposal would come from you; I waited respectfully to see. It may have been well known to you that you went to Springfield for the purpose of agreeing on the plan of campaign; but it was not so known to me. When your appointments were announced in the papers, extending only to the 21st. of August, I, for the first time, considered it certain that you would make no proposal to me; and then resolved, that if my friends concurred, I would make one to you. As soon thereafter as I could see and consult with friends satisfactorily, I did make the proposal. It did not occur to me that the proposed arrangement could derange your plan, after the latest of your appointments already made. After that, there was, before the election, largely over two months of clear time.

For you to say that we have already spoken at Chicago and Springfield, and that on both occasions I had the concluding speech, is hardly a fair statement. The truth rather is this. At Chicago, July 9th, you made a carefully prepared conclusion on my speech of June 16th.; twentyfour hours after I made a hasty conclusion on yours of the 9th.; you had six days to prepare, and concluded

speak from the same stand; so that he and you in concert might be able to take the opening and closing speech in every case.

I cannot refrain from expressing my surprise, if it was your original intention to invite such an arrangement that you should have waited until after I had made my appointments, inasmuch as we were both here in Chicago together for several days after my arrival, and again at Bloomington, Atlanta, Lincoln and Springfield, where it was well known I went for the purpose of consulting with the State Central Committee and agreeing upon the plan of campaign.

While under these circumstances I do not feel at liberty to make any arrangement which would deprive the Democratic candidates for congress, State officers and the Legislature from participating in the discussion at the various meetings designated by the Democratic State Central Committee, I will, in order to accommodate you as far as it is in my power to do so, take the responsibility of making an arrangement with you for a discussion between us at one prominent point in each congressional district in the state, excepting the second and sixth districts, where we have both spoken and in each of which cases you had the concluding speech. If agreeable to you I will indicate the following places as those most suitable in the several congressional districts at which we should speak, to wit, Freeport, Ottawa, Galesburg, Quincy, Alton, Jonesboro and Charleston.

I will confer with you at the earliest convenient opportunity in regard to the mode of conducting the debate and the times of meeting at the several places subject to the condition that where appointments have already been made by the Democratic State Central Committee at any of those places I must insist upon your meeting me at the times specified. Very respectfully, Your Obd't Servant   S. A. DOUGLAS.

2 Whether Lincoln and Douglas dined at Clinton or Decatur is uncertain.

3 The story that Justice Sidney Breese of the Illinois Supreme Court was about to become a candidate had appeared in the Republican press.

on me again at Bloomington on the 16th.; twentyfour hours after I concluded on you again at Springfield. In the mean time you had made another conclusion on me at Springfield, which I did not hear, and of the contents of which I knew nothing when I spoke; so that your speech made in day-light, and mine at night of the 17th. at Springfield were both made in perfect independence of each other. The dates of making all these speeches,[4] will show, I think, that in the matter of time for preparation, the advantage has all been on your side; and that none of the external circumstances have stood to my advantage.

I agree to an arrangement for us to speak at the seven places you have named, and at your own times, provided you name the times at once, so that I, as well as you, can have to myself the time not covered by the arrangement. As to other details, I wish perfect reciprocity, and no more. I wish as much time as you, and that conclusions shall alternate. That is all. Your obedient Servant

A. Lincoln—

P.S. As matters now stand, I shall be at no more of your exclusive meetings; and for about a week from to-day a letter from you will reach me at Springfield.   A. L.

[4] This clause is inserted above the following deletion: "The contents of all these speeches and the dates of making them."

To Henry Asbury[1]

Henry Asbury, Esq   Springfield,
My dear Sir   July 31. 1858.

Yours of the 28th. is received. The points you propose to press upon Douglas, he will be very hard to get up to. But I think you labor under a mistake when you say no one cares how he answers. This implies that it is equal with him whether he is injured here or at the South. That is a mistake. He cares nothing for the South —he knows he is already dead there. He only leans Southward now to keep the Buchanan party from growing in Illinois. You shall have hard work to get him directly to the point whether a teritorial Legislature has or has not the power to exclude slavery. But if you succeed in bringing him to it, though he will be compelled to say it possesses no such power; he will instantly take ground that slavery can not actually exist in the teritories, unless the people desire it, and so give it protective teritorial legislation. If this offends the South he will let it offend them; as at all events he means to hold on to his chances in Illinois. You will soon learn by the papers that both the Judge and myself, are to be in

Quincy on the 13th. of October, when & where I expect the pleasure of seeing you. Yours very truly A. LINCOLN.

[1] ALS, ORB. Henry Asbury was an attorney of Quincy, Illinois. Accompanying the original letter is a signed statement by Asbury dated July, 1883, stating that, "The main Question I had urged Mr. Lincoln to put to Judge Douglas . . . was the Question 2 at Freeport 'Can the people of a United States territory in any lawful way against the wish of any citizen of the united States exclude Slavery from its limits prior to the formation of a state constitution.' "

To John C. Bagby[1]

John C. Bagby, Esq. Springfield,
Dear Sir July 31– 1858–

Yours of the 27th. is just received. You will see by the papers that Judge Douglas and I have agreed to meet at one place in each congressional district, and the first comes off at Ottawa on the 21st. of August; so that, of course I can not be at Rushville on that day. Judge Trumbull is expected home soon; and I will try to get him to be with you on the 21st.; though I have no certain information what the chance will be. I have some expectation of being at Beardstown on the 12th. and, if so, I should be pleased to see you. How stands Dr. Adams Dunlap[2] now?

Please write again. Your Obt. Servt. A. LINCOLN

[1] ALS-P, ISLA. John C. Bagby was a resident of Rushville, Illinois.
[2] Contemporary sources give the name as "Adam" not "Adams" as Lincoln spells it. Adam Dunlap was prominent in Schuyler County politics.

To Stephen A. Douglas[1]

Hon. S. A. Douglas: Springfield,
Dear Sir July 31. 1858.

Yours of yesterday, naming places, times, and terms, for joint discussions between us, was received this morning. Although, by the terms, as you propose, you take *four* openings and closes to my *three*, I accede, and thus close the arrangement. I direct this to you at Hillsboro; and shall try to have both your letter and this, appear in the Journal and Register of Monday morning. Your Obt. Servt. A. LINCOLN—

[1] ALS, ICHi, and Debates Scrapbook, ORB. Douglas' letter of July 30 (DLC-RTL) is as follows:

Bement, Piatt Co. Ill.
Dear Sir: July 30th, 1858
Your letter, dated yesterday, accepting my proposition for a joint discussion at one prominent point in each Congressional district as stated in my previous letter was received this morning.

The times and places designated are as follows:

Ottawa, Lasalle Co,	August	21st	1858.
Freeport, Stevenson [sic] Co.	"	27th	"
Jonesboro, Union Co.	September	15 "	"
Charleston, Coles Co.	"	18 "	"
Galesburg, Knox Co.	October	7 "	"
Quincy, Adams Co.	"	13 "	"
Alton, Madison Co.	"	15 "	"

I agree to your suggestion that we shall alternately open and close the discussion. I will speak at Ottawa one hour, you can reply, occupying an hour and a half, and I will then follow for half an hour. At Freeport you shall open the discussion and speak one hour, I will follow for an hour and a half and you can then reply for half an hour. We will alternate in like manner at each successive place. Very resp' Y'r ob't Serv't,   S. A. DOUGLAS
Hon. A. Lincoln, Springfield, Ill.

Definition of Democracy[1]

[August 1, 1858?]

As I would not be a *slave*, so I would not be a *master*. This expresses my idea of democracy. Whatever differs from this, to the extent of the difference, is no democracy.   A. LINCOLN—

[1] AD-F, ISLA. The date which has been assigned to this document is apparently pure conjecture. The manuscript is associated with no speech or occasion known to the editors. It was given by Mrs. Lincoln to her friend Myra Bradwell of Chicago, who together with her husband, Judge James B. Bradwell, succeeded in having Mrs. Lincoln released from the institution in which she was confined as insane in her later years. The scrap of paper is unsigned, but a signature clipped from another document has been pasted below the definition.

To Jediah F. Alexander[1]

J. F. Alexander, Esq   Springfield,
My dear Sir   Aug. 2. 1858.

I should be with Judge Douglas at your town on the 4th. had he not intimated in his published letter, that my presence would be considered an intrusion. I shall soon publish a string of appointments following his present track, which will bring me to Greenville about the 11th. of Sept. I hope to have Judge Trumbull with me. Yours truly   A. LINCOLN

[1] ALS, IHi.

To Burton C. Cook[1]

Hon: B. C. Cook   Springfield,
My dear Sir   Aug. 2. 1858–

I have a letter from a very true friend, and intelligent man, insisting that there is a plan on foot in La Salle and Bureau, to run

Douglas republicans for Congress, and for the Legislature in those counties, if they can only get the encouragement of our folks nominating pretty extreme abolitionists. It is thought they will do nothing if our folks nominate men, who are not very obnoxious to the charge of abolitionism. Please have your eye upon this.

Signs are looking pretty fair. Yours very truly   A. LINCOLN

1 ALS, ORB. Burton C. Cook of Ottawa, Illinois, state senator from LaSalle County since 1852, had been a Democrat but became a Republican during the anti-Nebraska movement.

To Joseph T. Eccles[1]

J. T. Eccles, Esq   Springfield,
My dear Sir   Aug. 2. 1858

I should be at your town to-day with Judge Douglas, had he not strongly intimated in his letter, which you have seen in the newspapers, that my presence, on the days or evenings of his meetings would be considered an intrusion. Before long I shall publish a string of appointments following upon his present track, which will bring me to Hillsborough about the 9th. of September. Yours truly   A. LINCOLN

1 ALS, owned by Foreman Lebold, Chicago, Illinois. There is also a forged copy of this letter in the New York City Public Library.

To Joseph Gillespie[1]

Hon: J. Gillespie   Springfield,
My dear Sir   Aug. 2. 1858

I should be with Judge Douglas at your town on the 6th. had he not strongly intimated in his published letter that my presence would be considered an intrusion. I shall soon publish a string of appointments following on his present track, which will bring me to Edwardsville about the 13th. of Sept.

On saturday I accidentally heard old A. G. Herndon remark that they had got to their new Buchanan paper here forty subscribers from Montgomery county. This last for yourself only. Yours as ever   A. LINCOLN.

1 ALS, owned by Frank E. Porter, Jr., Kansas City, Missouri.

To Abraham Jonas[1]

A. Jonas, Esq   Springfield,
My dear Sir   Aug: 2. 1858–

Yours of the 30th. July is just received. My mind is at once made up to be with you at Augusta on the 25th. of August, unless

I shall conclude it will prevent my being at Freeport on the 27th. when and where, by appointment, I am to meet Judge Douglas. I suppose there will be no difficulty in getting from Augusta to Freeport in due time. Yours very truly A. LINCOLN—

[1] ALS, IHi.

To C. W. Michael and William Proctor[1]

C. W. Michael & ⎱ Esqs   Springfield,
W Proctor ⎰   Aug. 2. 1858

  Gentlemen Yours of the 29th. July is received. Judge Douglas considers my presence at his appointments as an intrusion; and so I have concluded to not be present at them. I have written Judge Kellogg[2] what I now say to you, that if you are pretty confident you can give me a respectable audience, at Lewistown, on the 17th. and will so notify me, I will try to be there. Yours very truly

        A. LINCOLN

 [1] ALS, owned by Arthur S. Wright, Canton, Illinois. C. W. Michael and William Proctor of Lewistown, Illinois, wrote that it would be desirable for Lincoln to follow Douglas at Lewistown on August 16 (DLC-RTL).
 [2] William Kellogg, former member of the legislature from Fulton County and judge of the Tenth Circuit, elected to Congress 1857-1863.

To Lyman Porter[1]

Col. Lyman Porter   Springfield,
My dear Sir   Aug. 2. 1858.

  You are quite aware, no doubt, of the contest I am engaged in; and I suppose you equally well know, I would be glad of your help. If you can *not* give it, burn this, and think no more of it. If you can give it, I shall be very grateful; and, in which case I will thank you to consult with friends, and try to fix up about Representatives in your county.

  Please write me at all events Yours truly A. LINCOLN

 [1] ALS, owned by C. L. Porter, Lafayette, Indiana.

To Henry C. Whitney[1]

Dear Whitney   Springfield August 2d. 1858

  Yours of the 31st.[2] is just received. I shall write to B. C. Cook at Ottawa and to Lovejoy himself on the subject you suggest.

  Pardon me for not writing a longer letter. I have a great many letters to write.

I was at Monticello Thursday evening. Signs all very good. Your friend as ever

A. LINCOLN

¹ ALS-F, ISLA, and copy, DLC-HW. The facsimile from Whitney's *A Souvenir of Abraham Lincoln* (1891), like other facsimiles in the same source, is so poor as to suggest forgery, but there seems little reason to doubt that the original was once extant.

² Whitney wrote from Chicago that "a large body of Republicans & many Democrats acting in concert with them" were planning to run Churchill Coffing as an independent candidate for Congress in the Third Congressional District and "republicans of the [Hugh T.] Dickey stamp for the legislature—those candidates to be understood as Douglas men. . . ." (DLC-RTL).

To Daniel S. Dickinson¹

Hon: D. S. Dickinson   Springfield, Ills.
Sir   Aug. 3. 1858

In March 1857 I saw upon the Railroad train, being taken from Chicago to Alton, to the Penitentiary there, a man of gentlemanly appearance by the name of Hyde. He accosted me and conversed some as to the chance of obtaining a pardon. A year after he addressed me the inclosed letter from the prison. You see he mentions your name. Do you really know him? If our Governor could learn that he has been respectable, and is of respectable connections, perhaps he would pardon him. Please answer.

Pardon the liberty I take in addressing you. Several years ago I knew you slightly at Washington. Your Obt. Servt.

A. LINCOLN

¹ ALS-F, ISLA. Daniel S. Dickinson, U. S. Senator from New York, 1844-1851, replied noncommittally on August 19 that he had known Alfred Hyde in business dealings but not intimately (DLC-RTL).

To William H. Grigsby¹

Wm. H. Grigsby, Esq.   Springfield,
My dear Sir: Aug: 3. 1858

Yours of the 14th. of July, desiring a situation in my law office, was received several days ago. My partner, Mr. Herndon, controls our office in this respect, and I have known of his declining at least a dozen applications like yours within the last three months.

If you wish to be a lawyer, attach no consequence to the *place* you are in, or the *person* you are with; but get books, sit down anywhere, and go to reading for yourself. That will make a lawyer of you quicker than any other way. Yours Respectfully,

A. LINCOLN.

¹ ALS, owned by John G. Oglesby, Elkhart, Illinois. William H. Grigsby, nineteen years of age and a native of Missouri, who was employed by G. L. Thomas, Bookseller and Stationer, at Pekin, Illinois, wrote Lincoln, July 14, 1858, applying to study in the Lincoln & Herndon law office (DLC-RTL). Probably he was related to the Grigsby family whom Lincoln had known in Spencer County, Indiana, but his letter does not specify.

To Henry E. Dummer¹

Friend Dummer   Springfield, Aug: 5. 1858

Yours, not dated, just received. No accident preventing, I shall be at Beardstown on the 12th. I thank you for the contents of your letter generally. I have not time now to notice the various points you suggest; but I will say I do not understand the Republican party to be committed to the proposition "No more slave States." I think they are not so committed. Most certainly they prefer there should be no more; but I know there are many of them who think we are under obligation to admit slave states from Texas, if such shall be presented for admission;² but I think the party as such is not committed either way. Your friend as ever   A. LINCOLN

¹ ALS, IHi.
² The resolution of annexation by which Texas was admitted to the United States provided that new states in addition to Texas not exceeding four might be formed out of the territory with the consent of Texas.

To John M. Palmer¹

Hon. J. M. Palmer   Springfield,
Dear Sir: Aug. 5, 1858.

Since we parted last evening no new thought has occurred to [me] on the subject of which we talked most yesterday.

I have concluded, however, to speak at your town on Tuesday, August 31st, and have promised to have it so appear in the papers of to-morrow. Judge Trumbull has not yet reached here. Yours as ever,   A. LINCOLN.

¹ Tarbell (Appendix), p. 334.

To Gustave P. Koerner¹

Hon. G. Koerner   Springfield,
My dear Sir   Aug. 6. 1858

Yesterday morning I found a drop letter from Gov: Bissell, urging, partly in consequence of a letter from you, that my late speeches, or some of them, shall be printed in pamphlet form both in English and German. Having had a good many letters to the same effect, I went at once to the Journal office here, and set them to work to print me in English, fifty dollars worth of my last speech at Springfield (July 17) that appearing, by what I hear to be the most "taking" speech I have made.[2] For that sum they will furnish about 7000; they will, at the same time print some more, on their own account, and keep the type standing for a while. I also wrote to Judd yesterday, to get the same speech done up there in German. When I hear from him I will write you again.

Some things are passing strange. Wednesday morning, Douglas' paper here, the Register, went out crowing over the defeat of Blair, at St. Louis; and Blair's paper, the, Missouri Democrat, comes back next day, puffing, and encouraging Douglas![3]

Please write me, on receipt of this, and let me know if you have any recent news from Madison. Every place seems to be coming quite up to my expectation, except Madison. Your friend, as ever

A. LINCOLN—

1 ALS, CtWat.
2 This eight-page pamphlet (Monaghan 12) furnished the text of this speech in the debates scrapbook. *Vide supra*, July 17, note 1.
3 Francis (Frank) P. Blair, Jr., editor of the *Missouri Democrat*, was elected to Congress in 1856 and served till March 3, 1859. In 1858 he lost the election to John R. Barret, but successfully contested and served from June 8 to June 25, 1860.

To Joseph O. Glover[1]

J. O. Glover, Esq.   Springfield,
My Dear Sir: Aug. 9. 1858.

Yours of the 4th, in answer to mine addressed to Mr. Cook,[2] is received, and for which I thank you.

I have written Lovejoy[3] the same as I wrote Mr. Cook, and he answers substantially as you do.

Things look reasonably well down this way. Friends write me from all the places where Douglas is speaking, and they all say he gains nothing. This shows at least that he does not scare and cowe our friends where he goes.

I shall be glad of a line from you at any time. Yours truly,

A. LINCOLN.

1 Ottawa *Daily Republican Times*, July 23, 1908. Glover was mayor of Ottawa, Illinois, and Lincoln's host on August 21, the day of the debate with Douglas.   2 Burton C. Cook. *Vide supra*, August 2.   3 Owen Lovejoy.

To Albert Parker[1]

Albert Parker, Esq   Springfield,
My dear Sir   Aug. 10. 1858

Yours of the 7th. is just received. I am greatly hurried, for which reason you will pardon me for not writing a longer letter. As to the law-question. As the consideration of the notes, Gridley[2] will insist they were given because of his acting as agent for the makers of the notes, in purchasing the land; and I rather think this will make out a legal consideration.

As to politics I am doing what I can for the cause. They have a meeting at Tremont on Saturday the 14th. and I wish you would go down and mingle with your old friends upon that occasion.

Again let me beg you to excuse the shortness of this letter. Yours very truly   A. LINCOLN

[1] ALS-P, ISLA. Albert Parker wrote from Chenoa, Illinois, that although he was now living in Livingston County, he expected to return to Tazewell County before the election and work for the cause (DLC-RTL).

[2] According to Parker's letter, Asahel Gridley as agent for the Illinois Central had sold the company's land in Livingston County to settlers, taking their notes payable to himself, and was suing the purchasers, who had no assurance of deeds to their property. Parker asked, "Cannot the collection of Gridley's notes be staied until the parties get deeds?"

To Alexander Sympson[1]

Alexr. Sympson, Esq.   Springfield,
Dear Sir   Aug: 11, 1858

Yours of the 6th. received. If life and health continue, I shall pretty surely be at Augusta on the 25th.

Things look reasonably well. Will tell you more fully when I see you. Yours truly   A. LINCOLN

[1] ALS-P, ISLA. Alexander Sympson of Carthage, Illinois, wrote that he had heard Lincoln was to speak at Augusta on August 25, and if so would "give it all the publicity I can. . . ." (DLC-RTL).

Speech at Beardstown, Illinois[1]

August 12, 1858

I made a speech in June last,[2] in which I pointed out, briefly and consecutively, a series of public measures leading directly to the nationalization of slavery—the spreading of that institution

[1] *Illinois State Journal*, August 19, 1858; Rushville *Schuyler Citizen*, August 18, 1858. The *Journal* gives the most complete available report, but the *Citizen* adds a summary of Lincoln's remarks on Negro equality. No contemporary report has been found, however, confirming the statement of Horace White that the passage on the Declaration of Independence which constitutes the major portion of the extant text of the speech at Lewistown, August 17 (*vide infra*, n.1), was actually delivered at Beardstown.   [2] *Vide supra*, June 16.

over all the Territories and all the States, old as well as new,
North as well as South. I enumerated the repeal of the Missouri
Compromise, which every candid man must acknowledge conferred upon emigrants to Kansas and Nebraska the right to carry
slaves there and hold them in bondage, whereas, formerly they
had no such right. I alluded to the events which followed that repeal—events in which Judge Douglas' name figures quite promi-
nently. I referred to the Dred Scott decision, and the extraordinary
means taken to prepare the public mind for that decision—the efforts put forth by President Pierce to make the people believe they
had indorsed, in the election of James Buchanan, the doctrine that
slavery may exist in the free Territories of the Union—the earnest exhortation put forth by President Buchanan to the people to
stick to that decision whatever it might be, [laughter] the close
fitting niche in the Nebraska bill wherein the right of the people
to govern themselves is made "subject to the Constitution of the
United States"—the extraordinary haste displayed by Mr. Douglas
to give this decision an endorsement at the Capital of Illinois. I
alluded to other occurring circumstances which I need not repeat
now, and I said that though I could not open the bosoms of men
and find out their secret motives, yet, when I found the framework
for a barn or a bridge, or any other structure, built by a number
of carpenters—Stephen and Franklin and Roger and James—and
so built that each tenon had its proper mortice, and the whole
forming a symmetrical piece of workmanship, I should say that
these carpenters all worked on an intelligent plan, and understood
each other from the beginning. This embraced the main argument
in my speech before the Republican State convention in June.
Judge Douglas received a copy of my speech some two weeks before his return to Illinois. He had ample time to examine and reply to it if he chose to do so. He did examine it, and he did reply
to it, but he wholly overlooked the body of my argument, and
said nothing about the "conspiracy charge," as he terms it. He
made up his speech of complaints against our tendencies to negro
equality and amalgamation. [Laughter.] Well, seeing that Douglas had had the process served on him, that he had taken notice
of such service, that he had come into court and pleaded to a part
of the complaint, but had ignored the main issue, I took a default
on him. I held that he had no plea to make to the general charge.
So, when I was called on to reply to him twenty-four hours afterwards, I renewed the charge as explicitly as I could. My speech
was reported and published on the following morning, and of
course Judge Douglas saw it. He went from Chicago to Blooming-

ton, and there made another and longer speech, and yet took no notice of the "conspiracy charge." He then went to Springfield and made another elaborate argument, but was not prevailed upon to know anything about the outstanding indictment. I made another speech in Springfield—this time taking it for granted that Judge Douglas was satisfied to take his chances in the campaign with the imputation of the conspiracy hanging over him. It was not until he went into a small town (Clinton) in DeWitt county, where he delivered his fourth or fifth regular speech, that he found it convenient to notice this matter at all. At that place (I was standing in the crowd when he made his speech,) he bethought himself that he was charged with something; [laughter;] and his reply was that "his self-respect alone prevented his calling it a falsehood." Well, my friends, perhaps he so far lost his self-respect in Beardstown as to actually call it a falsehood! [Great laughter— Douglas had called it "an infamous lie."] But now I have this reply to make: That while the Nebraska bill was pending, Judge Douglas helped to *vote down* a clause giving the people of the Territories the right to *exclude* slavery if they chose; that neither while the bill was pending, nor at any other time, would he give his *opinion* whether the people had the right to exclude slavery— though respectfully asked; that he made a report, which I hold in my hand, from the Committee on Territories, in which he said the rights of the people of the Territories in this regard are "held in abeyance," and can not be immediately exercised, [Mr. Lincoln here read the passage referred to, from an official document in the Senate;] that the Dred Scott decision expressly denies any such right, but declares that neither Congress nor the Territorial Legislature can keep slavery out of Kansas; and that Judge Douglas *indorses that decision.* All these "charges" are new; that is, I did not make them in my original speech—they are additional and cumulative testimony. I bring them forward now, and dare Judge Douglas to deny one of them. Let him do it, and I will prove it by such testimony as will confound him forever. [Loud applause.] I say to you, gentlemen, that it would be more to the purpose for Judge Douglas to say that he did *not* repeal the Missouri Compromise; that he did *not* make slavery possible where it was impossible before; that he did *not* leave a niche in the Nebraska bill for the Dred Scott decision to rest in; that he did *not* vote down a clause giving the people the right to exclude slavery if they wanted to; that he did *not* refuse to give his individual opinion whether a Territorial Legislature could exclude slavery; that he did *not* make a report to the Senate in which he said that the rights of

the people in this regard were "held in abeyance" and could not
be immediately exercised; that he did *not* make a hasty indorsement of the Dred Scott decision over at Springfield; that he does
not now indorse that decision; that that decision does *not* take
away from the Territorial Legislature the power to exclude slavery, and that he did *not* in the original Nebraska bill so couple the
words *State* and *Territory* together, that what the Supreme Court
has done in forcing open all the Territories for slavery, it may
yet do in forcing open all the States—I say it would be vastly
more to the point for Judge Douglas to say he did *not* do some of
these things, did *not* forge some of these links of overwhelming
testimony, than to go vociferating about the country that possibly
he may hint that somebody is a liar! [Deafening applause.] I repeat and renew, and shall continue to repeat and renew this
"charge" until he denies the evidence, and then I shall so fasten it
upon him that it will cling to him as long as he lives.

He showed that Douglas had no foundation for charging him
with being favorable to negro equality; it was a false logic that
assumed because a man did not want a negro woman for a *slave*,
he must needs want her for a *wife*. From copious statistics he
showed that where slavery existed, the *white* race was mixed with
the *black* to an alarming degree, and thus proved that his policy
of keeping them separate was decidedly more to be approved than
that of Judge Douglas' who would bring them in contact.[3]

[3] From the *Schuyler Citizen*.

Speech at Havana, Illinois[1]

August 14, 1858

A QUESTION OF MUSCLE

I am informed, that my distinguished friend yesterday became
a little excited, nervous, perhaps, [laughter] and he said something about *fighting*, as though referring to a pugilistic encounter
between him and myself. Did anybody in this audience hear him
use such language? [Cries of yes.] I am informed, further, that
somebody in *his* audience, rather more excited, or nervous, than
himself, took off his coat, and offered to take the job off Judge
Douglas' hands, and fight Lincoln himself. Did anybody here witness that warlike proceeding? [Laughter, and cries of yes.] Well,
I merely desire to say that I shall fight neither Judge Douglas nor
his second. [Great laughter.] I shall not do this for two reasons,
which I will now explain. In the first place, a fight would *prove*

nothing which is in issue in this contest. It might establish that Judge Douglas is a more muscular man than myself, or it might demonstrate that I am a more muscular man than Judge Douglas. But this question is not referred to in the Cincinnati platform, nor in either of the Springfield platforms. [Great laughter.] Neither result would prove him right or me wrong. And so of the gentleman who volunteered to do his fighting for him. If my fighting Judge Douglas would not prove anything, it would certainly prove nothing for me to fight his bottle-holder. [Continued laughter.]

My second reason for not having a personal encounter with the Judge is, that I don't believe he wants it himself. [Laughter.] He and I are about the best friends in the world, and when we get together he would no more think of fighting me than of fighting his wife. Therefore, ladies and gentlemen, when the Judge talked about fighting, he was not giving vent to any ill-feeling of his own, but merely trying to excite—well, *enthusiasm* against me on the part of his audience. And as I find he was tolerably successful, we will call it quits. [Cheers and laughter.]

TWO UPON ONE

One other matter of trifling consequence, and I will proceed. I understand that Judge Douglas yesterday referred to the fact that both Judge Trumbull and myself are making speeches throughout the State to beat him for the Senate, and that he tried to create a sympathy by the suggestion that this was playing *two upon one* against him. It is true that Judge Trumbull has made a speech in Chicago, and I believe he intends to co-operate with the Republican Central Committee in their arrangements for the campaign to the extent of making other speeches in different parts of the State. Judge Trumbull is a Republican, like myself, and he naturally feels a lively interest in the success of his party. Is there anything wrong about that? But I will show you how little Judge Douglas's appeal to your sympathies amounts to. At the next general election, two years from now, a Legislature will be elected which will have to choose a successor to Judge Trumbull. Of course there will be an effort to fill his place with a Democrat. This person, who-ever he may be, is probably out making stump-speeches against me, just as Judge Douglas is. It may be one of the present Democratic members of the lower house of Congress—but who ever he is, I can tell you he has got to make some stump speeches now, or his party will not nominate him for the seat occupied by Judge Trumbull. Well, are not Judge Douglas and this man playing *two upon one* against me, just as much as Judge Trumbull and I are playing *two upon one* against Judge Douglas? [Laughter.] And if it happens that there are two Democratic aspirants for Judge Trumbull's place, are they not playing *three upon one* against me, just as we are playing *two upon one* against Judge Douglas? [Renewed laughter.]

¹ Chicago *Daily Press and Tribune,* August 20, 1858. This is the most complete report available, but the *Tribune* specifies that following these introductory remarks Lincoln spoke for two hours, touching on "negro equality and amalgamation," and "the conspiracy to Africanize the American continent."

Speech at Bath, Illinois¹

August 16, 1858

In commencing his speech today, in a grove adjoining Bath, where a large and most respectable audience greeted him, Mr. Lincoln said he had many things since coming into Mason County to remind him that he had ceased to be a young man. Among the old men, he had met more than half a dozen who were in the same company with him 27 years ago in the Black Hawk war—a war which truly was not a very extensive one, or calculated to make great heroes of men engaged in it. But here are these old men now, some of them on the stand with him; and on this very spot, 22 years ago, he (Mr. L.) had with his own hands staked out the first plat of this town of Bath, then a wooded wilderness. But what more reminded him of his advancing age, was the number of young men around him, now, and for years past, voters, who were the sons of his friends of early years, and who are now of the age he was when he first knew their fathers. Here at least he expected to be heard with can[dor] and respectful attention—and he was so heard, throughout an address of more than two hours' duration.

The Republicans at their Springfield Convention of June 16th, said he, had chosen to put him forward as candidate for U.S. Senator—as their standard bearer in the campaign. He appreciated the honor, but felt the responsibility of the task. Recurring to the great disturbing question of the day, Slavery, he stated his belief that Douglas had never in his life once intimated that there was any wrong in slavery; and that if that gentleman were here, he would not, even to secure every voter present, make this admission. And yet, he was trying to wrap himself up in the cloak of Henry Clay, a statesman in defence of whose principles Lincoln had battled all his life. Not a shred of that cloak would he allow to Lincoln. But this old son of Kentucky, a son of whom all the Western States may be proud, read extracts from Mr. Clay's speech of 1847, and

from another of 20 years before, 1827, delivered before the Colonization Society, in which that statesman spoke in favor of the ultimate emancipation of slavery, and pronouncing the institution the
greatest of evils. Mr. L. contrasted these remarks of the old patriot,
with the sentiments and political course of Douglas on this question, and showed clearly that nothing but the most brazen impudence would dare to take the name of Clay on his lips, by a man
so destitute of his principles.

[1] Chicago *Daily Press and Tribune*, August 21, 1858.

Speech at Lewistown, Illinois[1]

August 17, 1858

At two o'clock, Judge Kellogg[2] introduced Mr. Lincoln, who was
again greeted with vociferous applause. After the noise had sub-
sided, he commenced and delivered the ablest, and, as I think, the
most powerful argument ever heard in Old Fulton. The speech

[1] Chicago *Press and Tribune*, August 21, 1858. The fragmentary text of this
speech as given in the *Press and Tribune* was widely copied in other papers.
Although there are reports in other papers originating from other correspondents, only this one gives a verbatim transcription of any considerable portion of
the speech.

Taking the *Press and Tribune* report at face value, it would seem that the
reporter whose initials "G.P." appear at the end, wrote his story at the scene of
the speech and transcribed verbatim the peroration on the Declaration of Independence. Since "G.P." cannot be identified, however, Horace White's statement
to Herndon in 1865 deserves to be considered. White, a *Tribune* reporter maintained in 1865 that he had reported the speech as printed in the *Press and Tribune*, and that it was actually part of the speech delivered at Beardstown on
August 12 (*supra*), which "inasmuch as my report of the Beardstown meeting
had already been mailed I incorporated . . . in my letter from Lewisto[w]n
two or three days [actually five days] subsequently." (Herndon, II, 418). To
offset this recollection of later years is the fact that in none of the reports of the
Beardstown speech which have been found, is there any reference to the peroration on the Declaration of Independence, the passage to which White referred in his 1865 statement. White's account also casts some doubt on the
verbal accuracy of the passage by maintaining that he had written it from
memory the day after it was delivered. "After I had finished writing I read it
to Mr. Lincoln. When I had finished the reading he said, 'Well, those are my
views, and if I said anything on the subject I must have said substantially that,
but not nearly so well as that is said.' " (*Ibid.*, 417-18).

It is conceivable that White's Lewistown report and the passage from the
Beardstown speech were treated as one story under the Lewistown date line.
The mystery of the initials "G.P.," however, has not been solved, and the fact
that the reports of the Beardstown speech in all other papers make no reference
to the passage on the Declaration of Independence leaves considerable doubt
concerning White's 1865 statement.

In any event, the passage in question was widely copied in the Republican
press, and two years later was reprinted in Republican campaign organs as a
high spot in Lincoln's oratory (*The Railsplitter*, October 10, 1860; *Wigwam*,
October 31, 1860).   [2] Congressman William Kellogg.

was two hours and a half long, yet there seemed to me to be more listeners at the conclusion than at the beginning. Among other things, Mr. Lincoln examined the pretensions of Douglas to the giant mantle of Henry Clay. He said he would lay no claim to the support of the Old Line Whigs of Illinois, because he had been the life-long friend and Douglas the life-long enemy of the great and brave Kentuckian, unless he could show from Mr. Clay's printed speeches that he stood upon the very ground occupied by that statesman, and that Douglas's position was as opposite to it as Beelzebub to an Angel of Light. In proving this point—reading extract after extract from the speeches and letters of Henry Clay, contending nobly and greatly for the "ultimate emancipation of the slave"—Mr. Lincoln remarked that he believed Douglas was the only statesman of any note or prominence in the country who had *never said to friend or enemy whether he believed human slavery in the abstract to be right or wrong.*

"All others," said he, "North and South, have at some time or another declared themselves in favor of it or against it. All others have said either that it is right and just, and should therefore be perpetuated, or that it is wrong and wicked, and should be immediately swept from civilized society, or that it is an evil to be tolerated because it cannot be removed. But to Judge Douglas belongs the *distinction* of having never said that he regarded it either as an evil or a good, morally right or morally wrong. His speech at Bloomington would leave us to infer that he was opposed to the introduction of slavery into Illinois; but his effort in Lewistown, I am told, favors the idea, that if you can make more money by flogging niggers than by flogging oxen, there is no moral consideration which should interfere to prevent your doing so."

LINCOLN ON THE DECLARATION OF INDEPENDENCE

I cannot close this letter without giving your readers a passage from Mr. Lincoln's noble and impressive apostrophe to the Declaration of Independence. This was truly one of the finest efforts of public speaking I ever listened to. It gave to his auditors such an insight into the character of the man as ought to carry him into the Senate on a great surge of popular affection. In my poor opinion, Mr. Lincoln is not only one of the foremost men in the Northwest in the nobility and excellence of his character, the clearness and scope of his intellect, but the peer of any man who has sat in the Senate since the mighty shadows of Webster and Clay ceased to darken the threshold of the Capitol.

* * * *³ The Declaration of Independence (said Mr. L.) was formed by the representatives of American liberty from thirteen States of the confederacy—twelve of which were slaveholding communities. We need not discuss the way or the reason of their becoming slaveholding communities. It is sufficient for our purpose that *all of them* greatly deplored the evil and that they placed a provision in the Constitution which they supposed would gradually remove the disease by cutting off its source. This was the abolition of the slave trade. So general was conviction—the public determination—to abolish the African slave trade, that the provision which I have referred to as being placed in the Constitution, declared that it should *not* be abolished prior to the year 1808. A constitutional provision was necessary to prevent the people, through Congress, from putting a stop to the traffic immediately at the close of the war. Now, if slavery had been a good thing, would the Fathers of the Republic have taken a step calculated to diminish its beneficent influences among themselves, and snatch the boon wholly from their posterity? These communities, by their representatives in old Independence Hall, said to the whole world of men: "We hold these truths to be self evident: that all men are created equal; that they are endowed by their Creator with certain unalienable rights; that among these are life, liberty and the pursuit of happiness." This was their majestic interpretation of the economy of the Universe. This was their lofty, and wise, and noble understanding of the justice of the Creator to His creatures. [Applause.] Yes, gentlemen, to *all* His creatures, to the whole great family of man. In their enlightened belief, nothing stamped with the Divine image and likeness was sent into the world to be trodden on, and degraded, and imbruted by its fellows. They grasped not only the whole race of man then living, but they reached forward and seized upon the farthest posterity. They erected a beacon to guide their children and their children's children, and the countless myriads who should inhabit the earth in other ages. Wise statesmen as they were, they knew the tendency of prosperity to breed tyrants, and so they established these great self-evident truths, that when in the distant future some man, some faction, some interest, should set up the doctrine that none but rich men, or none but white men, were entitled to life, liberty and the pursuit of happiness, their posterity might look up again to the Declaration of Independence and take courage to renew the battle which their fathers began—so that truth, and justice, and mercy, and all the humane and Christian virtues might not be extin-

³ Asterisks in the source.

guished from the land; so that no man would hereafter dare to limit and circumscribe the great principles on which the temple of liberty was being built. [Loud cheers.]

Now, my countrymen (Mr. Lincoln continued with great earnestness,) if you have been taught doctrines conflicting with the great landmarks of the Declaration of Independence; if you have listened to suggestions which would take away from its grandeur, and mutilate the fair symmetry of its proportions; if you have been inclined to believe that all men are *not* created equal in those inalienable rights enumerated by our chart of liberty, let me entreat you to come back. Return to the fountain whose waters spring close by the blood of the Revolution. Think nothing of me—take no thought for the political fate of any man whomsoever—but come back to the truths that are in the Declaration of Independence. You may do anything with me you choose, if you will but heed these sacred principles. You may not only defeat me for the Senate, but you may take me and put me to death. While pretending no indifference to earthly honors, I *do claim* to be actuated in this contest by something higher than an anxiety for office. I charge you to drop every paltry and insignificant thought for any man's success. It is nothing; I am nothing; Judge Douglas is nothing. *But do not destroy that immortal emblem of Humanity—the Declaration of American Independence.*[4]

[4] Two concluding paragraphs of "G.P.'s" report contain nothing more about the speech.

Fragment: Notes for Speeches[1]

[c. August 21, 1858]

When Douglas ascribes such to me, he does so, not by argument, but by mere burlesque on the art and name of argument—by such fantastic arrangements of words as prove "horse-chestnuts to be chestnut horses." In the main I shall trust an intelligent community to learn my objects and aims from what I say and do myself, rather than from what Judge Douglas may say of me. But I must not leave the judge just yet. When he has burlesqued me into a

[1] NH, IV, 212-24, and AD, NNP. Nicolay and Hay date this fragment [October 1, 1858?]. While a fixed date cannot be given, obviously the arguments and much of the language of the fragment are duplicated in Lincoln's reply to Douglas in the Debate at Ottawa, August 21, and the last three paragraphs appear in his speeches at Bloomington, September 4, and Edwardsville, September 11. Presuming that Nicolay and Hay found the manuscript of the fragment intact as printed in the *Complete Works*, one concludes that it was composed prior to or between August 21 and September 11. Only two pages of the manuscript have been located, however, as indicated in the succeeding footnote. Presumably the manuscript was dispersed after Nicolay and Hay had access to it.

position which I never thought of assuming myself, he will, in the most benevolent and patronizing manner imaginable, compliment me by saying "he has no doubt I am perfectly conscientious in it." I thank him for that word "conscientious." It turns my attention to the wonderful evidences of conscience he manifests. When he assumes to be the first discoverer and sole advocate of the right of a people to govern themselves, he is conscientious. When he affects to understand that a man, putting a hundred slaves through under the lash, is simply governing himself, he is more conscientious. When he affects not to know that the Dred Scott decision forbids a territorial legislature to exclude slavery, he is most conscientious. When, as in his last Springfield speech, he declares that I say, unless I shall play my batteries successfully, so as to abolish slavery in every one of the States, the Union shall be dissolved, he is absolutely bursting with conscience. It is nothing that I have never said any such thing. With some men it might make a difference; but consciences differ in different individuals. Judge Douglas has a greater conscience than most men. It corresponds with his other points of greatness. Judge Douglas amuses himself by saying I wish to go into the Senate on my qualifications as a prophet. He says he has known some other prophets, and does not think very well of them. Well, others of us have also known some prophets. We know one who nearly five years ago prophesied that the "Nebraska bill" would put an end to slavery agitation in next to no time—one who has renewed that prophecy at least as often as quarter-yearly ever since; and still the prophecy has not been fulfilled. That one might very well go out of the Senate on his qualifications as a false prophet.

Allow me now, in my own way, to state with what aims and objects I did enter upon this campaign. I claim no extraordinary exemption from personal ambition. That I like preferment as well as the average of men may be admitted. But I protest I have not entered upon this hard contest solely, or even chiefly, for a mere personal object. I clearly see, as I think, a powerful plot to make slavery universal and perpetual in this nation. The effort to carry that plot through will be persistent and long continued, extending far beyond the senatorial term for which Judge Douglas and I are just now struggling. I enter upon the contest to contribute my humble and temporary mite in opposition to that effort.

At the Republican State convention at Springfield I made a speech. That speech has been considered the opening of the canvass on my part. In it I arrange a string of incontestable facts which, I think, prove the existence of a conspiracy to nationalize slavery. The evidence was circumstantial only; but nevertheless it seemed inconsistent with every hypothesis, save that of the existence of such conspiracy. I believe the facts can be explained to-day on no other hypothesis. Judge Douglas can so explain them if any one can. From warp to woof his handiwork is everywhere woven in.

At New York he finds this speech of mine, and devises his plan of assault upon it. At Chicago he develops that plan. Passing over, unnoticed, the obvious purport of the whole speech, he cooks up two or three issues upon points not discussed by me at all, and then authoritatively announces that these are to be the issues of the campaign. Next evening I answer, assuring him that he misunderstands me—that he takes issues which I have not tendered. In good faith I try to set him right. If he really has misunderstood my meaning, I give him language that can no longer be misunderstood. He will have none of it. At Bloomington, six days later, he speaks again, and perverts me even worse than before. He seems to have grown confident and jubilant, in the belief that he has entirely diverted me from my purpose of fixing a conspiracy upon him and his co-workers. Next day he speaks again at Springfield, pursuing the same course, with increased confidence and recklessness of assertion. At night of that day I speak again. I tell him that as he has carefully read my speech making the charge of conspiracy, and has twice spoken of the speech without noticing the charge, upon his own tacit admission I renew the charge against him. I call him, and take a default upon him. At Clifton, ten days after, he comes in with a plea. The substance of that plea is that he never passed a word with Chief Justice Taney as to what his decision was to be in the Dred Scott case; that I ought to know that he who affirms what he does not know to be true falsifies as much as he who affirms what he does know to be false; and that he would pronounce the whole charge of conspiracy a falsehood, were it not for his own self-respect!

Now I demur to this plea. Waiving objection that it was not filed till after default, I demur to it on the merits. I say it does not meet the case. What if he did not pass a word with Chief Justice Taney? Could he not have as distinct an understanding, and play his part just as well, without directly passing a word with Taney, as with it? But suppose we construe this part of the plea more broadly than he puts it himself—suppose we construe it, as in an answer in chancery, to be a denial of all knowledge, information, or belief of such conspiracy. Still I have the right to prove the conspiracy, even against his answer; and there is much more than the evidence of two witnesses to prove it by. Grant that he has no knowledge, information, or belief of such conspiracy, and what of it? That does not disturb the facts in evidence. It only makes him the dupe, instead of a principal, of conspirators.

What if a man may not affirm a proposition without knowing it to be true? I have not affirmed that a conspiracy does exist. I have only stated the evidence, and affirmed my belief in its existence. If Judge Douglas shall assert that I do not believe what I say, then he affirms what he cannot know to be true, and falls within the condemnation of his own rule.

Would it not be much better for him to meet the evidence, and show, if he can, that I have no good reason to believe the charge? Would not this be far more satisfactory than merely vociferating an intimation that he may be provoked to call somebody a liar?

So far as I know, he denies no fact which I have alleged. Without now repeating all those facts, I recall attention to only a few of them. A provision of the Nebraska bill, penned by Judge Douglas, is in these words:

It being the true intent and meaning of this act not to legislate slavery into any Territory or State, nor exclude it therefrom, but to leave the people thereof perfectly free to form and regulate their domestic institutions in their own way, subject only to the Constitution of the United States.

In support of this the argument, evidently prepared in advance, went forth: "Why not let the people of a Territory have or exclude slavery, just as they choose? Have they any less sense or less patriotism when they settle in the Territories than when they lived in the States?"

Now the question occurs: Did Judge Douglas, even then, intend that the people of a Territory should have the power to exclude slavery? If he did, why did he vote against an amendment expressly declaring they might exclude it? With men who then knew and intended that a Supreme Court decision should soon follow, declaring that the people of a Territory could not exclude slavery, voting down such an amendment was perfectly rational. But with men not expecting or desiring such a decision, and really wishing the people to have such power, voting down such an amendment, to my mind, is wholly inexplicable.

That such an amendment was voted down by the friends of the bill, including Judge Douglas, is a recorded fact of the case. There was some real reason for so voting it down. What that reason was, Judge Douglas can tell. I believe that reason was to keep the way clear for a court decision, then expected to come, and which has since come, in the case of Dred Scott. If there was any other reason for voting down that amendment, Judge Douglas knows of it and can tell it. Again, in the before-quoted part of the Nebraska bill, what means the provision that the people of the "State" shall be left perfectly free, subject only to the Constitution? Congress was not therein legislating for, or about, States or the people of States. In that bill the provision about the people of "States" is the odd half of something, the other half of which was not yet quite ready for exhibition. What is that other half to be? Another Supreme Court decision, declaring that the people of a State cannot exclude slavery, is exactly fitted to be that other half. As the power of the people of the Territories and of the States is cozily set down in the Nebraska bill as being the same: so the constitutional limitations on that power will then be judicially held to be precisely the same in both Territories and States—that is, that the Constitution permits neither a Territory nor a State to exclude slavery.

With persons looking forward to such additional decision, the incorting a provision about States in the Nebraska bill was perfectly rational; but to persons not looking for such decision it was a puzzle. There was a real reason for inserting such provision. Judge Douglas inserted it, and therefore knows, and can tell, what that real reason was.

Judge Douglas's present course by no means lessens my belief in the existence of a purpose to make slavery alike lawful in all the States. This can be done by a Supreme Court decision holding that the United States Constitution forbids a State to exclude slavery; and probably it can be done in no other way. The idea of forcing slavery into a free State, or out of a slave State, at the point of the bayonet, is alike nonsensical. Slavery can only become extinct by being restricted to its present limits, and dwindling out. It can only become national by a Supreme Court decision. To such a decision, when it comes, Judge Douglas is fully committed. Such a decision acquiesced in by the people effects the whole object. Bearing this in mind, look at what Judge Douglas is doing every day. For the first sixty-five years under the United States Constitution, the practice of government had been to exclude slavery from the new free Territories. About the end of that period Congress, by the Nebraska bill, resolved to abandon this practice; and this was rapidly succeeded by a Supreme Court decision holding the practice to have always been unconstitutional. Some of us refuse to obey this decision as a political rule. Forthwith Judge Douglas espouses the decision, and denounces all opposition to it in no measured terms. He adheres to it with extraordinary tenacity; and under rather extraordinary circumstances. He espouses it not on any opinion of his that it is right within itself. On this he forbears to commit himself. He espouses it exclusively on the ground of its binding authority on all citizens—a ground which commits him as fully to the next decision as to this. I point out to him that Mr. Jefferson and General Jackson were both against him on the binding political authority of Supreme Court decisions. No response. I might as well preach Christianity to a grizzly bear as to preach Jefferson and Jackson to him.

I tell him I have often heard him denounce the Supreme Court decision in favor of a national bank. He denies the accuracy of my recollection—which seems strange to me, but I let it pass.

I remind him that he, even now, indorses the Cincinnati platform, which declares that Congress has no constitutional power to charter a bank; and that in the teeth of a Supreme Court decision that Congress has such power. This he cannot deny; and so he remembers to forget it.

I remind him of a piece of Illinois history about Supreme Court decisions—of a time when the Supreme Court of Illinois, consisting of four judges, because of one decision made, and one expected to be made, were overwhelmed by the adding of five new judges to their number; that he, Judge Douglas, took a leading part in that onslaught, ending in his sitting down on the bench as one of the five added judges. I suggest to him that as to his questions how far judges have to be catechized in advance, when appointed under such circumstances, and how far a court, so constituted, is prostituted beneath the contempt of all men, no man is better posted to answer than he, having once been entirely through the mill himself.

Still no response, except "Hurrah for the Dred Scott decision!" These things warrant me in saying that Judge Douglas adheres to the Dred Scott decision under rather extraordinary circumstances—circumstances suggesting the question, "Why does he adhere to it so pertinaciously? Why does he thus belie his whole past life? Why, with a long record more marked for hostility to judicial decisions than almost any living man, does he cling to this with a devotion that nothing can baffle?" In[2] this age, and this

[2] From this point to the end, the text has been corrected from two pages of autograph manuscript in the Pierpont Morgan Library. A third page of manuscript held by the Morgan Library in association with these two may have formed part of the same manuscript. Nicolay and Hay, however, include it with another fragment (c. May 18, 1858, *supra*), presumably for sufficient reasons, and the present editors have followed their predecessors in the absence of sufficient evidence to the contrary. The Morgan Library has all three pages dated [June 18—November 4, 1860], which date cannot be supported by the contents of the pages.

country, public sentiment is every thing. *With* it, nothing can fail; *against* it, nothing can succeed. Whoever moulds public sentiment, goes deeper than he who enacts statutes, or pronounces judicial decisions. He makes possible the inforcement of these, else impossible.

Judge Douglas is a man of large influence. His bare opinion goes far to fix the opinion of others. Besides this, thousands hang their hopes upon forcing their opinions to agree with his. It is a party necessity with them to *say* they agree with him; and there is danger they will repeat the saying till they really come to believe it. Others dread, and shrink from his denunciations, his sarcasms, and his ingenious misrepresentations. The susceptable young hear lessons from him, such as their fathers never heared [*sic*] when they were young.

If, by all these means, he shall succeed in moulding public sentiment to a perfect accordance with his own—in bringing all men to indorse all court decisions, without caring to know whether they are right or wrong—in bringing all tongues to as perfect a silence us his own, as to there being any wrong in slavery—in bringing all to declare, with him, that they care not whether slavery be voted down or voted up—that if any people want slaves they have a right to have them—that negroes are not men—have no part in the declaration of Independence—that there is no moral question about slavery—that liberty and slavery are perfectly consistent—indeed, necessary accompaniaments—that for a strong man to declare himself the *superior* of a weak one, and thereupon enslave the weak one, is the very *essence* of liberty—the most sacred right of self-government—when, I say, public sentiment shall be brought to all this, in the name of heaven, what barrier will be left against slavery being made lawful every where? Can you find *one* word of his, opposed to it? Can you *not* find many strongly favoring it? If for his life—for his eternal salvation —he was solely striving for that end, could he find any means so well adapted to reach the end?

If our Presidential election, by a mere plurality, and of doubtful significance, brought one Supreme Court decision, that no power can exclude slavery from a Teritory; how much much [*sic*] more shall a public sentiment, in exact accordance with the sentiments of Judge Douglas bring another that no power can exclude it from a State?

And then, the negro being doomed, and damned, and forgotten, to everlasting bondage, is the white man quite certain that the tyrant demon will not turn upon him too?

[553]